# Personnel Management in Britain

**Industrial Relations in Context**

General Editor: George Sayers Bain

**Titles available**

*Industrial Relations in Britain*
George Sayers Bain (ed.)

*Labour Law in Britain*
Roy Lewis (ed.)

*Employment in Britain*
Duncan Gallie (ed.)

*Personnel Management in Britain*
Keith Sisson (ed.)

# PERSONNEL

## M·A·N·A·G·E·M·E·N·T

## in Britain

*Edited by*
Keith Sisson

Basil Blackwell

First published 1989

Basil Blackwell Ltd
108 Cowley Road, Oxford, OX4 1JF, UK

Basil Blackwell Inc.
432 Park Avenue South, Suite 1503
New York, NY 10016, USA

*British Library Cataloguing-in-Publication Data*
Personnel management in Britain
  1. Great Britain. Personnel management
  I. Sisson, Keith  II. Series
  658.3 ′00941
ISBN 0-631-14185-5
ISBN 0-631-14186-3 Pbk.

*Library of Congress Cataloging-in-Publication Data*
Personnel management in Britain/edited by Keith Sisson.
    p.  cm. – (Industrial relations in context)
  Includes bibliographies and index.
  ISBN 0-631-14185-5 – ISBN 0-631-14186-3 (pbk.)
    1. Personnel management – Great Britain.  I. Sisson, Keith.
II. Series.
HF5549.2.G7P47  1989     89-30076
658.3 ′0094 – dc19     CIP

Typeset in 10 on 11½ pt Times
by Joshua Associates Ltd, Oxford
Printed in Great Britain by T J Press Ltd, Padstow

# Contents

## PART V   THE WAGE–WORK BARGAIN

## PART VI   PARTICIPATION AND INVOLVEMENT

# Contributors

*William Brown*, Professor of Industrial Relations, University of Cambridge

*David Buchanan*, Senior Lecturer in Organizational Behaviour, Department of Management Studies, University of Glasgow

*Ron Collard*, Director, London Personnel, Coopers and Lybrand

*Barrie Dale*, Lecturer in Production Management, School of Management, University of Manchester Institute of Science and Technology

*P. K. Edwards*, Deputy Director, Industrial Relations Research Unit, University of Warwick

*Arthur Francis*, Senior Lecturer, School of Management, Imperial College of Science, Technology and Medicine

*Ewart Keep*, Research Fellow, Industrial Relations Research Unit, University of Warwick

*Mick Marchington*, Lecturer in Sociology/Industrial Relations, School of Management, University of Manchester Institute of Science and Technology

*Bruce Partridge*, Lecturer in Organizational Behaviour, School of Management, University of Leeds

*Robert Price*, Head of Policy and Co-ordination, ESRC.

*Gerry Randell*, Professor of Organizational Behaviour, Management Centre, University of Bradford

*Philip Sadler*, Principal, Ashridge Management College

*Keith Sisson*, Professor of Industrial Relations and Director of Industrial Relations Research Unit, University of Warwick

*Stuart Timperley*, Senior Lecturer in Organizational Behaviour, London Business School

*Barbara Townley*, Lecturer in Industrial Relations, School of Industrial and Business Studies, University of Warwick

*Tom Watson*, Senior Lecturer in Organizational Behaviour, School of Industrial and Business Studies, University of Warwick

# List of figures

# List of tables

# Foreword

'Industrial Relations in Context' is a new series of books which complements the well-established 'Warwick Studies in Industrial Relations'. The latter continues as a vehicle for disseminating research undertaken at Warwick University's Industrial Relations Research Unit. The new series is designed for the purposes of teaching and wider dissemination. Its rationale is the need for an analysis of current problems and issues in British industrial relations which is systematically informed by the relevant research and scholarship, and by an awareness of recent trends and developments and the wider social, economic, political and international contexts of industrial relations.

The series aims at providing a clear, comprehensive, authoritative, and up-to-date analysis of the entire field of employment relations. It is intended for students doing diploma, undergraduate, or postgraduate courses in personnel management and industrial relations at colleges, polytechnics, or universities, as well as for those studying industrial sociology, labour economics and labour law. It should also be of interest to those in adult education, to those seeking membership of professional bodies like the Institute of Personnel Management, to industrial relations practitioners in both unions and management, and to the general reader who wants to find out more about industrial relations in Britain today.

The hallmarks of the series are clarity, comprehensiveness, authoritativeness and topicality. Each chapter of each volume is an original essay that brings together the relevant theoretical and empirical work. Each is stamped with the views of the authors who are leading experts in the field. Each emphasizes analysis and explanation as well as description. Each focuses on trends over the past two or three decades (unless a longer time perspective is required to develop the argument) and says something about likely future developments. And in each case the complete text is welded into a coherent order for teaching purposes by an editor who combines a distinguished research record with a proven ability to communicate to a wide audience.

The series began with the publication in 1983 of *Industrial Relations in Britain*, edited by George Bain, a general text covering trade unions, management, collective bargaining, industrial conflict, the labour market, labour law, and state intervention in industrial relations. It continued in 1986 with the publication of *Labour Law in Britain*, edited by Roy Lewis, and, more recently in 1988, with the publication of *Employment in Britain*, edited by Duncan Gallie.

*Personnel Management in Britain* is the latest volume to be published. Personnel management, as Keith Sisson points out in his preface, has been regarded as being more or less synonymous with the techniques and activities associated with, if not necessarily performed by, specialist personnel managers. Consequently, unlike other areas of industrial relations, the treatment has been massively prescriptive; there has been little or no empirical information about, let alone analysis of, what happens in practice. In surveying the changes in the actual practice of personnel management, and the discussion and debates taking place about them, the authors of the following chapters have gone a very long way towards remedying these deficiencies. The result is the most up-to-date, comprehensive and authoritative account of personnel management in Britain.

*George Sayers Bain*

# Preface

In conforming to the model of the other texts in the series, this volume represents, in two major respects, a significant departure from the way personnel management has been treated in the past. First, whereas most texts have regarded personnel management as being more or less synonymous with the techniques and activities associated with, if not necessarily performed by, specialist personnel managers, this collection is primarily concerned with personnel management as a system of employment regulation: the ways in which people in work organizations are selected, appraised, trained, paid, disciplined, and so on. Second, and perhaps even more importantly, although it raises and throws considerable light on a great many policy issues – in particular, the significance for personnel management of the wider economic, political and social context – the book is not directly prescriptive as most textbooks in the area have been; the objective is to understand the ways in which people in work organizations in Britain are actually selected, appraised, trained, paid, and disciplined, rather than with offering seemingly 'universal' solutions to the problem of managing the employment relationship. The aim, as well as contributing to the growing debate about the significance of the management of people in Britain, is to meet the demands of teachers and students, at every level, for the breadth and depth of description, explanation and analysis they have come to expect in other areas of industrial relations.

Breaking with tradition is never easy. In this particular case, the major problem has been to overcome what is perhaps the most unfortunate legacy of the prescriptive tradition that has dominated the study of personnel management. In many areas, while there is no shortage of texts telling managers what to do, there is a lack of information about what actually happens in practice. It is small wonder that students, especially at post-experience level, become confused and frustrated; the gap between so many of the prescriptions offered by the textbooks and the reality of personnel management in the typical organization in Britain is enormous. It is to the great credit of the authors that, despite the lack of information, they have kept to the brief and have sought to piece together as comprehensive a picture as they have been able to. The hope must be that younger scholars will begin to follow their example and take up the challenge of writing descriptively and analytically about personnel management. For, contrary to the conventional wisdom, it is the analysis that informs policy-making that is desperately lacking in this area.

To quote one example among many, there has only been one large-scale survey of manpower planning or, as it is becoming known, human resource planning in Britain. This was carried out more than a decade ago and was restricted to a number of fairly basic questions. There is virtually no information available whatsoever about the links between human resource planning and business planning. Yet most pundits stress the vital importance of business planning to human resource planning and vice versa.

The 16 chapters in the book deal with six major themes. The two chapters in part I offer an overview of trends and developments in personnel management, as well as a perspective and, to borrow a phrase from Roy Lewis' preface to *Labour Law in Britain*, are as much a conclusion as an introduction. The chapters in part II, which are concerned with the design of organizations, deal with issues which have too often been neglected in personnel management textbooks, largely because they are usually outside the control of personnel managers, and yet which provide the essential context in which they work. The chapters in the other four parts deal with themes which, although dealt with differently from previous studies, will be readily recognizable: employee resourcing, employee development, the wage–work bargain, and participation and involvement.

Clearly, had this volume not been part of a wider series, there would have been a strong case for including consideration of an even wider range of issues. Roy Lewis' *Labour Law in Britain* deals with many of these issues, such as the contract of employment, health and safety, sickness and social security, and occupational pensions, on the grounds that it is extremely difficult to divorce discussion of these from the legal framework. Similarly, George Bain's *Industrial Relations in Britain* covers in some detail British management's attitude and approach to trade unions, since they are critical to an understanding of the institutions and processes of joint regulation.

Readers will notice the universal 'he/his' has been used throughout the text. This convention is adopted simply for semantic clarity and in no way reflects on the presence or absence of female practitioners in personnel management and in the workforce at large. I trust female readers will not be offended by this.

As well as the authors, many people helped to make this book possible. Special thanks are due to George Bain, and to René Olivieri (of Basil Blackwell) for their support and their patience; to colleagues in the Industrial Relations Research Unit (George Bain, Margaret Morgan and Bob Price) and the Institute of Employment Research for compiling the data that appear in the tables in the appendix to chapter 2; to Annemarie Flanders for doing the bulk of the copy-editing and for preparing the final versions of the bibliographies; to Mary Robinson for preparing the manuscript for printing; and to Jackie McDermott for producing the index.

*Keith Sisson*

# PART I
Introduction

# 1 Personnel Management in Perspective

*Keith Sisson*

The term personnel management is used here to describe the policies, processes and procedures involved in the management of people in work organizations. As will be seen from the book's list of contents, the term covers the design of organizations, as well as planning, recruitment and selection, appraisal, training and development, remuneration, discipline, and participation and involvement. Very often such activities have come to be associated with a group of specialist personnel managers, above all in Britain, where they have had their own professional organization, the Institute of Personnel Management (IPM), an examination scheme covering membership, and codes of ethics. Specialist managers are not necessarily required to perform these activities, however, and are not present in every work organization. Indeed, the survey evidence suggests that they are the exception rather than the rule in most workplaces (Millward and Stevens, 1986: 20–3) and they are not even universal in the divisional and head offices of large enterprises that dominate employment in Britain (Marginson et al., 1988: 52–4). Moreover, even where such specialists are employed, other managers are likely to be intimately involved in the design and performance of these activities. For personnel management is inevitably an important part of the job of any manager who has to get things done by people; it is, in other words, an 'element' function. In short, and viewed from the perspective of the first two volumes in this series – *Industrial Relations in Britain*, which was mostly concerned with the joint regulation of the employment relationship, and *Labour Law in Britain*, which was concerned with its legal regulation – the present volume is concerned with the regulation for which managers are primarily, if not exclusively, responsible.

Accepting these definitions, this and the following chapter attempt to give an overview of personnel management in Britain. In contrast to the traditional approaches to the subject, which tend to see things largely in universalistic terms, this chapter argues that the actual practice of personnel management is deeply rooted in specific contexts. In particular, it seeks to show how the 'opportunism' or 'pragmatism' which might be said to characterize the practice of personnel management in Britain in many organizations is related to key structures inherited from the past. Chapter 2 considers the pressures on British management to change, and discusses the nature and extent of the changes taking place.

## TWO TRADITIONS: TWO APPROACHES

Although the study as well as the practice of personnel management might be said to be in a state of transition, the literature is dominated by two main approaches. The first, and by far the most important in terms of the number of contributions, is intended for managers, and students of management, and is largely concerned with the techniques of personnel management. The second, which draws on a very different tradition, is essentially a critique: personnel management is seen largely as a set of controls which are imposed on workers in order to maximize the surplus value of their labour power. Each of these has had a profound influence on how personnel management is viewed, and so needs to be considered in some detail before moving on to discuss actual practice.

### The Prescriptive Approach

The bulk of the literature is intended primarily, if not exclusively, for a management audience and, in particular, for the specialist personnel manager. Although in recent years more emphasis has been given to the disciplines and philosophy that underpin it (Thomason, 1981; Torrington and Chapman, 1983; Torrington and Hall, 1987), personnel management is considered in this literature to be about what the *personnel* manager does and, even more importantly, should be doing. In other words, the tradition is, first and foremost, prescriptive in approach. The emphasis is on information it is thought will help the personnel manager to do the job better and above all, on the techniques of personnel management; how to do manpower planning, how to recruit and select, how to devise training programmes, how to design payment systems and pay structures, how to draw up disciplinary codes and procedures, and so on.

In many works there is no explicit set of ideas – let alone theoretical framework – underpinning the approach, and the reader has to take on trust the prescriptions offered. Closer inspection, however, reveals, implicitly, if not explicitly, a very particular set of ideas. Originally these ideas were grounded in the 'human relations' tradition of sociology, in psychology and social psychology, but in recent years they have come to be grouped together under the subject heading of organizational behaviour.

Seen from this perspective, work organizations are no different in kind from other types of organization. Stripped of their essentials, they are continuous, if not permanent, bodies which have common goals and which are composed of individuals performing a range of differentiated, and yet mutually indepen-dent, tasks and functions in a co-ordinated manner – differentiation and co-ordination being necessary because they are 'a means of goal achievement' (Porter, Lawler and Hackman, 1975: 88). Like other types of organization, there is not only a great deal of mutual dependence between the tasks and functions performed internally; the work organization is an 'open' system in constant exchange interaction with the environment from which it receives 'inputs' and to which it transmits 'outputs' (Torrington and Chapman, 1983: 19). A central problem for complex organizations, it is argued (see, for example, Thomson, 1967), is in coping with uncertainty; individuals and groups in the organization do not determine the 'system's' outcomes by themselves. In the case of the business organization, for example, it is the market that is seen to set the key parameters within which decisions have to be made.

Perhaps even more influential than the perspective on organization is the particular view of the individual that underpins the approach. Here the main source of ideas is the work of Maslow (1943), Herzberg (1966), McGregor (1960) and other associated with the so-called 'neo-human relations' school. Again at the risk of oversimplification, the view of the individual as 'economic man' motivated simply by financial self-interest, inherited from the 'scientific management' approach associated with Taylor (1911), is rejected. Instead, the individual is seen as having a number of needs. According to Maslow (1948), the individual has a hierarchy of needs: physiological, safety, love, esteem and self-actualization. Only when the physiological needs have been satisfied, will the other needs come into play and then in sequence. Herzberg (1966) talks in terms of 'hygiene' and 'motivator' needs. The first are lower order and include acceptable levels of pay, appropriate working conditions, and tolerable discipline; the second are higher order or growth needs and include independence, responsibility and, perhaps most crucially, recognition of the contribution made. In more recent formulations (see, for example, Vroom, 1964; Porter, Lawler and Hackman, 1975), the individual is seen as having complex needs, which reflect not only inner needs but also perceptions and evaluations of situations; in this case individual expectations are also regarded as being important.

The most explicit and influential formulation of the prescriptive implications of these ideas for managers – indeed, it has become almost part of the staple diet of most management courses – is McGregor's (1960) work. Two contrasting styles or approaches are presented: theory $X$ and theory $Y$. Theory $X$, which holds that individuals have an inherent dislike of work, that they must be controlled and directed, that they have little ambition, must be rejected; it brings about resentment and resistance and so is self-defeating. Instead, managers should start from the premises of theory $Y$, which holds that work is as natural as rest or play, that direction and control are not the only means of ensuring that the organization meets its objectives, and that there is a high degree of creativity to be harnessed. The conclusion is that managers should seek to move away from the highly centralized hierarchies associated with traditional forms of organization, design jobs that are as interesting and meaningful as possible, and generally promote the maximum participation and involvement of individuals.

The emergence of this body of ideas has been highly significant in the attempt to establish the specialist activity of personnel management as a profession akin to medicine or the law. First, in providing a body of theoretical knowledge to underpin the practical skills of personnel management, it has made it possible to introduce training and education schemes on which qualifying examinations can be built. Second, it has enabled personnel specialists to claim some legitimacy for the view that personnel management is 'different from other staff jobs' (Miller, 1975); employees as well as employers are seen as the 'clients' of the *professional* personnel specialist and, in maintaining the highest standards of integrity – often based on codes of ethics – he or she also performs an important public service which earns the right to claim some of the independence which goes with the traditional professions.

This is an especially important consideration in Britain, in particular, where the functional divisions within management and their organization into 'professional' bodies are so pronounced (Armstrong, 1984), and where occupational identity is closely linked to status. In an attempt to raise the status, as well as the standard of personnel management, the IPM plays an extremely influential role in the education and training of personnel managers in Britain. As well as a large number of courses and conferences, the IPM is responsible for two major education programmes. One, the Certificate in Personnel, is offered by some 70 colleges of higher and further education and provides a basic introduction to personnel management practice. The other, the Professional Education Scheme, is offered by some 90 colleges and universities and, it is claimed, is of degree level. The scheme is in two parts: part one for which colleges themselves are responsible for examining, and part two, involving courses in 'Employee Relations', 'Employee Resourcing' and 'Employee Development', which has a national syllabus and is externally examined by IPM-appointed examiners. Some indication of the importance of the IPM's education and training activities is revealed by the number of student members: in 1987 there were more than 8,000 such members (IPM, 1987).

As the next section will show, many of the assumptions of the prescriptive approach have been severely criticized in recent years. Thus, to begin with, it has been suggested that the empirical grounding of some of the theories is extremely dubious. Even within its own terms, of seeking to help managers to do the job better, there are major weaknesses. There is, above all, little or no information given about what actually happens in practice, and usually very little discussion of the problems managers experience in applying the techniques. Although considerable emphasis is placed on the interaction with the environment, attention is rarely given to the wider society in which the organization operates. Trade unions and the law, for example, are seen largely as external constraints on what goes on in the workplace, and there is scarcely any appreciation of the interaction between them and management practice. Even the implications of differences in organization structures, which have received considerable attention in business history and economics, following the pioneering work of Chandler (1962, 1977) and Williamson (1975), are ignored; one organization, as noted earlier, is much like another. Similarly ignored are differences in ownership structures, in the composition of management, and in market structures – all of which, it can be argued, have a profound effect on management practice and on the practice of personnel management in particular. In short, and in keeping with the professional aspirations of many personnel managers, the prescription is universal and so is the analysis.

## The Labour Process Approach

The second approach draws on a very different sociological tradition from the first. Although in recent years it has come to be associated with the work of Braverman (1974) and the school to which his work has given rise, its point of departure is Marx and his analysis of capitalism. As with the first approach, there is a distinctive perspective on organizations. The shape and form of work organizations are man-made and the implication is that they do not have to be like they are. The view that work organizations have common goals or are presided over by managers who seek to pursue the interests of the organization as a whole is also rejected as, at best, a myth and at worst, conscious distortion or mystification. Essentially, work organizations are seen as hierarchical and authoritarian in structure, where the few exploit the many in the pursuit of greater profit. Evidently, the message of the approach, which is, first and foremost, a critique of the status quo, is not intended primarily for a management audience, but for workers; and the main purpose is to enlighten them about the 'sad, horrible and heart-breaking way', to quote from Sweezy's foreword to Braverman's pioneering text (1974: xii), in which the majority of people are required to spend their working lives.

From this perspective, the policies, processes and procedures typically involved in the management of people are to be seen, first and foremost, as instruments of management control. In Edwards' (1979: 16–21) formulation, for example, there are three main types of control: simple or direct control by either supervisor or manager; technical controls in which the nature and pace of work is dictated by machines or the process of production or operations; and bureaucratic controls which take the form of rules and procedures. Thus, the policies, practices and procedures involved in selection, training and development, appraisal, pay systems and pay structures constitute a network of bureaucratic controls – or 'rule of law' – that either supplements or replaces the simple and technical controls and are seen largely as a response to changes in size and complexity and workers' success in opposing previous forms of control. All groups of employees, from the bottom to the very top of the organization, are affected; only the type of emphasis of control differs and depends primarily on the nature and extent of the discretion that employees enjoy.

The image of the specialist personnel manager associated with the prescriptive approach also gets pretty short shrift. Far from being the independent professional, let alone the workers' champion, personnel managers are seen as misguided, if not mischievous. Braverman himself, for example, is totally unsparing in his criticism:

Work itself is organized according to Taylorian principles, while personnel departments and academics have busied themselves with the selection, training, manipulation, pacification, and adjustment of 'manpower' to suit the work processes so organized. Taylorism dominates the world of production; the practitioners of 'human relations' and 'industrial psychology' are the maintenance crew for the human machinery. (1974: 87)

Clearly, then, this approach is very different from the first. Although in many respects the analysis is much more sophisticated, however, it is not beyond criticism. To begin with, it is a moot point whether it is appropriate to place so much emphasis on control as the central focus of management activity. Clearly, control is profoundly important but, arguably, is a means to an end rather than an end in itself. Moreover, as later sections will discuss, direct control through the employment relationship is not necessarily management's preferred option and, indeed, may come to assume less significance in the future, with the growth in such developments as subcontracting and franchising which will be discussed in chapter 2.

Some of the criticisms levelled at the prescriptive approach also apply. With relatively few exceptions (see, for example, Friedman, 1977), there is little or no empirical underpinning and examples are used, often in a partisan way, to illustrate theory rather than to test it. Similarly, although there are numerous statements denying it, the impression given is that, allowing for differences in the stages of capitalism, in size and technology, things are always and everywhere the same. Management, it is recognized, does not have matters all its own way and workers' opposition is seen as a powerful constraint. Even so, like the prescriptive approach, scarcely any attention is paid to specific differences in business structures and institutions such as trade unions and collective bargaining; or to the interaction between management and trade unions in specific contexts and the opportunities and constraints this produces. In short, managers would appear to have little choice in the way they manage people and, even if they do, it is at the margin and makes no material difference.

## PERSONNEL MANAGEMENT IN PRACTICE

The point of presenting these two approaches in a critical way is not to deny that they have any validity at all. Patently, personnel management does involve the application of techniques and managers will want to know how to do things better. Uncomfortable though the implications may be, even most managers, if pressed, would also accept that it is difficult to refute much of what the labour process theorists have to say. Individuals possess far fewer rights as employees than they do as citizens; and the assumptions of theory $X$, as the textbooks readily admit, continue to hold considerable sway over many managers. Rather it is to suggest that these approaches offer only partial views of personnel management and are not the complete picture by any means. Work organizations are to be found in a range of different sectors; they employ people in many different jobs; and, even within the same sector, they come in different shapes and sizes. As this section will attempt to show, even the limited evidence available would suggest that the approach adopted to personnel management and the role of personnel managers can differ significantly from one organization to another, let alone from one country to another; it is also deeply rooted in a specific historical and institutional as well as market context.


## A Variety of Practice

In Britain, one obvious distinction is whether or not a trade union is recognized for the purposes of collective bargaining. Other things being equal, this raises fundamental questions about the emphasis managements place, consciously or not, on individualism and collectivism in their approach. Thus, where the management does not recognize a trade union, it is likely to emphasize the relationship with the individual; where it does recognize a trade union, it is likely to put the emphasis on the relationship with the trade union and relations with individuals are no longer central.

In practice, of course, it is perfectly possible for managers to combine elements of both dimensions in their approach. Indeed, it is on the basis of the combination of these elements that it is possible to suggest a number of models or ideal-types of management approach or style. Figure 1.1 gives the details.

Although these are only models or ideal-types, they do highlight some of the main observable differences in the practice of personnel management in Britain. Certainly, it is not difficult to think of organizations in Britain which approximate to at least three of the categories. A candidate for the 'traditional' category might be the Grunwick photo-processing company which was the centre of a major dispute over trade union recognition in 1976–7; the evidence before the Committee of Inquiry (Rogaly, 1977) suggested that there had been considerable exploitation of the mainly immigrant labour-force. Several varieties of the 'sophisticated human relations' type can be identified: IBM (Peach, 1983) and Marks and Spencer (Tse, 1985), both of which do not recognize trade unions but have large personnel departments and highly developed practices designed to secure the commitment of the individual employee through training and development, counselling and appraisal, might be regarded as long-standing examples. Similarly, there are a number of varieties of the 'consultative' type; there is the traditional 'Whitley' model of industrial relations in the public sector with its extensive procedures for both consultation and negotiation (Clegg, 1979: 104–15) there are the examples of Cadbury-Schweppes (Child, 1964; Whittaker, 1986) and ICI (Roeber, 1975) in the private sector; there are the more recent examples of the Japanese subsidiaries set up in Britain and, in particular, the Nissan subsidiary on Teesside whose initiatives in selection, training, appraisal and job evaluation, as well as collective bargaining and joint consultation, have received widespread publicity (see, for example, IRRR, 1985: 2–7).

Surprising as it may seem in the light of the support of public policy for collective bargaining in the 1960s and 1970s, and the case made for 'management by agreement' (see, for example, McCarthy and Ellis, 1973), the one type

FIGURE 1.1   *Models of management style*

| | **Management style in handling employee relations** | |
|---|---|---|
| | *Individualism high* | |
| Sophisticated human relations | | Consultative |
| *Collectivism low* | | *Collectivism high* |
| Traditional | | Constitutional |
| | *Individualism low* | |

**Traditional**
Labour is viewed as a factor of production, and employee subordination is assumed to be part of the 'natural order' of the employment relationship. There is often a fear of outside union interference. Unionization is opposed or unions kept at arm's length.

**Constitutional**
Somewhat similar to the traditionalists in basic value structures, especially for unskilled and semiskilled workers, but unions have been recognized for some time and accepted as inevitable. Employee relations policies centre on the need for stability, control and the institutionalization of conflict. Management prerogatives are defended through highly specific collective agreements, and careful attention is paid to the administration of agreements on the shopfloor. The importance of management control is emphasized with the aim of minimizing or neutralizing union constraints on both operational (line) and strategic (corporate) management.

**Sophisticated human relations**
Employees (excluding short-term contract or subcontract labour) are viewed as the company's most valuable resource. Firms adopting this style often deliberately have above-average pay, and clear internal labour market structures with promotion ladders; periodic attitude surveys are used to harness employees' views. Emphasis is placed on flexible reward structures, employee appraisal systems linked to merit awards, internal grievance, disciplinary and consultative procedures and extensive networks and methods of communication. The aim is to inculcate employee loyalty, commitment and dependency. As a by-product these companies seek to make it unnecessary or unattractive for staff to unionize.

**Consultative**
Similar to the sophisticated human resource companies except that unions are recognized. The attempt is made to build 'constructive' relationships with the unions and incorporate them into the organizational fabric. Broad-ranging discussions are held and extensive information provided to the unions on a whole range of decisions and plans, including aspects of strategic management; the 'rights of last say', though, rests with management. Emphasis is also placed on techniques designed to enhance individual employee commitment to the firm and the need to accept change (share option schemes, profit-sharing, briefing or cascade information systems, joint working parties, quality or productivity circles/councils).

*Sources:*   J. Purcell, 'Employee Relations Autonomy within a Corporate Culture', *Personnel Management*, February 1986, 39; see also J. Purcell and K. Sisson, 'Strategies and Practice in the Management of Industrial Relations', *Industrial Relations in Britain*, ed. G. S. Bain (Oxford: Blackwell, 1983), 95–120.

of which there are few, if any, examples in Britain is the 'constitutional'. As will be argued below, for examples of this type, which would seem to depend on a highly developed legal framework coupled with a structure of single-employer bargaining, it is necessary to look to the US, where it has been the predominant pattern in highly unionized companies since the 'New Deal' legislation of the 1930s (Kochan, Katz and McKersie, 1986).

Interesting though it may be to speculate about examples of these models, most organizations in Britain, it can be argued, do not conform to any of them. There is a considerable body of evidence, much of which will be found later in this and subsequent chapters, to suggest that, for the want of a better way of putting it, the approach is '*ad hoc*' (Thurley, 1981: 26) or 'pragmatic' or 'opportunistic' (Purcell and Sisson, 1983: 116). Certainly the approach is very different from the impression to be gained from the prescriptive texts and, as recent survey evidence suggests (Millward and Stevens, 1986; Purcell et al., 1987), also stands in contrast with the practice in foreign-owned companies.

Thus, although the typical large organization in Britain is likely to have a range of personnel policies, there is usually little integration between them; there is also unlikely to be an explicit philosophy or strategy towards the management of people and little integration of personnel policies with business planning more generally. As chapter 5 suggests, there may be little manpower planning and, if it is done at all, it is likely to be largely about numbers with little qualitative input. Most organizations rely on the interview for selection, as the survey evidence in chapter 6 suggests – even in the case of managerial employees – and there is little use of tests. The use of appraisal is growing, chapter 7 finds, but it continues to be one of the most controversial and problematic techniques in personnel management. Training, the recent survey evidence discussed in chapters 8, 9, and 10 suggests, is seen as a cost rather than an investment and very little is done. As chapter 12 points out, status differences between manual and non-manual employees and between male and female employees are marked. The communications programmes discussed in chapter 14 are of relatively recent origin as are the experiments with task participation such as quality circles, discussed in chapter 15.

## A Variety of Roles

The picture that emerges from the survey evidence also suggests that the role played by personnel managers is in strong contrast to that which appears in the textbooks. Here the impression given, even in those texts that draw on survey evidence (see, for example, Torrington and Hall, 1987: 24), is of a very rounded or 'generalist' portfolio of activities: personnel managers are (and, by implication, should be) involved in a wide range of activities: the design of organizations, employee resourcing, employee development, discipline and reward, and participation and involvement, as well as in dealing with trade unions and the impact of legislation. The survey evidence (Daniel and Millward, 1983; Millward and Stevens, 1986; Marginson et al., 1988; Sisson and Scullion, 1985) suggests there is much greater variability to the job. Certainly, although there may be a number of 'generalists', it cannot be assumed that the majority of personnel managers are necessarily involved in a wide range of activities, or that the nature and extent of their involvement is the same from one organization to another or, perhaps even more importantly, from one level to another in the same organization. Moreover, although many personnel managers, both at workplace and higher levels in the organization, are not without influence, it would appear to be within the relatively narrow confines of management–trade union relations. Indeed, it would appear that they pay for their relative influence in this area by being excluded from other areas (Millward and Stevens, 1986: 47; Marginson et al., 1988). It is where they are involved in key development activities involving senior managers that they wield most influence (Sisson and Scullion, 1985).

One typology that captures the variety of the roles that personnel managers can play has been developed by Tyson and Fell (1986: 21–7). There is the 'clerk of the works' who is largely involved in routine matters; record-keeping, preparing letters and documents on instructions, first-interviewing of some applicants for employment, and visiting the sick. They will report to a senior line manager or personnel manager and are unlikely to have any qualifications. The second is the 'contracts manager', who is most likely to be found in organizations with strong trade unions and a traditional industrial relations background. They will be involved in policy-making but of a relatively short-term time-scale; their main activity is likely to be the making and interpretation of procedures and agreements. In some organizations, consequently, they may exercise considerable power and authority which comes from their ability to resolve day-to-day problems, and from their intimate knowledge and personal relationships with shop stewards and trade union officers, as well as senior line managers. 'Architects', the third type, are likely to be intimately involved in policy-making as a member of the senior management team and have a seat on the board of directors. Certainly they will regard themselves as 'business managers' first and 'personnel managers' second and will have a broad portfolio which encompasses not just dealing with trade unions but the organization's entire human resources, as well as the design of the structure of the organization. They are likely to be highly qualified, both academically and in experience, although they may not be members of the IPM; they will have worked in personnel and may have considerable experience as a line manager at some time in their career.

Tyson and Fell (1986) are primarily concerned with differences between organizations. In practice, however, and even though they counsel against mixing the different 'types', their typology is equally, if not more, relevant in understanding the differences in the role of personnel managers from one level to another in the multi-establishment organizations which dominate employment in this country. Thus, many personnel managers employed at workplace level are likely to fall into the 'clerk of the works' category, whereas the senior personnel manager is likely to be a 'contracts manager'; most senior personnel managers working at divisional and central headquarters are likely to be 'contracts managers' or 'architects'. In other words, the personnel manager's job can be very different depending on the level in the organization as well as the type of organization.

The position of the IPM is also not quite what it seems. At first sight, as Torrington and Hall (1987: 17) point out, personnel management in Britain exhibits many of the hallmarks of the profession listed by Millerson (1964): a permanent organization (the permanent headquarters staff of the IPM totalled nearly 100 in 1987 and the combined income from subscriptions and other activities was of the order of £3.7 million); skills based on theoretical know-ledge; education and training provisions; qualifying examinations; codes of ethics; and a claim to be in the public good. The two regular monthly publications which the IPM supports, the *Digest* and *Personnel Management*, are not only an important source of general information, but also play a key role in the IPM's appointments service, bringing in a profit of nearly £800,000 in 1986 (IPM, 1987).

Even so, and perhaps not surprisingly given that personnel management is usually an element in the job of every manager, personnel managers have been singularly unsuccessful in achieving the exclusivity that goes with the traditional professions. Relatively few organizations make membership a condition of employment or accept as binding the edicts of the IPM. Also large numbers of personnel managers do not belong to the IPM. Indeed, only a half of those managers who spend a major part of their time on personnel even have the word 'personnel' in their title; and, of those that do, the personnel specialists, less than half have any qualification and only about one quarter are members of the IPM (Daniel, 1983: 26; Millward and Stevens, 1986: 25–7). Even less than half of the personnel managers employed in the corporate and divisional headquarters of the larger enterprises in the private sector are IPM-qualified (Marginson et al., 1988: 54).

It is doubtful too if many personnel managers see themselves and what they do as 'professional' in the strict sense of the term. Thus, Tyson and Fell (1986: 53) draw on unpublished research (Tyson, 1979) to suggest that the notion of being a professional, in the sense of having one's prime loyalty to the occupation, is nowhere so important as a number of studies have suggested; the organization is the source of status and rewards. Even Mackay and Torrington (1986), who otherwise would appear to incline towards the 'professional' model, are forced to conclude, on the basis of their survey of personnel managers, that things are not quite perhaps what they hoped:

> There is little reference to a mediating role between employer and employee. The role of the personnel practitioner as the 'in-between' person seems to have gone. Personnel managers appear to be managers first and personnel people second. (pp. 161–2)

To paraphrase Thurley's (1981: 26) summary of what is said to be wrong with personnel management as a specialist activity in Britain, many personnel managers are caught in a mismatch between a pretentious abstract model of what they should be doing, and the reality of a relatively fragmented and routine set of activities which receive little recognition. They cope with this situation by using professionalism in an instrumental fashion, but in reality conform to local organizational norms (Watson, 1977). In internalizing the problem, however, they have failed to generate or be associated with a serious debate about the fundamental issues of personnel management in Britain.

## International Comparisons

At the international level, what little evidence there is suggests that the differences in personnel management would appear to be especially marked. In the USA, for example, the large companies might be said to fall into two main groups (Kochan, Katz and McKersie, 1986). The first group, which includes long-standing examples such as IBM and Hewlett-Packard, and more recent cases such as Procter and Gamble, and Du Pont, pursue policies of the kind associated with the 'human relations' approach referred to in figure 1.1. Indeed, these are the real-life cases from which the model for that approach was derived. They almost invariably do not recognize trade unions and have large personnel departments and highly developed practices designed to secure the commitment of the individual employee through training and development, counselling and appraisal (Foulkes, 1980, 1981). The second group, which includes the major vehicle manufacturers, Chrysler, Ford and General Motors, are the real-life cases on which the 'constitutional' model in figure 1.1 is based. Most have recognized trade unions since the 'New Deal' legislation of the 1930s. Managerial prerogative has been fiercely upheld, but detailed collective agreements cover most aspects of the employment relationship, including job mobility and fringe benefits.

A recent development has been the attempt on the part of some members of the second group to graft on some of the elements of the 'human relations' approach to the 'constitutional' approach to create a hybrid 'new industrial relations' model in order to meet the threat of Japanese competition. General Motors' so-called 'Saturn' experiment, in which novel production methods have been accompanied by single-status arrangements, pay for knowledge, gain-sharing and problem-solving groups, is a good example (Kochan, Katz and McKersie, 1986).

Japan, the second country to be considered, also has a 'dual' system or structure. In this case, however, the differences are between the large *keiretsu* or linked groups such as Mitsubishi, Sumitomo, Nissan and Toyoto, and the many small firms, which are often involved in a subcontracting relationship with them. Most attention has focused on the three so-called 'pillars' of the employment system that prevails in the large companies and affects between a quarter and a third of the total labour-force (Okochi et al., 1973; Thurley, 1982). The first is 'life-long' employment; permanent employees, as opposed to the large number of temporary or secondary workers the typical organization also employs, are recruited straight from high school or university in a highly competitive selection process and then promoted within the internal labour-market through a process of appraisal, on-the-job-training and development. The second is the pay system; pay reflects age and length of service, as well as job and merit, and a considerable element of the total package is related to the performance of the company. The third is the system of enterprise unionism; although there are a number of industrial federations and centres, they have much less power than in Western Europe or the USA and the key unit is the workplace or company.

In discussion of the situation in West Germany, the third country to be considered here, most attention has focused on the system of co-determination; companies with more than five employees are obliged by law to have a works council and those with more than 2000 to have a supervisory board on which trade unions have representatives (see, for example, Commission on Industrial Relations, 1974). Recent studies, however, have drawn attention to other features. One is the provisions for training; West Germany has a tripartite system of training in which government, employers' organizations and trade unions are involved (Coopers and Lybrand, 1985). The combined effect of the system of co-determination and these provisions, a leading authority (Streeck, 1985) has argued, has been to encourage employers to develop far-reaching manpower planning and training strategies; manpower planning is built into the investment analysis process and a number of companies have, in effect, committed themselves to a guarantee of employment for the existing workforce; while, even during the recent depression, employers have trained beyond their immediately perceived needs.

The extent to which the practice of personnel management in Britain is different from other countries is a matter for debate; not enough is known about the detailed practice to make a definitive judgement. Certainly, a number of commentators have argued that the practice *is* different and, what is more, that the difference is significant. For example, in a famous article in the journal of the Institute of Personnel Management, appropriately entitled 'Personnel Management in the UK – A Case for Urgent Treatment?', Thurley (1981) not only lists a number of comments and criticisms made down the years of personnel management as a specialist activity: Flanders' (1970) strictures about the lack of planning; the ambiguous role of personnel specialist managers in many organizations and their lack of credibility cited in the works of Legge (1978), Watson (1977) and Marsh (subsequently published in 1983); and the contradictory nature of personnel policies to which Batstone (1980) had drawn attention. More significantly for the present discussion, he talks in terms of personnel policy having developed in an '*ad hoc*' way'; of UK manufacturing organizations being 'inefficient in using human resources'; of 'poor labour and machine utilization'; of the growth of non-productive personnel due largely to the problems of maintaining control. He even suggests that personnel management in Britain is a victim of 'stunted growth' and queried whether personnel managers were 'working against the grain of British culture and values'. All this, he suggests, appears to be in strong contrast with other countries, notably Japan and the US, where there is a closer relationship between personnel management and business strategy.

## THE LEGACY OF HISTORY

Thurley may or may not be correct in suggesting that personnel managers are working 'against the grain of British culture and values'. Certainly there are grounds for arguing that the practice of personnel management in any country is deeply rooted in the past. Thus, in understanding the 'pragmatism' or '*ad hoc*ery' associated with many British organizations, it is significant that not only was Britain the first country to industrialize, but also that the process of industrialization was relatively autonomous and market-based. In contrast to Germany, Japan and the USA, where industrialization came later and involved large-scale operations and advanced technology from the very beginning, the large organization was relatively late in developing in Britain, and came about largely as a result of the merger and acquisition of family-owned firms with different histories and traditions. Similarly, the shift from personal or entrepreneurial to professional control by career managers occurred at a later stage in the process of industrialization in Britain, and the finance function assumed far greater significance than in many other countries due to the need to raise money internally (Chandler, 1976; Hannah, 1976; Armstrong, 1984). Crucially, too, the institutions into whose hands ownership gradually passed were not, as in Japan and West Germany, the banks, which therefore have a strong stake in the business and a concern for its long-term development, but the investment trusts and the pension funds, which have to have primary regard to the short-term return on their investments (Scott, 1979).

In combination, it can be argued, these structural features constitute a major barrier to managements in Britain investing in the long term and, in particular, in people. For, despite the CBI's recent report on relations between the City and industry, there is a considerable body of evidence to suggest that the relative absence of the kind of long-term relationship between banks, stockholders and company managements which is found in West Germany and Japan forces companies to take the short-term view of the trade-off between investment and profit (Dore, 1985; Keep, forthcoming). Added to this, the growth in the number of large diversified companies reliant on financial control systems which simply count the cost of what is done (Fox, 1988), rather than the opportunity cost of what is not done, has not only tightened the squeeze on subsidiary managers, but also poses a considerable threat, in the form of takeovers, to other companies.

Trade union structure is both an important legacy of the past and a key influence on management. As Hyman (1983: 36) points out in the first volume of this series, a highly complex and diverse structure has emerged. The relatively protracted nature of industrialization, coupled with the continued need for skilled craftsmen due to the demand for non-standard goods in export markets, made it possible for craft unions to establish themselves in the key sector of engineering before the coming of the second wave of trade union membership among semi- and unskilled workers towards the end of the nineteenth century. The ability of the craft unions to maintain the tradition of their unilateral regulation of employment was important not only for the development of collective bargaining – and, in particular, its massive informality – but also for the so-called internal labour-market. As figure 1.2 shows, whereas in most other countries, the main port of entry is at the bottom and employees have an opportunity to work their way through, in Britain the internal labour-market has been highly structured. One implication, it can be argued, is that British management, especially in manufacturing, has been unable to maximize its returns from training.

The apparent success of employers and craft unions in coming to an accommodation reinforced the *laissez-faire* approach of the state in the sphere of employment. Responsibility for education was given to local authorities and the assumption was that vocational training was a matter for individual employers and employees. Crucially, too, there was little direct regulation of the employment relationship by the state to pressurize employers into adopting a wide range of standards; the labour codes that were a prominent feature of many other countries are noticeable by their absence, though since the mid-1960s a limited 'statutory floor' of employment rights has evolved. Legislation dealing with trade unions and collective bargaining also proceeded down a particular path. In most other countries a series of positive rights was established: the right to belong to a trade union, the right to strike and so on; in Britain, however, legislation took the form of the introduction of immunities for trade unions from common law liabilities. Uniquely among industrialized economies, then, collective bargaining was allowed to develop its own

FIGURE 1.2   *Types of internal labour market*

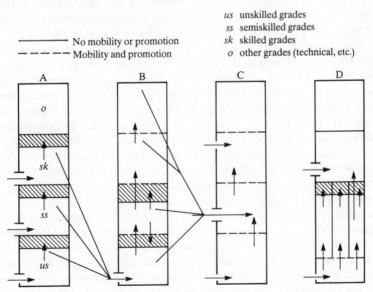

Source: D. Robinson, 'External and Internal Labour Markets', *Local Labour Markets and Wage Structures*, ed. D. Robinson (London: Gower, 1970), figure 2.6.

informal logic more or less unregulated by the legal framework (Kahn-Freund, 1983).

Much of the ambiguity that crops up regularly in discussions of personnel management as a specialist activity in Britain (see, for example, Legge and Exley, 1975; Tyson, 1980; Purcell and Grey, 1986) can also be put down to the very particular development of the function. First, following Thomason (1981, 15–23) and Tyson and Fell (1986, 18–21), there was the 'welfare' tradition which grew out of the industrial betterment movement associated with many of the Quaker companies at the turn of the century. This gave rise to the IPM itself. The IPM began life in 1913 as the Industrial Welfare Society founded predominantly by female welfare workers; and the notion of the personnel manager being a member of the 'loyal opposition' or 'the corporate conscience' representing the interests of workers to management thus became institutionalized (Niven, 1967). Second, there was the 'manpower control tradition', which reflected the growth of large bureaucratic organizations in the 1920s and 1930s – ICI is often quoted as an example. This emphasized the need for policies and procedures covering both management–employee and management–trade union relations. Third, there was the 'professional tradition', which grew primarily out of the quest for status on the part of personnel managers themselves in the post-Second World War period. This emphasized the possession of specialist knowledge and expertise; it also manifested itself in the IPM becoming a 'qualifying' association with what even strong supporters (Cowan, 1988) have argued is an unnecessarily restrictive membership. Fourth, there was the 'industrial relations tradition' which reflected the rise in workplace bargaining in the 1960s and 1970s, especially in manufacturing. This emphasized the importance of managing the relationship with trade unions and brought to the fore the 'contracts manager' referred to earlier.

As will be clear from the previous discussion, a number of organizations have been able to escape the full impact of this past. Organizations in the service sector, for example, did not experience the relationship with the craft unions that led to the development of highly structured internal labour-markets. Even companies in manufacturing have not been total prisoners. Foreign-owned enterprises such as IBM and Ford developed fairly distinctive approaches. Even some British-owned companies did so, suggesting that managers do have choice in the way they manage. The Quaker-owned companies such as Boots, Cadbury, Lever Brothers, and Rowntree-Mackintosh are examples; ICI is another. Significantly, however, in each case there would appear to be special factors at work to do with sector, foreign ownership, or the philosophy of the pioneers of the business.

To sum up, then, the practice of personnel management is far more complicated than the impression given in many texts which adopt either the prescriptive or labour process approaches. There is considerable variety from one organization to another and from one country to another. The practice of personnel management is deeply rooted in a specific historical context and this holds for the dominant 'pragmatic' or 'opportunistic' model in Britain, as it does for practice in other countries.

# Bibliography

Armstrong, P. 1984. 'Competition Between the Organisational Professions and the Evolution of Management Control Strategies'. *Work, Employment and Unemployment*. Ed. Thompson, K. Milton Keynes: Open University Press, 97–120.

Batstone, E.V. 1980. 'What have Personnel Managers Done for Industrial Relations'. *Personnel Management*, June, 36–9.

Braverman, H.A. 1974. *Labor and Monopoly Capital: The Degradation of Work in the Twentieth Century*. New York: Monthly Review Press.

Chandler, A. 1962. *Strategy and Structure: Chapters in the History of the Industrial Enterprise*. Cambridge, MA: MIT Press.

—— 1976. Ed. Hannah, L. *Management Strategy and Business Development: An Historical and Comparative Study*. London: Macmillan.

—— 1977. *The Visible Hand: The Managerial Revolution in American Business*. Cambridge, MA: Harvard University Press.

Child, J. 1964. 'Quaker Employers and Industrial Relations'. *Sociological Review*, 12: 293–315.

Clegg, H.A. 1979. *The Changing System of Industrial Relations in Britain*. Oxford: Blackwell.

Commission on Industrial Relations. 1974. *Worker Participation and Collective Bargaining in Europe*. Study No. 4. London: HMSO.

Coopers and Lybrand. 1985. *A Challenge to Complacency: Changing Attitudes to Training: A Report to the Manpower Services Commission and the National Economic Development Office*. Imprint, Sheffield: MSC.

Cowan, L. 1988. 'Change and the Personnel Profession'. *Personnel Management*, January, 32–6.

Daniel, W.W. 1983. 'Who Handles Personnel Issues in British Industry?'. *Personnel Management*, December, 25–7.

—— and Millward, N. 1983. *Workplace Industrial Relations in Britain: The DE/PSI/SSRC Survey*. London: Heinemann Educational.

Dore, R.P. 1985. 'Financial Structures and the Long-Term View'. *Policy Studies*, 6: Pt 1, July.

Edwards, R. 1979. *Contested Terrain: The Transformation of the Workplace in the Twentieth Century*. London: Heinemann.

Flanders, A. 1970. *Management and Trade Unions: The Theory and Reform of Industrial Relations*. London: Faber.

Foulkes, F. 1980. *Personnel Policies in Large Non-Union Companies*. Englewood Cliffs, NJ: Prentice-Hall.

—— 1981. 'How Top Non-Union Companies Manage Employees'. *Harvard Business Review*, 59: September/October, 90–6.

Fox, J. 1988. 'Norsk Hydro's New Approach Takes Root'. *Personnel Management*, January, 37–9.

## 20    Bibliography

Friedman, A.L. 1977. *Industry and Labour: Class Struggle at Work and Modern Capitalism*. London: Macmillan.

Hannah, L. 1976. 'Strategy and Structure in the Manufacturing Sector'. Ed. Hannah, L. *Management Strategy and Business Development: An Historical and Comparative Study*. London: Macmillan, 184–202.

Hertzberg, F. 1966. *Work and the Nature of Man*. Cleveland, Ohio: World Publishing.

Hyman, R. 1983. 'Trade Unions: Structure, Policies, Politics.' Ed. Bain, G.S. *Industrial Relations in Britain*. Oxford: Blackwell.

Industrial Relations Review and Report. 1985. 'Nissan: A Deal for Teamwork and Flexibility?'. 344: May, 2–7.

Institute of Personnel Management. 1987. *Annual Report*. London: IPM.

Kahn-Freund, O. 1983. *Labour and the Law*. 3rd edn. Ed. Davies, P. and Freedland, M. London: Steven.

Keep, E. forthcoming. 'Corporate Training Strategies – the Vital Component?'. Ed. Storey, J. *New Perspectives on Human Resource Management*. London: Routledge & Kegan Paul.

Kochan, T.A., Katz, H.C. and McKersie, R.B. 1986. *The Transformation of American Industrial Relations*. New York: Basic Books.

Legge, K. 1978. *Power, Innovation and Problem-Solving in Personnel Management*. London: McGraw-Hill.

—— and Exley, M. 1975. 'Authority, Ambiguity and Adaptation: The Personnel Specialist's Dilemma'. *Industrial Relations Journal*, 6, 51–65.

Long, P. 1984. 'Would You Put Your Daughter in Personnel?'. *Personnel Management*, April, 16–20.

McCarthy, W.E.J. and Ellis, N. 1973. *Management By Agreement: An Alternative to the Industrial Relations Act*. London: Hutchinson.

McGregor, D.C. 1960. *The Human Side of the Enterprise*. New York: McGraw-Hill.

Mackay, L. and Torrington, D. 1986. *The Changing Nature of Personnel Management*. London: IPM.

Marginson, P., Edwards, P.K., Marten, R., Purcell, J. and Sisson, K. 1988. *Beyond the Workplace: Managing Industrial Relations in the Multi-Establishment Enterprise*. Oxford: Blackwell.

Marsh, A. 1983. *Employee Relations Policy and Decision Making*. Aldershot: Gower.

Maslow, A. 1943. 'A Theory of Human Motivation'. *Psychological Development*, 50, 370–96.

Miller, K. 1975. *Psychological Testing*. Aldershot: Gower.

Millerson, G. 1964. *The Qualifying Associations*. London: Routledge & Kegan Paul.

Millward, N. and Stevens, M. 1986. *British Workplace Industrial Relations 1980–1984: the DE/PSI/ACAS Surveys*. Aldershot: Gower.

Niven, M. 1967. *Personnel Management 1913–1963*. London: IPM.

Okochi, K., Karsh, B. and Levine, S.B. Eds. 1973. *Workers and Employers in Japan: The Japanese Employment System*. Tokyo: University of Tokyo Press.

Peach, L. 1983. 'Employee Relations at IBM'. *Employee Relations*, 3, 17–20.

Porter, L.W., Lawler, E.E. and Hackman, J.R. 1975. *Behaviour in Organisations*. Tokyo: McGraw-Hill Kogakusha.

Purcell, J. 1986. 'Employee Relations Autonomy within a Corporate Culture'. *Personnel Management*, February, 38–40.

—— and Gray, A. 1986. 'Corporate Personnel Departments and the Management of Industrial Relations: Two Case Studies in Ambiguity'. *Journal of Management Studies*, 23, 205–23.

— and Sisson, K. 1983. 'Strategies and Practice in the Management of Industrial Relations'. *Industrial Relations in Britain*. Ed. Bain, G.S. Oxford: Blackwell, 95–120.

—, Marginson, P., Edwards, P.K. and Sisson, K. 1987. 'The Industrial Relations Practices of Multi-Plant Foreign Owned Firms'. *Industrial Relations Journal*, 18: Summer, 130–7.

Robinson, D. 1970. 'External and Internal Labour Markets'. *Local Labour Markets and Wage Structures*. Ed. Robinson, D. London: Gower, 28–67.

Roeber, J. 1975. *Social Change at Work: the ICI Weekly Staff Agreement*. London: Duckworth.

Rogaly, J. 1977. *Grunwick*. Harmondsworth: Penguin.

Scott, J. 1979. *Corporations, Classes and Capitalism*. London: Hutchinson.

Sisson, K. and Scullion, H. 1985. 'Putting the Corporate Personnel Department in its Place'. *Personnel Management*, December, 36–9.

Streeck, W. 1985. 'Industrial Relations and Industrial Change in the Motor Industry: An International View'. Public Lecture, University of Warwick: Industrial Relations Research Unit.

Taylor, F. W. 1911. *The Principles of Scientific Management*. New York: Harper.

Thomason, G. 1981. *A Textbook of Personnel Management*. London: IPM.

Thomson, J. D. 1967. *Organizations in Action*. New York: McGraw-Hill.

Thurley, K. 1981. 'Personnel Management in the UK – a Case for Urgent Treatment?'. *Personnel Management*, August, 24–8.

— 1982. 'The Japanese Model: Practice, Reservations and Surprising Opportunities'. *Personnel Management*, February, 36–9.

Torrington, D. and Chapman, J. 1983. *Personnel Management*. London: Prentice-Hall International.

— and Hall, L. 1987. *Personnel Management: a New Approach*. London: Prentice-Hall International.

Tse, K. 1985. *Marks and Spencer*. Oxford: Pergamon.

Tyson, S. 1979. 'Specialists in Ambiguity: Personnel Management as an Occupation'. PhD thesis, University of London.

— 1980. 'Taking Advantage of Ambiguity'. *Personnel Management*, February, 45–8.

— and Fell, A. 1986. *Evaluating the Personnel Function*. London: Hutchinson.

Vroom, V. 1964. *Work and Motivation*. New York: Wiley.

Watson, T. J. 1977. *The Personnel Managers*. London: Routledge & Kegan Paul.

Whittaker, A. 1986. 'Managerial Strategy and Industrial Relations: A Case Study of Plant Relocation'. *Journal of Management Studies*, 23: November, 656–78.

Williamson, O.E. 1975. *Markets and Hierarchies: Analysis and Anti-Trust Implications*. New York: Free Press.

# 2 Personnel Management in Transition?

*Keith Sisson*

However personnel management in Britain is characterized, one thing is very clear. In recent years British management has come under increasing pressure to change, and the main source of this pressure has been the product market. The nature and extent of the competition facing British management, especially in manufacturing, have transformed in recent years. A second source of pressure has been the government. The election of three successive Conservative governments, in 1979, 1983 and 1987, committed to a radical change in the management of the economy, has not only brought about a very different political context, but has also had a direct and immediate impact on the public sector where, privatization notwithstanding, more than one quarter of the labour-force is employed. Together, these changes in the economic and political context have, in turn, had a dramatic impact on the labour-market and the trade unions which organize it.

Having considered the implications of these changes in more detail, this chapter goes on to consider whether personnel management in Britain is in a state of transition. Particular attention is given to two related themes which appear in discussions of what is happening to personnel management in Britain: the emergence of the so-called 'flexible' organization, and the adoption of a 'human resource management' approach. The fourth section considers the changes in the role and status of personnel managers and the fifth and final section reflects on likely developments in the foreseeable future.

## THE CHANGING CONTEXT

### The Economic Context

Clearly Britain has always been involved in competitive markets. In recent years, however, the nature of this competition has changed and its intensity has grown enormously. One consideration has been the rise of a number of countries – first Japan, and then South Korea, Taiwan and others – able to take advantage of modern technology and relatively cheap labour, to challenge the industrial supremacy of the traditional producer countries. Another has been the development of wider markets such as the European Economic Community; trade barriers have come down and inward investment is encouraged to take advantage of the larger market. Above all, there has been the growth of a truly international economy. Technology has played a part: improved communications, for example, have drastically reduced the time and expense involved in trading between continents. The major factor, however, has been the emergence of a large number of multinational companies which operate on a world-wide basis. Production, in particular, is increasingly organized with the world market in view, and is located where it is most cost-effective; while multiple-sourcing of products and services, whereby one unit replicates the output of others, is used to encourage internal competition in the drive for maximum performance. On top of these came a number of further factors: the breakdown of a number of international trade treaties, such as Bretton Woods, providing for stable exchange rates; major economic shocks such as the surge in oil prices in 1973; and the depression of the late 1970s and early 1980s – all of which have served to increase the volatility of trading.

Britain has not been unique in experiencing these competitive pressures, but the impact has been especially marked. Britain, relatively speaking, is an extremely open economy, reflecting the domination of market principles inherited from earlier times; the methods used by some of our EEC partners to deal with the threat of Japanese imports, for example, are noticeable by their absence in Britain. Manufacturing, in particular, is heavily rooted in mature industries, such as steel, engineering and shipbuilding, and textiles, where competition has been especially sensitive to price. Traditional methods of working, and low levels of investment and technology have contributed to comparatively poor performance; while the inferior training provision for both management and workforce has made it especially difficult to move up-market as manufacturers in some of these industries in other countries have been able to do (see, for example, the discussion of the British and West German experience in Streeck, 1985). The abolition of exchange controls in 1979 also opened up the possibility of alternative and competing overseas investment opportunities.

In their study of the reaction of US employers to the changes in and intensification of international competition, Cappelli and McKersie (1987: 443–4) suggest that management has responded in two ways. One approach might be described as 'asset management'. This involves shifting the firm's capital away from high-cost/low-profit businesses to those that are more profitable; in the extreme case it means selling all or part of the business and transferring the assets to an alternative line of business in the same or another country. The second approach involves the attempt to improve the 'value added' produced by employees. In this case the assets are not moved, but attempts are made to reform existing practices and arrangements either with or without new technology and production systems.

British employers, like their US counterparts, have pursued both these strategies. The evidence for asset management is very clear. There have been large-scale closures, divestment and diversification. An increasing number of companies have taken advantage of the abolition of exchange controls in 1979 to invest overseas. One recent study (Mervis and Co., 1986), for example, estimates that in North America alone British-owned companies made 812 acquisitions in the period 1978–85. Indeed, although it is difficult to show – changes in the Companies Act of 1981 mean that companies no longer have to give a breakdown of their employment by country – it is highly likely that many large British-owned companies now employ more people overseas than they do in the UK.

In the case of the value-added approach, many of the changes have been production driven and have been designed to cut costs. In some cases new technology has been introduced, such as computer aided manufacture (CAM) and computer aided design (CAD) systems. In others, new systems of production scheduling have been introduced; 'just-in-time' (JIT) systems, which are designed to achieve substantial reductions in stock and inventories, is one of the best known examples (for further details, see Hill, 1985).

In terms of the impact on personnel management, the introduction of such systems has not simply meant cost-cutting or pressure on numbers. To paraphrase Paul Roots (1986), who was the Industrial Relations Director of the Ford Motor Company, British management is increasingly being obliged to undertake a far more thorough-going review of their approach to the management of people. Substantial reductions in numbers – more than 40 per cent in some 5 years in the case of his own organization – have meant that managers simply cannot carry on in the same way. Reductions in staff, often accompanied by the introduction of new technology or new production methods, mean that there is a need for greater flexibility: both functional (skills, tasks and jobs) and numerical (patterns of working time and new forms of employment). Such flexibility has profound implications for training and development, pay and reward structures, communication systems and so on. As will be argued in the following section, above all, the package of changes requires a great deal more than compliance from employees: it requires their co-operation and commitment.

If the pressures to improve value-added in some organizations might be described as *production* or *cost* driven, in others they have been *marketing* driven. Good examples here might be Jaguar Cars and British Airways. The problem which Jaguar Cars faced was not so much one of cost but of quality; sales, especially in the lucrative North American market, had declined because of the poor reputation for reliability that the once-famous marque had acquired in the 1970s. The problem which British Airways faced was to maintain and, if possible, increase the number of passengers on its aircraft; competition from other international carriers placed a premium on customer service. In both cases, then, the achievement of better quality or improved service demanded substantial investments in communications and training, and then, perhaps even more critically, on changing the style of managers.

## The Political Context

Important though the changes in the economic context have been, they are not the only consideration. Throughout the post-Second World War period successive governments, accepting the argument that 'man-mismanagement' – to borrow a phrase from Fox (1974) – has been a significant contributory factor in Britain's relatively poor economic performance, have applied both direct and indirect pressures in an attempt to bring about change. Indirect methods have included, among many others, the setting-up of a Royal Commission and such quasi-government agencies as the Advisory, Conciliation and Arbitration Service (ACAS), National Economic Development Council (NEDC), the Manpower Services Commission (MSC), the Equal Opportunities Commission (EOC), the Commission for Racial Equality (CRE), and, in the 1960s and 1970s, different types of pay review bodies – all of which have produced reports and publications seeking to change some aspect of the management of people. The main direct pressure has taken the form of legislation. Indeed, it was to legislation on contracts of employment, training, redundancy, discipline and dismissal, equal opportunities, health and safety, pensions, trade unions and collective bargaining, that many personnel managers attributed the increase in the importance of their function in the 1970s (Brown, 1981: 33) and the 1980s (Millward and Stevens, 1986: 41).

It was the return of the Conservative government in 1979, however, that brought about a radical change in the political context. Anxious to avoid the failures of the past, the Conservative governments have sought to introduce an enterprise culture in which individuals and organizations, rather than governments, are held responsible for economic performance. The Keynesian demand management policies, which had dominated successive government economic policies throughout the post-war period, have been firmly rejected in favour of a monetarist approach. The maintenance of full employment is no longer the major policy objective; levels of employment are to find their own or 'natural' level through the operation of the forces of demand and supply in the labour-market. Tripartitism, under which governments had sought to involve the participation of representatives of employers and trade unions, is no more. Having identified excess money as the major cause of inflation in the economy, the government's chief policy instrument has become the control of the money supply. The public sector borrowing requirement (PSBR), in particular, is seen as a main target and every attempt is being made to reduce it through cuts in public expenditure.

In its role of legislator, the government has effectively abandoned the commitment of its predecessors to collective bargaining as the most effective method of determining pay and conditions; trade unions – and the collective bargaining for which they are responsible – are seen as major factors in the stickiness of the response of wages to changes in demand and supply. Thus, as Lewis (1986: 5–11) points out in the second volume in this series, the 1980 Employment Act repealed the provisions of the 1976 Employment Protection Act for a procedure for trade union recognition and did away with the same Act's support for the arbitration of terms and conditions; following its denouncement of two International Labour Organization Conventions – No. 94 dealing with labour clauses in public contracts, and No. 26 dealing with minimum wage-fixing – the government also repealed the statutory Fair Wages

Resolution of 1946 and limited the scope of wage council orders. Both the 1980 and the 1982 Employment Acts reinforced the right of individuals to dissociate from trade union membership and imposed stringent requirements for maintaining a closed shop or union membership agreement. There have also been attempts to limit the ability of trade unions to mount industrial action in support of collective bargaining. Following the 1980 and 1982 Employment Acts, trade unions no longer enjoy immunity from the common law where there is picketing other than at the place of work; secondary action, action to uphold union- and recognition-only practices, and 'official' industrial action which has not been approved by secret ballot, have also been outlawed. The definition of a trade dispute on which the immunities depend has been narrowed as well.

In order to deregulate or free up the labour-market, the government has also reduced the nature and scope of individual employment protection available under previous legislation. Thus, the eligibility of employees to claim unfair dismissal and to apply to industrial tribunals has been severely restricted – with the service qualification being increased from six to twelve months and then to two years; the burden of proving reasonableness has been shifted from the employer; and the 'basic' award component has been restricted. In addition, the entitlement to statutory guaranteed pay has been restricted, and maternity provisions weakened. Small businesses have also been exempted from certain aspects of the Health and Safety at Work Act and the long-standing limitations on women's hours of work under the Factories Acts have been repealed (Lewis, 1986: 13–19).

In the case of the nationalized industries, the government has pursued a vigorous policy of privatization. From relatively small beginnings, involving Cable and Wireless, and Amersham International, the government has moved on to privatize large public sector corporations such as British Telecommunications, British Gas and British Airways. Electricity and Water are to follow shortly. In those sectors where privatization has not yet been deemed appropriate, notably steel, coal, railways and the Post Office, external financial limits have been used to ensure substantial cost-cutting and improvements in efficiency. In the case of steel, in 1980, and coal, in 1985–6, the government has been prepared to countenance major industrial conflicts as part of the process of restructuring.

The role of the government as the good or model employer has also effectively been abandoned in both the public services and the remaining public enterprises in favour of a more contingent approach. Thus in the public services, the civil service, local government, and the National Health Service, the government has used the system of cash limits, first introduced in the 1970s to control public expenditure, to bring about changes in working practices; budgets have not been maintained in real terms and in some cases reduced at the same time as services have to be maintained or increased. Second, local authorities and health service authorities in particular have been required to tender and, where appropriate, to subcontract to the private sector such activities as refuse collection, catering or cleaning, previously performed by their direct employees. Third, the government has sponsored a number of specific initiatives in an attempt to improve performance. In the civil service and the educational sector, for example, there has been the introduction of appraisal and merit pay. In the National Health Service, there has been the introduction of general managers at unit, district and regional levels following the recommendations of the Griffiths Report in 1984. A National Health Management Board with a personnel director has also been established.

## Trade Unions and the Labour Market

The most obvious impact of the changing economic and political environment has been the very considerable increase in unemployment which seems only likely to fall with the dramatic decline in the number of young people entering the labour market in the 1990s. Throughout the 1970s unemployment averaged less than 1 million, or 4 per cent of the labour-force; throughout the period 1982–6 it has averaged 3 million or approximately 12 per cent of the labour-force – and this does not take into account changes in the definition of unemployment, which probably excludes some 300,000 or so, plus young people on the Youth Training Scheme and other community programmes (see table 2.3 in the appendix to this chapter).

There have also been very significant and interrelated structural changes in the patterns of employment of those in work (see tables 2.4 to 2.9 in the appendix to this chapter). One is the shift in employment from manufacturing to services; the share of manufacturing employment fell from 28.0 per cent in 1980 to 22.2 per cent in 1986, while the share of the service sector grew from 60.4 to 67.0 per cent over the same period. A second change has been the shift from manual to non-manual occupations; in 1981 the balance between the two categories shifted in favour of non-manual workers for the first time. A third change has been in the gender of the labour-force: in 1951 women accounted for only 33.2 per cent of the labour-force; by 1985 that figure had grown to 44.3 per cent with further increases projected until 1990 and beyond, following the substantial decline in the number of young people entering the labour-force anticipated in the early 1990s. The decline in public sector employment is also beginning to show up in the statistics; its share fell from 29.2 per cent in 1980 to 26.6 per cent in 1986, with further falls likely as the government's privatization campaign proceeds. Further details can be found in the tables in the appendix to this chapter.

Trade union membership, which was on the increase throughout the 1970s, has also declined significantly in the early 1980s. Absolute union membership for 1986 has been estimated to be of the order of 10.3 million, whereas in 1979 it was nearly 13.3 million; the density of membership, the proportion of the eligible labour-force in membership has declined from 54.4 per cent in 1979 to 41.6 per cent in 1986. The main losses have been suffered by unions whose members have been in declining occupations, such as the Transport and General Workers, and the General Municipal and Boilermakers, or those, such as the National Union of Miners and the National Union of Railwaymen, whose industry or sector is in decline. By contrast, unions such as the Banking, Insurance and Finance Union have considerably increased their membership.

Again, further details will be found in the appendix to this chapter (tables 2.10–2.12).

## TOWARDS THE FLEXIBLE ORGANIZATION?

One of the two related themes that appear in discussions of what is happening or supposed to be happening to personnel management in the light of this changing context is the emergence of what might be termed the 'flexible' organization. Handy (1984: 79–89) has written in terms of the 'federal' organization (in which there is greater decentralization), the 'contractual' organization (in which there is a move from wages to fees), and the 'professional' organization (in which there is an increase in the number of highly qualified experts and co-ordinators). Others, notably Atkinson (1984), have suggested that the labour-force may come to be divided into 'core' and 'periphery' groups. In this case three types of flexibility are said to be involved: numerical flexibility – under which the employer increases the non-standard forms of employment, such as temporary, part-time and subcontracting work, and/or varies the hours of 'core' workers; functional or task flexibility – under which the employer seeks to break down traditional demarcations, usually among 'core' workers, and to move towards greater interchangeability between tasks and jobs; and financial flexibility – under which the employer seeks to relate a greater element in the pay packet to performance through bonus systems and profit-sharing.

Certainly there is a growing body of evidence to confirm that, even though the large multi-establishment enterprise continues to dominate the British economy (Channon, 1973, 1978; Hill and Pickering, 1986; Marginson et al., 1988; see also table 2.1 in the appendix to this chapter), there has been a very considerable decentralization internally. As chapter 3 will explain in greater detail, in an attempt to deal with the problems of accountability and control in the large and complex organizations that continue to dominate the British economy, many managements have abandoned the highly centralized functional structures which, along with the loose 'holding company' structure, were the characteristic forms of internal organization of the past. In their place they have introduced arrangements that emphasize the separation of strategic from operating management, the disaggregation of the enterprise into quasi-independent divisions and business units, and the decentralization of responsibility for day-to-day operations.

Similar developments have taken place in the public sector. British Rail and the Post Office, for example, have been divided into a number of profit-responsible sectors or divisions. In the National Health Service, the introduction of 'general managers' has involved a considerable devolution of cost responsibility to individual units such as hospitals. In schools, head-teachers are being asked to take similar responsibilities for their budgets.

There would also appear to have been considerable developments in numerical, functional and financial flexibility. In the case of numerical flexibility, increases are reported, first, in the non-standard forms of working such as part-time, temporary and subcontract working (Atkinson and Meager, 1986; Marginson et al., 1988); and, second, in flexible working arrangements such as 'minimum–maximum' hours contracts, which predefine the range of hours to be worked within the day or week, and 'annual hours' agreements, which guarantee annual salaries in return for the freedom to vary the number of hours worked in a given period within the scope of the standard working hours of the year as a whole (Brewster and Connock, 1985: 60–81). In the case of functional or task flexibility, a wide range of initiatives are reported: the 'combination' of jobs – with the elimination of differences within and between crafts; 'team' working involving interchangeability and flexibility between jobs; 'balanced labour-force' techniques designed to deal with shortages and surpluses by having workers in one craft or occupation supplement those in another; the ending of 'trade' supervision under which craftsmen would accept instructions only from a supervisor who had completed an apprenticeship in the same trade; and a breakdown of the distinction between blue- and white-collar jobs – especially craftsmen and technicians (IRRR, 1984: 2–9). In the case of financial flexibility there appears to have been a considerable increase in the incidence of profit-sharing and share-ownership (Poole, 1986); there has also been a marked increase in the number of 'management buy-outs', under which the managers of a company or a subsidiary buy the equity from the existing shareholders either with a view to maintaining total control or, as is more likely, with a view to a flotation on the Stock Market in two or three years' time (Clutterbuck and Devine, 1987).

One particularly noteworthy development, because it would seem to have considerable potential in the private service sector, is franchising. Instead of owning the subsidiary units or outlets and employing people directly, the parent company subcontracts the operation to an individual or group of individuals who set up their own business. Depending on the size of the operation, these individuals remain self-employed or go on to become direct employers in their own right (Felstead, 1988).

Clearly, then, there have been changes in the direction of the 'flexible' organization, but there is a need to keep them in perspective. For example, the decentralization that appears to have taken place in many large multi-establishment enterprises is nowhere as straightforward or as far-reaching in its implications as may at first appear. The autonomy that the managers of individual units are now supposed to have is not unqualified. Certainly unit managers may appear to have greater autonomy as far as operating decisions are concerned, but they are not free agents. Even in apparently highly decentralized organizations a framework of planning and budgetary controls is laid down or agreed with enterprise or divisional headquarters, and unit managers are held strictly to account for their financial performance (Goold and Campbell, 1986; Edwards, 1987). Indeed, units within the same enterprise are increasingly encouraged to compete with one another in ways reminiscent of the internal subcontracting of the nineteenth century. The evidence also suggests that many of the decisions that appear to be taken in the unit emanate from higher levels in the organization (Marginson et al., 1988).

On the face of it, there is also little evidence to suggest major changes within the operating unit. Although cases are reported of a reduction in the number of management tiers, hierarchical structures continue to predominate. As chapter 4 points out, the evidence suggests that relatively few British managements have experimented with new forms of working; autonomous working groups, for example, remain very rare.

Closer inspection of the evidence on numerical flexibility also gives grounds for treating some of the more exaggerated claims with caution. Thus, much of the increase in temporary and part-time working can be explained by the decline of manufacturing and the growth of services, which have always employed large numbers of these types of workers. Also, the increases in subcontracting turn out to be concentrated in areas where it has long been the practice in some organizations to subcontract, such as catering, construction, cleaning, maintenance and transport (Pollert, 1987). Examples of subcontracting in mainstream activities are more rare (Marginson et al., 1988). Similarly, there would appear to be relatively few cases of 'networking', which combines homeworking with self-employment, pioneered by Rank Xerox; and even in this case the numbers are relatively small (Judkins and West, 1982).

Further analysis also suggests that the developments taking place do not necessarily reflect a deliberate strategy of moving towards a 'core' and 'peripheral' labour-force. Much of what is happening, as proponents of the 'core–periphery' model themselves have had to recognize (Atkinson and Meager, 1986), is largely an *ad hoc* reaction to events. Crucially, too, it is beginning to emerge that a number of recent developments reflect 'supply-side' rather than 'demand-side' considerations. In other words, the growth of these non-standard forms of employment does not so much represent a conscious and changing strategy to the employment relationship on the part of British management, much as advocates of the 'core–periphery' model would seem to imply, but a response to changes in the labour supply, especially among young people, and a growing realization of the need to find alternative supplies of labour, in particular from among the ranks of middle-aged married women.

The second area of flexibility – functional or task flexibility – has so far occasioned less controversy, but raises as many problems of interpretation as does numerical flexibility. On the face of it, there have been considerable changes in working practices. Even so, the precise nature and extent of these changes is open to question as are the more radical claims for changes in job structures and job descriptions. Indeed, the detailed study of manufacturing by Cross (IRRR, 1988: 2–10) suggests that relatively little by way of major change has, in fact, taken place. In particular, few managements have moved beyond the amalgamation of some aspects of the work of engineering maintenance crafts; examples of the amalgamation of maintenance and production jobs are extremely rare.

The growth in profit-related pay has also taken place along fairly traditional lines, namely profit-sharing, savings-related share option schemes, executive share option schemes, and Personal Equity Plans under various Finance Acts; the more radical ambitions of the Chancellor of the Exchequer, Nigel Lawson, to make a sizeable element of the pay packet dependent on performance have been frustrated largely by the opposition of management (IRRR, 1986c: 2–6). Moreover, the implications of extending share-ownership to employees are far from obvious. Certainly individual employees might be thought to have a greater stake in the company. But this stake reflects their rights as shareholders and not as employees; and it does not necessarily follow that managers will act any differently from the past. Indeed, for there to be major changes, it would seem necessary for there to be some fusion of shareholder and employee rights involving new forms of decision-making.

## FROM PERSONNEL MANAGEMENT TO HUMAN RESOURCE MANAGEMENT?

Unlike the 'flexible' organization, the second theme in discussions of present trends in personnel management in Britain – the adoption of a human resource management approach – has been received with considerable disquiet by some personnel specialists (see, for example, Armstrong, 1987; Torrington and Hall, 1987: 14–16; Fowler, 1987). A major problem, as Guest (1987: 506) points out, is that the term 'human resource management' can mean very different things to different people: a simple retitling – perhaps designed to give the personnel specialist greater status; an attempt to reflect a reorganization of the approach to personnel management; or a very particular approach such as might be associated with the 'human relations' type discussed in chapter 1. It can even be used, regardless of the specific policies involved, to refer simply to a more strategic and integrated approach to personnel management.

At first sight, the language and concepts involved, certainly in the case of the particular approach associated with the 'human relations' type, would appear to be very much at odds with the harsh realities of highly competitive and unregulated labour-markets in which individuals are going to have to live by their wits and fend for themselves. Thus, to paraphrase Guest (1987: 507), responsibility for personnel management, instead of being primarily relegated to specialist managers, is assumed by senior line managers. Indeed, the management of people becomes a key, if not *the* key element in the strategic planning of the business; and attempts are made to integrate policies both with one another and with business planning more generally. By implication, a different time-span is involved; whereas personnel management might be said to deal with the short term, human resource management is concerned with the long term. There is also a shift in focus as well as time-span. The main emphasis is on management–employee relations rather than management–trade union relations; and the objective is to maximize the commitment of employees through the adoption of organic and devolved structures in which the individual is encouraged to develop the habits of self-discipline and initiative.

One explanation for the discrepancy, bearing in mind the quote from Braverman in chapter 1, is that the human resource management approach is simply a piece of ideology designed to make unilateral management action more palatable; if employees can be persuaded that the organization really cares and has their interest at heart, then they are more likely to let management have its way. In similar vein, it might be argued that the human resource management approach is essentially anti-union; and even if those adopting it do not intend to withdraw recognition from trade unions, nonetheless the effect will be to undermine the collectivism on which trade unions and collective bargaining so much depend. After all, as proponents of this interpretation point out, in North America the approach has come to be associated, first and foremost, with a strategy of union avoidance.

Even so, these interpretations would not appear to be the complete explanation. Paradoxical as it may seem, the implication of many of the changes outlined in the previous section is that compliance is no longer enough and, more than ever before, management really does need the commitment of a larger number of its employees, albeit not necessarily the majority (Walton, 1985).

The introduction of the 'just-in-time' system of production offers a good illustration of the point. As Tailby and Turnbull (1987) have observed, the introduction of this system requires not only fundamental changes in the organization of work – the exact quantity of raw materials, components and subassemblies, all of uniform quality, have to be detailed 'just-in-time' for the next stage – but also changes in the practice of personnel management. In particular, indirect tasks, such as routine maintenance and responsibility for quality, have to be allocated to direct workers, with considerable implications for training, payment and supervision. Similar changes have to be made in the operation of suppliers as well. The overall effect is to bring about a set of relationships that are much more mutually interdependent than in the past. The exercise of initiative becomes essential. This explains why the idea of the neo-human relations approach would appear, many years after it was first developed, to be beginning to be taken seriously in some organizations.

As far as evidence for the approach is concerned, retitling is certainly very fashionable. Recent examples of organizations appointing 'Human Resources' Directors, as opposed to 'Personnel' Directors or 'Employee Relations' Directors, include British Airways, the engineering companies, GKN, TI and Whitbread (brewing, public houses and restaurants). As the next section will consider in more detail, there is also recent survey evidence (Mackay and Torrington, 1986: 164–5) to confirm some of the well-publicized examples, such as in the then-British Leyland, of a shift in the responsibility for the handling of personnel issues from specialist to line managers. A greater emphasis on management–employee relations, as opposed to management–trade union relations, is also evident. As chapters 6 and 7 will show, more organizations appear to be using selection testing and appraisal, and manual as well as non-manual workers are affected. In pay systems, too, as chapter 11 will argue, there is more emphasis on the individual. Especially significant, as it would appear to be a departure from a long-established practice of 'the rate for the job', is the introduction of merit pay based on systematic performance or appraisal. As chapter 12 will discuss, in a number of companies this development has been closely associated with changes in the status of the individual employee following the harmonization of the terms and conditions of manual and non-manual employees; and, albeit in a relatively small number of cases, including those of Cummins Engines, Pilkington (the glass manufacturers) and Whitbread, there has even been the introduction of fully-integrated single status salary structures (IRRR, 1986b: 2–7).

Developments in participation and involvement, which will be discussed in chapters 14, 15 and 16, also suggest a greater focus on the individual. On the face of it, many British managements seem no longer prepared to communicate solely through the trade union channel. One particularly noteworthy development, because it also has important implications for the role of the first line managers, which will be discussed in chapter 9, has been the growth in face-to-face forms of communication such as 'team briefing'. The Industrial Society alone claims to have helped no less than 400–500 organizations to introduce team briefing in recent years (IRRR, 1986a: 2–9). A second development has been the growth in direct forms of participation such as 'quality circles'. Here too, recent estimates suggest a very considerable growth from a handful of organizations in the late 1970s to at least 400 in 1985 (IDS, 1985: 1–12).

Management–trade union relations also appear to be undergoing change. Although few British managements appear to be taking advantage of the economic situation to withdraw recognition from trade unions, as chapter 16 points out, there has been a considerable increase in the tendency to consult with trade unions rather than to regulate matters jointly. In particular, so-called 'new-style' (sometimes known as 'no strike' or 'single union') agreements have received considerable publicity (Bassett, 1986). As the descriptions suggest, such arrangements have involved the recognition of a single trade union and the introduction of machinery to prohibit industrial action. This usually involves an exhaustive disputes procedure, including a final stage in which an arbitrator is required to choose between the final negotiating positions of the two parties.

Here too, then, there have been changes. Several notes of caution have to be introduced, however, if there is to be any realistic appraisal of what is taking place. Even a moment's thought serves as a reminder that organizations making such changes are the exception rather than the rule. The number of managements reported to have introduced single status arrangements or new style agreements is extremely small. Impressive though they may appear to be at first sight, the figures for team briefing and quality circles have also to be kept in proportion: set against the total number of establishments – 11,000 in manufacturing alone – the 400 or 500 organizations introducing these initiatives are a small minority.

It is also difficult to say whether these and other changes are being introduced as part of an integrated approach, to which senior line managers are committed, or whether they are essentially piecemeal reactions to changing economic circumstances. It is one thing, for example, to introduce team briefing as part of an overall approach designed to secure the commitment of employees, such as would appear to be the case in Jaguar, Grattans (in mail order) and others (NEDC/MSC, 1987). It is quite another if it is done because it is the 'flavour of the month' or because the organization is going through a particularly difficult period in the market-place and the management hopes that the 'bad' news will help persuade employees to moderate their next pay claim.

One recent survey (Marginson et al., 1988), for example, found that although a significant number of large enterprises claimed to have an overall policy or approach to the management of people, less than one half put it in writing and less than a quarter gave copies to their employees. Questioned further, few managers could describe the policy in adequate terms, while subsequent analysis could find little correspondence between descriptions of the policy or approach and what was reported to happen in practice.

Perhaps the biggest single reason for questioning whether the human resource management approach is being widely adopted, however, arises when the issues of training and development are considered. Chapters 8, 9 and 10 will present evidence from a clutch of recent reports to suggest that, with very rare exceptions, British management continues to give training and development relatively low priority and undertake little of it. Furthermore, it is not simply operator training that is being neglected; many British organizations, it emerges, make comparatively little provision for the training and development of their managers who might have been seen as a prime target for the human resource management type of approach.

As chapter 8 points out, despite the emphasis which has been placed on equal opportunities in recent years, the levels of training provision for women are especially poor. Recent research suggests that Britain's record on training for clerical workers, of whom some three-quarters are women, is extremely poor compared with that of other countries in terms of both quality and quantity and data published by the Equal Opportunities Commission suggests that of those 16–18 year-olds given day release by the employers, only one in five was female.

In any evaluation of current trends it is tempting to offset the deficiencies in the training record of British management against the initiatives being taken in other areas. Yet training and development, it can be argued, are of a very different order of magnitude. It is not simply that the organization that does not train is likely to find itself dependent on the vagaries of the external labour-market, as many are beginning to find even with the record levels of unemployment. The evidence of the international comparisons quoted in chapter 1 would seem to suggest that the organization which does train has considerable incentive to develop the many other complementary aspects of human resource management, if only to maximize the return on its investment. By contrast, the organization that does little training and development would appear to have scarcely any incentive to do so. Furthermore, the 'excellence' literature (see, for example, Peters and Waterman, 1982; Peters and Austin, 1985; Kanter, 1984) would seem to imply that if the organization is seen by its employees to be investing in training and development, the message that it views people as the most important resource is likely to be taken seriously. Indeed, it is the structuring of attitudes, rather than the acquisition of specific skills, made possible by training and development that is seen as important for success by the companies quoted in this literature. Again, by contrast, the organization that does little training and development would appear to have far greater difficulty in convincing employees of the seriousness of its commitment and hence in winning their loyalty.

## THE CHANGING ROLE AND STATUS OF PERSONNEL MANAGERS

In view of the occupational interest involved, it is perhaps not surprising that there has been considerable debate not only about the impact of the changing context on personnel management as a set of activities, but also about the implications for the role and status of specialist personnel managers. Here a major problem in interpreting the different viewpoints arises from the dominance of the prescriptive tradition discussed in chapter 1. Time and time again, what appears at first sight to be a difference of fact turns out to be a difference of value judgement and reflects whether the result is seen to be 'good' or 'bad'. Thus, those such as Torrington and his colleagues (Torrington and Hall, 1987: 14–18; MacKay and Torrington, 1986: 175–80; Torrington, forthcoming, 1989), who might be said to incline to the 'generalist' or 'professional' model of personnel management, would appear to see many of the developments as a threat, especially those associated with human resource management. Those such as Brewster and Connock (1985: 160–2), Tyson and Fell (1986: 132–6), and Armstrong (1987), however, who regard the role as more varied and complex, see them as bringing opportunities.

A second problem is that, again at first sight, much of the evidence appears to be in conflict. Thus, as Legge (1988) points out in her survey of surveys, there is evidence to support both what she calls 'the fall of personnel management' and the 'business as before' arguments. In the case of the 'fall of personnel management' argument, it is possible to find case study evidence (Manning, 1983; Purcell, 1985; Purcell and Gray, 1986; Storey, 1987) consistent with the view that, with the changing economic and political climate, and the rise of the 'macho manager', the position of personnel managers has been considerably undermined. In the case of the 'business as before' argument, it is possible to point to the survey evidence (Millward and Stevens, 1986: 20–3; Marginson et al., 1988) to suggest that there has been relatively little change in the representation of personnel (apart, perhaps, from a decline in board level representation) and, for that matter, trade union representation. Even the influence of personnel appears to be maintained (Millward and Stevens, 1986: 45; Marginson et al., 1988: 60–3), albeit within the relatively narrow area of management–trade union relations.

As Legge (1988) recognizes, in fact, there is no conflict of evidence: the reality is that in some organizations personnel managers have experienced a substantial reduction in their influence in the way the 'fall of personnel management suggests', whereas as in others it is a case of 'business as before'. Much depends, as in the case of the flexible organization and the human resource management approach discussed in the previous sections, on the specific situation. Certainly business strategy and organization structure, which is discussed in more detail in chapter 3, are one important set of considerations (Sisson and Scullion, 1985; Marginson et al., 1988). The role of personnel managers in the single business 'critical function' type organizations, especially at divisional and central headquarters, is likely to be very different from that of personnel managers in the highly diversified multi divisional or 'M' form type. Size and ownership are another set of considerations; the size of establishment is important in explaining both the presence and the qualifications of workplace personnel managers (Millward and Stevens, 1986: 23–7); and foreign-owned companies are more likely to have qualified personnel managers sitting on the main board and involved in a wider range of human resource management-type policies, than their British-owned counterparts (Purcell et al., 1987). Industrial relations history is also important. It is difficult, for example, to understand the role played by personnel managers in the engineering industry without taking into account the long-standing practice of multi-employer bargaining through the Engineering Employers' Federation coupled with a highly decentralized system of workplace bargaining involving local management and shop stewards.

Thus, it is in manufacturing and, in particular, in engineering that some of the significant developments associated with the 'fall of personnel management' argument have been taking place. One development (see, for example, Millward and Stevens, 1986: 45; Storey, 1987: 22–4), is that the initiative in personnel matters has shifted from the personnel manager to the line manager. Common to many organizations, whether they are simply reacting to the economic situation or undertaking more wide-ranging change, is the assumption or re-assumption by first line managers of responsibility for such matters as absence, appraisal, discipline, grievances, which had gravitated to the personnel department. At workplace level, it means that line managers rather than personnel managers of the 'contract manager' type take overall responsibility and in some cases take the lead in negotiations with shop stewards. At the company level in those organizations which are inclining towards the 'human resource management approach', it can mean senior line managers and even the chief executive take the initiative in chairing personnel policy committees, and are identified with programmes of major change such as 'customer care' and 'working with pride' campaigns.

In some organizations the talk is of the line, rather than personnel, 'owning' the 'people' problem. Storey (1987: 16–17) gives two graphic examples which are both taken from the engineering industry. In one case the manufacturing director continually tells his people, 'the line manager is king' and plans are afoot to have all the specialist functions, including engineering and personnel, report directly to the production manager. In the second case, production managers are quite clear in stating that the 'working with pride' campaign is more acceptable because it emanates from the manufacturing director and not his personnel counterpart.

Paralleling this development is the closer integration of the personnel manager with line managers. Again, a common development, regardless of the extent of the overall changes, is that personnel specialists should be 'managers first and personnel people second' (Mackay and Torrington, 1986: 162); by implication the notion of the personnel specialist somehow or other acting as an intermediary between management and workforce is being firmly rejected – if ever, indeed, this really was the case. In some organizations it can mean a great deal more. At workplace level, it can mean the personnel manager becoming a fully-accepted member of the management team with a shared responsibility for general management. At company level, it can mean the personnel manager assuming the role of the internal consultant. Even if he or she is not a member of the main board – and many are not members of the board even though they may have the title 'director' (Marginson et al., 1988: 56–7) – they are likely to be working very closely with the chief executive and directors and becoming involved in the strategic management of the business; they are likely to be involved in the provision of a consultancy service to both line and personnel specialists in subsidiary divisions and businesses. Their influence is likely to be especially strong, as the previous chapter pointed out, where they are intimately involved in management succession and development.

Outside manufacturing, notably in the large 'critical function' type organizations in retailing and in services more generally, these changes will be noticeable by their absence. Few, if any, recognize trade unions other than in respect of their distribution of workers and so the 'contracts manager' is a very rare species. Personnel managers are either 'architects' or 'clerks of the works'. Similarly, the notion that line managers should not be primarily responsible for personnel, or that personnel managers should not be fully integrated with line management would be met with incredulity: it was ever thus, many would say, in their organization.

Changes in the role of personnel managers, if they have taken place in these organizations at all, have had little to do with the economic and political context, and much more to do with some of the underlying trends and developments in the nature of personnel work. One, the greater complexity and fragmentation of personnel work, is double-edged in its implications. To begin with, it manifests itself in a growth in the demand for experts – in compensation, communications, management development, pensions administration and relocation, as well as some of the more traditional specialisms such as selection, training and employee relations. Typically, for example, even where the headquarters staff of the large multi-establishment enterprise may be small, it is likely to be divided into sections such as 'Employee Relations', 'Training and Development' and 'Compensation and Benefits'. The corollary of this greater specialization, however, is that it often ceases to be cost-effective for the individual organization to employ such specialists directly, and so the use of outside consultants, which has always been extensive in personnel work, is growing (Mackay and Torrington, 1986: 102–3).

Another development is what Tyson (1987: 530) has termed the 'balkanization' of the personnel role. By this he means that the specialist activity of personnel management is not only being subdivided into a variety of different roles or types, but also that they are increasingly relatively self-contained with little, if any, passage between them. In terms of career path, for example, although some 'clerks of the works' and 'contracts' managers' may force themselves into consideration for the post of 'architect', it is doubtful, except where there is graduate entry, if they are in the majority; an identification with relatively low level administrative routine or with 'firefighting' is likely to be seen as a barrier to promotion rather than the necessary steps to be followed. 'Architects', it seems, are increasingly coming from two main sources: either from the ranks of line management – a number of organizations, including ICI, Shell and Unilever, have appointed line rather than personnel managers to the most senior personnel post in recent years; or, as is regularly revealed in the biographies of 'the man of the moment' column in *Personnel Management*, from outside the organization. In Tyson's words,

> Top personnel executives in the 1960s and 1970s were the old retainers, who had served the organization for many years and knew its traditions and decision-making habits. The executive of the 1980s and 1990s is more likely to have short service, and to be expecting to move quickly in and out of different jobs, including consultancy, and line management. (1987: 531)

## CONCLUDING REMARKS

Both the nature and extent of the changes taking place give grounds for questioning whether there has as yet been a radical shift in the practice of personnel management in Britain – it is striking how often the same few organizations are cited as examples of innovation. Even so, the pace of change could begin to quicken. Superficially, the idea of the 'flexible' firm – especially of the 'core–periphery' variety – would appear to have considerable attractions from the employer's point of view. For, at one and the same time, it would appear to enable the employer to satisfy two apparently conflicting objectives necessary to stay competitive: the minimization of costs and the increased investment in employees in order to ensure greater commitment. By reducing the number of permanent employees, an organization can not only keep overhead costs to a minimum, but also concentrate scarce resources on the essential 'core' whose co-operation and commitment it cannot do without.

It is not as simple as this, however. One problem, as Pollert (1987) points out, is that distinguishing between a 'core' and a 'periphery' labour-force is far more difficult than is made out; a group of workers may be 'peripheral' in the sense they possess no specific skills and yet the jobs they perform may be vital to the success of the business because, say, they are in close contact with customers. Subcontracting, in particular, has far fewer benefits in practice than is supposed, which is why employers shifted to permanent employment over the last century. In effect, the main employer loses control over the employment discipline and reward and so on. In theory, control is exercised through the commercial contract with the subcontractor, but this can take some time to work its way through. The opportunity to substitute one subcontractor for another, for example, is not as straightforward as it might seem. The presumption is that it will be possible to find another subcontractor who will provide a better service, but if the main contractor is required to accept tenders on the basis of lowest cost, the chances of this happening are relatively remote. In short, and as some health authorities, for example, have found to their cost, managing a commercial relationship can be far more difficult than managing the employment relationship.

The widespread adoption of the human resource management approach is also far from assured. Certainly relatively few managements seem prepared to take the fundamental step of withdrawing recognition from trade unions. The likely opposition of 'professional' personnel managers is one consideration, but not a major one. The opposition of trade unions is another but, as experience in the USA has shown, not insurmountable. Much more important are the cost implications of such a shift in approach. For, although they may not be fully recognized, the existing situation is not entirely without benefits for managements. Trade unions fulfil a number of important managerial functions; they perform an agency function – management escapes the time-consuming and costly process of dealing with employees individually and separately; they 'voice' the grievances and complaints of employees; and, through the legitimacy they give to procedures, they help to manage discontent and so make a major contribution to discipline.

Attractive though the alternative of doing without trade unions may be in theory, it carries a number of implications. There would have to be radical changes in the style and approach of individual managers; there would have to be substantial investments of time and resources in people management. It is a moot point whether most British managements would be able, let alone willing, to go down this path. Certainly, given the structural considerations outlined in chapter 1 and, in particular, the structure of ownership which militates against taking the long-term view, few, if any, British managements would probably be able to commit themselves to the kind of employment security involved, and certainly not to the 'life-long' employment that has come to be regarded as one of the main pillars of the approach of the large Japanese companies.

Looking to the future, then, there is likely to continue to be considerable variety of practice. Indeed, if anything, the variety is likely to grow; one consideration is the break-up of the dominant public sector model; another is the growth in alternative forms of contracts such as franchising. Thus, to return to chapter 1, there are likely to be a number of organizations practising the human relations approach and their number may grow, although not perhaps as much as some commentators have suggested. The number of organizations practising the consultative approach could also grow if more managements come to terms with the realities described in the previous paragraphs. Most large organizations, however, are likely to continue to be 'opportunistic' or 'pragmatic' in their approach and are unlikely to adopt a dominant or overall philosophy. As for the smaller organizations a number, especially those in high technology industries, may well follow the human resources approach. Far more, however, especially in the service sector, are likely to follow the traditional model. Labour will continue to be treated as a commodity to be hired and fired as appropriate.

It follows from this that the role of personnel managers is also likely to continue to vary from organization to organization and from level to level in the same organization. The 'generalist', of course, will survive. In the smaller enterprises in particular, and in the larger workplaces of the multi-establishment enterprises, size dictates that, if there is going to be a personnel manager, he or she is going to have to be a generalist. Generalists are also likely to continue to dominate the IPM because of the occupational identity and status it gives them. However, despite Torrington's (forthcoming, 1989) vigorous defence in his parallel drawn with the general (medical) practitioner, it is difficult to envisage that the generalist or professional personnel manager will ever be the dominant role model, even if, as chapter 10 discusses, management itself becomes more 'institutionalized' and 'professionalized'. Given the analysis of the previous section, those who make it to senior positions are likely to be 'architects' who have been either line managers or experts in a particular field, while the relatively few generalists who join them will need to demonstrate that they are 'managers first and personnel people second'. Moreover, with the likelihood of line managers playing a far more active role in personnel management, the proportion of the generalists who are essentially clerks of the works is likely to increase with inevitable consequences for the status of this group as a whole. In short, it will be the policies of the organization that determine the role of personnel managers, as it has been in the past, rather than an idealized model of what personnel managers ought to be.

# Appendix

TABLE 2.1 *Establishment size in manufacturing industries in the United Kingdom, 1951–1984*

|  | 1951 | 1979 | 1984 |
|---|---|---|---|
| % of employees working in establishments with: | | | |
| 500 and more employees | 44.3 | 54.1 | 44.9 |
| 1000 and more employees | 30.8 | 40.9 | 31.8 |
| 1500 and more employees | 23.6 | 32.9 | 25.3 |

*Source*: For 1951 the data are from *Census of Production for 1951: Summary Tables* (London: HMSO, 1956) pt. 1, table 4; for 1979 the data are from Business Statistics Office, *Business Monitor: Report on the Census of Production, 1979: Summary Tables*, PA1002 (London: HMSO, 1982), table 6, and for 1984 from ibid. 1984 (London: HMSO, 1987)

TABLE 2.2 *Enterprise size in manufacturing industries, 1958–1984*

| Enterprise size (number of employees) | | 2,000 and over | 5,000 and over | 10,000 and over | 20,000 and over | 50,000 and over |
|---|---|---|---|---|---|---|
| Number of | 1958 | 469 | 180 | 74 | 32 | 8 |
| enterprises | 1979 | 406 | 174 | 83 | 34 | 9 |
|  | 1984 | 282 | 104 | 47 | 18 | 5 |
| Number of | 1958 | 5805 | 3788 | 2224 | 1398 | 467 |
| establishments owned | 1979 | 7911 | 5242 | 3446 | 1995 | 720 |
|  | 1984 | 5581 | 3542 | 1926 | 943 | 289 |
| Proportion of | 1958 | 45.8 | 34.3 | 24.8 | 17.3 | 7.3 |
| employees working | 1979 | 55.6 | 44.7 | 34.9 | 24.4 | 12.7 |
| for these enterprises | 1984 | 44.7 | 33.5 | 24.9 | 16.4 | 7.8 |

*Source*: For 1958, Business Statistics Office, *Historical Record of the Census of Production 1907–1970* (London: HMSO, 1978), table 10; for 1979 the data are from Business Statistics Office, *Business Monitor: Report on the Census of Production 1979: Summary Tables*, PA1002 (London: HMSO, 1982), table 13, and for 1984 from ibid. 1984 (London: HMSO, 1987), table 12

TABLE 2.3 *Employment and unemployment in the United Kingdom, 1948–1995*

| Year | Employment | | Registered unemployment[a] | |
|---|---|---|---|---|
| | Number (*millions*) | Annual average compound growth rate (%) | Number (*millions*) | Rate[b] (%) |
| 1948–68 | 23.6 | 0.6 | 0.3 | 1.4 |
| 1968–79 | 24.5 | 0.2 | 0.9 | 3.5 |
| 1968–70 | 24.4 | −0.1 | 0.5 | 2.2 |
| 1970–73 | 24.3 | 0.3 | 0.7 | 2.7 |
| 1973–79 | 24.6 | 0.3 | 1.1 | 4.2 |
| 1980 | 25.3 | c | 1.7 | 6.9 |
| 1981 | 24.3 | c | 2.4 | 9.9 |
| 1982 | 23.9 | c | 2.8 | 11.4 |
| 1983 | 23.6 | c | 3.0 | 12.4 |
| 1984 | 24.0 | c | 3.0 | 12.5 |
| 1985 | 24.5 | c | 3.2 | 12.9 |
| 1986 | 24.6 | c | 3.2 | 11.1 |
| 1987–90 | 25.6 | 1.5 | 2.6 | 10.3 |
| 1990–92 | 26.3 | 0.6 | 2.3 | 9.1 |
| 1992–95 | 26.6 | 0.4 | 2.2 | 8.7 |

*Source*: Data for the period 1981–95 are from the Institute for Employment Research, *Review of the Economy and Employment* (Coventry: IER, University of Warwick, 1987), tables A1 and A2 and *Review of the Economy and Employment: Occupational Update* 1988 (Coventry: IER, University of Warwick, 1988) table 1; data for the year 1980 are from the Institute for Employment Research, *Review of the Economy and Employment* (Coventry: IER, University of Warwick, Summer 1983), table 2.3; data for the period 1949–79 are unpublished, and were supplied by the IER on a comparable basis to those for later years

*Notes*:  [a] The estimates for years up to 1979 are based on the Department of Employment's definition of registered unemployed; subsequently, they are the number of claimants to benefit; in 1982 the number of registered unemployed was 3.1 million compared with 2.8 million claimants

[b] Percentage of employees in employment plus the unemployed

[c] Not applicable

TABLE 2.4  *Civilian economic activity rates by age and sex in Great Britain,*
*1951–1991 (%)*

|  | 1951 | 1961 | 1971 | 1981 | 1986 | 1991 |
|---|---|---|---|---|---|---|
| **Males** | | | | | | |
| Under 20 | 83.8 | 74.6 | 69.4 | 72.4 | 73.7 | 75.8 |
| 20–24 | 94.9 | 91.9 | 87.7 | 85.1 | 84.5 | 83.9 |
| 25–44 | 98.3 | 98.2 | 95.4 | 95.7 | 93.9 | 94.0 |
| 45–64 | 95.2 | 97.6 | 93.2 | 85.6 | 79.6 | 79.7 |
| 65+ | 31.1 | 24.4 | 17.6 | 9.2 | 7.4 | 5.6 |
| All ages | 87.6 | 86.0 | 80.5 | 76.5 | 73.4 | 73.1 |
| **Females** | | | | | | |
| Under 20 | 78.9 | 71.1 | 65.0 | 70.4 | 71.1 | 74.2 |
| 20–24 | 65.4 | 62.0 | 60.2 | 68.8 | 69.2 | 69.2 |
| 25–44 | 36.1 | 40.8 | 50.6 | 61.4 | 67.2 | 68.4 |
| 45–64 | 28.7 | 37.1 | 50.2 | 52.5 | 52.4 | 54.1 |
| 65+ | 5.3 | 5.4 | 6.3 | 3.7 | 2.7 | 2.4 |
| All ages | 34.7 | 37.4 | 43.9 | 47.6 | 49.2 | 49.9 |
| **Males and females** | | | | | | |
| All ages | 59.6 | 60.5 | 61.9 | 61.7 | 60.8 | 61.1 |

*Source*:  P. Elias, 'Labour Supply and Employment Opportunities for Women', R. M. Lindley
(ed.), *Economic Change and Employment Policy* (London: Macmillan, 1980), table 6.1,
updated by Peter Elias on a comparable basis from data published in *Employment
Gazette* (May 1987)

*Note*:  Before 1971 the age group 'under 20' consisted of 15–19 year olds, except for married
women for whom it is 16–19 years; from 1981 the age group consists of 16–19 year olds

TABLE 2.5  *Employment by sector in the United Kingdom, 1954–1995*
*(share of total employment, %)*

| Sector | 1954 | 1975 | 1980 | 1987 | 1990 | 1995 |
|---|---|---|---|---|---|---|
| Primary and utilities [a] | 10.6 | 5.5 | 5.3 | 4.2 | 3.8 | 3.6 |
| Manufacturing | 34.7 | 30.6 | 28.0 | 21.5 | 19.7 | 19.2 |
| Construction | 6.1 | 6.5 | 6.4 | 6.3 | 6.8 | 6.6 |
| Distribution, transport and communications | 24.7 | 24.9 | 26.1 | 27.1 | 27.3 | 27.0 |
| Business and miscellaneous services | 9.1 | 12.8 | 14.7 | 20.2 | 21.3 | 23.5 |
| Non-marketed services [b] | 14.9 | 19.6 | 19.6 | 20.7 | 20.1 | 20.1 |
| Public sector | 24.3 | 29.0 | 29.2 | 25.6 | | |
| Whole economy | 100.0 | 100.0 | 100.0 | 100.0 | 100.0 | 100.0 |

*Sources*:  Date from Institute for Employment Research, *Review of the Economy and Employment* (Coventry: IER, University of Warwick, 1987), table A4. Data for the 'public
sector' category for 1954 and 1975 are from A. W. J. Thomson and P. B. Beaumont,
*Public Sector Bargaining* (Farnborough, Hants: Saxon House, 1978), 115; the data for
1980 and 1987 are from *Economic Trends*, no. 410 (December 1987), 98–107

*Notes*:   [a] Agriculture, forestry and fishing: mining and quarrying; and gas, electricity and water
[b] Medical and dental services; religious organizations; private domestic services; and
national and local government

TABLE 2.6 *Occupational change in the United Kingdom, 1971–1995*

| WOC | Occupation | 1971 level | Change (thousands) | | | Change (% p.a.) | | | 1995 level |
|---|---|---|---|---|---|---|---|---|---|
| | | | 1971–81 | 1981–86 | 1986–95 | 1971–81 | 1981–86 | 1986–95 | |
| 1 | Managers and administrators | 582 | 150 | 52 | 151 | 2.3 | 1.4 | 2.0 | 935 |
| 2 | Education professions | 802 | 195 | 31 | 138 | 2.2 | 0.6 | 1.4 | 1,166 |
| 3 | Health welfare professions | 731 | 272 | 144 | 205 | 3.2 | 2.8 | 1.8 | 1,351 |
| 4 | Other professions | 848 | 224 | 184 | 226 | 2.3 | 3.2 | 1.9 | 1,483 |
| 5 | Literary, artistic, sports occupations | 159 | 40 | 51 | 79 | 2.3 | 4.6 | 3.1 | 328 |
| 6 | Engineers, scientists, etc. | 458 | 142 | 93 | 142 | 2.8 | 2.9 | 2.1 | 836 |
| 7 | Technicians, draughtsmen | 425 | 46 | 75 | 77 | 1.0 | 3.0 | 1.5 | 623 |
| 8 | Clerical occupations[a] | 2,709 | 10 | 26 | 170 | 0.0 | 0.2 | 0.7 | 2,915 |
| 9 | Secretarial occupations[b] | 841 | 101 | 40 | 61 | 1.1 | 0.8 | 0.7 | 1,043 |
| 10 | Sales representatives | 429 | −36 | 18 | −33 | −0.9 | 0.9 | −0.9 | 379 |
| 11 | Other sales occupations | 1,061 | 64 | 101 | 60 | 0.6 | 1.7 | 0.6 | 1,287 |
| 12 | Supervisors[c] | 207 | 115 | 13 | 64 | 4.5 | 0.9 | 2.0 | 400 |
| 13 | Foremen[d] | 577 | −13 | −94 | 37 | −0.2 | −3.6 | 0.9 | 507 |
| 14 | Engineering craft occupations (module)[e] | 1,504 | −155 | −121 | −8 | −1.1 | −1.9 | −0.1 | 1,220 |
| 15 | Engineering craft occupations (non-module)[f] | 525 | −56 | −31 | 41 | −1.1 | −1.4 | 1.0 | 478 |

| | | | | | | | | |
|---|---|---:|---:|---:|---:|---:|---:|---:|
| 16 | Construction craft occupations | 813 | −56 | 93 | 109 | −0.7 | 2.3 | 1.4 | 959 |
| 17 | Other craft occupations | 374 | −99 | −64 | −19 | −3.0 | −5.2 | −1.0 | 193 |
| 18 | Skilled operatives | 990 | −209 | −84 | −74 | −2.3 | −2.2 | −1.3 | 623 |
| 19 | Other operatives | 4,962 | −980 | −467 | −284 | −2.2 | −2.5 | −0.9 | 3,230 |
| 20 | Security occupations | 253 | 65 | 7 | 31 | 2.3 | 0.4 | 1.0 | 355 |
| 21 | Skilled personal service occupations | 2,165 | 219 | 172 | 257 | 0.9 | 1.4 | 1.0 | 2,812 |
| 22 | Other personal service occupations | 1,757 | 159 | 120 | 171 | 0.9 | 1.3 | 0.9 | 2,207 |
| 23 | Other occupations | 972 | −352 | −73 | −197 | −4.4 | −2.5 | −4.8 | 350 |
| 1 − 12 + 20 | Non-manual occupations | 9,505 | 1,388 | 835 | 1,371 | 1.4 | 1.5 | 1.3 | 13,101 |
| 13 − 19 + 21 − 23 | Manual occupations | 14,639 | −1,542 | −549 | 33 | −1.1 | −0.9 | 0.0 | 12,579 |
| 1 − 23 | All occupations[g,h] | 24,143 | −155 | 286 | 1,403 | −0.1 | 0.2 | 0.7 | 25,677 |

Source: Institute of Employment Research, *Review of the Economy and Employment* (Coventry: IER, University of Warwick, 1987), tables A17, A18 and A19

Notes:
[a] Stores clerks; other clerks and cashiers (not retail); office machine operators; telephonist receptionists
[b] Receptionists; typists
[c] All supervisory occupations in unit groups, in 1981 Census of Population, 45.02 to 73.00 (except 60.02–60.06, which are classified as foremen)
[d] All occupation unit groups, in 1981 Census of Population, described as 'foremen' (also including supervisors in 60.02–60.06)
[e] Press and machine tool setters; centre lathe turners; setter operators; toolmakers; precision instrument makers; production fitters; electricians; sheet metal workers; metal plate workers; welders; pattern makers; moulders; die casters
[f] Watch repairers; motor mechanics; radio and TV mechanics; plumbers; gas fitters
[g] Excluding HM Forces
[h] Components may not sum to totals because of roundings

TABLE 2.7  *Male and female employment in the United Kingdom,*
          *1951–1995*

|  | 1951 | 1961 | 1971 | 1981 | 1987 | 1992 | 1995 |
|---|---|---|---|---|---|---|---|
| Males (m) | 13.7 | 14.6 | 13.7 | 12.5 | 11.9 | 12.3 | 12.2 |
| Females (m) | 6.8 | 7.9 | 8.4 | 9.3 | 9.9 | 10.6 | 10.8 |
| Total (m)[a] | 20.6 | 22.6 | 22.1 | 21.9 | 21.8 | 22.8 | 23.0 |
| Male (% of total)[b] | 66.5 | 64.6 | 62.0 | 57.1 | 54.6 | 53.9 | 53.0 |
| Female (% of total)[b] | 33.0 | 35.0 | 38.0 | 42.5 | 45.4 | 46.1 | 47.0 |

*Source*:  Data for 1981, 1987, 1992 and 1995 are from the Institute of Employment Research, *Review of the Economy and Employment* (Coventry: IER, University of Warwick, 1987), table 2. Data for 1951, 1961 and 1971 are unpublished and were supplied by the IER on a comparable basis to those for later years
*Notes*:   [a] Excluding those in HM Forces and those in private domestic services
          [b] Percentages may not add to 100 because of roundings.

TABLE 2.8  *Average weekly hours worked for all employees in the United Kingdom,*
          *1951–1990*

| Sector | 1951 | 1961 | 1971 | 1980 | 1990 |
|---|---|---|---|---|---|
| Manufacturing | 43.6 | 42.4 | 39.3 | 38.3 | 36.8 |
| Financial and professional services | 41.4 | 38.8 | 34.8 | 34.4 | 32.4 |
| Miscellaneous services | 40.8 | 39.9 | 35.4 | 33.5 | 31.5 |
| All industries and services[a] | 44.4 | 43.0 | 39.0 | 37.4 | 35.4 |

*Source*:  For 1951–1980 the data are from R. A. Wilson, 'Average Weekly Hours 1948–81', an unpublished paper presented at a conference on 'Hours of Work and Employment', University of Warwick, 16–17 September 1982. The projections for 1990 are from Institute for Employment Research, *Review of the Economy and Employment* (Coventry: IER, University of Warwick, Summer 1983), 51–2
*Note*:    [a] Excluding central and local government

TABLE 2.9 *Self-employment and part-time employment[a] in the United Kingdom, 1951–1995*

|  | 1951 | 1961 | 1971 | 1981 | 1987 | 1992 | 1995 |
|---|---|---|---|---|---|---|---|
| Self-employment (m) | 1.64 | 1.63 | 1.84 | 2.1 | 2.9 | 3.3 | 3.4 |
| Part-time employment (m) | 0.73 | 1.94 | 3.39 | 4.6 | 5.3 | 5.9 | 6.3 |
| Total employment (m) | 20.55 | 22.57 | 22.12 | 21.9 | 21.8 | 22.8 | 23.0 |
| Self-employment (% of total) | 8.0 | 7.2 | 8.3 | 9.6 | 11.7 | 12.6 | 12.9 |
| Part-time employment (% of total) | 3.5 | 8.6 | 15.3 | 21.0 | 24.3 | 25.9 | 27.4 |

*Source*: For 1951–71 unpublished data supplied by the Institute of Employment Research. For 1981, 1986, 1990, 1992 and 1995 data are from Institute of Employment Research, *Review of the Economy and Employment: Occupational Update* (Coventry: IER, University of Warwick, 1987), table A5

*Note*:   [a] Those working 30 or less hours per week (excluding meal breaks and overtime)

TABLE 2.10 *Union density in Great Britain and the United Kingdom, 1948–1987*

|  | 1948 | 1968 | 1979 | 1987 |
|---|---|---|---|---|
| Aggregate union density UK | 45.2 | 44.0 | 54.4 | 41.9[a] |
| Aggregate union density GB | 45.0 | 42.7 | 53.2 |  |
| Male union density GB | 55.4 | 51.4 | 63.1 |  |
| Female union density GB | 24.3 | 27.5 | 39.0 |  |
| Manual union density GB | 50.3 | 49.8 | 62.5 |  |
| White-collar union density GB | 33.0 | 32.6 | 43.6 |  |

*Source*: G. S. Bain and R. J. Price, 'Union Growth', G. S. Bain (ed.), *Industrial Relations in Britain* (Oxford: Blackwell, 1983), tables 1.1, 1.2 and 1.3

*Note*:   [a] The union membership figure for 1987 is a rough estimate. Total membership as a proportion of the TUC's membership (9,243,297) was 114.018 in 1986; hence the TUC's membership figure for 1987 (9,126,911) was increased by 14.018% to give a total union membership figure of 10,406,321

TABLE 2.11    *TUC unions with 100,000 and more members at 1986*

|  | Membership | |
| --- | --- | --- |
|  | 1979 | 1986 |
| Transport and General Workers Union | 2,228,536 | 1,377,944 |
| Amalgamated Engineering Union | 1,299,224 | 857,559 |
| General, Municipal,.Boilermakers and Allied Trades Union | 1,132,575 | 814,084 |
| National and Local Goverment Officers Association | 753,226 | 750,430 |
| National Union of Public Employees | 691,770 | 657,633 |
| Association of Scientific, Technical and Managerial Staffs | 491,000 | 390,000 |
| Union of Shop, Distributive and Allied Workers | 470,017 | 381,984 |
| Electrical, Electronic, Telecommunication and Plumbing Union | 420,000 | 336,155 |
| Union of Construction, Allied Trades and Technicians | 347,777 | 249,485 |
| Amalgamated Union of Engineering Workers (Technical, Administrative and Supervisory Section) | 358,673 | 241,000 |
| Confederation of Health Service Employees | 212,930 | 212,312 |
| Society of Graphical and Allied Trades '82 | 260,248 | 199,594 |
| Union of Communication Workers | 203,452 | 191,959 |
| National Union of Teachers | 248,896 | 184,455 |
| Banking, Insurance and Finance Union | 131,774 | 158,746 |
| National Communications Union | 125,723 | 155,643 |
| Civil and Public Services Association | 223,884 | 150,514 |
| National Graphical Association (1982) | 136,462 | 125,587 |
| National Union of Railwaymen | 180,000 | 125,000 |
| National Association of Schoolmasters/Union of Women Teachers | 122,058 | 123,945 |
| National Union of Mineworkers | 253,142 | 104,941 |

*Source*:  Various issues of *TUC Report*

TABLE 2.12  Number and size of unions in the United Kingdom, 1950–1985

| Number of members | 1950 | | | | 1960 | | | | 1985 | | | |
|---|---|---|---|---|---|---|---|---|---|---|---|---|
| | Number of unions | Total membership ('000s) | Percentage of All unions | Percentage of All membership | Number of unions | Total membership ('000s) | Percentage of All unions | Percentage of All membership | Number of unions | Total membership ('000s) | Percentage of All unions | Percentage of All membership |
| Below 500 | 327 | 56 | 46.5 | 0.6 | 308 | 51 | 47.4 | 0.5 | 168 | 26 | 45.1 | 0.3 |
| 500–9,999 | 285 | 746 | 40.5 | 8.1 | 249 | 661 | 38.3 | 6.7 | 134 | 321 | 35.9 | 2.9 |
| 10,000–24,999 | 42 | 638 | 6.0 | 6.9 | 44 | 718 | 6.8 | 7.3 | 15 | 250 | 4.0 | 2.3 |
| 25,000–99,999 | 33 | 1,679 | 4.6 | 18.2 | 32 | 1,782 | 4.9 | 18.2 | 32 | 1,460 | 8.6 | 13.6 |
| 100,000 and over | 17 | 6,116 | 2.4 | 66.2 | 17 | 6,590 | 2.6 | 67.3 | 24 | 8,668 | 6.4 | 80.9 |
| Total | 704 | 9,235 | 100.0 | 100.0 | 650 | 9,802 | 100.0 | 100.0 | 373 | 10,716 | 100.0 | 100.0 |

Source:  See, for example, Employment Gazette, XCV (February 1987), 85

# Bibliography

Armstrong, M. 1987. 'Human Resource Management: A Case of the Emperor's New Clothes'. *Personnel Management*, August, 30–5.

Atkinson, J. 1984. 'Manpower Strategies for Flexible Organisations'. *Personnel Management*, August, 28–31.

—— and Meager, M. 1986. 'Is Flexibility Just a Flash in the Pan?'. *Personnel Management*, September, 26–9.

Bassett, P. 1986. *Strike Free*. Oxford: Blackwell.

Brewster, C. and Connock, S. 1985. *Industrial Relations: Cost-Effective Strategies*. London: Hutchinson.

Brown, W.A. Ed. 1981. *The Changing Contours of British Industrial Relations*. Oxford: Blackwell.

Cappelli, P. and McKersie, R.B. 1987. 'Management Strategy and the Redesign of Work Rules'. *Journal of Management Studies*, 24: September, 441–62.

Channon, D. 1973. *The Strategy and Structure of British Enterprise*. London: Macmillan.

—— 1978. *The Service Industries: Strategy, Structure and Financial Performance*. London: Macmillan.

Clutterbuck, D. and Devine, M. 1987. *Management Buyouts*. London: Hutchinson.

Daniel, W.W. and Millward, N. 1983. *Workplace Industrial Relations in Britain: The DE/PSI/SSRC Survey*. London: Heinemann Educational Books.

Edwards, P.K. 1987. *Managing the Factory*. Oxford: Blackwell.

Felstead, A. 1988. 'Towards An Explanation of the Franchise Phenomenon'. The Franchise Project, Research Paper No. 3, Nuffield College, Oxford.

Fowler, A. 1987. 'When Chief Executives Discover Human Resource Management'. *Personnel Management*, January, 3.

Fox, A. 1974. *Man Mismanagement*. London: Hutchinson.

Goold, M. and Campbell, A. 1986. *Strategic Decision Making: the Corporate Role. Vol. 1 Strategic Management Styles*. London Business School: Centre for Business Strategy.

Guest, D. 1982. 'Has the Recession Really Hit Personnel?'. *Personnel Management*, October, 36–9.

—— 1987. 'Human Resources Management and Industrial Relations'. *Journal of Management Studies*, 24: September, 503–22.

Handy, C. 1984. *The Future of Work*. Oxford: Blackwell.

Hill, T. 1985. *Manufacturing Strategy: The Strategic Management of the Manufacturing Function*. London: Macmillan Educational.

Hill, C.W.L. and Pickering, J.F. 1986. 'Divisionalization, Decentralization and Performance of Large UK Companies'. *Journal of Management Studies*, 23: January, 26–50.

Incomes Data Services. 1985. 'Ever Increasing Circles'. Study 352: December, 1–12.

Industrial Relations Review and Report. 1984. 'Flexibility Agreements – the End of Who Does What?', 316: March, 2–7.

—— 1986a. 'Team Briefing: Practical Steps in Employee Communication', 361: February, 2–9.

—— 1986b. 'Integrated Payment Structures', 367: May, 2–7.

—— 1986c. 'Responses on Profit Related Pay', 380: November, 2–6.

—— 1988. 'Changes in Working Practices in UK Manufacturing 1981–88', 415: May, 2–10.

Judkins, D. and West, D. 1982. *Networking – the Distributed Office*. London: Rank Xerox.

Kanter, R. M. 1984. *The Change Masters*. London: Allen & Unwin.

Legge, K. 1988. 'Personnel Management in Recession and Recovery: A Comparative Analysis of What the Surveys Say'. *Personnel Review*, 17: 2.

Lewis, R. 1986. 'The Role of Law in Employment Relations'. *Labour Law in Britain*. Lewis, R. Ed. Oxford: Blackwell, 3–43.

Long, P. 1984. 'Would You Put Your Daughter in Personnel?'. *Personnel Management*, April, 16–20.

Mackay, L. and Torrington, D. 1986. *The Changing Nature of Personnel Management*. London: Institute of Personnel Management.

Manning, K. 1983. 'The Rise and Fall of Personnel'. *Management Today*, March, 74–7.

Marginson, P., Edwards, P.K., Martin, R., Purcell, J. and Sisson, K. 1988. *Beyond the Workplace: The Management of Industrial Relations in Large Enterprises*. Oxford: Blackwell.

Marsh, A. 1983. *Employee Relations Policy and Decision Making*. Aldershot: Gower.

Meager, N. 1986. 'Temporary Work in Britain: its Growth and Rationales'. IMS Report No. 106, University of Sussex: Institute of Manpower Studies.

Mervis, J.P. and Co. 1986. *Survey of Acquisitions in the US by British Companies, with Emphasis on 1984–85*. London: J.P. Mervis and Co.

Millward, N. and Stevens, M. 1986. *British Workplace Industrial Relations 1980–1984*: the DE/PSI/ACAS Surveys. Aldershot: Gower.

National Economic Development Office/Manpower Services Commission. 1987. *People: the Key to Success*. London.

Peters, T. and Austin, N. 1985. *A Passion for Excellence*. London: Fontana Paperback.

—— and Waterman, R.H. 1982. *In Pursuit of Excellence*. New York: Harper & Row.

Pollert, A. 1987. '"The Flexible Firm": A Model in Search of Reality (Or A Policy in Search of a Practice)?'. Warwick Papers in Industrial Relations, No. 19.

Poole, M. 1986. 'Profit-Sharing and Share Ownership Schemes in Britain'. *Employee Relations*, 8, 45–50.

Purcell, J. 1985. 'Is Anyone Listening to the Corporate Personnel Department'. *Personnel Management*, September, 28–31.

—— and Gray, A. 1986. 'Corporate Personnel Departments and the Management of Industrial Relations: Two Case Studies in Ambiguity'. *Journal of Management Studies*, 23: 205–23.

—— Marginson, P., Edwards, P.K. and Sisson, K. 1987. 'The Industrial Relations Practices of Multi-Plant Foreign Owned Firms'. *Industrial Relations Journal*, 18: Summer, 130–7.

Roots, P. 1986. 'Collective Bargaining: Opportunities for a New Approach'. Warwick Papers in Industrial Relations. University of Warwick: Industrial Relations Research Unit, No. 5.

Sisson, K. and Scullion, H. 1985. 'Putting the Corporate Personnel Department in its Place'. *Personnel Management*, December, 36–9.

Storey, J. 1987. 'Developments in the Management of Human Resources: An Interim Report'. Warwick Papers in Industrial Relations, No. 17.

Streeck, W. 1985. 'Industrial Relations and Industrial Change in the Motor Industry: An International View'. Public Lecture. University of Warwick: Industrial Relations Research Unit.

Tailby, S. and Turnbull, P. 1987. 'Learning to Manage Just-in-Time'. *Personnel Management*, January, 16–19.

Thomason, G. 1981. *A Textbook of Personnel Management*. London: Institute of Personnel Management.

Torrington, D. forthcoming. 'Human Resource Management and the Personnel Function'. Storey, J. Ed. *New Perspectives on Human Resource Management*. London: Routledge & Kegan Paul.

—— and Chapman, J. 1983. *Personnel Management*. London: Prentice-Hall International.

—— and Hall, L. 1987. *Personnel Management: a New Approach*. London: Prentice-Hall International.

Tyson, S. 1980. 'Taking Advantage of Ambiguity'. *Personnel Management*, February, 45–8.

—— 1987. 'The Management of the Personnel Function'. *Journal of Management Studies*, 24: September, 523–32.

—— and Fell, A. 1986. *Evaluating the Personnel Function*. London: Hutchinson.

Walton, R.E. 1985. 'From Control to Commitment in the Workplace'. *Harvard Business Review*, 63: March/April, 76–84.

# PART II
## The Design of Organizations

# 3 The Structure of Organizations
## Arthur Francis

Work organizations take many forms. Solicitors' practices, worker co-operatives, and owner-managed small engineering companies, for example, differ considerably and systematically in their organizational structures; they vary in the way in which labour is divided, activities co-ordinated, and decisions taken, and they differ in the amount of power, influence, and status enjoyed by organizational members. There are also differences between the structures of larger scale organizations. Universities are organized on a different basis from the civil service, and civil service organizational structures differ from those in many business concerns. Within the business sector variations are also considerable. For example, one multinational corporation, the Hanson Trust, operates with a headquarters executive staff of 20 in the UK and 12 in the USA (Goold and Campbell, 1986: 161); Imperial Tobacco, which is a recent Hanson Trust acquisition, employed 800 in its head office operations (*Guardian*, 8 September 1987). Differences of this magnitude do not result from overmanning, but rather they imply the use of different principles in shaping their organizational arrangements.

The purpose of this chapter is to set out the range of organizational forms adopted by business enterprises, and the circumstances in which each type is likely to be chosen. Though the bulk of material in this chapter concerns business organizations – for it is within these that most people in Britain are employed – many of the principles underlying the arguments and research findings reported here are applicable across a wider range, including public sector and voluntary organizations.

## THE DIMENSIONS OF ORGANIZATIONAL STRUCTURE

### Specialization

Organization becomes necessary when a product or service is so large or complex that more than one person's effort and/or skills are required to produce it. One fundamental element, therefore, is the way in which the tasks necessary for the completion of the product or service are divided up between organizational members. Though this issue will be discussed in the following chapter on job design, it should be noted here that a key dimension of organizational structure, and an important influence on the choices made about other aspects of that structure, is the nature of the division of labour within the enterprise. One well-established measure of this within survey-based organizational research is that of 'specialization', measured by the number of different occupational types or functional departments within an enterprise (Pugh et al., 1969). This measure can be misleading, however, as it fails to distinguish between two quite different phenomena. One is where the task to be performed is rather simple, requires little expertise, and hence relatively few occupational types are involved – for example in routine assembly work. The other is where the task may be complex, but is performed by flexible multiskilled workers, each person performing a range of operations, and occupational labelling is deliberately reduced to a minimum. The specialization dimension relates to this second phenomenon and should measure the extent to which work is organized on the basis of fragmented tasks performed by specialized workers or of more complete tasks performed by workers who are multiskilled and flexible.

## Standardization and Formalization

Two further important organizational dimensions relate to the extent to which organizational relationships and procedures are standardized and formalized, that is, subject to standard procedures and rules for doing things, some of which may be written down. Examples of formalization are written policies, procedures, rules, job definitions and standing orders.

## Tall or Flat?

Until relatively recently, it was generally believed that the optimum number of people a manager could supervise was between six and eight. It is now known that there is no such optimum figure. The size of the span of control depends on a variety of factors discussed later in the chapter.

This span also determines, to some extent, the number of levels in the managerial hierarchy. An organization of a given size with a short span of control will, by simple arithmetic, have more managerial levels than one of an equivalent size with a longer span of control. Therefore the extent to which an organization may be 'tall' or 'flat' is a fourth dimension along which organizational structures vary.

## Centralization

Though decisions vary in importance, and therefore some get made at higher levels in the organization than others, organizations do appear to differ systematically in the extent to which they centralize or decentralize their decision-making. In one organization, for example, an operator may be allowed, and even encouraged, to decide how a job is done, whereas in another this decision will have been centralized with detailed procedures laid down for the way tasks should be carried out. Capital expenditure and budgeting decisions involving specific amounts of funds will be made higher up the managerial hierarchy in some firms than others.

As one recent survey (Goold and Campbell, 1986) has established, differences in the nature and extent of centralization are especially marked in the case of the large multi-establishment enterprise. At one extreme, there were enterprises such as BOC (industrial gases), Lex (automotive services) and STC (telecommunications), which saw an essential role for corporate management in developing the strategy of the subsidiary businesses and its co-ordination from one business to another. At the other extreme, there were enterprises such as BTR (services), Tarmac (construction), Hanson Trust and GEC. Here there appeared to be little or no formal strategic planning process at headquarters; responsibility for strategy was devolved to the subsidiary businesses, with close monitoring of performance against budget and strong personal incentives for managers to meet targets. In between there were enterprises such as Courtaulds (textiles), ICI, the Imperial Group (now part of Hanson Trust), Plessey (telecommunications) and Vickers (engineering), which had established planning processes, but left a great deal of initiative to subsidiary managers in drawing up the plans.

## Organizational Types

So far five separate dimensions of organization structure have been identified. Are these dimensions independent, in the sense that an organization will take up a position on one dimension independent of the position it takes on any other, or are they linked in some way? For example, does an organization which is highly standardized also have a very formalized structure with centralized decision-making? Perhaps surprisingly, research has shown an inverse correlation between centralization and the degree of standardization and formalization. It appears that management view these as alternative forms of control. When organizations are standardized and formalized, there is less need for senior managers to be involved in detailed decision-making because junior staff are constrained to carry out senior management's wishes by the rules and procedures surrounding their decision-making process. Hence the formalized organization is decentralized in its decision-making.

Other research has indicated that all five dimensions are related. One early and influential study (Burns and Stalker, 1966: 5–6) suggested that there seemed in practice to be just two divergent systems of management and forms of organizational structure. Though subsequent research has shown this view to be rather too simple, leading to the development of a more sophisticated and complex view of organizational types (discussed later), this early idea of two extreme types illuminates a wide variety of possibilities.

The researchers label their two types 'mechanistic' and 'organic' and describe the differences thus:

In mechanistic systems the problems and tasks facing the concern as a whole are broken down into specialisms. Each individual pursues his task as something distinct from the real tasks of the concern as a whole, as if it were the subject of a sub-contract. 'Somebody at the top' is responsible for seeing to its relevance. The technical methods, duties, and powers attached to each functional role are precisely defined. Interaction within management tends to be vertical, i.e. between superior and subordinate. Operations and working behaviour are governed by instructions and decisions issued by superiors. This command hierarchy is maintained by the implicit assumption that all knowledge about the situation of the firm and its tasks is, or should be, available only to the head of the firm. Management, often visualised as the complex hierarchy familiar in the organisation charts, operates a simple control system, with information flowing up through a succession of filters, and decisions and instructions flowing downwards through a succession of amplifiers.

Organic systems are adapted to unstable conditions, when problems and requirements for action arise which cannot be broken down and distributed among specialist roles within a clearly defined hierarchy. Individuals have to perform their special tasks in the light of their knowledge of the tasks of the firm as a whole. Jobs lose much of their formal definition in terms of methods, duties, and powers, which have to be redefined continually by interaction with others participating in a task. Interaction runs laterally as much as vertically. Communication between people of different ranks tends to resemble lateral consultation rather than vertical command. Omniscience can no longer be imputed to the head of the concern.

## Grouping of Activities

The final structural dimension is the way activities are grouped. When organizations are involved in the production of two or more products or services, management has to choose whether to group activities around each organizational function, around each product or service, or some combination of the two. In the first of these possibilities, the organization is structured around the main departmental functions of the business: research and development, production, sales and marketing, accounts and finance, etc., with each department handling the complete range of the firm's products or services. The alternative is for each product to have its own range of departments, headed by a product manager. Each arrangement has its costs and benefits, discussed in the next section, and an increasingly popular organizational form is that of the matrix, which attempts to obtain the benefits of both functional and product organization while minimizing the costs. In this organizational form there are both functional department heads and product heads, each providing leadership in their own area, with individuals working on particular products or services being responsible to both managers, to the former for the technical content of their work and to the latter for the progress and co-ordination of the provision of the product or service.

The question of functional, product, or matrix form of organization is one which has to be addressed both at plant and enterprise levels. It is at enterprise level, however, that the decisions have greatest impact, because they determine the overall shape of the organization. It is also at this level that the terminology is most developed. Enterprises which are organized around the main departments are known as functional or, to adopt Channon's (1978) refinement, critical function organizations and are often referred to as 'U' form in type; while those which are divided into divisions, defined either by product or geography, are known as 'M' form organizations (see Williamson, 1975, for further details, see also figure 3.1 for examples).

In terms of practice, although there has been considerable decentralization in recent years, especially in the nationalized industries, where British Rail and the Post Office have been divided into sectors or divisions, in the public sector most organizations are of the functional or critical functional type; personnel, for example, is usually a critical function, and decision-making about pay and conditions of employment is highly centralized. In the private sector, the multidivisional or 'M' form type is increasingly the dominant pattern and very few multi-establishment enterprises, usually single business enterprises such as Marks and Spencer or Ford, are of the functional or critical functional type. Thus, Hill and Pickering (1986: 29) found that of 144 enterprises surveyed in the early 1980s, all of which were among the 500 largest UK companies, no less than 80 per cent were organized along divisional lines. Overall, some 38 per cent were divided on the basis of product divisions and nearly 10 per cent on the basis of geographical divisions. Furthermore, 20 per cent had a

FIGURE 3.1   *Types of organization structure*

**Multi-Divisional**

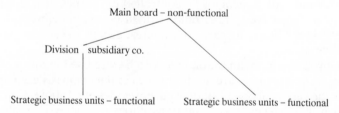

**Critical Function – Manufacturing**

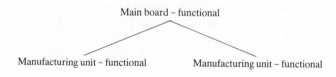

**Critical Function – Retail**

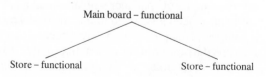

mixture of product and geographical divisions and almost 12 per cent had a mixture of product and international divisions.

## APPROACHES TO ORGANIZATION THEORY

The development of understanding of organizations has not progressed smoothly nor has knowledge developed in a cumulative fashion. Indeed, the current state of knowledge is still characterized by lively debates about which are the most fruitful and insightful ways of understanding organizational processes and the factors influencing the development of organizational structures. To a very considerable extent, the conflict and confusion which are the subject of much debate within organizational studies are due to the fact that the organization of an enterprise serves a number of different purposes. As mentioned above, one such purpose is the co-ordination of the many different activities necessary to create the product or service produced by the enterprise. To this end, the objective is to structure the organization so that information can be transmitted, stored and processed to enable appropriate decision-making. But most individuals at work also have social needs and the structure of the organization is likely to have an effect on levels of commitment to the enterprise and levels of motivation to work. Hence the structure of an organization may also be influenced by concerns to socialize its members, and to maintain a degree of institutional commitment. Thirdly, organizations are likely to contain within them, or be controlled by, particular interest groups with particular objectives. Organization structures may therefore also, to some extent, reflect the desire by particular interest groups to exercise power and control over others.

The approaches to organization theory to be discussed in this section owe their origins, in large measure, to differences in the emphasis each approach places on the variety of organizational purposes identified above. Contingency theory as well as agency theory and transactions cost analysis emphasize the co-ordination and decision-making functions of the organization to which writers in the 'scientific principles' tradition first drew attention. The socio-technical systems approach focuses much more on motivational and organizational commitment aspects; while the so-called radical critique explores the extent to which organization structures reflect and, possibly, amplify coercive social relations in wider society. Each of the first four approaches will be discussed in rough date order; the radical critique will be considered last.

### Scientific Principles

Until about twenty years ago, any manager who attended a course in business administration would have been instructed in the one best way to organize the business. Several simple principles would have been enunciated, many of which had been borrowed from centuries of practice in the Armed Forces. In a paper entitled 'Scientific Principles and Organization', published in 1938,

Urwick, a famed international management consultant, summarized the current set of beliefs in the form of eight principles. As late as 1957, Brech (1957: 374), a noted British exponent of this classical management school, quoted these eight principles 'because of their importance and long-standing acceptance'. They are:

1  All organizations and each part of any undertaking should be the expression of a purpose, either explicit or implied – the *Principle of the Objective*.
2  Formal authority and responsibility must be coterminous and coequal – the *Principle of Correspondence*.
3  The responsibility of higher authority for the acts of its subordinates is absolute – the *Principle of Responsibility*.
4  There must be a clear line of formal authority running from the top to the bottom of every organization – the *Scalar Principle*.
5  No superior can supervise directly the work of more than five or, at the most, six subordinates whose work interlocks – the *Principle of the Span of Control*.
6  The work of every person in the organization should be confined as far as possible to the performance of a single leading function – the *Principle of Specialization*.
7  The final object of all organization is smooth and effective co-ordination – the *Principle of Co-ordination*.
8  Every position in every organization should be clearly prescribed in writing – the *Principle of Definition*.

*Contingency Theory*

The second approach, contingency theory, grew out of attempts in the late 1950s to test the validity of the 'scientific principles' by empirical research. One group of researchers, led by Woodward (1965), investigated the extent to which a sample of over 100 firms in the South East of England had organization structures which accorded to these principles. They measured the organization structures and the business performance of all the firms in their sample and, despite over half the firms having organization structures which departed significantly from the eight classical principles of management, found no relationship between organization structure and performance. Had Woodward and her researchers given up at this point, organization theory might well have disappeared off the business school agenda, but persistent analysis of the data led to the discovery that use and non-use of the eight classical principles were not randomly distributed, but were associated with the type of technology used in each firm. The researchers went further. Having established what kind of structure a firm with a particular technology was likely to have, they then measured the extent to which the structure fitted the technology, and how well that firm performed. Their results showed that firms which had adopted a structure appropriate to their production technology performed on average better than those with an inappropriate structure.

Burns and Stalker (1961), who were the authors of a second study, were not teachers of management, but were familiar with the precepts of classical management theory. They were unsurprised to discover that one of the plants in their study, a rayon mill, was organized in this manner. Within the second plant surveyed, an engineering concern, on the other hand, they found that positions and functions in the management hierarchy were ill-defined, and that this was so because of the deliberate policy of the head of the concern. Although there were considerable feelings of insecurity and stress among individuals in the organization, to the extent that cliques and cabals had formed and people spent much energy in internal politics, the firm was nevertheless a commercial and technical success. The researchers wondered if the firm's success would have been even greater if they had sorted out the organization structure and reduced the level of stress and anxiety, or, conversely, might the insecurity, stress, and anxiety be the mainspring of the management system and the cause of the success? These questions became the focus of a series of further investigations into nearly twenty other firms which led Burns and Stalker to their conclusions about mechanistic and organic types of organizational structure, the former being akin to Urwick's eight principles.

The importance of Burns' and Stalker's research findings has been two-fold. First, they set out a clear alternative to the classical management theorists' prescription for the structure of an organization. This finding, in conjunction with Woodward's results, put paid to the idea that there was 'one best way' to organize an enterprise, and led to the development of 'contingency' theory, the approach which suggests that the structure of organization most appropriate to a particular enterprise is contingent upon a number of features of that enterprise. Secondly, Burns and Stalker, along with Woodward, suggested that the rate of environmental change – in particular the rate of change in the technological basis of production and in the market situation – was the crucial contingent factor in determining what form of organization is most appropriate.

The most useful outcome of contingency theory has not been a set of measuring instruments and precise predictions about specific structural features for a particular task, its size and environmental attributes, however, but a conceptual and analytical framework which can be used by those involved in organizational design to aid them in their own analysis.

One of the most helpful formulations of the general findings of contingency theory is by Galbraith (1977), who focuses on the information-processing function of organization. To the extent that the organization exists to process information, 'uncertainty is the core concept upon which the organization design frameworks are based' (Galbraith, 1977: 36–7). Uncertainty, he defines as 'the difference between the amount of information required to perform the task and the amount of information already possessed by the organization'. The strength of the approach is that it captures within this general formulation of uncertainty the various attempts to measure those attributes of technology, task and environment identified by earlier researchers as having a significant influence on organization structure. Galbraith then goes on to synthesize the various findings of the researchers within the contingency theory tradition about the variety of structural forms an organization can take.

Galbraith's general argument is that, as the level of uncertainty facing an organization increases, it must adopt increasingly sophisticated organization structural devices. The nature of these various options is described below, but before turning to this it is worth mentioning the factors which, according to Galbraith, are likely to increase the level of uncertainty faced by an organization. He identifies three. One is the diversity of goals the organization is attempting to achieve. Such goals relate to the number of different products, different markets, different clients, etc. with which the organization is concerned. An increase in the number of goals will increase the amount of information which needs to be processed and hence increase the overall level of uncertainty. A second factor is the division of labour in the organization: those with a simple division of labour need to process less information, other things being equal, than those with many different categories of personnel. Hence an increase in the division of labour will increase the level of uncertainty. Thirdly, there is the level of goal performance needed to remain viable in the organization's chosen domain. 'The higher the level of performance', says Galbraith, 'the larger the number of variables that must be considered simultaneously when allocating resources, setting priorities, or determining schedules' (1977: 37).

Galbraith's approach becomes particularly interesting and insightful when he describes possible organizational responses to continuing uncertainty. He suggests that the organization faces a choice between two competing strategic responses. It can adopt the strategy of reducing the need to process more information, or it can increase the organization's capacity to process information. If management chooses the former strategy, which it may do by default, there are three alternative tactical responses which can be made. One, which he labels environmental management, is to attempt to modify the environment rather than the organization's internal structure. If, for example, a new competitive challenge arises, the organization could, instead of improving its own performance, choose to mount an advertising campaign to attempt to convince its environment (i.e. its customers) that its own performance was adequate. Another environmental management technique might be to engage in vertical integration, by buying either the prior or subsequent stage in the production chain, thus containing or reducing the level of uncertainty which the core organization faces.

A second tactic, within the overall strategy of reducing the need for information processing, is to create slack resources. It is this particular tactic that is the one most likely to be adopted by default. If, for example, the demand facing the organization fluctuates fairly widely, one response would be to attempt to predict the fluctuations, or to be responsive to the fluctuations, so that production levels rose and fell in accordance with demand. This may require a great deal of information processing. The 'slack resource' option is to cope with the fluctuations by producing for stock in the periods of low demand and allowing a backlog of orders to build up during peak demand. Another way of coping with higher levels of uncertainty by the use of slack resources would be to reduce the level of performance. Galbraith cites the example of the aircraft company engaging in wing design. Under pressure, the company could increase the amount of time or man–hours scheduled to do the design, or increase the weight of the wing. 'In each case more resources would be consumed. These additional resources are called slack resources' (Galbraith, 1977: 50).

Of course, each of these tactics incurs cost. To advertise heavily, or to buy up other companies in the production chain, is expensive, and an even greater expense may be incurred from postponing the day when the relatively poor performance is found out and the competition puts the poorly performing company out of business. Using slack resources costs money too. Goods built for stock incur interest charges. Extra man–hours scheduled to design the wing add to labour costs. Using backlogs of work and waiting lists as a substitute for market intelligence or flexible production schedules may lose orders to competitors, perhaps for ever. The question for the organization designer is whether these costs are greater or smaller than those incurred by creating and maintaining a more sophisticated organization capable of processing the information needed if these other tactics are not to be used.

The third tactic within the strategy of reducing the need for information processing is that of creating self-contained task units. This organizational response was adopted recently by a Swedish pump manufacturer. For very many years the company had dominated world markets for a particular type of pump, producing a wide range of specifications and sizes of this one specific product. Recently, however, the Japanese had entered the market and were beginning to gain a considerable share of it. They were competing keenly with the Swedish company on both price and delivery date of the pumps which were usually made to customer order. Up to this time, the company had been organized on traditional functional lines – sales, design, production and accounting, and within production a single machine shop, assembly shop and testing shop. This structure made efficient use of both machinery and the specialized skills of the sales force, the designers, the accountants and other specialists but, with very many varieties of pump going through the one system, co-ordination between the functions over one order was cumbersome and the lead time between receipt of an order and delivery to the customer was lengthy. The Swedish company responded to the Japanese challenge by setting up a self-contained task unit or 'factory within a factory', to make the middle size range pums which constituted the bulk of the company's production. Thus, when enquiries came in for pumps of that particular size, costings, designs and production methods could be ascertained more speedily, and production control exercised more tightly. Though more expensive in terms of duplicated production facilities and slack resources in the form of extra staff, this self-contained task unit was expected to be quicker in getting the goods delivered to the customer.

The shift from functional to product organization is also found at corporate level. Chandler's (1966) careful historical study of the development of the largest US corporations documents how the majority of them eventually abandoned functional corporate structures in favour of product-divisional arrangements. As Chandler says:

> The inherent weakness in the centralized, functionally departmentalized operating company ... became critical only when the administrative load on the senior executives increased to such an extent that they were unable to handle their entrepreneurial responsibilities efficiently. This situation arose when the operations of the enterprise became too complex and the problems of coordination, appraisal, and policy formulation too intricate for a small number of top officers to handle both long-run, entrepreneurial, and short-run, operational administrative activities. (1966: 332–3)

The response was to divisionalize the business, with duties officially split between divisional managers responsible for the short-run, operational activities of each business unit and the head office who would continue to handle the long-run, entrepreneurial responsibilities.

The alternative strategy to that of reducing the need for information processing is to increase the information-processing capacity of the organization. Galbraith (1977) suggests two tactics to achieve this: invest in vertical information systems and create lateral relations. The former tactic maintains the integrity of the managerial hierarchy and the principle of information only flowing through officially defined reporting relationships. It acknowledges that, as uncertainty increases and the flow of information passing along these channels becomes more intense, then the capacity of the individuals in the various authority positions becomes overloaded. One technique to reduce this overload is to appoint 'assistants to' people in key positions to help them cope with the required increase in information processing. A second technique is to increase the number of clerical staff assisting those in the hierarchy. A third is the introduction of computer-based management information systems.

The creation of lateral relations is the most radical organizational change and one which many organizations have been adopting in the late 1970s and the 1980s. It goes wholly against classical management principles and for that reason was often greeted with incredulity when the idea was first introduced to managers or management students. One of the classical principles was that communication should go exclusively up and down the hierarchy, and that if two people in different departments, but at the same hierarchical level, wished to communicate, they should do this only via their superiors who in turn passed the information up the hierarchy. The advantage of maintaining this principle is that all those who might have relevant information about the problem, and in particular the senior managers in the enterprise who are assumed to have the broader picture, are kept informed about problems arising and decisions which are being made. The disadvantage, however, is the slowness at which information can be transmitted down, and the possibility of distortion when passed through so many stages. To give official sanction to communication between two lower level individuals or groups so that they can by-pass the hierarchy increases the speed and accuracy of communication, though it reduces the amount of control the more senior managers have over what is going on, and lessens their ability to contribute their own wider knowledge and possibly greater experience.

There are a variety of mechanisms available to encourage lateral relations. The simplest is to allow direct contact between two people who share a problem. If, however, a large volume of contact is needed between two subtasks such as, to use the example of the Swedish pump factory, the designers and the production engineers, then a liaison role can be created to handle the interdepartmental contacts. Alternatively, if the volume of liaison work is large and likely to continue for some time, the organizational strategy of creating an integrating role might be used. As Galbraith (1977: 53) puts it 'the function of the role is to represent the general manager in the inter-departmental decisions for a particular brand, product line, project, country, or geographical unit. These roles are called product managers in commercial firms, project managers in aerospace, and unit managers in hospitals'. Another mechanism, particularly useful if several departments are involved and the need for intense lateral communications is likely only to be short-term, for example when a new product is to be launched, is to set up a task-force or team, comprising members from the departments involved either on a part-time or a full-time basis. Finally, a very common mechanism used to maintain lateral relations is the use of meetings, either on a scheduled and formal, or *ad hoc* and informal, basis. Though such meetings may often be a substitute for action, it may be that, as in Burns' and Stalker's 'organic' organizations which created insecurity and anxiety in their members, but also had a high performance, the extensive use of 'meetings, bloody meetings' actually increases efficiency.

The ultimate in complexity is the matrix organization which attempts to achieve the advantages of the functional and the product forms without incurring the full disadvantages of either. As figure 3.2 shows, the matrix is made up of two superimposed forms of organization: the functional organiza-

FIGURE 3.2    *Matrix organization*

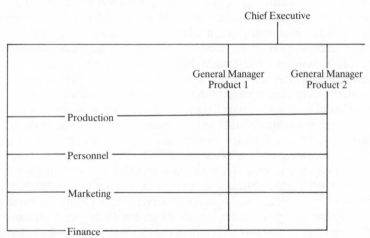

tion and a system of product or project management. Any individual in the organization is responsible to a functional manager for the technical aspects of the work and to a product or project manager for the way in which the task in hand is co-ordinated with other tasks relating to the same product or project. To return yet again to the pump factory, had they chosen to adopt a matrix organization, they would have retained their existing functional organization and management, but superimposed product managers for each of the main ranges of pump. A designer would be responsible both to the chief designer for the way in which the design office ran, for overall standards in design, for information and encouragement about developments in pump technology, and so on, and to the product manager for medium-range pumps, for scheduling the work, for finding out information about particular cost and quality standards to be worked to, and for liaison with the production facilities as the pump went into production.

A rapidly increasing number of companies in the UK are introducing some form of matrix organization. As production technologies have become increasingly complex and automated, as products themselves have become more sophisticated, and as markets have become increasingly competitive in both price and non-price terms, the level of uncertainty facing many enterprises has risen and there is, consequently, a need to process much more information. Moving to a matrix form of organization has been a common response to this, though in many cases the change has needed much preparation, staff training, and careful induction.

## Socio-technical Systems Theory

Organizations are not only concerned with the processing of information in order to exercise efficient co-ordination, they serve other functions too. People are not just 'canny calculators', they have social and other needs which they may expect the organization to meet. There has been an important strand in the development of organization theory which has been concerned with this particular issue. If the developments sketched out above had their genesis in classical management theory, then the strand to be discussed now has its roots in the work of Mayo and the 'human relations' approach arising from this research. The Hawthorne experiments, to which Mayo was consultant, must be familiar to every management student. In these studies (Roethlisberger and Dickson, 1939) a group of female workers engaged in electrical wiring work was subjected to a series of changes in their environment, such as the level of lighting, length of rest breaks, and length of working day, and the effect on their level of output was carefully monitored. With every environmental change, output went up, and more surprisingly, continued to rise even when all environmental conditions were returned to their original level. Mayo's conclusion was that what was important to the women in the study was not the external conditions of their working environment, but their social relationship with each other, with their supervisor, and with the researchers. Because they had been fully involved in the design and setting up of the research, the women had become committed to its objective – that of working out ways of achieving higher productivity – and had responded by producing that higher productivity. The implication was that organizations should be designed not just to be efficient processors of information, but to enable strong positive social relations to be formed within work groups, and between work groups and management. In this way, it was hoped that a strong positive commitment to the firm and norms of high productivity would be established. Eventually, this approach came to be systematized in the form of socio-technical systems theory.

The socio-technical systems approach resulted from the researchers of a team from the Tavistock Institute in London into the organization of coal mining (Trist et al., 1963). Concerned that levels of productivity with new mining machinery were much lower than expected, the National Coal Board called in the Tavistock researchers to advise immediately following the nationalization of the mines at the end of the Second World War. As a result of intensive research in several pits, the researchers concluded that the form of work organization adopted when the new technology was introduced had disrupted the previous pattern of social relations. In non-mechanized pits small groups of miners worked together, each worker having a range of skills, each group sharing a common paynote, and the groups were self-selecting and worked out for themselves who did what job. With the introduction of face conveyors and the longwall method of coal abstraction, the size of work groups increased from half a dozen to up to 50. Moreover, an elaborate division of labour was involved, with each worker doing a specialized and fragmented task that required little skill.

There were several problems with this arrangement. The previous small groups required no managerial co-ordination and hence there was no tradition of middle management within the organization to co-ordinate these very large groups of workers with their fragmented jobs. Even if the organization had the structure to provide this co-ordination, it is likely that the miners, having for so many years operated in a highly autonomous way, would have resisted co-ordination and control by a managerial hierarchy. Moreover, underground conditions made managerial control from a distance difficult to exercise. Thirdly, the payment system was now inappropriate for the new method of working. Previously each small group had worked almost on a subcontract basis, being paid for each ton of coal removed. Attempts to manage the new large groups on this subcontract basis ran into difficulty because it involved a great deal of time in haggling over prices for specific tasks, and, with no common denominator for fixing rates, different criteria were used for measuring performance – tonnage, yardage, cubic measures, number of operations completed, and so on – and contradictory interests developed.

It was in response to this that the Tavistock researchers developed their approach. As Trist and his colleagues define it,

the concept of a socio-technical system arose from the consideration that any production system requires both a technological organization – equipment and process layout – and a work organization relating to each other those who carry out the necessary tasks. The technological demands place limits on the type of work organization possible, but a work organization has social and psychological properties of its own that are independent of technology. (1963: 6)

Using this perspective the research team suggested a different organization structure, known as the composite longwall method of working which was based on a self-selected group of men who allocated themselves to tasks and shifts and received a comprehensive payment on a common note. This form of work organization attempted to reintroduce an element of responsible autonomy and subcontracting into the organization structure.

The general principle emerging from socio-technical systems theory, therefore, is that organization structure has to meet social and psychological needs of various kinds, in addition to providing efficient channels of communication and authority; and these needs, as well as the level of uncertainty posed by the size, technology, and environment of the firm, must be considered by the organizational designer. To put this another way, structures of organization may be required which are not optimal for decision-making alone; the needs of the system as a whole must be optimized. Though this is an important insight into the functions of organization structure, it is only a partial view and in the last section of this chapter the limits to this view are challenged.

## Agency Theory and Transaction Costs Analysis

Organization theory has, until recently, nearly always taken for granted the existence of an organization and concerned itself only with the particular structure adopted. It has not been concerned with attempting to explain the circumstances under which organizations might be set up or disbanded. This particular question has become a central issue and is important for two reasons. Firstly, there have been interesting theoretical developments within industrial economics and organization theory which enable intelligent questions to be posed and plausible answers to be given about the determinants of organizational boundaries. Secondly, the question has become of great practical interest with the growth of a great deal of subcontract work, and large corporations deliberately shrinking by selling off parts of their enterprise.

It is the economists who have paid most attention to this type of question and the concept that is central to their analysis is that of the transaction. Organizational life is conceptualized as individuals and groups conducting transactions with each other and the question is, whether it is more efficient to conduct a transaction by means of making a contract in the market place (buying and selling) or by internalizing the transaction and handling it by means of a managerial hierarchy. Economists assume that all transactions between any two human beings will be conducted by means of market mechanisms unless there is some good reason for not doing so. The existence of large-scale hierarchical organizations, when apparently many of the transactions conducted within the enterprise could instead have been conducted in the market-place, is a puzzle for the profession.

One attempt to solve this puzzle (Alchian and Demsetz, 1972) is agency theory. In this model, there is a principal–agent relationship, in which the one party (the principal) delegates work to another party (the agent) who performs the work. The principal–agent arrangement may come about when, for a specific task, there is an advantage in co-operative effort or teams. If everyone in the team was happy with an equal share of the compensation, and all team members trusted each other to put in a similar level of effort or were not very concerned about minor degrees of free-riding, there would be no problem for the economist. However, because in many cases neither of these assumptions holds, there is a problem about metering effort and rewarding performance fairly. If a group of producers acting as a team were left to their own devices then, suggest the agency theorists, they would either spend a great deal of time attempting to monitor each other's performance and negotiating levels of compensation for each other or, worse still, the stresses caused by the difficulties of metering would either split the group or prevent the team from forming in the first place. Hence, they argue, the principal–agent arrangement comes into being with the principal doing the metering and rewarding. One major question addressed by agency theory has been that of what type of relationship might exist between the principal and agent, and what factors might determine the optimal contract which might govern that relationship. This question covers the employment relationship itself, the vertical integration of relationships within firms between divisions engaged in processes at various points down the chain of production, and relations between organizations.

An example of the application of agency theory is the work of Demski and Feltham (1978). As economists, they use the language of the market-place and speak of contracts, but the result of their analysis is very similar to the contingency theories. They suggest that when the principal knows what the agent has done, which would be the case when tasks are highly programmed (that is, there is a low level of uncertainty), then a 'behaviour-based' contract (when the principal monitors the actual behaviour of the agent) is most efficient. If the principal does not know what the agent has actually done, however, and only has knowledge about the outcome – the job is less programmed and involves a higher level of uncertainty – the agent may or may not have performed as agreed. In other words, there may be goal conflict between the principal and the agent because both are self-interested. Given self-interest and information asymmetry which arises from the technology of the agent's job, the principal has two options. One is to discover the agent's behaviour by investing in systems of scientific management, budgetary control, or simple supervision. The other option is to contract on the outcome of the agent's behaviour.

The choice between 'behaviour-based' and 'outcome-based' contracts depends upon the trade-off between the cost of measuring behaviour and the cost of transferring risk to the agent through an 'outcome-based' contract. If it is relatively inexpensive to monitor behaviour, or expensive to place risk on the agent, one would expect a 'behaviour-based' contract. While this analysis has immediate relevance to the design of payment systems, it also has substantial implications for the structure of the organization. Monitoring behaviour implies fragmented tasks, direct supervision, and a formalized, mechanistic organization, whereas emphasis on outcomes is likely to mean that workers are multiskilled, there is less direct supervision, and a less formalized, more organic form of organization structure.

Transactions cost analysis, developed primarily by Williamson (1975), takes the economist's perspective on organization a great deal further, and with more sensitivity to social behaviour. At the core of Williamson's analysis are the concepts of complexity, uncertainty, bounded rationality, small numbers, opportunism and 'information impactedness'. This last concept is a term coined by Williamson to describe a situation in which the one party to the transaction has less information relevant to the transaction than the other, and cannot obtain more information without incurring costs. Like the agency theorists, Williamson assumes that markets will be the preferred form of conducting transactions unless there are reasons why they should fail. They do fail, he suggests, when the transactions to be conducted involve high levels of complexity or uncertainty and when there are only small numbers capable of conducting the transaction either as buyers or sellers. His argument is that, when there is a high level of complexity or uncertainty, then because of the 'bounded rationality' condition (Simon, 1957), it will be difficult, expensive, or even impossible for each side of the transaction to have full knowledge of all the relevant details of that transaction. If, for example, a car assembler is planning a new car model and is considering buying in, rather than making, the gear-boxes, it may attempt to transact with a gear-box manufacturer to set up a contract for supply. But, because of the complexity of the product and the production process, and because of 'bounded rationality', the car assembler may not know whether the supplier has the capability to produce the gear-box in sufficient quantities by the launch date.

The supplier may be tempted to behave opportunistically (defined by Williamson as 'self-interest seeking with guile') and promise delivery by launch date, even if he knows this is impossible. He can do this, however, only if the 'small numbers condition' holds. Although this condition may not hold at the point when the assembler is setting up the contract (as there may be other potential gear-box suppliers), it does by the time delivery of the goods is expected, because at that stage only the contracted supplier is near to being able to supply, and the assembler cannot switch suppliers at this late stage. Thus the supplier will be tempted to win the contract by acting opportunistically and, because of complexity, uncertainty and bounded rationality, the assembler will not know of this. This is information impactedness and leads, suggests Williamson, to market failure. A firm will be unwilling to take this risk and will therefore make rather than buy-in the product. In other words, hierarchy has superseded market. Though the example here is of vertical integration, like agency theory, transactions cost analysis can be used to analyse the employment relationship and other inter-organizational relationships.

Three particular strengths of transactions cost analysis compared to agency theory are worth noting. It emphasizes bounded rationality, complexity and small numbers as the sources of market failure, rather than the difficulty of metering; it delineates hierarchy as the alternative to market, rather than merely discussing problems with the principal–agency relationship; and the treatment of hierarchy, and of mechanisms to develop consummate rather than perfunctory commitment by organizational members, goes much further than agency theory's specification of behaviour and 'outcome-based' contracts.


*The Radical Critique of Organization Theory*

Thus far the chapter has dealt with explanations that rest on the assumption that organizational structures reflect, either consciously or unconsciously, the preferences and interests of management whose objectives are to design organizations which optimize decision-making, co-ordination, and the commitment of organizational members. This core assumption within both contingency and socio-technical systems theory leaves them open to criticism on at least two counts: on the adequacy of their theoretical basis and on the quality of advice they give to management.

With regard to theoretical adequacy, sociological critiques of conventional organization theory have often drawn attention to one of its most questionable assumptions, namely that there is a common goal to which all organizational members are committed, and that the primary organizational problem is merely that of ensuring that appropriate information gets to individuals so that, as people of good-will, they can make an appropriate response. Williamson's transactions cost analysis replaces this assumption with the alternative that people behave opportunistically, but even his approach has been criticized for neglecting wider issues of power (Francis, 1983). The sociological critique of these assumptions points out that organizations are made up of individuals and groups who have their own goals and purposes, and who often attempt to subvert formal organizational goals in order to gain their own ends. Organizational structure is the result of an attempt by one powerful group (management) to impose structures on others (various groups of workers) in order to exercise tight control over them and to ensure that activities are co-ordinated in a way that efficiently meets management goals.

A persuasive example of this radical critique is developed by Marglin (1974) in a paper provocatively titled 'What Do Bosses Do?'. His thesis is that factory production and managerial hierarchies came into being at the time of the Industrial Revolution in Britain, not because of developments in spinning and weaving technology, but because they enabled merchants and capitalists to exploit labour more efficiently. Prior to industrialization, most spinning and weaving was done by independent contractors working on a putting-out basis. This arrangement posed several problems for the merchants. They found it difficult to prevent the spinners and weavers from cheating them and they could not use the price mechanism to raise output because most craftsmen had a strong preference for leisure. Payment was on a piece-work system and, if the price per unit was raised, the craftsmen would work less.

According to Marglin, the merchants set up factories for these and not for technological reasons. His argument is given weight by the historical evidence; many early factories used identical equipment to that found in the cottage-based industry. Factory workers were offered the all-or-nothing choice of a 14-hour day, six-day week and many merchants did not recruit skilled workers to their factories, relying instead on unskilled labour provided by women and children from the workhouses.

This line of argument has several implications for discussions about the structure of organization. Firstly, it poses a different explanation from agency theory or transactions cost analysis for the switch from market to hierarchy. If the switch was made because of the power and preferences of the merchants, as Marglin suggests, rather than because hierarchy was more efficient than market, as agency theory or transactions cost analysis would suggest, then the question arises about the extent to which hierarchies today have resulted from the exercise of power in a similar way. The implication of Marglin's analysis is that there is far more opportunity for work to be done by independent contractors than the current situation permits. Secondly, it poses a different explanation for the complexity of organizational structure. Marglin argues that the merchants and capitalists, in order to provide for themselves a niche in the labour process, deliberately fragmented work and instituted managerial co-ordination rather than direct co-ordination between workers in order to safe-guard their own role. Again, to the extent that this process still operates, it implies that much work could be organized in a more co-operative rather than managerially-directed manner with no loss of efficiency.

Elements of this argument are contained within the more widely-known writing of Braverman (1974). His argument is that technology has developed within the kind of process described above, and so the technology itself embodies the interests of capital. Technologies could have been developed which were suitable for use by skilled spinners, weavers, and other home-workers in small-scale production. However, there was no market for this kind of technology, partly because such people did not express a demand for it and partly because they would not have had the capital to buy it. Instead, the demand was for technology suitable for large-scale factory production and this was what was developed. This makes it difficult now to envisage how things could be done in any other way. Moreover, the technology was developed to fit in with the capitalists' need to maintain their niche in the labour process and so, argues Braverman, it was designed deliberately to deskill labour. With labour deskilled by the technology, more extensive managerial hierarchies had to be developed. Indeed, the process goes further. As a result of fragmenting labour and instituting managerial control at the expense of work-group control, informal social controls in the workplace broke down and the hierarchy had to be elaborated still further to exercise control and ensure higher levels of effort.

The radical critique also invites questions about the quality of advice offered to management within conventional theories of organizational structure. Such advice is limited, the critique would suggest, because it neglects consideration of many of the issues posed above and, worse still, encourages management to design structures which build in inherent conflicts. Sophisticated management may already be aware of these deficiencies, but even they may learn something from Marglin and Braverman.

## THE ORGANIZATION OF THE FUTURE

A number of forecasts have been made recently about trends in organizational structure based on current practice in successful US, Japanese and UK businesses (Atkinson, 1984; Kanter, 1984; Peters and Waterman, 1982; and Pinchot, 1985). As chapter 2 pointed out, one concern is the development of the flexible organization and, in particular, of core–periphery structures, in which the firm focuses strongly on its own core activities and moves the rest to the periphery, by subcontracting for example. A strong pressure for this development has been the rise in the fixed costs of labour, due to rising labour cost rates and, in some countries, greater employee protection through government legislation. Companies are therefore concerned to minimize the number of direct long-term employees. Ways of doing this include the use of primary and secondary labour markets within the firm; employment of people on short-term contracts; use of agency staff; giving contracts to self-employed individuals (who may perform the work at home); subcontracting work to small firms; and increasing the amount of out-sourcing (Atkinson, 1984). Each of these tactics increases the flexibility of the core firm to adjust labour utilization and output in response to market fluctuations.

Another pressure on firms to adopt the core–periphery structure may come from technological developments. For example, it may be that in high-technology industries tasks are so complex that there is a greatly increased use of self-contained task units. It is possible to co-ordinate such task units by managerial hierarchy, but it may be more efficient to do so through the market-place, for example, by treating its units as subcontractors or independent suppliers from whom the core firm out-sources components or services. Of course, it may not be the core firm which initiates these organizational changes. Technological developments may bring into the market-place independent suppliers who pose so severe a competitive challenge to the core firm's own internal source of supply that it is forced to switch to out-sourcing.

Another technological pressure is the increased availability of information technology. Transactions cost analysis would suggest that, if information technology provided all parties to the transaction with adequate information, the chances of 'information impactedness' and 'opportunism' occurring are much reduced, and the market recovers its advantage over hierarchy as the preferred method of handling the transaction. One consequence might be a fragmentation (rather than 'peripheralization') of organizations as various units are uncoupled from the managerial hierarchy to trade with each other.

The second major shift in organizational structure which has been identified – change within the core firm to enhance its ability to manage rapid and effective product and process innovations – is partly stimulated by techno-logical developments, though the competitive challenge from Japan is also frequently cited as a pressure for this type of organizational change. Peters and Waterman (1982: 9) characterize this shift in terms of the 'seven-S variables' which 'any intelligent approach to organizing has to encompass, and treat as interdependent'. The suggestion is that, although the first three of these seven

'S's – strategy, structure and systems – must always be given attention, the critical variables in the future will no longer be these 'rationalist' factors but the latter four – 'shared values', 'skills', 'style', and 'staff'. Organizational structures in the future must place value on people rather than systems, and provide a context which generates a high level of motivation. The result is an organization which approximates to Burns' and Stalker's concept of the organic system of management, though for Peters and Waterman, and others writing on this topic, the issue is more one of developing an appropriate culture rather than structure.

This theme, which enhances the human resource management approach discussed in chapter 2, is pursued both by Kanter (1984) and Pinchot (1985) in their analysis of conditions which encourage entrepreneurial activity. For Pinchot, the notion of 'intrapreneurship' (entrepreneurial activity within the firm) is an essential ingredient of successfully innovating organizations. Like Kanter, he also suggests a series of organizational factors which are needed to encourage this activity: structures which allow intrapreneurs to stay with their 'intraprise' throughout the entire innovation process ('no handoffs'), the use of cross-functional teams, corporate slack, and decentralized decision-making ('the doer decides'). Kanter's treatment is more sophisticated and discursive, but follows a similar line. In almost every case the suggested structures are the antithesis of the bureaucratic, mechanistic organization.

From this, one can forecast that organizations of the future will take many forms. There will doubtless continue to be monolithic organizations, mechanistically structured, producing standard goods for stable markets, in which cost-minimization through economies of scale and strict management control will be the key criteria for success. But there is likely to be a range of other organizational types, linked together in a wide variety of different ways through a combination of contractual and managerial arrangements. Some of these, especially those carrying out core tasks and using specialist staff, will be organized for innovation, using structures based on the Peters and Waterman, Pinchot, and Kanter models of what is required for intrapreneurship. In these, management will exercise control through encouraging shared values and a participative management style. Other organizations, performing the more mundane 'peripheral' tasks, may be little changed from today.

It remains to be seen how the numerical balance will shift between organizations of different types, and whether flexible, innovation-centred organizations will have as benign a structure as some commentators now predict. In any event, organizational structures do not simply emerge in response to technological and market changes. They are, as has been indicated in this chapter, designed by individuals and groups with particular objectives in mind, and their implementation is a matter of negotiation, formal or informal. Corporate and line management, the personnel function, trade unions and organizational members in general will all play important roles in shaping the organization of the future and their respective influence and preferences will be crucial. The task of the organization theorist is not to predict, but to provide an analytical framework which can assist each of these groups to shape their preferences in an intelligent manner.

# Bibliography

Alchian, A.A. and Demsetz, H. 1972. 'Production, Information Costs, and Economic Organization'. *American Economic Review*, 62, 777–95.

Aldrich, H.E. 1979. *Organizations and Environments*. Englewood Cliffs, NJ: Prentice-Hall.

Atkinson, J. 1984. 'Manpower Strategies for Flexible Organizations'. *Personnel Management*, August, 28–31.

Braverman, H. 1974. *Labor and Monopoly Capital: The Degradation of Work in the Twentieth Century*. New York: Monthly Review Press.

Brech, E.F.L. 1957. *Organization: The Framework of Management*. London: Longman.

Burns, T. and Stalker, G.M. 1961. *The Management of Innovation*. London: Tavistock 2nd edn. 1966.

Chandler, A.D. 1966. *Strategy and Structure*. New York: Doubleday.

Channon, D. 1978. *The Service Industries: Strategy, Structure and Financial Performance*. London: Macmillan.

Child. J. 1973. 'Strategies of Control and Organizational Behavior'. *Administrative Science Quarterly*, 18: March, 1–17.

Demski, J. and Feltham, G. 1978. 'Economic Incentives in Budgetary Control Systems'. *Accounting Review*, 53: April, 336–59.

Francis, A. 1983. 'Markets and Hierarchies: Efficiency or Domination?'. *Power, Efficiency and Institutions*. Eds. Francis, A., Turk, J. and Willman, P. London: Heinemann, 105–16.

Galbraith, J. 1977. *Organization Design*. Reading, Mass.: Addison-Wesley.

Goold, M. and Campbell, A. 1986. *Strategic Management Styles*. Vol. I of *Strategic Decision Making: The Corporate Role*. London: London Business School, Centre for Business Strategy.

*Guardian*. 1987. 'Imperial to Cut HQ Staff'. 8 September.

Hill, C.W.L. and Pickering, J.F. 1986. 'Divisionalization, Decentralization and Performance of Large UK Companies'. *Journal of Management Studies*, 23: January, 26–50.

Kanter, R.M. 1984. *The Change Masters: Corporate Entrepreneurs at Work*. London: Allen & Unwin.

Lawrence, P.R. and Lorsch, J.W. 1967. *Organization and Environment*. Cambridge, Mass.: Harvard University Press.

Marglin, S. 1974. 'What Do Bosses Do? The Origins and Functions of Hierarchy in Capitalist Production'. *The Division of Labour*. Ed. Gorz, A. Brighton: Harvester Press, 13–54.

Perrow, C. 1970. *Organizational Analysis: A Sociological View*. Belmont, CA: Wadsworth.

Peters, T.J. and Waterman, R.H. 1982. *In Search of Excellence*. New York: Harper & Row.

Pinchot, G. 1985. *Intrapreneuring: Why You Don't Have to Leave the Corporation to Become an Entrepreneur*. New York: Harper & Row.

Pugh, D., Hickson, D., Hinings, R. and Turner, C. 1968. 'Dimensions of Organizational Structure'. *Administrative Science Quarterly*, 13: June, 65–104.

——, Hickson, D. and Hinings, R. 1969. 'The Context of Organizational Structures'. *Administrative Science Quarterly*, 14: March, 91–114.

Roethlisberger, F.J. and Dickson, W.J. 1939. *Management and the Worker*. Cambridge, MA: Harvard University Press.

Simon, H.A. 1957. *Administrative Behavior: A Study of Decision-Making Processes in Administrative Organization*. New York: Macmillan.

Thompson, J. 1967. *Organizations in Action*. New York: McGraw-Hill.

Trist, E.L., Higgin, G.W., Murray, H. and Pollock, A.B. 1963. *Organizational Choice*. London: Tavistock.

Williamson, O.E. 1970. *Corporate Control and Business Behavior*. Englewood Cliffs, NJ: Prentice-Hall.

—— 1975. *Markets and Hierarchies: Analysis and Antitrust Implications*. New York: Free Press.

Woodward, J. 1965. *Industrial Organization: Theory and Practice*. London: Oxford University Press.

—— Ed. 1970. *Industrial Organization: Behaviour and Control*. London: Oxford University Press.

# 4 Principles and Practice in Work Design

*David A. Buchanan*

The ways that tasks and roles are determined and allocated form the building blocks of organizations. Traditionally, tasks and roles have been determined, at least implicitly, according to the principles of 'scientific management'. There have, however, been pressures to reject that approach, and to develop other methods to improve both the quality of working life and employee performance by increasing variety, meaning and autonomy in work. Attempts to discover the elusive common ground for the simultaneous satisfaction of human and organizational goals through the judicious manipulation of job characteristics have been described as the search for 'person–environment fit' (Lawler, 1976: 225). The practice of work design assumes that a fit can be found, and has been defined as 'specification of the contents, methods, and relationships of jobs in order to satisfy technological and organizational requirements as well as the social and personal requirements of the job holder' (Davis, 1966: 21).

There are four main work design techniques based on theories of human motivation which emphasize the need for interesting and meaningful work experience and which indicate the richness and complexity of the human motives influencing performance at work. *Job rotation* involves moving employees systematically from task to task. *Job enlargement* concerns giving each employee several tasks, and is also known as horizontal enlargement. *Job enrichment* incorporates inspection, supervisory and other activities into the individual job, and is also known as vertical enlargement. *Autonomous group working* involves the creation of self-managing multiskilled teams.

This chapter describes and illustrates how work is designed and explains the theories and assumptions on which these designs are based. Where appropriate, practical examples are drawn from British, European, Scandinavian and American experience with work design applications. The chapter argues that the pressures on management to change its approach to the design of work in the 1980s and 1990s are different from and more urgent than those which encouraged the quality of working life movement in the 1960s and 1970s. The chapter further argues that effective work design strategies for the future need to be more radical in their organizational effects and need to be formulated as part of an integrated employment and rewards package. Initial approaches to work design involved tinkering with individual jobs only and these techniques had weak and limited effects. Broadly-based organizational strategies are now necessary to develop and sustain the high levels of skill, commitment and performance fundamental to continued international competitiveness and economic growth.

## THE TRADITIONAL APPROACH

The key figure in the development of traditional approaches to designing work was F.W. Taylor. An engineer from Philadelphia who trained as a machinist, Taylor was appalled by the inefficiency of the industrial practices he witnessed and set out to demonstrate how managers and workers could benefit by adopting a more 'scientific' approach. He felt that inefficiency was caused by what he called *systematic soldiering*, or the deliberate restriction of output by workers anxious to sustain their employment. Soldiering was easy because management control was weak, and because discretion over work methods was left to individual workers who wasted time and effort with inefficient working rules of thumb. Managers expected their employees to have the appropriate skills for the work they were given, or to learn what to do from those around them. Notions of systematic job specifications, clearly established responsibilities, and training needs analysis were not appreciated. Taylor sought to change that.

Taylor (1911) argued that manual and mental work should be separated. Management, he claimed, should specialize in planning and organizing work, and workers should specialize in actually doing it. Taylor regarded this as a way of ensuring industrial harmony, as everyone would know clearly what was expected of them and what their responsibilities were. He also saw the clear advantages in making individuals specialize in activities in which they would become expert and highly proficient.

His technique for designing manual jobs involved the following steps. First, decide the optimum degree of *task fragmentation*, breaking down complex jobs into their simple component parts. Second, determine the most efficient way of performing each part of the work. Studies are carried out to discover the *one best way* of doing each of the fragmented tasks, and to design the layout of the workplace and tools to be used so that unnecessary movements are eliminated. Finally, select and train employees to carry out the fragmented tasks in exactly the one best way, and reward them for above-average performance.

Clearly, task fragmentation can have a number of advantages for the organization that applies it. Individual workers do not need to be given expensive and time-consuming training, and those who leave or who prove to be unreliable can easily be replaced. Specialization in one small task makes people work very fast at it. Less skilled work is lower paid work. And it is easier to observe and control workers doing simple activities.

But task fragmentation also has disadvantages for those subjected to it. The work is repetitive and boring. The contribution of the individual to the work of the organization as a whole is comparatively meaningless. Monotony can lead to apathy, dissatisfaction and carelessness. The individual develops no special skill or knowledge that might lead to promotion or to better work in another organization. One of the main criticisms of Taylor's work is that it lacked any sustained attention to human needs other than those concerning money and rest. His approach to job design appeared to create efficient ways of working, but created fragmented and dissatisfying jobs that were unlikely to develop employee skills, commitment and high performance in the long run. Subsequent research has suggested that the expression of human needs at work is richer and more complex than Taylor's methods have assumed.

It is often argued that many people prefer the simplified types of work that Taylor's approach produces. This argument cannot be generally accepted for two main reasons. First, there are probably not enough people available with the high level of tolerance of boredom required to carry out simple and meaningless tasks efficiently. Most people have higher levels of ability and higher expectations of working life. Second, they have a physiological need for sensory stimulation, for changes in the patterns of information that feed to the senses to sustain arousal. When we do not receive that stimulation, our sensory equipment 'switches off'. And there are several ways in which poor psychological well-being can affect the performance of an organization, through the costs of absenteeism, labour turnover, careless accidents and sabotage.

Even so, Taylorism and scientific management have been more widely accepted and applied through the rest of this century than in Taylor's lifetime (he died in 1915). From a survey of 24 American firms around the middle of the century, Davis et al. (1955) found that the work design principles of maximum specialization and repetitiveness were still popular. In an influential critique of scientific management and the dehumanization of work, Braverman (1974) demonstrates how Taylor's approach has been extended to clerical and administrative work as well as manual manufacturing tasks, creating what has been called 'office factories'.

Modern techniques of work design have been developed and applied mainly in the second half of this century as antidotes to Taylorism. But the impact of those techniques has not been nearly as powerful or pervasive as the influence of scientific management on management practice. Why has Taylorism retained its popularity? There are perhaps two reasons. First, it is a plausible, easy and cheap set of techniques which appear to work. Managers in Britain seem to prefer common-sense, practical ideas to more complex and sophisticated techniques, especially those based on 'social science', an enterprise which is widely regarded with suspicion and scepticism. Task specialization in assembly work reduces work in progress and throughput times, takes less space, and simplifies production control. These clear, 'hard', short-term gains from Taylor's approach may outweigh the less certain and less quantifiable longer-term costs and disadvantages, which rest on 'soft' arguments about the nature of human reactions to work. It is always easier to blame workers who have the wrong skills, wrong attitudes and wrong values, than to blame a systematically prepared job specification.

A second, less obvious and to managers less acceptable, explanation is that Taylor's approach to work design perpetuates the higher status and authority of managers, who work in clean offices, do no manual work, take all the responsibility and the decisions, and take home higher financial rewards. Groups of office and shopfloor workers who have discretion over the performance of meaningful sections of an organization's operations are a greater threat to managerial legitimacy than individual workers who have little or no idea of how their fragmented tasks contribute to the work of the organization as a whole.

It is therefore wrong to dismiss scientific management methods as disused and outdated. Some organizations have departed from that approach and adopted some of the techniques discussed later in this chapter. But Taylor's ideas have become a central feature of the taken-for-granted organizational recipe that many managers apply to the design and redesign of work without serious question or challenge.

## PRESSURES FOR CHANGE

Why should managers have any interest in approaches to the design of work that depart from the simple and practical methods of Taylor's scientific management? Humanitarian considerations may become part of the justification for using more sophisticated work design methods, and most managers would of course deny that they disregard the well-being, both physical and psychological, of their employees. But the evidence overwhelmingly shows that managers do not take action to improve working conditions, improve health and safety, or improve the quality of working life, unless they are convinced that there will be an adequate return on the time and money invested in such measures, or (in the case of safety at work, for example) they are forced to do so by legislation (Asplund, 1981).

### Early Developments

Management interest in work design is thus primarily a financial interest. Until the late 1970s, the main considerations were the costs of low productivity, absenteeism and labour turnover. Those aspects of worker behaviour were attributed to dissatisfying repetitive work and work design techniques seemed to offer solutions. The British Industrial Fatigue Research Board produced the first systematic findings which demonstrated that Taylor's methods and fragmented jobs could adversely affect labour productivity and costs (Vernon et al., 1924). They examined several types of light, 'short-cycle', work in the boot and shoe, and tin can industries. The work cycle is simply the time taken to complete one operation and begin the next. The tasks that they investigated had work cycles from less than one second to one minute. The Board discovered, not surprisingly, that the workers found these tasks boring, and that output could be increased by 20 per cent by *job rotation* which simply involved moving workers from one task to another every half hour. They argued that it would be possible to find the optimum rotation interval for different tasks.

Job rotation was thus the first work design technique to be advocated as an antidote to scientific management methods. Job rotation does not involve changes to job content or methods. It concerns the way in which work and workers are organized. The work of the British National Institute of Industrial Psychology was partly responsible for developing this simple concept further. In the early 1930s the Institute was involved in consultancy work with a company that made wireless sets, Kolster-Brandes, where the problems of repetitive work in assembly had arisen (Harding, 1931). That work produced the first reported experiment in *job enlargement*.

Job enlargement involves the recombination of tasks separated by scientific management techniques and an increase in work cycle. It is therefore slightly more radical than job rotation in which the basic tasks remain the same. Although the British research had demonstrated before the Second World War that Taylor had gone too far with the specialization of work and that productivity could be improved by enlarging jobs, these techniques became popular only in the 1950s. In the period of economic growth following the Second World War, management in the Western industrialized nations became more aware of the hidden costs of monotonous work which created dissatisfied workers. Yet research has failed to show that unhappy workers are less productive than contented ones, and the relationship is more complex than common sense suggests. But unhappy workers are more likely to seek work elsewhere, be absent and turn up late more often, and create their own variety at work through interesting and creative diversions and forms of sabotage. Job rotation and enlargement offered simple ways of reducing the costs of turnover, absenteeism and mischief.

One influential American study of the experience of work in the early 1950s was conducted by Walker and Guest (1952) and took the form of an attitude survey of 180 automobile assembly workers from which they identified six key characteristics of mass production work: mechanical pacing, repetitiveness, minimum skill requirement, no choice of tools or methods, minute subdivision of product, and surface mental attention. Workers in jobs with high ratings of those characteristics had higher absenteeism rates than in those jobs without those features.

The first report of successful job enlargement in practice also came from Walker (1950) and stemmed from work in the Endicott plant of IBM in 1944. The jobs of machinists were enlarged to include machine set-up and inspection of finished products leading to improved product quality, reduced scrap, less idle time for men and machines, and a 95 per cent reduction in set-up and inspection times. A number of other successful job enlargement applications, mainly North American, were reported during the 1950s (Buchanan 1979: 26). The technique was relevant to white-collar office work as well as to manual tasks, and applications continued to be reported sporadically throughout the 1960s and into the 1970s. But the technique may not have been as widespread in practice as it appeared to be from the literature. A survey which covered 276 of the 500 largest corporations in the USA found in 1969 that over 80 per cent of them had never used or considered job enlargement (Schoderbek and Reif, 1969).

One European company which used job enlargement extensively was Philips which replaced the continuous assembly line in their television plant at Eindhoven in Holland with groups of workers each performing enlarged tasks (van Beek, 1964). Philips also used the technique in one of their Australian plants with operators completing whole mobile radios instead of performing a fragmented part of the subassembly operation (Pauling, 1968); and in the plant at Hamilton in Scotland, where operators moved from a conveyor-paced assembly line to the manufacture of complete fan heaters (Thornely and Valantine, 1968).

Workers on assembly lines perform meaningless and repetitive tasks. Each worker also has to work at the same pace as the others so that the line as a whole moves continuously and smoothly in a 'balanced' manner. The same applies to fragmented administrative routines, all the stations on the line have to be staffed for the work to flow. Job enlargement offers more variety and a potentially more meaningful contribution for the worker. But it also overcomes the management problems of balancing the work rates at the various operations in the line. Workers on enlarged tasks are not so completely dependent on each other's output and 'line balancing' is not a problem. The absence of one worker does not mean that work stops altogether and production planning and labour use can be more flexible.

Another management advantage concerns the identification of incompetent operatives. It is often hard to trace faults in work that comes off an assembly line back to one of the dozen people involved at different stages. With enlarged jobs, output is clearly traceable to the individual responsible. The technique of job enlargement can therefore be used to control employees as well as to give them more responsibility and discretion. Job enlargement thus offers managerial benefits beyond improvements in the quality of work experience.

## Autonomous Groups

Developments in work design techniques beyond job rotation and enlargement have been significantly influenced by the development of a 'humanistic' psychology whose most popular and influential figure has undoubtedly been the American psychologist Maslow. As chapter 1 pointed out, Maslow (1943) argued that human beings have seven innate needs. *Physiological*, or survival, needs concern sunlight, sex, food and water. *Safety* needs concern freedom from threat from the environment, animals and other people, and the desire for shelter, security, order and predictability. *Love* needs concern relationships, affection, giving and receiving love, and the desire for feelings of belongingness. *Esteem* needs concern strength, achievement, adequacy, confidence, independence, *and* the desire for reputation, prestige, recognition, attention, importance, appreciation, and for a high self-evaluation based on capability and respect from others. *Self-actualization* needs concern the development of the human capability to the fullest potential. *Freedom of inquiry and expression* needs concern social conditions that permit free speech, and encourage justice, fairness and honesty. And finally, *the need to know and understand* concerns the desire to gain and to systematize knowledge, to satisfy curiosity, to learn, experiment and explore.

Maslow also claimed that these needs are organized in a loose hierarchy. A person does not pay much attention to love and esteem needs, for example, unless physical and safety requirements are more or less satisfied. The ultimate human goal is self-actualization, the needs for freedom of inquiry and to know and understand being prerequisites for the satisfaction of all the other needs.

The theory is vague, it cannot easily make predictions about human behaviour, it makes some predictions that are inconsistent with the facts, and is more like a social philosophy than a psychological theory. Yet Maslow's influence is clearly stamped across the work design theories and practices of the latter half of the twentieth century and is a key facet of the 'quality of working life movement' that emerged in the 1960s and 1970s. Thus, one of the most powerful and enduring approaches to work design, drawing on Maslow's expression of human need, is based on the experience of management consultants working at the Tavistock Institute of Human Relations in London. The Tavistock consultants were responsible for the concept of the *composite autonomous work group* or 'self-managing multiskilled team' first developed in a textile mill in north-west India (Rice, 1958).

The work of a second Tavistock consultant, Trist, in the north-west Durham coal mines in Britain in the early 1950s, confirmed the social and economic advantages of self-managing work groups with 'responsible autonomy' (Trist et al., 1963). The traditional miner had a 'composite work role'. He was a 'complete collier' who worked unsupervised and was responsible for all face tasks. As each miner could perform all or most aspects of the work, the coal-getting cycle was 'self-regulating'. But what Trist et al. found in Durham was different. Mechanical conveyors increased the length of coal face which could be mined simultaneously. Longwall mining methods displaced the composite autonomous collier by introducing mass production techniques underground. Each shift performed one distinct phase of the mining sequence which involved undercutting and blasting the coal, loading it onto a conveyor, and advancing the roofwork for the next cycle. Each group of miners carried out specific and narrowly defined tasks and were paid on different bases. A lot of productive time was lost in arguments over pay rates for the different groups for 'non-standard' work, such as that made necessary when the previous shift had not finished its part of the cycle. The coal-getting cycle was no longer self-regulating but required constant management effort to co-ordinate.

In some pits, however, composite autonomous work groups had developed spontaneously as bad conditions had made longwall mining dangerous. These 'composite shortwalls' were worked by multiskilled groups on a common pay scheme which were responsible for the whole coal-mining cycle on any shift. They were self-selecting and leaderless groups, had over 40 members, and made their own task and shift allocations. The level and continuity of their production were significantly better than on comparable longwalls and absenteeism was markedly lower.

The Tavistock approach to work design has been translated into the psychological requirements that job content should meet (Emery et al., 1965: 5–9). From these considerations, one of Trist's colleagues, Emery (1963), compiled a list of 'hypotheses about the ways in which tasks may be more effectively put together to make jobs' (see also van Beinum, 1966). Seven of these hypotheses concern individual task content and the rest concern the organization of work groups. This approach appears to demonstrate that the design of work is not determined by the technology in use.

Autonomous group working has been used extensively in Scandinavia, notably by the Swedish car manufacturers Saab and Volvo. Pehr Gyllen-hammar (1977: 15), President of Volvo, explained that, 'we decided ... to bring people together by replacing the mechanical line with the human work group. In this pattern, employees can act in cooperation, discussing more, deciding among themselves how to organize the work – and, as a result, doing much more. In essence, our approach is based on stimulation rather than restriction. If you view the employees as adults, then you must assume that they will respond to stimulation; if you view them as children, then the assumption is that they need restriction. The intense emphasis on measurement and control in most factories seems to be a manifestation of the latter viewpoint.'

Valéry (1974) estimated that over 1000 experiments had been started in Sweden. Many failed. The Scandinavian quality of working life movement relied on the publicity given to the car manufacturers which became manage-ment tourist attractions. Experience in the rest of Europe has also been apparently limited to a few well-publicized companies such as Philips (Philips Report, 1969; den Hertog, 1976) and Fiat (Ruehl, 1974). The technique has not been popular in North America (see Butteriss and Murdoch, 1976) although more applications have recently been reported (Manz and Sims, 1984). There have been few applications in Britain either (Carby, 1976) although it was used by Shell (Hill, 1971), Scottish and Newcastle Breweries, and some others (Butteriss and Murdoch, 1975).

The composite autonomous work group is a powerful technique in the tool-kit of work design, but unlike job rotation and enlargement it is based on a theory of motivation, rather than on simplistic notions of monotony and variety. One possible reason for the comparative unpopularity of the Tavistock approach is that it comes as part of a package of *socio-technical systems* theory, analysis and design which has a comparatively rich, but complex and impenetrable language. Another possible reason for its lack of popularity is that it directly interferes with the status and responsibilities of lower ranks of managers whose supervisory duties may be absorbed by self-managing groups.

## Enriched Jobs

In 1970, General Motors opened one of the most advanced car assembly plants in the world at that time in Lordstown, Ohio, to make the Chevrolet Vega. The car and the plant were designed for each other. The body had a third of the components of comparable automobiles and was assembled by automatic welding devices and robots. The plant was designed to produce one hundred vehicles an hour, with single operation cycle times as low as 20 seconds. This was publicized as 'the pattern of vehicle production of the future'. By January 1972, incomplete and damaged cars were being made faster than they could be repaired. By February 1982 the Union of Auto Workers had lodged over 5000 grievances about work standards, job losses and 'speed up' in the plant. Management complained about sabotage and neglect. Cars were being made with broken windscreens and mirrors, cut upholstery, keys broken in locks and washers in carburettors. Welding machines were mysteriously reprogrammed to weld bodies in the wrong places, and some cars left the line with all their doors locked. The workers' grievances were not resolved, and the result was a strike which lasted a month, affected 7800 workers in the plant and 8800 other workers indirectly, cost the company an estimated $160 million in lost production, and cost the workers around $11 million in lost wages.

'Blue-collar blues' was the explanation (Gooding, 1970a,b) and Lordstown was a typical example. The workforce had an average age of 24 and their aggression and industrial action indicated their rejection of the monotony of the assembly line. This and subsequent unrest at Lordstown and elsewhere prompted General Motors to change the plant layout and work assignment practices, to appoint a Vice-President of Personnel Development responsible for worker motivation (Wild, 1975), and to develop a programme of employee involvement, suggestion schemes and team problem-solving (Weil, 1981).

The source of the ideas underpinning its programme was Herzberg, whose *job enrichment* technique was widely publicized through his (1968) article in the *Harvard Business Review* with the desperate title 'One More time: How Do You Motivate Employees?'. Whatever criticism it might attract, it is important to note that this technique is derived from an empirically based theory of work motivation. In the early 1950s, Herzberg and colleagues at the Psychological Service of Pittsburg had interviewed 203 accountants and engineers and asked them two 'critical incident' questions. They were asked to recall events which had made them feel good about their work and events which had made them feel bad about it. Analysis of these critical incidents suggested that factors which led to satisfaction were in different categories from those which led to dissatisfaction at work. The characteristics of work which led to satisfaction were called 'motivators' or 'content factors' and were achievement, recognition, responsibility, advancement, growth in competence, and the work itself. The events which led to dissatisfaction were called 'hygiene factors' or 'context factors' and were salary, company policy, supervision, status, security, and working conditions. Herzberg called this a 'two-factor theory' of motivation. Improvements in 'hygiene', he argued, can overcome dissatisfaction, but do not increase satisfaction and motivation. The enrichment of jobs to increase motivation and performance must focus on the 'motivators', and Herzberg suggested the application of seven *vertical job loading factors*. Herzberg's theory is summarized in figure 4.1.

These vertical job loading factors involve removing some controls on employees, increasing individual accountability for work, giving employees

FIGURE 4.1    *Frederick Herzberg's approach to job enrichment*

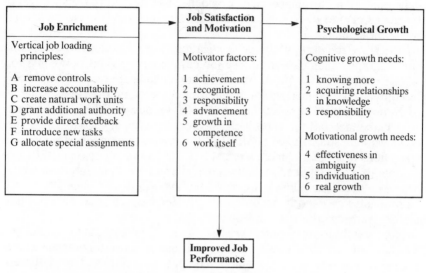

*Source:*  Buchanan (1979: 43); based on Herzberg (1966, 1968)

complete or natural units of work and additional authority, freedom or discretion, providing feedback on performance directly to the individual rather than through supervisors, introducing new and more difficult tasks, and assigning specialized tasks at which employees can become experts.

Herzberg (1966) argued, with Maslow, that humans need 'psychological growth', and that job enrichment was necessary to provide this. He suggested that people have two types of growth needs, to develop understanding and motivation, and these are listed on the right of figure. 4.1. These needs resemble those listed by Maslow, are equally vague, and attract similar criticisms. The technique of job enrichment through use of the loading factors, however, does not rely on this aspect of the theory, as the figure implies.

Herzberg's two-factor motivation theory has not been able to withstand subsequent criticism. The two factors appear to arise through the psychological defence mechanism called 'projection'. When we are happy and successful, we tend to credit ourselves. But when we are unhappy, at work or elsewhere, we tend to 'project' the blame onto people and circumstances beyond our influence. Studies of work motivation that have used other methods thus do not reveal a split between motivator and hygiene factors. Job satisfaction probably has a single dimension, but with Herzberg's motivator factors having a more powerful influence than hygiene. Improving the motivational content of a job is thus more likely to produce the desired results than improving its hygiene context.

Job enrichment has been vastly more popular in practice than autonomous group working on both sides of the Atlantic and there is a vast literature on both the background theory and applications (Buchanan, 1979: 52–60). The technique is easy to understand, and it suggests ways of improving employee motivation and performance which do not necessarily involve higher wages (a hygiene factor) and which leave organization structures and management roles and authority intact.

In the USA, the best publicized applications were in American Telephone and Telegraph which carried out 19 job enrichment projects between 1965 and 1969 affecting over 1000 blue- and white-collar employees (Ford, 1969). The company was concerned about the rising costs of employee dissatisfaction and turnover which were attributed to monotonous jobs. One of the company's personnel staff was reported as saying, 'our company has lost too many people who are still with us!' (Ford, 1969: 16). In Britain, the best publicized applications of job enrichment were at ICI. Paul and Robertson (1970) give accounts of eight applications between 1967 and 1968, mainly with white-collar employees including sales representatives, design engineers, foremen and draughtsmen (who in accordance with Herzberg's advice were not told that they were experimental subjects).

More recently, job enrichment was used at the enquiry unit at the Driver and Vehicle Licensing Centre in Swansea in Britain, when staff complained that they could not deal with the number of public enquiries. The staff were involved in determining the changes in this application. Each staff member was made responsible for all the case work arising from an enquiry and dealt with the problems personally, with only back-up from the manager (Asplund, 1981: 101–2).

Herzberg's approach has three other noteworthy features. First, like Taylor, Herzberg believes that the 'tyranny of the group' suppresses the satisfaction of individual needs. The target of job enrichment is thus individual jobs. Second, in contrast to the 'participative management' movement, Herzberg argues that employees should not be involved in deciding the types of enrichment to which they are subjected as they are not always competent to contribute to the discussion and decision. Third, Herzberg is a 'psychological universalist' (Lupton, 1971; 1976). Everyone is potentially a motivation-seeker or self-actualizer, and this is an indication of mental health. Hygiene seekers are mentally unhealthy and have been blocked at the hygiene level by some unfortunate past experience. This position is not consistent with the facts of individual differences. It is not reasonable to question the psychological well-being of everyone who rejects increased work-load and responsibility.

The more recent job enrichment approach developed by Hackman and Oldham (Hackman et al., 1975) attempts to overcome the universalist criticism. Their *job characteristics model* is summed up in figure 4.2. Their *implementing concepts* are very similar to Herzberg's vertical job loading factors, and the model attempts to separate clearly the main features of work, the *core job dimensions*, from employee experience, the *critical psychological states*, which are confused in Herzberg's concept of motivator factors.

The model thus sets out a causal chain, from job enrichment implementing concepts, through job dimensions and psychological states, to desirable personal and work outcomes. The main difference between this and Herzberg's

FIGURE 4.2     *The job characteristics model*

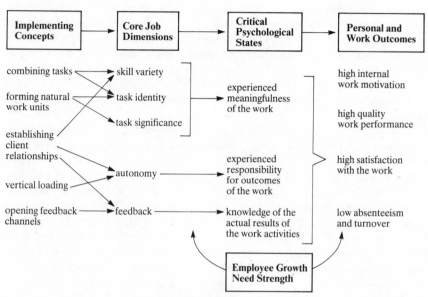

*Source:*  Hackman, Oldham, Janson and Purdy (1975); © 1975 by the Regents of the
University of California; reprinted from the *California Management Review*,
17: 4, 63, by permission of the Regents

approach is that the causal chain works for people with high 'growth need strength', which is not assumed to reflect mental health. This approach still does not work, however, for those with low growth need strength, low need for self-actualization, or for those who in Herzberg's terms are neurotic hygiene seekers.

## LOOKING BACK: AN ASSESSMENT

The theory and practice of work design have convincingly demonstrated that there are few 'technical necessities' behind the design of most jobs. Technological determinism in the design of work is an unrealistic perspective which can serve as a cover for management laziness, or as an excuse for ill-formed and disguised social and political motives. It is necessary, in the interests of skilled, motivated and effective performance to identify and evaluate the work design options that are available in the unique circumstances of each case. The evidence suggests that this is rarely done.

Experience also shows that the application of improved work design techniques is not restricted to low grade manual jobs. They have been applied effectively to several white-collar occupations. As scientific management and new technologies increasingly affect administrative and clerical activities, work design will become a more important issue for these occupations.

Numerous problems have been attributed to inappropriate work design, such as dissatisfaction, passivity, apathy, carelessness, instrumental attitudes to work, lack of co-operation and initiative, indiscipline, sabotage, absenteeism and turnover, poor time-keeping, poor quality and output, waste, interruptions to workflow, stress, psychosomatic disorders, alcoholism and drug abuse. These outcomes affect the individuals concerned, increase the costs of their employers and increase social costs in the form of health care and other benefits.

It is perhaps surprising, therefore, that the incidence of work design applications in Britain has been comparatively low. There was little national interest in the topic until the early 1970s when the costs of absenteeism and turnover were recognized as a serious problem. The Department of Employment commissioned a review of the field (Wilson, 1973) and a Tripartite Steering Group on Job Satisfaction was formed in 1973 with representatives from the government, the CBI and the TUC. The IPM conducted a survey of British practice (Carby, 1976) which revealed the advantages of the techniques in resolving a range of operational, behavioural and personnel problems. Carby's survey indicated, however, that work design was employed primarily for operational reasons, and that only 20 per cent of applications had been initiated by personnel management.

Interest waned in the late 1970s. Unemployment was rising steeply and there was increased concern about any kind of working life, regardless of its quality. Management became preoccupied with resisting the direction in which the industrial democracy debate was moving (Bullock, 1977), which would have put employee representatives on supervisory boards of directors of large companies.

Despite the publicity given to the topic and to a few publicized cases like ICI, British management and trade unions do not appear to have embraced work design enthusiastically. Many managers today regard autonomous groups and job enrichment as quaint relics of a past decade. Why should managers resist attempts to improve the quality of working life and performance of their employees, if work design techniques do not affect their own status? Many managers do, however, see in these approaches a threat to their vested interest in their occupation, and to managerial prerogative. Few managers question the fundamental structure of capitalism. The majority of people in Britain appear to accept that there is a broad consensus in support of our social and economic structure, regardless of its obvious inequalities in status and financial rewards. This is a view which sees industrial relations as a forum in which real conflicts of interest are legitimately resolved by parties with fluctuating but broadly comparable power and influence to pursue their aims. Inequalities are thus matters for negotiation, not revolution, from this perspective.

Why have trade unions resisted attempts to improve the quality of working life of their members? Work design techniques can be regarded as part of a capitalist plot to resolve 'the labour problem', to control workers and to extract co-operation from them while maintaining their subordinate financial and political position at work and in society as a whole. And increased loyalty to an employer is likely to weaken the attachment of members to their union. Taylor's original approach to task fragmentation meant minimum skill, minimum knowledge, minimum pay and dependence on management. Scientific management gives managers an aura of respectability and legitimacy in an exploitative relationship which sustains management status and control over work methods and the pace of work. Job enrichment can be a cosmetic attempt to increase skill, discretion and commitment without interfering with management authority in any significant way. Autonomous group work can be similarly cosmetic.

One of the most recent and persuasive proponents of this view is Braverman (1974) who regards capitalist management practice as a means of increasing management control over work and workers, or over 'the labour process'. French trade unions in particular, such as the communist Confederation Générale du Travail and the socialist Confederation Français du Travail, believe that it is better for them not to co-operate with capitalism in any way that might strengthen it and thus undermine their own ideology and support. Work design applications are rare in France (Jenkins, 1981).

German trade unions have, in contrast, welcomed attempts to improve both industrial democracy and the quality of working life. They have collaborated with capitalism in a long-term and expensive quality of work life programme supported by government funds (Jenkins, 1978).

British trade unions have adopted sceptical and fluctuating views between those extremes. Osbaldeston and Hepworth (1975) claimed that lack of union interest had inhibited the incidence of work design projects in Britain, and Banks (1974), Head of Research of the Amalgamated Union of Engineering Workers, argued that work design techniques benefit only management. British trade unions are preoccupied with pay, job security and involvement in management decision-making, probably in that order. Work design projects can sound like more work for the same cash and are thus rejected.

Work design techniques can be seen as genuine and sincere attempts to satisfy human needs, and to improve both the performance of an organization and the quality of working life of its employees. But Carby (1976), among others, found that as jobs at the bottom of an organization changed through work design, the 'ripple effects' were often felt at levels and functions in the management structure beyond the first line supervision of the jobs immediately affected. Management style and skills are likely to be affected when subordinates increase their knowledge and discretion. Such managerial implications of work design, however limited, can be seen as embryo approaches to worker participation which might evolve into more significant forms of industrial democracy, and present even more fundamental challenges to managerial legitimacy and authority.

The approaches to work design examined here have as yet had little impact on overall organization structures. They have not altered or threatened structures of management planning, organization and control. Managers can rest easy on this evidence. But this limited impact is a weakness which needs to be remedied. Work design applications have also shown that there is no necessary contradiction between a quality work experience and organizational effectiveness. But work design has tended to be regarded and applied as an isolated management technique aimed at local organizational problems and at individual jobs and work groups, 'rather than realising that it must be part of the whole company philosophy, through all levels, if it is to be really successful' (Weir, 1976: 6). These techniques have been used to address a limited range of problems, mainly concerning absenteeism and turnover, and have had limited success.

As the problems facing British industry have deepened, the focus of work design strategies must be widened to achieve a more significant and effective impact. The lack of management and union enthusiasm for work design in Britain is regrettable because, as the final section argues, these techniques offer a basis for solutions to the more pressing problems of British industry and commerce in the 1980s and 1990s.

## LOOKING FORWARD: TRENDS AND PROSPECTS

There has been a revival of interest in work design in the 1980s, due to pressures that are more intense than and different from those that have caused concern for the previous half century. Work design has so far been applied as a response to problems of turnover and absenteeism, and does not represent an enlightened management response to the challenges of developing technology and an emergent post-industrial value system. There was a widespread belief in the 1970s that improving the quality of working life was an appropriate goal for an affluent, educated, industrial society. That belief has also waned in the face of a worsening economic climate, and was never popular with British managers. The concern with work design in the late 1980s and into the 1990s is likely to be based on pressures arising from stiffer *trading conditions* in domestic and international markets, from the realization that *stress* has more impact on job performance than dissatisfaction, and from the introduction of *new technologies* in computing and information systems based on the ubiquitous microchip, all of which lead to a rethink of work flows and work roles in manufacturing and administrative contexts.

### The Economic Context

As chapter 2 pointed out, stiffer trading conditions have reduced whatever slack British companies had in costing, pricing and delivery. The comparatively sheltered domestic and international markets of the 1950s and 1960s have become fiercely competitive. Fluctuations in interest and exchange rates and commodity prices have become volatile and unpredictable, and can make or break profits on export trade. Companies which fail to meet customers' demands for cost, quality and delivery find their business quickly lost to competitors. The public sector has also been affected by the pressure to trim budgets.

A deskilled, unmotivated, uncommitted and inflexible workforce is not competitive when such careful attention to costs, quality and delivery schedules is fundamental to capturing and retaining changing and unpredictable markets. For these reasons, the effective management of human resources has become even more of a key factor in sustaining competitive advantage, and work design has become a more crucial management consideration (Taylor, 1983).

It is important, however, not to put too much emphasis on the link between job satisfaction and performance. Although common sense suggests that an unhappy worker is an unproductive one, it does not necessarily follow. Discontented workers may show up late and quit their jobs more often, but they are not automatically less efficient on the job. The relationship may run the other way. People may gain and improve job satisfaction by being productive. Unhappy workers may sustain their efforts in the hope of promotion out of their jobs, or into another organization. Individual job performance is affected, positively and negatively, by a range of other factors, such as incentive payment systems, production scheduling, availability of materials, equipment breakdown, and so on.

*Stress*

The potentially adverse implications of stress induced by paced, repetitive, meaningless work have been appreciated for some time (Kornhauser, 1965; Karasek, 1979), but it is only in the mid-1980s that this topic has started to receive widespread management attention. The current costs of stress-related illness in Britain are estimated at around $9 billion a year, compared with $66 billion in America (*Economist*, 7 July 1984), and are shared by companies and health services. Coronary heart disease accounts for about half of those costs, but stress also leads to mental breakdowns, alcoholism, ulcers and drug dependence. The symptoms include irritability, fatigue, apathy, indecision, anxiety, and overeating and drinking. These effects can clearly have an adverse influence on employee behaviour and performance.

It has become fashionable for US companies in particular to run health and fitness programmes for employees to help reduce stress. Two Canadian insurance companies claim to have reduced absenteeism by over 20 per cent and improved productivity by giving over 1000 employees a free fitness course. PepsiCo runs fitness courses for their head office staff in New York. British managers appear to be less concerned about the health of their employees (Marshall and Cooper, 1983), although the Trustee Savings Bank and ICI have introduced schemes to reduce stress among managers. Stress, however, can affect employees at all levels in an organization, not just at management level. And if stress is caused by the pattern of duties and responsibilities an individual performs, then the remedies may lie with work design, and not with diet sheets, lunchtime aerobic exercises, transcendental meditation or jogging.

New technologies have also unfortunately created new sources of stress for those who have to operate them. Work at computer terminals can cause eye strain, headaches, and arm and shoulder pains. Administrative workers can suffer from anxiety and frustration when their work at a terminal is interrupted by computer breakdowns and telephone calls. When interruptions are expected, employees work more intensely to avoid piling up a backlog of work and this increases the stress under which they work (Johansson and Aronsson, 1984). One simple answer is to design into the work planned breaks from the routine of the computer terminal. Job rotation would also alleviate this problem.

Recent studies in Japanese offices and factories using new computing technologies confirm the high incidence of eye fatigue and shoulder pain, and also attribute nervous and digestive disorders to working with advanced automation, particularly among women (Shaw, 1984). A group called the Committee for the Protection of Women in the Computer World has been formed and has conducted studies on how computerization is affecting the health of women workers. One study investigated the conditions and health of workers using Japan Airlines' computerized reservations system, introduced in 1970. The computer operators, mostly women, wear headsets and sit at terminals where they make and confirm reservations, checking with the schedules on the visual display screen. This led to eye strain, and to complaints that they were not able to talk to colleagues or to control their work. The company's solutions were to give the more intensive jobs to men, and to put those with eye strain onto other work. The Council of Civil Service Unions in Britain has recently asked the government to arrange for the redeployment of pregnant women following research which links work at computer terminals and word-processors with miscarriages and stillbirths (McCrone, 1984).

*The Impact of Technology*

The adverse effects of computer technologies on employment and skill levels have been widely assumed and publicized, but have been grossly exaggerated as has been the extent of the resistance to their introduction. The research consistently shows that these technologies are not likely to create mass unemployment (Sleigh et al., 1979; Green et al., 1980; Evans, 1980; Tucker, 1984). Their use will alter both the occupational structure and the patterns of skills required and could create many new jobs through the creation of new products and services (Williams, 1984). Although microchips are comparatively cheap, computing devices of all kinds are still expensive, their benefits take time and effort to achieve, and their impact on the economy as a whole is likely to be slow. Failure to adopt these new technologies can, on the other hand, cost jobs if overseas competitors innovate and capture British markets (ACARD, 1979).

The extent to which new technologies will replace human skills, effort and jobs has also been exaggerated. Computing devices clearly replace human manual effort in many ways. Computer-aided draughting, for example, means that traditional manual draughting skills are no longer required. Word-processors reduce the paper handling skills of typists. Accounting packages for computers replace the drudgery of routine mental arithmetic once performed by rooms full of clerks. Machine tool operators have no wheels and levers to turn on computer numerically controlled machine tools. Machined components can be inspected with computer co-ordinate measuring machines which check dimensions with a computer controlled probe which replaces the various hand-held measuring devices traditionally used in engineering inspection. Robots are widely used to perform traditional manual tasks in paint spraying, welding and assembly.

Recent research has confirmed the views expressed by Davis and Taylor (1975 and 1976) more than a decade ago. First, technical change opens up new opportunities for work design and does not close the available options. These new technologies do not bring with them any new form of technological determinism and their implications depend to a large extent on the organizational strategies and choices of the managers who decide to apply them. Second, technical change may replace manual skills and effort, but can increase the demands made on human cognitive and social skills (Sorge et al., 1982; Wilkinson, 1983; Buchanan and Boddy, 1983a; Wall, 1984).

To put this another way, sophisticated, flexible, expensive equipment needs sophisticated, flexible, expensive people to operate it. The effective and safe operation of these new technologies requires very careful attention to work design. Noble (1979), for example, described how quality, precision machining in engineering, even with computer numerically controlled machine tools, requires 'close attention to the details of the operation and frequent manual intervention'; he noted moreover that the 'invisibility' of the functions of computer-based devices and the high costs of error place a premium on skilled and motivated human intervention. As Noble (1979: 44) pointedly says, 'what will a machine operator, "skilled" or "unskilled" do when he sees a $250,000 milling machine heading for a smash-up? He could rush to the machine and press the panic button, retracting the workpiece from the cutter or shutting the whole thing down, or he could remain seated and think to himself, "Oh look, no work tomorrow".' Perrow (1983) offers entertaining but frightening evidence of the disastrous consequences of ignoring work design in sophisticated and computerized aircraft, ship navigation and nuclear power generation control systems. Buchanan and Bessant (1985) identify a similar need for skilled, experienced, rapid and motivated response to production problems in a computer-integrated chemicals processing plant.

The limited extent to which computerized devices can replace people at work is also evident in the service sector. As the manager of a large international hotel in Scotland put it, 'These systems have not made staff redundant. The critical thing for us in the hotel business is that having computers does not run the hotel. There are problems involved. You can imagine on a busy checkout day where you have got 160 businessmen and the computer goes down at the front desk, suddenly they are left with nothing. There is no information on the guests or rooms or anthing else. There are backup systems, but there is no point in us blaming the computer. Social skills are needed to cope with that and to combat anything that gives an indication it is computerized. Frankly guests do not want that in a hotel.'

Technology can replace manual skills, but they can also *complement* social and problem-solving skills. Indeed, Buchanan and Boddy (1982) argue that the effectiveness of word-processing technology is reduced where work design is inflexible, overcontrolled and prevents typists and authors from experimenting with the capabilities of the technology to improve the typing service. An effective work design in this case has to take into account the interdependence of typists and authors, and the ways in which the new technology can complement typists' skills and 'author knowledge'. Similarly, Rosenbrock (1982) argues that engineers fail to design systems that could complement or enhance human skills and exploit human adaptability. Attempts to use new technologies to replace human skills entirely can thus go wrong. Buchanan and Boddy (1983b) argue that lack of attention to the potential contribution of human intervention in the operation of computer-controlled equipment can create 'distanced' tasks in which human presence is required to carry out 'residual activities' that the equipment cannot perform alone, but in which the degree of human intervention is limited. Operators in these circumstances become apathetic and careless, develop no skills through their work experience, are not able to assist with maintenance and repairs on the sophisticated equipment they supervise, and are not promotable: all consequences of work design decisions, not just technical necessities.

*Concluding Remarks*

To what extent will work design theory and techniques help organizations to develop the skilled, motivated, committed and flexible workforces necessary for them to survive the pressures of competition, employee stress and technological change over the next decade? Work design can form the *basis* for solutions to these problems, but should be regarded as an incomplete solution on its own. Work design techniques cannot be applied in isolation. They should be applied as part of an *integrated employment package*. Even limited changes in work design can have implications for related management functions and levels. It was apparent to many commentators in the mid-1970s that the individual job and the work group were not the appropriate units of analyses and that the wider issue of organizational design had to be tackled (Wild, 1975; Lupton, 1976; Davis, 1976; Buchanan, 1979). If work design techniques are to have a significant impact on the experience of work and organizational performance, then they will have to be more radical than those currently in use, and will need to be more closely integrated with other employment policies.

# Bibliography

Advisory Council for Applied Research and Development (ACARD). 1979. *Techno-logical Change: Threats and Opportunities for the United Kingdom*. London: HMSO.
Asplund, C. 1981. *Redesigning Jobs: Western European Experience*. Brussels: European Trade Union Institute.
Atkinson, J. 1984. 'Manpower Strategies for Flexible Organizations'. *Personnel Management*, August, 28–31.
Banks, A. 1974. 'Autonomous Work Groups'. *Industrial Society*, July/August, 10–12.
Beek, H.G. van. 1964. 'The influence of Assembly Line Organization on Output, Quality and Morale'. *Occupational Psychology*, 38: July and October, 161–72.
Beinum, H. van. 1966. *The Morale of the Dublin Busmen*. London: Tavistock Institute.
Braverman, H. 1974. *Labor and Monopoly Capital: The Degradation of Work in the Twentieth Century*. New York: Monthly Review Press.
Buchanan, D.A. 1979. *The Development of Job Design Theories and Techniques*. Aldershot: Saxon House.
—— and Bessant, J. 1985. 'Failure, Uncertainty and Control: The Role of Operators in a Computer Integrated Production System'. *Journal of Management Studies*, 22: 3, 292–308.
—— and Boddy, D. 1982. 'Advanced Technology and the Quality of Working Life: The Effects of Word Processing on Video Typists'. *Journal of Occupational Psychology*, 55: 1, 1–11.
—— and Boddy, D. 1983a. *Organizations in the Computer Age: Technological Imperatives and Strategic Choice*. Aldershot: Gower.
—— and Boddy, D. 1983b. 'Advanced Technology and the Quality of Working Life: The Effects of Computerized Controls on Biscuit-Making Operators'. *Journal of Occupational Psychology*, 56: 2, 109–19.
Bullock. 1977. Committee of Inquiry on Industrial Democracy. *Report*. Cmnd 6706. London: HMSO.
Butteriss, M. and Murdoch, R.D. 1975. *Work Restructuring Projects and Experiments in the United Kingdom*. Report 2. London: Work Research Unit.
—— and Murdoch, R.D. 1976. *Work Restructuring Projects and Experiments in the USA*. Report 3. London: Work Research Unit.
Carby, K. 1976. *Job Redesign in Practice*. London: IPM.
Cockroft, D. 1980. 'Microelectronics: The Employment Effects and the Trade Union Response'. *Microelectronics and Society*. Ed. Jones, T. Milton Keynes: Open University Press, 72–94.
Davis, L.E. 1966. 'The Design of Jobs'. *Industrial Relations*, 6: 1, 21–45.
—— 1976. 'Developments in Job Design'. *Personal Goals and Work Design*. Ed. Warr, P. London: Wiley, 67–80.
—— and Taylor, J.C. 1975. 'Technology Effects on Job, Work, and Organizational Structure: A Contingency View'. *The Quality of Working Life, Problems, Prospects*

*and the State of the Art*, Vol. 1. Eds. Davis, L.E. and Cherns, A.B. New York: Free Press, 220–41.

—— and Taylor, J.C. 1976. 'Technology, Organization and Job Structure'. *Handbook of Work, Organization and Society*. Ed. Dubin, R. Chicago: Rand McNally, 379–419.

—— Canter, R.R. and Hoffman, J. 1955. 'Current Job Design Criteria'. *Journal of Industrial Engineering*, 6: 2, 5–11.

*Economist*. 1984. 'You Can Tell a Company by the People It Keeps'. 7 July, 61–2.

Emery, F.E. 1963. 'Some Hypotheses about the Ways in which Tasks May be More Effectively Put Together to Make Jobs'. London: Tavistock Institute of Human Relations. Reprinted in Hill, P. 1971. *Towards a New Philosophy of Management*. Aldershot: Gower, 208–10.

—— Thorsrud, E. and Lange, K. 1965. 'Field Experiments at Christiana Spigerverk'. Industrial Democracy Project Paper Number 2, Phase B. Tavistock Institute Document T807. London: Tavistock Institute of Human Relations.

Evans, J. 1980. *The Impact of Microelectronics on Employment in Western Europe in the 1980s*. Brussels: European Trade Union Institute.

Ford, R.N. 1969. *Motivation through the Work Itself*. New York: American Management Association.

Gooding, J. 1970a. 'Blue Collar Blues on the Assembly Line'. *Fortune*, July, 68–71.

—— 1970b. 'It Pays to Wake Up the Blue Collar Workers'. *Fortune*, September, 132–5.

Green, K., Coombs, R. and Holroyd, K. 1980. *The Effects of Microelectronic Technologies on Employment Prospects*. Aldershot: Gower.

Gyllenhammar, P.G. 1977. *People at Work*. Reading, MA: Addison-Wesley.

Hackman, J.R., Oldham, G.R., Janson, R. and Purdy, K. 1975. 'A New Strategy for Job Enrichment'. *California Management Review*, 17: 4, 57–71.

Harding, D.W. 1931. 'A Note on the Subdivision of Assembly Work'. *Journal of the National Institute of Industrial Psychology*, 5: 5, 261–4.

Hertog, F.J. den. 1976. 'Work Structuring'. *Personal Goals and Work Design*. Ed. Warr, P. London: Wiley, 43–65.

Herzberg, F. 1966. *Work and the Nature of Man*. London: Staples Press.

—— 1968. 'One More Time: How Do You Motivate Employees?'. *Harvard Business Review*, 46: 1, 53–62.

——, Mausner, B. and Synderman, B.B. 1959. *The Motivation to Work*. New York: Wiley.

Hill, P. 1971. *Towards a New Philosophy of Management*. Aldershot: Gower.

Jenkins, D. 1978. *The West German Humanization of Work Program: A Preliminary Assessment*. Occasional Paper 8. London: Work Research Unit.

—— 1981. *Work Reform in France: A Ten-Year Record of Continuous Progress*. Occasional Paper 15. London: Work Research Unit.

Johansson, G. and Aronsson, G. 1984. 'Stress Reactions in Computerized Administrative Work'. *Journal of Occupational Behaviour*, 5: July, 159–81.

Karasek, R.A. 1979. 'Job Demands, Job Decision Latitude, and Mental Strain: Implications for Job Redesign'. *Administrative Science Quarterly*, 24: 2, 285–308.

Kornhauser, A. 1965. *Mental Health of the Industrial Worker: A Detroit Study*. New York: Wiley.

Lawler, E.E. 1976. 'Conference Review: Issues of Understanding'. *Personal Goals and Work Design*. Ed. Warr, P. London: Wiley, 225–33.

Lupton, T. 1971. *Management and the Social Sciences*. Harmondsworth: Penguin.

—— 1976. '"Best Fit" in the Design of Organizations'. *Task and Organization*. Ed. Miller, E.J. London: Wiley, 121–49.

McCrone, J. 1984. 'CCTA Faces Call to Bar Use of VDUs During Pregnancy'. *Computing*, 18 October, 6.

Manz, C.C. and Sims, H.P. 1984. 'Searching for the "Unleader": Organizational Member Views on Leading the Self-Managed Group'. *Human Relations*, 37: May, 409–24.

Marshall, J. and Cooper, C. 1983. *Coping with Stress at Work*. Aldershot: Gower.

Maslow, A. 1943. 'A Theory of Motivation'. *Psychological Review*, 50: 4, 370–96.

Noble, D.F. 1979. 'Social Choice in Machine Design: The Case of Automatically Controlled Machine Tools'. *Case Studies on the Labour Process*. Ed. Zimbalist, A. New York: Monthly Review Press, 18–50.

Osbaldeston, M. and Hepworth, A. 1975. 'White Collar Work Structuring: The European Experience'. Paper presented to the European Institute for Advanced Studies in Management seminar on 'Personnel Research in Europe', Brussels, 25–7 March.

Paul, W.J. and Robertson, K.B. 1970. *Job Enrichment and Employee Motivation*. Aldershot: Gower.

Pauling, T.P. 1968. 'Job Enlargement: An Experience at Philips Telecommunication of Australia Limited'. *Personnel Practice Bulletin*, 24: 3, 194–6.

Perrow, C. 1983. 'The Organizational Context of Human Factors Engineering'. *Administrative Science Quarterly*, 28: 4, 521–41.

Philips Report. 1969. *Work Structuring: A Survey of Experiments at NV Philips, Eindhoven, 1963–68*. Eindhoven, NV Philips.

Rice, A.K. 1958. *Productivity and Social Organization*. London: Tavistock Publications.

Rosenbrock, H.H. 1982. 'Technology Policies and Options'. *Information Society: For Richer, For Poorer*. Ed. Andersen, N.B., Earl, M., Holst, O. and Mumford, E. Amsterdam: North-Holland.

Ruehl, G. 1974. 'Work Structuring, Part 1'. *Industrial Engineering*, January, 32–7.

Schoderbek, P.P. and Reif, W.E. 1969. *Job Enlargement: Key to Improved Performance*. Ann Arbor: Bureau of Industrial Relations, Graduate School of Business Administration, University of Michigan.

Shaw, C. 1984. 'When the Risks Look Higher than Your Wages'. *Computing*, 12 July, 22–3.

Sleigh, J., Boatwright, B., Irwin, P. and Stanyon, R. 1979. *The Manpower Implications of Micro-Electronic Technology*. London: HMSO.

Sorge, A., Hartmann, G., Warner, M. and Nicholas, I. 1982. 'Computer Numerical Control Applications in Manufacturing'. *Information Technology: Impact on the Way of Life*. Eds. Bannon, L., Barry, U. and Holst, O. Dublin: Tycooly International, 99–113.

Taylor, D. 1983. *Learning from Japan*. London: Work Research Unit.

Taylor, F.W. 1911. *Principles of Scientific Management*. New York: Harper.

Thornely, D.H. and Valantine, G.A. 1968. 'Job Enlargement: Some Implications of Longer Cycle Jobs on Fan Heater Production'. *Philips Personnel Management Review*, 12–17.

Trist, E.L., Higgin, G.W., Murray, H. and Pollock, A.B. 1963. *Organizational Choice: Capabilities of Groups at the Coal Face under Changing Technologies*. London: Tavistock Publications.

Tucker, O. 1984. 'Studies Reassess IT's Effect on Jobs'. *Computing*, 4 October, 26.

Valéry, N. 1974. 'Importing the Lessons of Swedish Workers'. *New Scientist*, 62: 4 April, 27–8.

Vernon, H.M., Wyatt, S. and Ogden, A.D. 1924. *On the Extent and Effects of Variety in*

*Repetitive Work*. Medical Research Council Industrial Fatigue Research Board Report 26. London: HMSO.

Walker, C.R. 1950. 'The Problem of the Repetitive Job'. *Harvard Business Review*, 28: 3, 54–8.

—— and Guest, R.H. 1952. *The Man on the Assembly Line*. Cambridge, MA: Harvard University Press.

Wall, T. 1984. 'What's New in . . . Job Design?'. *Personnel Management*, April, 27–9.

Weil, R. 1981. *General Motors Corporation: Organization Development by Improving the Quality of Working Life*. Occasional Paper 18. London: Work Research Unit.

Weir, M. 1976. *Redesigning Jobs in Scotland*. Report 5. London: Work Research Unit.

Wild, R. 1975. *Work Organization: A Study of Manual Work and Mass Production*. New York: Wiley.

Wilkinson, B. 1983. *The Shopfloor Politics of New Technology*. London: Heinemann.

Williams, V. 1984. 'Employment Implications of New Technology'. *Employment Gazette*, 92: May, 210–15.

Wilson, N.A.B. 1973. *On the Quality of Working Life*. Department of Employment Manpower Papers 7. London: HMSO.

# PART III
Employee Resourcing

# 5 From Manpower Planning to Human Resource Planning?

*Stuart Timperley and Keith Sisson*

Depending on how it is defined, manpower planning appears to have moved in and out of fashion over the last 30 years, both as an area of activity and as a subject of study, reflecting the changing context described in chapter 2. Thus the early traditions of manpower planning owed much to the circumstances of the 1950s and 1960s: unemployment was low; economic growth appeared to be continuous and there was a considerable increase in public spending, notably on an expansion of higher and further education, in keeping with a growing working population; organization structures were highly centralized and relatively stable, with the emphasis on promotion and upward mobility; and the main concerns were recruitment and retention. In the 1980s the context has changed – and so have the concerns. Overall unemployment has grown and, although it has declined from record levels and there are substantial skill shortages, continues to remain stubbornly high. Competition has intensified. Senior managers in the large enterprises especially are continuously rethinking their business strategies; there has been considerable diversification and decentralization of operations to semi-autonomous business units. Rationalization and restructuring are the order of the day; and 'competence, commitment and the capacity to change' (MSC/NEDO, 1987) are the key concerns.

It is with the changing nature of manpower planning that this chapter is primarily concerned. It begins by considering how a number of influential commentators have defined manpower planning. In view of the abundance of technical terms and models, the second section then goes on to discuss the main stages typically involved in the process. The third section examines the evidence for the practice, while the fourth and final section considers the prospects for the future and the possibility that manpower planning may evolve, at least in some organizations, into a less quantitative and yet more strategic approach to the management of human resources generally.

## WHAT IS MANPOWER PLANNING?

In his attempt to summarize the variety of definitions of manpower planning, Thomason (1975) suggests that there was broad agreement on the *steps* involved in the development of a manpower plan, and these were seen to be the following: deciding what *data* are relevant to the decision required; collecting and collating these to transmit to decision-makers; allocating competent persons to decision-taking roles; developing criteria to use in judgements about data; taking decisions about manpower unilaterally or through negotiation; controlled implementation of the decisions and the use of feedback. He did distinguish between two approaches, however, each reflecting a level of management decision: those associated with corporate decision-making – with the emphasis on broad policies and strategies; and those that were more sceptical about formal planning procedures – with the emphasis on the skill requirements of manpower policy-makers (especially their bargaining skills).

Thomason's own approach is interesting in that it focuses as much on the process and context of manpower planning as it does on content. It is particularly fascinating to see the role that negotiated agreement is deemed to play in manpower planning and decision-making. Given the industrial relations climate of the mid-1970s, however, his emphasis is understandable.

The issues of what is needed, how it is communicated, who decides, what gets emphasized, and how things are decided and implemented provide a useful framework for examining the organizational contexts within which manpower planning activities take place. Even so, there are significant variations in these processes within different organizations, although as Timperley (1972) has pointed out, there are patterns to be identified in the way they are introduced. The different organizational contexts can operate across a range of dimensions: the extent of centralization or decentralization; the structural characteristics of the organization; and the degree of organizational complexity, size, and culture or style.

The business strategy literature is helpful in highlighting the different forms that strategic planning can take in relation to different organizational types (see, for example, Goold and Campbell, 1986). Planning in large complex organizations with multiple markets, products and geographical regions will often tend to be dominated by sophisticated corporate planning departments and equally sophisticated planning techniques such as 'portfolio planning' and 'scenario planning' (for further details, see Argenti, 1974; Haspeslagh, 1982). Shell, for example, has developed its own strategic planning matrix now widely used in other organizations. In smaller organizations, where there are entrepreneurial traditions and where ownership is centralized, planning and policy issues appear more likely to be dealt with in an *ad hoc*, intuitive and personalized fashion (Goffee and Scase, 1985). In both cases the pattern of planning processes is well documented (see, for example, Scott, 1971) and provides an important reference point for understanding that the content of manpower planning has to take into account the reasons for its introduction (political and economic), the methods chosen to introduce it (formal or informal), the resources given to it, sponsors, the links with other personnel tools or with formal strategic planning processes, and the type of organization.

Irrespective of context, there seems to be some agreement about what manpower planning involves; any differences appear related more to scope and emphasis than detailed content. Four influential works on manpower planning between 1971 and 1984 have been selected to illustrate both agreement on the major components and the differences in emphasis.

In 1971 one of the most influential commentators on manpower planning, A.R. Smith, who was Director of Statistics for the Civil Service, suggested that it covered three main types of activity: demand work – analysing, reviewing and attempting to predict the quantity and type of manpower needed by an organization to achieve its objectives; supply work – attempting to predict the action necessary to ensure that the manpower needed is available when required; and designing the interaction between demand and supply so that skills are utilized to the best possible advantage, and the legitimate aspirations of the individual are taken into account.

Bramham (1975), another influential figure, developed a fairly pragmatic approach to the subject area, and in particular distinguished between the short-term function of manpower planning and its longer-term productive function. He saw these as interrelated, with the short-term functions providing information about current manpower resources and capabilities in order to develop contingency plans to cope with sudden changes in the business environment. The more important function is, however, the one related to anticipating and predicting the future. Further, effectiveness in performing these two functions was seen as dependent on the quality of awareness of the manpower environment, the quality of information on business plans and objectives, and knowledge of present manpower resources.

The development of a 'practitioner' perspective on manpower planning evolved during the 1970s, and reflected the recognition of emerging problems (such as low productivity, declining promotion prospects, industrial relations, pay, and worsening age profiles) and the desire, especially by specialist personnel managers, to be seen to be addressing these questions. Such an approach is exemplified by Armstrong (1979) who produced a number of contributions to the personnel literature related to best practice, problem-solving, and optimum solutions. Specifically, the key points of emphasis in this type of approach were the *recruitment* and *retention* of appropriate manpower, efficient *utilization* of resources, and anticipation of problems related to *surplus* or *deficit*.

The problem-driven approach was obviously attractive to practitioners looking for specific help in dealing with a myriad of manpower issues. The growth of the personnel profession in the 1970s was very rapid and, though increased sophistication was apparent in the technical sense, there were clear pressures emerging organizationally for greater success in dealing with the problems. This emphasis on *action* mirrored the approach of Armstrong (and others) to manpower planning in that it was defined in terms of 'areas of interrelated activity'. Essentially five areas of activity were highlighted:

1 the *demand forecasting process* which estimates manpower needs by reference to corporate and functional plans, and forecasts of future levels of activity (involving ratio-trend analysis, work study and econometric models);

2 the *supply forecasting process*, which assesses the manpower likely to be available from within and outside the organization (involving analysis of labour turnover, promotion and transfer effects, sources of supply, and existing manpower resources);

3 assessment of *productivity changes* likely to be affected by, say, reward systems, or technological changes;

4 the *determination of manpower requirements* through adjusting the demand forecast to take account of productivity changes, labour turnover, absence, and changes in employment practice; and

5 the *development of plans for action* – in particular recruitment plans (how many, where from, when); training plans to ensure skill supply; productivity plans for improving productivity; retention plans to reduce avoidable wastage; redevelopment plans for retraining or transferring existing employees, and redundancy plans to deal with enforced wastage and its timing.

The 'problems' referred to above had traditionally become the territorial area of personnel management, but in the 1980s it appears that this pattern might be changing, and that manpower planning might develop as a mainstream issue driven by the needs of organizations and their top executives for the 'right' people performing the 'appropriate' tasks. Perhaps the best indication of this is the work of Bennison and Casson (1984), which is an excellent reference on the current state of manpower planning. This they see as a framework with a number of sequential steps – forecasting manpower needs for the future; estimating the ways in which it is to be supplied (wastage, flow and labour markets); and establishing whether supply will be enough to cope with demand. This framework, related to level of demand, rate of loss, and replacement policy, is seen as being common to most problems and, together with the associated analytical techniques, is put forward as the key to a manpower planning approach with four very specific steps: drawing a 'map of the system' to demonstrate and to understand how manpower behaves; developing key indicators of 'problems' with the aid of data on manpower stocks, flows, age distribution, length of service; estimating future demand as a result of likely business developments; and quantifying the rate of loss by examining types of wastage.

What can be discerned from this examination of the nature of manpower planning is that there appears to be general agreement on a number of specific components. There is, for example, the dominant theme that acquiring, utilizing, developing and retaining manpower are key parts of the process. There is the clear sense that manpower should be planned on the same basis as other corporate resources, that its planning should be integrated into the corporate planning process, and that the manpower plan should reflect overall organizational objectives. As a later section will argue in more detail, the process of evolution has some way to go before manpower planning is seen as a key element in strategic planning. Even so, we might conclude that the move to make manpower planning broader in scope and more problem-centred is likely to be important in a world where strategy implementation is increasingly seen as being closely identified with the quality and performance of human resources.

## THE PROCESS OF MANPOWER PLANNING

Although manpower planning has been related to a variety of activities from simple forecasting techniques to the whole range of activities in the personnel function, there is a pervasive view of the 'sequencing' of the major stages, namely analysis and investigation; forecasting of demand and forecasting of supply; the development of plans; and implementation and control. In simple terms, the first and second relate to the area of *prediction* and the third and the fourth to the area of *control*. Figure 5.1 illustrates the four stages and also provides a framework for looking in more detail at what is involved.

### Analysis

On the face of it, there has been a significant increase in the sophistication of information systems in recent years, which has provided high quality, relevant information on manpower matters. Such information, now often computerized, would normally include quantitative data on age, length of service, job and job moves, salary and salary progression, experience and qualifications, and qualitative data relating to potential, performance, and skills. Thus computerized payrolls, occupational and job classifications, and the development

FIGURE 5.1    *The process of manpower planning*

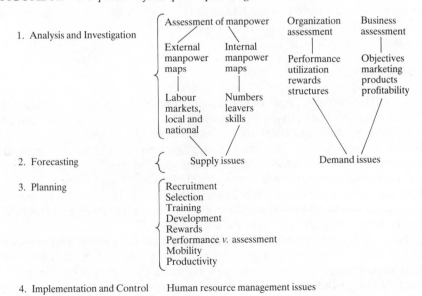

of manpower inventories have become standard parts of the information systems of many organizations. In theory, then, this provides organizations with the tools to draw the manpower maps referred to by Bennison and Casson and to understand better the workings of internal and external labour markets; whether or not they do so, however, is a moot point because there is little or no empirical evidence available.

Productivity and performance are the other main elements in the analysis. Clearly, if organizations have strategic plans that are based on assumptions about performance, then the base point of current utilization needs to be assessed and understood before steps can be taken (either through technology investment or labour productivity change) to implement those plans. Given the significance of labour costs, the issue of performance has become critical for many of today's organizations and it might be expected that a great deal of attention is being paid to the measurement of performance, the analysis of reasons for performance levels, and the processes by which performance can be improved. Certainly, as other chapters point out, attention is being paid to the impact of work structure and job design on performance; methods of working have been changed and new reward systems introduced.

In addition to analysing the manpower situation it is increasingly recognized that the organizational and business contexts provide a critical reference point for planning processes. To equate the supply and demand aspects of manpower is inadequate, as this perpetrates its misuse or underuse. Similarly, to perpetrate current organizational structure, culture or processes and current business activities and practices is also unsatisfactory. As chapter 3 has pointed out, there has been an upsurge of interest in the 'cultures' of organizations, and the need for cultural change, together with a questioning of business portfolios and the need to develop into new markets, or products, services, technologies and regions. Clearly, if drawing a manpower 'map' is deemed to be necessary for future planning, then drawing a cultural 'map' or portfolio 'map' would appear to be equally appropriate.

*Forecasting Supply*

Probably because of the operational research emphasis, a point brought out at various stages by both Bryant (1965) and Lawrence (1973), the traditions of manpower planning draw heavily on the work related to forecasting supply. Indeed, the forecasting of internal supply might be said to be the centre-piece of manpower planning and it is here that one sees the development of models and the use of indices or measures to highlight what is happening and what, given certain assumptions, will happen in the future. Three areas of supply forecasting will be examined to illustrate this: labour turnover and stability, mathematical techniques, and manpower models.

*Measures of labour turnover and stability.* There has been much debate about the best ways to measure labour turnover or wastage. Indeed, the measure that many organizations still appear to use – the British Institute of Management (BIM) Wastage Index – has been heavily criticized. Essentially, this index calculates the number of people leaving during a time period, divided by the average number of people employed during that same time period, multiplied by 100. This gives a simple measure but presents problems when even a little complexity sets in. A simple example will illustrate:

Case 1. In September 1984 Company *A* employs 1000 salesmen; by September 1985, 400 have left. Turnover Rate $= \frac{400}{1000} \times 100 = 40\%$

Case 2. In September 1984 Company *B* employs 1000 salesmen; by September 1985, 50 have left but are replaced 8 times during the year. Turnover Rate $= \frac{400}{1000} \times 100 = 40\%$

Thus the same turnover rate emerges from what are two entirely different situations – a clear indication that the BIM Index is useful only as a very general guide.

In an attempt to understand better the process of wastage, Bowey (1974) developed the concept of a stability index which focused on employees who do not quit. Here the number of people with more than, say, one year's service is divided by the total currently employed, and multiplied by 100 to give a stability measure. The same case examples illustrate the technique:

Case 1. In September 1984 Company *A* employs 1000 salesmen; by September 1985 400 have left = stability rate of 60%

Case 2. In September 1984 Company *B* employs 1000 salesmen; by September 1985 400 have left = stability rate of 95%

This highlights the importance of stability, focuses attention on those who stay, and allows a more detailed assessment of the problem.

Wastage, however, remains central. Among many approaches to this issue, the question of length of service is particularly important, and has led not only to improved forecasting techniques but to an improved understanding of the underlying processes of wastage over time. It is possible to develop a frequency distribution of leavers by length of service by plotting members leaving over various time periods to produce a wastage curve. A typical example is shown in figure 5.2.

The extension of this approach, based originally on work at the Tavistock Institute by Rice, Hill and Trist (1950), allows labour turnover to be identified as a quasi-stationary process with three major phases being identified:

1 *induction crisis*, namely the first period of service, a fragile relationship and where many people choose to stay;
2 *differential transit*, where wastage declines and people think about settling or, perhaps, plan to leave;
3 *settled connection*, where wastage is low and intermittent, and when people have basically decided to stay.

The policy implication is that there are inherent predictabilities in the process, allowing wastage to be expected and, therefore, forecast.

FIGURE 5.2    *Frequency distribution of leavers by length of service*

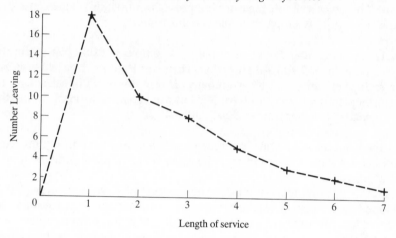

*Mathematical techniques.* Bartholomew (1969) has provided a detailed discussion of many of the mathematical techniques available, and his approach is also worthy of comment. Essentially, Bartholomew uses the concept of renewal to discuss the labour turnover process. He initially considered that the problems of labour turnover process, with wastage being made up by means of a self-renewing aggregate, could be solved given certain assumptions and predictions about recruitment needs. In terms of predicting manpower requirements for new or expanding organizations, he suggested that an adequate supply of manpower was initially required, and also that the rate of required replacement would need to be much larger than for a more traditional organization. The later development of the approach by Bartholomew has been concerned with the development of a theory of a multi-stage renewal process, where the size of the stages is fixed, and the transfer rates are treated as random variables. Applications of this theory have been discussed by Bartholomew with reference to the prediction of manpower needs in a newly established organization, the behaviour of a contracting organization, and the forecasting of recruitment, wastage and promotion rates in simple hierarchical organizations.

The significance of this sort of theorizing about manpower planning problems is that it does draw attention to the areas in which detailed information is required. Thus the suggestion that it would be useful to know how propensity to leave depends on grade and length of service in the organization and seniority within grade is particularly apt, and certainly his approach is useful in highlighting the problem of understanding the relationship between organizational policies and the attitudes and behaviour of individuals. This understanding is essential if the predictive element in manpower planning is to become more sophisticated.

*Models*. The development of early manpower models, in particular those relating to the Royal Navy, Royal Air Force and the National Coal Board, has been well documented by Lawrence (1973). Since then a variety of models has been developed including:

1 *'renewal' or 'pull' models*, where people are assumed to be 'pulled through' as a vacancy occurs through recruitment or promotion and where vacancies in any grade are defined by outflows (wastage or promotion use of grade);
2 *linear programming models* for recruitment and deployment;
3 *'camel' models* based on assessing promotion chances in a hierarchy using age distribution and estimates about the future size of the manpower system; and *Markov* or *'push'* models which model the flow of people.

Taking one of these as illustration, Markov models were used by Young (1976) in the prediction of future manpower structures. The basis of this approach can be understood by reference to two demographic models of staffing: the first is a model of staff wastage based on the 'log normal law of distribution', and the second is a model of the hierarchical staff structure of institutions based on 'status profile analysis'. The log normal law of wastage asserts that staff leave an organization according to a clearly definable pattern of length of service, that this pattern may be recognized early in service, and survival rates deduced, from which losses of staff can be predicted; if total staff requirments are known, then recruitment needs can be predicted. The second approach is based on the assumption that recruitment, promotion and wastage patterns of staff are stable over reasonable periods of time, so the probability that someone in a particular grade at any time will be in some other grade at a later time can be established from the detailed recent career histories of staff; using these probabilities the possible distribution of the numbers of staff in each status or category (the status profile of the organization) at future dates can be inferred from the status profile at one particular time and thus institutions pass through staffing cycles. This process involves the expansion and contraction of organizations and considers the effect this has on promotion and wastage, and the subsequent behavioural effects of such changes.

*Forecasting Demand*

As will be argued in more detail later, one of the great problems with manpower planning is that it has typically struggled, outside the more predictable sectors and organizations, either to influence strategic planning in a formal sense, or to become integrated enough with strategic decision-making processes to respond other than in a short-term fashion. Typically, most of the approaches to manpower planning deal with lists of factors emanating from the strategic plan and assume a direct link with manpower requirements. Such factors would usually include the general pattern of trading and production, product demand, technology and administrative changes, capital investment plans, market strategies, acquisitions, divestments, mergers, product diversification, centralization–decentralization, and budgets; and the problem is to establish what these factors mean in manpower terms, and more pertinently how the organization then goes about planning to ensure that requirements are met. But this is essentially a reactive approach involving short-term plans and accommodations; it clearly focuses on the manpower elements of implementing strategic change, but it still remains difficult apparently for manpower analysis and supply forecasts to influence strategic planning at the formative stage, and this must be a major question in evaluating the success of manpower planning. Where impact has tended to come is in the link between prediction and control, or between forecasting, planning and implementation. It is here that there are likely to be interesting new approaches based on the needs of business organizations to respond more quickly, more creatively, and more efficiently to changes in the business environment.

*Manpower Plans*

The results of analysis and the outcomes of forecasting provide the basis for the establishment of manpower plans in several key areas. Increasingly, the starting point for the development of manpower plans is the needs of the business within the climate of the 1980s which require compatibility between organizational requirements and manpower resources. Clearly this is not a simple administrative process, since the issues raised by increasingly rapid changes in the needs of businesses create the necessity for equally rapid changes in the manpower system. Thus, any plans developed in the key manpower areas need to be both broad in principle and flexible in execution. Before examining in more detail some of the central issues in these areas, we need to stress that the main problem is to develop plans to deal with issues in specific areas to ensure that they are well integrated. It is no use, for example, changing the nature of promotion systems and criteria and yet recruiting new people on the basis of the old systems. One useful way of looking at this problem is to examine all the possible manpower flows in organizations and then to look at the potential impact on these flows of plans and activities in some of the key manpower areas. Figure 5.3 illustrates such flow patterns and lists the manpower policy areas that could have an influence on the rate, nature and direction of such flow. The remainder of this section examines the issues involved in developing plans for some of the major manpower areas.

*Recruitment and selection.* The ability of an organization to choose its employees is one of the major factors influencing organizational performance. Despite unemployment, competition for high quality people at, say, graduate level remains high as the quality of intake of potential future senior managers is taken more seriously in more and more organizations. Certainly decisions taken at the recruitment and selection stage clearly influence the future manpower structure and quality.

Dimensions of recruitment and selection planning can typically relate to the following: degree of internal versus external recruitment; criteria for recruitment; entry levels for recruitment (balance between 'bottom end' entry, specialist entry, senior entry); range of recruitment avenues; 'signals' given to

FIGURE 5.3    *Manpower flow and its influences*

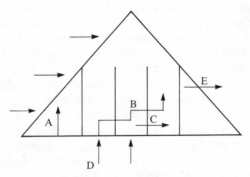

| Flow Patterns | Affected By |
| --- | --- |
| A  Upward mobility (narrow) | Promotion criteria (specific)<br>Age structure/Opportunity<br>Formalized structure |
| B  Upward mobility (broader) | Promotion criteria (flexible)<br>Development<br>Generalist culture |
| C  Lateral mobility | Development<br>Task/Problem culture<br>Compensation |
| D  Recruitment | Promotion opportunities<br>Growth<br>Internal/External philosophies<br>Organizational reputation<br>Compensation<br>Training/Development |
| E  Wastage (voluntary/involuntary) | Promotion opportunities<br>Corporate growth/Contraction<br>Age structure<br>Compensation (or lack of)<br>Training (or lack of) |

recruits about the organization; the balance between quantitative and qualitative selection methods; scope of selection processes; and degree to which selection is a mutual matching process.

*Promotion opportunities.* Considerable attention has been paid in recent years to the problem of sustaining opportunities for promotion in a situation of rationalization, low voluntary wastage and reduction of hierarchical levels. The effects on morale of declining opportunities in a traditional sense have been dramatic, especially at middle levels in organizations, and there has been a shift of emphasis away from narrow upward mobility and towards either lateral mobility, with its implications of extending the development of the individual, or on performance in the current job with related changes in reward systems to reinforce this.

It would appear sensible for organizations to evaluate the nature of past practice in the area of promotion and to contrast this with human resource requirements of the organization now and in the foreseeable future as dictated by the strategic development of the business. It is, for example, quite clear that for many organizations – in such fields as financial services, textiles and brewing – the requirements for managerial staff are quite different from even five years ago. Diversification typically creates two problems: the efficiency needs of the mainstream business and the creative needs of newer developing businesses. The first relates to providing people who can perform in what is a cost-oriented and internally-focused culture, the second to providing those who can perform in a market-oriented and externally-focused culture. This creates not only specific manpower requirements, but also raises problems about people becoming locked into 'sub-organizational' cultures. The development of a planning approach to this issue is of potential benefit – essentially it involves linking manpower flows (actual and desired) to performance needs and career and promotion plans.

Other issues relevant to the development of promotion plans for organizations would include interpreting the likely effect of structural changes or promotion opportunities; the need to move from, say, length of service criteria and attitudinal assessment to performance criteria and behavioural assessment – as this is typically driven by the link between increased pressure in the business environment and the need for major organizational change; the balance to be achieved between internal promotion and external requirement; the problems of achieving an equitable base for promotion opportunities and decisions; barriers to upward mobility – formal and informal; creating realistic expectations in respect of future promotion opportunities; and ensuring that the link between promotion prospects and wastage is understood and that decisions taken in the promotion area take account of wastage implications.

*Rewards*. The ability to recruit and to retain are affected by the quality of reward. What has given increased significance to the link is the pressure on cost control in many organizations, and an assumed need for increased performance. Personnel policy traditions in this area are associated with increased sophistication and formalizing reward systems in relation to grading systems, job evaluation procedures, and appraisal systems. The Hay–MSL system of job evaluation that appears to dominate many organizations has had one major effect in bringing order to what were often chaotic systems. Yet such a system now finds itself under increasing pressure as organizational need to obtain speedy structural change, and even speedier performance change, has become high priority. The interest being shown in incentives, bonuses, merit, and profit-sharing and share options is testimony to this.

The need for a more flexible approach in compensation, driven by strategic changes, raises a number of questions, such as: the relationship between reward and ability to attract the right people; reward as a trade-off for promotion; the need to retain people and to ensure that the reward system supports this rather than hinders it; obtaining an effort/reward relationship that fits the emerging needs of the organization.

*Manpower plans and business plans*. The three areas provide examples of the need to address manpower needs in a coherent and integrated fashion. Using the dimension of manpower flow, it is clear that the types of plans and policies developed in such areas as recruitment, promotion and compensation not only affect the nature, rate and direction of manpower flow, but also impact on the plans in other areas. Thus, a change in recruitment policy would impact on promotion and create different pressures for rewards. Changes in promotion policy would impact on rewards and recruitment. Not only, therefore, is it necessary to think within a planning framework, but also in terms of the interrelatedness of plans in each of the corporate personnel policy areas.

It is for these reasons that there has been a significant move in manpower planning to incorporate the integration of personnel plans with the needs of the business, and in addition to address consideration of manpower questions within the relationship between corporate strategy and organizational structure. To take one example, if the strategy of a business requires the development of an organization designed to provide for innovation, not only will the structural characteristics of the new organization be different from those of an operating organization, but the people requirements will be equally different. Similarly, if an organization creates a matrix structure, the requirements for matrix managers will differ from those of functional managers. This then creates pressure for planning processes that are able to ensure that the organizational requirements for manpower are met, not least the need for bigger investment in training and development. In the circumstances, then, it is perhaps not surprising that for practitioners the current challenge lies in demonstrating the significance of manpower planning to the strategic needs of the organization. Just as the personnel function faces a crisis of identity based on the need to find areas of contribution, so too does manpower planning need to be seen to be closely integrated with strategic planning and strategy implementation. The final section in the chapter will return to this issue.

*Implementation*

The stages considered so far – analysis, forecasting, and the formulation of plans – are clearly necessary in any attempt at planning. Important though they are, however, they are not sufficient to guarantee success. The most sophisticated techniques and the best-laid plans are likely to be to no avail unless those ultimately responsible have the will and ability to implement the outcome.

Surprisingly, this final stage, implementation, has received little, if any, attention in the manpower planning literature. Certainly there is a recognition of the need to have the confidence and commitment of decision-makers and of chief executives in particular; there has also been some discussion about the most appropriate location for the manpower activity (Institute of Personnel Management, 1975: 27–9; Bennison and Casson, 1984: 302) – with the personnel and management services (or corporate planning) departments both having their advocates. As with the planning literature more generally, however (see, for example, Taylor's comments, 1986: 17), scarcely any attention is paid to the problems that are involved in implementing plans; the assumption seems to be that manpower planning is a rational process and that, as long as they are presented and communicated properly, the plans will be accepted automatically. Only recently, and then in literature dealing more generally with the management of change (Kanter, 1983; Pettigrew, 1985), has there been any serious discussion of the difficulties that even supposedly powerful chief executives have in translating plans into action and the way they seek to overcome them.

## MANPOWER PLANNING IN PRACTICE

It will already be clear from some of the comments in previous sections, which draw largely on the prescriptive texts, that the practice of manpower planning can be very different from the theory. There is a problem, however, in evaluating the practice of planning. Of all the topics considered in this book, planning is probably the one about which least is known in practice. There is only a small number of case study collections (Institute of Personnel Management, 1972; MSC/NEDO, 1978), all of relatively large organizations, such as the Civil Service, the Royal Air Force, National Westminster Bank, Ford, and International Computers, who appear to practise manpower planning fairly successfully and to experience few problems.

At first sight, the only one major survey, carried out by the IPM as long ago as 1975, suggests that such activity is also widespread. Of the 308 respondents, all of whom were senior personnel specialists drawn from a wide range of establishment sizes in manufacturing and service industries, 88 per cent claimed to take stock of manpower, 82.8 per cent engaged in determining the demand for it and 64.2 per cent in forecasting supply; 76.6 per cent decided actions to match future needs; and 71.4 per cent saw the four processes as an integrated procedure (IPM, 1975: 24–5). Even the majority of the 72 organizations which admitted to not doing manpower planning said they were likely to become involved in the near future.

Closer inspection of the survey results, however, suggests that the activity was far from being as well-established or extensive as at first appeared. To begin with, more than half of the establishments which practised manpower planning said they had introduced it less than five years ago (IPM, 1975: 37). Activity was also very partial. Thus, of those practising manpower planning only slightly more than half (59.3 per cent) prepared forecasts for the organization as a whole; the remainder did forecasting for specific categories only, either throughout the entire organization or in certain divisions or establishments. The evidence also suggested that forecasting was mainly confined to white-collar employees; whereas 90.6 per cent of respondents said they produced forecasts for managers; 73.3 per cent for technicians; 66.1 per cent for sales personnel; and 58.1 per cent for supervisors, only 30.7 per cent and 21.9 per cent said that they did forecasts for skilled and unskilled operations; even fewer, 14.6 per cent, said that they did forecasts for apprentices (Institute of Personnel Management, 1975: 41). These results, incidentally, were irrespective of the size of the organization.

The uses to which the organizations put manpower planning were also relatively limited. The most frequently quoted purpose, which 71.4 per cent of the 236 respondents mentioned, was to determine recruitment needs. Only slightly more than two-thirds mentioned the assessment of training and development needs. Less than a half mentioned anticipating and avoiding redundancies, assisting in career planning and forecasting skill changes; and less than 30 per cent mentioned helping in industrial relations negotiations (Institute of Personnel Management, 1975: 35).

The only recent information about the nature and extent of manpower planning comes from the findings of the Mackay and Torrington (1986) survey of personnel management practice. Again, the superficial impression is that manpower planning is regarded as one of the most important personnel activities, and the one activity that has increased in importance to the greatest extent (Torrington and Hall, 1987: 159; Mackay and Torrington, 1986: 151). Even so, it emerged that only two-thirds of the respondents claimed that there was a manpower plan covering their establishment (Torrington and Hall, 1987: 159).

Even the advent of computerization, which has received considerable attention in the personnel journals (see, for example, Malloch, 1986), does not seem to have had the impact that might have been expected. More than a half of the respondents in the Mackay and Torrington survey (1986: 27) said the use of the computer in their organization had not affected the work of the personnel function in the area of manpower planning at all and only 11.7 per cent said that it had affected it a great deal. Relatively few claimed that the computer was used to model personnel activities with 'what if ...' type questions (Mackay and Torrington, 1986: 25).

Certainly there is no doubting the sombre mood of commentators on manpower planning. The talk is of a 'lack of application of manpower planning' (Torrington and Hall, 1987: 159) and of 'the lack of manpower policies in many organizations, and the brittle nature of these policies in others' (Bennison and Casson, 1984: 6). Purkiss, who was Director of the Institute of Manpower Studies for a number of years, has been even more forthright:

> Manpower planning has a reputation for being academic, if not tedious. It has been written about for over twenty years, every new book the definitive version. It failed in the 1960s and 1970s. It belongs to the world of calculation, computers and big bureaucracies. (Bennison and Casson, 1984: ix)

As has been indicated in the previous section, the traditional view of manpower planning as a highly precise technology seems to have been rejected. Instead, manpower planning is seen as 'a loose assemblage of ideas, tools, and techniques, which can be applied as necessary to the individual needs of a particular organization, and reflect its particular circumstances' (Bennison and Casson, 1984: 298).

Much of the emphasis in the explanation for this state of affairs focuses on the technical difficulties experienced in forecasting – especially in forecasting demand in the rapidly changing context of the 1970s and the 1980s. Torrington and Hall (1987: 158) paraphrase the example given by Lord Bowden in a lecture in 1978 appropriately entitled 'Is Manpower Planning Necessary? Is it Possible? What Next?':

> In 1972 and 1973 Mr Barber, the then Chancellor of the Exchequer, tried to reflate the economy. Restrictions on credit were removed so that the demand for television sets suddenly and dramatically increased. We began to import television sets from Japan as we were unable to make sufficient ourselves. In the expectation that this demand would continue, and using money borrowed from the government, a large factory was built to make television sets north of Manchester. It was several years between the time that some enterprising managers identified increasing demand for television sets and the time that the factory started to produce them in quantity. At the same time there was an economic crisis and a change of government. Mr Barber and then Mr Healey took measures to cut non-essential spending, and the demand for television sets dramatically fell by a factor of five. The factory closed just as it had started to work.

Important though these difficulties of forecasting have been, they are not the only considerations. In this regard it is interesting to note the views of the respondents in the 1975 Institute of Personnel Management survey referred to above. As suggested by table 5.1, which lists their reactions to reasons given for the absence of manpower planning, three main reasons would seem to be important: first, a lack of understanding of what manpower planning is; second, a lack of data in forecasting manpower demand and supply; and, third, the non-existence of a corporate plan.

The last point is especially noteworthy. All the prescriptive texts say how essential corporate planning is. The respondents in the Institute of Personnel Management survey (1975: 38) agreed, and the great majority (80 per cent) claimed that their organizations did corporate planning. Yet their reactions to the question about the reasons for the absence of manpower planning suggest that perhaps all was not well.

Though there is no survey evidence for it, the impression is that there has been a decline in corporate planning. For example, in the one hundredth issue of *Long Range Planning*, which has been the main publication in the field, the editor (Taylor, 1986: 17) talks in terms of a general disillusionment with corporate planning, of corporate planning departments being closed down, and of a shift to strategic management, as opposed to strategic planning, for which senior line managers are themselves responsible.

There is also some evidence to suggest that, where it does take place, the form of corporate or strategic planning could be an important consideration. The Goold and Campbell (1986) survey, which has already been referred to in this and previous chapters, for example, suggested a wide range of practice. Of the 16 enterprises in the survey, relatively few – BOC, BP, Cadbury-Schweppes, Lex, STC, United Biscuits – indulged in the formal process of strategic planning. Courtaulds, ICI, Imperial, Plessey and Vickers, which the

TABLE 5.1  *Reactions to reasons given for absence of manpower planning(N = 308)*

|  |  | Strongly disagree to disagree | Strongly agree to undecided |
|---|---|---|---|
| (a) | Manpower planning is not for small and medium-sized companies | 81.5 | 18.5 |
| (b) | Manpower planning is seen as an interference by line managers | 51.0 | 49.0 |
| (c) | Manpower planning is seen as 'redundancy planning' by unions | 50.6 | 49.4 |
| (d) | Change in government policy often frustrates planning efforts | 75.3 | 24.7 |
| (e) | Technology is too static to justify manpower planning | 84.7 | 15.3 |
| (f) | Manpower planning suffers from a lack of data in forecasting manpower demand and supply | 23.1 | 76.9 |
| (g) | Manpower planning suffers from a lack of readily applicable planning techniques | 45.8 | 54.2 |
| (h) | Manpower planning suffers from a lack of personnel qualified for planning | 33.5 | 66.5 |
| (i) | Manpower planning suffers from a lack of involvement by top management | 35.1 | 64.9 |
| (j) | Manpower planning suffers from a lack of understanding of what manpower planning is | 16.9 | 83.1 |
| (k) | Manpower planning suffers from the non-existence of a corporate plan | 24.1 | 75.9 |

*Source*: IPM *Manpower Planning in Action*. (London: IPM, 1975)

authors labelled the 'strategic controllers', had established planning procedures, but left the primary responsibility for doing it to the businesses. A third major group, notably those with a large number of businesses, such as BTR, Hanson Trust, GEC and Tarmac, claimed that discussion of business strategy was more or less continuous, but had no formal planning process as such. Instead, considerable emphasis was placed on the annual budgeting process in which the main focus was on financial control – on the sanctioning of expenditure, agreeing targets, and monitoring of performance against targets. Fairly strict short-term pay-back criteria of two to four years were also applied to investment decisions. Clearly if these 'financial controllers' are the dominant model – no hard data are available, but the financial success which these companies have enjoyed has encouraged a great deal of emulation and the number of enterprises with diversified interests is growing – it is not too difficult to understand why it is such a problem for managers to undertake meaningful medium-term or long-term planning of any kind, let alone manpower planning.

## TOWARDS HUMAN RESOURCE PLANNING?

To suggest, in the light of the evidence presented in the previous section, that there are signs of the emergence of an all-embracing approach towards the management of human resources may appear far-fetched. Paradoxically, however, the very conditions that have rendered the highly mathematical models of the manpower planners virtually redundant are also placing a premium on developing a more strategic approach to the management of people. The evidence of successful companies (Peters and Waterman, 1982; Peters and Austin, 1985; Kanter, 1983), and especially the Japanese competition, suggests that markets, machinery and the money are available to everyone: success goes to those organizations which are able to recruit and develop the right people and not just at the top. This means planning resources not only in quantitative terms, which has tended to be the main preoccupation with manpower planning, but on qualitative terms as well. It means seeking to integrate the full range of policies with one another and with business planning. Also, and perhaps more idealistically, it means seeking to achieve some fit between organizational and individual goals. One attempt to show such a model diagrammatically is that of Schein (1977) which appears in modified form in figure 5.4.

A particular reason for raising these issues is that NEDO and the MSC have recently joined forces to promote a more strategic approach in a major campaign entitled 'People: The Key to Success'. Chief executives, who are the main target for the campaign rather than personnel specialists, are being invited to a series of workshops up and down the country to discuss both the need for adopting a more strategic approach, and how this might be introduced. They are being told that 'the development of people, as well as the development of products and processes, must now be a core element in business strategy' (1987: 5) and that what an organization requires from its people are 'competence, commitment and the capacity to change'. Then they are shown how to go about developing a more strategic approach: they have to take stock of their existing situation, prepare plans covering a wide range of activities, which fit with their business planning, and allocate responsibilities for carrying out actions. An 'action pack', which includes a video and a suggested form of a presentation to the board, is also available.

In an attempt to reinforce the message, a number of brief case studies have been prepared, showing how several commercially successful British companies have gone about the development of the contribution made by people. Not surprisingly, the precise details are very different and reflect the specific circumstances of each case. There is a common theme, however, and it is the development of a more strategic approach. The full list – British Aerospace (Military Aircraft Division), Crane Packing, Don and Low Textiles, Grattan,

# Bibliography

Argenti, J. 1974. *Systematic Corporate Planning*. Sunbury on Thames: Nelson.

Armstrong, M. 1979. *Case Studies in Personnel Management*. London: Kogan Page.

Bartholomew, D.J. 1969. *Stochastic Models of Social Processes*. London: Wiley.

Bennison, M. and Casson, J. 1984. *The Manpower Planning Handbook*. Maidenhead: McGraw-Hill.

Bowey, A.M. 1974. *A Guide to Manpower Planning*. London: Macmillan.

Bramham, J. 1975. *Practical Manpower Planning*. London: IPM.

Bryant, D.T. 1965. 'A Survey of the Development of Manpower Planning'. *British Journal of Industrial Relations*, 3: November, 279–90.

Goffee, R. and Scase, R. 1985. 'Proprietorial Control in Family Firms'. *Journal of Management Studies*, 22: January, 52–6.

Goold, M. and Campbell, A. 1986. *Strategic Decision Making: the Corporate Role*, Vol. 1, Strategic Management Styles. London: London Business School, Centre for Business Strategy.

Haspeslagh, P.C. 1982. 'Portfolio Planning: Uses and Limits'. *Harvard Business Review*, January–February.

Institute of Personnel Management. 1972. *Company Practice in Manpower Planning*. London: IPM.

—— 1975. *Manpower Planning in Action*. London: IPM.

Kanter, R.M. 1983. *The Change Masters*. London: Allen & Unwin.

Lawrence, J. 1973. 'Manpower and Personnel Models in Britain'. *Personnel Review*, 2: 4–26.

Mackay, L. and Torrington, D. 1986. *The Changing Nature of Personnel Management*. London: IPM.

Malloch. 1986. 'Manpower Modelling with Spreadsheets'. *Personnel Management*, May, 44–6.

Manpower Services Commission/National Economic Development Office. 1978. *Case Studies in Company Manpower Planning*. London: NEDO.

—— 1987. *People: The Key to Success*. London: NEDO.

Peters, T. and Austin, N. 1985. *A Passion for Excellence*. London: Fontana Paperback.

—— and Waterman, R.H. 1982. *In Search of Excellence*. New York: Harper & Row.

Pettigrew, A.M. 1985. *The Awakening Giant*. Oxford: Blackwell.

Rice, A.K., Hill, J.M. and Trist, E.L. 1950. 'The Representation of Labour Turnover as a Social Process'. *Human Relations*, 3: 349–72.

Schein, E.H. 1977. 'Increasing Organizational Effectiveness Through Better Human Resource Planning and Development'. *Sloan Management Review*, 19: Fall, 1–20.

Scott, B.R. 1971. *Strategies of Corporate Development*. Cambridge, MA: Harvard University Press.

Smith, A.R. 1971. 'The Nature of Corporate Manpower Planning'. *Personnel Review*, 1: 44–55.

Taylor, B. 1986. 'Corporate Planning for the 1990s: The New Frontiers'. *Long Range Planning*, 19: 13–18.

Thomason, G.F. 1975. 'Manpower Planning'. *Handbook of Personnel Management*. Ed. Thomason, G.F. London: IPM.

Timperley, S.R. 1974. 'Towards a Behavioural Approach to Manpower Planning'. *Personnel Review*, 2: Winter.

Torrington, D. and Hall, L. 1987. *Personnel Management: a New Approach*. London: Prentice-Hall International.

Young, A. 1976. 'Demographic and Ecological Models for Manpower Planning'. *Manpower Planning*. Ed. Bartholomew, D.J. Harmondsworth: Penguin, 145–61.

# 6 Recruitment and Selection

*Tom Watson*

Recruitment and selection are triggered by vacancies which may be the result of retirement, resignation, promotion, transfer, or dismissal of an incumbent. Vacancies may also be created when additional or new work has to be undertaken or significant changes occur in technology, procedures, or circumstances. Each vacancy, by whatever process it arises, provides an opportunity to review the use of personnel. The issues to be faced in such a review are treated in other chapters, notably chapter 5, and will not be discussed further here: it will be assumed throughout this chapter, however, that such a review will have taken place before any recruitment is undertaken.

Recruitment and selection are the processes by which organizations solicit, contact, and engender interest in potential new appointees to vacant positions in the organization, and then in some way establish their suitability for appointment. This definition does not include the process of negotiating the terms on which a new incumbent will be accepted into the position, but clearly recruitment and selection would not be regarded as having been successful until this process, too, had been satisfactorily concluded. Moreover, these processes are not in practice separate and distinct: the first statement made about remuneration or conditions of employment may also be the opening phase of the bargaining which leads to the offer and acceptance of appointment.

It is, of course, true that for positions covered by collective agreements the bargaining takes place between management and unions. It is not part of the recruitment process, but nevertheless can affect recruitment considerably. Even in such circumstances some negotiation may still take place, as for example when a recruit is offered 'guaranteed' overtime.

Stress has been laid on recruitment and selection as processes which involve negotiation because it leads to the view that it is the task of managers to influence these processes to the advantage of the organization; it is also a reminder that other parties are involved with different interests. Though they would probably clothe it in different language, this notion is quite familiar to, and underlies some of the recruitment practices of, many British managers. They know that practical success depends on understanding what influences potential employees. It is therefore curious that British textbooks on personnel management tend to ignore the multiple roles of candidates and the impact of external influences on them in relation to seeking and accepting employment (for example, Torrington and Chapman, 1983: 478; Higham, 1983; Courtis,

1985). This issue is treated briefly by Thomason (1981: 154–8), and Atkinson and Purkiss (1983: 13–19) and is given thorough treatment in relation to graduates by Herriot (1984: 97–131).

This chapter will review the processes of recruitment and selection, drawing on surveys and other evidence and the author's knowledge of present practice and will comment on it from the perspective outlined above.

## ANALYSING THE NEED

Before any active steps are taken to recruit, it is assumed that the review mentioned above will have taken place, and that it will have shown the need to make a new appointment. One of the consequences of economic stringency in recent years is that this review is much more likely to have been carried out than was the case in easier times. Measures aimed at maintaining control of staff and labour costs by requiring all new appointments or replacements to be justified, are now very common. They usually have the virtue of causing the nature of an appointment to be reviewed so that there is less likelihood of an unthinking perpetuation of existing practice, and this must reduce the danger of organizational calcification. However, this tighter control can also be counterproductive if a departmental manager were to tolerate an unsatisfactory state of affairs rather than take corrective action that could lead to the reduction of his work group if the organization were 'freezing' all vacancies.

Following this review, the next step towards recruitment is to define what kind of employee is required by describing and analysing the job and drawing up a job description and personnel specification. This process is now commonly carried out fairly formally, due no doubt to the influence of the Industrial Training Boards in the 1960s and 1970s. The information which is collected is used as a basis for seeking internal candidates or for advertising or notifying the vacancy to recruitment sources, for giving job details to candidates, and for briefing or reminding selectors of what is required. Job descriptions typically include the following information:

1  job title, reference, and other identifying data;
2  reporting relationships;
3  the purpose, aims or objectives of the job;
4  the key tasks;
5  main contacts inside and outside the organization.

They may also include additional useful information such as:

6  limits of authority over expenditure, working methods, sales, information, equipment, personnel matters, and so on;
7  particular problems, difficulties, distasteful aspects, and constraints;
8  working conditions and hours;
9  remuneration and benefits.

These items are derived from a range of texts, such as Courtis, 1985:8; Torrington and Chapman, 1983: 381–5; Thomason, 1981: 187–92; ACAS, 1981: 4, 17; Cuming, 1978: 71–3; Grant and Smith, 1977: 30–4; Armstrong, 1977: 86–8; Fraser, 1971: 53–61; Denerley and Plumbley, 1968: 19–22, which are taken to be representative of usual good practice in Britain.

None of the sources above mentions two very important items which could be added to the list as a reminder that recruitment and selection take place in a dynamic environment. The first item, the date of preparation of the document, may seem relatively trivial. It earns specific mention here because it is a reminder that such documents can quickly become obsolete. The second item, a prediction of the future changes likely to impinge on the job, may be difficult to estimate. However, as Burns and Stalker (1961) and Lawrence and Lorsch (1967) have shown, uncertainty and change are contingencies which call for changes in roles and organization if they are to be faced successfully.

Whatever system of headings is used, the purpose will be to identify and describe those aspects of the job which are crucial to success. This description will then provide a useful basis for identifying the critical attributes to be sought in candidates for appointment by revealing the particular demands which a job will make on the incumbent. This is not a mechanical process: the process of deduction requires imagination and the conclusions will be based on opinions and probability rather than certainty. People often feel 'certain' of their uncertain conclusions in such circumstances. It is, therefore, valuable to have systematic ways of approaching this problem in order to constrain the effects of bias and prejudice.

Two such aids are used fairly extensively in Britain (Mackay and Torrington, 1986: 41) and are summarized in the 'Seven Point Plan' (Rodger, 1970) and the 'Five-Fold Framework' (Fraser, 1971: 64–80) and also in the ACAS Advisory Booklet No. 6 (ACAS, 1981). Rodger's Seven Point Plan is 'a series of questions gathered together under seven headings':

1 physical make-up (health, physique, appearance, bearing, speech);
2 attainments (education, training, experience, degree of success in each);
3 general intelligence;
4 special aptitudes (mechanical, numerical, verbal, drawing, music, manual dexterity);
5 interests (intellectual, practical, social, artistic, physically active);
6 disposition (acceptability, influence, dependability, self-reliance);
7 circumstances (domestic, family, special).

Rodger formulated his questions so that they relate to people, but made it clear that the answers have to be interpreted in relation to the demands of a job or occupation. The questions thus serve to link the form in which job demands are specified to the way in which candidates will be assessed. If it is not clear what is to be expected from a suitable candidate it is probable that there is a deficiency in the job analysis which should, therefore, be explored further.

Munro Fraser's 'Five-Fold Framework' was developed specifically as an aid to selection interviewing. It can be viewed as a development of the 'Seven Point

Plan' and there is considerable overlap between the two check-lists. The five areas are:

1  impact on others (appearance, speech, manner, self-confidence);
2  acquired knowledge or qualifications (education, training, work experience);
3  innate abilities (speed of perception, special aptitudes);
4  motivation (goals, consistency, initiative, practical effectiveness);
5  emotional adjustment (ability to stand up to stress).

Fraser recommends the use of rating scales in relation to each of these headings, suggesting a grading in which 'A' indicates the top 10 per cent, 'B' the next 20 per cent, 'C' the mid 40 per cent, 'D' the next 20 per cent lower and 'E' the bottom 10 per cent on each characteristic. This practice and variations of it are widely used in the design of interview report forms.

Comparison of the two lists reveals the difficulty that can be experienced in classifying quite familiar ideas. Fraser's 'impact on others' is largely concerned with first impressions. It therefore overlaps Rodger's 'physical make-up'. Examination of Rodger's 'disposition' shows it to be largely concerned with 'impact on others' considered over a longer period. Rodger did not use the heading 'motivation' but some motivational issues are covered under 'interests' and 'disposition' and possibly 'attainment' (particularly if 'attainment' is considered in relation to 'circumstances'). Fraser (1971: 75) uses the heading 'motivation' but his notes of guidance place more emphasis on the strength of the motivation than on its direction. At the stage of specifying the person likely to succeed in a job, it would seem important to identify the particular pattern of motives likely to be satisfied by the job and necessary for success; specifying the pattern will involve estimating, probably very crudely, the relative and absolute strength of the motives which are identified. Neither check-list pulls all of this together.

## METHODS OF RECRUITMENT

Having identified the characteristics of the person required for the vacancy, the next stage is to consider how to reach such people and to enlist their interest in the job. This requires consideration of the channels available for communication, the possible sources of information about such people, and the most cost-effective way of using either. These channels and sources overlap and Courtis (1985: 15) puts them in a single list: advertising; employment agencies and job centres/job points/Professional and Executive Register (PER); registers; selection consultants; search consultants (headhunters); outplacement consultants; introductions by existing staff or unions; people already known; people who have left the organization; people who applied last time; other 'volunteers' such as casual callers and correspondents; and university milkround/schools contacts. In terms of order of priority, one might expect an organization to look inside, ask friends and contacts; and then, after that, think about advertising or consultants.

Internal candidates may be sought by searching the records, asking managers or supervisors for recommendations, or internal advertisements on notice-boards and/or in-house journals. It is difficult to know how extensively or how effectively the first method is used. Its success will depend very much on the quality of the records and whether they are kept in a way which facilitates this kind of search. Keeping and searching manual records is very labour-intensive and error-prone and it is to be hoped that computerization will ease the problem. However, just as the cost of clerical time discouraged the elaboration of manual records in ways which would have assisted the search for internal candidates, it seems possible that, for a while at least, the Data Protection Act 1984 may inhibit companies from storing more than essential short-term operating information in computer-processable form. Skills not necessary, and therefore underutilized in a present job, maybe of key importance in a vacancy to be filled, but may be unrecorded.

Asking supervisors and managers for recommendations is similarly de-pendent on the quality of their information, but is likely to be able to tap much more complex and up-to-date information. The danger is that this richer information is even more vulnerable to bias. Internal advertising is one way of reaching current employees who have unexpected and unrecorded skills or experience. It may have the disadvantage of producing large numbers of applications which are expensive to process, but this risk can be reduced by improved information for human resource management to reduce the need for general notices. As will be elaborated below, careful drafting of announce-ments will also reduce the number of unsuitable applications. In some cases, internal advertising may not be optional: unions such as the National and Local Government-Officers negotiate agreements that for positions above basic entry grades internal advertising shall be the primary method of seeking applicants.

If there are not suitable internal candidates, an organization's records of former employees or applicants for other jobs may enable a vacancy to be filled quickly and economically. Again, the quality of the records will be of key importance; the Data Protection Act may be inhibiting, and, depending on the time likely to elapse between the last contact and the possibility of another relevant vacancy, the chance that the person will be satisfactorily employed elsewhere, and not interested in being considered, may be too high to justify much investment in retaining information.

Casual callers and candidates who send unsolicited applications may prove to be useful candidates on occasion. An organization might even be able to encourage enquiries, but unless it had a very high rate of labour turnover (which would seem to call for corrective action rather than cheap recruitment) the low probability that such approaches would match needs suggests that this is not a particularly worthwhile course of action. However, the reputation which a company enjoys for treating applicants courteously is likely to affect its ability to attract candidates when it wishes to do so, and this should guide the handling of casual applicants. Courtis (1985) points out that consultants take such applicants seriously: their case is of course different, because applicants are their stock-in-trade.

Contacts made through present employees may lead to very satisfactory appointments. The information made available to the candidate before accepting appointment may be more comprehensive and, as Wanous (1980: 71–8) has shown in the United States, realistic job previews can reduce turnover. However, the practice may be regarded as unacceptably paternalistic and, as Massey-Ferguson discovered, if the current workforce is not a fair cross-section of the local population, it may be held to be 'indirect discrimination' under the Race Relations Act. In some industries, printing is an example, a union may exercise tight control over entry by agreement or custom and practice, in which case management may only be able to recruit through the union. Management has, of course, lost control in such circumstances, but recruitment will not be expensive and appointments may be no less satisfactory.

Employment agencies and job centres can be useful subcontractors of recruitment work. As Courtis (1985: 16–17) reminds us, they vary in quality and their work is influenced by the quality of the brief they are given. He groups the Professional and Executive Register (PER) with the agencies. PER advertising stresses its similarity with selection consultants. This is fair because it offers a similar service to employers, but also throws light on the issue of acceptability mentioned earlier. Professional and managerial candidates, who would have had little or no contact with job centres, are likely to prefer to deal with a consultancy rather than a job centre.

Some management consultants and psychologists had earlier offered a consultancy service related to selection, but selection consultancy really began to grow in a significant way in the mid-1950s. The development followed a trend begun in the United States, but the British pioneers did not believe that the UK was ready for US-style head-hunting or search consultancy in which promising candidates are sought out and approached directly. Developments in Continental Europe were even slower, being hindered by legislation banning employment agencies. This legislation was intended to protect workers from having to pay anyone to find them a job, as in France and West Germany, but was broadly drawn and was construed to forbid the establishment of any agency which maintained records of possible candidates.

Selection consultants sell their services on the basis of offering:

1  skills in recruitment, advertising, and selection which may be in short supply in the client firm;
2  detailed and current knowledge of particular labour markets;
3  access to a large file of candidates which may save advertising costs; and
4  brokerage between employer and applicants so that jobs can be advertised without revealing the employer's identity and potential applicants need not have their identity revealed to the employer unless the post seems interesting after a fairly detailed discussion with the consultant.

It is argued that these factors will produce more appropriate candidates than would be prepared to apply directly to the employer. As with agencies competence varies. The best test is probably to get the opinion of a former client for whom the consultants have handled a similar task recently. Courtis (1985: 18) suggests reviewing Executive Grapevine to identify firms claiming appropriate expertise: he then suggests some useful questions to test their professionalism.

Search consultancy, which appears to have considerably strengthened its grip on senior management recruitment since 1980 (Heidrich and Struggles, 1985), is very labour-intensive and so the fees for an assignment are correspondingly high. In consequence, it is mainly used for positions at very senior levels, though here again acceptability may be a significant factor. To apply for a job may suggest that the candidate needs to change, and this would not be reassuring to potential future colleagues. The process must therefore be managed so that the prospective candidates can discuss the possibility of joining the organization without having to make an application. If the discussions are not fruitful, they can withdraw gracefully and nobody suffers the ignomiy of being rejected or having their current positions undermined. Interestingly, head-hunting of a 'do-it-yourself' kind has long been practised at the highest levels in the public sector. Advertisements for some very senior positions in the public sector often indicate the willingness of the body concerned to have interesting names suggested by third parties.

Selection and search consultancy raise some interesting ethical problems. The purpose of most recruitment is to lure good employees away from other employers. Employers may not like it, but publicizing the availability of jobs shows employees the opportunities that are open to them. 'No poaching' agreements limit the freedom of workers for the short-run economic advantage of employers, though it might also be argued that the longer term effects are not in the employers' interests either because they inhibit the development of a labour market in which critical skills are in adequate supply. In the case of selection and search consultants the problem is narrowed and sharpened. Both would normally begin an assignment by meeting a considerable proportion of the managers with whom the new person will have to work in order to understand the client organization's requirements. The difficulty arises because this means that they meet and be able to form an opinion of the competence of a group of exactly the sort of people their next client may be seeking. Naturally, the current client will want some reassurance that the consultant will not exploit this privileged access. The ethical selection consultant may undertake not to initiate any approach to the current client's employees, but is likely to point out that if any of these employees reply to an advertisement their applications will be treated no less favourably. They will be recommended to the other client if they seem suitable and the consultant will not inform their present employer (the current client). An advantage that will probably be pointed out to the client is that the consultant is free to consider anybody who replies to an advertisement or who has already agreed to details being kept on file. The client generally agrees that it would be unsatisfactory for the strongest candidates to be withheld because they were employed by another of the consultant's clients. The ethical search consultant, on the other hand, will reassure the client that no employee will be put forward for another job during the assignment and during some specified period afterwards, and that no direct competitor of the client will be accepted as a client during this period. The client thus has stronger protection with the search consultant than the selection consultant for a period of, probably, up to two years, and continually if the organization is large enough to be able to retain the search consultant regularly. Even so, some large companies are rumoured to retain head-hunters continuously as an insurance policy to reduce the chance of the opposition getting to their best people.

Schools, colleges, polytechnics, universities, 'outplacement' consultants who assist individuals with career planning or are retained by employers to help place· staff made redundant, and registers may all prove to be fruitful sources of candidates. Registers ask for a relatively small fee if someone from their list is appointed; some universities have recently asked visiting recruiters to pay a fee or have charged for interviewing rooms; otherwise these sources do not involve the direct payment of a charge. This is not to imply, however, that recruitment through these channels is free or even cheap. As in the other cases, careful thought is necessary to achieve cost-effectiveness. There are more than forty universities in the UK and a similar number of polytechnics, some with more than one location. The travel and accommodation costs incurred in sending recruiters to visit all of them are considerable. Briefing their careers advisers to understand the ethos and requirements of the employing organization can also be quite expensive. For these reasons a number of employers have concentrated on buidling up a strong relationship with a small number of institutions which seem best able to assist them. Good reasons for choosing particular institutions may be geographical, the existence of particularly relevant or good courses, prestige, or the competence of the careers staff.

Advertising is probably the recruitment channel which first comes to mind if internal candidates are not available to fill a job (although appropriate advertising may be necessary in internal recruitment too).

Recruitment advertising is expensive. Fordham (1983: 48) considers that revenue from this source saved a large sector of the newspaper industry from financial collapse. Selling space to recruiters has become big and sophisticated business. They are being courted as never before. In 1957 *The Times* did not accept display advertisements for jobs, and refused to allow the pioneer selection consultants Management Selection Limited to advertise under their initials MSL; in May 1985 it was offering bottles of champagne to job advertisers.

In this new climate it is very easy to spend too much on recruitment advertising. Cuming (1978: 79) expressed strong opinions about wasteful advertising in the NHS, coupled with the suggestion that employers could get some coverage of 'stories' relating to job opportunities in the local press and use local direct mail shots much more cheaply as ways of reaching people who might not be reading the 'situations vacant' columns. The force of Cuming's comments is underlined by a news item in *Personnel Management* (May 1985, 57) which reports a two-year trial period for restrictions on advertising designed to save the National Health Service £4 million.

To achieve cost-effectiveness in advertising it is necessary to consider the choice of media; the content of the advertisement; its presentation; and, finally, a simple but effective system of response analysis to monitor the results. These are discussed in turn below.

The aim of advertising will generally be to attract a sufficient number of suitably qualified applicants so that a good appointment can be made, and to do this at minimum cost. Effectiveness is the first consideration, and cost the second. When the Civil Service advertises a national competition for posts it has to be fair to all suitable candidates and takes steps to publicize the competition widely. In other cases, such as medical appointments at consultant level in the NHS, it is a statutory requirement that the appointment be advertised in more than one journal. These are special cases and it will be more usual to aim close to the minimum coverage necessary, though this may be very wide in a difficult case. The question is, therefore, how can the organization reach the people it needs? Recruitment officers are nowadays deluged with readership information by the press and advertising agents. Courtis (1985: 26) points out that 'the media which people read often bear no resemblance to the ones they look at for jobs'. An old example should make this clear. In the 1950s there was a shortage of draughtsmen. The majority of draughtsmen read the *Daily Mirror* and there would always be a considerable number of copies of that paper in a large drawing office. In addition there was very often one copy of the *Daily Telegraph* which passed from hand to hand so that the jobs column could be scanned. The question is therefore not, what do they read? but, where will they see a job advertisement? Knowing the market and analysing the past responses to advertising will give the best guidance. The *Daily Express* (2.32 million) and *Daily Mail* (1.98 million) both have larger circulations than the *Daily Telegraph* (1.44 million) but carry much less job advertising (15 per cent, 11.4 per cent and 35 per cent respectively). The difference is partly explained by the difference in the social class profile of the readers of these papers but the habit of non-readers to consult the paper when searching for jobs has assisted the *Daily Telegraph* to maintain its ascendency in job advertising.

In addition to the press, trade and specialist publications, there are other possibilities for the recruiter to bear in mind. Some companies use slides at the local cinema. These do not seem likely to reach very large audiences at present, but may meet special needs. Posters are not widely used but may well be effective for some grades of staff when used on the London Underground trains or in similar situations. Television is relatively expensive and little used at present. However, the point made by Courtis in relation to the local press could be even more important in relation to television. At the present time, job losses and job creation are national news. When numbers of new jobs are created, this is reported, naming the employer and the location: such very wide publicity can produce large numbers of applications which may be expensive to process. Television advertising through Prestel (Ray, 1980: 66–9) or Oracle and similar networks may become useful to recruiters.

It seems likely, however, that recruiters will not rush to use new media. The *Sunday Telegraph* was launched during a job advertising boom. Initially, it offered very favourable terms to prestigious advertisers whose example was likely to be followed by others. One such advertiser declined to support the new paper on the grounds that if an additional place were created where people would look for jobs it would become necessary to use it and this would increase the costs of reaching the people who were already being recruited through the existing Sunday papers. It is interesting to note that in March 1985 the *Sunday Times* had 15.7 per cent, the *Observer* 3.7 per cent, and the *Sunday Telegraph* only 0.2 per cent of recruitment advertising in the quality papers (*Personnel Management*, May 1985: 57).

Other media worth a brief mention are radio, television, careers exhibitions or conferences, films, and video cassettes. Radio can compete directly with local papers and can be very effective in persuading people to make a preliminary contact. It has the disadvantage that the listener has to create any record that is needed, so the message which has to be recorded or remembered is best kept very simple. The other media seem most likely to be of value for large-scale recruitment, recruitment when a requirement is likely to remain unchanged over a number of years, or collaborative recruitment to a profession. Video cassettes have been supplied to universities in this latter connection for use in careers advisory work.

The message contained in the advertisement is crucial. The essence of preparing an effective message was given very pithily by Parkinson (1986: ch.2) who argued that the ideal advertisement produced only one applicant but that applicant would be ideally qualified for the job. To achieve this, the message would balance the attractive and unattractive features of the job. It would avoid stating the requirements in terms of vague qualities which most people would claim to possess such as initiative, integrity, intelligence, and tact. Instead it would set out a realistic thumbnail sketch of the job from which the reader would be able to deduce the skills and qualities required. The difficulties and unpleasant features would not be minimized and the pay and benefits would be set out clearly. Allowing for the humorous exaggeration this advice is based on a more searching analysis of some of the key issues than is found in most contemporary texts: Fordham (1983) and Courtis (1985) are exceptions.

Overall, an effective advertisement is likely to include:

1  information concerning the organization;
2  the location of the job;
3  significant developments which may have their impact on the job;
4  job preview;
5  qualifications and experience required;
6  outline of the remuneration and benefits; and
7  instructions for responding.

People usually want to know who the advertiser is before revealing their own identity. Horror stories used to be told about people applying to their current employers who had advertised under a box number. Agencies and consultants now offer protection to both parties and the box number has almost disappeared from recruitment advertising. In specifying the requirements, it is useful to keep in mind both the ideal and the minimum candidate (Courtis, 1985: 37) and to consider whether it is desirable to encourage or discourage candidates near the minimum. The employer's policy and the statutory requirements concerning the employment of disabled people need to be kept in mind.

Many companies are reluctant to state clearly what pay they are offering, though this coyness seems to have diminished over recent years and the intermediaries provide a way of separating salary information from company identity in an initial advertisement. Courtis (1985: 38–9) demolishes four stock arguments for coyness: first, if a company has a sound pay structure it does not have to worry about jealousy among existing employees; second, existing employees know more about supposedly secret salaries than management cares to acknowledge; third, if you do not reveal the salary you will not meet some of the most promising potential candidates; and fourth, appointments are frequently made at salaries below the advertised maximum starting salary. Furthermore, at times when there is a shortage of particular skills employers may be inhibited from advertising salaries either by agreement or a shared belief that this will lead to an escalation of salary costs. In West Germany after the Second World War there was legislation prohibiting the inclusion of salaries in job advertising. Some organizations circumvented this by arranging that the diagonal measurement across a display advertisement for a managerial position was directly proportional to the salary in Deutschmarks but it is not known how widely this convention was understood.

If people are not sure how they are required to respond, they may not do so at all, or may do so in an inconvenient way. The illiterate, the highly literate but very busy, and those who may use the telephone a great deal in their work may use the telephone in the first instance. Firms using graphologists may ask for hand-written applications. If application forms are to be used, applicants can be discouraged from writing long letters; if they are not to be used, the task of comparing initial letters can be made easier by asking for specific information to be included. In either case the selector is left to decide how to interpret the failure of candidates to follow the instructions.

A final and very important consideration when drafting copy and planning supporting illustration is to be aware of the considerable range of relevant legislation and to avoid infringing any of it. Wording (and, of course, illustration) which states or implies an intention to discriminate against some candidates in ways which contravene the Sex Discrimination Act or the Race Relations Act are obviously to be avoided, and guidance on such points is readily available from the Equal Opportunities Commission (1977). Ray (1980: ch. 10) discusses not only these Acts but nine others from the Criminal Justice Act 1925 to the Control of Pollution Act 1974 'which prohibits the use of loudspeakers in the street for advertising purposes'.

An advertisement can deliver its message only when it has caught attention. Recruitment advertisements can be seen to be trying to do this in several ways. The first is size. This may convey more about the importance and resources of the employing organization than it does about the specific vacancy or vacancies that are being advertised: it may also indicate the scale of the recruitment need. The Army is one of the few organizations with the resources and the need to use both full-page advertisements in the national press and quite substantial commercials on television. The economy campaign in the NHS referred to earlier is aimed very largely at reducing expenditure on the features which attract attention. In journals where the majority of the advertising is for NHS jobs only, lineage or semi-display advertising is to be used. Logos which are also used as eye-catching devices are banned (*Personnel Management*, May 1985, 57). Other aspects of presentation that assist an advertisement to draw attention are the use of artwork, special type, and the position on the page or within the publication. Competent space sales managers recognize the value of the positions facing editorial matter and charge a premium which may be worth paying because the advertisement has a better chance of being noticed by people who are not actively job hunting, as well as those who are.

The style in which an advertisement is written can be significant in two ways: it affects the impression which is created and it can also affect costs. Ray (1980: 150–3) discusses indifferent, interesting, influential, impressive, and gimmicky styles. The indifferent should be avoided but each of the others can be appropriate, though they have to be matched to the circumstances with increasing care as one progresses through the list. Costs are inflated when the copywriter uses an unnecessarily verbose style or adds redundant phrases such as 'Applications are invited for the post of' when the heading 'Computer Programmer' serves quite well on its own.

Consideration of the cost-effectiveness of advertisements requires the setting up of a monitoring procedure. Analysing the responses is, of course, different from merely counting them. Two hundred replies to an advertisement might sound impressive, but if the applicants are not suitable the advertisement is of less value than another which produces two applicants and both are appointable. It is common practice to ask candidates to quote a reference number which indicates both the position being sought and the publication in which the advertisement was seen: it is better practice to analyse the sources of the short-listed and appointed candidates.

Employers may feel the need for outside help in presenting their recruitment message. Ray (1980: ch. 16) reviews the role of agencies in recruitment advertising. A good agency will have a range of skills which only the largest employer could hope to match. It will have experience with a wider range of media and will have up-to-date knowledge of costs, print and artwork requirements, copy dates and so on; and it will be able to relieve the recruiter of the tedious and very detailed administrative work necessary to ensure that his instructions are correctly carried out by a range of different publications, and that their bills are correct.

It has been stated above that the recruiter must know his market. This is fundamental. As recruitment has become more professional, more data have become available about trends in the job market. As a public relations and publicity device, Hay–MSL have been publishing an index of recruitment advertising for managerial staff since 1960. This was based on an analysis of the advertisements in six publications and for a time gave the best available impression of general trends in this job market. A wider analysis is now prepared by the *Guardian* and very detailed analyses are published by Media Expenditure Analysis Ltd. All of these are reported in *Personnel Management*, which also reports data from search consultants. Any tendency to rely on any one of these as indicating the state of a job market should be corrected by considering two headlines in the Recruitment Report (*Personnel Management*, 1983: 45–6): one based on advertising said 'Demand for executives highest since 1974' the other based on head-hunters' data declared 'Executive jobs down'. There is clearly an ebb and flow between the channels that are being used for recruitment as well as fluctuations in the number of vacancies to be filled. This has recently been confirmed by a study of works managers which showed a strong trend away from outside recruitment towards promotion from within (Stirling et al., 1985). The implication, if this trend continues, is that recruitment from outside by the larger companies will be aimed at a younger age group and the main consideration will be to potential and not short-term job requirements.

An organization setting up a unit in a new location may find that successful recruitment of a new labour-force requires activities beyond those discussed above. It may have to convince the local community that its employment practices, the nature of its work, and its impact on the district are consistent with it being accepted as a good citizen. Much of this will be done in discussion with trade unions, but it will probably also be necessary to cultivate the goodwill and support of civic, social or religious leaders, depending on the context. That this is merely a special case of a general issue is illustrated by the Annual Report for 1984 of the Civil Service Commission which reports that careers in the Civil Service have become less attractive to able undergraduates. This is reported to be influenced by 'how well-regarded the employment is seen to be by the community as a whole' (*Personnel Management*, 1985: 16).

Finally it is worth comment that this chapter is relatively unusual among chapters in British texts on personnel management in devoting so much space to recruitment (cf. Pratt and Bennett, 1985; Torrington and Chapman, 1983; Thomason, 1981; Cuming, 1978; Grant and Smith, 1977; Armstrong, 1977; Fraser, 1971). The justification is that recruitment provides the candidates for the selector to judge. Selection techniques cannot overcome failures in recruitment; they merely make them evident.

## THE SELECTION PROCESS

Selection is a decision-making process. Torrington and Chapman (1983: 70) point out that it is a reciprocal process with both candidates and employers making decisions. They claim that with one exception (French, 1974: 267), which turns out to be a single sentence and diagram, there is no discussion of this issue in major US personnel management texts. It does emerge in the literature of industrial and organizational psychology (Rodger, 1971; Wanous, 1980) and is basic to the preceding discussion of recruitment and to the comments on realistic job previews and self-selection below. Makin and Robertson (1983: 21, 24) have also aired this issue in the personnel management literature.

Selection processes require the collecting and ordering of the data, opinions, and inferences on which the decisions will be based. What follows will be largely concerned with the methods employers use. The methods selected are influenced by the employers' view of what is required to provide a satisfactory basis for decision-making and awareness of the appropriateness of particular techniques to provide what is sought.

Parkinson (1986) in another of his pithy oversimplifications suggests that all selection methods can be reduced to two basic methods and combinations or elaborations of these. Each method requires asking the candidate only one question. In the Chinese method the candidate is asked 'what do you know?': the English method is to ask 'who is your father?'. The 'English method' is blatantly discriminatory. The question does not have to be asked aloud and is an encapsulation of much racial and class discrimination. The United States version of the question is 'where did you go to school?' which can be used in an elitist discriminatory way familiar in Britain. The Civil Service Commission is said still to be concerned that Oxbridge graduates are over-represented in the higher grades of the Civil Service. The 'Chinese method' is the basis of attempts to collect objective information about job-relevant knowledge, skills and abilities. It can also be used in ways which are as discriminatory as the 'English method' if the information collected is not job-relevant or consists of biased subjective judgements. McIntosh and Smith (1974) reported that the level of racial discrimination had declined since the passing of the 1967 Race Relations Act, but it was still substantial and considerably exceeded the level indicated by official complaints. A point worth underlining is that the adoption of systematic selection techniques designed to reduce racial and sex discrimination by focusing on valid job-relevant selection criteria would probably also reduce the number of selection errors affecting members of groups who are not discriminated against at present.

*Reliability and Validity*

Before examining the techniques used to collect the data used in making selection decisions, there are some general principles to consider. Rodger told generations of his students that in considering the use of any psychological technique they should check that it is technically sound, administratively convenient and politically acceptable. This roughly means that it should really work, be cost-effective, and not run into so much resistance that it will be impossible to introduce with any hope of success. This is sound advice in relation to any managerial or administrative technique. Comments will be made on administrative convenience and political acceptability below. Technical soundness is, however, fundamental and will be considered separately before moving on to more detailed consideration of data-gathering techniques.

The two key requirements for selection methods to be technically sound are 'reliability' and 'validity'. Reliability means that the method should not be influenced too much by chance factors, and should be consistent in the results it gives if used to assess a person on more than one occasion. Validity means that the method measures the characteristic or ability that it purports to measure and what is more important from a practical point of view, predicts the future behaviour or performance that it is required or assumed to predict. These qualities can only be established by practical empirical testing. For example, during the later stages of the Second World War, it was discovered that a 10-minute test of mental arithmetic was a better predictor of recruits' ability to pass an army driving test than was an elaborate procedure using a simulated driving cab to measure the precision and speed of typical driving responses (Semeonoff, 1948). The simulated cab seems more likely to be useful (this is called having higher 'face validity') but properly controlled comparisons of scores and driving test results showed that the arithmetic test had higher 'predictive validity': it worked better. If the scores gained in a selection test, or awarded by a panel of interviewers, for a group of candidates are compared with a measure of their performance on the job, the correlation between these two sets of scores is a measure of the validity of the predictor. This measure, the coefficient of validity, can only be interpreted in relation to the group of candidates from whom it was obtained. A test may have different validities for males and females, or for different ethnic groups, which means that selection procedures to be used with mixed groups of applicants should be separately validated for each constituent subgroup. A strict interpretation of the anti-discrimination legislation in Britain would seem to call for this if it is to be shown that selection criteria are job-related. Up to the present time this has not been demanded in Britain, but litigation in the USA has included some highly technical arguments on validation.

There are probably at least three reasons why validation of tests has not been widely practised in Britain (Sneath et al., 1976). Firstly, the users have not realized the need, or had assumed that tests acquired through reputable agencies were already validated (not understanding that validity is affected by the context in which the test is used). Secondly, true predictive validation is a very lengthy process. It requires candidates to be tested, but selected on grounds other than the test results. These should remain unknown to anyone who will assess the candidates in any way so that the assessor's judgement is not influenced by knowledge of the test results. The results are reviewed and the validity of the test calculated when a sufficiently large group of candidates has been in employment long enough for there to be good measures available of their performance in the job. Because this process takes so long it is often replaced by applying the test to a group of existing employees whose performance is already recorded. This is known as concurrent validation. It is less satisfactory because test performance may have been influenced by experience of the job; the motivation of present employees and applicants taking the test may be different; and the variability of the validation group may have been reduced by promotions and separations. Thirdly, validation of measures to predict job performance requires that criteria of job performance are available which are themselves valid and reliable. These may not be available for service or advisory jobs. Even in production and sales jobs, where performance seems more readily measurable, there may be differences in the volume or quality of production which are attributable to the condition of equipment rather than worker performance, and sales volume can be influenced by the special factors in a particular territory as well as by an employee's selling skills.

Brotherton (1980) has drawn a distinction between measures of 'organizational performance' and 'job performance' and emphasized that successful non-discriminatory selection requires validation based on job performance. It is clear, however, that many employers are looking to select personnel for careers and so are trying to predict something much more complex than performance in a specific job. The validation of such predictions will necessarily be an even lengthier and more difficult task.

*Methods of Selection*

The methods of collecting information about candidates can now be considered. Comments will be offered on five groups: letters of application, application forms, references, interviews, tests and assessment centres.

*Letters of application*. These are probably of little significance in selection for many manual jobs. If they are used at all, they probably serve only to provide a statement of the candidate's interest, identity and address, and possibly an indication of literacy if this is a requirement of the job. They probably also include some statement of previous experience which could assist a selector.

It must be true that millions of decisions to reject candidates are made every year on the basis of letters alone, yet there seems to be practically nothing in the contemporary British personnel literature on this subject. McIntosh and Smith (1974) showed discriminatory responses to application letters, Knollys (1983: 237) acknowledges that letters can be of critical importance, and Duxfield (1983; 247) is of the opinion that 'good potential salesmen are often poor performers in the art of letter-writing'. This all suggests a need for some systematic research, particularly as the Manpower Services Commission, careers consultants, outplacement consultants, and careers teachers are engaged in training applicants to write better letters.

*Application forms*. The usefulness of letters to the selector will overlap with the usefulness of application forms. In particular, both can state claims to education, experience, and qualifications which can be compared with the recruitment specification. A candidate has more freedom of choice over what is presented in a letter. This may be either an advantage or a disadvantage to the selector. The possible disadvantage is that candidates may be difficult to compare because they have submitted different patterns of information. This is turned to advantage by some selectors who try to give a clear picture of the job in an advertisement which invites concise statements of relevant information. Candidates are then judged on their grasp of what is likely to be relevant. Some recruiters combine the advantages by inviting applicants to request a form and further particulars. The selector then does not have to make any decisions until information is available in a convenient format. However, a good letter and *curriculum vitae* (CV) can make a form unnecessary and thus reduce postage and printing costs.

Graphology, the study of handwriting characteristics in order to assess aspects of the personality or character of the writer, is claimed to provide a way of deriving additional information from application letters. It has been used in the Netherlands for a considerable period, but its use is controversial in Britain. *Personnel Management* has featured the subject on a number of occasions recently and in the March 1985 issue Lynch reports that it is being used in Britain, citing Petrofina, Warburgs, Price Waterhouse Associates and a leading advertising agency as users. A cautionary note from Fletcher of the British Psychological Society is printed alongside, and the editor seems to be sitting on the fence. Graphology is worth using if it can be shown that there is a series of characteristics which are a basis for valid predictions and which can be applied with some objectivity by any suitably trained selector.

Application forms have several purposes. Edwards (1983: 64) lists seven which should be taken into account in designing an application form. They may be paraphrased as:

1  selection of candidates for interview;
2  foundation for planning interview;
3  basic personnel record;
4  candidate file for other possible vacancies;
5  labour market analysis;
6  analysis of advertising and recruitment sources; and
7  improvement of public relations.

These might be considered to have been arranged in order of importance. It is economical to collect the factual information required for preliminary selection by using application forms: interviews can then be used to investigate the most promising candidates more fully. The data to be collected should, of course, be derived from the job analysis and employee specification. Because jobs vary, some organizations use different forms for distinct groups of employees, such as technicians, clerks, managers, from whom they may need to collect different information. Indeed, it can prove economical to have supplementary questionnaires for single specific appointments.

There has been considerable interest in the USA in attempting to apply the rigorous methods used for validating tests to the validation of items of biographical data as predictors of job success; Owens (1976) quotes work dating back to 1925. However, this seems not to have been carried over into practice on a large scale: a 1983 survey of 437 firms showed only 11 per cent using the weighted application forms such work is intended to generate (Mathis and Jackson, 1985: 245). Jewell (1985) points out that, of the items which had statistical significance in one study, 'a number of questions fall into the EEOC's suspect group'. One of these, 'marital status', would be considered dubious in Britain. The approach and its jargon label 'biodata' are being discussed in Britain: Torrington and Chapman (1983: 72) point out that not only will validation take time and require large samples, but also it may not be acceptable because 'it smacks of witchcraft to the applicants who might find it difficult to believe that success in a position correlates with being, *inter alia*, the first born in one's family'.

*References*. There would appear to be wide variation in the practices followed by companies when they take up references. Some ask for no more than a few perfunctory ticks on a short proforma, whereas others ask a series of searching open-ended questions that require careful thought. As a first generalization, it would be reasonable to say that the public services are more likely to use a searching procedure than manufacturing companies. Among commercial concerns, subsidiaries of US companies are more likely to have a carefully thought-out enquiry procedure than British companies. The present trend, while not dramatic, appears to be to tighten up the reference enquiry and, where it is possible to obtain candidates' permission, to take up references earlier in the selection process. The advantage of doing so is that some of the candidates who seem suitable when judged by their own account of themselves can be eliminated without incurring the cost of an interview. Economic stringency also seems to be causing some employers to present their require- ments to referees much more carefully. For example, in 1985 the Atomic Energy Authority told the referees of graduate applicants what proportion of candidates it intended to interview, and asked them to frame their reports with this in mind.

An effective reference procedure needs to make clear what the selector wants. It should ask for information the referee can reasonably be expected to supply, and should make it as easy as possible for this to be done. Early in the selection process the selector can check critical facts and solicit opinions. There will always be a problem in assessing what weight to attach to opinions given by someone nominated by the candidate. A useful check which some companies do is to ask for supporting evidence. Later in the selection procedure it is possible to ask referees about any points that remain doubtful. Companies often do this by telephone rather than by letter, and a personal meeting is also used when the significance of the appointment justifies it. Some companies invariably take up references and do so very carefully. Experience suggests that having being informed that references will be taken up encour- ages candidates to avoid making claims that will not hold up. It has also shown that the candidate who seems excellent when assessed by the techniques reviewed above may turn out to have feet of clay.

*Interviews*. Employment interviewing is like sex and driving: most people rate themselves highly, the consequences of mistakes can be serious, when something goes wrong there is a tendency to blame the other party, and nonetheless most of us continue to do it. Other parallels include the small amount of rigorous research in relation to the importance of the topic and the large amount of prescriptive advice that is available.

Three main types of approach to interviewing may be identified (Torrington and Chapman, 1983: 86–7); the 'biographical' in which the interviewer questions the candiate about incidents in previous experience; the 'problem-solving' in which the interviewer presents the candidate with a hypothetical 'what if' type problem and asks for the candidate to offer his or her solution; and the 'stress' interview in which the interviewer may become aggressive and put the candidate under some pressure, perhaps criticizing an aspect of their career or performance. Typically, a single interview may involve elements of each of these approaches.

No evidence is available on the different approaches to the interview. As far as the form of the interview is concerned, the Mackay and Torrington (1986: 39) survey of personnel managers quoted in previous chapters suggests that the single interviewer was very much the norm in the case of manual workers. In the case of non-manual and managerial employees, however, the single interview was less in evidence. In the case of non-manual employees the predominant form was for a line manager and a personnel specialist to be involved. In the case of managers, the panel interview was the single most important type; indeed, no less than a third of respondents confirmed this.

If the survey evidence suggests that the interview is the most widely-used method of selection, it also confirms that it is the most abused. It is not simply that the interview is subjective. The research evidence (see, for example, the review in Wanous, 1980) suggests that interviewers are systematically prone to adopting certain stereotypes; they deem people from a particular background to be of a certain 'type'; they emphasize similarities with themselves; they tend to give undue emphasis to first impressions – the 'primacy effect'; they adopt different standards depending on the criterion – the 'contrast effect'; and they tend to give overwhelming importance to negative features – selection, in other words is essentially a process of rejection.

*Testing.* A selection test is no more than a method of collecting a sample of behaviour under standardized conditions; the behaviour sample may be written or spoken answers to questions or the carrying out of a mental or physical task. This sample is then taken to be representative of how the person will generally behave or used to predict how the person will perform in the future in some job. Part of the debate about tests is therefore a debate about whether the samples used provide a sensible basis for the generalizations and predictions made. This is an alternative way of raising the key issues of validity and reliability which have been discussed above (and, therefore, relates to all selection techniques).

Tests are variously classified according to what they purport to test (intelligence, aptitude, skill, trade knowledge, personality) or by the way they are carried out or administered (performance tests, paper and pencil tests, questionnaires, group tests, individual tests). In all cases, if the results are to be a satisfactory sample in the sense that they can be compared with results obtained from other people on the same test, three requirements must be met: first, the subject must fully understand what is required; second, the subject must be motivated to perform in the way that the interpreter of the test will be assuming to be the case: that is, motivated to achieve the best possible result on a test of ability, or to reply openly and honestly to a personality questionnaire; and finally, the test must be administered under standardized conditions and every subject must be given exactly the same instructions. If these conditions are not met, it is not safe to generalize or make predictions from the test results.

Occupational testing began in a systematic way in Europe and Britain shortly before the First World War. It quickly spread to the USA and was there given a tremendous boost by the success of the Army Alpha and Army Beta tests in classifying and allocating recruits. Testing continued and developed in Britain and Europe but not as rapidly as it did in the USA, where a culture which emphasized a combination of quantification, objectivity, and a pragmatic approach led to the rapid development and application of a wide range of tests, particularly paper and pencil tests for simultaneous administration to groups of people. The European tradition was more inclined to qualitative approaches to individual psychology and that is reflected in the tests which were developed (Drenth, 1978: 144). Also since individual tests are more expensive to administer, their economic appeal to employers is probably not as great.

Despite a growing interest in the use of testing in this country – over 50 companies contributed to the cost of developing a British personality questionnaire by the consultants Savill and Holdsworth (Savill and Holdsworth, 1987) – it is debatable whether there has been a significant increase in practice since the 1960s and 1970s when IPM surveys suggested that less than one half of 696 respondent organizations used psychological tests (IPM, 1968) and just over 60 per cent of 281 respondent organizations used tests of any kind (Sneath et al., 1976). Thus, Mackay and Torrington (1986: 42) suggest that in the case of manual and non-manual employees only one-quarter of the organizations used tests of any kind. In the case of managers only one-fifth reported using tests.

A study carried out in 1985, which draws on a survey of 108 organizations in *The Times* 'Top 1000' companies (Makin and Roberts, 1986) confirms the much larger survey carried out by the IPM (Gill, 1980) in conjunction with the British Institute of Management at the beginning of the decade in suggesting that the great majority of companies rely almost exclusively on the interview and references in selecting managers. Nearly two-thirds of the organizations in the sample never used psychological tests and over 70 per cent never used cognitive tests of critical reasoning or perceptual ability. The proportion of organizations using assessment centres (discussed below), although on the increase, was also exceedingly low at 21 per cent.

Given that no test is perfect, how imperfect can a test be and still be useful? Critics of tests (and other selection methods) make perfectly justified comments about the shortcomings of tests but do not stop to carry out a hard-nosed evaluation of the costs and benefits. The value of a test depends on the accuracy of its prediction (validity), but also on the proportion of applicants that are capable of performing the job satisfactorily (if all were satisfactory there could be no gain from using a test, only costs incurred) and finally the proportion of applicants it would be necessary to take to fill all vacancies (the higher the proportion that have to be taken the lower the value of a test). Some texts provide tables of the interaction of these factors which show that tests with low validities can have considerable practical value (McCormick and Ilgen, 1980).

Physical tests, which have received relatively little attention in the selection literature, are also subject to the problems of validity and reliability. For example, in one study of reliability two medical examiners testing the same items by the same methods achieved only 16 per cent agreement. In another study of pilots who were re-examined after passing the Civil Aeronautics Administration fitness examination, 43 per cent were found to have a disqualifying defect. A study of the validity of the physical screening procedure for RAF pilots compared 106 pilots who met the standards with 106 who had defects. After ten years half of each group were still flying and there was no statistically reliable difference in their accident rates. Some of these findings might be accounted for at least in part as resulting from the wise use of clinical judgement by medical practitioners.

*Assessment centres*. These are essentially an amalgam of several of the methods discussed above. They seem to be in fashion again but are by no means new, having been invented by the German and British armies during the Second World War. The British version, the War Office Selection Board (WOSB) was considered a success (Vernon and Parry, 1949) and a useful model for selecting fairly large numbers of graduates for the civil service (Vernon, 1950). The Civil Service Selection Boards (CSSB) were followed up for 36 years and the boards' final assessment had a very high correlation with the positions being held at the end of the study (Anstey, 1977).

The essence of these group selection methods or assessment centres is that they use a variety of techniques, and observe the candidates in interaction over a period of two or three days (Macrae, 1970; Toplis and Stewart, 1983). It was the work of Douglas Bray at American Telephone & Telegraph which focused most attention on the industrial applications. Toplis and Stewart (1983) sound a note of caution. Copying the superficial features of an assessment centre may not improve selection: the key feature of the successful major studies is that they were based on very careful studies of the jobs or careers for which people were being selected. CSSB was based on a whole series of complex and interrelated exercises which simulated in some detail the type of work undertaken by senior and junior civil servants. In addition, the candidates were interviewed by panels and individual members of the assessment team and completed ability, aptitude and personality tests.

## CONCLUDING REMARKS

On the face of it, the pressures on British management to adopt recruitment and selection procedures that are sound and defensible, as well as job-related, have grown considerably in recent years. Most obviously, legislation, dealing in particular with sex and race discrimination, requires organizations to develop procedures which, at the very least, are defensible against the charge that individual applicants have been unfairly treated. The competitive situation described in chapter 2 is also important: there is a premium on having the required number of people with the appropriate levels of attainment at the right time; while the costs of mistakes in recruitment and selection, which have always been considerably underestimated, have risen proportionately with the decline in the size of workforces. The prospects of a tightening labour market for some groups, especially among the young in the South East, mean that the manner in which people are recruited and selected is likely to have a significant impact on the perceptions of organizations as 'good' or 'bad' employers.

Surprising as it may seem, however, the message of the survey evidence is that much of British management does not give the issues the attention that they deserve and does not make use of many of the techniques and procedures available. In recruitment, they continue to place a great deal of reliance on word-of-mouth. In selection, they place a near-total reliance on the application form to preselect and on the interview, supported by references, to make the final decision; testing and assessment centres, let alone some of the more recent developments such as the use of biodata, are noticeable by their absence. Significantly, too, all groups are affected from the bottom to the very top of the organization. Indeed, contrary to what might have been expected, testing in particular is even less in evidence in the case of managers than other groups. Habits, it seems, die hard.

# Bibliography

Advisory, Conciliation and Arbitration Service (ACAS). 1981. *Recruitment and Selection*. Advisory Booklet No. 6. London: ACAS.

Anstey, E. 1977. 'A 3-Year Follow-Up of the CSSB Procedure, with Lessons for the Future'. *Journal of Occupational Psychology*, 50: September, 149–59.

Armstrong, M. 1977. *A Handbook of Personnel Management Practice*. London: Kogan Page.

Atkinson, S. and Purkiss, C. 1983. 'Recruitment and Mobility of Labour'. *Recruitment Handbook*. 3rd edn. Ed. Ungerson, B. Aldershot: Gower, 10–22.

Brotherton, C. 1980. 'Paradigms of Selection Validation'. *Journal of Occupational Psychology*, 53: March, 73–9.

Burns, T. and Stalker, G.M. 1961. *The Management of Innovation*. London: Tavistock.

Courtis, J. 1985. *The IPM Guide to Cost-effective Recruitment*. 2nd edn. London: IPM.

Cuming, M.W. 1978. *Personnel Management in the National Health Service*. London: Heinemann.

Denerley, R.A. and Plumbley, P.R. 1968. *Recruitment and Selection in a Full-Employment Economy*. London: IPM.

Drenth, P. 1978. 'Principles of Selection'. *Psychology at Work*. 2nd edn. Ed. Warr, P.B. Harmondsworth: Penguin, 140–64.

Duxfield, T.S. 1983. 'Sales Staff'. *Recruitment Handbook*. 3rd edn. Ed. Ungerson, B. Aldershot: Gower, 239–47.

Edwards, B.J. 1983. 'Application Forms'. *Recruitment Handbook*. 3rd edn. Ed. Ungerson, B. Aldershot: Gower, 64–82.

Equal Opportunities Commission (EOC). 1977. *Guidance on Employment Advertising Practice*. Manchester: EOC.

Fordham, K.G. 1983. 'Job Advertising'. *Recruitment Handbook*. 3rd edn. Ed. Ungerson, B. Aldershot: Gower, 46–63.

Fraser, J.M. 1971. *Introduction to Personnel Management*. London: Nelson.

French, W.L. 1974. *The Personnel Management Process*. 3rd edn. Boston, MA: Houghton Mifflin.

Gill, D. 1980. 'How Britain Selects Its Managers'. *Personnel Management*, October, 49–52.

Grant, J.V. and Smith, G. 1977. *Personnel Administration and Industrial Relations*. 2nd edn. London: Longman.

Heidrich and Struggles. 1985. Consultants publicity leaflet.

Herriot, P. 1984. *Down from the Ivory Tower*. Chichester: Wiley.

Higham, T.M. 1983. 'Choosing the Method of Recruitment'. *Recruitment Handbook*. 3rd edn. Ed. Ungerson, B. Aldershot: Gower, 23–38.

Jenkins, J.F. 1983. 'Management Trainees in Retailing'. *Recruitment Handbook*. 3rd edn. Ed. Ungerson, B. Aldershot: Gower, 248–64.

Jewell, L.N. 1985. *Contemporary Industrial/Organizational Psychology*. St. Paul, MN: West.

Knollys, J.G. 1983. 'Clerical Staff'. *Recruitment Handbook*. 3rd edn. Ed. Ungerson, B. Aldershot: Gower, 230–8.

Lawrence, P.R. and Lorsch, J.W. 1967. *Organization and Environment*. Boston, MA: Harvard University Press.

McCormick, E.J. and Ilgen, D. 1980. *Industrial Psychology*. Englewood Cliffs, NJ: Prentice-Hall.

McIntosh, N. and Smith, D.J. 1974. *The Extent of Racial Discrimination*. PEP Broadsheet No. 547. London: PEP.

Mackay, L. and Torrington, D. 1986. *The Changing Nature of Personnel Management*. London: IPM.

Macrae, A. 1970. *Group Selection Procedures*. London: NFER.

Makin, P.J. and Robertson, I.T. 1983. 'Self Assessment, Realistic Job Previews and Occupational Decisions'. *Personnel Review*, 12: 3, 21–5.

—— and Robertson, I.T. 1986. 'Selecting the Best Selection Techniques'. *Personnel Management*, November, 38–43.

Mathis, R.L. and Jackson, J.H. 1985. *Personnel*. 4th edn. St. Paul, MN: West.

Miller, K.M. and Hydes, J. 1971. *The Use of Psychological Tests in Personnel Work*. London: Independent Assessment and Research Centre.

Owens, W.A. 1976. 'Background Data'. *Handbook of Industrial and Organizational Psychology*. Ed. Dunnette, M.D. Chicago, Ill.: Rand-McNally, 609–44.

Parkinson, E.N. 1986. *Parkinson's Law*. London: Sidgewick & Jackson.

Personnel Management. 1985. 'Two-Year Trial Period for Cuts in NHS Recruitment Ads'. *Personnel Management*, May, 57.

Pratt, K.J. and Bennett, S.G. 1985. *Elements of Personnel Management*. 2nd edn. Wokingham: Van Nostrand Reinhold (UK).

Ray, M. 1980. *Recruitment Advertising*. London: IPM.

Rodger, A. 1970. *The Seven Point Plan*. 3rd edn. London: NFER.

—— 1971. 'Recent Trends in Personnel Selection'. *NIIP Bulletin*, Spring, 3.

—— 1983. 'Using Interviews in Personnel Selection'. *Recruitment Handbook*. 3rd edn. Ed. Ungerson, B. Aldershot: Gower, 161–77.

Saville and Holdsworth. 1987. Consultants publicity booklet.

Semeonoff, B. 1948. Private communication.

Sneath, F., Thakur, M. and Medjuck, B. 1976. *Testing People at Work*. IPM Information Report 24. London: IPM.

Stirling, I., Hill, T.J. and Boothroyd, H. 1985. Private communication.

Thomason, G. 1981. *A Textbook of Personnel Management*. 4th edn. London: IPM.

Toplis, J. and Stewart, B. 1983. 'Group Selection Methods'. *Recruitment Handbook*. 3rd edn. Ed. Ungerson, B. Aldershot: Gower, 178–94.

Torrington, D. and Chapman, J. 1983. *Personnel Management*. 2nd edn. London: Prentice-Hall.

Vernon, P.E. 1950. 'The Validation of Civil Service Selection Board Procedures'. *Occupational Psychology*, 24: April, 75–95.

—— and Parry, J.B. 1949. *Personnel Selection in the British Forces*. London: University of London Press.

Wanous, J.P. 1980. *Organizational Entry*. Reading, MA: Addison-Wesley.

# 7 Employee Appraisal

*Gerry Randell*

Employee appraisal can be seen as the *formal* process for collecting information from and about the staff of an organization for decision-making purposes. From an analysis of many organizations' procedures and a detailed review of the literature on the topic, one overriding purpose of this decision-making emerges, *to improve people's performance in their existing job*. When this purpose is not explicitly stated, it is clearly implied that the scheme is aimed at least to maintain the level of effectiveness of people at work and, hopefully, to add to their performance and satisfaction.

Consequently, employee or staff appraisal can be defined as the process whereby current performance in a job is observed and discussed for the purpose of adding to that level of performance. Even though this is a simple definition of an everyday managerial activity, it is a controversial topic. In the above description three contentious issues are implied:

1  What and how are observations made?
2  Why and how are these observations discussed?
3  What determines the level of performance in a job?

When these issues are misunderstood and their implications mis-applied, employee appraisal can be seen as 'dysfunctional' in that it can detract from performance and satisfaction. Such outcomes have been observed and discussed by McGregor (1957) in the US and Rowe (1964) and Pym (1973) in Britain. This chapter aims to help the understanding of the key issues and implications of employee appraisal. It tries to achieve this first through a historical review; by a conceptual analysis of the process of employee appraisal and, finally by deriving from this implications for practice so that schemes can be designed which bring about increased performance and satisfaction.

The more the above issues are analysed, the more complex they appear to be. The literature abounds with different analyses and conclusions. What adds to the confusion is the fact that work organizations are dynamic. It is not the purpose of this chapter to review the topic of organization analysis, but when deciding exactly how an employee appraisal scheme should be designed, consideration must be given to the nature of the organization and the way it is intended to change. This point can be illustrated through a review of the development of employee appraisal as a managerial technique over the last two centuries of industrial and organizational change.


## THE DEVELOPMENT OF EMPLOYEE APPRAISAL

The formal observation of an individual's performance at work by an appointed member of the organization and the communication of this observation to the individual for the purpose of improving his or her performance probably began in Scotland in the early 1800s. Robert Owen hung a multi-coloured block of wood over employees' machines in his New Lanark textile mills; the front colour indicated the superintendent's assessment of the previous day's conduct, from white for excellent through yellow, blue and then black for bad. As Cole (1925) reports, Owen believed that letting employees know what was thought of them through his 'silent monitors' would have the effect of recognizing the worthy and encouraging the less able to improve. To add to the pressure, Owen also recorded yearly assessments in a 'book of character', which might be seen as the beginning of annual staff reporting. It is these twin objectives of concern for satisfaction and performance that is now known as employee or staff appraisal, or performance appraisal or performance review, or similar terms to be found in contemporary personnel management systems.

One of the great problems of staff appraisal over the years since Owen's time is how these two criteria have been diluted or even lost. Even Owen, with all his human concern, saw that work was both about profit and human well-being. In his essay to factory managers (quoted by Cole, 1925) he said 'many of you have long experienced in your manufacturing operations the advantages of substantial, well-contained and well-executed machinery. If then, due care as to the state of your inanimate machines can produce such beneficial results, what may not be expected if you devote equal attention to your vital machines, which are far more wonderfully constructed?'. Perhaps hanging signs over employees' machines or desks in the 1980s may not be a way of achieving *equal* care and attention for people and work, but this review will continue to explore how 180 years of personnel management in Britain has helped the understanding and practice of what is required to help people to be better at their jobs.

The literature of performance appraisal is sparse during the remainder of the nineteenth century. Owen's utopian dreams were replaced by the realities of 'scientific management', for at the turn of the century performance measurement began to receive a great deal of attention through the work of Taylor and the 'scientific management' movement. Although extremely well-intentioned, the use of quantitative measures to understand and to increase productivity at work ran into difficulties with the inept application of otherwise useful concepts. In his testimony before a US Government Special House Committee in 1912, Taylor (1964) was vehement that work measurement was just a part of the whole philosophy of 'scientific management' and could and should not be regarded as an end in itself. Further, as the Hawthorne studies carried out by Mayo and his colleagues in the 1920s in the USA subsequently revealed (Roethlisberger and Dickson, 1939), even apparently objective measures of work performance were influenced by subjective factors and social control.

No doubt many attempts at performance appraisal were widespread in work organizations in the first half of this century and probably reached a pinnacle, as often is the case, by the effects of mobilization of people for war. In the inter-war years, the techniques of time and motion study matured into the discipline of 'work study' and were then incorporated into 'production engineering', but, as will be seen later, the legacy of attempts for precision in measuring work performance remained.

Many people gained their first management responsibilities and experience through work in government and the armed forces during the two World Wars. The special circumstances of this work led to great advances in the techniques of personnel management, notably in the field of selection. Even so, the systematic study of performance for the purpose of improving performance received scant attention. Vernon and Parry (1949) devote two pages to performance assessment in the military setting and say about 'gradings or assessments' that 'such judgements are extremely liable to be biased by the social qualities or conformity to discipline etc. of the people being graded' (1949: 107). The Royal Navy form S206 of 1940 gave 21 attributes to be graded using 9-point scales as well as extensive provison for narrative information. Such assessment and reporting procedures were probably appropriate for that kind of organization at that stage in its development for the kind of work that it was expected to do. No doubt forms of a similar kind were introduced to British and American work organizations as officers returned to civilian managerial life. It took a little time to realize that such approaches were inappropriate for both post-war organizations and post-war people. It was this realization of inappropriateness that began the attack on the concepts and practice of staff appraisal in the 1950s.

The attack was spearheaded by an article by McGregor (1957). This 'uneasy look' was followed by his 'critique' in 1960, where he saw the main purposes of appraisal as 'administrative', 'informative', and 'motivational' and concluded that 'it appears to be something of a tribute to the adaptability of human beings that these procedures work at all!' (1960: 88). This conceptual attack was followed by an empirical study in Britain by Rowe (1964) which exposed considerable reluctance by managers to use mainly personality trait-based appraisal procedures. These findings were further supported by Stewart's (1965) study illustrating the ineptness of appraisal interviewers.

Undoubtedly, the classic compendium of relevant work in this period was *Performance Appraisal* edited by Whisler and Harper in 1962. Their own review of the history and the work of their colleagues led them to conclusions which still have much relevance for current practice. They observed that 'many appraisal systems have failed simply because staff people responsible for planning the systems have become engrossed in trying to achieve technical perfection' (1962: 437); and that 'concentration on specific job-related activities and forms of behavior is the best substitute for quantitative perform-ance standards where the latter cannot be formulated' (p. 438).

While McGregor was making his attack, Maier (1952, 1958) was trying to give support to and guidelines for an approach to appraisal that would help it to be regarded as an essential feature of personnel management. Maier (1952) had already set out his philosophical position which he had developed on the basis of the earlier work of social psychologists who were studying 'democratic leadership'. He had also foreseen how these concepts should be put into practice by saying 'skills must supplement this knowledge. In order to develop skills, practice on the job, interviews with trainees, and role playing are needed' (1952: 18). Later that decade, Maier further recognized the place of skill in management: 'the skill of the interviewer is one of the more important determiners of the success of this plan; and since the interviews are conducted by all supervisors at all levels, this skill factor becomes a general managerial requisite' (1958: 1). Maier went on to contrast three styles of appraisal interviewing in great detail; he brushed aside the use of evaluation ratings with what he thought could be regarded as an 'insincere suggestion' (1958: 175) and condemned the use of personality trait approaches. 'When a person's traits are discussed from the point of view of appraisal, a deficiency in a desirable characteristic takes the form of devaluation of the individual' (1958: 206). Instead he strongly advocated the 'problem-solving' approach to appraisal interviewing and training for it using role-playing. Regrettably, Maier did not give any insight into exactly how such skills should be inculcated or acquired, nor did he display any awareness of just how difficult it was to bridge the gap between theory and practice in staff appraisal. Also, Maier's deep concern about the skills of management has not been carried forward by his colleagues or students, a point that will be returned to later as a key issue in understanding how to bring about improvement in performance and the leadership of organizations.

In Great Britain a more positive approach to staff appraisal was first shown in the 1970s by Randell (1972) in Fisons Limited, and by Anstey (1976) in the civil service. Randell had developed the point about skill being an essential component of management in an earlier article (1971) and had subsequently used the opportunity of helping a company with their staff appraisal scheme to formulate a 'skills approach' to staff development. Together with Packard, Shaw and Slater of Fisons (1972), he first presented a conceptual analysis of staff appraisal which cut through all the conflicting issues of purposes and measurement. Although an oversimplification of the process – the three elements of development, reward and potential were separated out – it did facilitate the adoption of thorough training as the way to cope with the problems of staff appraisal, starting at the top of the organization and working progressively through all managers and supervisors who have responsibility for the work of staff. Perhaps reflecting the nature and needs of their employing organization, Anstey, Fletcher and Walker (1976) emphasized assessment and reporting in their account of staff appraisal. They saw that the way forward in the subject was to take a 'dynamic' approach. Although they agreed with separating discussion of pay from development, they were against any further 'fragmentation' on grounds of extra complications and costs of time and effort. They were, however, strong on the need for training and, in particular, the use of practice interviews under guidance from trained tutors. Anstey et al. concluded:

> a good appraisal scheme may help a manager to achieve, more of the time, the good relationships and the good results from the staff which he already experiences some of the time. It will help staff to improve their performance and develop their potential. It will be regarded by managers and staff as demanding, and at times exhausting, but worthwhile. A bad scheme will be regarded as a futile piece of bureaucratic machinery. (1976: 197)

The growth of interest in performance appraisal in the 1960s and 1970s is further illustrated by the publication in both Britain and the USA of several surveys of companies' practices and managers' opinions of employee appraisal. In Britain, there were two surveys by the BIM and three by the IPM. In the USA, the more influential surveys were carried out by the US Bureau of National Affairs and the National Conference Board. The first BIM study (Haeri, 1967) was based on 170 companies and showed just how diverse were the purposes of the schemes and how important to them were the rating of personality traits. The second (Haeri, 1969) was a detailed study of four of the original sample and the main conclusions were that 'if one appraisal scheme tries to cover (1) review of performance (2) appraisal of potential (3) appraisal of salary, and at the same time indicate adequately the training needs for the individual being assessed, then that scheme is in danger of falling between several stools. Indeed it may result in not achieving any of these objectives satisfactorily' (1969: 1).

The first IPM study (Gill et al., 1973) was based on 360 British companies ranging from 16 with less than 500 employees to 62 with more than 20,000. Of these 74 per cent had a 'systematic' appraisal scheme and 26 per cent had no scheme at all. The authors noted trends away from trait assessment towards both organizational and personal development. They reported that even though an appraisal interview was regarded as an essential part of the process, only half the companies appeared to recognize the importance of training line managers in appraisal interviewing – 'an area which is notoriously susceptible to human error and mishandling' (1973: 11).

The second IPM survey (Gill, 1977) was a similar study of 288 companies also randomly selected. This time 82 per cent of the sample reported on a company staff appraisal scheme. The key trends noted were towards emphasis on current performance rather than future performance, a shift back towards personality trait rating (34 per cent of sample rather than 18 per cent found in 1973), and 84 per cent of companies were using an appraisal interview as an integral part of the scheme, but still only 56 per cent of the companies were providing any kind of training in interviewing. Gill (1977: 65) went on to say that 'of the companies which do provide training, less than half use role playing as a technique and even then only 22 per cent always do so. Since role playing is the method most commonly used in practice interview sessions, it seems probable that many companies do not include practice interviews in their training'. She concluded that 'failure to consult, lack of commitment from the top, unequal standards, over elaborate paperwork and inadequate feedback are seen as some of the main faults of appraisal systems or reasons why they fail' (1977: 65).

The third IPM survey, by Long (1986), covered 306 organizations, of which 18 per cent had no formal appraisal schemes. Her main findings were that there had been a substantial overall increase in systems for appraising non-management employees; the shift in emphasis in performance review towards concern for current rather than future performance had continued; appraisal for performance-related pay had remained at about 40 per cent of schemes, with only 15 per cent of organizations carrying out a salary review at the same time as the performance review; and there had been a sharp increase of 22 per cent in the number of organizations providing appraisal skills training to 78 per cent of the sample surveyed.

In the USA, the study by the National Industrial Conference Board (Habbe, 1951) was based on nine case studies of companies which were thought to reflect 'a fair cross section of current thinking and current practice in this important area'. Although this report was mainly concerned with the merit-rating aspect of appraisal, it did show considerable insight into the problems of getting appraisal schemes accepted and the importance of training, particularly the usefulness of role-playing. A more statistical survey was carried out by the Bureau of National Affairs (1974) which showed that 85 per cent of the organizations sampled saw the main purpose of appraisal for salary adjustments, 64 per cent for promotion decisions, 57 per cent for counselling and setting goals, and 55 per cent for training and development. Another Conference Board survey (Lazer and Wickstrom, 1977) picked up a shift towards counselling and performance feedback with 73–82 per cent of the organizations seeing the purpose of their appraisal scheme concerned with this, while only 63–70 per cent saw it concerned with salaries, 50–66 per cent with promotion, and 54–60 per cent with training and development.

The 1983 Bureau of National Affairs survey of 244 organizations showed how more widespread appraisal schemes are in the USA in particular for first-line supervisors (91 per cent of organizations surveyed) and also the predominance of compensation-linked performance reviews (86 per cent).

The problem with such surveys is that they only display the current *conventional* wisdom. To discover what is really good practice requires the application of more conceptual ability by the researchers. In recent years the main output of textbooks on performance appraisal has been in the USA rather than in Britain. After the Whisler and Harper classic (1962), probably the next most impressive text was by Cummings and Schwab (1973). Their analysis is thorough and at a high level of abstraction. They attempt to integrate both ability and motivation development into a single model of performance determinants. They are succinct on measurement techniques, leaning heavily towards objectives setting and self-appraisal procedures. They are extremely thin on training managers to appraise, however, saying 'managers should be given specialized skill training along the lines [eight short guidelines] just suggested' (1973: 116).

In Britain, Williams (1972) has produced a useful descriptive overview of contemporary appraisal practices. This wide-ranging account touches on most of the main theoretical and practical issues and, by implication, advocates taking an eclectic and pragmatic approach to installing a staff appraisal system. By comparison, Stewart and Stewart (1977), while being also far-ranging, end each chapter with a crisp prescription for each of the issues raised. For example, they advocate that no more than five points should be used on a rating scale, and 'real-life counselling' and 'live appraisal of real tasks' should be the preferred methods for appraisal training.

In this period two attempts also appeared to aid the task of developing appraisal skills. Based on work within International Computers Ltd, Schollick and Bloxsom (1975) produced a programmed text on the concepts of effective staff appraisal interviews. This entertaining book is well founded on the appraisal literature and is only prescriptive insofar as it inculcated into the user the concept that the main criterion for a successful appraisal interview is the acceptance by the appraisee of the plan of action, and the ultimate criterion of successful appraisal is improved performance. In contrast, the approach taken by Beveridge (1975) to the staff appraisal interview is much more discursive. 'Appraisal is properly a learning process. Through their interaction in the appraisal they [manager and subordinate] each learn how to make a more effective contribution to the adequate performance of the work. If this does not happen, appraisal merely serves a cataloguing purpose' (1975: 50).

Also far-ranging and thorough is the work of Fletcher and Williams (1985) who place their analysis in both an historical and economic context and also relate performance appraisal to the wider issues of career development. But this breadth dilutes the depth of their conclusions, for they do not adequately tackle the conflicts between evaluation and development in appraisal, nor do they stress just how important interpersonal skills are to successful appraisal schemes.

Unlike the British trend towards more person-centred, skills-based approaches to staff appraisal, American texts display a distinct leaning towards work-centred, mechanistic systems-based procedures, with hardly a reference to the interpersonal skills training that is required to support a staff appraisal scheme. Thus, Latham and Wexley (1981) devote most of their book to the criterion problem and to measuring work performance. They give a detailed account of the use of 'Behavioral Observation Scales' (BOS), including the legal aspects of using them in the US, and conclude with many guidelines about 'making the system work'. Carroll and Schneier (1982) follow a very similar line, concentrating on the use of 'Behaviorally Anchored Rating Scales' (BARS). They take more of a contingency approach, arguing the need to match appraisal systems to organizational and individual differences. But they conclude that in future more emphasis should be put on interpersonal and behavioural rather than psychometric issues. In a more insightful text DeVries et al. (1981) analyse the history and use of performance appraisal under all the main issue headings. With a slight tone of despair, they conclude that their analysis at least showed the need for appraisal systems to be constantly adaptive to changing economic and social developments. To achieve this, they advocate that performance appraisal should be broken down into its manageable parts, each serving a critical purpose, and that these parts should be planned according to the particular needs and resources of any given organization.

The observation that can be made from this review of recent literature is what little advance has been made since the first wave of work in the 1960s. At the end of the preface to their collection of readings, Whisler and Harper (1962: vi) say that 'the one best way in performance appraisal still eludes us'. The same can be said today, and to help the way forward this pattern of issues will now be made explicit.

## ISSUES IN EMPLOYEE APPRAISAL

As can be seen from a review of the surveys and analysis of research, the term 'employee or staff appraisal' means different things to different people. What can be said is that its use has grown to include all those formal processes for observing, collecting, recording and using information about the performance of staff at their jobs. Unfortunately, an emotive tone has also grown up around the term and many organizations prefer to use the term 'staff' or 'employee development' or 'job appraisal review' to minimize hostility to the process. The previous section has also shown that confusion and controversy still surround this topic. There are many unresolved issues, which will now be considered in detail.

### Conflicts of Purpose

The overriding purpose of employee appraisal is the improvement of the performance of people in their jobs. However, this broad purpose can be interpreted in many ways both from a theoretical and a practical standpoint. For example, following Randell et al. (1972), the main functions of appraisal, each of which can be seen to a greater or lesser degree in all schemes, can be summarized as follows: to enable the organization to share out the money, promotions and perquisites apparently 'fairly', i.e. *evaluation*; to discover the work potential, both present and future, of individuals and departments, i.e. *auditing*; to construct plans for manpower, departmental and corporate planning, i.e. *succession planning*; to discover learning needs by exposing inadequacies and deficiencies that could be remedied, i.e. *training*; to ensure that employees reach organizational standards and objectives, i.e. *controlling*; to develop individuals: by advice, information and through shaping their behaviour by praise or punishment, i.e. *development*; to add to employees' job satisfaction through understanding their needs, i.e. *motivation*; to check the effectiveness of personnel procedures and practice, i.e. *validation*.

Behind these operational purposes lie more significant theoretical issues. An examination of an organization's employee appraisal scheme can indicate a great deal about how the organization 'sees' their staff and how they should be managed and developed. So the overall broad purpose of performance improvement can both be influenced by theories about people at work and contribute to those theories. In practice, the format of an employee appraisal scheme is perhaps determined more by how senior managers who design the system see the *causes* of work performance than by specific objectives for the scheme.

Beliefs about the determinants of human behaviour at work can be grouped in four ways which encompass the academic theories about the probable causes of performance. These theories can be seen to be reflected, more often implicitly rather than explicitly, in the various approaches to staff appraisal.

If it is believed that it is the past that is the main determinant of the present and the future, then this is given emphasis in an information-gathering and decision-making procedure through some kind of comprehensive assessment of past strengths and weaknesses. Implicit is the view that if good performance is observed and then rewarded, the chances of it being repeated are increased, while poor performance is discouraged or even punished to decrease the chance of it happening again.

Psychologists will notice a connection with the ideas of 'reinforcement theory' associated with the work of Skinner (1972). These concepts have been very influential in all branches of psychology and have been very usefully and practically set out under the general descriptive heading of 'behaviour modification' by Martin and Pear (1978), and more explicitly in relation to changing managers' work by Goldstein and Sorcher (1974) under the term 'behaviour modelling'. This 'past patterns of behaviour' approach has been taken to the limits of atheoretical pragmatism by Rackham and Morgan (1977) in their work on interactive skills development. The approaches to staff appraisal based on these ideas usually lead to an emphasis on providing praise and recognition, and even in special circumstances to 'token economies', where immediate rewards are handed out for extra effort and performance. As Skinner (1972) has pointed out, it takes a great deal of skill on the part of the manager to shape human behaviour through appropriate 'schedules of reinforcement'. When this can be achieved, however, it can be a very powerful approach to developing performance at work.

If the 'here and now' is seen as the most important source of causes of behaviour, then such factors as understanding and learning will be the focus of observation and decision-making in an employee appraisal procedure. These beliefs fit in with the more 'cognitive' theories in psychology, such as those of Festinger (1957) and Lawler (1973), and can be elaborated through using the additional concept of 'equity' as put forward by Adams (1964). The point about much of this work is that it is how the member of staff *perceives* the work situation that is important, rather than what actually exists. Techniques for getting a better match between what a member of staff perceives and what actually exists have been put forward by Mager and Pipe (1970), but their rather pragmatic approach does not get much reference in the appraisal literature, sound and useful as it is. Evidence for the usefulness of this approach comes from studies by Meyer et al. (1965) in the General Electric Company. They surveyed 92 employees who heavily criticized the existing mechanistic pay-related appraisal system. On the basis of their survey, they developed alternative 'Work Planning and Review' discussions that took place more frequently, had no summary judgements or ratings or discussion of pay, and instead discussed specific work goals that could be immediately achieved. A controlled follow-up study showed that the staff who experienced the 'WP and R' method had significantly better attitudes to their work than those who experienced the GEC traditional appraisal scheme. The attractiveness of this approach to many practitioners is its non-evaluative and non-threatening tone.

If the 'pull' of future events desired by individuals is seen as the pervading influence, then employee appraisal schemes will emphasize the work that has to be achieved for the organization and the reward and promotion prospects and opportunities for the individual. The more advanced 'expectancy' theories such as those of Vroom (1964), and concepts of self-actualization and self-fulfilment, for example Maslow (1970), fit in with such approaches to employee appraisal. Further, the enthusiasm towards objective-setting procedures can be explained in terms of belief in future-oriented theories of human behaviour. The practical aspects of objectives setting have been well organized by Odiorne (1965, 1979) and are widely used. The theoretical aspects have been set out by Locke and Latham (1984) who wisely integrate the use of goal-setting with behavioural observation scales in appraisal interviewing to counteract the relative paucity of truly objective indices of work performance.

As a footnote, it is important to point out that 'management by objectives', which is often associated with this school of thought, has been widely criticized because of its unhealthy emphasis on quantitative rather than qualitative or behavioural objectives. However, a more fundamental theoretical criticism can be made of objectives or goal-setting as a method for performance improvement. Just setting targets does not necessarily change behaviour. It may provide pressure to change, but unless a person *knows* what to do differently, it is chance that determines whether or not the appropriate behaviour is produced. This is why there has been the trend away from quantitative target-setting procedures in appraisal towards more qualitative behavioural objectives, as it is now realized that target setting, like financial budgets, is a method of *control* rather than development.

Many senior managers are inclined towards beliefs about human behaviour that can be regarded as transcending time. They believe that if an individual values, and is committed to, a certain doctrine, then all their behaviour stems from this. Such doctrines are usually religious or political in nature, but not necessarily so, as can be seen by membership of certain semi-secret societies: the phrase 'is he one of us?' can be the key question asked in employee appraisal. The theories underpinning this approach to understanding and predicting human behaviour are more sociological, or even philosophical, than psychological. It could be that there is a pervading influence of the ideas of Jung (1958), or just the influence of age, as many psychologists, such as

Skinner (1971), Maslow (1965), Argyris (1964), and Herzberg (1968), turn in their later years to higher levels of abstraction to explain human behaviour. These rather abstract ideas are a long way from the day-to-day problems of employee appraisal and perhaps best understood and placed in context by sociologists such as Sorokin (1966).

The above analysis of the *theoretical* basis of staff appraisal shows that the stated explicit purposes can be in conflict. However, what can be seen is that *implicitly* there are just two main purposes for all staff appraisal schemes. The first is to add to the individuals' capacity for their existing job, and the second is to maintain, and if possible, add to their motivation for their job. The above section is mainly concerned with the motivational theories behind staff development, none of which adequately explains how people come to put the effort that they do into their work. Where the theories can help is to signal to a manager just what should be done *next* for a member of staff that increases the chances of their most pressing need being met. People's motivation is maintained or enhanced by having their needs met, or at least worked upon, by another individual or their employing organization. Theoretical standpoints can either hinder or help this process.

This chapter is concerned with changing individual behaviour at work, over and above that which would change through ordinary work experiences and the passage of time, through the personnel management techniques that can be termed 'employee appraisal'. As the above analysis has shown, there are many conflicting purposes involved, so it is not possible to advocate or prescribe any particular technique. All those that exist can have their place in the overall scheme of employee appraisal; what is used, how and when, will have to be decided by the designers. Getting such decisions appropriate to the needs of the organization, and of the employees, is one of the key problems of personnel management.

This conflict of organizational needs and employee needs can be looked at another way, from either a *macro* or *micro* point of view. If a work organization is analysed in terms of its economic purpose or historical structure, then its development is seen in those terms. If, however, it is seen as an organization of people assembled around a set of purposes (e.g. making things or money or providing a service), then its development is seen through changes in behaviour of its people. Clearly, some kind of balance is required between organizational and individual needs. The achievement of such a balance must be at the upper limits of skilled management.

## Methods of Assessment

An analysis of the various approaches to employee appraisal to be found in Britain reveals that the main area of controversy is the part that the evaluation or measurement of work performance plays in the process. On the one side are railed those managers who are philosophically inclined towards McGregor's (1960) Theory $X$ or Likert's (1961) System 1. They see, as Likert would put it, that the leading variable is work. People go to work to work and if the amount of work that is performed is assessed, and the person told about how much more they could and should do, then more work will result.

Alternatively, this 'work-centred' position can be explained by the observation that many managers have had some kind of systematic, or even scientific, education. Such managers would argue that if employee appraisal is about changing performance at work, its organization should begin by defining the headings under which performance can be assessed, then it should devise measurements of those categories, apply the 'treatment' (i.e. some kind of employee development process), and, finally, re-assess to see if the 'treatments' have taken effect. It is this paradigm that underpins most employee appraisal schemes in Britain today. It can be called the *performance control approach* to appraisal.

A complication in the *performance control approach* is defining what it is that should be assessed. Managers who are inclined to more abstract sets of beliefs about the determinants of work performance tend to be disposed to scales that attempt to measure the personality traits regarded as crucial to effective work. Examples appear in many employee appraisal forms, such as integrity, honesty, determination, drive, initiative and other labels of human behaviour that are used in everyday life but lack precise psychological meaning. These kinds of staff appraisal schemes result in an individual being told at an annual interview to go and get more 'integrity' and perhaps show a bit more 'initiative', so that things are better next year!

Locke and Latham (1984: 89) summarize the position by saying 'performance is typically appraised in one of three ways: by the use of trait scales, by objective outcome measures, or by Behavioral Observation Scales'. Trait scales are inherently ambiguous and are not recommended. Outcome measures can be extremely useful when they are available and relevant to the job. 'Behavioral Observation Scales' are always recommended, so that the means as well as the ends receive proper attention. Consequently, a key question to be faced by designers of employee appraisal schemes is whether any kind of assessment or quantitative evaluation should take place within the scheme. As has been pointed out, this decision is more often determined in practice by the background or training of the designers rather than on any conceptual analysis of the purpose of the staff appraisal procedure. The need to measure is the basis of methodology in science, but, as it happens, not in technology. Managers trained in scientific disciplines find it difficult to accept that change, albeit less certain, can be arranged to take place in other ways.

The further observation can be made that measurement-based methodology is more appropriate to the raw material of the 'hard' sciences and technologies than to the 'soft' behavioural sciences. Here the raw material is people. Unlike inanimate objects, they can have their own views, and, in particular, feelings, about the processes of measurement and change to which they are subjected. If the process is seen as inept or unfair, they can feel strong resentment and reject the whole procedure. Unfortunately, in performance assessment, the probability that the measurement process is inept and unfair is very high because the technical problems in designing rating scales and the observational problems involved in using them are considerable; this makes it virtually certain that the assessment process is seen as uncertain by the appraisees. Hence the many references to the need for accuracy in ratings, which abound in the appraisal literature.

So the key question must be, why take this approach if it creates so many problems? If 'assessment' is the main purpose of the procedure, as data are required to feed some kind of control or merit-rating scheme, the risks may be seen as acceptable. Under such circumstances, the stages and techniques set out by Bailey (1983) would appear to be the least that should be attempted. These are the establishment of dimensions for performance measurement, and controlling subjectivity in judgement and ratings. If the purpose is employee development, i.e. bringing about committed behaviour change, the dangers in going through an assessment stage are not likely to be justifiable no matter how technically competent the measurement devices are.

A further important point about the use of assessment of employees arises from its relationship to organization development. Many managers see an employee *development* scheme as a means to *organizational* development. Where the ability and willingness to change behaviour exist, setting organizational objectives and quantitative criteria of performance could well work as a strategy for bringing about change in performance through the pressure of an assessment method. However, if the causes of non-obtained objectives and poor performance are *behavioural*, such *structural* solutions are not likely to work. It can be argued that to solve organizational problems requires organizational solutions, and to solve behavioural problems requires behavioural solutions. This is why the techniques of target setting and management by quantitative objectives can be effective with able and committed staff but ineffective with inept and alienated staff. In such circumstances, to attempt to change individual behaviour through the means of a so-called employee development procedure with targets or rating scales is highly misguided. All it does is let employees know how poor their performance is, rather than what they should do to correct it, probably with alienation rather than motivation being the outcome.

This is not to say that methods of assessment do not have their place in personnel management. They clearly are crucial to many organizational *control* activities, e.g. payment systems, production and sales planning and manpower-planning. It is their place in the sequence of personnel management procedures that is important to get right. Traditionally in employee appraisal the sequence is seen as from *performance assessment* to *performance change*. What is being argued here is that it should be from *performance development* to *performance assessment*. In other words, employee appraisal should be development-led rather than assessment-led.

Consequently this section argues that there may be no need to have any formal scheme for the assessment of employee performance at all. If this is so, all the difficulties of designing rating scales and ensuring their accuracy in use disappear!

The alternative to rating can be called *qualitative assessment*. At the most simple level, all that a qualitative approach demands is the diagnosis of what an individual should be doing differently *next* in their job. This can be checked and discussed with the individual in an interview and this diagnosis turned into an 'action plan'. Randell et al. (1972) call this agreed next action a '*development step*'. All manner of observation forms and scales could be used in this process, as long as they aid the diagnosis and commitment to an action plan. With a skilled observer/interviewer as a manager, all the support that is required, at this simple level, is a blank sheet of paper. In practice, however, some kind of paperwork procedure is required for all the kinds of formal employee appraisal that take place within an organization.

*Forms and Reporting*

As the previous sections imply, the kind of support system that is designed for an employee appraisal procedure more often than not reflects the beliefs of the designers about the determinants and control of behaviour at work, rather than serving the main purposes of the scheme. The literature already quoted abounds with examples of forms and paperwork. Such systems often become ends in themselves: their biggest indictment comes when managers are heard to say to a member of staff that the time has come to complete an appraisal form as 'they have to'.

In many cases there is no need for more than a blank sheet of paper. However, to lay down guidelines, give support, and to signal organizational sanction of time and effort, something more than that is usually required. What, exactly, bearing in mind the different purposes of appraisal, is appropriate to the current needs of the organization? As the diversity and history of the design of employee appraisal systems reveal, getting the design right is fraught with difficulty, and requires great care to match the objectives, the commitment and skill of the managers and managed, who are going to use it.

One of the first design decisions that has to be made is how the different purposes of a scheme are to be separated in time, training and paperwork. Many workers in the field (Maier, 1958; Sokolik, 1970; Randell, 1973) have argued for separation of purposes into separate procedures, for example 'reward review', 'potential review' and 'performance development'. Others, for example Anstey et al. (1976) and Stewart and Stewart (1977), advocate integration and attempting to achieve as much as possible in a single procedure.

A further aspect of diversification is designing separate procedures for different types and levels of staff. Such separation, if done ineptly, may cause misunderstandings among the various levels, but can, if the organization is flexible, provide useful variations of approach. A less obvious variation is having schemes for people of the same grade, but different levels of ability. This has quite a long history, going back to Miner (1965) and then Steinmetz (1969), who both analyse and prescribe ways to manage the unsatisfactory performer. Cummings and Schwab (1973) went further and identified how the separation of development and evaluation could be adapted to three kinds and levels of appraisal – DAP (developmental action programme); MAP (maintenance action programme); and RAP (remedial action programme).

It is probable that with growing understanding of the concepts of appraisal and increasing sophistication in techniques, this trend to designing different kinds of systems and paperwork for different types and levels of staff will become more strongly apparent and applied. In the meantime, the exhortation that appears frequently in the literature to 'keep it simple' would appear the best current advice on form design.

The other main use for forms is the vehicle for transmission of information to other managers, and to the 'files'. This use is of considerable concern to the larger, perhaps more bureaucratic, organization. Smaller organizations may not see this as much of a problem, as there is sufficient general knowledge about the individuals making up the company. There has been much debate about open versus closed reporting, as Anstey et al. (1976) display in their work based on the British civil service. Such difficulties as who should see, sign, countersign and file the forms, cause considerable heart-searching and discussion in many organizations.

Clearly in large organizations, where staff may be spread among different locations and are relatively mobile between them, some kind of central file is an important personnel management need. However, if care is not applied, this central file can become more important to the appraisal system than the behavioural effects on the employees involved. The issue is how to meet the needs of a report with the need for open, frank and purposeful discussion between a manager and member of staff.

The main problem to be resolved is whether or not the system requires regular reports. Again, at the lowest level of reporting a note on the file that a formal meeting has taken place between a manager and a member of staff may well be sufficient. Also, at the extremes of performance some kind of report will be important. If performance is so poor that a formal warning to the member of staff has to be given, then a central record of this is necessary, for any subsequent stages in a disciplinary procedure. If performance is outstanding, then some kind of formal recognition may be desirable, or important for a procedure for identifying management potential. But for the usual range of interactions between a manager and a member of staff, it is probably better for no detailed report to be submitted at all on the appraisee. However, what may be justifiable is some kind of self-report by the managers, if just for their own files, commenting on the level of skill they displayed, what they think they achieved and how they could do better in future in managing that particular employee.

### The Significance of Interpersonal Skills

An issue that has run through the whole history of employee appraisal is the place of interpersonal skills in the process. The survey and analysis of practice has shown that attempts to resolve the problems of employee appraisal by the design of systems and forms have not been successful. The complexity of the process explains why such simplistic approaches probably fail. The alternative is to regard purposeful interactions between managers and staff as nothing more nor *less* than a high-level sensorimotor skill. Even though Maier (1958) laid the foundations for this skills approach to staff development, the American practice since then has been to emphasize systems and assessment techniques, whereas in Britain the skills approach was taken up by Randell and his colleagues (Randell et al., 1972, 1984; Wright and Taylor, 1984). Although most workers in the field recognize the need for training support for employee appraisal procedures, they seem reluctant to start from the premise that it is the skill that is crucial and the systems and forms should be designed in support. Perhaps it is the practical implications of regarding employee appraisal as primarily a skill that deter organizations from taking this approach. For skills can only be acquired by people who want to obtain them; can only be learned by practice with some kind of guidance or feedback from skilled tutors; and cannot be acquired easily in a matter of days. On the contrary, the long-term development of the skill can be achieved only by training managers in how to be their own source of guidance and feedback, that is to be a 'self-tutor', which is perhaps the most difficult kind of training of all.

Not only have the difficulties of taking a skills approach to staff appraisal been underestimated, so too have the benefits. It has been argued by Randell (1978) that training in the skills of staff appraisal can be used as the vehicle for getting managers to develop their skills of interviewing that form the basis of all interpersonal decision-making at work. Many writers in Britain such as Argyle (1981) and Randell (1981) have argued, following Maier's (1958) original plea, that these skills should form the basis of all management training. A conceptual structure for inculcating such skills in managers has also been propounded by Randell (1980). A very full manual of exercises for interview skills training has been assembled by Hackett (1978). It is probably the shortage of skilled tutors that now hinders the advance of this skills-based approach to employee appraisal. A detailed analysis of what is required by tutors to be effective trainers of managers in staff development skills has been set out by Taylor (1976). A thorough analysis of the concepts and practice of interpersonal skills training for managers has been provided by Taylor and Wright (1986). In the US this skills approach to staff development has been taken up by Sashkin (1981) who asserts that not only are such skills necessary to effective implementation of performance appraisal, but they are basic to long-term sound management practice. In a highly detailed and descriptive way, Whetton and Cameron (1984) also give a useful account of management skills, but although they emphasize the key concepts, they fall short on how the motor component of such skills can be inculcated.

Viewed from the vantage point of the later 1980s, the struggles to comprehend the concepts and apply the processes of employee appraisal can be understood in the light of the attempts to understand the whole activity of personnel management. As has been previously stated, appraisal of some kind or other is essential for effective management. This view first emerged at a NATO Conference in Brussels in 1971, and in his introduction to the published proceedings Tilley (1974) notes overlapping methods for increasing managerial effectiveness among appraisal systems, interviews, management by objectives and the activity of leadership. It is as a part of 'leadership' that employee appraisal should now be seen.

More recently, in Britain in particular, similarities have been noticed between what is required for successful 'leadership' on the part of a manager and what is required for effective appraisal. Alban-Metcalfe (1984) has called these activities the 'micro-skills of leadership', and they are seen to form an essential part of *any* effective interpersonal behaviour between managers and staff. This 'skills' based view is now known as the 'Bradford Approach' to development and has been described by Randell et al. (1984), and Wright and Taylor (1984). The theoretical and practical implications of this approach are wide-ranging. As Wright and Taylor say:

> We would rather supply managers with a set of behavioural tools from which they can select the one most appropriate to handle a particular leadership situation, than develop a grand theory which explains everything but has few real practical implications. Unfortunately much of modern leadership theory seems to fall into the latter category. (1984: xi)

The powerful implication of this position is that employee appraisal can be used, if an organization is so inclined, to be the vehicle for the development of what most of them search for – better leadership for their human resources, which results in more effective use of the capacities and inclinations of their employees.

## *Evaluation*

The evaluation of the effectiveness of any process or technique of personnel management is both highly desirable and exceedingly complex. Such validation studies are notoriously difficult to design and it is especially difficult to generate data of sufficient quality to enable causal conclusions to be drawn. There is the further complication of 'bias of auspices', when the promulgators of the concepts and training produce evidence of its effectiveness themselves. Obtaining 'independent' evaluation data is methodologically more respectable, but difficult to achieve in practice. Nevertheless, even though data generated from such studies may be suspect for validation purposes, the act of carrying them out can have two important beneficial effects. By authorizing a survey into the effectiveness of a staff appraisal scheme, an organization can signal how seriously it is taking its application and effects. Second, by completing a questionnaire, or by being interviewed, a manager can be reminded of the main principles, purposes, and practices of the procedure, and hopefully be encouraged in their further application.

Problems arise when these twin aims of maintaining the process and evaluating its effectiveness become entwined. The designers of a scheme require the data for their systems' development, whereas senior managers require evidence that the scheme is working. In practice, it is extremely difficult to disentangle these two aims. Fletcher and Williams (1985) allow the two requirements to merge. In a survey of seven organizations, totalling 5,940 appraisees and 1,332 appraisers, they give six indices describing details of the process, one on overall assessment of the scheme by the appraisee (9 per cent on average against it), and two on outcomes (30 per cent of appraisees saying the appraisal interview had increased job satisfaction and 40 per cent saying it had resulted in improved job performance). No information was given about the training the appraisers had received in appraisal skills.

The trouble with such overviews is that they do not help the real issue. The long history of employee appraisal and the conceptual analysis given in this chapter should be convincing enough for any manager that it is a necessary and useful part of personnel management; what is not known is just how effective a particular technique or application really is. As Meyer et al. (1965) displayed, different kinds of appraisal procedures can have different effects in the same organization. What then is required is detailed study of the effects and effectiveness of a particular scheme.

An example of this is a study carried out within the British civil service and reported by Anstey et al. (1976). It involved the detailed analysis of 3239 post-facto questionnaires from appraisees and 564 from appraisers. The study concentrated on the effects of the appraisal interview and showed that 51 per cent of appraisees reported 'encouraged performance' as a result of the interview, 79 per cent of appraisers reported 'useful outcomes' and only 6 per cent of respondents 'saw no value in it'.

In an ingenious study carried out within Fisons, a 3-stage hierarchical/corroborated evidence design involved questionnaires from 640 managers. As reported by Allinson (1977), the 103 managers who had received appraisal *skills* training not only reported on themselves, but were also reported upon by their own managers and staff. The three overlapping and interlocking samples provided a total of 220 corroborating questionnaires and their analysis showed that the managers had improved in their skill on all the nine rating scales of 'before' and 'after' behaviour as a result of the training. Managers in mid-career, in particular, seemed to gain most from such skills training. It did emerge, however, that the appraisal scheme raised hopes and expectations in employees about being managed more skilfully.

At the simplest level of evaluation, it would appear that most organizations which undertake training in the structure and content of their appraisal scheme at least ask participants at the end of the course to give their 'reaction' to the training. Although reactions data are scientifically suspect, they can have considerable social significance. If senior managers say that such training works for them and authorize further investment of money and staff time in it, then this will be interpreted by staff as hard evidence for the effectiveness of the procedures. As far as line-managers are concerned, such evidence is regarded as far more 'significant' than any statistical tests. If this outcome is widely felt, then the climate can be established for the delicate and sensitive skills of interpersonal interaction to grow and develop within an organization. It is this that could well be the main use of evaluation studies of employee appraisal within an organization, rather than the generation of suspect validation data.

## THE NEED FOR A CONTINGENCY APPROACH

It can be not unfairly concluded that the study of employee appraisal has turned full circle. Robert Owen can be seen as one of the first great leaders of industry who, in his early work, and within the constraints of his time, skilfully balanced the needs of profit-making and human well-being to develop an effective work organization. F.W. Taylor, although working from a different philosophical base and in a different economic climate, attempted much the same. Douglas McGregor, spurred on by Alfred P. Sloan of General Motors, was working under different conditions again, but at a similar level of managerial balance and success. Today, all these efforts and themes can be recognized in the work of contemporary leadership theorists. Leaders are currently judged mainly on how well they make use of and develop the human resources of their organization. As can be seen from the information and analysis in this chapter, employee appraisal is one of the major processes available to them to achieve this. However, the problem of choosing the appropriate approach to human resources development remains. As has been emphasized in this chapter, to be successful, an employee appraisal scheme has to reflect the current needs and skills of the appraisers and appraisees of the organization. This is not easy as there are invariably many different expressions of needs and skills, and the vested interests of groups and individuals colour their perception.

This can be vividly illustrated by the debate about the appraisal of teachers in Britain. It would appear from statements and interviews in the press that the Department of Education and Science requires an assessment-led reporting scheme, based on a 5-point rating scale where a teacher rated 1 gets a substantial increase in salary and a teacher rated 5 is encouraged to leave the profession. The contrary view is taken by a Working Party of teachers who suggest a skills-led development scheme. In their report (Suffolk Education Department, 1985) they conclude 'the very last thing our schools need at this time is the debilitating discouragement handed down by untrained assessors operating mechanistic schemes' (p. 87). Further, 'without adequate training of appraisers, an appraisal system will fail or be counterproductive. Indeed, without a commitment to this training, it would not be profitable to set up an appraisal system!' (p. 25). In contrast, the American approach is to set up a large research project, directed by a committee of teachers, administrators, union representatives and university-based researchers to produce a set of standards for evaluation of educational personnel. In their first report (Joint Committee on Standards for Educational Evaluation, 1986) they say 'personnel evaluation problems are different depending on the type of personnel action contemplated. Among the examples are licensure and certification, recruitment and selection, assignment and promotion, tenure and merit, recertification and dismissal, position analysis and reduction in force, and feedback for professional growth' (p. 4). They then go on to produce 30 standards for rating scales to meet all these purposes, implying that all these can be achieved in a simple appraisal scheme.

TABLE 7.1 *Types of employee development*

| Radical Staff Development | Passive Staff Development |
|---|---|
| 1. Establish quantitative or operational performance criteria | 1. Agree a staff reporting policy based on fixed interval reports and discussions of staff performance |
| 2. Design behaviourally anchored scales to assess the criteria | 2. Design a comprehensive form, usually through meetings of widely representative committees |
| 3. Establish training in staff assessment concepts and include rating exercises | 3. Prepare a thorough manual describing the scheme and distribute it widely throughout the organization |
| 4. Introduce the staff assessment and reporting procedure, by decree, and supply a set of authoritative guidelines or manual of operation | 4. According to the agreed wishes of the staff, establish the distribution and filing of the reports |
| 5. Give recognition and/or reward to those who are assessed as excellent and assurance to those who are regarded as adequate | 5. Establish training opportunities for learning needs arising from the scheme |
| 6. Give counselling and, if necessary, warnings, to those who are assessed as inadequate | |
| 7. Provide opportunity for re-assessment and arbitration | |
| 8. Provide training opportunities for learning needs arising from the reports | |
| 9. File all data arising from the system | |

TABLE 7.1 *cont*

| *Dynamic Staff Development* | *Active Staff Development* |
|---|---|
| 1. Agree a quantitative target – objective setting management policy<br>2. Brief managers on 'management by objectives' concepts and techniques, preferably incorporating behavioural standards as well as quantitative<br>3. Distribute MBO paperwork systems and exhort managers to use them<br>4. Monitor procedure by reviewing targets and the realism of objectives set | 1. Agree a 'performance improvement' policy based on a 'work review and action plan' (WRAP). This plan leads to a capacity development step being taken by a member of staff, hopefully with commitment but, failing that, compliance and a 'motivation development step' being taken by the manager, hopefully with sincerity, but failing that, reluctance<br>2. Gain acceptance of the policy at all levels in the organization, particularly with the trade unions and staff associations<br>3. Establish a workshop in the interpersonal skills of staff development, and make sure that the managers who most need the training attend the course first, and all others subsequently<br>4. Design paperwork procedures, *supportive* of the staff development system, probably of a narrative kind<br>5. Establish training opportunities for learning needs arising from the scheme<br>6. Establish reporting channels that will enhance change and commitment, both by the individual members of staff and the management of the organization<br>7. Monitor progress, and change the content and emphasis of the scheme according to the follow-up data that are generated |

So how should an appraisal scheme be designed to take into account the demands of the organization, the expectations of the appraisees and the skills of the appraisers? The main conclusion of this chapter is that a contingency approach is needed. The other main conclusion is that employee appraisal can only be effective if appraisers possess the interpersonal skills required for its practice. It is of little use designing and improving any personnel management system if the participants in it are unable or unwilling to work it *skilfully*. Of course, as the contingency approach implies, the nature and timing of the skills training depends on the existing skills and attitudes of the employees; if they are not ready or prepared for it, a 'shake-up' approach may be required. Or, if sufficient skill exists, a very direct approach can be taken. To help designers of employee appraisal schemes to decide what is appropriate for their organization, four approaches, described in simple and rather prescriptive terms in Table 7.1, are put forward. In practice, a particular scheme may turn out to be a 'blend' of these approaches.

*Radical Staff Development* might be for organizations where employees are inclined to be inept and alienated and where the objective is to provide a psychological shake-up. It is a very 'organization-work centred' approach to appraisal, and not to be undertaken lightly. Various variations of this approach can be seen in practice; it could even be regarded as the 'traditional' approach that emerges when a committee of tough-minded managers decides upon an appraisal scheme for their organization. However, many of the attacks on appraisal are directed at schemes like these, for they are known to produce within employees reactions of antagonism or alienation.

*Passive Staff Development* might be appropriate for those organizations that are working satisfactorily but where the maintenance of performance is regarded as important and where some provision is thought necessary to cope with the occasional ineffective or highly able member of staff. Such an approach can lead to a 'cosy' rather bureaucratic system. If care is not taken, a great deal of paperwork can be generated, with not much use made of it. One of its main virtues is the comfort it can provide by letting employees know where they stand and by giving a channel of communication into the central personnel administration.

*Dynamic Staff Development* might be for organizations where able employees are already highly committed to short-term organizational object-ives, and where the organization is growing and changing rapidly. This approach may well be appropriate for a relatively young organization, where the selection procedure has attracted very able and highly motivated employees. A danger here is over-stressing the staff with unrealistic or inappropriate objectives, so that the commitment turns to break-down and alienation.

*Active Staff Development* might be for those organizations that have a satisfactory level of performance, where morale and industrial relations are sound, and where there is a desire to increase productivity and job satisfaction as much as possible within the constraints of economic conditions and existing quality of staff. It is this approach that demands most of the management of an organization in time, effort and cost, which is probably why it is not chosen as often as it should be. It is built upon the interpersonal skills of bringing about behaviour change, rather than the pressure of forms or reporting procedures. It works from the premise that employees *want* to get better at their jobs and to see their employing organization improve and succeed. If this is not the case, the approach is inappropriate, and a more 'shake-up' policy may have to be chosen. The task for personnel managers is to diagnose what approach is most appropriate for their organization, and to take astute steps to get it accepted and applied.

# Bibliography

Adams, J.S. 1964. 'Inequity in Social Exchange'. *Advances in Experimental Social Psychology*. Vol. 2. Ed. Berkowitz, L. New York: Academic Press, 267–99.

Alban-Metcalf, B.M. 1984. 'Micro-skills of Leadership: A Detailed Analysis of the Behaviour of Managers in the Appraisal Interview'. *Leaders and Managers: International Perspectives on Managerial Behavior*. Ed. Hunt, J.G., Hosking, D., Schriesheim, C.A. and Stewart, R. New York: Pergamon, 179–99.

Allinson, C.W. 1977. 'Training in Performance Appraisal Interviewing: An Evaluation Study'. *Journal of Management Studies*, 14: 179–91.

Anstey, E., Fletcher, C. and Walker, J. 1976. *Staff Appraisal and Development*. London: Allen & Unwin.

Argyle, M. Ed. 1981. *Social Skills and Work*. London: Methuen.

Argyris, C. 1964. *Integrating the Individual and the Organization*. New York: Wiley.

Bailey, C.T. 1983. *The Measurement of Job Performance*. Aldershot: Gower.

Beveridge, W.E. 1975. *The Interview in Staff Appraisal*. London: Allen & Unwin.

Bureau of National Affairs. 1974. *Management Performance Appraisal Programs*. Personnel Policies Forum Survey 104. Washington, DC: The Bureau.

— 1983. *Performance Appraisal Programs*. Personnel Policies Forum Survey 135. Washington, DC: The Bureau.

Carroll, S.J. and Schneier, C.E. 1982. *Performance Appraisal and Review Systems*. Glenview, Ill.: Scott, Foresman.

Cole, G.D.H. 1925. *Robert Owen*. London: Benn.

Cummings, L.L. and Schwab, D.P. 1973. *Performance in Organizations: Determinants and Appraisal*. Glenview, Ill.: Scott, Foresman.

DeVries, D.L., Morrison, A.M., Schullman, S.L. and Gerlach, M.L. 1981. *Performance Appraisal on the Line*. New York: Wiley.

Festinger, L. 1957. *A Theory of Cognitive Dissonance*. Evanston, Ill.: Row, Peterson.

Fletcher, C. and Williams, R. 1985. *Performance Appraisal and Career Development*. London: Hutchinson.

Gill, D. 1977. *Appraising Performance: Present Trends and Next Decade*. London: IPM.

— Ungerson, B. and Thakur, M. 1973. *Performance Appraisal in Perspective*. London: IPM.

Goldstein, A.P. and Sorcher, M. 1974. *Changing Supervisor Behavior*. New York: Pergamon.

Habbe, S. 1951. *Appraisal of Job Performance*. New York: National Industrial Conference Board.

Hackett, P. 1978. *Interview Skills Training*. London: IPM.

Haeri, F.H. 1967. *Management Appraisal Practices*. Information Summary 133. London: BIM.

— 1969. *Performance Appraisals: What Managers Think*. Information Summary 136. London: BIM.

Herzberg, F. 1968. *Work and the Nature of Man*. London: Staples Press.

Joint Committee on Standards for Educational Evaluation. 1986. *Standards for Evaluations of Educational Personnel*. Kalamazoo: Western Michigan University Press.

Jung, C.C. 1958. *The Undiscovered Self*. Boston, MA: Little, Brown.

Latham, G.P. and Wexley, K.N. 1981. *Increasing Productivity through Performance Appraisal*. Reading, MA: Addison-Wesley.

Lawler, E.E. 1973. *Motivation in Work Organizations*. Monterey, Cal.: Brooks Cole.

Lazer, R.I. and Wickstrom, W.S. 1977. *Appraising Managerial Performance: Current Practices and Future Directions*. New York: The Conference Board.

Likert, R. 1961. *New Patterns of Management*. New York: McGraw-Hill.

Locke, E.A. and Latham, G.P. 1984. *Goal Setting: A Motivational Technique that Works*. Englewood Cliffs, NJ: Prentice-Hall.

Long, P. 1986. *Performance Appraisal Revisited*. London: IPM.

McGregor, D. 1957. 'An Uneasy Look at Performance Appraisal'. *Harvard Business Review*, 35: 3, 89–94.

—— 1960. *The Human Side of Enterprise*. New York: McGraw-Hill.

Mager, R.K. and Pipe, P. 1970. *Analyzing Performance Problems*. Belmont, CA: Fearon.

Maier, N.R.F. 1952. *Principles of Human Relations*. New York: Wiley.

—— 1958. *The Appraisal Interview*. New York: Wiley.

Martin, G. and Pear, J. 1978. *Behavior Modification: What It is and How to Do It*. Englewood Cliffs, NJ: Prentice-Hall.

Maslow, A.H. 1965. *Eupsychian Management*. Homewood, Ill.: Irwin Dorsey.

—— 1970. *Motivation and Personality*. 2nd edn. New York: Harper & Row.

Meyer, H.H., Kay, E. and French, J.R.P. 1965. 'Split Roles in Performance Appraisal'. *Harvard Business Review*, 43: 1, 123–9.

Miner, J.B. 1965. *The Management of Ineffective Performance*. New York: McGraw-Hill.

Odiorne, G.S. 1965. *Management by Objectives: A System of Management Leadership*. New York: Pitman.

—— 1979. *Management by Objectives II: A System of Managerial Leadership for the 80's*. Belmont, CA: Fearon Pitman.

Pym, D. 1973. 'The Politics and Rituals of Appraisals'. *Occupational Psychology*, 47: 231–5.

Rackham, N. and Morgan, T. 1977. *Behaviour Analysis in Training*. Maidenhead: McGraw-Hill.

Randell, G.A. 1971. 'The Motor Skills of Man-Management'. *Management Decision*, 9: 31–9.

—— 1973. 'Performance Appraisal, Purposes, Practices and Conflicts'. *Occupational Psychology*, 47: 221–4.

—— 1978. 'Interviewing at Work'. *Psychology at Work*. 2nd edn. Ed. Warr, P.B. Harmondsworth: Penguin, 165–86.

—— 1980. 'The Skills of Staff Development'. *The Analysis of Social Skill*. Eds. Singleton, W.T., Spurgeon, P. and Stammers, R.B. New York: Plenum, 131–46.

—— 1981. 'Management Education and Training'. *Management Skills. The Study of Real Skills*. Vol. 3. Ed. Singleton, W.T. Lancaster: MTP, 239–53.

—— Packard, P.M.A., Shaw, R.L. and Slater, A.J. 1972. *Staff Appraisal*. London: IPM.

—— Packard, P.M.A. and Slater, A.J. 1984. *Staff Appraisal: A First Step to Effective Leadership*. 3rd edn. London: IPM.

Roethlisberger, F.H. and Dickson, W.J. 1939. *Management and the Worker*. Cambridge, MA: Harvard University Press.

Rowe, K.H. 1964. 'An Appraisal of Appraisals'. *Journal of Management Studies*, 1: 1, 1–25.

Sashkin, M. 1981. *Assessing Performance Appraisal*. San Diego, CA: University Associates.

Schollick, N. and Bloxsom, P. 1975. *Staff Appraisal, Self Appraisal*. London: Godwin.

Skinner, B.F. 1971. *Beyond Freedom and Dignity*. New York: Knopf.

—— 1972. *Cumulative Record: A Selection of Papers*. 3rd edn. New York: Appleton-Century Crofts.

Sokolik, S.L. 1970. *The Personnel Process*. Scranton, NJ: International Text Book Co.

Sorokin, P. 1966. *Sociological Theories of Today*. New York: Harper & Row.

Steinmetz, L.L. 1969. *Managing the Marginal and Unsatisfactory Performer*. Reading, MA: Addison-Wesley.

Stewart, R. 1965. 'Reactions to Appraisal Interviews'. *Journal of Management Studies*, 2: 1, 83–99.

Stewart, V. and Stewart, A. 1977. *Practical Performance Appraisal*. Aldershot: Gower.

Suffolk Education Department. 1985. *Those Having Torches . . . Teacher Appraisal: A Study*. Ipswich: Suffolk Education Department.

Taylor, D.S. 1976. *Performance Reviews: A Handbook for Tutors*. London: IPM.

—— and Wright, P.L. 1988. *Developing Interpersonal Skills through Tutored Practice*. Bradford: Human Resources Research Group.

Taylor, F.W. 1964. *Scientific Management*. London: Harper & Row.

Tilley, K.W. Ed. 1974. *Leadership and Management Appraisal*. London: English Universities Press.

Vernon, P.E. and Parry, J.B. 1949. *Personnel Selection in the British Forces*. London: University of London Press.

Vroom, V.H. 1964. *Work and Motivation*. New York: Wiley.

Whetton, D.A. and Cameron, K.S. 1984. *Developing Management Skills*. Glenview, Ill.: Scott, Foresman.

Whisler, T.L. and Harper, S.F. Eds. 1962. *Performance Appraisal: Research and Practice*. New York: Holt, Rinehart & Winston.

Williams, M.R. 1972. *Performance Appraisal in Management*. London: Heinemann.

Wright, P.L. and Taylor, D.S. 1984. *Improving Leadership Performance*. Englewood Cliffs, NJ: Prentice-Hall.

# PART IV
# Employee Development

# 8 A Training Scandal?

*Ewart Keep*

The term training and development can be defined as forms of activity aimed at the improvement of the human capital within an organization – the term development in everyday use being differentiated from training by its usually being reserved to describe the activities involved in producing supervisors or managers. Training and development can be viewed by the parties involved as either a cost or as an investment. The complexity of the policy issues that arise from conceptualizing training and development in either of these ways results from the different, and often conflicting, perspectives of the three main parties involved in the process, namely governments, employers, and employees or their representatives. For governments, the main concern is with ensuring a 'better educated, better trained, more adaptable workforce' (Department of Employment, 1981: 4) as a means of aiding national wealth creation. For employers, the concern is with improving the capacity of existing employees to perform a reasonably well-defined set of activities. Generally, the employer will be primarily concerned to invest in specific rather than general training; that is to say, training that is specific to his organization's activities rather than training that is also likely to be of use to other employers. Unlike governments, in their role as co-ordinators of training policy at an aggregate national level, the individual employer can also opt to pursue the alternative strategy of increasing the skills within his workforce by recruiting new employees who have been previously trained elsewhere. Finally, there are the employees. Here the prime interest is likely to be in maximizing the returns to the individual from skill acquisition, either in financial terms or as 'net advantages' of a more general kind. It is the interplay between these varied interests that helps to explain the nature and level of training and development that actually takes place in any society.

In this chapter the main focus is on the employer, although the position of the other two parties is not neglected. For the employer, the objective of the expenditure that training and development entail is to modify the behaviour of employees; in the words of Heseling (1966: 45), training is a 'sequence of experiences and opportunities designed to modify behaviour in order to attain stated objectives'. More often than not, training is associated with the process of ensuring that employees acquire the requisite knowledge and skills to perform present and future jobs in the organization. For example, it may be the skills that are required to perform a complicated set of manual operations, or the knowledge of a fairly complex group of clerical and administrative procedures that are essential to the operation of distribution. Secondly, and perhaps less obviously, training can be primarily concerned with motivation; that is to say, with changing employees' attitude or approach to the tasks that they are required to perform. Indeed, in the great majority of work situations the approach of employees is integral to the task to be performed. For instance, production employees who give no thought to quality are likely to damage the reputation of the business, however fast they work; retail assistants who are rude to the customers are less likely to make a sale.

There can be significant differences in the sophistication of training and development programmes. For example, Oatley (1970: 75) distinguishes between formal and informal training and learning experiences on the job. Formal training is that which takes place in the 'classroom' and informal that which takes place on the job. Learning by experience speaks for itself, although it is important to point out that the degree of structure involved in experiential learning can vary significantly, from 'sitting next to Nellie' to sophisticated coaching or mentoring systems. Clearly, none of these forms is exclusive and, indeed, they are likely to be combined in most cases – be it a relatively unskilled production job, with a brief induction programme followed by a period of working under the guidance of another experienced employee, or a senior management post which may involve various off-the-job training courses and rotation through a variety of management functions taking several years.

Torrington and Chapman (1984: 285) suggest that there are six main activities involved in a programme of training and development: assessment of needs; the specification of training objectives; the design of a training programme; the choice of instruction methods; conduct of the training; and the evaluation of the results of the training. It is with these activities that the bulk of the traditional personnel management literature is concerned (see, for example, Singer and Ramsden, 1972; Beach, 1975; Greenlaw and Biggs, 1979; Pigors and Myers, 1981; Yoder and Staudohar, 1982; Guest and Kenny, 1988; Flippo, 1984; Hall and Goodale, 1986). The prescriptive approach, as portrayed in this body of literature, looks neat and simple. The reality of training in Britain is not quite so straightforward.

All employees, including the most senior executives of an organization, are likely to be subject, at one stage or another of their working lives, to training and development of some form. The chapters that follow deal specifically with the training and development of supervisors and managers. The present chapter is concerned with the training of the vast bulk of employees who fall outside these categories, an area of activity that is often loosely described as vocational training. The first and second sections discuss the extent and nature of such training. British management, it is emphasized, has historically placed little emphasis on training and this is, in part, attributed to two of the distinctive characteristics of training in Britain: the dominance of a particular form of exclusive craft apprenticeship system and the 'voluntarist' nature of vocational training and education. The third section summarizes the main arguments in the increasingly intense debate about how to improve Britain's training performance, and the fourth considers what kinds of changes are taking place in managerial attitudes and practice.

## INPUTS AND OUTPUTS: THE EXTENT OF TRAINING PROVISION

The attitude and approach of British management to training and develop-
ment would appear to be ambivalent, and the linkage between attitudes and practice less than clear (Mangham and Silvers, 1986: 18). Certainly research has tended to show that British managerial attitudes towards training are not entirely consistent. The 1985 MSC-sponsored IFF survey cited below tended to indicate positive general attitudes towards training, though with some reservations about the success of management training; whereas a survey undertaken by Mangham and Silvers (1986) which was specifically devoted to management training appeared to uncover much less favourable managerial perceptions of the value of training and development.

Be that as it may, at one level there seems to be little doubt about the significance that British management claims to attach to training and develop-
ment. In a study of some 500 employers throughout Britain employing over 25 people, which was carried out for the Manpower Services Commission (MSC) by IFF Research Ltd, no less than 89 per cent said that they regarded training as an essential investment; 88 per cent felt training was necessary to maximize productivity and profits; and 95 per cent said that they recognized that changing needs meant that their workforces must be trained to update old skills or learn new ones (MSC, 1985: 2). Almost half the respondents (49 per cent) claimed that training was a formal section of their establishment's business plan and that there was a training budget. Over half the sample claimed that training was a regular item on the board's agenda; was discussed at regular pay reviews; and that their company had a formal written training policy (1985: 5).

Yet the same survey revealed that, despite these very positive attitudes towards training and the apparent development of corporate frameworks within which training can take place, British management does not actually do very much of it. For example, although expenditure on training is only a crude measure of activity, the comparative information that has recently become available suggests that the amount spent by British employers is considerably less than in other countries. Leading employers in Japan, West Germany and the USA, it has been suggested, spend of the order of 3 per cent of turnover on training (IMS: 1984). In contrast the IFF survey found that on average the employers surveyed invested only £200 per employee per annum on training, which added up to only 0.15 per cent of turnover; that 24 per cent of establishments had provided no training of any kind in the past 12 months; and that 69 per cent of employees had received no training during this period (MSC, 1985: 2). A similar picture emerges in a survey carried out by the Industrial Society in 1985. Nearly two-thirds of the 130 or so respondents, who came from the public as well as the private sector, reported that they spend less than 0.5 per cent of their annual turnover on training, with another

23 per cent reporting training expenditure of between 0.5 per cent and 1 per cent (Industrial Society, 1985: 2).

In terms of a breakdown by sector, both surveys confirm that there was generally greater training activity in services than in manufacturing. The IFF survey carried out for the MSC suggested that overall expenditure in services and manufacturing was about equal, whereas the service establishments employed only 39 per cent of the employees in the survey and manufacturing 61 per cent; services were also responsible for training a larger absolute number of employees (MSC 1985: 10). Similarly, the Industrial Society survey suggested that there were very few employers in manufacturing who spent more than 1 per cent of their turnover on training. Indeed, only one such employer was found. By contrast, the survey identified three employers in the finance sector who were spending more than 1 per cent of turnover on training and also 1 per cent on research. The same survey (Industrial Society, 1985: 33) also revealed that the public services (local government, hospitals and water authorities) had a poor record as far as training expenditure was concerned: of eleven respondents, not one single authority spent more than 0.5 per cent on training.

An analysis by occupation reveals a very clear picture. The Industrial Society survey (1985: 6) suggests that the bulk of training and development expenditure is concentrated on managers and supervisors, followed by technical and professional employees; industrial training for blue-collar employees comes bottom of the list, although it consumes a significant amount of funds in the heavy manufacturing sector. In more detail, the survey (1985: 6) pointed out that whereas nearly 97 per cent of respondents reported that they trained their managers, 89 per cent that they trained technical and professional employees, and 89 per cent secretarial and clerical employees, only 62 per cent trained manual employees.

The occupational bias depicted by the results of this survey perhaps requires some qualification. While they reveal the claimed relative order of priority being afforded to the training of different occupational groupings, they tell us little about the appropriateness, quality or availability of that training. For example, the survey appears to indicate a relative emphasis being placed by British employers on the training of their secretarial and clerical employees. Yet research recently undertaken by the National Institute of Economic and Social Research (NIESR) shows that Britain's record on clerical training is extremely poor, in terms of both quality and quantity, compared with that of France or West Germany (Steedman, 1987).

Also, despite the relatively high ranking British employers believe they afford clerical and secretarial training, another traditional feature of the levels of British vocational training provision has been the relatively poor opportunities available to women, who make up 74 per cent of the clerical workforce (EOC, 1986: table 3.4). This is partly a reflection of the concentration of female employment in areas such as clerical work, catering and cleaning, the distributive trades, and unskilled factory work (Cantor, 1985: 21; Cockburn, 1987: 7), where, at least in the past, the provision of vocational training has not been particularly intensive. Data published by the EOC (Benett and Carter,

1983) indicate that of those 16–18 year-olds given day release by their employers, only one in five was a girl. In the traditional heartland of British vocational training, the apprenticeship system, women have accounted for only a tiny proportion of the training places.

On a wider front, the recent collapse of the apprenticeship system offers another and quite startling illustration of how little training is now generally taking place in Britain. Historically, and for reasons that will be discussed in the following section, the major concentration so far as manual workers have been concerned has been on the training of apprentices; indeed, it is no exaggeration to suggest that in much of manufacturing, apprentice training has been more or less synonymous with training (Norris and Thomas, 1982: 78). According to figures supplied by the MSC (*New Society*, 8 August, 1986), in 1964 there were some 240,000 apprentices in British manufacturing industry; by 1979 the figure had dropped to 155,000 and by 1986 it had declined even further to only 63,700. In engineering, intake levels have fallen from a high point of 27,000 apprentices in the late 1960s and early 1970s, to 16,500 new apprentices and 7,500 technician trainees in 1978, and since then to only 7,000 new apprentices and 2,000 new technicians in 1986. Even allowing for the substantial reduction in employment in manufacturing and the changing demands of technology that have taken place during this period, the decline in the number of apprentices is little short of astonishing.

Britain's poor vocational training performance is thrown into sharp relief by a number of detailed international comparisons that have been published in recent years. Mention has already been made above of recent work by the NIESR comparing clerical training in Britain and France. Earlier studies by the same organization indicate that Britain trails its European rivals across a broad front of training activity. As Prais (1985: 43) has pointed out, as far as qualifications are concerned the essential difference between Britain and other countries such as West Germany lies not so much in the proportion with university degrees or their equivalent, but in the proportion with intermediate qualifications, such as apprenticeships, City and Guilds and secretarial qualifications. Prais draws attention to the fact that less than one third of the labour-force in Britain has vocational qualifications, whereas in Germany two-thirds have them. He points out that per head of workforce Germany trains each year twice as many mechanics, electricians and construction workers, with Germany's lead being even greater in the training of office workers and those employed in the distributive trades (Prais and Wagner, 1981). Prais also argues (1985: 42) that there is no evidence to suggest that the training and qualifications in Germany are in any way inferior to those in Britain for specific occupations.

One final aspect of the limited extent of training provision in Britain is the associated absence of adequate manpower planning information (Wellington, 1986; IMS, 1984: 88–9). As Hayes and Fonda point out (IMS, 1984: 88–9) in Germany, Japan and the USA the systematic collection, analysis and dissemination of manpower and training information are regarded as highly important to the success of their vocational training systems. In contrast, as chapter 4 explained, British employers have traditionally shown only limited interest in developing manpower planning systems. The absence of adequate manpower planning information in Britain makes it harder for individual employers to evaluate their training needs or to deploy skills within their workforces to best effect. At a wider level, the lack of accurate and detailed information on current training provision and future skill requirements makes it difficult for the education system and external training agencies to meet the needs of employers, or to tackle the skill shortages which, despite current high levels of unemployment, are constantly being reported.

The view painted so far of British training is a bleak one, but it is one that has not gone entirely unchallenged by some employers (Wilson, 1987). They argue that some of the international comparisons of training expenditure made by using data from officially-sponsored reports such as the IFF's 'Adult Training in Britain' (MSC, 1985) are misleading, in that they do not compare like with like, and confuse the percentage of company turnover spent on adult training with the percentage of Gross National Product (GNP) allocated to adult training. The gap that exists between Britain and West Germany, at least in terms of adult training, they argue, is relatively small. The real problem is the vocational training of young employees. Wilson (1987) also suggests that concern at the rapid fall in the number of apprentices in the engineering industry may be misplaced, and questions the real scale and importance of reported skill shortages in the industry.

The existence of this continuing debate is to some extent an indication of the paucity of reliable data on the British training effort, and serves as a warning to the dangers of trying to draw hard and fast conclusions from what have often been essentially 'snapshot' views of training activity at home and abroad. Nevertheless, the weight of existing evidence, however incomplete, does tend to suggest that, at least in overall terms, Britain does not currently enjoy the fruits of the sort of a coherent vocational education and training system developed by many of our overseas competitors.

To sum up then, despite expressions of support in principle, the balance of evidence suggests that in general British companies' training expenditure is not high, and that this tendency is particularly marked in the case of manufacturing. Compared with groups such as managers and supervisors, the training of manual workers is very much the poor relation. Female workers tend to receive less training than their male colleagues. The industrial training that has taken place has traditionally been concentrated on the apprentice. Young workers not on apprenticeship schemes have normally received little or no training (Holland, 1985: 16); the same has gone for adult manual workers. Detailed information about employers' training needs is often lacking.

## THE NATURE OF VOCATIONAL TRAINING

As the international comparison produced by Hayes and his colleagues (IMS, 1984) shows, training arrangements differ markedly from one country to another and their development has been deeply rooted in the varying patterns and processes of industrialization. For example, West Germany possesses what is termed a 'dual system' under which the authorities and employers share the costs of comprehensive vocational training provision for the young, with the education system playing a major role in providing pre-vocational and vocational training. This dual system is overseen by regional chambers of commerce and industry to which employers are legally obliged to belong. The trade unions play an active role within the system in helping to determine the structure and contents of training provision (Lawler, 1985) and these training structures operate within the broader context of an industrial relations system that places considerable emphasis on worker/management co-determination. This is significant because the process of co-determination plays an important part in shaping companies' training and manpower planning policies.

The Japanese vocational education and training system is very different. The education system is expected to lay a broad, non-specialized foundation of knowledge and attitudes that will underpin future training. It is not required to provide very much at all in the way of pre-vocational or vocational training. One very noticeable feature of Japanese education is that a very high proportion of young people (42 per cent of males and 34 per cent of females according to Goodridge and Twiss, 1986) enter higher education.

Training, on the other hand, is very largely the responsibility of the individual company, with only limited state-sponsored public sector provision (IMS, 1984: 44–54). Because of the division of responsibility with the education system, Japanese firms expect to have to equip their workforces with the skills that they require. Companies generally place a heavy emphasis on highly-structured on-the-job training, including job-rotation and mentor coaching. The value of training is stressed at every level within companies' managements, and 'figures largely in any expression of the philosophy of business management' (Brown and Read, 1984: 53). As a result training is normally an integral part of the company's business plan.

Historically, vocational education and training in Britain has also had its distinctive characteristics. The educational side of vocational provision will be considered in a later section. What follows below concentrates on the peculiarities of Britain's vocational training system. Commentators have identified a wide variety of structural characteristics that it has been suggested have contributed to the distinctiveness of British vocational training. These have ranged from the low level of educational qualifications held by British managers to the relative failure of British engineers and technologists to assume the same dominance within management as have their colleagues in West Germany, Japan and France. What follows focuses on two character-istics that in particular stand out. Firstly, vocational training has often been virtually synonymous with a distinctive form of exclusive craft apprenticeship system. Secondly, British training arrangements have been characterized by a failure to evolve and maintain a coherent national institutional framework for vocational training. Each of these characteristics will be considered in turn and an attempt made to assess their contribution to Britain's training record.

## *The British Apprenticeship System*

It is no exaggeration to say that historically vocational training in Britain could, to all intents and purposes, be almost entirely equated with the apprenticeship system. Precise details of the apprenticeship system have differed from industry to industry and between occupations, but broadly speaking there was a fairly common pattern after the Second World War. An apprenticeship almost invariably involved young people of school-leaving age, the vast majority of whom were male. It entailed an attachment to an individual employer. It involved considerable 'on the job' experience under varying degrees of supervision, supplemented in more recent years by elements of 'off the job' instruction in a college of further education or perhaps a government training centre. It was relatively exclusive in terms of the skills that were acquired; the skills being those of a very specific occupation rather than a range of occupations. It was also time-served; that is to say, the duration of the apprenticeship was not dictated by what had to be learnt or by the pace at which the trainees acquired the requisite skills and knowledge, but pre-determined by a fixed length of time. Finally, there were very rarely tests of competence to ensure that the knowledge and skills had been correctly learnt; it was enough for the apprentice to have 'served his time' and reached the end of the apprenticeship.

The most distinctive feature of this traditional model of the apprenticeship system was its exclusive nature. This is important in helping to explain why so few apprentices were trained. Patently trade unions had a vested interest in restricting the number of trainees in order to force up the price of skilled labour. Although employers were constantly complaining about this, there was little real incentive for them to do anything about it. Not only was the structure of the training arrangements which the unions imposed upon them far from satisfactory, but the skills that individual craftsmen were able to exercise were tightly controlled by job demarcations within the work-place. Furthermore, the ethos of the apprenticeship was as much about indoctrinating the individual in the 'arts and mystery' of the trade as it was about teaching specific skills that the employer could use. In many ways it was as if the employer was providing the training for the benefit of the individual and the trade union rather than himself. In other words, although the system was relatively costless, the employer reaped few of the direct benefits normally associated with skills training and hardly any of the attitudinal benefits.

The exclusive nature of the traditional model of apprenticeship also goes some way towards explaining why employers did little training for semi- and unskilled workers. In the great majority of cases the demarcations associated with the craft apprenticeship system meant that there was relatively limited opportunity for the employer to promote the semi- and unskilled worker to what the apprenticeship system defined as a skilled job. It was also difficult, if not impossible, to promote semi- and unskilled workers to supervisory and managerial positions because of the refusal of craftsmen to work under anyone who had not completed an apprenticeship in the same trade. Taken together, these two considerations meant that there was little incentive for employers to give these workers any training beyond what was necessary to perform the immediate task (MSC, 1977: 11).

The foregoing may appear to place all the responsibility on the trade unions, but it is important not to forget that the attitudes that supported this apprenticeship system often became equally deeply ingrained among employers. Indeed, in the first half of the nineteenth century, when trade union power was relatively weak, it was employers who helped introduce earlier, inflexible models of the handicraft trade apprenticeship into new industries such as engineering (More, 1980) and then perpetuated the system, not simply from innate conservatism, or as a result of trade union imposition, but because the lack of standardization in product markets rendered unprofitable the replacement of the craft system by mass production techniques (More, 1980: 157). Moreover, nineteenth-century British employers' attitudes towards their responsibility to train their workforces were, to say the least, ambivalent (Perry, 1976: 33).

In the twentieth century, employers' attitudes changed somewhat, and they began to point to the difficulties caused by the entrenched traditions of the craft apprenticeship system. However, despite their criticisms (MSC, 1977: 11), for a long time they did little to mount any very serious challenge to that system.

The willingness of employers to live with the constraints imposed by a system of exclusive craft apprenticeships becomes clear when one considers their reaction to attempts by government to encourage the training and retraining of adult workers through the Training Opportunities Scheme (TOPS). In the year 1978–9 the MSC estimated that only 70,187 workers went through TOPS courses, and of these less than 10 per cent attended courses directly sponsored by employers. Moreover, successive MSC annual reports commented on the reluctance of employers to offer jobs to people who had passed through TOPS skills, training courses. Taylor (1980: 50) pointed to 'doubts among companies that the end-product was good enough for their needs,' and continued;

> Industry prefers the time-served apprentice every time; in some parts of Britain, companies insist, when recruiting to meet skills shortages, that they will only take workers who have gone through the traditional system. Firms will refuse to take on TOPS trainees, many of whom must disguise where they learnt their skills in order to get a job in their chosen trade.

It was only in 1981, during the depths of the recession, as part of the MSC's New Training Initiative, that employers and unions finally faced up to these problems and committed themselves to a reform of the apprenticeship system. The aim of the resulting reforms has been to secure an end to limits on the age of entry to apprenticeship schemes, and the replacement of qualifications based on serving a set training period by training to specific, tested standards. Progress towards these objectives has been somewhat slower than the MSC had originally envisaged, but as the final section of this chapter indicates, significant progress has been made in a number of sectors.

Unfortunately, as figures given earlier indicate, these reforms have apparently done little to check the very sharp decline in the number of apprentices actually in training in Britain.

In the light of the influence which the traditional craft apprenticeship has had within manufacturing in Britain, it becomes easier to understand the marked difference, referred to in the previous section, in the levels of training activity between the manufacturing and services sectors. The internal labour-markets that are usually found within banks and retail organizations offer far greater flexibility in the deployment of skills. Consequently, there has been more scope for managements in these organizations to secure an adequate return on their investment in training, not simply in terms of the acquisition of skills, but also in terms of the attitudinal benefits of training.

## A Voluntarist System?

Britain is often said to have a 'voluntarist' system of vocational education and training. As far as education is concerned, this has meant that although the government has been involved in the setting of overall policy objectives and a broad legislative framework within which they can operate, offering guidance on the curriculum, and providing much of the finance, it has not directed the curriculum, run the schools and colleges, or employed the teachers. Such matters have largely been the responsibility of local authorities, examination boards, the governing bodies of the educational institutions, and the teachers themselves. Furthermore, the expectation has been that serious vocational education would take place after the age of 16 and therefore outside the period of compulsory school education, and that it would largely be the responsibility of the individual on a 'self-help' basis.

In the case of vocational training, the implications of the 'voluntarist' tradition might be summed up in terms of the expectations of the Conservative government elected in 1983:

> it is for employers to make the necessary investment in training for the work that they require. It is for trainees to show enterprise in taking up training opportunities, perhaps financing their own training by means of a government loan. The government's own role is information provision, encouragement of training standards, setting-up pump-priming courses in new technologies, and provision of training assistance to the unemployed and disabled. (IMS, 1984: 68)

In practice, the division of responsibilities between the various parties involved in training has not proved quite so simple. In particular, the role of government has varied considerably in the post-Second World War period.

Prior to the early 1960s employers were left to their own devices and the 'training and the supply of skilled manpower was left to the play of market forces' (Stringer and Richardson, 1982: 23). However, as Lindley has argued

(1983: 343), growing concern in the late 1950s and early 1960s about the facilities for, and the organization of, training and retraining was fuelled by worries about the impact of the imminent increase in the number of school-leavers entering the job market. This concern about the adequacy of British training provision, especially when compared with that of Britain's West European competitors (Stringer and Richardson, 1982: 23), led to the passage of the Industrial Training Act in 1964. In the words of the White Paper on Industrial Training: Government Proposals (Ministry of Labour, 1962: 4), the main aims of the Act were: '(i) to enable decisions on the scale of training to be better related to economic needs and technological development; (ii) to improve the overall quality of industrial training and to establish minimum standards; and (iii) to enable the cost to be more evenly spread'. Industrial Training Boards (ITBs) were established in the major industries with the statutory authority to operate a levy/grant system on employers. Under this system a levy or payroll tax was imposed on all employers within the industry and grants paid out to those achieving acceptable volumes and levels of training. By 1972 there were 27 ITBs in existence and 12 million employees in establishments subject to levy/grant schemes. The levies, which ranged from 0.04 per cent for the Electrical Supply industry, to 3.8 per cent for parts of the Air Transport and Travel industry, reached a grand total in 1970–1 of £208 million, including grants of £5 million from the Department of Employment.

It is generally accepted that the ITBs did much good work (MSC, 1981). As well as forcing many employers to begin to take training seriously, they encouraged the setting-up of training departments where none had previously existed; they were responsible for improvements in manpower planning; they sponsored the training of groups other than apprentices, including technicians and managers (for details, see chapter 9); they pioneered and promoted new training methods; and they helped to raise standards in most areas.

Even so, there was considerable criticism of many of the ITBs. Despite the new initiatives taken, the work of the majority of ITBs continued to be dominated by the apprenticeship system; and although efforts at apprentice-ship reform were instituted, they were relatively marginal in effect. Little progress was made in improving training and retraining opportunities for adult workers (Norris and Thomas, 1982: 69). Added to this, there were complaints 'from industries saddled with poorly organized training boards, by firms (especially small ones) feeling that the levy–grant system affected them unfairly, and by educationalists who saw the influence of industrial training upon technical colleges and colleges of further education as tending to undermine their broader educational purpose' (Lindley, 1983: 344). Economists, such as McCormick and Manley (1967) and Lees and Chiplin (1970), were also critical, arguing that the Industrial Training Act ignored the important distinction between specific and general training.

One result of this criticism was the 1973 Employment and Training Act. Instead of operating a simple levy–grant system, ITBs were now empowered to give exemption from these arrangements to employers who were deemed to be doing adequate training. The government also undertook to contribute towards the operating costs of the ITBs. In addition, there was a major reorganization of the employment and training services agencies leading to the establishment of the Manpower Services Commission. The creation of the MSC provided a central focus for policy development; and, once established, the MSC began to sponsor initiatives that were designed to deal with some of the continuing weaknesses of the ITB levy–grant–exemption schemes. In particular, the MSC began to initiate policies to deal with the problems of youth unemployment and the training of adult skilled workers – both of which the ITBs had apparently had grave difficulty in tackling.

In the event, the passage of the 1973 Employment and Training Act did not fully assuage employers' criticisms of the ITB system. There was also a growing general frustration at the apparent inability of the ITBs to deal with many of the problems that began to emerge in the 1970s; in particular, the need to secure a sufficient supply of general or cross-sectorally 'transferable skills', the difficulties in meeting many instances of skill shortages that were highly occupation-specific and geographically-based, and, above all, the growing problem of youth unemployment. Employers were also disenchanted with what they perceived as the growing subordination of the boards to the MSC (Stringer and Richardson, 1982: 27–8). The deciding factor, however, in sealing the fate of the ITBs was the economic philosophy of the incoming Conservative government: training was a matter for individuals and their employers; and there was little that the government should or, indeed, could do.

The third phase of post-war government policy was therefore ushered in by the 1981 Employment and Training Act, which saw the abolition of all but six of the ITBs. The passage of the 1981 Act did not in fact signal a total end to direct government intervention. For, as the following section will describe in greater detail, by 1981 the problem of youth unemployment had reached such proportions that the government was under considerable pressure to revamp the Youth Opportunities Programme (YOP), originally introduced under the previous Labour government.

More recently, the often limited effectiveness of the voluntary training arrangements that have replaced the ITBs has become increasingly apparent, and this has led to a re-opening of the debate about the ability of employers to provide adequate levels of training without the backing of a statutory training system. In point of fact, many of the Non-Statutory Training Organizations (NSTOs) were established by employers simply as the price to be paid for the abolition of their industry's ITB (Coopers and Lybrand, 1985: 13; Green, 1986: 27) and were in any case never intended as direct replacements for the boards. Most NSTOs have confined themselves to disbursing MSC training grants, disseminating information, and acting as 'ginger-groups' for training activity (Rainbird and Grant, 1985). All are dependent upon the goodwill of companies in their industry, since in areas where the ITBs have vanished, training is now a purely voluntary activity which companies can choose to opt out of at any time. The relative ineffectiveness of voluntary arrangements in securing change and improvement in employers' training performance has led to public criticism by senior MSC officials ( *The Times*, 25 March 1986; *Times*

*Educational Supplement*, 1 August 1986) and even to the threat of the reimposition of some form of statutory training levy or tax.


## THE DEBATE INTENSIFIES

The relatively detailed information that has recently become available about Britain's poor international record in the field of vocational education and training has served to intensify the long-standing debate that has existed in this area. As Lindley (1983: 343) has pointed out, the core of the debate centres on how both the quality and quantity of vocational education and training can be improved. In practice, however, the precise form of the debate has been dependent upon the major policy concerns of the day. As the previous section has pointed out, in the period leading up to the passage of the Industrial Training Act in 1964, the major concerns were the perceived inadequacies of the traditional apprenticeship system and the problems that were expected to arise from shortages of specific skills, as well as alarm at the rising numbers of school leavers entering the job market. In the late 1970s and early 1980s the major concern was centred on the rapid acceleration in youth unemployment and the political consequences that this entailed. Clearly youth unemployment remains a major issue. In recent years, however, it has become increasingly difficult to ignore the wider weaknesses of the system and, in particular, the growing body of evidence linking investment in education and training with economic success.

One strand of the debate centres on the educational system. As Parkes and *Educch* Russell (1983) point out, the distinctive British tradition of semi-autonomous educational institutions; a multiplicity of local education authorities, often at odds with central government; and a profusion of examining and validating bodies had been the subject of adverse comment for many years. It is only recently, however, that pressure for change has reached a level that presents serious challenge to the traditions of this system. The mounting pressure has stemmed in part from the political imperatives generated by large-scale youth unemployment, but also reflects concern by employers at the economic consequences of an education system that has tended to emphasize early specialization and academic rather than practical values to the detriment of technical and vocational subjects. Such a fragmented and academically-oriented education system was seen as being artificially divorced from the business of training and insufficiently responsive to the needs of employers.

The result of mounting concern has been a series of measures in the education sector aimed at promoting greater central influence and control over educational institutions, allied with attempts to foster an increased emphasis upon vocational and pre-vocational elements within the curriculum. At secondary level the MSC has developed with great rapidity, since its launch in 1983, the Technical and Vocational Education Initiative (TVEI). TVEI originated as a five year pilot scheme designed to test new methods of developing a technical and vocationally-oriented curriculum within secondary schools. Together with the policies outlined in Sir Keith Joseph' White Paper, 'Better Schools', it was hailed by government ministers (Young, 1985: 6) and senior MSC officials as the centrepiece of their strategy to introduce work-related preparation as a widespread and permanent feature in secondary education. Accordingly, in early July 1986 the government announced its intention to extend existing TVEI pilot projects into a national scheme covering all state secondary schools. This extension commenced in the autumn term of 1987 and will be phased over a number of years.

The Department of Education and Science (DES) has introduced in parallel a number of its own initiatives aimed at increasing pre-vocational elements within the secondary school system, including a Certificate of Pre-Vocational Education (CPVE). More controversial has been the decision to establish a number of City Technology Colleges (CTCs) in inner-city areas to be financially sponsored by employers. In addition, recent proposals, such as a compulsory national core curriculum and the devolution of budgetary control to the heads of individual schools, have signalled a clear intention on the part of the government to reduce the power of local education authorities.

Beyond the secondary sector, other initiatives have included the establishment of a National Council for Vocational Qualifications (NCVQ) charged with the task of rationalizing and simplifying the current profusion of vocational courses and qualifications. Within non-advanced further education the percentage of funding controlled by the MSC has risen from 8 per cent in 1984–5 to 16 per cent in 1986–7 in order, in the words of the chairman of the MSC, 'to gear technical and vocational education more closely to the real needs of local labour markets' (Nicholson, 1985: 35). At the level of higher education a limited 'switch' away from the humanities towards science and technological subjects has been promoted, and greater liaison between employers and educational institutions encouraged.

A great deal of change has occurred within the education sector in recent years. At a time when the government has been attempting to 'roll back the frontiers of the state', many of these changes have represented a major increase in the powers of central government and an unprecedented increase in central direction of the education system. It is, however, open to question whether these developments amount to a coherent overall strategy on the part of government, or whether they simply represent a series of hastily introduced, fairly unco-ordinated, *ad hoc* initiatives (Keep, 1987). Nevertheless, the pace and scale of the changes reflect the growing sense of urgency with which the creation of a national system of vocational education and training has been viewed.

A second strand in the debate about the development of a national system of vocational educaton and training has been concerned with the need for the systematic provision of vocational training for young school leavers. As the previous section made clear, unlike some other countries, notably France and West Germany, Britain has never possessed such a system. Training for work was regarded as the responsibility of the employer, and British employers traditionally offered little if any training to those of their young employees who were not apprentices. The implications of this situation for those school leavers who were able to find work were serious; for example, in 1979 the MSC estimated that nearly 40 per cent of school leavers that found jobs received no training at all from their employer, and another 20 per cent received training for eight weeks or less. From the point of view of governments in the late 1970s and early 1980s, however, a far more serious problem was posed by the growing number of school leavers who were unable to find a job. Not only was some form of work experience or preparation deemed to be essential if such individuals were to make themselves attractive to potential employers; it also provided an extremely convenient means of removing a large, and politically embarrassing, group from the ranks of the unemployed.

The first tentative steps towards resolving this problem were taken in 1978 with the introduction of the Youth Opportunities Programme (YOP), which replaced a patchwork of earlier schemes and which was designed to give unemployed school leavers a period of limited work experience. In 1978 one in eight school leavers were going into YOP. By 1982 that proportion had climbed to more than half the entire school leaver population. The pressures engendered by a four-fold increase in places over the five years of the programme's life led to problems with the quality of the work experience places and the widespread misuse of YOP youngsters as substitutes for paid adult labour (Finn, 1983: 19; St John-Brooks, 1985: 2).

Following the Conservative government's endorsement of the MSC's 'New Training Initiative' in 1981, the Youth Training Scheme was introduced to cover all unemployed minimum age school leavers in 1983. YTS was designed to counter the criticisms that had undermined YOP and 'to equip unemployed young people to adapt successfully to the demands of employment; to have a fuller appreciation of the world of industry, business and technolgy in which they will work; and to develop basic and recognized skills which employers will require in the future' (Department of Employment, 1981: 7). Initially a one-year period was envisaged to include on-the-job training and planned work experience, together with a minimum of 13 weeks off-the-job training or a period of further education. Subsequently, and with effect from September 1986, the duration of YTS was extended to two years for young people leaving school at the age of 16.

Some idea of the impact of YTS can be gained by studying the provisional estimates produced by the MSC for the year 1986 (MSC, 1986: 13); of the total 16-year-old population of 860,000 some 45 per cent (390,000) were involved in full-time education, 27 per cent (230,000) were involved in YTS, 12 per cent (100,000) were unemployed, and 16 per cent were either employed, or seeking work and not claiming benefit.

Clearly, it has been no mean achievement to launch a scheme with this scale of coverage in such a short space of time. More to the point, it can also be argued that the advent of YTS has acted as a catalyst for promoting greater coherence within British training provision (Bevan and Hutt, 1985) and the MSC accord it a major role in encouraging wider changes in companies' general attitudes towards training. Representative of this view of YTS is the following passage from the MSC Corporate Plan for 1983/87:

*only* represents a major step towards the fulfilment of the New Training
objective for vocational preparation, but will also contribute substantially to
m of occupational training and provide the basis of knowledge and practical
ice that will allow adults to train and re-train during the course of their
g lives. (1983: 15).

YTS has certainly led to the introduction of training of young people in many
sectors where little or no opportunity previously existed, and has also
encouraged the development of training to defined standards of competence
and a move away from time-based training (MSC, 1986: 8). Another
important feature is the support that YTS has given to off-the-job training and
to periods in further education.

Even so, critics argue that YTS is largely a palliative for youth unemployment and that it falls a long way short of the acceptable national scheme that is
needed. The first point that can be made is that YTS was an *ad hoc* development, planned, in both its one- and two-year forms, at great speed and with
little thought being given to its place within wider patterns of vocational
education and training provision for the young (Keep, 1986). Partly as a result
of the rush to get the scheme into operation, the quality of the training
provision has sometimes been variable.

Also, as originally conceived by the MSC Youth Task Group's planners,
YTS was expected to cover both employed and unemployed youngsters, but
evidence shows that relatively few employers have bothered to register their
normal youth training intakes under the scheme (Roberts et al., 1986: 46). In
some cases employers have preferred to keep YTS provision separate from
the training given to their own young employees (Rainbird and Grant, 1985;
Roberts et al., 1986: 46) and have even, on offering employment to YTS
trainees, then removed them prematurely from the scheme. Indeed, in the year
1985–6, 50 per cent of YTS trainees quit the scheme early, the most common
reason being to take up a full-time job (*MSC Youth Training News*, February
1987), and less than 11 per cent of trainees on the scheme have formal
employed status (*Transition*, November 1987). In response to this the MSC
has been forced to create a 'Working with YTS' campaign in order to convince
employers to extend YTS to cover employed youngsters. This problem tends
to reinforce evidence from a considerable body of research (Bevan and Hutt,
1985: 10; Williams, 1985: 260; Rainbird and Grant, 1985: 29; Coopers and
Lybrand, 1985: 12; Tomlinson, 1985; Sako and Dore, 1986) which indicates
that employers have so far seen YTS as a palliative for youth unemployment,
rather than as an attempt to establish a coherent, high quality vocational training system that would form an integral part of their companies' training structures. Certainly it should be pointed out that apprentices in the West German
'dual system' do not leave their apprenticeships to take up a job.

Therefore, while YTS's potential long-term impact on vocational training
for the young should not be underestimated, the scheme still has some way to
go before it can seriously be said to offer an equivalent to the vocational
education and training package on offer to youngsters in West Germany or
Japan. For this to happen, the attitudes of a large number of employers

towards the scheme will need to be modified. Moreover, in terms of this importance as an area of government intervention in, and financing of, training which runs counter to the general policy of employer responsibility, it is important to note that the government has made clear its intention to shift an increasing proportion of the cost of YTS onto employers. West German companies foot over 80 per cent of the annual £5 billion bill for the 'dual system', whereas currently British employers are putting about £0.8 billion into YTS as against a government contribution of £1.1 billion.

The third strand to the debate is concerned with how to influence employers to adopt a more positive attitude towards training at work, particularly towards the training and retraining of adult workers. The government's public commitment to a voluntarist policy of allowing employers to determine the amount of training that takes place, leaves it with little else beside exhortation as a means of influencing employers' decisions in this area. An idea of the range of proposals being canvassed can be gained from an examination of the report prepared by Coopers and Lybrand Associates for the MSC and NEDO (1985). It includes proposals for encouraging employers' belief in the value of training through education; the use of case studies and inter-firm comparisons (with the possible requirement that the amount spent on training be published in companies' annual reports); the introduction of a 'Queen's Award for Training'; and the adoption of the concept of the 'training employer' along the lines of the 'equal opportunity' employer; reducing employers' training costs through further tax concessions (training costs are already a tax allowable reduction); grants and compensations for 'poaching'; and enabling employers to obtain increased benefits from training by improving the operation of the training 'market' in terms of the availability of advice and information, the services provided by local education establishments, and the introduction of a 'coherent and comprehensive' structure of qualifications.

More controversially, the Coopers and Lybrand report (1985: 25–30) discussed a number of proposals for increasing the pressure on employers to invest in training. Such pressure might be applied by sectoral bodies, such as the Non-Statutory Training Organizations (NSTOs), or local ones, which would have the power to recommend the withholding of grants, as is done by the chambers of commerce in West Germany; by individuals who might be given an 'individual training credit' which would confer an entitlement to training and which would operate in a similar way to pension entitlements; by trade unions who might be afforded representation on workplace training committees with comparable rights and duties to those of the health and safety committees set up under the 1974 Health and Safety at Work Act; and, finally, by government, which might pass legislation requiring employers to provide training for key groups, such as the under-18s or those made redundant, or obliging them through a form of remissible training tax or levy to undertake a minimum level of expenditure, either on a sectoral basis, as under the 1964 Industrial Training Act, or nationally, as in France, with penalties for underspending.

Not surprisingly, it is the proposal for a levy/grant system or a remissible training tax that arouses most heat. Opponents argue that there are a number of reasons for not adopting such measures. First, there are the problems of deciding the basis of the financial levy or tax; if, as under the earlier Industrial Training Act, it is set on a sectoral basis, it would be difficult to cope with demands that cut across sectors. If, on the other hand, it is set on a national basis, as in France, there is the danger that the specific needs and circumstances of individual industries or occupations will be ignored. Secondly, it is suggested that any such system would be difficult to monitor and, if it is to be done properly, would entail a considerable oncost. Thirdly, and more fundamentally, critics argue that previous experience in Britain under the Industrial Training Act and in France since 1972 suggests that the results are likely to be out of all proportion to the costs. A tax or levy might stimulate an initial upsurge of interest in training by employers, but in all likelihood this would tend to fade away; and in the medium and longer term employers will simply undertake that training which is easiest to organize, rather than that which is really needed.

Those in favour of a levy or tax argue that exhortation is not enough. They also point to past experience. Voluntarist training arrangements in Britain prior to 1964 failed to produce an adequate level of training, or flexible training arrangements. The introduction of the ITBs was an acknowledgement of the scale and persistence of this failure, as well as an implicit acceptance by policy-makers that simply exhorting firms to undertake more training would not be enough (Lindley, 1988: 344). The apparent virtual collapse of training in many sectors following the 1981 abolition of the ITB levy/grant systems confirms that a specific set of circumstances combine in Britain to militate against employers seeing training as an investment.

To begin with, as chapter 1 underlined, the structure of ownership in the UK more or less obliges many employers to take a short-term view. Despite assertions to the contrary in the CBI City/Industry Task Force's recent report 'Investing in Britain's Future' (CBI, 1987), the balance of evidence suggests that British financial institutions and the stock market exert great pressure on businesses to produce good short-term results at the expense of long-term investment for the future. At the same time many of the financial institutions are themselves subject to similar short-term pressures, as competition among investment fund managers forces them to maximize the immediate return on their investments (Whittam Smith, 1985). The recent merger boom has meant that companies have been forced to concentrate on producing good short-term results for fear of disappointing City analysts, hence seeing their share prices drop, and thus laying themselves open to a hostile takeover bid. The result of all this, according to the Director-General of the BIM, has been to produce 'an inordinate emphasis on the short term' (*Guardian*, 30 January 1986) and other commentators have suggested that 'it is doubtful whether many publicly quoted companies can any longer contemplate courses of action that, while beneficial for the long-term health of the enterprise, would depress profits in the short term' (Whittam Smith, 1985). It is important to note that in both West Germany and Japan these sorts of pressures are largely absent, due to differing structures of ownership and the tendency for a long-term relationship to exist between companies, their banks, and their share-holders.

The two areas of British company activity which arguably have been hardest hit by these pressures have been research and development, and training. Both are areas where investment is unlikely to provide a substantial return within the horizons of annual or half-yearly results. As was remarked by Coopers and Lybrand in 'A Challenge of Complacency' (1985: 14), 'investment managers do not perceive training activity to be significant when assessing a company's worth'. The result has been a powerful incentive to British managements to treat training as a cost that needs to be minimized, rather than as an investment.

At the same time, the absence of a long-established national system of vocational education and training, as in West Germany, or of flexible internal labour-market structures, as in Japan and the USA, exposes individual employers who would otherwise train to the constant threat of seeing their investment in skilled labour being poached by rivals who have opted not to train. In short, implicit in the arguments of those who advocate some form of training tax is acceptance of the view that there is a market 'failure', which necessitates government intervention in order to bring about greater efficiency and equity.

At first sight, the prospect of reimposition of some form of training tax or levy so soon after its abolition would hardly appear to be practical politics. Even so, it cannot be ruled out completely, even by the present or a future Conservative government. There is now a widespread consensus that Britain needs a coherent system of vocational education and training. Employers share that view; and it could even be said that they have been one of the prime instigators in intensifying the debate, especially about the perceived short-comings of vocational education. An essential ingredient of any such vocational education and training is the active involvement of employers in the provision of training, not only for young workers, but also for adults. If employers are not seen to play their part, the pressure for further action to force them to do so is likely to grow; for the alternative, which is for the government itself to play an even larger role in both the funding and provision of training, is likely to prove even more unacceptable.

One development that may stimulate such a debate is the MSC's major research project on the funding of vocational education and training, which was due to be published during 1988. The results of this study, which has examined the contributions made by companies, local and central govern-ment, and individuals to the financial support of education and training provision, are likely to fuel discussions about the balance of responsibility that exists between state and employer. It also seems probable that in the wake of its publication there will be renewed discussion of the relative merits of statutory enforcement of the duty to train upon employers as against the present voluntary system. A former MSC chairman, Bryan Nicholson, has already predicted that statutory mechanisms to back adult training 'are going to be explored in the future' (Pickard, 1987: 11). Whether there is any evidence of employers being willing and able, of their own accord, to assume the responsibilities the government would wish them to is the subject of the next section.

## CHANGES IN MANAGEMENT PRACTICE

Certainly there is evidence of a number of changes in managerial practice. One recent survey (IRRR, 1985: 2–8), for example, suggests that there have been major changes in the apprenticeship system in the building, chemicals, electrical contracting, electrical supply, engineering and printing industries. The changes include the revision of existing modular arrangements to allow for greater flexibility and transferability of skills, greater emphasis on practical experience, the incorporation of certain elements of YTS into the first year of the apprenticeship, and training based on the achievement of standards rather than on age or length of service criteria. Coupled with this last point has been the substitution of the traditional 'wage for age' pay systems by 'wage for stage' scales. The introduction of standards-based training, supporters argue, is particularly significant. It makes it possible to establish national standards – for intake, for performance and for training – in a number of cases in conjunction with the City and Guilds of London Institute (CGLI), one of the nationally-recognized examination organizations for arts and crafts. As the IRRR survey concludes, 'it remains to be seen – although hopes are high – whether the new approach and quality of training produces in sufficient numbers a more flexible and highly trained generation of craft workers able to meet industry's needs in the late 1990s and beyond'.

A number of individual employers, including British Shipbuilders, Cadbury-Schweppes, Babcock Power, Esso and Whitbread, have also taken the opportunity provided by the recession to break down some of the barriers in the internal labour-market which, as a previous section argued, have not only stood in the way of flexibility and transferability, but have also discouraged investments in training. As one review of flexibility agreements introduced in the early 1980s found (IRRR, 1984: 2–9), the trend has included moves to 'combine' jobs by eliminating differences within and between crafts; 'team' working involving complete interchangeability and flexibility between individual jobs; 'balanced labour-force techniques' designed to deal with shortages and surpluses by having workers in one craft supplement those in another; the ending of 'trade supervision' under which craftsmen would only accept instructions from a supervisor who had completed an apprenticeship in the same trade; and the blurring of the distinction between blue- and white-collar jobs, especially between craftsmen and technicians. Of necessity, such changes have involved considerable retraining of exisiting employees, most of which has been specific to the individual employer (NEDO, 1985).

Paradoxical as it may seem, the recession has been an important catalyst in promoting training and development more generally. As chapter 2 pointed out, under the pressure of intense international competition many British manufacturing companies have been obliged to make radical changes in their working arrangements, with the introduction of new technology or new production methods. Either way, the effect of these changes, coupled with the substantial reductions in manpower that have usually been involved, has been very similar: management has been forced to introduce training programmes to equip existing employees with the requisite skills and knowledge to operate the new working arrangements.

In other examples quoted in chapter 2, such as British Airways and British Rail, similar developments have been 'market-led'. Attempts to promote 'customer first' or 'customer care' campaigns, again under the pressure of intense competition, have been shown to require substantial investments in training if they are to stand any chance of success (Sacker, 1987).

The use of training to achieve substantial attitudinal changes, which is the important distinguishing characteristic of this second set of examples, is also associated with many of the developments in participation and involvement which will be considered in part V of the book. Strictly speaking, attendance at a team briefing session with a first line supervisor or taking part in a quality circle meeting might not be regarded as 'training'. Yet, as is more and more recognized to be the case in Japan, such activities are 'prominent and effective ways of developing employees' attitudes' and are to be considered to have 'contributed significantly to Japan's superior record of adjustment to recession' (IMS, 1984: 49).

Chapters 14, 15 and 16 will deal in greater detail with the nature and extent of these developments. It is significant to note here, however, that the Industrial Society alone reckons to have helped to introduce team briefing in some 400 organizations in recent years (IRRR, 1986a: 3). There has also been a significant increase in the number of organizations with quality circles; from next to nothing in 1978 (Rolls-Royce claims to be the pioneer in Britain) to 100 in 1981 and to 400 in 1986 (IDS Study, 1985: 1).

The various training and development initiatives described above have also helped to encourage the adoption of new learning methods. Perhaps the most important of these is 'open' or 'distance' learning, which has been adopted by employers such as Jaguar Cars, British Telecom, the Rover Group and British Steel. 'Open learning', which usually involves the individual trainee in running a software package on a computer, has a number of advantages over traditional instruction methods such as lectures. For instance, fully standardized training programmes can be tailor-made precisely to suit the specific tasks or circumstances which the individual trainee will be expected to tackle; the individual can learn at his or her own pace in the relative privacy of the training unit; feedback, through interactive computer software, is usually instantaneous; and the time at which the training takes place is much more flexible.

Perhaps even more fundamental for the long-term viability of training activity, the initiatives have led employers to recognize the importance of carrying out audits of the skills, training and experience of their existing employees, and of developing personnel databases to record this information. Good examples would be British Rail and British Steel (Ballin, 1986: 25). As chapter 5 and an earlier section above observed, such basic 'house-keeping' activities have been noticeable chiefly by their absence in many British organizations. Yet such information is not only essential if the individual employer is to develop a clear picture of the organization's human resources; it is also necessary if employers are to be able to articulate their needs to the MSC and other organizations concerned with education and training, with sufficient precision to allow the planning of numbers and activities.

To conclude this section, then, there are not only signs of training activity on the part of management, but many of the developments are of considerable significance. Even so, it would be wrong to make too much of what is going on. For example, although engineering employers have revamped the arrangements for apprenticeship training, the number of apprentices remains extremely small – scarcely 8,000 out of a total manual workforce of 800,000 that was covered by the relevant agreement in 1985 (IRRR, 1985: 2). Or, to take another example, the figures for the number of organizations introducing team briefings and quality circles look impressive enough, but they pale into insignificance when placed against the total number of employers in Britain. Finally, employers' worries about the persistent reoccurrence of widespread skill shortages, despite high levels of unemployment, are an indication that there are still considerable problems with skill supply in Britain.


## CONCLUSION

This review of vocational training in Britain has identified a number of issues: the importance of the role of employers; the interrelationship between training and vocational education; the relatively low levels of education and training opportunities offered to the broad mass of the workforce; and the concentration of this limited training effort on certain groups of employees. The structural features that underlie this situation have been examined and an attempt made to explain them in the light of two distinctive characteristics of training in Britain: the traditional monopolization of training by a pattern of exclusive craft apprenticeships, and the persistent failure to evolve and maintain a coherent national system for the delivery of vocational education and training.

It is hardly surprising that vocational education and training continues to maintain a high profile as the focus of a national policy debate (IRRR, 1986b). The skills and adaptability of the workforce have come to be viewed as one of the major determinants of competition, both at interfirm and international levels (Cassels, 1985: 439; Chandler, 1987: 795). The general perception that Britain has lagged behind competitors in this area has led to concern that, in the long term, British firms will become increasingly unable to compete with overseas rivals, particularly where competition turns on non-price factors such as reliability of delivery and product quality and design. Training and education are now seen as one of the major structural problems that underlie the relative weakness of the British economy.

At another level, debate has focused upon training partly as a result of wider changes in employment practices that it is alleged are taking place in Britain. In recent years a great deal has been heard about a general movement by British organizations towards the adoption of a human resource management (HRM) approach to the motivation and deployment of their workforces. If the concept has any validity, then it might be reasonable to expect that the willingness of employers to treat their employees as assets, and to invest in their training and development, would be a prerequisite for its success. The efforts of companies such as Jaguar Cars and British Steel arguably offer examples of this new approach.

A great deal of wider change at national level has already resulted from this debate. These changes have occurred in both vocational education and training, and have embraced structural delivery mechanisms, the form and contents of courses and qualifications, the introduction of new types of provision, and the re-apportioning of responsibilities. One very recent example of these continuing alterations has been the decision to remove responsibility for Jobcentres and services to the unemployed from the MSC, to concentrate its activities on training, and to rename it the Training Commission. The stated aim of all these developments is the creation of a coherent system of vocational education and training, and the importance of a number of the most far-reaching of these changes has been discussed in the course of this chapter.

It is apparent that the pace of change is unlikely to diminish significantly in the foreseeable future. The momentum of political interest in the area and the influence of government and tripartite agencies look set to ensure a continued emphasis on the issue of vocational education and training. One small example of this is the recent MSC/NEDO 'People – The Key to Success' campaign, which is aimed at chief executives and senior managers, and which attempts to put the case for organizations placing greater emphasis upon the development of the skills and enthusiasms of their employees.

Yet despite the scope and pace of developments, and the considerable political and economic pressure that has built up behind them, it is perhaps most appropriate to draw this discussion of the training debate to a close by underlining the formidable scale of the problems that still remain to be tackled. In view of the deep-seated and seemingly intractable nature of many of the factors that impede progress in this area, such as the pressure for short-term profits that arise out of the distinctive structure of ownership in the UK, it is hardly surprising that progress has been relatively slow and limited. Much remains to be done, particularly in terms of creating a coherent and comprehensive system of provision. The distance still to be travelled is highlighted by Geoffrey Holland, the Director of the MSC, when he points out (Kennedy, 1987: 56) that seven out of ten of the workforce that will be employed in the year 2000 are already in employment; that seven out of ten of those that left at the minimum school-leaving age had few, if any, qualifications; and that seven out of ten of this group have been offered no systematic training opportunity since leaving school. It is not surprising that training has acquired a higher profile than almost any other area of personnel management activity.

# Bibliography

Ballin, M. 1986. 'How British Steel Tempered the Job Cuts'. *Transition*, January, 24–6.

Beach, D.S. 1975. *Personnel: The Management of People at Work*. London: Collier-Macmillan.

Benett, Y. and Carter, D. 1983. *Day Release for Girls*. Manchester: Equal Opportunities Commission.

Bevan, S. and Hutt, R. 1985. 'Company Perspectives on the Youth Training Scheme'. Report No. 104. Falmer: University of Sussex, Institute of Manpower Studies.

Brown G.F. and Read, A.R. 1984. 'Personnel and Training Policies – Some Lessons for Western Companies'. *Long Range Planning*, 7: 2, 48–57.

Cantor, L. 1985. 'A Coherent Approach to the Training of the 16–19 Age Group'. *Education and Economic Performance*. Ed. Worswick, G. D. N. Aldershot: Gower, 13–24.

Cassels, J.S. 1985. 'Educating for Tomorrow – Learning, Work and the Future'. *Royal Society of Arts Journal*, 133: June, 438–49.

Chandler, G. 1987. 'Britain's Industrial Crisis: Sacred Cows or Real Solutions?'. *Royal Society of Arts Journal*, 135: October, 792–803.

Cockburn, C. 1987. *Two-Track Training*. London: Macmillan.

Confederation of British Industry (CBI). 1987. *Investing in Britain's Future: Report of the CBI City/Industry Task Force*. London: CBI.

Coopers and Lybrand Associates. 1985. *A Challenge to Complacency: Changing Attitudes to Training*. London: MSC/NEDO.

Department of Employment. 1981. *A New Training Initiative: A Programme for Action*. Cmnd 8455. London: HMSO.

Equal Opportunities Commission (EOC). 1986. *Women and Men in Britain: a Statistical Profile*. London: HMSO.

Finn, D. 1983. 'The Youth Training Scheme – A New Deal?'. *Youth and Policy*, 1: Spring, 16–24.

Flippo, E.B. 1984. *Personnel Management*. 6th edn. New York: McGraw-Hill.

Goodridge, M. and Twiss, B. 1986. *Management Development and Technological Innovation in Japan*. Sheffield: MSC.

Green, S. 1986. 'A Critical Assessment of RVQ'. *Personnel Management*, July, 24–9.

Greenlaw, P.S. and Biggs, W.D. 1979. *Modern Personnel Management*. Eastbourne: W. B. Saunders.

Guest, D. and Kenny, T. 1983. *A Textbook of Techniques and Strategies in Personnel Management*. London: IPM.

Hall, D.T. and Goodale, J.G. 1986. *Human Resource Management: Strategy, Design and Implementation*. London: Scott, Foresman.

Hesseling, P.G.M. 1966. *Strategy Evaluation Research*. Assen, Netherlands: Van Gorcum.

Holland, G. 1985. 'More Adult Training in Britain'. *Public Money*, December, 11.

Incomes Data Services (IDS). 1985. *Ever Increasing Circles*. Study No. 352. London: IDS.

*Industrial Relations Review and Report* (IRRR). 1984. 'Flexibility Agreements – The End of Who Does What?'. 316: March, 2–9.

—— 1985. 'Apprentice Training'. 354: October.

—— 1986a. 'Team Briefing: Practical Steps in Employee Communication'. 361: February, 2–9.

—— 1986b. 'Training Developments – A Review'. 375: September, 12–14.

Industrial Society. 1985. *Survey of Training Costs: New Series No. 1*. London: Industrial Society.

Institute of Manpower Studies (IMS). 1984. *Competence and Competition: Training and Education in the Federal Republic of Germany, the United States and Japan*. London: MSC/NEDO.

Keep, E. 1986. 'Designing the Stable Door: A Study of How the Youth Training Scheme was Planned'. Warwick Papers in Industrial Relations No. 8. Coventry: University of Warwick, Industrial Relations Research Unit.

—— 1987. 'Britain's Attempts to Create a National Vocational Education and Training System: A Review of Progress'. Warwick Papers in Industrial Relations No. 16. Coventry: University of Warwick, Industrial Relations Research Unit.

Kennedy, C. 1987. 'Who are the Unemployed?'. *The Director*, November, 55–6.

Lawler, G. 1985. 'Land of Youth Opportunity'. *Times Higher Education Supplement*, 14 January.

Lees, D. and Chiplin, B. 1970. 'The Economics of Industrial Training'. *Lloyds Bank Review*, 94: April, 29–41.

Lindley, R. 1983. 'Active Manpower Policy'. *Industrial Relations in Britain*. Ed. Bain, G. S. Oxford: Blackwell, 339–60.

McCormick, B.J. and Manley, P.S. 1967. 'The Industrial Training Act'. *Westminster Bank Review*, February, 44–56.

Mangham, I.L. and Silvers, M.S. 1986. *Management Training: Context and Practice*. Claverton Down: University of Bath, School of Management.

Manpower Services Commission (MSC). 1977. *Training for Skills: A Programme for Action*. London: MSC.

—— 1981. *A Framework for the Future: A Sector by Sector Review of Industrial and Commerical Training*. London: MSC.

—— 1983. *MSC Corporate Plan 1983/87*. Sheffield: MSC.

—— 1985. *Adult Training in Britain*. Sheffield: MSC.

—— 1986. *Labour Market Quarterly Report*. June. Sheffield: MSC.

Ministry of Labour. 1962. *Industrial Training: Government Proposals*. Cmnd 1892. London: HMSO.

More, C. 1980. *Skills and the English Working Class, 1870–1914*. London: Croom Helm.

National Economic Development Office (NEDO). Electronics EDC Employment and Technology Task Group. 1985. *Retraining for Electronic Skills*. London: NEDO.

Nicholson, B. 1985. 'Managing Change in Education and Training'. *BACIE Journal*, March/April, 31–5.

Norris, C. and Thomas, H. 1982. 'Industrial Training Policy in Great Britain'. *The Politics of Industrial Training Policy*. Eds. Anderson, M. and Fairley, J. Edinburgh: University of Edinburgh, Department of Politics, 65–89.

Oatley, M. 1970. 'The Economics of Training'. *British Journal of Industrial Relations*, 8: March, 1–21.

Parkes, D. and Russell, R. 1983. 'Continental Comparisons'. *Times Higher Education Supplement*, 21 January.

Perry, P.J.C. 1976. *The Evolution of British Manpower Policy, from the Statute of Artificers 1563 to the Industrial Training Act 1964*. London: The Author.

Pickard, J. 1987. 'Ironing Out Quibbles on a Quango'. *Transition*, October, 10–11.

Pigors, P. and Myers, C.A. 1981. *Personnel Administration: A Point of View and a Method*. 9th edn. New York: McGraw-Hill.

Prais, S.J. 1985. 'What Can We Learn from the German System of Education and Vocational Training?'. *Education and Economic Performance*. Ed. Worswick, G. D. N. London: Gower, 40–51.

—— and Wagner, K. 1981. 'Some Practical Aspects of Human Capital Investment: Training Standards in Five Occupations in Britain and Germany'. *National Institute of Economic and Social Research Review*, November, 46–65.

Rainbird, H. and Grant, W. 1985. 'Employers' Associations and Training Policy'. Coventry: University of Warwick, Institute of Employment Research (mimeo).

Roberts, K., Dench, S. and Richardson, D. 1986. 'Firms' Uses of the Youth Training Scheme'. *Policy Studies*, 6: January, 37–53.

Sacker, F. 1987. 'Customer Service Training in Context'. *Personnel Management*, March, 34–7.

St. John-Brooks, C. 1985. *Who Controls Training? The Rise of the MSC*. Fabian Tract 506. London: Fabian Society.

Sako, M. and Dore, R. 1986. 'How the Youth Training Scheme Helps Employers'. *Employment Gazette*, June, 195–204.

Singer, E.J. and Ramsden, J. 1972. *Human Resources: Obtaining Results from People at Work*. London: McGraw-Hill.

Steedman, H. 1987. 'Vocational Training in France and Britain: Office Work'. Discussion Paper No. 14. London: National Institute of Economic and Social Research.

Stringer, J. and Richardson, J. 1982. 'Policy Stability and Policy Change: Industrial Training 1964–1982'. *Public Administration Bulletin*, 39: 22–39.

Taylor, R. 1980. 'The Training Scandal'. *Management Today*, July, 46–51.

Tomlinson, J. 1985. 'Stalled on the Road to Recovery?'. *Times Educational Supplement*, 22 February.

Torrington, D. and Chapman, J. 1984. *Personnel Management*. London: Prentice-Hall International.

Wellington, J. 1986. 'Industry Expects …'. *Times Educational Supplement*, 10 January.

Whittam Smith, A. 1985. 'Long and Short Pressures on Management'. *Daily Telegraph*, 16 November.

Williams, S. 1985. 'The Shape of Education for Tomorrow's Society'. *Policy Studies*, 5: April, 4–13.

Wilson, T. 1987. 'Opinion'. *Transition*, May, 3–4.

Yodor, D. and Staudohar, P.D. 1982. *Personnel Management and Industrial Relations*. 7th edn. Englewood Cliffs, NJ: Prentice-Hall.

Young, D. 1985. 'Start at the Beginning'. *Industrial Society*, June, 3–5.

# 9 The Problem of Supervision

## Bruce Partridge

This chapter deals with one of the key figures in work organizations – the supervisor. Many commentators have stressed the importance of the supervisor. Thus, the survey by Daley et al. (1985) seeking to account for differences in productivity between British and West German manufacturing first found no great differences on average in many areas such as direct manning levels, nor were there any significant differences in the age of machinery or in normal machine running speeds. There was a question as to whether the new machinery in British firms was as advanced or as technologically sophisticated as in German firms but the authors felt that the greater part of the productivity gap came from a lack of machine-feeding devices, frequent machine breakdowns, poor maintenance procedures, inadequate control of the quality of raw materials and similar deficiencies in basic production techniques – all of which were related to the performance of the supervisor. Echoing an earlier NEDO (1981) study, they went on to identify key differences in the role and capabilities of the supervisor with the German *Meisters* being far more technically competent than their British counterparts. The lower technical competence of those directly responsible for production in the British firms meant that machines were not used as effectively as they might be because their full capacity was not so well understood. The superior German productivity performance was also attributed to the *role* played by their *Meister*, which helped to achieve greater co-ordination, better use of equipment and tighter detailed control with relatively smaller overheads.

If supervision can be seen to be part of the productivity problem of British industry, it has also attracted considerable attention as a problem in its own right. In the USA and in Europe, as well as in Britain, the exact position and role of the supervisor in the organization and in the management hierarchy have been recognized as major organizational problems (Thurley and Wirdenius, 1973). One hundred years ago the supervisor could be typically characterized as 'the man in charge' with complete authority in the workplace. He was not only the labour contractor; he was also responsible for planning and allocating work, working methods, quality control, safety and wages (Child, 1975; Edwards, 1979; Melling, 1980; Smith, 1878). By the 1940s the growth of specialized management functions and personnel had changed the position of the supervisor. He had come to be characterized as 'the man in the middle' (Gardner and Whyte, 1945; Fletcher, 1969; Roethlisberger, 1945) caught between the opposing forces of management and the shopfloor, and torn by competing demands and loyalties. The continued development of centralized functional departments prescribing frameworks of formal procedures, as well as the growth of shopfloor bargaining which led to the development of the shop steward's role at the expense of that of the supervisor (Partridge, 1977) led to a different characterization of the latter as 'the marginal man' (Wray, 1949). The supervisor no longer occupied a position of special importance, but merely transmitted management decisions in which he played no active part. The supervisor has even been called 'the man on the outside' (Hill, 1976) with very little role to play and 'the man on the way out' with the eventual disappearance of the role being predicted (Fletcher, 1973).

The main purpose of this chapter is to clarify the task logic of the supervisor's role. For without a proper understanding of this task logic, organizations risk making inappropriate decisions about the content of the supervisor's role and about the recruitment, selection and training of supervisors. Such inappropriate decisions will add to the considerable pressures that supervisors already experience and will further reduce their capability to tackle their complex task.

The chapter begins by discussing the nature of managerial work. The second section then considers whether or not it is appropriate to consider supervisory work as managerial and in what respects it is different. The third and final section goes on to evaluate a number of possible ways in which the supervisor's role might develop and the implications for the recruitment, selection and training of supervisors.

## THE NATURE OF MANAGERIAL WORK

To understand the task logic of the supervisor's role, it is necessary to describe what management is. Here lies a major problem. Despite over 75 years of management education and research, the nature of management itself remains elusive (Stewart, 1984). The predominant approach to its understanding is the rational-bureaucratic school where the manager is seen to be a rational actor who is in charge and who can control the organization. As chapters 3 and 4 have pointed out, although Taylor (1911) introduced the science of work as a managerial function, it was Weber, Fayol and Brech who articulated the *rational* design of the administrative structure of management control. Weber (1947) emphasized that the rational-bureaucratic type of organization became predominant because it gave rise to greater control and efficiency. Control became an organizational problem as the scale of production increased, and firms integrated vertically, bringing together what were formerly small independent groups linked through the market. These combined trends created problems of co-ordination and complexity.

Fayol (1949) identified constituent functional elements of the management control process – planning, organizing, co-ordinating, commanding and controlling, and formulated a set of principles of how to organize in order to achieve control. Brech (1963) suggested that effective control required the unambiguous definition of what must be done, who is to do it and to whom each is responsible: the science of work was being extended up the management hierarchy. Firms developed methods of organization and control that were more formalized and more consciously contrived than simple personal control by the foremen: the control became more bureaucratic and embedded in the production technology and in formal systems and procedures (Edwards, 1979).

Barnard's (1938) contribution marks the beginning of the behavioural studies of management and organization. The 'human relations' approach to management suggested that control could be enhanced through person-oriented supervision rather than task-centred supervision: the emphasis for first line managers was to become leaders and motivators of the workforce. The 'human relations' school tried to resolve a control dilemma: uncertainty for management could be reduced by taking discretion away from the workforce but, as the production technology became more sophisticated and the competitive environment demanded more flexibility from the production process, management found that it was potentially more technically effective for workers to have discretion. A very effective form of collective shopfloor protest was to exercise *no* discretion at all and work to rule. The problem for management was how to control the exercise of workers' discretion so that it was exercised in a manner and direction which management desired or preferred.

It can be argued that control is less controversial if it is not so visible (Gouldner, 1954) and certainly the emphasis upon control has been played down by recent pundits of management such as Dale and Drucker (Willmott, 1984). The work of March and Simon is important in emphasizing less visible mechanisms of control as they suggest that decision-makers could be controlled not by the giving of direct orders but rather by controlling the premises of their decisions through the organization's information systems (March and Simon, 1958; Perrow, 1979).

This brief overview of the evolution of management thought emphasizes that management is concerned with control. However, this is only the objective or purpose of management, but it does not really clarify what managers do, nor does it catch the essence of the role. Studies of managers' behaviour and activities give a very different picture which challenges the premise of a rational actor in control.

Studies of managers' behaviour show a remarkable consistency – managerial work across all levels from chief executive to foreman is characterized by pace, brevity, variety and fragmentation (Burns, 1961; Carlson, 1951; Guest, 1956; Kotter, 1982; Mintzberg, 1973; Stewart, 1967). Managerial work is hectic and fragmented requiring the ability to shift continuously from relationship to relationship, from topic to topic, from problem to problem; it is far removed from the rational, academic staff image of the studied, analytical ordered pattern of a professional. The way in which managers perform their jobs looks less systematic, more informal, less reflective, less well organized and more frivolous than the above theory suggests. Yet despite the divergence of the rhetoric from the reality there is an underlying logic to the process.

One model which can be used to help explain the task logic of the manager's role is that of Mintzberg (1973). His model was initially developed to describe the activities of chief executives, but it has also been applied to the activities of middle managers (Costin, 1970; Rashid, 1986) and also of shop stewards (Partridge, 1977). Mintzberg lists ten activities or roles which managers undertake in discharging their responsibilities for the performance of a particular organizational unit. The ten activities are: *figurehead*, *leader*, *liaison*, *monitor*, *disseminator*, *spokesman*, *entrepreneur*, *disturbance-handler*, *resource-allocator*, *negotiator*. Mintzberg classifies these activities in three general categories. The first three activities are classified as 'inter-personal', the next three as 'informational' and the final four as 'decisional'.

In the *figurehead* role managers represent their unit in formal matters mainly of a symbolic or ceremonial nature; for example, the presentation of a retirement present to one of the unit's members. In the *leader* role managers guide and motivate subordinates, giving the unit direction and purpose, and seeking to integrate subordinates' individual needs and organizational goals. In the *liaison* role the manager is developing a network of reciprocating contacts outside the unit which involves the trading of favours and information. The networks are primarily horizontal between managers of equivalent task units whose work flows are interdependent.

In the *monitor* role managers seek information to develop their understanding of the unit and its environment, in particular to detect changes, to identify problems and opportunities. Managers have to develop their own information systems because the formal organization system provides historical aggregated data whereas the manager is more interested in current signals and triggers. In the *disseminator* role managers pass information inwards from the organizational environment to subordinates; this information is not just from superiors but from anywhere within the organization or indeed outside. The disseminator role is the sharing of information gathered through the monitor and liaison roles. In the *spokesman* role managers pass information from the unit up the formal authority hierarchy, speaking on behalf of the unit and its members. The manager is seen as the specialist on the unit's task.

In the *entrepreneur* role managers are initiators of change, designers of controlled change, exploiters of opportunities, with the emphasis on improvement of the unit's performance. In the *disturbance-handler* role managers respond to unexpected disturbances and crises where there is no clear programmed response with the implication that the manager rather than a subordinate has to handle it. Examples given by Mintzberg include conflicts between subordinates, conflict with other units and the potential loss of resources. In the *resource-allocator* role managers supervise the allocation of unit resources between the different sub-tasks and projects within the unit. This involves planning and scheduling, and allows for flexibility and incremental adjustment within the unit's overall budget. In the *negotiator* role the manager is involved in negotiations with superiors and other unit managers for resources.

In order to explain the task logic of the manager's role and why managers must pursue Mintzberg's ten activities, it is useful to refer to the *time span of discretion* (Gray, 1976; Jaques, 1956, 1967, 1976). A job can be divided into prescribed and discretionary elements. The prescribed elements allow the job-holder no choice; they must be carried out in the prescribed manner and subject to externally defined criteria and observable control; they are visible and tangible and are monitored by superiors. The prescribed elements correspond to role formalization. The discretionary elements, by definition and in contrast to the prescribed elements, have no prescribed method of doing them and are difficult to evaluate. The job-holder may be given specific objectives, but the means of achieving these objectives may be left unspecified and so the job-holder has some discretion or choice in how to go about achieving them. This discretion can make it difficult to monitor or evaluate the performance of the job-holder in terms of specific elements; the best that can be done is to evaluate overall performance for a given period. The discretion is not allowed to continue indefinitely, however, without being subject to a superior's review. The review period is the time span of discretion (TSD): the TSD of a job is defined as the longest period which can elapse before the superior can be sure that the job-holder has not been exercising marginally substandard discretion. TSD has been offered as a measure of the authority of a particular job – the longer the TSD the more authority and responsibility there is in the job.

The problem is that managers do not normally produce any individual tangible output from their work which makes it extremely difficult to measure performance objectively. They may well be responsible for the performance of their units, but it is almost impossible to determine the individual contribution of the manager. As Child and Partridge (1982) and Thurley and Wirdenius (1973) have pointed out, managerial roles are not well defined and are highly variable, so there is usually no basis for standardized criteria of performance; therefore it is not possible to assess managerial performance straightforwardly by reference to objective and standard measurements. Various managerial objectives have been suggested, for example POSDCORB (Gulick, 1937) (planning, organizing, staffing, directing, co-ordinating, reporting and budgeting), but as Mintzberg and others (Carlson, 1951; Kotter, 1982; Stewart, 1967) have shown, it is extremely difficult to map managers' day-to-day activities to these broad objectives: an activity may be related to more than one objective. Similarly, the systems view of organization (Katz and Kahn, 1966) emphasizes that a desired end can often be attained by different routes or there may not be a clear relationship between inputs and outcomes. If there is more than one way of achieving a desired end, managers can choose how they go about attaining their objectives; if managers cannot be evaluated in the daily activities of the role, it is difficult to judge them other than on general longer-term performance. Hence the relevance of the time span of discretion.

But the question remains as to why there is *so much* managerial discretion. Managers are formally responsible for the performance of their organizational unit, but it is not always clear what factors determine such performance. Clearly identifiable factors may be within the authority of the manager to control. Indeed, this should be so if authority and responsibility are to match according to the classical administrative principle (Fayol, 1949; Gulick, 1937). Yet it is not always possible to design managerial jobs in such a way. The complexities and the interdependencies of the work flow may make it extremely difficult to disaggregate overall system tasks into simpler discrete sub-tasks or problems (Sayles, 1964, 1979). Other units and departments support, feed, control, influence, interface and impact on the manager's own unit. Lateral relations are critical because of the system of workflows in the organization. This is the paradox of management: it is concerned with the vertical hierarchies of authority and responsibility, but the work flows horizontally through the organization making any vertical delineation of this horizontal flow somewhat arbitrary.

In short, the managerial task cannot be explicitly formalized except at a very general abstract level. Indeed, if it could be explicitly formalized, then the task could to a great extent be computerized or administered by a lower level clerk using a standard operating procedure. As it cannot be so explicitly defined, flexibility and adaptability have to be built into the system. This is not to argue that managers are needed because of imperfections in the system (Braybrooke, 1964): it is not possible to design the perfect complete system. Design is incomplete even where there are no changing environmental conditions: the internal dynamics of the organization (Katz and Kahn, 1966) may not make it worthwhile to be complete. It makes more sense for the formal system to have flexibility and adaptability built in, rather than attempt to be totally complete. Dealing with unexpected crises as well as changing circumstances in the organization's environment also requires flexibility and adaptability. Rather than struggle to design the perfect system, it is simpler and easier to allow managers to be able to adapt incrementally within the overall framework. The formal system has an informal system built into it, not one which runs counter to it but complements it. Managers are there to cover what cannot be defined or prescribed – by definition it must be discretionary and hence becomes part of the informal system of the organization. The informal system has long been acknowledged (Burns, 1961; Dalton, 1959; Stryker, 1954) but it tends to be seen as in opposition to the formal system.

This is not to suggest that managers necessarily comprehend the nature or logic of the role they must perform. Management education with its predominant emphasis on the bureaucratic rational model of management does not prepare potential managers for their roles (Whitley et al., 1981; Peters and Waterman, 1982; Stewart, 1984). Nor do organizations formally induct or socialize new recruits into the nature or logic of the managerial role. Pfeffer (1981) notes the difficulties that organizations might face if they did acknowledge the organizational politics. Changes in the norms and values of managerial culture and ideology would be involved, which would adversely affect motivation and could lead to challenges from other stakeholders of the organization. Pfeffer also points out that, because knowledge is power and power is seen as a zero-sum game, established managers are reluctant to share their insights gained from hard-won experience. Sayles (1979) and Stephenson (1985) go further and suggest that many managers retreat from the complex reality and resort to various simplistic stereotypes of the managerial role, including the Machiavellian politician, the complete bureaucrat, the sophisticated (quantitative) technician and the rejectionist cynic. New managers therefore have great difficulty in learning the task logic of their organizational role: they are neither educated nor socialized into the logic but may, if they are lucky, stumble across it in the course of their careers.

## IS THE SUPERVISOR A MANAGER?

Brown (1960) defined supervision as that component of the production job which the operator is unable to do without leaving his work station, whilst Jaques (1976) regarded the supervisor as an assistant to a full manager who performs certain delegated functions without severing the manager's direct authority over employees. Both Brown and Jaques were concerned with distinguishing the boundary between supervisory and managerial roles; both were clear that the logic of the supervisor's role was not a managerial one. The supervisor was limited to exercising discipline, making technical decisions and offering recommendations about subordinates, whereas the manager could appoint subordinates and determine their work and was accountable for their performance. Yet, when these technical decisions are examined, it emerges that the supervisor is dealing with a number of other departments such as planning and scheduling, maintenance, personnel, quality, tool-room, and industrial engineering, as well as coping with the complexities of the role outlined earlier. In short, there is no indication in the writings of Brown and Jaques about the experience at Glacier Metals of the uncertainties, complexities or the dynamics involved in the supervisor's role, and the distinction between supervisory and managerial roles appears to be arbitrary. Certainly the Glacier supervisors were not satisfied that either Brown or Jaques understood the role of the supervisor (Laner and Crossman, 1976).

Some commentators (for example, Lennerlof, 1966) have concentrated on the supervisor's formal right to make a decision. But a supervisor's authority is only partly laid down in written form in job descriptions, procedures and the like (Lennerlof, 1966). Supervisors have to rely on verbal statements from superiors and sometimes have to infer their authority from their superiors' behaviour. These cues are not without their contradictions and are open to different interpretations. Even when the formal authority system specifically denotes one individual as the decision-maker, decisions in practice are usually formed by means of a complicated ongoing interaction process. It is possible for supervisors to influence decisions for which they have no recognized authority. Abell (1975) likewise distinguishes between the formal authority to make a decision and influence over the decision and regards influence as the more significant concept. Patten (1968) argues that both influence and authority are important in understanding the supervisors' role. Child and Partridge (1982: 43) found that supervisors' authority and influence were highly correlated.

It is also not surprising that attempts to evaluate supervisory performance have run into the same difficulties as attempts to evaluate managerial performance (Bates and Hosking, 1977; Child and Partridge, 1982; Rodger, 1965; Thurley and Wirdenius, 1973). Supervisors do not normally produce any tangible output which can be identified, let alone measured; their roles appear to be ill-defined and variable, and so do not offer a secure foundation upon which to base any standardized criteria of performance. Their role depends upon co-operation with and from others and upon the quality of the organizational policies and procedures within which they have to operate (Bates and Hosking, 1977). Thurley and Wirdenius (1973) cast grave doubt on whether there is any real purpose in attempting to measure supervisory effectiveness.

In what ways is the supervisor's role different from that of other managers? One clear distinction is that, unlike other manages, supervisors have non-managerial subordinates. One of the pressures outlined above was that managerial subordinates have discretion: their superiors are dependent upon them for the achievement of their responsibilities, but do not necessarily have effective control over them. On the face of it, the supervisor's role should be somewhat easier given the deskilling of the shopfloor and the removal of discretion from the shopfloor highlighted by Braverman (1974). Penn (1982), however, gives examples from the engineering and textile industries where the shopfloor have been able to resist deskilling and retain discretion by maintaining exclusive access to the production technology by excluding management from the utilization and operation of the machinery. Penn, and also Jones (1982) and Sethi et al. (1984), indicate that technological innovations have created new opportunities for new skills, and new opportunities for workers to regain discretion. It is the shopfloor operators of new technology who have the most experience and familiarity with the new technology, far more so than management and are therefore able to exploit the opportunities to enhance their own discretion (Yankelovich and Immerwahr, 1983). Detailed case studies have documented the continued existence of discretion on the shopfloor even without new technology (Crozier, 1964; Roy, 1954).

The Birmingham supervisors in the Child and Partridge (1982: 92) study felt that they were under pressure, that they were caught in the middle, that the shopfloor could exert pressure which suggests that the shopfloor still has a major amount of discretion. Fifty-six per cent of these supervisors agreed that supervisors in their own firm were pushed about from above and below at the same time. The supervisors were prepared to *trade* with their workers: for example, when there was insufficient work for employees within a given section, the formal policy was for the spare employees to be moved temporarily to other sections that were short of labour, but employees resented this policy and so supervisors would often attempt to find work in order to avoid having people moved out of their section. Some supervisors attempted to maintain their own discretion for trading with the shopfloor.

Being caught in the middle indicates pressure from above, which raises questions about the discretion supervisors have in dealings with their superiors. Management is not a unitary body. Child and Partridge (1982: 92) reported that 49 per cent of the supervisors in their study experienced receiving conflicting instructions from different sections of management. Production planning instructions could be at variance with the type or quantity of materials that storekeepers were able to release; if there were more than one customer service department, there might be conflicting demands for priority of output for goods, especially if there was a shortage of labour or a breakdown, and there were also the perennial problems of balancing output against quality, maintenance and safety. The supervisor has to absorb these conflicts on behalf of the section, and to decide which demands to satisfy in which order and then to pass this on to the section; that is, the supervisor is there to protect the operators from external conflicts, to interpret them, translate them and simplify them into schedules and directives. In this type of situation, of course, whatever the supervisor does is 'wrong' because it is impossible to satisfy incompatible expectations. But the supervisor can choose how to respond to the conflicting role expectations by activating different role priorities (Pugh, 1966). The supervisor also has scope for discretion, and can play one management party off against another.

Studies of supervisory authority have been broadly consistent. The NIIP (1951) found that supervisors had considerable authority over the volumes of production, quality, general discipline and allocation of overtime, but that they had negligible authority over design or alteration to design, purchasing materials or tools, costing and fixing or altering rates of payment. The BIM (1976) found that supervisors had some authority over safety, quality, materials handling, allocating jobs, discipline and grievance handling, but that supervisors had little authority over production scheduling, the introduction of new working methods, maintenance of plant and equipment, cost control, or recruiting and promoting of employees. Child and Partridge (1982) found that supervisors had considerable authority over job allocation, requisitioning sundries, overtime, discipline, dealing with wage queries, and repair of equipment, but little or no authority in deciding whether new work was to come into the section, determining manning levels, promoting employees, specifying or purchasing new equipment or in vetting new recruits. From these studies, supervisory authority looks very limited, but this should not be surprising as the supervisor is near the bottom of the authority hierarchy.

Moreover, studies caution against dismissing the responsibilities performed by supervisors. Boyd and Scanlon (1965) and Sasser and Leonard (1980) suggest that supervisors' responsibilities are still significant and that they may even have increased in recent years, whilst the NIIP (1957) suggest that, although specialist departments and formal systems may have absorbed some traditional supervisory functions, management still depends upon the co-operation of the supervisor at the point of operation for both the provision of adequate information and for the effective co-ordination and performance of these functions. Child and Partridge (1982) report that supervisors perceived that their burden of responsibility had increased in recent years:

> The job used to be one of just disciplining the men, now there are a whole host of extra responsibilities which the supervisor carries. I don't mind the extra responsibility as it makes the job more interesting. (p. 46)

Much of the problem of supervision stems from the fact that the organizational task logic of the role is barely understood (Page, 1977). This uncertainty about the appropriate role of supervisors derives from the way in which a clearly recognizable occupational position (Thurley and Wirdenius, 1973) has over the years become submerged within the evolving idiosyncratic organizational structures of different firms. The role has not developed in a systematic, consistent or even logical manner, but has shrunk randomly and inconsistently (Child and Partridge, 1982; Thurley and Wirdenius, 1973). Functions and responsibilities have been taken away from the supervisor in a piecemeal and *ad hoc* fashion. The 'scientific management' school challenged the traditional role of supervision and argued for its breakdown into its component parts, into 'functional foremanship' (Taylor, 1911); traditional supervisory activities such as selection, production scheduling, quality control, and costing were taken away from the supervisor, becoming the responsibility of new functional departments with 'scientific' procedures under the charge of appropriately qualified staff personnel. A separate development in Britain was the introduction of personnel departments to reform and restrict what was perceived to be the abuse and arbitrariness of supervisory power over workers (Child, 1969). Indeed the supervisor was often singled out as the culprit for much of the contemporary industrial unrest and hostility to the employers.

These developments were further encouraged by the growth in scale and complexity of manufacturing firms which strengthened the arguments in favour of reallocating activities previously under the supervisor's control to specialist experts (Melling, 1980). At the same time, the application of new management methods often associated with updated technology had a significant impact on the supervisor's role. Management control became embedded in the technology itself, with work becoming machine-paced rather than under the direct control of the supervisor, giving rise to 'technical control' (Edwards, 1979). The supervisor's role also suffered from the encroachments of 'bureaucratic control' where the supervisor's formal autonomy has been curtailed by company policies and procedures covering such areas of shopfloor work as job design, promotion, performance evaluation and rewards systems. Functions and responsibilities have been taken away from the supervisor and those that remain severely constrained by bureaucratic systems and procedures.

The supervisor's role has not so much been designed as evolved by accident in the sense that supervisors' responsibilities are precisely those which have not been formalized, proceduralized or taken over by a specialist function. In other words, the supervisor's role can be seen as an historic relic, comprising those bits and pieces which have been left behind or which cannot be found a home elsewhere.

Yet, as the supervisors' role shrinks, it cannot be said that it is better understood, particularly by supervisors' superiors. A review of managerial roles in the USA concluded that the largest gap in the organizational hierarchy lay between the first line supervisors and their immediate superior (Nealey and Fiedler, 1968). A study of British supervisors (Child and Partridge, 1982) similarly found evidence of considerable disagreement between individual supervisors and their own managers about supervisors' authority and influence, and doubted whether the supervisor's own manager fully understood the pressures and conflict that their supervisors had to cope with and had at best only a distant understanding of what their supervisors actually did. Managers inhabited an orderly paper world of plans, targets and variances which the supervisors struggled to turn into some semblance of reality.

This situation is partly caused and exacerbated by the closing down of promotion opportunities from supervision into management so that fewer production managers have first line experience. The danger is increased that managers will make decisions about the supervisor's role without fully understanding the implications for the role; the most likely outcome is that supervisors will tend to withdraw from their work roles either because of conflicting role pressures or because of the development of a bureaucratic role (Thurley and Wirdenius, 1973). 'If on the basis of a poor understanding of the part supervisors are playing, management were to set out to develop supervisors' roles formally into a reflection of their own, this would run the risk of leaving a vacuum in which the necessary degree of informal interpretive flexibility for handling contingencies and disturbances could go by default' (Child and Partridge, 1982: 199). The uniqueness of the supervisors' position is that they are located at the interface of the management control system and the shopfloor: they are the ones who have to translate plans and policies into action.

Without a proper understanding of the logic of this organizational role, management not only risks making inappropriate decisions about the content of the role, they also run the risk of making inappropriate decisions about the recruitment, selection and training of supervisors, which will increase the role pressures on the supervisors as they struggle to make some sense of the inconsistencies and reduce their capability to tackle their role.

## WHAT OF THE FUTURE?

There have been suggestions that increasing automation will make the supervisor's role redundant (Crossman, 1960; Leavitt and Whisler, 1958) as control systems become more incorporated into the technology (Edwards, 1979). Responsibility for routine supervisory tasks, it is argued, will be given to the workgroups which will have the freedom to elect their own leaders, who will carry responsibility *vis-à-vis* management for arranging the groups' internal organization, allocation of work and people to jobs or equipment, and even possibly inspection and routine maintenance. The immediate benefits include economy in management resources and improvement of vertical communication by abolishing one level in the hierarchy. An additional benefit is the potential contribution to the social goals of improving the quality of working life and enhancing democracy at shopfloor level.

In practice, however, the attempt to abolish the role of supervisors altogether has run into considerable difficulties suggesting that supervisors perform a greater range of indispensable services than management had realized (Swedish Employers' Confederation, 1975). A review (Schlesinger and Walton, 1976) of work restructuring programmes in the USA also concludes that a particularly troublesome problem was the appropriate reformulation of the first line supervisory role. Moreover, the logic of the role, particularly highlighted by the new demands on production, suggests that whereas tiers of middle managers might be made redundant, the supervisor cannot be as that is the role by definition which is at the interface of the task and the control systems, and the role will therefore become *more* important (Zalewski, 1966).

The evidence suggests that supervisors can serve either as important catalysts for change or as a focus of resistance to change (Weir and Mills, 1973). In the past, part of the supervision problem has been associated with the low status of the production function within management (Lockyer, 1976; Nicholson, 1976), but its importance is now, albeit belatedly, being recognized (Abernathy et al., 1983; Hayes and Wheelwright, 1984; Skinner, 1985; Little, 1985) due to the competitive advantage that West German and Japanese firms have in manufacturing. Competition has not just changed the status of production management, it has also changed the very objectives of the process. Traditionally, production management has been concerned with the efficient utilization of a given technology: once the production system had been implemented, the primary concern was to ensure that it did not drift out of control in terms of cost and quality. But under the leadership of Japan and Germany the emphasis is now changing. Production management has to keep on *improving* performance: costs have to be reduced in line with the experience curve; quality and reliability have to be improved beyond the level of just acceptable quality; the production system must be able to handle a greater heterogeneity of products; and break-even levels have to be reduced together with set-up costs and inventory levels (Abernathy et al., 1983; Hayes and Wheelwright, 1984; Ohmae, 1983; Peters and Waterman, 1982; Sethi et al., 1984).

Manufacturing is also being recognized as a major element of competitive strategy after having been neglected for so long (Skinner, 1985). Increasingly, there are demands for flexibility, adaptability and innovation (Jelinek and Goldhar, 1984) in which the supervisor has a crucial role to play. In many organizations, for the foreseeable future, manufacturing will require more troubleshooters, more training specialists and more preventive maintenance, which will mean enhancing the supervisors' role, not downgrading it (Little,1985). Sasser and Leonard (1980) report one company's attitude: 'our supervisors can probably have more influence on our productivity, quality, etc. ... than any other group in the company.' Similarly, new forms of work organization, coupled with many of the developments in personnel practice discussed in other chapters, have added considerably to the list of jobs and responsibilities of the supervisor – section or team leader, cross-trade supervisor, the supervisor as quality circle leader, the supervisor as communicator and counsellor (Ferdows and de Meyer, 1984; IDS Study 386, 1987).

Given the recognized leadership of Japan and West Germany in manufacturing management, what can be learnt from them about the role of the supervisor? In Germany the *Meister* is expected to be familiar with every detail of the section's work, as well as to liaise with other departments; the emphasis is on showing others how to do the work better (Fores et al., 1978). The *Meister* also has the responsibility for training his workgroup; indeed, the *Meister* is the only one with formal authority to train workers on the job. Part of the difference between German and British supervisors is that the *Meister* is clearly a first line manager who can and is expected to make decisions which in Britain may well be the prerogative of staff specialists: German firms have lower proportions of staff personnel compared to British firms (Maurice et al., 1980). The *Meister* is also far more technically qualified than the British supervisor: he will have completed an apprenticeship, had years of experience as a skilled worker, and taken an appropriate course with sets of formal examinations (Lawrence, 1980). The *Meister* is seen as a powerful position with authority deriving from technical competence and from the fact that he alone knows what is going on (Fores et al., 1978).

In Japan, as in Germany, supervisors have a position of considerable status (Hayes and Wheelwright, 1984): most have at least ten years' experience and a proven reputation as an excellent worker before being promoted. The supervisor benefits from having direct access to high levels in the production hierarchy, and from having job responsibilities defined very broadly. In both Japan and Germany, organizations devote far more effort to developing the technical skills of their workforce, including supervisors, to improve the skill base continually, which contrasts with the traditional process of deskilling in the US and Britain.

In Sweden supervisors have become increasingly and actively involved in the introduction of new working methods and work organization. The supervisory role that is evolving in Sweden is based on the following assumptions (Swedish Employers Confederation, 1975): (1) that employees and workgroups will always need a leader; (2) that supervisors will have to meet new demands as production situations develop; (3) that groups of production workers will increasingly handle 'fire-fighting' problems which will relieve supervisors of routine tasks; (4) that supervisors will have to learn to consult with workers and to handle co-ordination between workgroups; and (5) that supervisors must be given the scope and backing to perform in this way by top management, including appropriate development and training. Supervisors in Sweden have become increasingly involved in complex technical problems regarding processes, methods and equipment; their experience and practical knowledge have made it possible for them to help make significant improvements in such areas (Swedish Employers' Confederation, 1975).

In contrast, in Britain there has been a tendency for supervisors to concentrate on the personnel and human-relations aspects of the role rather than the task content (Child and Partridge, 1982). This is partly a reflection of the prevailing management ethos (Child, 1969; Mant, 1979) but it is also a reflection of the recruitment and training processes: supervisors generally do not have skilled backgrounds and neither do they have much technical training once recruited. A leadership reorientation may be necessary for British supervisors when it is realized that employees have discretion and that trading and trust are necessary facets of any managerial role, including that of the supervisor (Breton and Wintrobe, 1982). The leadership dimension of supervision has traditionally received a great deal of attention but with the emphasis on the 'consideration' or employee-centred aspects of leadership, whereas the German and Japanese supervisors seem to be more concerned with the task-centred aspects and 'initiating structure'.

Caution is needed before simply transferring management practices and policies between different societies and cultures (Sethi et al., 1984). However, the evidence from Germany, Japan and Sweden suggests that there are two main ways forward. The first is to *develop into a first line managerial role*. This involves a transformation from first line supervision to first line management, such that they can control or at least influence the major parameters of their sections, such as the selection and training of their subordinates, working on technical improvements and having a greater share in the determination of work methods, layouts and choices of equipment. This model moves the supervisor closer to the German *Meister* (Fores et al., 1978; Lawrence, 1980). The greater decentralization of authority and responsibility in this model could be more economical in staff roles – German firms have lower proportions of staff personnel than British firms (Maurice et al., 1980).

The second way is to *develop into a technical role*. This can involve either the supervision of craft skills such as in maintenance work or in craft production, or the supervision of technical and scientific areas of work. The role can thus be defined either occupationally or professionally. Either variant of this role requires expert knowledge of a technical or craft nature which is unlikely to be available to superiors, and as such would be relatively impervious to organizational rules of a bureaucratic kind.

The question arises of whether the supervisors are ready, willing and able to play a managerial role and fulfil the logic of their role. The motivation of supervisors does not seem to be a problem; Bates and Hosking (1977) report that it is the *task content* of the role that attracts supervisors to the job, whilst Child and Partridge (1982) argue that the problem of supervision is not the task content, but the status of the supervisor; in other words, supervisor dissatisfaction is focused on the status, not the task content, of the role. More importantly, profiles of supervisors (Bates and Hosking, 1977; BIM, 1976; Child and Partridge, 1982; Government Social Survey, 1968; IPM, 1975; NIIP, 1951) all raise fundamental questions about the lack of educational qualifications, both school-leaving and technical qualifications, and the lack of training on the job, although the majority of supervisors feel that such qualifications are not necessary (Bates and Hosking, 1977) or that they consider personal qualities and experience to be of greater importance in carrying out the role (Child and Partridge, 1982).

The logic of the role has major implications for the recruitment and selection of supervisors as well as their training. The traditional approach to supervisory recruitment and training has been to disaggregate the role down into its constituent tasks, subtasks and activities (Brech, 1963) in order to emphasize the skills or attributes required to perform each constituent element. The result of such an approach has been to produce extensive if not exhaustive lists of attributes and skills that a supervisor is presumed to need (George, 1979; Sartain and Baker, 1972). The approach has two major weaknesses: the lists are too exhaustive and demanding – it is virtually impossible to recruit and/or train such perfect specimens; they also divert attention from the logic of the role. Certainly supervisors have not been generally enthusiastic about the training they have been given under this approach (Bates and Hosking, 1977).

The focus on recruitment and training should be holistic, looking at the whole role and not just the constituent elements within the role. A primary objective of management is to *improve* the technical processes of production; this suggests that supervisors would benefit from having technical expertise and detailed understanding of the technology. This in turn implies that management should try to increase recruitment from amongst skilled workers and to provide for more technical training for existing supervisors. There is now at least a belated recognition in Britain of the benefits to be gained from having technically more qualified supervisors (Daly et al., 1985; NEDO, 1981) and a scheme is being considered for joint certification of engineering supervisors by the Engineering Industry Training Board and the City and Guilds of London Institute. The North-East London Polytechnic has launched a four-year course in manufacturing studies with the aim of producing foremen who will have the opportunity to rise rapidly through line management. The Staff College at Henley has recently introduced a special programme for supervisors based on the *Meister* model in Germany. Several major companies, including Ford, Gallager, British Bakeries, Glaxo and MEL (Philips) have also sought to introduce major changes in the way supervisors are selected and developed (Shepherd, 1980; IRRR, 1984; IDS, Study 386, 1987). However, even in companies who are strongly supporting supervisory training (Shepherd, 1980) there remains a strong tendency both to recruit supervisors on the basis of personal characteristics rather than technical background, and to emphasize recruitment from amongst manual workers.

To sum up, then, the logic of the role requires the supervisor to be able to handle complexities, conflicts, ambiguities and uncertainties. This cannot be handled solely through training: training will only be effective if the appropriate attributes are there to begin with, which emphasizes the need for careful recruitment and selection. The fact that promotion channels are being blocked to supervisors (Child and Partridge, 1982) means that fewer line managers above the level of the first line supervisor have had first line experience which, in turn, means that senior managers are becoming increasingly dependent upon the supervisors as the only managers to have had practical experience with the production technology. This increases the urgency for management to recognize the organizational task logic of the supervisor's role and to act on it; otherwise there is the prospect that production performance in Britain will continue to lag behind that of competitor countries.

# Bibliography

Abell, P. 1975. 'Organizations as Bargaining and Influence Systems: Measuring Intra-Organizational Power and Influence'. *Organizations as Bargaining and Influence Systems.* Ed. Abell, P. London: Heinemann, 10–40.

Abernathy, W.J., Clark, K.B. and Kantrow, A.M. 1983. *Industrial Renaissance.* New York: Basic Books.

Barnard, C. 1938. *The Functions of the Executive.* Cambridge, MA: Harvard University Press.

Bates, D. and Hosking, D. 1977. *Factors which Influence the Success of Supervisory Training.* Watford: Engineering Industry Training Board.

Boyd, B.B. and Scanlon, B. 1965. 'Developing Tomorrow's Foremen'. *Training Directors' Journal,* 19: 44–5.

Braverman, H. 1974. *Labor and Monopoly Capital.* New York: Monthly Review Press.

Braybrooke, D. 1964. 'The Mystery of Executive Success Re-examined'. *Administrative Science Quarterly,* 8: 533–60.

Brech, E.F.L. 1963. *The Principles and Practice of Management.* 2nd edn. London: Longman.

Breton, A. and Wintrobe, R. 1982. *The Logic of Bureaucratic Conduct.* Cambridge: Cambridge University Press.

British Institute of Management (BIM). 1976. *Front Line Management.* London: BIM.

Brown, W. 1960. *Explorations in Management.* London: Heinemann.

Burns, T. 1961. 'Micropolitics: Mechanisms of Institutional Change'. *Administrative Science Quarterly,* 6: 257–81.

Carlson, S. 1951. *Executive Behaviour: A Study of the Work Load and the Working Methods of Managing Directors.* Stockholm: Strombergs.

Child, J. 1969. *British Management Thought.* London: Allen & Unwin.

—— 1975. 'The Industrial Supervisor'. *People and Work.* Ed. Esland, G., Salaman, G. and Speakman, M.A. Edinburgh: Holmes McDougall, 70–87.

—— and Partridge, B.E. 1982. *Lost Managers.* Cambridge: Cambridge University Press.

Costin, A.A. 1970. 'Management Profiles in Business and Government'. MBA dissertation, McGill University, Montreal. Cited in Mintzberg, H. 1973. *The Nature of Managerial Work.* New York: Harper & Row.

Crossman, E.R.F.W. 1960. *Automation and Skill.* London: HMSO.

Crozier, M. 1964. *The Bureaucratic Phenomenon.* Chicago: Chicago University Press.

Dalton, M. 1959. *Men Who Manage.* New York: Wiley.

Daly, A., Hitchens, D.M.W.N. and Wagner, K. 1985. 'Productivity, Machinery and Skills in a Sample of British and German Manufacturing Plants'. *National Institute Economic Review,* February, 48–61.

Edwards, R. 1979. *Contested Terrain: The Transformation of the Workplace in the Twentieth Century.* London: Heinemann.

Fayol, H. 1949. *General and Industrial Management.* London: Pitman.

Ferdows, K. and de Meyer, A. 1984. *The State of Large Manufacturers in Europe.* Fontainebleau: INSEAD.

Fletcher, C. 1969. 'Men in the Middle: A Reformulation of the Thesis'. *Sociological Review*, 17: 3, 341–54.

—— 1973. 'The End of Management'. *Man and Organization.* Ed. Child, J. London: Allen & Unwin, 135–57.

Fores, M., Lawrence, P. and Sorge, A. 1978. 'Germany's Front Line Force'. *Management Today*, March, 86–9, 158.

Gardner, B.B. and Whyte, W.H. 1945. 'The Man in the Middle: Position and Problems of the Foreman'. *Applied Anthropology*, 4: 1–28.

George, C.S. 1979. *Supervision in Action.* Reston, VA.: Reston.

Gouldner, A. 1954. *Patterns of Industrial Bureaucracy.* New York: Free Press.

Government Social Survey. 1968. *Workplace Industrial Relations.* London: HMSO.

Gray, J. 1976. *The Glacier Project: Concepts and Critiques.* London: Heinemann.

Guest, R.H. 1956. 'Of Time and the Foreman'. *Personnel*, 32: 478–86.

Gulick, L.H. 1937. 'Notes on the Theory of Organization'. *Papers on the Science of Administration.* Ed. Gulick, L.H. and Urwick, L.F. New York: Columbia University Press.

Hayes, R. and Wheelwright, S. 1984. *Restoring our Competitive Edge.* New York: Wiley.

Hill, S. 1976. *The Dockers: Class and Tradition in London.* London: Heinemann.

Incomes Data Services (IDS). 1987. *Supervisors of Manual Workers.* Study No. 386. London; IDS.

*Industrial Relations Review and Report* (IRRR). 1984. 'Training for Change at Gallaher – The Role of the Supervisor'. 333: December, 9–12.

Institute of Personnel Management (IPM). 1975. *Profile of a Supervisor.* London: IPM.

Jaques, E. 1956. *Measurement of Responsibility.* London: Tavistock.

—— 1967. *Equitable Payment.* Harmondsworth: Penguin.

—— 1976. *A General Theory of Bureaucracy.* London: Heinemann.

Jelinek, M. and Goldhar, J. 1984. 'The Strategic Implications of the Factory of the Future'. *Sloan Management Review*, Summer, 29–37.

Jones, B. 1982. 'Destruction or Redistribution of Engineering Skills? The Case of Numerical Control'. *The Degradation of Work? Skill, Deskilling and the Labour Process.* Ed. Wood, S. London: Hutchinson, 179–200.

Katz, D. and Kahn, R. 1966. *Social Psychology of Organizations.* New York: Wiley.

Kotter, J.P. 1982. *The General Managers.* New York: Free Press.

Laner, S. and Crossman, E.R.F.W. 1976. 'The Current Status of the Jaquesian Time-Span of Discretion Concept'. *The Glacier Project: Concepts and Critiques.* Ed. Gray, J. London: Heinemann.

Lawrence, P. 1980. *Managers and Management in West Germany.* London: Croom Helm.

Leavitt, H.J. and Whisler, T.L. 1958. 'Management in the 1980's'. *Harvard Business Review*, 36: 6, 41–8.

Lennerlof, L. 1966. *Dimensions of Supervision.* Stockholm: Swedish Council for Personnel Administration.

Little, A.D. 1985. *The Strategic Benefits of Computer-Integrated Manufacturing.* Cambridge, MA: Arthur D. Little.

Lockyer, K. 1976. 'The British Production Cinderella: 2 – Effects'. *Management Today*, June, 70–1.

Mant, A. 1979. *The Rise and Fall of the British Manager.* London: Pan.

March, J.G. and Simon, H.A. 1958. *Organizations.* New York: Wiley.

Maurice, M., Sorge, A. and Warner, M. 1980. 'Societal Differences in Organizing Manufacturing Units: A Comparison of France, West Germany and Great Britain'. *Organization Studies*, 1: 59–86.

Melling, J. 1980. '"Non-Commissioned Officers": British Employers and their Supervisory Workers'. *Social History*, 5: May, 183–221.

Mintzberg, H. 1973. *The Nature of Managerial Work.* New York: Harper & Row.

National Economic Development Office (NEDO). Gauge and Tool Sector Working Party. 1891. *Toolmaking: A Comparison of UK and West German Companies.* London: NEDO.

National Institute of Industrial Psychology (NIIP). 1951. *The Foreman.* London: Staples.

—— 1957. *The Place of the Foreman in Management.* London: Staples.

Nealy, S.M. and Fiedler, F.E. 1968. 'Leadership Functions of Middle Managers'. *Psychological Bulletin*, 70: 5, 313–29.

Nicholson, T.A.J. 1976. 'The British Production Cinderella: 1 – Causes'. *Management Today*, June, 66–9.

Ohmae, K. 1983. *The Mind of the Strategist.* Harmondsworth: Penguin.

Page, M. 1977. 'The Supervisor: An Endangered Species'. *Works Management*, July, 74—6.

Partridge, B.E. 1977. 'Activities of Shop Stewards'. *Industrial Relations Journal*, 8: 4, 28–42.

Patten, T.H. 1968. 'The Authority and Responsibilities of Supervisors in a Multi-Plant Firm'. *Journal of Management Studies*, 5: 61–82.

Penn, R. 1982. 'Skilled Manual Workers in the Labour Process, 1856–1964'. *The Degradation of Work: Skill, Deskilling and the Labour Process.* Ed. Wood, S. London: Hutchinson, 90–108.

Perrow, C. 1979. *Complex Organizations.* 2nd edn. Glenview, IL.: Scott, Foresman.

Peters, T. and Waterman, R.H. Jr. 1982. *In Search of Excellence.* New York: Harper & Row.

Pfeffer, J. 1981. *Power in Organizations.* Boston, MA: Pitman.

Pugh, D. 1966. 'Role Activation Conflict: A Study of Industrial Inspection'. *American Sociological Review*, 31: 6, 835–42.

Rashid, S. 1986. 'An Activity Analysis of Unit General Managers'. MA dissertation, Nuffield Centre for Health Studies, University of Leeds.

Rodger, A. 1965. 'The Criterion Problem in Selection and Guidance: Part 1'. *Occupational Psychology*, 39: 77–82.

Roethlisberger, F.J. 1945. 'The Foreman: Master and Victim of Double Talk'. *Harvard Business Review*, 23: 283–98.

Roy, D. 1954. 'Efficiency and "The Fix": Informal Intergroup Relations in a Piecework Machine Shop'. *American Journal of Sociology*, 60: November, 255–66.

Sartain, A.Q. and Baker, A.W. 1972. *The Supervisor and His Job.* New York: McGraw-Hill.

Sasser, W.E. and Leonard, F. 1980. 'Let First Level Supervisors Do Their Jobs'. *Harvard Business Review*, 58: 2, 113–21.

Sayles, L.R. 1964. *Managerial Behavior.* New York: McGraw-Hill.

—— 1979. *Leadership.* New York: McGraw-Hill.

Schlesinger, L.A. and Walton, R.E. 1976. 'Work Restructuring in Unionized Organizations: Risks, Opportunities and Impact on Collective Bargaining'. Industrial Relations Research Association. *Proceedings of the Twenty-Ninth Annual Winter Meeting.* Eds. Stern, J. and Dennis, B. Madison, WI.: IRRA, 345–51.

Sethi, S.P., Namiki, N. and Swanson, C.L. 1984. *The False Promise of the Japanese Miracle.* Boston, MA: Pitman.

Shepherd, R. 1980. 'Off the Line into Management: An Exercise in Selection and Training'. *Personnel Management*, December, 20–4.

Skinner, W. 1985. *Manufacturing: The Formidable Competitive Weapon.* New York: Wiley.

Smith, F. 1878. *Workshop Management: A Manual for Masters and Men.* London: Wyman.

Stephenson, T.E. 1985. *Management: A Political Activity.* London: Macmillan.

Stewart, R. 1967. *Managers and Their Jobs.* London: Macmillan.

—— 1984. 'The Nature of Management? A Problem for Management Education'. *Journal of Management Studies*, 21: 3, 323–30.

Stryker, P. 1954. *A Guide to Modern Management Methods.* New York: McGraw-Hill.

Swedish Employers Confederation (SEC). 1975. *Job Reform in Sweden.* Stockholm: SEC.

Taylor, F.W. 1911. *The Principles of Scientific Management.* New York: Harper & Row.

Thurley, K.E. and Wirdenius, H. 1973. *Supervision: A Reappraisal.* London: Heinemann.

Weber, M. 1947. *The Theory of Social and Economic Organization.* Tr. Henderson, A.M. and Parsons, T. New York: Free Press.

Weir, D. and Mills, S. 1973. 'The Supervisor as a Change Catalyst'. *Industrial Relations Journal*, 4: 4, 61–9.

Whitley, R., Thomas, A. and Marceau, J. 1981. *Masters of Business? Business Schools and Business Graduates in Britain and France.* London: Tavistock.

Willmott, H. 1984. 'Images and Ideals of Managerial Work'. *Journal of Management Studies*, 21: 3, 349–68.

Wray, D.E. 1949. 'Marginal Men of Industry: The Foremen'. *American Journal of Sociology*, 54: 4, 298–301.

Yankelovich, D. and Immerwahr, J. 1983. *Putting the Work Ethic to Work.* New York: The Public Agenda Foundation.

Zalewski, A. 1966. 'The Influence of Automation on Management'. *Employment Problems of Automation and Advanced Technology.* Ed. Steiber, J. New York: Macmillan.

# 10 Management Development

*Philip Sadler*

The term 'development' is used here to describe a range of processes and experiences including formal education and training courses, whether in-company or provided by external institutions; training on the job; and activities such as project work, secondment and job rotation. The field which is covered excludes undergraduate courses in management and business studies, but embraces all developmental activities at postgraduate or post-experience level. 'Management' is used to denote a wide range of activities concerned with achieving results through people in organizations in both public and private sectors and embraces directors, senior, middle and junior managers as well as both general managers and the managers of specialist functions.

The chapter begins with an account of the emergence and growth of management development activities in the post-Second World War period. The next section deals with the principal methods of management development. A third section assesses the current state of thinking about management development and the chapter concludes by looking at the development of managers for the future.

## THE ORIGINS AND GROWTH OF MANAGEMENT DEVELOPMENT IN BRITAIN

Formal management development hardly existed in Britain before the Second World War, apart from courses leading to the qualifications of professional bodies. This is in sharp contrast to the USA where, beginning with the Wharton School at Pennsylvania University, approximately 20 business schools were established between 1881 and 1910 and a further 180 by 1930. A few companies ran short internal courses, but there were virtually none designed specifically for managers by educational institutions. The main exceptions were the technical colleges that ran courses leading to the examinations of the Institute of Industrial Administration; the Regent Street Polytechnic, which offered part-time courses for managers; while the Manchester College of Science and Technology and the London School of Economics both began to offer full-time postgraduate courses for managers in the 1930s. There were, in addition, undergraduate courses in commerce, business or industrial economics, the first of which was pioneered by Birmingham University at the turn of the century.

*Early Initiatives*

Interest in management development grew, albeit slowly, in the years following the Second World War. An attitudinal climate had grown up during the war, which accorded a new respect to 'scientific' management. This received additional emphasis as family firms increasingly gave way to professionally managed concerns and as the post-war drive for increased productivity got under way. At the same time the expansion of higher education meant an increased supply of graduate recruits for industry, which led to the growth of graduate-entry training schemes for potential managers. This in turn led to the growth of in-company courses. By 1960, according to the Rose Report (Rose, 1970) at least 400 largish companies ran management courses and about 50 of these had their own residential centres.

Another early post-war initiative was the Urwick Report (1947) which established a National Scheme of Management Studies for the commercial and technical colleges. This scheme was jointly sponsored by the then Ministry of Education and the British Institute of Management and was launched in 1949. It provided for part-time courses leading to a Diploma and those who were successful in the examinations were admitted to Graduate Membership of the BIM. By 1960 these courses were being offered in over 60 colleges and had about 1,000 students enrolled. In 1961 this scheme was replaced by the Diploma in Management Studies (Committee for the Diploma in Management Studies, 1968). Today the DMS is administered by the Council for National Academic Awards. The course is offered at all polytechnics and at some colleges of higher education. Many colleges offer specialized versions of the Diploma to meet the needs of particular industries in subjects ranging from Agriculture to Transport and Physical Distribution and from Local Government to the Distributive Trades.

A third development in this early post-war period was the growth of independent management centres devoted to the development of middle and senior managers. In 1947 the Administrative Staff College (now the Management College) at Henley was founded and, in 1959, Ashridge Management College. Consultancy-based centres such as the Urwick Management Centre (Urwick, Orr and Partners) and the Sundridge Park Management Centre (PA Consulting) were also established during this period. By 1960 some 30 independent centres of various kinds had come into existence and were offering a wide variety of courses.

Further impetus was given by the Industrial Training Boards established by the Industrial Training Act of 1964 (Lynch, 1970). Although the policies and practices adopted by the individual boards varied considerably, almost all gave grants for management training and development, many published detailed recommendations on the subject and some actually provided training courses.

The contribution of the boards was especially valuable in three areas. First, and most important, they encouraged the analysis of training needs, the preparation of job descriptions and job specifications for management development advisers, and the introduction of appraisal systems. Second, they sponsored a considerable amount of industry-specific activity, which had the advantage of bringing managers together from different organizations, while ensuring that the content was relevant to the participants. Among the boards that carried out pioneering work in this field were those in the shipbuilding and electricity supply industries. Third, by means of grants, the direct provision of courses and, perhaps most importantly, specialist advice and guidance, the boards were able to make a significant impact on the amount and quality of management development being carried out in small businesses. This work was particularly important in distribution and in the construction and foundry industries where small firms are prevalent.

*The Coming of the Business Schools*

Although management education was coming to be accepted as playing an important part in the development of experienced managers, the idea of the business graduate was slower to take root. For example, in the first of two highly influential reports dealing with management development published in the 1960s, the NEDC (1963) stated that in the past there had been too wide a gap between further education and the practical life of industry. There was also a shortage of case material and of fundamental research into the organization and management of people. There was difficulty finding qualified teachers (see also NEDC, 1963; 1972a, b). It was pointed out that in the US there were a number of business schools providing undergraduate and graduate courses, and that graduates from these schools had a more professional attitude to management than many British managers and were much sought after by business in the USA. The report concluded that there was a need in Britain for at least one very high level new school or institute on the lines of the Harvard Business School or the School of Industrial Management at the Massachusetts Institute of Technology.

The subsequent expansion of university-level management education in this country stemmed largely from the recommendations of the Franks Report published in the same year (Franks, 1963). After establishing that there were four great centres of industry and commerce (London, the Midlands, the North West and central Scotland) which he identified as 'natural growth points for business schools', Franks recommended the establishment of two schools within the university complexes of London and Manchester. Two rather than one, because no single institution could fully develop all aspects of certain subjects and two rather than more 'because qualified staff and finance' were limited. Lord Franks emphasized that these new high quality business schools should not displace the work already going on in other universities and colleges but that rather they must be complemented by an extension and greater concentration of present activities.

The Franks Report was accepted by industry, the academic world and the government. To put his recommendations into effect – in particular the launching in 1965 of the London and Manchester Business Schools in a 50/50 partnership with government – the Foundation for Management Education was established and industry subscribed £5 million in 1964. Since then, postgraduate business education in Britain has grown rapidly and some 40 institutions now offer postgraduate courses, producing about 1,500 business graduates annually. (This compares with some 800 institutions in the US, producing some 60,000 MBAs each year.) Almost all courses in the US span a two-year period, but in Britain the length of course varies from 9 to 23 months. Indeed, only London and Manchester offer the two-year intensive course on the American model. Most are condensed into a 10- or 12-month period. Many UK schools also offer part-time options, usually spread over a period of two or three years.

## Regional Management Centres

In 1971 the then Secretary of State for Education made public plans for 12 regional management centres to cover virtually all England and Wales. The aim of this initiative was to ensure a more controlled pace of development of management studies at the higher level and to avoid dilution of physical, human and financial resources (Lee, 1983). One or more polytechnics or colleges of further education were designated as the 'initiating institution' for each region and they were chosen on the basis of their existing track record in the management studies field. The Manpower Services Commission (MSC, 1978) subsequently became very active in this area.

## The Verdict of Two Decades of Activity: The Mant and Owen Reports

Two major reports published in 1969 and 1970 respectively make it possible to assess the impact of the management development activities described above (see also Central Training Council, 1971; Hardy, 1971; Lazell, 1969). The first of these was written by Mant (1969), who had been seconded from IBM to work with a steering committee of the British Institute of Management. The main findings of the Mant Report, which was published in 1969, were as follows. Each year only some 7 to 8 per cent of managers in British industry attended courses lasting one week or more. Most of these were 'mobile' managers in the fast stream of their company's promotion system. A much smaller proportion of 'non-mobile' experienced managers was receiving any formal training. There was growing concern about the gap in communication and relationships that was seen to be opening up between those experienced but untrained managers, and a new generation of managers with much better business or management education and quite different attitudes. A 'startling' number of people, particularly senior executives, were sceptical about the relevance of much of the post-experience management training available.

This scepticism was in Mant's view well founded, for the following reasons: most management education programmes for experienced managers were 'traditional' in content and form; little attention was being paid to transferring classroom learning to the workplace; there did not appear to exist a coherent theory of experienced manager action or learning as a basis for course design or evaluation. Where companies felt that they had coped successfully with problems of career-long motivation, 'obsolescence', and mid-career perform-ance improvement, it was a consequence of organizational changes, defining objectives and developing more appropriate styles of management rather than as a result of training. Where training had been successful, however, it had been closely linked to the job, usually by some form of project work based in the company and focusing on a real problem or issue. The most successful examples arose from collaborative efforts between companies and external institutions. As a result of these findings, Mant argued that it could not be accepted as 'received doctrine' that management education courses, of what-ever kind, should be 'built up'. It did, however, follow that more attention and more resources should be devoted to the development of better theories of management action and management learning.

Mant's report, which dealt with the education and training of the experi-enced manager, was followed a year later by the Owen Report (CIME 1970). This report was commissioned by the joint CBI/BIM Advisory Panel on Management Education at the request of the Council of Industry for Manage-ment Education, and arose from growing unease about some developments in the rapid expansion of undergraduate and postgraduate courses in business studies.

The report was based on a limited sample of companies confined to manu-facturing industry and gave evidence of widely different attitudes to business graduates. The 50 enterprises in the sample had recruited between them some 258 business graduates in the five years prior to the study. Of these, some 52 had resigned by the time of the survey. The sample fell broadly into three groups. Three firms stated flatly that they would never recruit a business graduate as they believed such training to be useless. Forty firms were doubtful about the value of postgraduate training. Some of these had not yet recruited business graduates but were considering doing so; the others had between them acquired 174 business graduates. They gave various reasons – because they were experimenting, because they felt they could not afford to ignore an important channel of recruiting or because an able member of staff had requested sponsorship. Finally, only seven companies recruited business graduates as a matter of clearly defined policy, believing they would make a real contribution to the success of the firm.

As far as postgraduate education was concerned, the report recommended that standards of entry to postgraduate courses should be higher and should take particular account of the qualities which will be needed by the business graduate if he or she is to succeed as a manager. A postgraduate course should ensure that the business graduate has a working knowledge of the various func-tions of management; understands how these functions fit together in the con-text of the total business; understands how to get things done through people; is aware of the economic and cultural environment of the enterprise; has the skills to do a practical job in one part of the business. Finally, the total output of the different specialisms from the schools should as far as possible match industry's need for those specialisms.

In the case of post-experience education, the report recommended that there should be an extended course for managers in mid-career who are moving from functional to general management; there should be short concentrated courses on the specialist techniques; courses should be available on a modular basis; and the business schools should be prepared to experiment in the field of post-experience education.

In general the report was fairly critical of the business schools. The calibre of the faculties at the schools should be improved. Expansion in numbers was needed less urgently than improvement in quality. The allocation of resources should take account of the continuing need to achieve at least two 'centres of excellence' (London and Manchester). The business schools should be encouraged to specialize. They should be encouraged to work together. They should be encouraged to develop as 'catalysts of industrial change'. There should be closer working links between industry and the schools.

*Renewed Interest*

After the depressions of 1974–5 and 1980–2 and a degree of retrenchment in the late 1970s and early 1980s, the late 1980s has seen renewed interest in management education and development reflecting the changing context discussed in chapter 2 and the debate over training in general referred to in chapter 7 (Ball, 1983, Barron, 1983, Leavitt, 1983; see also Department of Industry, 1977; Foy, 1979). The private sector management colleges offering 'Executive Programmes' have reported considerable activity. The MBA, having survived a period of intense scrutiny and criticisms earlier in the decade, appears to be going from strength to strength; scarcely a day goes by without an announcement by a university or polytechnic that it is launching a new programme.

Further impetus has been given by the commissioning and publication of a number of influential reports, by the BIM, the CBI, the Economic and Social Research Council, the MSC and the NEDC, reflecting the widespread concern about the quality of British management and the implications for economic performance. In 1986 there was a report by Mangham and Silver dealing with management training. In 1987 no less than three major reports appeared; one, by Mumford and his colleagues, dealt with the development of directors; a second, by Constable and McCormick, covered similar ground to the Mangham and Silver Report, but also considered the provision of management education and training more generally; the third, by Handy and a team of colleagues, compared management education and training and development in Britain with four major competitor countries – France, Japan, the USA and West Germany.

In many respects the Mangham and Silver (1986) Report, which is a major survey of the nature and extent of management training, anticipated many of the findings of Constable and McCormick. Over one half of British companies made no training provision for their managers, and even the larger companies with over one thousand employees figured in this group – one fifth of these were failing to train. Of those that did, the medium expenditure per annum was only £600 per manager – and senior managers were apportioned even less.

The report by Mumford and his colleagues (1987) draws on a survey of more than 140 directors of 45 organizations carried out in 1985 and 1986. The authors found that, although some organizations were able to point to considerable systematic management development activity among their directors – and could even claim a direct linkage between this and the subsequent level of performance by the recipients – others had no schemes at all. In some cases schemes had not met their full potential – indeed, occasionally they had failed completely. Overall, most directors interviewed seemed to feel that the formal processes of management development, where they existed, had not been very influential. More positively, most claimed to have learnt through a mixture of accidental and unstructured experiences.

The Constable and McCormick (1987) Report found that most of the 2.75 million managers in this country lacked formal education and training. Indeed, Constable and McCormick estimated that managers received on average only one day's training per year. The Handy (1987) Report put this and other findings into an international context. Although some organizations in Britain did a lot and did it well, the conclusion was that those in major competitor countries did more and did it better.

Both reports included a number of recommendations. Many are to individual organizations – the Handy Report, for example, suggests leading companies should commit themselves to a 'Development Charter' of good practice, including a standard of five days off-the-job training per year per manager. Other recommendations relate to the provisions for education and training. Perhaps the most far-reaching of these is Constable and McCormick's call for the establishment of a tradition of apprenticeship or 'articles of management' in the form of a new national Diploma in Business Administration, and an expansion in MBA programmes towards a target of 10,000 graduates a year by the late 1990s. They also recommended that access to both of these courses should be made more easily available to working managers through the provision of part-time, modular courses involving a careful melding of academic and work-based study.

## The Management Charter Initiative

A direct outcome of the Handy and Constable/McCormick Reports was the formation, by a number of large companies, of the so-called 'Management Charter Initiative' committed to improving the quality of management. Supported by the CBI and the Foundation of Management Education (FME), leading figures in the group have proposed the setting up of a management institute, complete with Royal Charter, to establish a set of management qualifications. In the words of Bob Reid, Chief Executive of Shell UK Ltd, and Chairman of the FME (Times Higher Education Supplement, 23 March, 1988), the initiative entails three principal tasks:

1   the founding of a mass movement of organizations committed to a Code of Practice promoting the development and application of high standards of modern management practice and business at all levels and in all sectors of the economy (the Management Charter Movement);
2   the development of a widely recognized system of professional management qualifications as a source of motivation to individuals undergoing continuous management development (Chartered Management);
3   the formation of a Chartered Institute of Management, under a Royal Charter, to direct and administer the Chartered Management movement and Chartered Management system on a permanent basis, and to advance the practice of professional management and its development.

The precise direction that the Management Charter Initiative has taken has proved to be extremely controversial. Critics (see, for example, the reports by Syrett, 1988a and Dixon, 1988) have argued that to see management as a 'profession' involving a set of measurable skills or 'competencies' is fraught with problems. On the face of it, it runs contrary to the philosophy of education by example rather than control which lay behind the setting up of the Management Charter Initiative in the first place; it ignores the immense diversity and complexity of managerial work which was discussed in chapter 9; and the espousal of universally-applied qualifications would seem to be at odds with the trend towards enterprise-specific development, often in co-operation with a university or polytechnic, which many organizations are pursuing. An added concern is that the initiative will become the creature of the larger companies and, rather than leading to new developments, will simply be used to legitimize the training and programmes already under way in these organizations.

Supporters of the ideas argue that there is a need to consolidate the initiatives begun with the Handy and Constable/McCormick Reports (see Syrett, 1988b). In particular, clearly defined qualifications are seen as important, especially given the numbers taking accountancy qualifications in Britain, in raising the status of management and in attracting young talent into management. In the words of Bob Reid (Syrett, 1988b) 'if the initiative is to be carried forward, it does require an architecture of qualifications easily understood by individuals so that they can identify what they should be studying once they have made the initial step. In this way, the whole revolution of self-development will be taken a stage further.' Any notion of exclusivity or restrictionism associated with the traditional professions is also firmly rejected; John Banham, Director-General of the CBI and a major protagonist of the Management Charter Initiative, has been quoted (Syrett, 1988b) as saying, 'I am not holding a candle for institutes or institutionalization . . . Professionalism and institutionalism are not synonymous.'

It remains to be seen how events unfold. One thing, however, is very clear. Together with the expansion in management education, especially in MBA programmes, referred to earlier, the activities of the Management Charter Initiatives have given a very considerable boost to both interest and activity in management development. The prospects for significant improvements in the performance of British management in this area are better than they have ever been.

## MANAGEMENT DEVELOPMENT METHODS AND TECHNIQUES

As management development activity has grown and matured, a range of learning methods and techniques has developed to supplement or take the place of the traditional 'talk and chalk' approach of the classroom (Pugh, 1966). At the same time it has become increasingly acknowledged that most management development takes place on the job and that planned job experience and career planning play an essential role in the process. This in turn has led in many cases to a much greater involvement by line managers in the development of their own subordinates by means of 'coaching' or 'mentoring' and considerable numbers of managers have been trained in the skills involved in the 'mentor' role, such as the assessment of strengths and weaknesses affecting individuals' performance, the diagnosis of training needs and counselling.

The major more formal approaches to learning are reviewed below.

### Sensitivity Training

Sensitivity training, sometimes known as 'T' Groups or the 'laboratory method' (for further details, see Seashore, 1968), was much more fashionable as a management learning vehicle in the 1960s and early 1970s than it is today.

The theory behind this approach, the objectives and methods of which have been summarized by Lippitt (1975), is that individuals can best learn interpersonal and group skills through actual 'here and now' experience which is analysed for the benefit of the learner. The method usually involves unstructured group situations, in which there is no set task as such and the sole agenda is the behaviour of the group, feedback to individuals about their impact on others, and opportunities to practise interpersonal skills, as well as more straightforward information-imparting sessions.

The term 'laboratory' training was first applied to this kind of learning in respect of the so-called 'human relations laboratories' sponsored by the National Training Laboratories at Bethel, Maine, USA beginning in 1947. More recently the term 'encounter group' has been used to describe a very similar type of programme. Underlying this approach to skills development there are several assumptions. Each participant is responsible for his or her own learning. The role of the teaching staff is to facilitate learning by helping participants examine and understand the experiences they have as members of the group. Learning results from having experience and then generalizing from it. The 'laboratory' provides a setting in which participants can examine their experience and draw valid generalizations from it. People learn best when they have established open, honest and direct relationships with each other, so that they communicate their true feelings and evaluations. The improvement in people's skills in working with each other results from being able to practise new behaviour and receive feedback as to the impact it produces on others.

Sensitivity training can be recommended to meet the training needs of individuals wishing to improve their interpersonal skills or can be used as a means of improving the effectiveness in working together in a real-life team.

'T' Groups have been subject to a great deal of evaluation, the results of which have been summarized by Seashore (1968). The findings show that attendance on sensitivity training programmes does in many instances lead to perceived improvements in managerial skills, although not everyone benefits equally. Many individuals report extremely significant changes in their lives as family members and citizens as well as workers. The incidence of serious stress and mental disturbance during training was estimated to be less than 1 per cent of all participants, and in almost all instances occurred in persons with a previous history of emotional problems. Anecdotes about breakdowns during sensitivity training are common, however, and anxiety raised by such 'horror' stories may be one reason for the undoubted decline in popularity of the technique, especially in Britain.

## The Case Method

The use of the case study method as an approach to the study of management was pioneered by the Harvard Business School. A case study is an account of situations and events drawn from real life and the material which has been selected and recorded has been chosen so as to provide a basis upon which learning can take place (Simmons, 1975). Each case will normally focus upon one or more key issues which either provoke an examination of general theoretical principles (e.g. what are the advantages and disadvantages of a highly decentralized organization structure) or which call for the solution of a specific problem or the taking of a specific decision (e.g. should Company *A* take over Company *B*?). Cases can, of course, vary in length and complexity and may deal with a single issue or a whole range.

Although the case study method has recently come in for considerable criticism, it offers two advantages as a tool for learning. First, there is a great deal of potential learning to be gained from the content of well-written cases in their own right. Few managers can experience situations involving key issues and decisions over a range of industrial and commercial situations in their own real life careers, yet by regarding a number of carefully chosen case studies they can vicariously acquire a great deal of managerial 'experience'.

The greater value, however, derives from the analysis of case material under the guidance of a skilled case method teacher. Normally, participants on a course are required to 'prepare' a case thoroughly in advance of a class, which means thinking about the issues involved, conceptualization of those issues and the forming of ideas about solutions to problems. Back in the classroom, the case is worked through and the skilled tutor will use the dynamics of a group-learning situation to maximum advantage by getting members of the group to challenge each other's assumptions, thought processes and ideas, so as to enhance their ability to distil the key facts and issues from a mass of information (much of it irrelevant) and to use concepts to aid the process of problem-solving and decision-taking. In other words, the ability to see the wood for the trees and to get to the essential core of any complex set of problems.

### The Use of Syndicates in Management Training

The so-called 'syndicate method' of management learning was pioneered in Britain by the Administrative Staff College (now the Management College) at Henley and has been adopted as a model by several other similar institutions in other parts of the world (Adams, 1975). The course within which this approach to learning was developed was the General Management Course, involving some 60–70 managers and lasting nine weeks.

Each course was divided into six 'syndicates' of 10–12 members and these groups were kept together for the duration of the whole course. This form of structure for learning was adopted from the military staff colleges on which in its early days Henley was largely modelled. In the military syndicates, however, all members are drawn from the same service (or at least from the armed services), whereas a key feature of the Henley syndicate is the mix of people from organizations of many kinds – public and private sector; industrial, commercial and administrative; governmental bodies and agencies, and trade unions.

Each Henley syndicate, therefore, has the following characteristics: its members are drawn from different types of organization and come from different functions; each syndicate has specified tasks to complete within certain stated time limits; for each task the syndicate is led by one of its number; each group is expected to evaluate and seek to improve its performance.

Syndicates are given two main types of task – to survey an area or aspect of management and formulate guidelines for action or to carry out an exercise, project or case study. To achieve these tasks, the syndicate members will need to co-operate in such ways as sharing out the task of reading the background material, going out on field visits where appropriate, and conducting interviews. Competitiveness between syndicates also forms part of the learning process.

The strong emphasis on the self-management of syndicates and the idea that much of the input which forms the basis of learning should come from the knowledge and experience of syndicate members themselves clearly mean that the relationship between course members and members of the teaching staff of the institution is different from the conventional one of teacher and student. Staff members in fact play two major roles. First, they are responsible for setting up the work to be done by all the syndicates in the particular subject area which is their specialization, and in respect of that work they will be available for consultation by all the syndicates. At the same time, they are also assigned to work with a particular syndicate for the duration of the course and will be available to both the group and its individual members as a consultant, adviser, resource and counsellor.

### Role-Playing

As the term implies, role-playing involves learning about behaviour and responses to behaviour by acting out a role. At one extreme this can involve a very complex process in which the learner is required to study and take the part of a real life or fictional person who is described in the exercise brief in great detail in terms of biographical background, personality and attitudes, usually in the context of a detailed case study. The issues raised in the case study are then explored, not by the impersonal and analytical process of classroom discussion, but via the much more emotional and experiential process of acting them out. Such situations can be deliberately manipulated by trainers in ways which simulate real-life conflicts and dilemmas, for example, by giving different actors in the same situation only partial information, or, indeed, information that is conflicting.

Role-playing is perhaps more commonly used, however, in a less complex way to enable people to practise such skills as selection interviewing, appraisal interview, counselling, negotiating, chairing meetings or conducting press conferences. Its value as a training technique for such applications has been greatly enhanced in recent years by the use of closed circuit television techniques. These not only enable an interview to take place with apparent privacy while in fact being observed by members of the same learning group located in another room, it also enables the role-playing activity to be recorded so that the learner can subsequently, during the playback of the interview or meeting, observe his or her own behaviour (and the response of others to it) in a way which offers most powerful opportunities for learning.

### Management Games

A management 'game' involves a scenario which simulates selected features of a management environment such as a number of companies competing in a given market (Elgood, 1984). It is also dynamic in the sense that the environment is developed through a series of sequential decisions in such a way as to provide opportunities for learning about the results of decisions, as well as for gaining insight into the underlying relationships between the various elements in the management situation being simulated. Most games today use computers to calculate the consequences of the decisions made by the participants, and so can be developed to a very high state of complexity and realism.

One factor which encourages the use of games in management development programmes is the sense of involvement in a real or lifelike situation which is experienced by the participants. A sense of excitement is generated and enjoyment and enthusiasm are normally high. Games are also normally played in teams, which reinforces additional lessons about the role of leadership, the need for effective organization, and the key importance of good teamwork. If the business game has a weakness as a teaching technique, it is the tendency to give undue emphasis to the rational and logical aspects of decision-making and problem-solving, glossing over the fact that decisions in real situations involve much higher levels of uncertainty as well as involving non-rational elements.

*Action Learning*

The approach to management learning known as 'Action Learning' has been developed and extensively practised by Revans (1971, 1975). This approach is based on a number of premises. First, all parties to the learning process must want to achieve. Second, the will to achieve will be directly related to the extent that the learning is seen as relevant to the solution of the real problems. Third, learning is a social process – human beings learn more effectively by learning together. Fourth, people need opportunities to try out in practice the ideas they have learned. Fifth, the last stage in learning consists of understanding why the successful idea or insight proved successful in solving the problem.

Revans argues that conventional higher education rarely meets these criteria and he set out to construct programmes for management development which did do just that, and which, in consequence, involved the following conditions: managers should be highly motivated volunteers; the programmes of study should be based on the study of real-life problems and on ones of significant importance; they would involve groups of managers who would work closely with each other, to support each other, teach each other and learn from each other; the programmes should lead to *action*.

The first programmes based on this approach, known as the 'Inter-University Programme', were held in Belgium in 1968. A consortium of 19 firms and 5 university management centres took part. The participating firms provided genuine problems which they were willing to discuss with senior managers from other enterprises. The senior managers taking part in the programme were exchanged between the firms for almost a year. For example, a logistics analyst from an oil company studied the future strategy of a bank and a manager from a steel works studied the roles of part-time insurance salesmen. Before moving into problem-solving in their host enterprises, the participating managers followed a basic introductory course covering such subjects as economics, systems theory, communication, learning theory. Having moved into their enterprises, the participants (who were allocated to the five university management centres for tutorial guidance) spent one day a week together at one of the centres where they discussed their progress with members of the academic staff. This model of action learning has been successfully used by Revans on many subsequent occasions and in many other countries. In Britain a particularly successful version of the approach has been used by the General Electric Company (Casey and Pearce, 1977).

## Management Self-Development

Whilst there is much about management that can be 'taught' or learned in contrived situations (obvious examples are various techniques and skills, and
knowledge of economics), there is equally obviously much that can be learned
from experience. The self-development approach to management development is concerned with seeking to help managers understand their own personal learning and development processes and thus to assume more control of,
and responsibility for, their own development.

There are various approaches to self-development but, according to Pedler
and his colleagues (1978, 1984), they tend to share three concepts. First, there
is the emphasis on 'development' as distinct from study or learning; second,
there is the emphasis on 'doing it oneself'; and, third, there is the emphasis
upon the development of the whole person.

Development is seen as a discontinuous process which proceeds by a series
of 'jumps' or 'steps' which are experienced as key events (even dramatic or
traumatic ones) in a person's experience. It is seen as passing through a series
of stages, each of which comes to an end through the experience of some form
of crisis. 'Doing it oneself' means the individual taking personal responsibility
for learning, which in turn involves such processes as selecting goals or objectives for learning, deciding how to set about achieving them, exercising the self-
discipline involved in keeping to these objectives and programmes of learning,
and evaluating what has been learned. The third aspect – the development of
the whole person – implies not simply producing more effective managers but
more effective human beings. It ties in with Maslow's concept of self-actualization – of developing to the full one's intellectual, creative and emotional
potential.

In practice, most systematic self-development work tends to be carried out
by people working together in groups so that the individuals participating can
provide each other with support and practical help as well as challenge and
stimulus. It is important that such groups achieve the right balance between
being supportive and providing challenge and opportunities for mutual critical
evaluation. The aim – to help people take more effective management action –
should never be out of sight.

The role of the management development adviser *vis-à-vis* individuals or
groups engaging in self-development activities is one calling for considerable
skills and sensitivity. He or she can do much to facilitate self-development and,
by working in an enabling and counselling mode rather than as a teacher, can
constitute a highly useful company-wide resource. It is also important that the
management development adviser should try to develop the kind of organizational climate within which self-development can most effectively take place.
This constitutes a climate in which experimentation is encouraged, which is
open and provides feedback, is tolerant of mistakes (and sees them as opportunities for learning), which respects the individual and encourages the questioning of the status quo, which gives individuals the maximum possible
autonomy and which, while providing a supportive setting, does not shirk

confrontation and facing up to major issues when necessary. It is possible to describe such a climate as a 'learning organization'.

## Distance Learning

The effective and flexible use of text combined with the use of modern educational technology (Cooper, 1984; Roed, 1984), especially video, makes it possible to produce 'packages' of learning material which can be studied in any location. This type of package, which was pioneered in Britain by the Open University, has been called 'distance learning', in the sense that the learner and the learning process are at a distance both from the trainer who has produced the material and the educational institution in which it has been originated. It is, of course, a development of the more traditional 'correspondence' course which has been used in education generally and in management education in particular for many years. More recently the term 'open learning systems' has been applied to the same type of approach.

The success of any distance learning course will reflect the skill which goes into the design of the training programme and the selection of the media used to deliver it. It is normally a process involving a multidisciplinary team of subject experts, media experts, graphic designers, editors and others, and it can be quite expensive. The implication therefore is that very large-scale distribution is required if distance learning is to be an economic proposition.

Some aspects of the total range of management subjects lend themselves more readily to distance learning than others, and in particular it is unlikely that there can ever be a real substitute for human interaction with other learners in the case of studies in the field of organizational behaviour.

Distance learning does, however, have some important advantages. More than most methods, it allows the learner to make progress at his or her own optimum speed for learning. It frees the learner from the constraints of normal course timetables, being flexible in time as well as space, and it enables study to take place in remote locations inaccessible to trainers.

## Collaboration between Industry and the External Institutions – Joint Development Activities

Forms of management development activity involving collaboration between industrial and commercial organizations on the one hand, and business schools/management colleges on the other, have become known as 'joint development activities' – a phrase originating in the Manchester Business School. Forms of joint development activity include: project work, in which managers learn as they set about real-life problems in the organization which employs them, while benefiting from tutorial advice and counselling from tutors from the schools and colleges; the contribution on a regular basis of industrialists on programmes at the schools as visiting lecturers and the reciprocal participation of business school tutors in in-company programmes;

consortia of companies running programmes in association with one or more business schools; secondment of managers for sabbatical periods to business schools and the reciprocal secondment of business school tutors to industry; and provision by industry and commerce of facilities for research into management and organizational problems and processes.

## CONDITIONS FOR EFFECTIVE MANAGEMENT DEVELOPMENT

As the first section pointed out, there has been considerable discussion and debate about the most appropriate conditions for effective management development. In recent years, however, a consensus has begun to emerge that those organizations with effective programmes share a number of characteristics. Briefly, these are that management education and training are perceived within the enterprise, especially by senior managers, as key activities; education and training needs are derived primarily from the strategic plan for the business; the design of education and training programmes and the selection of learning methods take into account the nature of managerial work; decisions about education and training take into account the needs and capacities of individual managers; education and training are seen as a continuous process in which job experience, career progression and opportunities for learning are linked together; and management education and training are systematically reviewed and evaluated to establish their cost-effectiveness. Each of these characteristics will be considered in turn.

### *Management Development as a Key Business Activity*

First, the commitment of top management to management development can be demonstrated in various ways. Increasingly, for example, they take an active part in in-company training programmes and lecture at the business schools where they become honorary or visiting fellows. They also accept that they still have things to learn themselves and find time to attend seminars to help keep abreast of new developments in management. Second, the executives responsible for management development are among the most able executives in the business with the potential to go right to the top. They are assigned to management development long enough to become professional at it and receive adequate education and training to prepare them for the task. The post, which is located in the organization structure so that it carries weight, authority and status, is not, however, regarded as a career job to be occupied by the same individual for 20 years.

Third, adequate resources are allocated to the management development function and the temptation to cut this allocation back in leaner times should be strongly resisted. This begs the question of what is meant by 'adequate resources', but there is no rule of thumb here. The size of the education and training task will vary over time, reflecting the analysis of education and training needs discussed below.

*Education and Training in Relation to Corporate Strategy*

Enterprises do not remain static. They grow, they diversify, they expand over-seas, they restructure themselves, they acquire subsidiaries and effect mergers. Not all these things will, of course, be planned or foreseen, certainly not in detail or in precise timing and sequence. In the well-managed enterprise, how-ever, they will reflect a corporate purpose or policy and a strategy for bringing it to fruition, which has profound implications for both the quantity and quality of managers required. In quantitative terms, this means having managers at each level to meet the changing needs of the enterprise. More importantly, in qualitative terms these managers must be capable of meeting the challenge, both internal and external, that the future will bring. It is the gap between today's level of managerial competence and the demands likely to be made on management in the future which defines the training need. At the individual level, it requires an appraisal of current performance and an assessment of the existing levels of knowledge, skill and other forms of competence possessed by individuals for comparison with the future requirements for managerial per-formance, knowledge and skills. At the level of the management team, it requires an objective and searching assessment of the collective capability of the management of a firm or of a division of an enterprise in such matters as achieving innovation, adapting to change, securing financial control, launching new products or services, and meeting competition – all those matters in fact which reflect the functioning of a management team rather than the perform-ance of individuals.

Inevitably, such an assessment is likely to identify not only education and training needs in the areas of interpersonal skills, communications, leadership, planning and handling information, but also in the less obvious fields of values and attitudes. For example, the failure of a management team to innovate suc-cessfully may reflect, more than anything else, a shared culture in which 'play-ing it safe', avoiding risk and prizing security are the dominant values. The need to change such a value system constitutes a training need just as much as the need to improve communications.

*Education, Training and the Nature of Managerial Work*

If education and training for management are to be more than a ritualistic act of faith, they need to be tailored to the nature of managerial work both in the sense of the content of managers' jobs and the characteristic processes by which these jobs are performed. As the previous chapter pointed out, Mintz-berg's (1973) analysis shows that managerial work is characterized by pres-sure; that the typical manager's day is broken up into a large number of separate activities; that managers deal with the concrete and specific rather than the abstract and the general; that they prefer to communicate verbally rather than on paper; that they operate within a complex network of relationships and are able to exercise power and influence over events. Mintzberg also identifies a number of key roles which managers in all types of organizations tend to play from time to time – roles such as leader, spokesman, negotiator and resource handler.

Such findings have had two important implications for management education and training. First, the design of training programmes is increasingly recognizing the nature of managerial work in the real world and reflecting this in terms of content, methods and training objectives. Managers require help, for example, in learning how to manage their own time. While many of the pressures of managerial work are unavoidable, managers need to learn how to reduce pressure through delegation, how to avoid fragmentation of effort through planning, how to think in abstract and conceptual terms when necessary, and how to express their thoughts in writing: all those things, in short, which tend to get crowded out by day-to-day pressures.

Second, in order to improve the manager's ability to perform managerial roles, the objectives of training programmes are being expressed in behavioural terms. This means giving attention to personal development and motivation, as well as to more conventional learning processes, such as the acquisition of skills and the ability to handle information. A corollary is that the learning methods being adopted involve active rather than passive processes, moving towards the abstract from a firm basis in concrete experience.

*Education and Training Related to Individual Need and Potential For Development*

Where management education and training is sponsored by business, the anticipated outcomes will be stated in terms of benefits for the business. These benefits can, however, be achieved only through the willing co-operation of individual managers who are motivated to learn and to apply what they have learned.

In order to achieve this, the needs of managers must be studied as well as those of the organization. The evidence suggests that two things are fundamental. First, managers should be able to perceive education and training as a way of achieving the things they variously want to achieve, such as personal development, career advancement, a sense of achievement, a sense of belonging, recognition, esteem, status, or other forms of satisfaction. If attendance on courses is unrelated to these needs, then managers will either find reasons for not attending them, or will attend them for the wrong reasons, such as taking an extra vacation at company expense.

Second, managers must be motivated to learn. This state of mind is quite different from merely being willing to be taught. It implies an active, searching, enquiring approach to learning, and one which, having been developed while attending a course, is capable of continuing back on the job, making a reality of the precept that management education is a continuous process.

As chapter 7 has pointed out, assessing the potential of the individual for development is a more difficult problem and the weaknesses of the traditional approaches are well documented. Appraisal of the individual's personal qualities and potential for higher management by an immediate superior is a highly subjective process in which personal bias and prejudice tend to cloud the issue. Once individuals are assessed as having high potential, they become marked out as 'crown princes', collect the best jobs and attend the most prestigious management courses until they arrive, through the reliable mechanism of the self-fulfilling prophecy, in top management jobs. At this stage it may be difficult to convince them that such a system does not necessarily produce the best senior managers. It is no answer, however, to rely solely on measured performance in relation to well-defined objectives or targets as a means of identifying potential top and senior managers. The requirements of jobs change a great deal between levels and functions and there is no reason to expect that the best field sales manager in the company (as measured by sales results) will one day make a good marketing director, let alone a good chief executive.

To avoid the division of managers into 'crown princes' and others on a more or less once-and-for-all basis, companies are increasingly looking to assessment centres not only to assess potential, but also to monitor the development of potential over time. The assessment centre may be operated by the enterprise, if it is a very large one, or offered as a service by an independent institute. It will provide an assessment of the strengths and weaknesses of individual managers, an indication of their suitability for various assignments and an appraisal of their suitability for positions of greater responsibility. Normally, such centres employ qualified psychologists experienced in vocation guidance, together with assessors experienced in line management. They wield a whole range of techniques, including psychological tests and group exercises as well as more conventional interviews. Experience in using such centres in the US, in companies such as A.T. & T. and Standard Oil, has been evaluated and is encouraging (Byham, 1970). There are indications that this approach will spread within Europe, despite a cultural aversion in some countries to psychological tests.

## Education and Training as a Continuous Process

People tend to see education and training as processes which happen to them and in which they have a more or less passive role. They also see formal courses of education and training largely as episodic processes, which begin on the first day of a programme and end on the last day, freeing the manager to return to 'the real world' and get on with the job until it is time for the next course. 'Learning', however, is not something that happens to people; it is something they do and something they can be active rather than passive about. Courses provide opportunities for learning, but so does the job itself, and so do other processes and activities, inside the organization or away from it, in which the individual manager becomes involved. Learning, therefore, does not begin when the course begins, nor stop when the course finishes. It proceeds continuously over time, changing from the informal to the more formal modes and back again.

In order to make this concept operational, however, certain conditions have to be satisfied. First, managers must not only be motivated to learn and be offered learning opportunities, they must also know how to take advantage of them, which means learning how to learn. Second, few people are capable of sustained learning without supporting relationships and a means of achieving knowledge of results and a sense of progress. Increasingly, these conditions are being created by means of close and continuing relationships between an organization and its managers on one hand, and an external centre of management education on the other. This again reduces the episodic nature of management education and gives it a continuity extending beyond the boundaries of formal education programmes, whether these take place within the company or externally.

*Evaluation and Review*

The evaluation of management education and training is especially difficult, because it is not normally possible to establish valid criteria of management performance. As in other instances where judgement has to be exercised in conditions of uncertainty, however, the provision of relevant data can be an important aid to decision-making. The relevant data in the case of management education include course participants' perceptions of the relevance of training programmes and their impact on performance, assessments of change in performance by superiors, measures of attitude change, and such performance measures as are available in a given managerial situation. The art of training evaluation has developed considerably in the past decade and organizations with large training budgets can avail themselves of the most up-to-date specialist knowledge in this field (see, for example, Warr, Bird & Rackham, 1970).

*Conclusion*

These, then, are the key features of a systematic approach to management development being undertaken in many companies. As the previous section pointed out, in many instances such companies are also working closely with one or more of the leading external institutions in the design of their management development programmes. Co-operation of this kind brings several advantages. First, the company gains access to a high level of professional competence in management education which it would find difficult to develop internally. Second, the external institutions gain added insight into the current issues and concerns of business organizations with consequently less risk that their approach will be seen to be unduly academic. Third, sustained relationships of this kind contribute to the realization of management development as a continuous process. This contribution is the greater the more the external institution becomes involved in the creation of opportunities for learning other than formal courses. Examples of such processes include supervised projects for groups or individuals, tutorials, jointly-manned researches and workshops on 'live' company issues.

There will, of course, remain some training needs which are best met by in-company programmes with little or no help from the management education centres. Equally, the broadening of horizons which results from participation in external courses should not be undervalued. Formal education of this kind is likely to continue to play a part in the professional and personal development of executives. In the next decade, however, the major developments are likely to be in the area of joint ventures between companies and the external institutions. They will pose problems and challenges for the business schools which may need to abandon some traditional academic values. As with business organizations, however, the ones which prove most adept at innovation and responsiveness to the needs of the market are likely to be the ones to survive.

## DEVELOPING MANAGERS FOR THE FUTURE

By its very nature, management development is concerned with the future. The process is concerned not only with helping managers improve their performance in their current tasks but also with preparing them for future tasks in a changed and changing environment. To be involved in management development, therefore, inescapably involves taking a view of the future and of the tasks and challenges facing tomorrow's managers and how people can best be helped to prepare for and adapt to them (AIESEC, 1978; Nind, 1979; London Business School, 1984; Sadler, 1984).

In the economic sphere there are important questions about the ability of Western countries to sustain economic growth, and there is a growing consensus that the turbulence and instability surrounding economic factors such as exchange rates and interest rates are likely to persist for some time. Attention has been drawn to the structural changes occurring in economic activity and in particular to the decline in manufacturing relative to services as a source both of gross domestic product and employment. By the end of the century, it is likely that at least three out of every four jobs will be in the service sector.

The typical manager in the year 2000 will be in charge of a service activity – a hotel, a bank, a hospital, a school. At the same time, the nature of the work that is to be managed is changing in another way. Economic activity is changing over time from being principally labour-intensive, via being capital-intensive, to being knowledge-intensive. The modern economy is characterized by rapid decline in highly centralized labour-intensive work organizations. Large factories employing thousands of people are beginning to be a feature of our industrial past in the same way that the sight of hundreds of farm labourers leaving the fields at dusk was a feature of our society before the Industrial Revolution. The need for capital-intensive production will remain high, but the production units involved will often be quite small in terms of the numbers of workers employed.

The fastest growing area will be the so-called 'knowledge-intensive' industries, with a proliferation of companies, mostly relatively small in terms of numbers employed, engaged in high technology manufacturing or highly specialized services such as management consulting or investment management. With the development of 'fifth generation' computers, the electronic office, new local and global communications systems, electronic funds transfer at point of sale (EFTPOS) in retailing and robotics in the factory, the nature of work and production in industry and commerce will undergo fundamental change.

Such powerful and important trends in the economic and technological spheres will in turn stimulate major social change. If writers such as Bell (1974) are to be believed, one important feature is likely to be a changed set of values, reflecting the emergence of society from a past in which it was organized primarily so as to ensure material survived through human work and production, and its moving towards a future where it will be organized so as to ensure an acceptable quality of life for its members and to promote leisure and consumption.

As these changes occur there will be related shifts in attitudes that will affect management. Obvious examples are such things as attitudes to work and to authority, expectations about careers and about rewards; new approaches to personnel policy and new styles of management will need to be developed in response.

These developments will take place in the real world and there is a danger that those involved in management development in colleges and management centres may become out of touch with the changing nature of managerial work (Sadler, 1984). The traditional model of the manager was set in the context of the manufacturing industry, and this is where most of the case material has been developed. Also, the management literature is almost exclusively concerned with issues to do with managing the traditional resources of capital and labour; it has little to say about the management of 'knowledge-intensive' organizations. There is an urgent need, for example, for more research into the processes involved in managing services, to build on the pioneering work of Richard Norman (1984), and into the problems involved in managing 'knowledge-workers' – the problems which were clearly identified by Drucker (1969) in *The Age of Discontinuity.*

The training needs of tomorrow's managers are, therefore, likely to involve the skills of leadership, motivation and managing change, with particular emphasis on managing an educated and articulate workforce; understanding of, and ability to use, information technology; the development of innovative, creative and entrepreneurial ability; sensitivity to environmental trends; and the development of the individual's ability to adapt to change personally, and to cope with the stress involved.

# Bibliography

Adams, J. 1975. 'The Use of Syndicates in Management Training'. *Management Development and Training Handbook.* Ed. Taylor, B. and Lippitt, G. 1st edn. London: McGraw-Hill.

AIESEC. 1978. *Management Education in the 80's.* (International Seminar, La Hulpe, Belgium). American Management Association.

Ascher, K. 1984. *Masters of Business? The MBA and British Industry.* London: Harbridge House Europe.

Ball, Sir James. 1983. 'Management Education in the United Kingdom'. *London Business School Journal*, 8: 1, 10–17.

Barron, Sir Donald. 1893. 'Management Education – Theory and Practice'. *London Business School Journal*, 8: 1, 3–9.

Bell, D. 1974. *The Coming of Post-Industrial Society.* London: Heinemann.

Byham, W.C. 1970. 'Assessment Centres for Spotting Future Managers'. *Harvard Business Review*, 48: July/August, 150–67.

Casey, D. and Pearce, D. Eds. 1977. *More Than Management Development: Action Learning at GEC.* Farnborough: Gower.

Central Training Council. Department of Employment. 1971. *Survey on Management Training and Development.* London: HMSO.

Committee for the Diploma in Management Studies. 1968. *The Diploma in Management Studies 1961–1968.* London: Department of Education and Science and Central Office of Information.

Constable, R. and McCormick, R.J. 1987. *The Making of British Managers: A Report for the BIM and CBI into Management Training Education and Development.* London: BIM.

Cooper, A. 1984. 'New Technologies in Management Education'. *Management Development and Training Handbook.* Ed. Taylor, B. and Lippitt, G. 2nd edn. London: McGraw-Hill.

Council of Industry for Management Education (CIME). 1970. *Business School Programmes: The Requirement of British Manufacturing Industry.* (Owen Report). London: BIM.

Department of Industry. 1977. *Industry, Education and Management.* London: DI.

Dixon, M. 1988. 'How Best to Find Out What Managers Need'. *Financial Times*, 6 April.

Drucker, P. 1969. *The Age of Discontinuity.* London: Heinemann.

Elgood, C. 1984. *Handbook of Management Games.* Aldershot: Gower.

Foy, N. 1979. 'Management Education – Current Action and Future Needs'. *Journal of European Industrial Training*, 3: 2, 1–28.

Franks, Lord. 1963. *British Business Schools.* London: BIM.

Handy, C.B. 1971. 'Exploding the Management Education Myth'. *European Business*, Spring, 79–86.

Lazell, H.G. 1969. 'Management Education: A Personal View'. Fifth Urwick Lecture, BIM.

Leavitt, H.J. 1983. 'Management and Management Education in the West: What's Right and What's Wrong'. *London Business School Journal*, 8: 1, 18–23.

Lee, J.G. 1983. 'Review of the History and Development of the Regional Management Centres'. Privately circulated document of the Foundation for Management Education.

Lippitt, G.L. 1975. 'Guidelines for the Use of Sensitivity Training in Management Development'. *Management Development and Training Handbook*. Ed. Taylor, B. and Lippitt, G. 1st edn. London: McGraw-Hill.

London Business School and Egon Zehnder International. 1984. *Management Resources: Present Problems and Future Trends*. London: LBS and Egon Zehnder.

Lynch, J. 1970. 'The Impact of the Industrial Training Act on Management Education'. *Management Education in the 1970s*. London: BIM.

Mangham, I. and Silver, M.S. 1986. *Management Training: Context and Practice*. London: Economic and Social Research Council.

Manpower Services Commission. 1978. *Management Development: Policy and Activities of the Manpower Services Commission*. London: MSC.

Mant, A. 1969. *The Experienced Manager: A Major Resource*. London: BIM.

Mintzberg, H. 1973. *The Nature of Managerial Work*. New York: Harper & Row.

Mumford, A., Robinson, G. and Stradling, D. 1987. *Developing Directors: The Learning Processes*. Sheffield: MSC.

National Economic Development Council (NEDC). 1963. *Conditions Favourable to Faster Growth*. London: HMSO.

—— 1965. *Management Recruitment and Development*. London: HMSO.

National Economic Development Office (NEDO). 1972a. *Second Report on the Supply of Teachers for Management Education*. London: NEDO.

—— 1972b. *The Training of British Managers: a Study of Need and Demand*. London: NEDO.

—— 1987. *The Making of Managers: A Report on Management Education, Training and Development in the USA, West Germany, France, Japan* (missing in our title) *and the UK*. London: NEDO. Prepared for publication by the National Economic Development Office (NEDO) on behalf of the National Economic Development Council (NEDC), the Manpower Services Commission (MSC) and the British Institute of Management (BIM).

Nind, P. 1979. 'The Challenge of the Eighties'. *Management Education in the Eighties*. Special issue of the *Business Graduate*, 9: 3, 34–5.

Norman, R. 1984. *Service Management: Strategy and Leadership in Service Businesses*. Chichester: Wiley.

Pedler, M. 1984. *Management Development and Training Survey*. London: BIM.

——, Burgoyne, J. and Boydell, T. 1978. *A Manager's Guide to Self-Development*. London: McGraw-Hill.

Pugh, D. Ed. 1966. *The Academic Teaching of Management*. ATM Occasional Papers No. 4. Oxford: Blackwell.

Read, B. 1988. 'Charter Flight'. *Times Higher Education Supplement*, 23 March.

Revans, R.W. 1971. *Developing Effective Managers*. London: Longmans.

—— 1975. 'Action Learning Projects'. *Management Development and Training Handbook*. Ed. Taylor, B. and Lippit, G. 1st edn. London: McGraw-Hill.

Roed, J. 1984. 'The Use of Audio Visual in Management Training'. *Management Development and Training Handbook*. Ed. Taylor, B. and Lippitt, G. 2nd edn. London: McGraw-Hill.

Rose, H. 1970. *Management Education in the 1970s: Growth and Issues.* London: HMSO.

Sadler, P. 1984. 'Educating Managers for the Twenty-First Century'. *Royal Society of Arts Journal*, 132: May, 355–61.

Seashore, C. 1968. *What is Sensitivity Training?* NTL News and Reports.

Simmons, D.D. 1975. 'The Case Method in Management Training'. *Management Development and Training Handbook.* Ed. Taylor, B. and Lippitt, G. 1st edn. London: McGraw-Hill.

Syrett, M. 1988a. 'Taking Licence with the Future of Management'. *Sunday Times*, 10 April.

—— 1988b. 'Enterprise Era Sets New Goals'. *Sunday Times*, 24 April.

Urwick Report. 1947. *Education for Management: Management Subjects in Technical and Commercial Colleges.* Report of a Special Committee appointed by the Minister of Education. London: HMSO.

Warr, P., Bird, M. and Rackham, N. 1970. *Evaluation of Management Training.* London: Gower.

# PART V
## The Wage–Work Bargain

# 11 Managing Remuneration

*William Brown*

The rewards from employment are far from clear-cut. For most employees, work offers a bitter-sweet mixture which cannot be simply added up: frustration, friendship, strain, status, boredom, satisfaction, and much else besides. These variable, unmeasurable, and very personal aspects of work are of profound motivational importance. Personnel policy is increasingly laying emphasis upon them in the design of jobs and careers, in training, and in policy on, for example, employee involvement.

Amid this complexity, pay and hours of work stand out as by far the most conspicuous part of the reward package. By their nature quantifiable, and thus generalizable across all manner of jobs and employees, pay and hours provide, however misleadingly, the only common language of reward. They provide the natural focus for collective bargaining and the obvious channel into which discontents over the more intangible aspects of work can be displaced. They may be only a part of the reward package, but they are the principal part open to transaction between employers and employees, and especially employee organizations. Consequently, the satisfactory management of employment requires the satisfactory management of remuneration as a necessary, if not a sufficient, precondition.

This chapter on remuneration is concerned with the problem of managing pay and, to a lesser extent, hours of work and fringe benefits; discussion of the significance of the differences between manual and non-manual workers is left to the next chapter. The intention is not to provide a technical guide – other works are cited for that purpose – but to make the reader sensitive to the tangled forces that affect management policy-making. The starting point is the labour-market, and the extent to which it guides or constrains management action. It is then argued that employees' notions of fairness are of crucial significance, which leads into a discussion of the job evaluation techniques used to manage them. After a brief acknowledgement of the importance of the wider institutional context, the chapter then discusses payment systems, by time and by results. It concludes with hours of work and fringe benefits.

## THE LABOUR-MARKET

In a perfect market for labour, management would have no discretion over what to pay. If pay fell below the 'going rate', or if the level of effort demanded rose above what was normal, then employees would, according to orthodox economic theory, start to leave, and the employer would then have to move back into line in order to remain in business. The management of pay would be a wholly passive routine. In practice, however, such circumstances are unusual, the closest being casual, unorganized, unskilled labour such as, for example, in seasonal catering jobs. For most employment, the labour-market is in varying degrees imperfect, often to such an extent that it has little explanatory value.

There is, in practice, little substance in the notion of a 'going rate' of pay. Surveys have been carried out of pay in many occupations in numerous local labour-markets in several countries. There is generally a substantial spread of pay to be found within the same occupation across the same labour-market. This applies whether one looks at gross earnings or at earnings standardized for hours worked. The median coefficient of variation of both individual and factory earnings in Britain and the USA is typically around 15 per cent (Brown et al., 1980). If one takes into account non-wage benefits, the spread of total benefits is even larger, for it is generally the firms that pay their employees higher wages that also give them better non-wage benefits (MacKay et al., 1971). Far from there being an obvious local market rate for a given occupation, firms are faced with a broad range of options for pay.

The generally sluggish and unequally priced nature of the labour-market stems partly from the behaviour of employees, and especially those who are older and more skilled. They tend to stick with the same employer for many years and, when they do move, it is rarely because of dissatisfaction with pay (Harris, 1966; Main, 1981). But employer behaviour also contributes. Many employers take pains to insulate their employees from the labour-market to some degree. By giving preference for promotion and training to existing employees, rather than recruiting from outside, firms encourage the view that individual improvement is to be sought within the firm rather than by job search outside. It is misleading to describe this practice as one of an 'internal labour-market', since there are no market-clearing mechanisms at work. Employees are encouraged to adapt their portfolio of skills and responsibilities in response to career and pay opportunities that are particular to their firm. It is an administrative and not a market process.

Many of the developments in training discussed in chapter 8 are tending to increase the imperfection of the labour-market. The rapid decline of apprenticeship and other forms of industry-wide training in Britain is leading to greater emphasis being placed on in-house, company specific training. One result is that employees are more than ever being recruited for their potential to acquire skills rather than for any skills that they might already possess. Another consequence is that job titles and job content are becoming increasingly specific to individual employers. Occupation and job descriptions, the essential language of the labour-market, are losing public meaning and precision so that it is becoming harder to match employees' capabilities to employer needs outside the confines of the firm. No market for any commodity can function satisfactorily without common terminology and trading standards.

There is a more fundamental reason for treating the market for labour as fundamentally different from markets for non-human things. This is, quite simply, that the act of hiring an employee is not sufficient to ensure that the job in question gets done in an acceptable way. Labour, unlike non-human goods, is sentient, and is not necessarily committed to the same objectives as the employer. The employee has to be motivated – by encouragement, threats, loyalty, discipline, money, competition, pride, promotion, or whatever is deemed effective – to work with the require pace and care.

Yet to this, the central issue of employee management – conventional economics – is wholly blind. Alfred Marshall, a founding father of the subject, fogged the issue for his successors with a convenient assumption. Drawing on farmers' anecdotes about the higher pay of workers in the North of England than in the South being a consequence of their greater 'average strength and energy', he established the general theory of 'efficiency earnings': that labour-markets would cause earnings to equalize once the 'exertion of ability and efficiency' of the workers, and also the equipment they were working with, was taken into account (Marshall, 1920). Because this was compatible with – indeed, essential for – conventional labour-market theory, it has remained largely unchallenged. As a result, economic analysis has ignored the significance of managerial competence in motivating employees. It is an omission which must be taken into account when considering the possible effect of the labour-market on company pay policy.

No systematic British data exist relating effort levels in different firms to earnings and, as we shall see, there are sound practical reasons for this. There has been some study by sociologists of the relationship between pay and effort *within* individual establishments (Baldamus, 1957; Behrend, 1984). These have noted the norms whereby managers and employees act as if there were an implicit 'effort bargain' between them that permits a trade-off between pay and effort: 'the definition of work obligations in everyday employment situations can usefully be understood as an example of negotiated order' (Hyman and Brough, 1975: 65). But this says nothing about the comparative terms of such 'bargains' in different establishments, and certainly not that the terms are identical nationwide. Modern-day managers of multi-plant firms, who have considerably better work study data than Marshall's turnip-carting farmers, report substantially different norms of effort prevailing over periods of many years in different factories with the same wage agreement and pay levels in different parts of the country. Far from seeing the trade-off between efficiency and pay as a matter to be left to the market, managers tend to see it as a focus for their attention. Within multi-plant concerns, the reduction of unit costs at laggardly sites is a constant but difficult management objective.

A more fundamental reason for questioning the way in which labour-market theory assumes away the problem of effort lies in the nature of the concept. Effort is essentially a subjective notion, assessed in terms of the strain felt by the individual doing the work. But this does not mean that it is wholly private. The amount of strain perceived is to a considerable extent socially conditioned. People feel less strain when doing something they enjoy, or feel committed to, or proud of, than when it seems boring, futile, or unappreciated. Herein lies the basis of much successful personnel policy.

More broadly, there are no objective means of comparing effort levels at different tasks such as, say, child-caring, stockbroking, rubbish collection, or soldiering. Societies differ markedly both among each other and between generations in the way effort is judged. But this absence of absolute values does not mean that there cannot be a parochial consensus, a negotiated order particular to a time and an organization. Nor does it deny the possibility of predictive calculations about the pace of working. Indeed, upon these two things depends the success of work study, to which we shall return. The essential point for the present argument is the fundamental weakness of a theory of the labour-market that assumes an unproblematic positive correlation between effort and pay.

The purpose of this discussion has been to qualify rather than to reject the idea of a price mechanism in the labour-market. Belief that there is a strong mechanism remains stubbornly central to the thinking of most macroeconomic policy-makers, but in the practical world of personnel managers it is more in evidence as a convenient excuse when they are under bargaining pressure to concede to comparability claims. They behave as if labour-market forces are generally fairly weak. It is true that many personnel managers use and participate in local pay surveys. The anxiety that prompts them to do this, however, often appears to be primarily that, if their firm's pay levels were to fall too far out of line, employees might become discontented and less productive, rather than that they will leave or that there will be serious recruitment problems. It is also true that there are times when the demand for a particular skill far exceeds the supply – recent examples have been provided by computer programmers, welders, deep-sea divers, and electronic engineers – and pay settlements temporarily reflect this. But such deliberate adjustment to market forces is surprisingly rare. Generally, it seems to be the case that the size of an individual's annual pay increase is more closely correlated with the increases achieved by other individuals of different occupations within the same firm, than to those of individuals of the same occupation in other local firms.

Managerial concern with competition focuses on the market for their product rather than that for their labour. The battle for competitive unit costs is generally not fought by recruiting and retaining labour that is in some sense technically competent, and doing so at the lowest wage rates possible, but rather by motivating the labour already employed to use and to develop its abilities, and to respond sympathetically to new methods of production (Rubery et al., 1986). The constraints to managerial pay policy presented by labour-market forces thus cannot be ignored, but they are easier to satisfy, and more forgiving of neglect, than are employees' conceptions of fairness.

## THE PROBLEM OF FAIRNESS

Pay deserves more respect as a source of disincentive than of incentive. The most ingenious of bonus schemes and the best of supervision are of little use if the underlying pay structure is felt to be unfair. Consequently, the prudent personnel manager devotes far less time to devising new pay incentives than to tending old notions of fairness. This section discusses the ways in which fairness features in perceptions of pay and leads on to the techniques of job evaluation that have been devised to cope with it.

There is nothing absolute about fairness in pay. It is a normative idea, the use of which varies from society to society and from generation to generation, from industry to industry and from workplace to workplace, much as does the notion of fairness of effort, or of a fair day's work. Fairness in pay is essentially concerned with the relationship between the pay of different individuals or groups; it is based on comparison. It is thus inextricably tied up with the valuation of social relationships and, of particular importance to individual motivation, with the way an individual perceives his or her work to be esteemed by others. This, in turn, has considerable significance for the individual's self-esteem. It is little wonder that arguments about fair pay arouse deep emotions, or that feelings of unfair treatment on pay issues lead to discouragement and dissent.

What sorts of comparisons matter in fairness arguments? There is no simple answer. Empirical studies have demonstrated how elusive, numerous and often contradictory are the reference groups with which individuals make their comparisons (Delafield, 1979; White, 1981a; Willman, 1982). One generalization that does seem fairly safe is that individuals appear to take comparisons more seriously when they are with those who are close to them, socially or geographically, than with those who are more distant. We have a far more discriminating and subtle evaluation of status within our own social class, our own workplace, or whatever, than elsewhere (Behrend, 1973). This is, after all, the part of our world upon which so much of our self-esteem depends. Consequently, employees tend to be far more upset if a pay differential deteriorates between themselves and others in their own department, than if a similar deterioration occurs with respect to their company directors, or another company altogether. For reasons that will be discussed later, the most salient group within which comparisons are made is usually that of the individual administrative or bargaining unit: that is, the group of employees covered by a particular set of pay arrangements.

The question of which points of comparison are felt to be most pertinent leads on to that of the criteria whereby those comparisons are judged to be fair. The most abiding basis for accepting the fairness of a pay differential is convention. Or rather, more negatively, it is a change in the status quo which provokes anxieties about unfairness. In the absence of good reason to do otherwise, we tend passively to accept as fair that to which we have become accustomed (Wootton, 1955). Collective bargaining consolidates this view of fairness because the use of traditional comparisons provides the basis for employers and trade unions to maintain a *modus vivendi*, a basis of settlement which preserves honour for both sets of negotiators (Ross, 1948). Historians of pay structures constantly stress their remarkable stability, over many years and much economic change (Routh, 1980; Phelps Brown, 1977).

Despite this deep foundation of conservatism, pay structures – the patterns of relative pay – do alter and can be made to alter. New jobs are introduced, occupations suffer from technological decline, organizational structures are altered, groups develop new bargaining strength, and so on. By what criteria are new pay relationships judged to be fair? Here the key issues seem to be those of legitimacy and consistency. Where trade unions are weak or non-existent, a new pay differential may be accepted as legitimate because management has decreed it. Under collective bargaining, however, it usually requires the use of formal negotiating procedures leading to an agreed settlement for the innovation to have sufficient legitimacy with the workforce to overrule past conceptions of fairness.

The principle of consistency refers to the normal sensitivity of any bureaucratic organization to the setting of precedents. Unless the criteria for establishing a new pay differential are clearly expressed at its initiation, and are adhered to subsequently, anomalies are likely to emerge which will provoke feelings of unfairness. Workforces appear to be able to accept with enduring equanimity some highly idiosyncratic internal pay structures, so long as they are internally consistent. But it only needs a single, slight inconsistency of treatment to generate an anomalous pay rate, for those concerned to begin to have doubts about the fairness of the whole pay structure.

The management of the fairness of pay is of great importance for the achievement of satisfactory labour productivity. Before thinking about positive incentives for employees, it is necessary to guard against the demoralizing effects of feelings of unfair treatment. The basis for managing fairness lies in the characteristics that have been outlined: its normative, relative, conservative, and parochial nature, and the importance of consistency and procedural rectitude. The fact that individuals on their own may be ambivalent and inconsistent in the ways they form conceptions of fairness does not prevent their collectively being marshalled into an orderly consensus. This is the purpose of job evaluation.

## JOB EVALUATION

Job evaluation is the generic term applied to a variety of ways in which, through more or less systematic analysis, the relative pay of different jobs within an organization can be established in a way that is broadly acceptable to the employees concerned. It can only be implemented within the individual unit and it must cover the whole of the unit, otherwise inconsistencies of job definition and pay rate will begin to creep in. Consequently, job evaluation schemes covering more than one employer are rare in Britain, being confined to industries such as jute and hosiery which have strong employers' associations. Particularly common in manufacturing industry and the nationalized industries, its incidence increases with establishment size, so that by 1980 over a half of the workplaces with 500 or more employees had job evaluation (Daniel and Millward, 1983).

The fact that the technique is generally applied to an individual unit has considerable significance. It is within the unit that the force of comparison is greatest and that attitudes to differentials are more sensitive. It is also within the unit, with its single management and union structures and its associated procedural framework, that it is possible to implement deliberate alterations of relative pay. A bargaining unit has the political infrastructure that permits the renegotiation of order. Furthermore, the visibility of different pay levels, and the understanding of different job contents, are far greater within the bargaining unit than outside. It was for these reasons that the Pay Board of 1972–4 drew a clear distinction between relative pay levels within individual units and those between them, terming the former 'differentials' and the latter 'relativities'. Pay structures are both more controllable and more in need of control within units than between them (Robinson, 1973; Pay Board, 1974).

The techniques of job evaluation are described in detail elsewhere (National Board for Prices and Incomes, 1968b; Belcher, 1974; Lupton and Bowey, 1983; Grant and Smith, 1984). The simplest and cheapest methods are those described as 'non-analytic'. In one of these, the 'ranking' method, either all or a selection of key jobs are described and then ranked in what is felt to be a 'fair' order. Those employees involved in this may be asked to compare random pairs of jobs as a means of arriving at a ranking. Once ranked, the jobs are split into distinct job grades for which pay rates can subsequently be negotiated. An alternative method, called 'grading' or 'classification', starts with the grades and then fits the separate jobs into them, again using the judgement of those concerned as to the nature of the various jobs, each taken as a whole.

The crudeness of this approach is its strength. It makes no pretence to do other than place the collective prejudices of the workforce on a consistent basis and, in workforces with strong traditions, that seems to work fairly well. It was, for example, the technique used in the 1950s by the (then) National Coal Board for producing a national grade structure for their employees out of the thousands of job titles inherited after nationalization. These two non-analytic methods accounted for about 40 per cent of schemes in operation in 1980 and 1984 (Millward and Stevens, 1986: 256).

The 'analytic' methods of job evaluation seek to break jobs down into component parts and to assess these separately. 'Factor comparison' is a method which usually identifies five different aspects of manual jobs: mental, physical, skill requirements, responsibility, and working conditions. Key jobs are examined, factor by factor, and are ranked within each factor. If the existing wage structure is thought to be reasonably acceptable, it is related to the factor rankings of each key job and the deduced factor values are then applied to the remaining jobs and to any new ones. Both the assumptions involved and the process of deduction are distinctly arbitrary. The technique accounts for less than 10 per cent of schemes.

The more sophisticated analytic technique, accounting for half in 1980 and 1984, is 'points rating' (Millward and Stevens, 1986: 256). This comes in many varieties, some extremely complex. They use varied factors, sometimes several of them, and sometimes they are broken down into subfactors and the subfactors into degrees. Within these categories, jobs are assessed on a scale of points, the number of points allocated to each factor indicating its weighting with respect to other factors. The final relative position of different jobs is determined by the total number of points they have scored. Clearly this is not an objective technique; the choice of factors and their weighting, quite apart from the assessment of points, are matters of judgement. What matters is that, in practice, the technique is found to be helpful in producing an acceptable and internally reasonable and consistent pay structure. The process of analysis helps to discipline and make more dispassionate the comparison of jobs to an extent denied by the non-analytic techniques.

A very different type of technique, examples of which have received considerable attention but little use, is that based upon a comprehensive theory of human behaviour. Jacques' (1961) 'time span of discretion' method uses as its yardstick the length of time between an employees' performance of a task and his supervisor's checking up on it. Underlying this is an ambitious theory linking fairness, responsibility, and income distribution. It has received little social science support, although the 'time span' measure itself has been a useful element in some points rating schemes. Another example is Paterson's (1972) 'decision band' method, based on the theory that identifiably different sorts of decision are involved in different jobs and that these correlate with organizational position and, again, fit into a general theory of fairness and income distribution. Perhaps the most interesting feature of these comprehensive theories is not their content, but the fact that they are considered necessary. Certainly it cannot be doubted that for these, as for many of the more complex points-rating schemes, the monolithic, jargon-ridden, and quasi-scientific character of the technique is effective in inhibiting dissent.

There are many circumstances, typically with weak or non-existent trade unions, where the grandeur of the job evaluation technique, or the unexceptional nature of its results, are sufficient for it to be implemented without employee involvement. But these are unusual. In 1980 two-thirds of the review panels attached to established job evaluation schemes included employee representatives, most of whom were appointed through trade union or staff association channels (Daniel and Millward, 1983).

Employee involvement is usually seen to be an essential feature for the establishment and maintenance of a job evaluation scheme. The seemingly endless committee meetings to discuss job descriptions, points ratings and factor weightings are doubly important. First, they provide a forum in which different employee interest groups can negotiate over differentials with each other. Many a personnel manager has commented on the value of the process for shop-steward training. This intra-organizational bargaining within employees on the union side, albeit muted by the constraints of the technique, is more significant than any bargaining that might occur between unions and employer at this stage; the latter starts in earnest when the job evaluation is complete. Secondly, as an elaborate participative ritual, job evaluation helps bestow legitimacy upon the resulting pay structure for the employees represented. Adding to this stabilizing inertia is usually a cumbersome procedure for the maintenance of the scheme and for the review of individual appeals for job regrading.

Job evaluation, it should be emphasized, is best seen as a procedural aid to pay determination that has to be maintained rather than as a one-off system to be installed and then insulated from individual and group pressures. It provides a flexible, disciplined, participative device for the management of the fairness of pay under what are usually changing circumstances. Hence the paradox, noted by Clark Kerr in 1950: 'the more exact, consistent, and rigid a job description and evaluation plan, the less its survival value under collective bargaining. The more self-executing the plan, the more it is self-defeating' (Kerr, 1977).

## The Institutional Context

Pay cannot be considered in isolation. It is part of a wider set of job rules, a larger structure of industrial government, and a broader package of motivation and control. This institutional context exercises a substantial constraint over managerial freedom in the choice of pay systems. Here the briefest of outlines will be given to some of its more important features.

The basic component of industrial government to which a payment system is attached is the administrative or bargaining unit. Other things being equal, the appropriateness and incentive effect of a payment system will be greater if it can be tailored to a unit which has been delineated to cover a relatively homogeneous group of employees, in terms of their occupation, or technology, or location, or union, or whatever is felt to be salient, not so much in terms of past divisions but future needs. In practice these characteristics usually have conflicting implications and the best outcome is a more or less adequate compromise. Indeed, industrial relations factors may have relatively little influence on the choice of bargaining units. The structure of financial controls within the organization may dictate that different profit centres are individually accountable for all aspects of costs, including the negotiation of pay. There is probably a growing tendency for firms to shape the pattern of their pay units to the circumstances of their product markets and their internal financial structures, rather than to the labour-market circumstances of their employees, as was more necessary when industry-wide agreements had greater significance.

The decision to alter the pattern of bargaining units in particular cannot be taken lightly. Their profound influence in shaping notions of fairness was discussed earlier; they shape conceptions as to what constitute 'fair' bases of pay comparison. There is ample evidence that changes in bargaining units alter not only the comparisons pursued by unions, but also the pay outcomes of negotiations (Brown and Sisson, 1975). Reshaping bargaining units, like the redrawing of national frontiers, generates a lingering confusion of new alignments and old loyalties.

Employment, like any other social activity, is governed by a complex network of rules. Many of these are no more than informal understandings and expectations. The rules defining the payment system constitute a small part of this, but it is an important part, because pay tends to be the main focus of transaction and of discontent. Because of this, a poorly controlled payment system can come to corrupt a far broader sphere of employment rules. It has been demonstrated, for example, that employees working under poorly controlled piecework systems, in their efforts to moderate pay anomalies, may manage to alter rules governing labour mobility, the speed of machines, quality standards, work study techniques, and much else besides (Brown, 1973). A poorly designed and inadequately maintained payment system may thus have far-reaching effects in weakening, not only employee motivation, but management's control over production as a whole.

Finally, pay has to be seen as only one part of a complex package of devices for the motivation and control of employees. Within a single workforce, as other chapters make clear, employers may use a variety of employment contracts, training opportunities, participative techniques, and supervisory methods to shape the expectations and degree of commitment of different categories of employee. The composition of the overall package has major consequences for employee behaviour, and the payment system is an integral part (Edwards and Scullion, 1982). Some illustrations of this will have to suffice: long-deferred payment by results incentives will be inappropriate for casual workers; a profit-related payment scheme is likely to be frustrated unless accompanied by access to business information and joint consultation; the opportunity of high overtime earnings at one level may discourage aspirations for promotion to more responsible jobs that lack overtime payment. In short, decisions on the choice of payment system have to be taken at the same time as larger decisions on overall employment strategy.

## PAYMENT BY TIME

There is no necessity for pay to play a central role in motivating employees. Although there is a great need to prevent pay from demotivating employees, its importance as a positive incentive is generally much exaggerated. According to the New Earnings Survey, over 75 per cent of British employees are paid on pure time rates with no element of performance-related pay (Bowey et al., 1982). For most of these people there will also be little opportunity for promotion. They work with whatever care and effort they bring to their job (and studies suggest that most individuals judge their own contribution to be considerable (Porter et al., 1975)) for a mixture of reasons that varies from individual to individual, from job to job, and probably, from day to day.

The need for money may be the central motive for being employed at all, but it is rarely enough to ensure that work is done well. More important even than the fear of dismissal may be a mixture of motives including the desire for the manager's approval, pressure from workmates, force of habit, pleasure in helping customers and clients, fear of doing a bad job, pride in exercising a skill, and much else. This is true even for those successful innovative managers whom political mythology might suggest are most in need of money incentives. Their exceptional achievements spring primarily from a desire to solve difficult problems, to do justice to the confidence placed in them, and to prove pet projects, and it is the less effective managers who appear to be more concerned with eventual rewards such as promotion and salary increases (Kanter, 1983).

There is a substantial literature on the nature of different pay systems and the circumstances appropriate to their use (see, for example, OECD, 1970; DE, 1971; Conboy, 1976; White, 1981b; Lupton and Bowey, 1983; Grayson,

1984; ILO, 1984). It is a reflection of the perennial nature of the problem that some of the best books on the subject are the oldest (Schloss, 1892; Cole, 1919).

Two preliminary observations are necessary. The first is that there is no such thing as the perfect payment system for a given situation. All will produce some difficulties and choice between different options is usually that between the least problematic. The second observation is that no payment system continues to operate satisfactorily for ever. They all lose their edge and develop anomalies with the passage of time. A certain amount of novelty appears to be a prerequisite for effective money incentives. Perhaps it is for any incentive. Certainly it is the case that,with growing familiarity, employees come to treat as an entitlement that which they once perceived as a reward. Time and changed circumstances tend to blur the rationale for once plausible grading structures. Minor loopholes become normal pathways. Consequently, most organizations periodically undertake a major overhaul of their payment systems, often switching into, or out of, a payment by results scheme of some sort. Few payment systems can last a decade without fundamental reform. Since personnel management is a fashion-conscious profession, it has a tendency to dress up such changes to appear more innovative than they are. Payment systems cannot, in short, be treated as mechanical constructs to meet fixed technical needs. They must be designed to meet the highly dynamic social task of eliciting labour productivity.

The majority of employees are paid according to a fixed rate per hour, shift, week, month or year. Their level of effort and quality of work is generally maintained by supervision, custom, or other social pressure. There has, in recent years, been a tendency in some industries to use work measurement as a basis for calculating and, sometimes, negotiating the work-load and pace of work. Often no more than a planning device, this can be made a central feature of the payment system, as it was under the name of 'measured daywork' in the 1970s (OME, 1973).

The supreme virtue of time rate payment systems is their simplicity. It is, however, a simplicity that is often denied in practice by three different sorts of response to bargaining pressures and changing circumstances. These are additional payments, grade drift, and grade proliferation. We shall look at these in turn.

A type of additional payment which was largely driven out by collective bargaining, but is now making a cautious reappearance, is that of the individual merit rate. These provide selected employees with extra pay in recognition of special management approval. More usual are additions linked to a more objective principle, such as length of service, or are designed to compensate for particular features of the job: dirty working conditions, excessive noise, danger, unusual technical complexity, responsibility for trainees, working away from home – the list could be long. To varying extents these additional payments all threaten the integrity of a time rate system by giving some discretion to a junior manager to base pay on something other than simply a job grade and a clock. The criteria used for the application of an additional payment – and equally important, the criteria for its removal when, for example, the cleanliness of working conditions improves – are liable to become dented by bargaining pressure and supervisory favour.

Grade drift is a term commonly applied to the tendency for individual jobs to bunch up, with the passage of time, into the higher levels of a grading structure. This typically occurs because individual managers, when dealing with a job grading decision that is marginal between two grades, generally give the benefit of the doubt to the employee concerned, and such actions become benchmarks for future decisions. It is thus common, in a grading structure that has not been overhauled for some years, to find the lowest grades quite empty and, within salary bands, to find most employees bunched up to the band maxima. Vigilant job evaluation procedures can mitigate this problem, but may not remove the need for a radical grade overhaul every decade or so.

The proliferation of job grades is another response to similar pressures. The introduction of a new job grade with a slightly higher pay rate is often used as an inducement to win employee acceptance of a slight alteration to an existing job, such as might arise from a new piece of equipment, or a reallocation of responsibilities, or extra training. In the mid-1980s many firms were augmenting their once sacrosanct craft rate with 'supercraft' grades. In time the multiplicity of job grades becomes a major irritant. Distinctions which were once introduced to facilitate change can themselves become serious sources of job demarcation. Since, however, the novelty of a job alteration fades quite quickly, it usually takes a fairly straightforward (if expensive) negotiation to shake the jobs back into a simpler grade structure. Many firms go through this process every few years; others cope better through the active use of job evaluation procedures.

It would be quite wrong to conclude that evidence of these complications of time rate systems was necessarily a sign of management failure – far from it. No bureaucratic system operates efficiently unless its rules are open to judicious bending and creative interpretation. This is of particular importance when so much job innovation is associated with productivity improvements. The fact that a time rate system has no formal allowance for productivity-related pay does not remove the fact that employees are often disturbed by innovation and require some compensation to accommodate to it. Typically, however, the shock of a work innovation is a passing experience. The disruption that it brings to an employee's sense of competence, work habits, and work friendships usually heals quite quickly and, while the job may have altered, it is rarely in the long run 'harder' in any tangible sense. By tacitly allowing some grade drift, or the creation of a new grade, in the knowledge that these aberrations will be 'restructured' away in a few years, the employer gives in effect a phased one-off payment to compensate for a fading one-off shock that has, however, continuing implications for improved productivity. It is vastly preferable to the sort of haggling over 'fair' cash shares from productivity improvements that caused so much difficulty in the late 1960s when official incomes policies had the effect of encouraging flimsy and divisive productivity deals.

A time rate system, when sensitively administered in these ways, and when backed up by a job evaluation procedure, provides a stable and acceptable pay structure which is a sound basis for managing employees' productivity. The absolute cash difference between different grade rates is of less importance than the fact of the difference between them. Grade structures tend, over the years, to dilate and contract, economy-wide, in response to business cycles and changing inflation rates (Behrend, 1984; Brown, 1976). There is no evidence that this has a marked effect upon their power as motivators. Employees appear to aspire for promotion less as a result of an economic calculation of the expected extra income, duly discounted, that might result, and more in response to the status rewards, among which the pay increase is important, partly as a symbol. The manager who gives detailed attention to perceptions of fairness within his organization, and keeps a broad awareness of prevailing pay trends outside, need have few anxieties about the employees' incentive for promotion.

## PAYMENT BY RESULTS

In payment by results systems a proportion of the employee's pay, typically between 10 and 20 per cent, is variable, linked to some measure of the output of the individual or of a wider group. The intention is that this should act as an incentive to work harder, or with less supervision. Such systems have been used since employment began. There are many guides to them and there has been much research into their effects (see, for example, Shimmin, 1959; NBPI, 1968a; Marriott, 1971; Lloyd, 1976; IDS, 1980; ILO, 1984). Payment by results systems come in numerous varieties, with pay linked to output in linear and non-linear, progressive and regressive, lagged, cushioned, contracted, and sometimes curious other ways. At best they offer a means of maintaining effort that is cheap to manage and popular with employees; at worst they provide the surest method imaginable of disrupting industrial relations.

The intention of payment by results is to raise and reward effort. But effort, as has been said above, cannot be measured. Consequently it is necessary to have a technique to link what is deemed to be an acceptable pace of work to the level of output. It is also necessary to be able to do this for the very different sorts of jobs that might be performed in the same workplace with sufficient consistency for similar workers to end up earning approximately the same bonus despite their different tasks. If this is not achieved they will consider the payment system unfair. The set of techniques used to establish this are variously called time and motion study, work study, and industrial engineering (DE, 1971; Whitmore, 1976). For convenience we shall use the term 'work study'.

At the heart of these techniques is the skill of 'effort rating' through which the work study engineer, considering the task as a series of short elements, repeatedly observes its performance by a trained worker. He times each element and simultaneously makes a judgement about the pace at which it is being performed, the latter being expressed as a percentage of a 'standard' effort. After rating a large number of cycles of the task, the work study engineer is then able to calculate a modal estimate of the time that would be taken by any adequately trained and practised worker putting in the sort of effort that is acceptable in that workplace (Brown, 1973). This provides a systematic method of gauging and thus of standardizing effort norms on different tasks. It makes it possible to predict how long jobs will take in future. Although norms do differ between different workplaces, as do the effort rating standards of work study engineers from different backgrounds, this does not matter as long as they are consistent within their own workplace and from one month to another (Lupton, 1961).

There are two ultimate justifications for this rather odd technique. The first is that, in the right circumstances, it can provide impressively accurate results and serve as the basis for satisfactory incentive schemes. The second justification is simply that there is usually no other practical way of predicting levels of output, and it is often necessary to do this for production engineering and cost control purposes as well as for payment.

Of the many impediments that prevent payment by results systems from performing as intended, two deserve special mention. The first is that workers often subordinate the maximizing of individual earnings to the social objective of minimizing conflict among themselves. As a result they may place informal restrictions on effort which reduce or even nullify the incentive (Whyte, 1955). The second major impediment is that errors and oversights may cause some job times to be 'slacker' than others, with the result that bonus earnings are seen to differ between individuals in ways that bear no relation to individual effort. These anomalies are likely to give rise to discontent and a loss of confidence in the fairness of the whole payment system. Unless contained this will result in the swamping of work study techniques by constant fragmented bargaining whenever jobs alter or groups feel their earnings are falling behind. Then it is not only the incentive effect that is corrupted but the control of production more generally (Brown, 1973).

This is not the place to discuss the design of payment by results systems; considerable thought has been given to the technical and industrial relations factors that enter into such decisions (Lupton and Gowler, 1969; Lupton and Bowey, 1983). Key variables in a scheme are the gearing of the reward to incremental changes in output; the length of time allowed to elapse before output levels are reflected in payment; and the size of the group to be covered by a common incentive payment. In any case, as was observed earlier, it is futile to seek either a perfect or a permanent payment by results system. Such choices are to some extent shaped by fashion, and during the 1980s this has favoured schemes encompassing larger groups of workers and with less frequent and smaller earnings fluctuations than would have been normal two decades earlier.

The payment by results schemes discussed so far try to relate pay more or less simply to workers' performance. But, increasingly during the 1980s, it is becoming popular to relate the bonus to some indicator that takes into account the market circumstances of the employer. By linking pay to a measure that fluctuates with external prices (both of raw materials and of product sales) or with company performance, it is felt that the worker is brought into closer contact with the risks and realities of the commercial world in which the company has to survive. The more a payment system focuses the employee's attention on the immediate task, the greater the danger that the pursuit of individual self-interest might undermine the efficiently co-ordinated management of the enterprise as a whole. On the other hand, incentives related to the performance of the enterprise as a whole may be too remote from anything over which the individual employee feels any degree of control. An incentive system that attempts to relate both to the immediate circumstances of the employee and also to the global circumstances of the firm runs the risk of confounding both objectives through complexity.

Schemes relating the incentive to some measure of the value (as opposed to quantity) of production have generally been more popular in the United States than in Britain. The Scanlon plan uses the relationship between the wage bill and the total value of sales as its indicator. The Rucker plan takes input costs into account by focusing on the relationship between the wage bill of the enterprise and total added value (for further details, see NBPI 1968a: 44–7).

Three developments have enabled British managers to give greater consideration to incentives related to commercial performance. The first is the growing sophistication of companies' internal accounting systems and the increased use of the notion of 'profit centres' within the firm. The second is the diminishing influence of industry-wide wage agreements, enabling managers to exercise greater discretion over pay within single-employer bargaining arrangements. The third is the concessions made by the Treasury, in a series of Finance Acts since 1978, for income tax relief on certain types of profit-related payment.

The first legislative stimulus in 1978 was for approved profit-sharing (APS) schemes which give employees a distribution of shares. Under this, the Inland Revenue require the company to establish a trust fund and periodically pay money into it. The trustees use this to buy shares in the company which are allocated to individual employees but held by the trustees on the employees' behalf. Such a scheme must be open to all full-time employees who have been with the company for at least five years. There are upper limits on the value of shares appropriated to a participant which, under the 1983 Finance Act, stood at 10 per cent of salary up to a limit of £5000.

The second major encouragement was the 1980 Save-As-You-Earn (SAYE) share option scheme. Under this the employee can enter a savings contract with an option to purchase shares in the company at the end of the contract at a price fixed when the contract was taken out. In addition, in 1984 a discretionary share option scheme was introduced which provided tax incentives to companies to grant options to selected employees. In 1987 the Chancellor introduced a far more radical scheme for tax relief on profit-related pay, if it could be demonstrated that pay was linked to an audited measure of profits.

A survey of over 1,000 companies in 1985 suggested that the use of schemes of one sort or another was spreading. Fifteen per cent had a scheme registered with the Inland Revenue, a further 6 per cent had a non-approved scheme applicable to all employees, and another 9 per cent had a selectively applied scheme. Over a half of publicly quoted companies of over 500 employees had an approved scheme and they were particularly common in the finance sector. Employers expressed general, if qualified, approval of the schemes, especially the APS ones stemming from the original 1978 legislation (Smith, 1986).

There was a marked rise in interest in employee share-ownership schemes in the mid-1980s, with macroeconomists such as Weitzman (1984) and Meade (1982) arguing their theoretical advantages for economic stability and fuller employment, with an increasing number of employee 'buy-outs', and with the government's stimulus of wider share-ownership through its denationalization programme. But experience has tempered much of the initial enthusiasm (Bradley and Gelb, 1986). Substantial employee shareholdings imply a measure of employee control over corporate decision-making that managers may find distasteful (see, for example, IRRR, 1986). Many companies have also found that, whether or not share-ownership gives employees a greater knowledge of the economic realities confronting their company, it certainly gives them a keen interest in its stock market performance and, faced with a take-over bid, they may change their shares into cash with a singular lack of loyalty.

## HOURS OF WORK

A continuing theme of this chapter has been that labour is not something that can be hired in predictable quantities and fuelled on cash incentives. The remarkable quality of employees, which successful personnel management seeks to utilize, is their potential. Suitably motivated, employees have the capacity to acquire new skills, accept changed responsibilities, and adjust to more potent technologies. On the other hand, when discouraged or poorly supervised, employees can, in most occupations, spend a great deal of time achieving very little. It is the productivity implications of this that make the consideration of working time far more than a matter of arithmetic. Here we consider the length of the normal working week, overtime hours in excess of that, and the number of working weeks in the year, which is another way of looking at paid holidays.

The length of the working week, more than any other term of employment in Britain, remains strongly affected by industry-wide agreements between employers' associations and trade unions. It has also, since the last century, been a powerful rallying issue for both sides. Employers have argued that its further reduction would seriously undermine competitiveness; unions have argued its reduction would generate large numbers of new jobs. In practice, it has generally done neither (Nyland, 1985; Ehrenberg and Schumann, 1982). Over the past 100 years the normal week for manual workers has fallen from around 55 hours to 39 hours. This has occurred in bursts, just after the two World Wars, in the early 1960s, and at the start of the 1980s. Each time the change seems to have acted as a stimulus to management to take in the 'slack' in work organization that has arisen from technological innovation in the intervening years. As a result, the postulated cost penalties and employment benefits of the change have been largely offset with improved labour productivity.

There can be no doubt that there will, from time to time, be further reductions in the length of the normal week. The 40-hour week proved relatively durable because of its arithmetical convenience for shift-working. But whatever the pace of its reduction, its application is being diffused by the use of flexible hours of working, by different patterns of shift-work, and by the continued growth of part-time employment (see, for example, Atkinson, 1984; Brewster and Connock, 1985). In addition, as companies become more confident in developing their own personnel and bargaining arrangements, they are less likely to follow the lead of the appropriate industry-wide agreement. They become more concerned with the effective use of labour within the hours that it is available than with the hours themselves. It may be that the normal working week is slowly fading as an issue of contention.

In Britain the normal week is, in any case, a less useful guide to working hours than in most countries because of the heavy use of overtime. Increasing since the Second World War as the normal week has been reduced, it has come to average four to six hours a week for manual men. The persistence of overtime is extraordinary. The approximately one-third of manual males in manufacturing who work some overtime have averaged eight to nine hours a week each, and they have done so throughout the massive redundancies of the early 1980s.

There are varied reasons for the persistence of overtime working or, to be more accurate, of overtime payments. In some industries it may be paid without being worked. In road haulage, for example, 'job-and-finish' arrangements provide the driver with a given number of hours for a trip and no one checks up how long he actually takes over it. In Fleet Street printing, before the managerial revolution of 1986, it was commonplace for overtime payments to be linked to the number of pages in the day's newspaper even though its production, for most workers, required no more hours work. More widespread is the sort of regular overtime that is, in effect, retained by junior management as a means of inducing workers to put in extra effort in a production crisis, with the *quid pro quo* that at other times they try to look busy when more senior management are in sight. One of the greatest problems created by institutionalized overtime arises from its voluntary nature, whereby overtime bans become an important and easy form of industrial sanction, used more than half as frequently as strikes (NBPI, 1970).

Paid holidays have increased substantially in the post-war period. In 1951, 95 per cent of manual employees who were subject to a national collective agreement were entitled to two weeks paid annual holiday or less; at the end of 1986, 100 per cent had an entitlement to four weeks or more. The average minimum entitlement for manual workers in 1987 was 22 days. Actual entitlements will be greater because of the common practice of giving extra days for extra years of service. Public and customary holidays ('bank holidays') have also increased in number, standing at eight days in 1987. The lack of any serious controversy accompanying these substantial concessions by employers' organizations and governments is in notable contrast to the bitter arguments over reductions in the normal working week.

There is no simple connection between the number of hours worked and the amount of work done or, more importantly, the amount of production or service achieved. A cut in hours may be accompanied by an improvement in organization that achieves reduced unit costs – some of the more respectable productivity agreements of the 1960s achieved this (NBPI, 1967). Conversely, extra unplanned hours in the form of overtime may amount to little more than the intrusion of leisure into working time, with rising marginal unit costs. Some firms 'bought-out' tea breaks in their early productivity deals, only to 'buy them back' some years later when they discovered that tea taken at the work bench can last longer than when taken in a canteen.

Extensive research by economists, particularly those interested in whether income tax increases act as an incentive or disincentive to work more hours, has produced conclusions of almost total agnosticism. As one review puts it, 'the most intellectually defensible position is that after a decade and a half of effort we can say very little about labour supply elasticities' (Brown, 1983). Perhaps the most that can be concluded is that, when well-planned and managed, small infrequent reductions in working hours have sufficient effect in refreshing workers to allow them, in conjunction with changing work technologies, to offset added wage costs with increased productivity.

## THE FRINGES OF REMUNERATION

Although, as was observed at the outset, pay is the most conspicuous aspect of the package of rewards from employment, other benefits are important. They also appear to be growing in importance. In manufacturing industry, for example, pensions, sick pay, time off with pay, benefits in kind and subsidized services were officially estimated to have risen from 11 per cent of average pre-tax remuneration in 1964 to 19 per cent in 1981 (Green et al., 1985). Such benefits are very unevenly distributed, with those on high incomes getting substantially larger benefits than the low paid, both absolutely and as a proportion of income.

As the following chapter shows, within organizations there is a systematic tendency for non-pay benefits to increase with job status. It is true that the 'harmonization' of manual and non-manual conditions is generally diminishing the once massive discrimination between them, but this mainly affects full-time adult men in reasonably secure jobs. Women, part-timers, and those in jobs of short tenure have much more limited non-pay benefits.

It has been argued that the disproportionate increase in non-pay benefits with ascending incomes reflects a conscious policy which attempts to conceal the full extent of inequality. But, against this, it is arguable that one managerial advantage of many non-pay benefits is precisely that although they are less conspicuous when viewed from outside organizations, they may be very visible within them. By clearly signalling status, within the social system of the organization, such 'perks' as company cars, differentiated catering, better furniture, and different working hours, emphasize the managerial authority structure. In this respect, a relatively cheap allocation of symbolic differentiators can be seen less as a means of rewarding employees than of reinforcing management.

The comparative lack of visibility of non-pay benefits outside the firm increases the difficulty of job search by their beneficiaries. Quite apart from the fact that many benefits are linked to length of service in some way, the higher one is in an organization, the harder it is to break away from it. Some might say that this reflects a reward for loyalty. Others might argue that employee attitudes do not shape but are shaped by the techniques of employee control and motivation and that, in the words of one hardened personnel manager, 'if you get them by their careers and pensions, their hearts and minds will follow'.

There is an inevitable lack of clarity about what constitutes fringe benefits (see, for example, Allen 1969; Bowey (ed.), 1982). A subsidized canteen may be more easily costed than a well air-conditioned building, but it is not necessarily more significant to the well-being of the workforce. Some firms make a virtue of benefits such as social facilities, nurseries, relocation expenses and compassionate leave that other firms would treat as part of a necessary personnel policy.

In Britain the state provides many benefits which in some other countries would be part of the responsibility of the employer – family allowance and health insurance, for example. There is currently a tendency for the state to withdraw from such commitments, however, and to legislate in such a way as to transfer the obligation to employers. Elements of this are to be found in recent policy developments on, for example, health and safety at work, maternity leave, pensions and training. There is no prospect of this shift of obligations going into reverse, although the energy with which common standards are enforced may alter with the political complexion of the government in power.

## CONCLUSION

A recurring theme of this chapter has been that the successful management of remuneration in an organization requires an internal structure of rewards that is consistent and acceptable to those covered, and that, if this is achieved, the level of those rewards need only be kept roughly comparable with those provided by other employers. At the heart of the issue is the task of managing productivity. While a highly productive workforce undoubtedly makes it easier for the employer to reward relatively generously, the two do not necessarily go together. Pay is only a part of the motivational package. A major requirement of remuneration systems is that they complement and uphold a stable social and managerial structure within the organization. The sources of productivity growth increasingly lie less in getting employees to work more productively, than in getting them to adapt to more productive ways of working. The potency of remuneration lies in its capacity, if mismanaged, to prevent this.

*Note*

The author was much helped by the comments of Dian-Marie Hosking, Paul Marginson and Peter Nolan.

# Bibliography

Allen, D. 1969. *Fringe Benefits: Wages or Social Obligation?* Ithaca, NY: Cornell University.

Atkinson, A.B. 1984. 'Manpower Strategies for Flexible Organisation'. *Personnel Management*, August: 28–31.

Baldamus, W. 1957. 'The Relationship between Wage and Effort'. *Journal of Industrial Economics*, 5: July, 192–201.

Behrend, H. 1973. *Incomes Policy, Equity and Pay Increase Differentials.* Edinburgh: Scottish Academic Press.

—— 1984. *Problems of Labour and Inflation.* London: Croom Helm.

Belcher, D.W. 1974. *Compensation Administration.* Englewood Cliffs, NJ: Prentice-Hall.

Bowey, A.M. Ed. 1982. *Handbook of Salary and Wage Systems.* 2nd edn. Aldershot: Gower.

Bowey, A.M., Thorpe, R., Mitchell, F.H.M., Nicholls, G., Gosnold, D., Savery, L. and Hellier, P.K. 1982. *Effects of Incentive Payment Systems: United Kingdom 1977–80*, Research Paper No. 36. London: Department of Employment.

Bradley, K. and Gelb, A. 1986. *Share Ownership for Employees.* London; Public Policy Centre.

Brewster, C. and Connock, S. 1985. *Industrial Relations: Cost-Effective Strategies.* London: Hutchinson.

Brown, C.V. 1983. *Taxation and the Incentive to Work.* Oxford: Oxford University Press.

Brown, W. 1973. *Piecework Bargaining.* London: Heinemann.

—— 1976. 'Incomes Policy and Pay Differentials'. *Oxford Bulletin of Economics and Statistics*, 38: February, 27–49.

—— and Sisson, K. 1975. 'The Use of Comparisons in Workplace Wage Determination'. *British Journal of Industrial Relations*, 13: March, 25–53.

—— Hayles, J., Hughes, B. and Rowe, L. 1980. 'Occupational Pay Structures under Different Wage Fixing Arrangements'. *British Journal of Industrial Relations*, 18: July, 217–30.

Cole, G.D.H. 1919. *The Payment of Wages.* London: Fabian Research Department.

Conboy, W. 1976. *Pay at Work.* London: Arrow Books.

Daniel, W.W. and Millward, N. 1983. *Workplace Industrial Relations in Britain.* London: Heinemann.

Delafield, G.L. 1979. 'Social Comparisons and Pay'. *Industrial Relations: A Social Psychological Approach.* Ed. Stephenson, G. and Brotherton, C.J. Chichester: Wiley, 131–51.

Department of Employment (DE). 1971. *Training for Work Study Practice.* London: HMSO.

Edwards, P.K. and Scullion, H. 1982. *The Social Organization of Industrial Conflict.* Oxford: Blackwell.

Ehrenberg, R.G. and Schumann, P.L. 1982. *Longer Hours or More Jobs?* Ithaca, NY: Cornell.

Grant, J.V. and Smith, G. 1984. *Personnel Administration and Industrial Relations.* London: Longman.

Grayson, D. 1984. *Progressive Payment Systems.* Occasional Paper 28. London: Work Research Unit.

Green, F., Hadjimatheou, G. and Smail, R. 1985. 'Fringe Benefit Distribution in Britain'. *British Journal of Industrial Relations*, 23: July, 261–80.

Harris, A. 1966. *Labour Mobility in Great Britain.* London: HMSO.

Hyman, R. and Brough, I. 1975. *Social Values and Industrial Relations.* Oxford: Blackwell.

Incomes Data Services (IDS). 1980. *Guide to Incentive Payment Schemes.* London: IDS.

*Industrial Relations Review and Report* (IRRR). 1986. 'Response on Profit-Related Pay'. 380: November, 2–6.

International Labour Organization (ILO). 1984. *Payment by Results.* Geneva: ILO.

Jacques, E. 1961. *Equitable Payment.* London: Heinemann.

Kanter, R.M. 1983. *The Change Masters.* London: Unwin Paperbacks.

Kerr, C. 1977. *Labor Markets and Wage Determination.* Berkeley, CA: University of California Press.

Lloyd, P.A. 1976. *Incentive Payment Schemes.* London: BIM.

Lupton, T. 1961. *Money for Effort.* London: HMSO.

—— and Bowey, A. 1983. *Wages and Salaries.* Aldershot: Gower.

—— and Gowler, D. 1969. *Selecting a Wage Payment System.* London: Kogan Page.

MacKay, D.I., Brack, J., Boddy, D., Diack, J.A. and Jones, N. 1971. *Labour Markets under Different Employment Conditions.* London: Allen & Unwin.

Main, B.G.M. 1981. 'The Length of Employment and Unemployment in Great Britain'. *Scottish Journal of Political Economy*, 28: June, 146–64.

Marriott, R. 1971. *Incentive Payment Systems.* London: Staples.

Marshall, A. 1920. *Principles of Economics.* London: Macmillan.

Meade, J.E. 1982. *Wage-Fixing.* Vol. 1 of *Stagflation.* London: Allen & Unwin.

Millward, N. and Stevens, M. 1986. *British Workplace Industrial Relations 1980–1984.* Aldershot: Gower.

National Board for Prices and Incomes (NBPI). 1967. *Productivity Agreements (1).* Report 36, Cmnd 3311. London: HMSO.

—— 1968a. *Payment by Results Systems.* Report 65, Cmnd 3627. London: HMSO.

—— 1968b. *Job Evaluation.* Report 83, Cmnd 3772. London: HMSO.

—— 1970. *Hours of Work, Overtime and Shiftworking.* Report 161, Cmnd 4554. London: HMSO.

Nyland, C.J. 1985. 'Worktime and the Rationalization of the Capitalist Production Process'. PhD thesis, University of Adelaide.

Office of Manpower Economics (OME). 1973. *Measured Daywork.* London: HMSO.

Organization for Economic Co-operation and Development (OECD). 1970. *Forms of Wage and Salary Payment for High Productivity.* Paris: OECD.

Paterson, T.T. 1972. *Job Evaluation.* London: Business Books.

Pay Board. 1974. *Relativities.* Cmnd 5535. London: HMSO.

Phelps Brown, E.H. 1977. *The Inequality of Pay.* Oxford: Oxford University Press.

Porter, L.W., Lawler, E.E. and Hackman, J.R. 1975. *Behaviour in Organizations.* Tokyo: McGraw-Hill Kogakusha.

Robinson, D. 1973. 'Differentials and Incomes Policy'. *Industrial Relations Journal*, 4: Spring, 4–20.

Ross, A.M. 1948. *Trade Union Wage Policy.* Berkeley, CA: University of California Press.

Routh, G. 1980. *Occupation and Pay in Great Britain 1906–1979.* Cambridge: Cambridge University Press.

Rubery, J., Tarling, R. and Wilkinson, F. 1986. 'Flexibility, Marketing and the Organisation of Production'. University of Cambridge, Department of Applied Economics (mimeo).

Schloss, D.F. 1892. *Methods of Industrial Remuneration.* London: Williams & Norgate.

Shimmin, S. 1959. *Payment by Results.* London: Staples.

Smith, G.R. 1896. 'Profit Sharing and Employee Share Ownership in Britain'. *Employment Gazette*, 94: September, 380–5.

Weitzman, M.L. 1984. *The Share Economy: Conquering Stagflation.* Cambridge, MA: Harvard University Press.

White, M. 1981a. *The Hidden Meaning of Pay Conflict.* London: Macmillan.

—— 1981b. *Payment Systems in Britain.* London: PSI and Gower.

Whitmore, D.A. 1976. *Work Study and Related Management Services.* London: Heinemann.

Whyte, W.F. 1955. *Money and Motivation.* New York: Harper & Row.

Willman, P. 1982. *Fairness, Collective Bargaining and Incomes Policy.* Oxford: Clarendon Press.

Wootton, B. 1955. *The Social Foundation of Wage Policy.* London: Allen & Unwin.

# 12 The Decline and Fall of the Status Divide?

*Robert Price*

The 'deep foundations of conservatism' referred to in the previous chapter, reinforced by powerful sentiments of 'fairness', have not only affected pay structures and differentials, but have also been at the root of the profound differences in the other terms and conditions of employment that have traditionally separated manual from non-manual or 'white-collar' workers. Throughout the world, non-manual work has carried with it an assumption of higher status and better terms and conditions of employment, providing, in particular, long-term job security and stability. Britain has been no exception. Indeed, the status divide in Britain has proved to be more durable than in many other countries. While some sections of the white-collar labour-force might not, for some periods, earn as much as some manual workers, their pay has been supplemented by better provisions for sick pay, longer holidays, a shorter working week and, often of greatest significance, a pension on retirement. Incremental pay scales, promotion prospects and a 'clean' working environment have also been traditional elements of non-manual employees' work experience, dividing them from the manual workforce.

Having examined the nature and extent of the status divide in Britain, this chapter will proceed to consider its origins and the reasons for its durability. It then goes on to discuss the pressures on managements to close the gap and to illustrate the argument with recent examples. The overall conclusion is that, while the introduction of single status is not a panacea or an end in itself, the direction in which personnel practice is moving under the impact of contemporary economic and social conditions means that it is increasingly a question not of 'whether', but of 'when', structures incorporating this principle are introduced.

## THE NATURE AND EXTENT OF THE STATUS DIVIDE

Table 12.1 summarizes the results of a postal enquiry carried out in 1968 by the Department of Applied Economics, Cambridge, into the terms and conditions of employment of manual and non-manual employees in manufacturing industry. The results show very clearly the distinctions made at that time between the two groups, and the very much less favourable conditions offered

TABLE 12.1 *Terms and conditions of employment (percentage of establishments where the condition applies)*

| Selected conditions of employment | Operatives | Foremen | Clerical workers | Technicians | Management Middle | Management Senior |
|---|---|---|---|---|---|---|
| Formal sick pay scheme available | 46 | 65 | 63 | 65 | 63 | 63 |
| Sick pay provided for more than three months | 49 | 58 | 55 | 57 | 65 | 67 |
| Coverage by formal pension scheme | 67 | 94 | 90 | 94 | 96 | 95 |
| Pension calculated as fixed amount per year of service | 48 | 18 | 16 | 14 | 13 | 12 |
| Holidays, excluding public holidays, of 15 days or more a year | 38 | 71 | 74 | 77 | 84 | 88 |
| Choice of time at which holidays taken | 35 | 54 | 76 | 76 | 84 | 88 |
| Time off with pay for domestic reasons | 29 | 84 | 84 | 86 | 92 | 93 |
| Period of notice of dismissal in excess of statutory requirements | 13 | 29 | 26 | 29 | 53 | 61 |
| Clocking on to record attendance | 92 | 33 | 24 | 29 | 2 | 4 |
| Pay deduction as penalty for lateness | 90 | 20 | 8 | 11 | 1 | — |
| Warning followed by dismissal for frequent absence without leave | 94 | 86 | 94 | 92 | 74 | 67 |

*Source:* Craig (1969) 'Men in Manufacturing Industry', Department of Applied Economics, University of Cambridge

to manual workers. They also illustrate the divisions within the non-manual category, particularly between managerial grades and the other groups. Commenting on these results, Wedderburn and Craig state:

> There is overall a greater similarity of treatment between the grades in respect of the more purely economic aspects of the terms of employment, such as sick pay and pension schemes, than in aspects controlling working hours and behaviour such as holidays, attendance recording and certain disciplinary penalties. (1974: 145)

This view was reinforced by the results of case studies undertaken to complement the postal enquiry which revealed that 'manual workers were in every case more closely bound by discipline than were staff' (1974: 146). For manual workers, rules were found to be stricter, penalties more frequent and severe, disciplinary procedures more frequently invoked, and less discretion was allowed to supervisors. Such differential treatment is symptomatic of the behavioural assumptions which underlie the status divide: manual workers are expected to be less reliable than their 'staff' counterparts because they are assumed to identify less strongly with the company or organization. They have to be placed under relatively stringent management controls because they cannot be relied upon to control themselves in a manner that accords with the interests of the company.

Despite the greater similarity noted in the economic aspects of the terms of employment, the evidence presented by Wedderburn and Craig for 1968–70 showed clearly that manual workers had a longer working week and shorter holidays than non-manual workers. In 1970, 60 per cent of non-manual employees worked less than 38 hours per week, while 65 per cent of manual workers worked more than 40 hours. Only half as many manual as non-manual workers had over three weeks holiday a year. Manual workers were also far more likely to suffer deductions from pay in respect of late arrival at work, and for taking time off in domestic emergencies. They also experienced greater irregularity of earnings associated with overtime, piece-rate payments and shift-working. Earnings data also showed that, while non-manual employees could typically expect increased earnings capacity over the bulk of their working lives, manual workers' earnings capacity tended to peak relatively early in their working life and then to level off and decline from age 40 onwards. The effect of incremental salary scales, merit increases and career progression for non-manual workers was to link non-manual pay more strongly to age, whereas the earnings capacity of manual workers was more closely linked to physical capacities. Very few manual workers were found to have the opportunity to cross the divide between manual and non-manual employment. A final area of inequality in the economic aspects of work referred to in the Cambridge study, and documented more fully at that time by government-sponsored research, was the insecurity engendered by a much greater likelihood of redundancy for manual workers, and their greater job mobility – motivated at least in part by the desire to improve their earnings capacity (Parker et al., 1971).

The Cambridge survey also showed that a majority of establishments had segregated canteen facilities, and that even where such facilities were nominally the same for all grades, 'in many firms it was customary for different occupational groups to use different facilities' (Wedderburn and Craig, 1974: 146). This type of segregation was also common in the provision of car-parking, toilet facilities and changing and rest facilities. Differential treatment in these symbolic areas of basic human functions is perhaps the clearest simple indication of the durability of the attitudinal assumptions underpinning the origins of the divide between manual and non-manual workers; it was still considered normal for manual workers to be treated as 'less worthy' of humane and comfortable conditions.

How far has the situation altered in the past two decades? For reasons that will be discussed further in a subsequent section, 'harmonization' of manual and non-manual conditions has been firmly on the bargaining agenda since the early 1970s. Progress has been patchy and variable, but the trend has been for a clear narrowing or elimination of differences in treatment. Recent survey evidence (ACAS, 1982; Roberts, 1985; ACAS, 1988), together with case study evidence from a variety of industries and firms, show continuing differences between the two groups in respect of payments for non-work periods – retirement pensions, sick pay, lay-off pay, short-time working and time off for domestic reasons; but there has been a strong trend towards equalization of treatment in hours, holidays, payment systems, facilities and fringe benefits.

On *pensions*, less than half of all manual employees were covered by an occupational scheme in the early 1980s, while nearly two-thirds of non-manual employees were so covered; it was still normal for the two groups to be covered by separate schemes within any individual enterprise, and for the entitlements to be better for non-manual staff (National Association of Pension Funds, 1981). Nevertheless, nearly one-third of firms in the 1988 ACAS sample had harmonized pensions within the previous three years and another 13 per cent were planning to harmonize pensions agreements (ACAS, 1982: 26). On *sick pay*, the Statutory Sick Pay provisions have stimulated a degree of harmonization of treatment between the two groups, but occupational schemes still cover more non-manual workers, and tend to provide better benefits (Labour Research Department, 1980). Here too, the ACAS sample identified some 40 per cent of companies as either having harmonized sick pay pensions or intending to do so (ACAS, 1982: 26). As far as the *variability of pay* is concerned, the gap between the two groups continues to be considerable; short-time working and lay-offs at reduced rates of pay still affect manual workers almost exclusively, and both overtime and payments by results show a far greater incidence among manual workers. For full-time manual males, overtime accounts for nearly a quarter of gross weekly earnings; and over a third of manual workers receive pay linked to output, while among non-manuals the proportion is between 12 and 18 per cent. Reductions in the *length of the basic working week* occurred across the board from mid-1979 to 1983, but have tended to remain stable since; these reductions still leave something of a gap at the aggregate level between manual and non-manual worker hours, but in many firms basic hours have been harmonized; Table 12.2 shows the extent of the hours gap in 1981. *Holiday entitlements* have been one of the

TABLE 12.2  *Hours of work*

*Average normal basic weekly hours for full-time adults – April 1981*

| | Manual workers | | Non-manual workers | |
|---|---|---|---|---|
| | M | F | M | F |
| All industries and services | 39.8 | 38.5 | 37.2 | 36.3 |
| All manufacturing industries | 39.8 | 39.0 | 37.7 | 36.8 |
| All non-manufacturing industries | 39.7 | 37.9 | 36.9 | 36.2 |

*Normal basic hours April 1981; percentage distribution for full-time adults*

| Percentage with normal basic hours in the range | Manual workers | | Non-manual workers | |
|---|---|---|---|---|
| | M | F | M | F |
| up to 30 | — | — | 4.4 | 6.8 |
| 30–45 | 2.4 | 15.3 | 17.0 | 24.0 |
| 35–39 | 21.4 | 22.7 | 58.0 | 59.8 |
| 39–40 | 70.4 | 60.1 | 16.1 | 8.4 |
| 40–45 | 4.0 | 1.6 | 3.2 | 0.9 |
| 45+ | 1.5 | 0.1 | 1.3 | — |

*Sources*:  NES April (1981) (Part C), tables 54–7; ACAS (1982) *Developments in Harmonisation*, Discussion Paper No. 1 (London: HMSO, p. 10)

most important areas of harmonization, with very considerable changes taking place during the 1970s. By April 1981, 87 per cent of manual men and 90 per cent of non-manual men had a basic entitlement of 20 days or more (DE, 1981); and a survey by the Policy Studies Institute in 1979 found that manual and non-manual entitlements were usually the same (PSI, 1980). The 1979 national engineering agreement provided for a move to a 25-day minimum holiday entitlement for manual workers by 1982, and the evidence for that industry is that this has resulted in a common basic entitlement for all employees (IRRR, 1986).

Other distinctions between manual and non-manual workers are of continuing significance, despite moves to eliminate or reduce them in many organizations. *Cashless pay* has been extended to many manual workers in the 1980s, but manuals are still much more likely to be paid weekly and in cash than non-manuals. This is an area in which Britain differs very markedly from other advanced industrial societies. Non-manual employees are still able to look forward to pay increases from *incremental progression* and *promotion* as well as from general annual reviews, while manual workers' pay increases tend to stem overwhelmingly from the annual pay round. Nevertheless, there has been a 'phenomenal increase in performance review among skilled manual workers' (IPM, 1986; IRRR, 1987c: 2–11), linking pay improvements in addition to any general increase to a worker's performance. Manual workers are still less likely to have fringe benefits such as *insurance*, *private health schemes*, *cars* and *cheap loans*, although it should be stressed that such benefits are often not universally offered to all grades of non-manual worker within any individual enterprise. *Flexitime* has tended to increase the numbers of non-manuals who are expected to clock in and out of work, but overall it is still the case that many companies operate a clocking system for manuals but not for staff workers. Finally, a Labour Research Department survey in 1981 showed that in respect of *redundancy*,

> non-manual workers are much more likely to be paid above the statutory minimum entitlement than manual workers; in 175 agreements studied, manual workers were often entitled to less notice, less favourable compensation, less income protection if alternative work was offered, and less favourable minor enhancements. (LRD, 1981)

This review of the surveys by Wedderburn and Craig (1974) and the Advisory, Conciliation and Arbitration Service (1982 and 1988) demonstrates both the durability of the status divide, and some of the changes that have been taking place in the extent of the differences between the two occupational groups. The evidence of change is unmistakable, but survey results presented in aggregate form cannot pick up the growing number of cases in which organizations have either opted for a fully integrated terms and conditions package on a new site, or for a radical change in favour of integration on an existing site or sites. The following sections seek to examine the origins and the durability of the status divide, and to explore the reasons for its recent decline and even, in some cases, disappearance.

## THE ORIGINS OF THE STATUS DIVIDE

Before proceeding to look at the pressures for change, it is instructive to reflect briefly on the origins of the distinction, and the operational and attitudinal assumptions which lie behind it. The emergence of 'non-productive' labour to assist employers with the book-keeping, design, merchandizing and supervisory functions of the growing industrial sector during the nineteenth century has been reviewed by many writers (Lockwood, 1958; Braverman, 1974). The growth in scale of the typical industrial enterprise made it impossible for the single entrepreneur to carry out all the functions associated with the control and management of the enterprise. The devolution of some or all of these functions to employees brought into being complex bureaucratic hierarchies, modelled frequently – as in the Weberian ideal-type – on military structures.

Two characteristic features of industrial and commercial bureaucracies as they emerged in the early periods of industrialization deserve particular comment here. First, the hierarchy of control, through which posts at successive levels were held responsible for the activities of the employees below them, was associated with non-manual status. These employees were the NCOs and junior officers of capital, and were expected to commit themselves to the success of the enterprise as defined by the owner-proprietor. Their privileged status was a natural consequence of their association with the control functions of the enterprise. Second, the creation of a number of tiers of bureaucracy was associated with the notion of 'career', through which loyal and competent performance at a lower level would be rewarded by preferment to the higher levels of the organization. A prerequisite of promotion would inevitably be the demonstration of an appropriate degree of commitment to the goals of the organization as defined by the principal power-holders – either the owner or the senior executive managers.

Non-manual staff have thus traditionally been expected to be motivated by something more than short term economic rewards; commitment and loyalty to the organization, whether public or private, were expected to be equally important, if not more so. Non-manual employees could be expected to exercise discretion and decision-making responsibilities in their work in ways which would be in accordance with the organization's objectives. The importance of that discretion being exercised in the interests of the enterprise was clearly greater at the higher levels of the hierarchy, and hence greater proximity to the functions of the employer brought with it higher social status and greater privileges in conditions of employment.

The key to the distinction between manual and non-manual workers is to be found in this association of non-manual work with the functions of the employer; proximity to authority, and hence a share in that authority, marked these employees out from their manual counterparts. Loyalty to the enterprise, a high level of personal identification with its fortunes, and a willingness to deliver services beyond the call of a standard job description, became stereotypical hallmarks of the 'staff' worker. In the public sector bureaucracies such as the civil service and local government, parallel distinctions emerged, although the greater proportionate size of the non-manual workforce, the absence of a 'production' environment, and the strong influence of the public service ethos tended to stimulate a rather closer relationship between the conditions of employment of the two groups of workers. For example, manual worker pensions and sick-pay arrangements were relatively generous in the public sector once a specific minimum period of employment was attained.

While the origins and the nature of the employment differentiation between manual and non-manual workers have been very similar in all industrial societies, the law has played a varying role in reinforcing the distinction. In Britain, the law's role has been very limited. As Bain and Price (1972) have shown, while the distinction between manual and non-manual workers was held to be significant in the provision of social insurance benefits and in the application of the Truck Acts in the early part of the century, legal distinctions ceased to have very much relevance during the inter-war period. In the countries of Northern and Central Europe, however, tight legal boundaries were drawn around white-collar work, and a privileged social and legal status conferred on these employees. The German categories of *Angestellte* (private sector white-collar employees) and *Beamte* (public sector employees) can be found in similar forms in many countries in Scandinavia and the old Austrian Empire. Special social insurance, taxation and legal regimes covering terms and conditions of employment were established for these groups of employees; and, as a broad generalization, they can be said to have displayed a closer identification with their employers, and a stronger sense of distance from manual workers than was the case in Britain (Lockwood, 1958; Bain and Price, 1972; Speier, 1934). While the legal entrenchment of these status differences has been of declining significance in the past 40 years, there are still areas in which it can be found (François, 1963). However, it is something of an irony that, while many European countries continue to have separate white-collar and manual worker union confederations, and separate seats on works councils and company boards for the two groups, the overall extent of the status divide has probably declined faster outside Britain than inside.

While profound differences of status and treatment did develop between non-manual and manual workforces, it should not be assumed that the non-manual group was internally homogeneous and undifferentiated, even in an era when it was much smaller, both absolutely and relatively, than it is today. In particular, a deep schism between male and female clerical workers emerged at a very early point. When women workers began to be taken on in large numbers in clerical and related functions, they were frequently employed on lower pay and under inferior conditions to their male counterparts. There was fierce opposition to the employment of women from male clerical workers precisely because it was considered to be a way of undercutting male pay rates and reducing male job opportunities. As Walby (1986: 154) shows, employers often responded to these fears by segregating female clerks in special grades with lower wages, fewer promotion opportunities, less job security and lower status. More generally, the rapid growth of the clerical labour-force in the early decades of the century inevitably resulted in a decline in the promotion prospects available to the average clerk, and this created a greater sense of distance between many clerks and their managerial superiors (Lockwood, 1958). As the non-manual labour-force expanded after the Second World War, its internal heterogeneity became increasingly marked. With the growth of higher education and the associated development of 'credentialism' in determining access to many upper-level non-manual jobs, notions of an internal community of interest and accessible ladders of promotion were steadily undermined.

It is a tribute to the power of custom and tradition that distinctions rooted in the latter part of the nineteenth century between 'white-collar' (itself a term redolent of the nineteenth-century counting house) and manual jobs, which derive essentially from the proximity of the former groups to the employer and which rest upon an assumed close identification of interest between them and their employer, should have persisted into the last decade of the twentieth century. For some considerable time, the majority of 'white-collar' workers have been female, and not typically wearers of collars; and whether male or female, most work in environments which do very little either to reflect or encourage a close identification with employers' interests – any more, that is, than might be found among their manual counterparts.

## THE DURABILITY OF THE STATUS DIVIDE

So why has the status divide proved to be so durable? Alan Fox in his influential contribution to the sociology of work has argued that the typical relationship between employers and workers in Britain has involved a 'low-trust' and 'contractualized' set of mutual expectations (1985: 92). As far as manual workers are concerned, British employers have typically sought to elicit acceptable levels of productive performance by what can loosely be described as the 'Taylorist' methods of work organization referred to in earlier chapters: linking pay to output through piecework systems to provide a direct economic incentive for productivity; close supervision; and the use of disciplinary procedures to enforce sanctions. With a relatively small group of well-known firms as exceptions, little weight has traditionally been attached to the development of a 'moral' involvement by employees with the enterprise. Senior management have been distant and uninvolved with the shopfloor, and employment conditions have been standardized and depersonalized. In Fox's own words,

> The . . . low-discretion work circumstances of most wage and lower salary earners cause them to feel excluded from more significant and responsible participation and therefore not really trusted. Their inferior rewards . . . confirm their sense of being low-status 'hands' who are not seen as full members of the higher corporate effort. The old terminology of 'hands' and 'staff' embodied this crucial distinction. (1985: 49–50)

Fox here includes lower-level non-manual employees within the area of low discretion work, implying that the historical conditions of manual employment have at some point also begun to apply equally to the lower levels of the white-collar hierarchy. This underlines vividly the ambiguity of the position of these groups. While they have continued to enjoy better conditions of employment than manual workers across a wide range of areas, they have increasingly been subjected to similar types of routinized and closely supervised work organization, with tight limits placed on the amount of personal discretion either expected or permitted. This relationship does not square with the attitudinal assumptions that were argued earlier to underpin the status divide. The contrast between 'hands' and 'staff' embodies the view that the 'staff' group consists of loyal 'employer's substitutes', motivated as much by personal commitment as financial incentives, and hence occupying a high-trust relationship with the employer.

The rapid expansion of the non-manual labour-force to the point where it is now larger than the manual workforce (52 per cent against 48 per cent at the 1981 Census: Price and Bain, 1983), bringing with it a massively increased internal heterogeneity and a sharp increase in the proportion of non-manual workers occupying routine jobs without significant career prospects, inevitably calls into question the continued relevance of sharp differentiation between manual and white-collar workers. However, while the assumptions built into the original distinction have been of questionable relevance for large sections of the non-manual labour-force for many decades, there has been little movement to bring together the terms and conditions of employment of the two groups until relatively recently.

The durability of the divide can be accounted for in a variety of ways, but the central element in any explanation must be the value to employers of a structure of control for some groups of employees based on a 'higher-trust', relationship, underpinned by a relatively privileged status within the enterprise. For non-production employees, few of whose contributions to the operation of the enterprise can be easily measured in profit-and-loss terms, and many of whom are still relatively closely related to senior management functions, a strategy of control based on what Friedman (1977: 78–9) has called 'responsible autonomy' can clearly be both effective and rational. By binding non-manual workers closer to the enterprise through privileged conditions, career perspectives (even if somewhat limited), and a degree of autonomy within the workplace, employers can expect to achieve a degree of both legitimacy and commitment.

The durability of the status divide can also be linked to the self-identification of non-manual employees as a distinctive group, as reflected in the structure of collective representation. With a few exceptions, such as the tally clerks in the London docks, non-manual workers in the early years of trade union organization established separate organizations from those representing the manual workers in the same industry (Lockwood, 1958). Since the early 1970s, some of the large general unions have been successful in developing or expanding 'white-collar' sections, but it remains the case that over 90 per cent of unionized white-collar employees are within non-manual organizations. As an early post-war American commentator summed it up:

> The white-collar worker wants to and manages to maintain his [sic] separate identity. This is a persisting situation; and union leaders will have to recognize it as such. (Strauss, 1954: 81)

The majority of non-manual workers have, of course, not joined unions at all; at the three high points in British union membership in 1920, 1948 and 1979, non-manual density reached 29, 33 and 44 per cent respectively. As Bain (1970) has indicated, employers were generally reluctant to recognize unions for non-manual workers up to the time when he was writing. A relatively brief period ensued in the 1970s when white-collar union bargaining was more readily accepted by employers, but the recession and social conditions of the 1980s have stimulated a return to the more negative approach characteristic of the earlier decades. The 1984 Workplace Industrial Relations Survey found that 26 per cent of private manufacturing establishments recognized unions for non-manual employees, as against 55 per cent recognizing manual unions; and in the private services, the proportions were 30 per cent against 38 per cent (Millward and Stevens, 1986: 63).

Employers' traditional reluctance to embrace collective representation on behalf of non-manual employees is closely associated with the beliefs that have sustained the divide between manual and non-manual workers. Non-manual staff were expected to be committed to the organization and to identify with its owners and managers. Since they were considered to form part of the managerial function of the organization, it was inappropriate for them to combine against that function. In Fox's terms, a 'high-trust' relationship was assumed to exist, within which collective bargaining had no place. And in many instances, as Bain (1970) documents, employers have gone out of their way to reinforce the notional 'high-trust' relationship by making special concessions in the face of a potential threat of unionization by non-manual staff.

The establishment of separate unions or staff associations catering for 'white-collar' workers has served to entrench further the divisions between the two groups over the long term. Where unions have bargained successfully on behalf of non-manual staff, they have fought to preserve a degree of separate identity and special status; the preservation of relative privilege over manual workers in the shape of pensions or sick-pay, or a more relaxed regime for timekeeping have been an important part of their *raison d'être*. And many white-collar workers have joined unions only because of an awareness of declining pay or status differentials, and a belief that collective representation would rectify that decline (Hyman and Price, 1983: 175–7). On the other hand, employers' desire to keep unions out of their organizations for non-manual staff has encouraged them to strengthen the status divide in order to 'buy' loyalty.

Comparing Britain with other European countries, where the move towards single status has been more rapid, suggests two additional features of the institutional framework which are important in helping to explain the durability of the status divide in Britain. One is the role of the state in employment affairs. Whereas in Britain the debate about state involvement has been over the most basic elements of employment protection, in many European countries, notably France and West Germany, there has been considerable pressure from governments to introduce and develop single status arrangements. In France and Sweden, for example, there has been legislation to underpin the principle of single status; and in West Germany, the state has consistently sought to harmonize key employment conditions, such as pay systems, holiday and sick pay entitlement. The second feature is the structure of collective bargaining. In France, Italy and West Germany, for example, the structure of multi-employer bargaining has provided an effective forum in which the broad principles informing comparative conditions of employment could be examined. In France, in particular, negotiations involving the equivalent of the Confederation of British Industry and the various union confederations have provided a framework for the introduction of single status arrangements covering entire industries or sectors. In Britain, by contrast, the decline of multi-employer bargaining and the considerable decentralization of collective bargaining to the individual unit has meant that no such framework exists; single status arrangements, as a later section will show, have to be introduced on a piecemeal basis.

## THE DECLINING DIVIDE

While the durability of the status divide as an important factor in the consciousness of both employers and employees alike cannot be doubted, it is clear that the cumulative effect of a number of different processes that have taken place over the past two decades in particular, has been to reduce substantially the utility and acceptability of the distinction between white-collar and blue-collar, and staff or works groups.

On the one hand, lower level clerical, secretarial, sales and technical functions have become increasingly routinized and often machine-dominated; entry requirements have been low, and labour supply has generally been good since the basic education system has provided most of the necessary training. Such routinization of non-manual work has tended to be associated with reduced career prospects; indeed, routinization has gone hand-in-hand with feminization, in such a way that employers have been able to rely on an assumed secondary labour-market role for women to reduce potential pressure for careers from a very large section of the lower levels of the non-manual labour-force. Meanwhile, the higher levels of non-manual employment have expanded dramatically in scale and complexity. In practice, entry to these positions is very often through the possession of graduate or professional qualifications and they are thus not open, even in theory, to employees on the lowest rungs of the ladder. In the final decades of the twentieth century, the traditional use of the non-manual label to describe a relatively small and homogeneous group, united in its close relationship to the seat of managerial or employer power, is dead. While some elements of the non-manual labour-force still do retain the traditional closeness to the locus of authority within the enterprise, the majority do not; and it is hardly surprising that this has led to a questioning of the relevance of traditional divisions and privileges.

On the other hand, new forms of work have emerged at the margins of the manual labour-force that serve to blur even further the traditional distinctions. In many traditional 'craft' areas, the application of microelectronic technologies has produced a range of jobs that are 'manual' in their day-to-day physical requirements, but demand 'non-manual' levels of technical training and expertise. The day of the 'craftician' has already dawned in some industries, and more generally, craft functions are becoming more closely aligned with technical functions. Even jobs that require relatively little technical training are being transformed by microprocessor applications into semi-technical, 'whitecoat', process control jobs (Boddy and Buchanan, 1986). The transition in printing from Linotype machines to visual display units and computer-controlled printing, and in retail distribution from shop assistants to check-out staff, both reflect vividly the blurring of old divisions.

It is important, however, to keep these changes in perspective. Despite its reduced share of the labour-force, manual work still consists overwhelmingly of jobs in cleaning, assembling, building, driving, processing and providing food and drink. Their manual content is as high as it has ever been, and the occupants of these jobs face the same limitations on personal discretion and on career progression that their precedessors have done. Similarly, there is still a considerable group of professional and managerial jobs for which the traditional notions of status and privileged relationships with the employer continue to be relevant. Nevertheless, the pressures to reduce the status divide from a range of sources outside the occupational changes discussed above are intense; these sources are worth examining in more detail.

### The Quality of Working Life

The early 1970s was a period of considerable turbulence in labour–management relationships throughout Europe (Barkin, 1975; Crouch and Pizzorno, 1978). The responses of unions, employers and the state to worker unrest were remarkably similar across all the major industrialized economies in their broad thrust, although they inevitably differed substantially in detail and in their effectiveness. On the one hand, a variety of initiatives were taken in the field of 'industrial democracy'; workers' representatives were placed on company boards, works councils' powers were strengthened, and workplace union rights to information, consultation and co-decision were extended. On the other hand, a range of measures were introduced that were intended to improve the 'quality of working life' for ordinary workers. Considerable effort went into exploring the potential for increasing the intrinsic interest of work tasks, by restructuring and reorganizing the workplace. To relieve boredom and the demotivating effects of unstimulating jobs, attempts were made to stimulate greater worker involvement in day-to-day decision-making on the shopfloor. In West Germany, major state-supported programmes for the 'humanization of work' (*Humanisierung der Arbeit*) were launched; in France, a programme was launched by the Minister of Labour seeking the '*revalorisation du travail manuel*' (increasing the value of manual work); in Sweden, the much discussed Volvo Kalmar experiment heralded a number of other initiatives around the Industrial Democracy Act of 1974, and the state-funded *Arbetslivscentrum* (Working Life Centre) began work on human-centred technology applications; even in Britain, the Work Research Unit of the Department of Employment provided a relatively low-key but significant stimulus to employer initiatives to extend worker participation and improve the content of dead-end jobs, and the Bullock Committee of Inquiry into board-level representation encouraged many employers to take voluntary steps to achieve greater involvement short of the unacceptable introduction of workers into the boardroom (Francis, 1986; Price and Steininger, 1987; Ramsey, 1985).

The common theme linking these initiatives was the apparent crisis of legitimacy reflected in the greater militancy of the workers of these countries. Workers' acquiescence to the discipline of the workplace could no longer be guaranteed; the long post-war boom and low levels of unemployment had eroded workers' willingness to defer to managerial authority. Fox's formulation of the problem for management is characteristically elegant:

Rising living standards, better education, and growing aspirations among ordinary men for self-respect and dignity have all contributed to a widening disinclination to accept without scrutiny the commands, policies and decisions of officially constituted authority. Increasingly men ask 'Why?'. (1985: 52)

Increasingly, too, management was coming to the view that acquiescence, or the passive assent to authority, was not enough. In the face of increased competition from newly industrializing nations of the Far East and Latin America, European industry had to win the hearts and minds of its employees to improve productivity and the quality of production. Quality of working life programmes and industrial democracy initiatives were regularly linked to the partial or full harmonization of terms and conditions of employment, as employers sought to come to grips with the re-establishment of legitimacy and authority within the enterprise. All these elements reflected a new willingness to re-examine social justice in the workplace, and to recognize the value of each individual to the business, as a means of creating a different, more stable and 'higher trust' relationship between employers and the workforce as a whole. In this perspective, traditional status distinctions were seen as divisive and anachronistic. More cynically, there was a strong current of employer opinion which held that the extension of staff conditions to manual workers could be expected to produce a 'non-manual' attitude to work, involving greater flexibility and commitment to company objectives. Whatever the precise motivation, however, the net effect was to give a major stimulus to harmonization of manual and non-manual conditions with a view to the creation of a new basis for social harmony within the enterprise.

*New Technologies*

The tendency for employers to seek to modify traditional 'low-trust' relationships with manual workers, and to attempt to achieve with them a relationship of integration and commitment very similar to that historically associated with non-manual employees, was further strengthened by the emergence of microprocessor-based technologies on a substantial scale at the end of the 1970s. Major changes to products and production systems were set in motion by the application of the microchip (Gill, 1985; Francis, 1986). This radical restructuring of the labour process, coinciding with a further 'oil shock' and a world recession, stimulated employers both to reduce their labour-forces and to seek maximum efficiency from those remaining. In this context, status differentials and job demarcations were increasingly viewed as obstructions to the efficient utilization of labour and the capacity of an enterprise to react flexibly to product market and technological changes. Harmonization has frequently been introduced as part of a package of measures to improve working practices and change payments systems, in order to derive optimal benefit from new capital equipment. New technology has also frequently had the effect of underlining the importance of winning workers' commitment to the objectives of the enterprise in a far more wholehearted way than has traditionally been the case; a willingness to be flexible and to exercise discretion and initiative in the interests of the enterprise have been seen to depend crucially on the development of a more 'unitary' relationship between workers and company – in short, to seek to put manual workers onto the same footing as was traditionally assumed to be the case with non-manual workers.

### *'Japanization'*

The steady growth in the penetration of European markets by manufactured goods from Japan and other nations in the Far East during the past two decades, and the more recent arrival in Britain of a number of major Japanese manufacturers such as Nissan, Toshiba, Hitachi, Komatsu and Isuzu have stimulated enormous – some would say obsessive – interest from British employers in Japanese personnel practice and production systems (Ackroyd et al., 1988). The apparent success of these companies in avoiding industrial relations conflicts and achieving high levels of worker commitment to quality and consistency of output has had a major impact on British companies' own thinking about systems of personnel management. The influential book by Pascale and Athos (1981) on the 'art' of Japanese management has been followed by a series of well-publicized success stories in the restructuring of traditional industrial relations systems (see, for example, Pegge, 1986; Trevor, 1988; Wickens, 1987).

While there is no clear evidence on the degree to which specifically Japanese practices have been adopted by British companies, there can be no doubt that the Japanese example has reinforced some of the most important themes already affecting domestic management thinking. The single-union 'no strike' deals at firms like Nissan, Toshiba and Hitachi have received wide media attention, but in practice the more influential changes have probably been those abolishing status distinctions such as separate canteens, car parks, and different types of clothing, and the introduction of quality circles and other group-based methods of involving workers in the quality of production. In its 1981 document, *The Will to Win*, the CBI was already contrasting the perceived unity of purpose of the typical Japanese enterprise with the 'unnecessarily divisive' distinctions, typical of British companies which could not be 'functionally justified'. 'British industry still suffers from too many social divisions, ranging from canteen facilities to pension provision, which bear no relation to work done.'

The central impact of Japanese practice has been to underline the apparent links between greater status equality, labour flexibility and a sense of personal commitment to the quality of the finished product. The continuing influence of Japan reinforces the declining acceptability of the status divide.

### *Human Resource Management*

A final stream of influence that has contributed to the declining significance of the status divide has come from the growth of a human resource management approach to corporate personnel policy. As chapter 2 indicated, the precise meaning of the term 'human resource management', and the ways in which it is said to differ from conventional personnel management techniques, are matters of continuing debate (Armstrong, 1987; Mackay and Torrington, 1986). There is little dispute, however, that a distinctive feature of the human resource management approach is the degree to which it focuses on the connections between overall corporate strategy and personnel policies. Strategic choices about the size, location and character of the labour-force are linked closely to the company's production, marketing and financial strategies: 'every aspect of employee management must be totally integrated with general business management and reinforce the desired company culture' (Fowler, 1987: 3).

This emphasis in human resource management on linking employee relations with the establishment and maintenance of a company culture is an important one. 'Old style' industrial relations and personnel management are characterized as managing the human environment in a relatively passive way; the job of the managers concerned is simply to keep up the supply of labour and to avoid disruption of production. By contrast, human resource management is credited with a strongly proactive role aimed at the integration of the employee into a harmonious and mutually supportive system of human relations. In Fowler's (1987: 3) view this amounts to 'a dominant emphasis on the common interests of the employer and the employee in the success of the business ... [to] release a massive potential of initiative and commitment within the workforce'.

Clearly such a framework of policy points strongly to the elimination of status divisions in order to give weight to the philosophy of common interests and commitment. In this way, too, contemporary management thinking is seeking to establish a new legitimacy through unitary or integrative personnel strategies based on the extension of 'non-manual' conditions to 'manual' employees.

Moves towards the implementation of human resource management strategies can be linked to the popular success among British managers of Peters' and Watermans' *In Search of Excellence* (1982) which has already been referred to in chapter 3. One of their key ingredients for corporate excellence is a 'people-oriented culture'. The use of the word 'culture' carries with it strong implications of value integration throughout an organization, of 'pulling together' and teamwork. It would be a mistake, however, to see the Peters and Waterman theme of 'productivity through people' as simply a return to the simple 'unitary' notions of traditional managements as described by Fox (1966; 1985). The traditional unitary approach can be seen as closely analogous to the authority structures of the military, in which commands flow from the top down, and subordinates are required above all to show obedience to those set in authority. In sharp contrast, the message of *In Search of Excellence* is to 'treat people as adults. Treat them as partners; treat them with dignity' (1982: 238). Instead of initiatives coming uniquely from the top of an organization, Peters and Waterman emphasize the importance of establishing structures which encourage employees to contribute positively to the company's success.

A people-oriented culture will embody an environment which releases employees' energies and initiative in support of the company's success. The job of human resource management is to align employees' objectives with those of the company. In their words:

> if you want productivity and the financial reward that goes with it, you must treat your workers as your most important asset.... There was hardly a more pervasive theme in the excellent companies than respect for the individual. We are talking about tough-minded respect for the individual and the willingness to train him, to set reasonable and clear expectations for him, and to grant him practical autonomy to step out and contribute directly to his job. (1982: 238–9)

On its own, *In Search of Excellence* might have had little impact. Coming as it did at a time when many other factors in the environment – technology, the Japanese example, interest in industrial democracy – were already stimulating managerial interest in new directions in personnel policy, the message of 'productivity through people' has reinforced the trend towards dismantling anachronistic structures and relationships. The themes of reducing hierarchy, increasing flexibility and providing scope for individual initiative that are at the heart of the Peters and Waterman recipe for excellence fell upon highly fertile ground in the circumstances of the early 1980s.

*Flexibility*

An important theme running through the sets of influences on management identified here is that of 'flexibility'. The introduction of new technologies and the associated changes in work organization, together with the need to cut labour costs in the face of international competitive pressures, have put a premium on securing maximum value from the labour-force while, at the same time, seeking to align labour supply more closely to production needs. This has led to a greater use of part-time and temporary workers, and to more subcontracting (ACAS, 1988; NEDO/IMS, 1986). For the 'core' workforce of full-time employees, the impact of flexibility has been to reduce demarcation between jobs, to increase the scope for individual merit payments and to extend the use of performance-related pay.

In the 1988 ACAS survey, between 45 and 51 per cent of firms had either relaxed demarcations to enable production workers to do routine maintenance tasks and to enable craftsmen to do work usually performed by other craftsmen, or had ended divisions between manual, technical and clerical staff (ACAS, 1988: 15). This type of functional flexibility between members of the full-time workforce, while increasing the use of part-time and temporary staff to achieve more numerical flexibility, has been a common approach in manufacturing and services sectors alike. It adds further weight to the case for dismantling the status divide, in order to achieve maximum permeability with the 'core' workforce; but it also underlines the likelihood that the new status divide in employment conditions will be between 'core' and 'periphery'.

The 1988 ACAS survey revealed only 14–15 per cent of firms where fully integrated job evaluation or payment systems had been introduced over the previous three years or were planned for the near future. This is a relatively low proportion, but it was linked to much higher proportions of 38–44 per cent of firms where new 'across-the-board' reward supplements based on merit, the acquisition of new skills or profitability had either been introduced or were planned. The extension of common rewards schemes is, thus, a significant feature of contemporary practice and is further eroding the distinctive identity of white-collar and manual occupational groups.

## TOWARDS SINGLE STATUS?

This chapter has argued that the origins of the status divide were located in the creation of an elite body of employees performing specific 'employer functions'; in a real sense, they were 'employers' substitutes' (Wedderburn and Craig, 1974). It was expected that the special status granted to these employees would be reciprocated by a high degree of commitment to, and co-operation with, the employer. This elite was distinguished by their style of dress and the locale of their work, as well as by their more favourable terms and conditions of employment. The functional basis of the distinction was thus linked to important normative and behavioural differences. Over time, the functional basis of the distinction has been substantially eroded, although employers have largely continued to operate as if the normative and behavioural differences were still relevant to the nature of their relationships with the two parts of the labour-force, and have thus continued to treat them differently.

The various factors that have been discussed in the previous section have been strongly influencing managements towards putting manual workers onto the same footing as non-manual workers, and seeking to establish similar normative and behavioural patterns for both groups. Such functional differences as do remain are considered to be largely irrelevant to the task of creating a committed and co-operative workforce or, as in the case of integrated pay structures, to pose major short-run technical problems involving job evaluation (IDS, 1988).

These themes were expressed strongly in the early examples of major single status deals in the 1960s, notably the ICI Weekly Staff Agreement and the Electricity Council's Status Agreement (Roeber, 1975; Wedderburn, 1966; Edwards, 1967). Both deals affected highly capital-intensive and technologically dynamic industries; both sought to link the abolition of status distinctions to greater flexibility in the use of labour, increased productivity and the creation of 'non-manual attitudes from manual workers' (Wedderburn, 1966). The aim of transforming manual worker attitudes to the employer and the workplace is even more strongly evident in the contemporary period (IDS, 1988). At Tioxide UK, for example, a single status deal in 1987 formed part of a radical restructuring of employee relations, involving the withdrawal of recognition of the TGWU, a totally new payments system including a profit-related element, and complete flexibility with no demarcation between jobs. As Kennedy puts it:

> traditional collective bargaining methods had begun to lose their relevance and no longer provided a satisfactory means of dialogue between the company and its employees. The need to foster attitudes of commitment, accountability and flexibility was clearly recognised, and means other than traditional collective bargaining were needed to bring this about. (1988: 51)

At Johnson and Johnson, harmonization had been conceived as an expression of the 'corporate credo' which stresses the need to respect the dignity of all employees and to recognize their merit. Equally significant was the company's belief that their ability to meet the challenge of the market-place would increasingly depend on the flexibility of the workforce:

> That seems most likely to come from a salaried workforce unencumbered by payments-by-results systems and able to switch effort from one product area to another on demand. (Mullins, 1986: 38)

At Hitachi in Hirwaun, the failure of the joint venture with GEC was linked to poor management and poor operator performance. The new management installed after the Hitachi buy out of the GEC share saw as its main task the turning round of a demoralized workforce. Two key principles were complete job flexibility and single-status conditions to 'facilitate the job flexibility change and to remove the general frustrations and distractions created by blue-collar/white-collar differentials' (Pegge, 1986: 43). At Ind Coope's Burton Brewery, the declining market, changes in customer tastes requiring flexibility and innovation, and intensified competition led management to set up a 'greenfield assessment' of existing operations. This was designed to integrate the capital investment programme with major changes in personnel policy. The key findings of the assessment were:

team working: this was fundamental to the key goal of flexibility;
harmonized terms and conditions to remove barriers to flexibility and to change;
a new industrial relations style based on co-operation and involvement;
demarcation and separate negotiations would cease;
retraining and redeployment supported by payments systems that helped, not hindered, change. (IRRR, 1987a: 3)

And at BICC Optical Cables, Whiston, a 'greenfield' spin-off from an existing cable plant in Manchester gave management the opportunity to establish a seven-grade integrated pay structure, common pay and performance review structures incorporating individual merit payments, and harmonized conditions of employment. Here, too, the new pay package was seen as establishing a fresh framework for employee relations, outside the industry agreement, and incorporating single-union and binding arbitration clauses (IRRR, 1987b: 13–15).

Each of these examples essentially involved the extension of non-manual conditions to manual workers in order to facilitate integration and flexibility. A key question that is posed by such policies is the response from non-manual employees; are the benefits in motivation and commitment from manual workers lost in reduced morale among their non-manual counterparts? In particular, where non-manual staff are unionized, a levelling up of benefits might have been expected to provoke demands for compensation. Perhaps surprisingly, the cases that have been documented reveal very few reactions of this type. The examples of Tioxide and Johnson and Johnson suggest why this may be. At Tioxide, management was acutely aware of the potential backlash from non-manual employees when they experienced a decline in their former differentials. To avoid this, new integrated pay scales were introduced in advance of the move to staff status, with performance-related merit increases to give 'headroom' for relatively well-paid groups; in addition, an across-the-board profit-sharing scheme was introduced, replacing the production bonuses that had gone only to manual workers. Non-manual staff were able to look towards potential benefits in pay, linked to both personal and company performance; they were not being required to stand still while others caught up. Harmonization in a generally dynamic environment is likely to reduce significantly non-manual concern at the loss of their privileged position. At Johnson and Johnson, piecemeal harmonization of selected elements of pay and conditions over the period 1974–82 had led to common pensions, sick pay, redundancy and holidays. Pay structures and job-evaluation arrangements were still separate, but the significance of the manual/non-manual divide had been eroded over the years and was thus much less an issue of principle. Johnson and Johnson's proposals also involved the replacement of individual incentive schemes for manual workers with group incentives and profit-sharing schemes on an across-the-board basis. As at Tioxide, non-manual staff were not being required to stand still, but could look forward to some improvement in their position. A further element in harmonization at Johnson and Johnson was the allocation of new responsibilities to supervisory staff, and retraining of these employees to meet the new requirements (Mullins, 1986: 41).

As far as non-manual workers are concerned, it would seem that the gradual narrowing of differences that was noted earlier has already reduced the perceived significance of the status divide; and that if harmonization is introduced as part of a much wider package of measures to change the personnel 'culture' of the organization, there is typically some scope for providing additional benefits that are attractive to non-manual employees.

A further advantage in introducing single status or harmonization of conditions as part of a wider package is that it allows productivity gains to offset some, or all, of the additional costs incurred. In the manner of the more genuine productivity deals of the 1960s (Donovan, 1968), the linking of flexibility elements to improvements in conditions can reduce labour costs per unit of output, and, over the longer run, can reduce the need to employ additional labour as output expands. In the Johnson and Johnson case, an initial estimate of 5 per cent increase in paybill costs over three years came down to 3 per cent through productivity gains; and, as in many similar cases, there were sizeable savings through the introduction of cashless pay. Wider experience seems to indicate that the potential productivity gains can only be secured if management organization is modified to ensure effective control of, for example, sickness absence and time-keeping. This reinforces the logic of setting harmonization/single status in the context of more thoroughgoing organizational change, including the development of new managerial control systems.

## CONCLUSIONS: THE END OF THE STATUS DIVIDE?

The abolition of status differentials and the introduction of a completely single status workforce are neither panaceas nor ends in themselves. They represent important elements in a process that has been affecting a growing proportion of British industry – and European industry more generally. This process begins with the product market, where ever sharper competitive pressures and rapid technological changes are placing a growing premium upon low-cost, high productivity production systems, and rapid adaptability in organization and production. These insistent product market pressures have been working through into major reassessments of personnel systems and the recruitment, motivation and rewards systems that companies have used for many decades. The outcome has been to call into question the logic of the traditional status divisions within the enterprise, based on nineteenth-century conditions and outdated assumptions about the nature of work, both 'manual' and 'non-manual'. But, in most cases, the strategic view of the organization's future has involved a very fundamental reassessment of the relationship between workers, managers and the enterprise, in which single status or harmonized conditions are simply one element. In a sense, harmonization is the outward sign of a strategy to create a new basis of trust and legitimacy for the relationship between employer and employee. Moving to 'higher-trust' relationships, securing employee 'commitment', removing perceptions of 'us and them', are all means of achieving maximum productive efficiency in order to meet the challenges of the product market more effectively. To quote Mullins:

> Future success will be with companies which are highly focused by technology and market expertise, which are able to adapt rapidly to changes in markets and technology. Such companies will have an overwhelming emphasis on cohesion and the fullest identification of their people with the overall business purpose.... They will be the companies which secure opportunities for business and individual growth. There will be no room in them for differences and divisions which consume energies and are unrelated to the work that has to be done. (1986: 41)

In this perspective, the decline of the status divide seems destined to be terminal. While there may continue to be some industries and organizations which do not feel the need to challenge traditional practices, increasingly it will be a question not of 'whether', but of 'how rapidly' new structures are developed. Costs, and the capacity to absorb them, will be an important factor here, as will the reaction of unions organizing on one side only of the status divide. Progress towards single status in the car industry has been relatively slow, for example, due to the likely cost in a very competitive product market. In West Germany, integrated pay and conditions agreements have been reached in recent years in most of the major industrial sectors, and this trend is likely to accelerate the parallel process in Britain. In essence, the demise of the status divide is a reflection of the 'new wave' in personnel management practice ushered in by the economic and technological circumstances of the 1980s and 1990s that provides much of the focus for this book.

# Bibliography

Ackroyd, S., Burrell, G., Hughes, M. and Whitaker, A. 1988. 'The Japanisation of British Industry?'. *Industrial Relations Journal*, 19: Spring 11–23.

Advisory, Conciliation and Arbitration Service (ACAS). 1982. 'Developments in Harmonisation'. Discussion Paper no. 1, March. London: ACAS.

—— 1988. 'Labour Flexibility in Britain'. Occasional Paper No. 41. London: ACAS.

Armstrong, M. 1987. 'Human Resource Management: A Case of the Emperor's New Clothes?'. *Personnel Management*, August, 31–5.

Bain, G.S. 1970. *The Growth of White-Collar Unionism*. Oxford: Clarendon Press.

—— and Price, R. 1972. 'Who is a White-Collar Employee?'. *British Journal of Industrial Relations*, 10: November 325–39.

Barkin, S. 1975. *Worker Militancy and Its Consequences*. New York: Praeger.

Boddy, D. and Buchanan, D.A. 1986. *Managing New Technology*. Oxford: Blackwell.

Braverman, H. 1974. *Labor and Monopoly Capital*. New York: Monthly Review Press.

Craig, C. 1969. 'Men in Manufacturing Industry'. Cambridge: Department of Applied Economics, University of Cambridge (mimeo).

Crouch, C. and Pizzorno, A. 1978. *The Resurgence of Class Conflict in Western Europe*. London: Macmillan.

Department of Employment (DE). 1981. 'Pattern of Holiday Entitlement'. *Employment Gazette*, 89: December 534–5.

Donovan. 1968. Royal Commission on Trade Unions and Employers' Associations 1965–1968. *Report*. Cmnd 3623. London: HMSO.

Edwards, Sir Ronald Stanley. 1967. *An Experiment in Industrial Relations: The Electricity Supply Industry's Status Agreement for Industrial Staff*. London: Electricity Council.

Fowler, A. 1987. 'When Chief Executives Discover HRM'. *Personnel Management*, January, 3.

Fox, A. 1966. *Industrial Sociology and Industrial Relations*. Research Paper 3, Royal Commission on Trade Unions and Employers' Associations. London: HMSO.

—— 1985. *Man Mismanagement*. 2nd edn. London: Hutchinson.

Francis, A. 1986. *New Technology at Work*. Oxford: Oxford University Press.

François, L. 1963. *La distinction entre employés et ouvriers en droit allemand, belge, français et italien*. The Hague.

Friedman, A. 1977. *Industry and Labour: Class Struggle at Work and Monopoly Capitalism*. London: Macmillan.

Gill, C. 1985. *Work, Unemployment and New Technology*. Cambridge: Polity.

Hyman, R. and Price, R. Eds. 1983. *The New Working Class? White Collar Workers and Their Organisations*. London: Macmillan.

Incomes Data Services (IDS). 1988. *Integrated Pay*. Study no. 411. London: IDS.

*Industrial Relations Review and Report* (IRRR). 1986. 'Holidays – 1986 Annual Survey'. 376: September 2–10.

—— 1987a. 'A Greenfield Strategy for Ind Coope's Burton Brewery'. 394: June 2–8.
—— 1987b. 'BICC Optical Cables Unit Goes "Into 2000"'. 398: August 12–17.
—— 1987c. 'Manual Workers' Appraisal: Growing Trend Surveyed'. 398: August 2–12.
Institute of Personnel Management (IPM). 1986. *Performance Appraisal Revisited*. London: IPM.
Kennedy, G. 1988. 'Single Status as the Key to Flexibility'. *Personnel Management*, February 51–3.
Labour Research Department (LRD). 1980. *Sick Pay: A Negotiator's Guide*. London: LRD.
—— 1981. *Bargaining Report 14*. May/June. London: LRD.
Lockwood, D. 1958. *The Blackcoated Worker: A Study in Class Consciousness*. London: Allen & Unwin.
Mackay, L. and Torrington, D. 1986. *The Changing Nature of Personnel Management*. London: IPM.
Millward, N. and Stevens, M. 1986. *British Workplace Industrial Relations 1980–1984: The DE/ESRC/PSI/ACAS Surveys*. Aldershot: Gower.
Mullins, T. 1986. 'Harmonisation: The Benefits and the Lessons'. *Personnel Management*, March 38–41.
National Association of Pension Funds (NAPF). 1981. *Survey of Occupational Pension Schemes, 1980*. London: NAPF.
National Economic Development Office (NEDO)/Institute of Manpower Studies (IMS). 1986. *Changing Working Patterns: How Companies Achieve Flexibility to Meet New Needs*. London: NEDO.
Parker, P.A.L., Hawes, W.R. and Lumb, A.L. 1971. *The Reform of Collective Bargaining at Plant and Company Level*. Department of Employment Manpower Papers 5. London: HMSO.
Pascale, R.T and Athos, A.G. 1981. *The Art of Japanese Management*. New York: Simon & Schuster.
Pegge, T. 1986. 'Hitachi Two Years On'. *Personnel Management*, October· 42–7.
Peters, T. and Waterman, R. 1982. *In Search of Excellence*. New York: Harper & Row.
Policy Studies Institute (PSI). *Shorter Working Time*. London: PSI.
Price, R. and Bain, G.S. 1983. 'Union Growth in Britain: Retrospect and Prospect'. *British Journal of Industrial Relations*, 21: March 46–68.
—— and Steininger, S. 1987. 'Trade Unions and New Technology in West Germany'. *New Technology, Work and Employment*, 2: Autumn 100–11.
Ramsey, H. 1985. 'What is Participation for? A Critical Evaluation of "Labour Process" Analyses of Job Reform'. *Job Redesign*. Ed. Knights, D., Willmott, H. and Collinson, D. Aldershot: Gower, 52–80.
Roberts, C. Ed. 1985. *Harmonisation: Whys and Wherefores*. London: IPM.
Roeber, J. 1975. *Social Change at Work: The ICI Weekly Staff Agreement*. London: Duckworth.
Speier, H. 1934. 'The Salaried Employee in Modern Society'. *Social Research*, February 111–33.
Strauss G. 1954. 'White-Collar Unions are Different'. *Harvard Business Review* September–October 73–81.
Trevor, M. 1988. *Toshiba's New British Company: Competitiveness Through Innovation in Industry*. London: PSI.
Walby, S. 1986. *Patriarchy at Work*. Cambridge: Polity.
Wedderburn, D. 1966. 'Staff Status: Its Meaning and Problems'. *IPM Digest 19*, November.

—— and Craig, C. 1974. 'Relative Deprivation in Work'. *Poverty, Inequality and Class Structure*. Ed. Wedderburn, D. Cambridge: Cambridge University Press, 141–64.

Wickens, P. 1987. *The Road to Nissan: Flexibility, Quality, Teamwork*. London: Macmillan.

# 13 The Three Faces of Discipline

*P. K. Edwards*

The apparently simple word 'discipline' covers a wide range of meanings: from the application of punishment, through a system of rules of behaviour, to morale and motivation, as expressed in such concepts as self-discipline and the professional discipline of doctors or lawyers. The last of these is widely seen as the desirable situation: 'the best discipline is self-discipline, the normal human tendency to do one's share and to live up to the rules of the game' (Strauss and Sayles, 1980: 218). This raises large questions of organizational functioning, which will be touched on in the concluding section of this chapter. Before then, however, some more narrowly defined issues of discipline will be addressed.

How is discipline to be defined? Sokolik (1970: 381) says that disciplinary action 'refers to the corrective action which is taken when the organizational discipline is found to have been significantly breached by one or more workers'. Ashdown and Baker (1973: 1) note the problems of this formulation: to include any breach of rules within the definition makes the topic impossibly broad, for any form of collective industrial action would qualify. Their solution is to see group behaviour as involving a widespread rejection of a current arrangement whereas 'individual indiscipline indicates merely a personal deviation from standards generally accepted by others'.

This narrows the focus to reflect what most people mean by discipline, namely the enforcement of rules of conduct. But there is a larger difficulty with these conventional approaches. Indiscipline is seen as the aberration of a few individuals from shared norms. Beach (1975: 599) says quite innocently that members of a group 'must reasonably conform to the code of conduct established by the leadership of the organization'. Cameron (1984) defines misconduct as a failure by employees to do what is required of them. And in the passages quoted above, Sayles and Strauss and Sokolik assume that there is no difficulty in deciding what an organization's disciplinary standards are and that these standards represent the shared values of all. It may be factually correct that most workers comply with rules, but it is a large jump to assume that the rules reflect shared values, and a still larger leap to say that anything that the 'leadership' demands must be obeyed.

Work organizations are systems of power, and rules reflect the use of power: the definition of acceptable standards of behaviour is a complex process involving differing interests. The identification of what the rule regarding some specific form of behaviour really is may also be uncertain. The use of the office telephone for private calls may be formally banned, but in practice the 'occasional' 'brief' call may be tolerated. The day-to-day understanding as to who has access to this perk (more leniency may be given to long-serving workers than to newcomers) and under what conditions is as much a 'rule' as is the formal edict. And reactions to punitive discipline for breaching the edict will be shaped by the strength of the understanding and by the politics of the organization: different patterns of politics can produce very different understandings, so that the day-to-day operation of discipline varies widely even though the formal rules and the associated disciplinary procedures may be identical.

Existing treatments often demonstrate awareness of such points, but these are rarely made central to the account. The texts quoted above do not see the making of rules as in any way problematic, and even Sokolik, who claims to analyse personnel management in the light of organizational realities, does not let these realities intrude into his discussion of the technicalities of discipline. Similarly, Thomason (1978) discusses it solely in relation to legal provisions on unfair dismissal, while Torrington and Chapman (1979) assume that the making of rules is unproblematic, with the drawing up of a procedure being simply a technical task. Ashdown and Baker (1973: 16) again display awareness of the limitations of this, and they cite differences between formal rules and what really happens. Yet they conclude that these 'underline the need for a clear, written statement of the standards of behaviour expected and the need for a joint review of these standards from time to time by management and worker representatives'. A piece of procedural advice is hardly sufficient to cope with the complexities of the negotiation and enforcement of rules of behaviour or with the interrelation of edicts and understandings.

Discipline thus has three faces. The first is the application of punishment for breaches of the rules. Second, there is the formulation of the rules themselves, together with the procedures to be followed in their application. Third is the creation in practice of the expectations, norms, and understandings that govern behaviour. The existing literature offers technical advice on the first two, embracing such matters as how to design a disciplinary procedure. This chapter tries to complement them by doing what Sokolik promises, namely examining this aspect of personnel management in relation to issues of conflict and control within organizations. Although not directly prescriptive, it aims to throw light on policy matters in two main ways. First, to the extent that procedures are treated in isolation from organizational politics, a policy prescription may be irrelevant, inoperable, or even counterproductive (for elaboration of this point in relation to control of absenteeism, see Edwards and Scullion, 1984). A consideration of the informal rules that govern behaviour will help in assessing how far a policy may fit into other parts of organizational life. Second, discipline is more important than a consideration of the technical issues may suggest. The disciplinary regime is important in setting the tone of a firm's relationship with its employees, and as the need for commitment is increasingly stressed, the place of the regime within personnel management as a whole takes on increasing significance. This is implied in references to the role of self-discipline, but to switch between these large issues and narrow questions of technique is not helpful. Building on a deeper conceptualization of the nature of discipline, this chapter tries to draw out some ways in which discipline, in the specific sense of the application of rules of individual conduct, connects with the wider issues of commitment and motivation.

The chapter begins by summarizing the development of discipline and changing approaches to its nature. The realities of day-to-day discipline may then be considered in the light of this context. Finally, current changes are considered in relation to the debate about self-discipline.

## DISCIPLINARY RULES AND PROCEDURES

### The Origins of Discipline

Employers have always needed to ensure the adequate performance of work tasks by their employees. Formal rules become necessary only when organizations became large and bureaucratic, with the result that the employer could not oversee operations personally. Pollard (1965: 181–9) has described the disciplinary problems of the early industrial employers: the new factories demanded regular attendance and the carrying out of tasks in the prescribed fashion if their complex division of labour was to work, whereas workers were accustomed to less regular and less routinized ways of working. The employers introduced strict rules on attendance and behaviour within the factory.

Writers who adopt what Henry (1983: 71) calls a consensus approach have seen such developments as characteristic of an authoritarian approach to discipline. Ashdown and Baker (1973: 5–7), for example, argue that managers saw their own authority as absolute, and imposed discipline in a harsh and arbitrary manner. Since the Second World War, the authors continue, managements have become aware that punitive discipline has adverse effects on morale and efficiency; they have also faced pressure from trade unions, legal restrictions on their powers, and difficulties of recruitment in tight labour markets. As a result, the aim of disciplinary action has become correction instead of coercion, and the administration of policy has been based less on the absolute authority of the employer and more on a democratic approach. Such an interpretation is not limited to 'consensus' theorists. An explicitly radical account of changes in work organization in America sees nineteenth-century work discipline as being based on 'arbitrary command' in which motivation was based on the dictum: 'perform your task correctly or be docked in pay, fired, or, on occasion, beaten'. Under bureaucratic systems of control that have developed since 1945, by contrast, punishment flows 'from the established organizational rules and procedures' and is no longer coercive in purpose or arbitrary in application (R. Edwards, 1979: 33, 142).

Such interpretations need to be treated with caution. They sit uneasily with evidence that in large parts of industry, notably cotton and steel and some areas of coal-mining, employers subcontracted sets of operations to skilled workers who were responsible for recruitment, payment, and discipline (Littler, 1982). Employers here exercised their authority at one remove. It is also hard to conceive of all workers being subjected to an identical form of discipline: skilled craftsmen were proud of their skills and independence, and would not have reacted meekly to harsh discipline. There is also evidence that standards of regular attendance were enforced slowly and unevenly. Industrialization was a lengthy process in which earlier forms of discipline and control could survive for considerable periods. In Birmingham, for example, it was not until the 1860s that employers were successful in eroding the tradition of taking Monday as a holiday (Reid, 1976). Finally, the connection between authoritarianism and paternalism should be noted. Recent interpretations of paternalism (e.g. Newby, 1977; Prude, 1983) are certainly critical of the view of paternalist employers as dominated by concern for the welfare of their workers. Paternalism was intimately tied up with strict rules of conduct. But it was also geared to gaining employees' compliance through material rewards and an ideology of the family firm. Managerial power was much in evidence but it was not used simply to coerce workers; firms were concerned to build up a degree of workforce commitment and did not rely on force alone as a means of discipline.

Neither should the shift to a corrective approach be exaggerated. One of the assumptions underlying the shift is that, as firms have grown increasingly bureaucratic, old and informal modes of discipline have become unworkable. But bureaucracy is not a product of the period since 1945. Rules emerged in many organizations before then. The railways (see Hudson, 1970; Bagwell, 1963: 20–8) and the Post Office (Clinton, 1984: 45–59) are good examples of organizations with formal and detailed rules specifying workers' duties long before then. Strict discipline and bureaucracy are not necessarily incompatible. As shown in detail below, moreover, many firms, particularly small ones, retain strict forms of discipline, while in larger ones the development of a 'corrective' approach is probably less advanced than consideration of formal policies might suggest. There is a need to be clear about what is meant by a corrective approach, for it can take several forms. The implication in many accounts of trends in the use of discipline and of the desirable characteristics of a modern disciplinary policy is that firms are increasingly adopting a low-key approach in which employees' needs are treated with consideration and rules are 'reasonable'. But correction can equally be based on strict rules, with anyone breaking them being subject to discipline. The rules, moreover, are still likely to be those of management. A corrective approach may not be as far removed from an authoritarian one as some observers suggest. This point may be considered further by looking in more detail at recent developments in disciplinary arrangements.

## *The Formalization of Procedures*

One of the outstanding features of the conduct of discipline in Britain is the speed with which formal arrangements have replaced informal ones. The idea that there has been a gradual shift to a corrective approach has to be balanced against evidence that formalization has occurred rapidly since 1970. Anderman (1972: 22–4) summarizes two studies carried out during the 1960s.

In 1967 the Ministry of Labour's National Joint Advisory Council (NJAC) produced figures from three enquiries. Of 45 members of the Engineering Employers' Federation, 73 per cent had formal procedures; a further 38 firms felt by the Ministry to have good personnel records returned a figure of 55 per cent; but a much larger number of firms, namely the 373 visited by Ministry officials in the course of their duties, recorded only 17 per cent with formal procedures. An unpublished Government Social Survey report of 1969 confirmed this picture, using a much more representative sample of 1100 establishments. Only 8 per cent had a formal procedure, although a further 34 per cent claimed to use 'normal' procedures, that is less formal arrangements that were not necessarily used in all cases, for disciplinary matters. Not surprisingly, formalization was most advanced in the larger plants: 2 per cent of those with fewer than 50 employees had formal procedures, compared with 19 per cent of those employing 500 or more workers.

In 1978, the IPM (1979: 7) surveyed 273 organizations and found a major change: 98 per cent had written disciplinary procedures for blue-collar workers. Since these tended to be large and sophisticated firms, this figure may exaggerate the growth of procedures. But the Workplace Industrial Relations Surveys, which cover all manufacturing and service establishments with at least 25 employees, confirm the general picture. In 1980, procedures for discipline and dismissal were present in 81 per cent of establishments, a figure that had risen to 90 per cent in 1984. They were more or less universal in plants with more than 200 employees, but even in plants with between 25 and 49 workers they were reported in 86 per cent of cases in 1984. Procedures have also been widely adopted by non-union firms (83 per cent of those with no recognized union having a procedure). The authors consider that the most appropriate comparison was the 8 per cent of plants in the 1969 survey with formal procedures; in 1980 the comparable figure was 80 per cent (Daniel and Millward, 1983: 160, 163; Millward and Stevens, 1986: 168–73). Small firms falling below the survey threshold remain, however, relatively informal: only one-third of those with fewer than 20 employees studied by Evans et al. (1985: 30) had a written disciplinary procedure.

Explanations of this growth focus above all on changing legal circumstances: it 'must to a considerable extent be attributed to the intervention of the law in matters relating to discipline (IPM, 1979: 7). The Industrial Relations Act 1971 introduced provisions relating to unfair dismissal, and this legislation has been widely seen as stimulating companies to reform their procedures. Employers interviewed in 1977 felt that the effect of employment protection laws had been to tighten up on recruitment and dismissal arrangements; although they claimed that management's power in discipline had been eroded, they also stressed an increase in the use of proper procedures and a decline in arbitrariness (Daniel and Stilgoe, 1978: 37).

The law was plainly not the only influence. As Henry (1983: 102) has argued, legal changes were part of a broader policy of intervention by the state which reflected a belief that formalized and standardized procedures would reduce the number of shopfloor grievances and strikes, thereby contributing to a more general process of industrial relations reform. Thus the NJAC had argued vigorously in favour of improved procedures that required management to specify what performance was expected, that gave employees a chance to improve their conduct, and that included the right of appeal (IPM, 1979: 52–5). The influence may not have been all one way. Authors of official and quasi-official reports looked to the practice of progressive firms in drawing up their recommendations. A manager interviewed by Henry (1983: 104) argued that the NJAC and other bodies consulted widely in industry and that they brought together existing practices saying 'this appears to be what industry does and finds acceptable and therefore this is what we will recommend'. It is unlikely that firms would have responded so rapidly had not legal provisions and advice on what constituted good practice been broadly congruent with ways in which they were already moving. The state's activities may have played more of an encouraging and facilitating role than one of an external force imposed on management.

The significance of formalization should not be exaggerated. It is true that the great majority of firms now operate procedures that contain explicit statements of rules of conduct, that have specified steps of disciplinary action ranging from a verbal warning to dismissal when rules are broken, that are based on encouraging workers to correct their conduct, and that contain arrangements for appeal. But these things refer only to the techniques of applying discipline. It should not be inferred that possession of a written document has necessarily altered actual practice in a dramatic fashion. Writing at the time of growing formality, a practising personnel manager castigated British managers' unthinking approach and their resistance to formalization, noting that arguments about a lack of flexibility were used as excuses to be inconsistent and capricious (Welch, 1978). This suggests that formalization may have been embraced with less enthusiasm than is sometimes suggested. As argued below, there is a greater variability in disciplinary practice than the widespread existence of procedures suggests, and even in firms whose practice is generally in line with the policy stated in the procedure, the actual conduct of discipline is more complex than appears at first sight.

*The Content and Operation of Procedures*

For discipline to be applied effectively, the rules must be clear. A benefit of formality is often felt to be that informality makes it difficult to ensure that rights and responsibilities are clear and known to all (e.g. Anderman, 1972: 24). Accordingly, most procedures specify the type of conduct which is likely to trigger disciplinary action. It is not, however, possible to be comprehensive: there will always be contingencies that cannot be predicted. Procedures typically do no more than indicate the type of action which is liable to be punished. Such actions fall into two types: very serious misconduct such as theft and violence which may lead to instant dismissal; and less serious offences such as excessive absenteeism or poor time-keeping which will be dealt with initially through warnings and, if performance does not improve, through increasingly severe sanctions. But the limitations of informality should not be exaggerated. In a nineteenth-century factory town expectations concerning behaviour at work would be widely known through the customs peculiar to a given trade. Little would have been gained from codifying these expectations in written rules. In the current circumstances there are benefits to be gained from having written rules; these may stem in part from the fact that written rules are likely to be clear and public, but equally important are the practical advantages to management, if accused of unfair dismissal, of being able to show that the firm had clear rules which were knowingly broken. Writing down the rules may be as much a precautionary measure as an attempt to ensure that discipline is fair and open.

The main types of action that lead to the operation of discipline seem to be common among small and large firms. Plumridge (1966: 139) found in a survey of 50 organizations that absenteeism was the most common reason, followed by 'incompetence and unsuitability'. Respondents to the IPM (1979: 28–31) survey listed time-keeping, unauthorized absence and poor work standards as the main issues. The mainly small firms studied by Evans et al. (1985: 27) gave time-keeping and absence together as the most common reason, followed by 'incompetence or incapacity in work performance'.

According to Ashdown and Baker (1973), absenteeism and lateness created the fewest problems in the 30 firms that they studied because standards of attendance were clear, evidence in the form of time-sheets was unambiguous, and managements and unions generally agreed that absenteeism needed to be contained. An American study, by contrast, argues that 'probably the single most difficult area of contract administration and enforcement involves the assessment of discipline for excessive absence' (Dilts et al., 1985: 97). It is unlikely that Anglo-American differences explain this flat disagreement. Two factors may be significant. First, Ashdown and Baker are concerned only with the processing of absence cases within the disciplinary procedure. Once an absence problem has reached this level, the question of how to progress it is reasonably straightforward. But the decision as to what level of absence warrants managerial action in the first place is likely to be at least as difficult as that on matters such as theft. Indeed, the decision may be more difficult, since theft, if proven, is plainly culpable whereas, with absence, questions arise as to how far health problems, as distinct from simple shirking, are responsible. Second, organizations are probably more 'absence conscious' than they were when Ashdown and Baker did their study. Part of this reflects the law on unfair dismissal, for it now has to be shown that an attendance record justifies dismissal and that the worker concerned was given the chance to improve. But it also reflects greater concern about absence levels (discussed below).

The operation of a procedure involves many levels of management. Most formal procedures start with action by the immediate supervisor, with higher levels being involved as more severe sanctions are applied. In only 2 per cent of companies surveyed by the IPM (1979: 41) did final authority to dismiss rest with the supervisor, compared with 32 per cent where it rested with the personnel manager and 39 per cent with the factory manager. Underlying these figures is the well-known tendency of the 1970s for authority in the area of discipline to be removed from the supervisor and placed in the hands of the personnel specialist. There may be something of a move in the opposite direction with the current popularity of decentralizing responsibility to line managers. Preliminary research findings from a current study suggest that this is the case; the study, being conducted by the author and Colin Whitston, has involved to date interviews in 25 organizations, together with detailed case-study work in three more. It appears to be quite common for the detailed handling of discipline, and related issues such as absence control, to be passed down to line managers. They, it is said, are the people who know the situation on the ground, and they should not expect personnel managers to solve their problems for them. This is not, however, a return to the old days when the shopfloor was the foreman's empire. The authority that line managers exercise exists within rules established from above; to the extent, moreover, that these managers are monitored on their performance, they cannot run their operations as their whims dictate but have to pursue goals laid down for them from above.

Decentralization highlights the role of the first line supervisor. As shown in chapter 9, they were at one time portrayed as 'men in the middle', caught between workers and management proper, and hence willing to bend or ignore rules. A more realistic view is that supervisors generally espouse broad managerial goals and that they do not differ fundamentally from other managers in seeing the need for discipline (see, especially, Armstrong, 1983; also Child and Partridge, 1982). They may be less prone to subvert rulings from above than to complain that they are not given sufficient support when they act to assert managerial rights (Edwards and Scullion, 1982a: 327–31). During the 1970s it was probably quite common for supervisors to feel that the authority to discipline was being taken away from them. At the same time, of course, they were having to negotiate the day-to-day application of the rules and in doing so may have promoted custom and practice that interpreted the silences of the formal rules or even supplanted them (Brown, 1973). They were thus central in the actual application of discipline. This remains true, although it is now a question of taking responsibility for matters previously handled by personnel specialists. Some organizations are aware of the issue and are making training in the handling of discipline a feature of supervisors' development. But there is little detailed evidence as to the reaction. It is, for example, possible that if the responsibilities are seen as out of line with the rewards offered, supervisors will not embrace their new duties with much enthusiasm. It also remains true that they will still have to interpret the application of discipline.

Another major influence on the operation of procedures is that of trade unions. Unions' formal involvement appears to be considerable. In the 1980 survey, 'in establishments where employees covered by the procedure were represented by trade unions or staff associations, managers reported that the procedure had been agreed with those bodies in the great majority of cases (91 per cent of those with unions, which amounted to 64 per cent of all establishments)' (Daniel and Millward, 1983: 165–7). The IPM (1979: 17) reported lower figures for the negotiation of procedures: only 38 per cent of respondents negotiated with unions representing blue-collar workers. This gap may reflect the difference between persuading the unions to work through a procedure and being willing to negotiate its content with them. Negotiation about the rules themselves appears to be less common still: 25 per cent of the IPM respondents reported agreeing the rules with the unions. It would also appear that unions rarely challenge the broad principles of disciplinary arrangements. A survey of 1400 stewards carried out in 1966 reported, 'when asked whether they considered their management reasonably fair in dealing with workers who break rules and disobey orders, 93 per cent of stewards said yes' (McCarthy and Parker, 1968: 48). Factory-level case studies support this picture, for attempts to bargain about disciplinary rules appear to be rare. Union representatives are, however, widely involved in the application of the rules. McCarthy and Parker (1968: 83) list 28 workplace issues and report how often stewards said they had discussed and settled matters relating to each issue: 67 per cent had at some time done so in disciplinary matters, with 34 per cent reported this as a standard practice (comparable figures for working conditions are 89 and 73 per cent, and for wage issues 83 and 56 per cent). Storey (1980: 129), in a survey of 96 organizations conducted in 1971 and 1978, reports a rather higher relative position for discipline, with discipline coming third in a list of 25 items that were put to management respondents: 63 per cent reported that they negotiated on the matter. It is tempting to infer an increase in negotiations about disciplinary issues that parallels the rise in formal procedures. The difference between the two surveys may not, however, be very great. The earlier one did not list discipline as such, but asked about three specific matters, reprimands by supervisors, suspensions, and dismissals. It is possible that stewards who had never discussed one of these three matters with management might have been involved in other disciplinary matters such as informing their members of the rules. The safest conclusion is that disciplinary issues are often discussed with shop stewards even though the rules themselves are rarely negotiated.

One view of stewards' behaviour is that attempts will always be made to challenge the application of discipline. This appears to be incorrect. First, it implies too narrow a role for the steward. As McCarthy (1966: 12) found in a study of 10 workplaces, stewards communicate managerial concern about breaches of rules to their members, give warnings about plans to tighten up, talk to members privately and warn them about their behaviour, and provide 'information as to the extent of breaches of rules'. Second, stewards will not take up cases that they consider to be unreasonable: they may try to persuade members that they are in the wrong, or they may go through the motions of defending them while making it clear to management that they do not agree with the members' claim (see, for example, Batstone et al., 1977: 108–9). Third, as noted above, they are likely to accept the general need for discipline, challenging management only if they feel that the rules have been applied unfairly. The managers interviewed by Henry (1983: 117–23) stressed the relationships of trust that can emerge with stewards and the private agreements that can be made about how a disciplinary case will be handled. This should not be taken as implying that stewards are simply quiescent. They can and do take up cases with great vigour in which they feel that an injustice has been done, and, as will be seen in more detail below, they and their members often have views about the day-to-day conduct of discipline that is at variance with the formal rules.

Finally, the role of outside agencies in procedures needs comment. The 1984 Workplace Industrial Relations Survey found that some third-party involvement was mentioned in more than half the establishments which had a disciplinary procedure (Millward and Stevens, 1986). But, as Upton (1987: 47, emphasis in original) concludes, 'only a minority of procedures provide for the use of an independent appeal procedure *which has been set up in advance specifically for the purpose*'. Much third-party intervention seems to involve an *ad hoc* reference to ACAS and, in contrast to the USA, Upton goes on, there is in Britain a reluctance to codify the final stages of a procedure by specifying independent adjudication as the final stage. Although there is dispute about the relative merits of American arbitration and the British industrial tribunals (Collins, 1982; Glasbeek, 1984), it seems clear that American arbitrators are more able to alter a managerial decision than are the tribunals: tribunals are constrained to accept any managerial action that a 'reasonable' employer might have taken, whereas arbitrators can look at a case in the round and use their own judgement as to appropriate penalties (Dickens et al., 1985).

This again highlights the fact that, despite the trend towards formalization, the substance of discipline in Britain has been changed less than might appear. As Dickens et al. (1985: 242) conclude, management, and not the unions or third parties, remains the dominant force in the application of discipline: in general, procedures operate 'without an independent element and without union agreement or involvement, other than in a representative capacity . . . the definitions of indiscipline remain managerially determined'. There may be a more 'corrective' approach than there was in the past, but it remains management that decides what is acceptable conduct.

## THE EXTENT AND PATTERN OF DISMISSAL

The lack of formality in dealing with discipline is indicated by the absence of statistics on how often disciplinary sanctions are applied (which again contrasts with the situation in the USA). The most extreme penalty of dismissal, being most visible, has, however, received some attention.

Daniel and Stilgoe (1978: 59) found that 83 per cent of their plants had had at least one dismissal for reasons other than redundancy over the previous year. Comparing their results with those of the 1969 Government Social Survey, they found a dramatic fall in the rate of dismissal. Most plants continued to have some dismissals, but fewer had very high rates. In both surveys, the higher rates were concentrated among the smallest plants, a pattern confirmed by Daniel and Millward (1983: 171), who estimated that the overall average rate of dismissals (for reasons other than redundancy) was 11 per 1000 people employed. Deaton (1984), analysing the 1977—8 Warwick Survey of manufacturing plants, found that there were four main influences on the dismissal rate. The risk was lowest in large plants, and where there was a high proportion of skilled workers, a high proportion of white-collar employees, and a high level of union density. The overall explanatory power of his model was, however, low ($R^2$ was 0.12), suggesting that dismissal rates are hard to predict. Deaton also aggregated his data across industries so that the association with wage levels could be assessed. He found that high earnings were linked with low dismissal rates, concluding that firms have a degree of choice: they can offer high wages so as to attract a high quality workforce, or provide only low wages and rely on dismissal to weed out unsuitable workers. Whether or not a specific argument about the 'quality' of workers can be sustained, it appears that firms differ in their employment policies. Some are far more dismissal-prone than others, and it is preferable to attribute these differences not to inherent differences between workers in their attitudes to work, but to the policies of the firms themselves. In the more progressive companies dismissal is a relatively rare sanction, employed when other means have failed. In others, dismissal or the threat of it remains an important form of control. A figure of one worker in every hundred being sacked each year for reasons other than redundancy can, in some ways, be seen as unduly high.

Popular attention has focused not on disciplinary practices, but on the operation of the unfair dismissals legislation, with worries being frequently expressed that it is difficult or impossible to sack anyone. Most dismissals do not, however, even enter the unfair dismissal system. Daniel and Stilgoe (1978: 62) found that only 26 per cent of their plants had been subject to formal unfair dismissal complaints, and they estimated that only one dismissal in 14 (7 per cent) led to a complaint. More recent evidence suggests that this figure may be something of an underestimate. As noted above, the 1980 survey gave a figure of 11 dismissals per 1000 employed, which represents about 278,000 dismissals for reasons other than redundancy each year. In 1980 there were approximately 33,000 claims for unfair dismissal in industrial tribunals, which is 12 per cent of all dismissals (Dickens et al., 1985: 31). One reason for the discrepancy may be that Daniel and Stilgoe surveyed establishments employing at least 50 workers. The chances of being involved in an unfair dismissal case increase as the size of a firm decreases, and excluding very small firms may have led to an underestimate; thus Dickens et al. (1985: 38) found from a survey of unfair dismissal cases that almost half the firms involved employed fewer than 100 workers, with a quarter employing fewer than 20. It remains true, however, that the great majority of dismissals do not lead to claims for unfair dismissal.

Detailed research by Dickens et al. on those cases that enter the industrial tribunal system suggests that employers' fears about the impossibility of sacking workers have been exaggerated. Less than a quarter of applicants who go to a hearing win their cases, and the typical remedy for this minority is a relatively small amount of money (the median amount in 1982 being £1200). The criteria for judging fairness are, moreover, restricted, being based on a judgement of what a reasonable employer would have done in the given circumstances. It has been held in cases of alleged theft, for example, that an employer does not have to prove beyond reasonable doubt that someone sacked for theft had in fact committed the offence; a reasonable belief is all that is necessary.

More important for present purposes than the law on unfair dismissal is the effect of the law on the handling of dismissal. As noted above, the law has been widely seen as an important influence on procedural reform; and it has also been seen as one factor in the reduction in rates of dismissal. But the effect may not be direct. Citing Daniel and Stilgoe's evidence, together with the results of a survey of 301 establishments each with fewer than 50 employees (Clifton and Tatton-Brown, 1979), Dickens et al. (1985: 257) conclude that managers generally attribute 'little effect to the unfair dismissal provisions in terms of inhibiting dismissal'. One indirect effect may be an improvement of disciplinary procedures, such that managements feel less need to rely on the ultimate sanction of the sack. Another seems to be increasing care in recruitment, which would have the result that fewer workers would be recruited who were subsequently found to be unsuitable.

It remains true, however, that dismissal or the threat of it is an important element in the overall system of control used in some firms. When considering the broad issue of labour control, the distinction between dismissal for disciplinary reasons and 'normal' labour turnover breaks down: people who quit 'voluntarily' during the first few months of service with a firm may do as much for reasons connected with the work that they are expected to do and the form of discipline to which they are subject, as for reasons associated with their personal characteristics. It is well known that most quits occur among workers with very short periods of service. A study of seven factories showed that at least one-third of leavers had been employed by their present firm for less than a year (Edwards and Scullion, 1982b: 63–73). More revealing, however, are variations between plants. In two clothing factories, over 40 per cent of leavers had been employed for less than six months. This was associated with very close managerial control of the work process, with disciplinary warnings for poor work performance being commonplace and with very strict control maintained of starting and finishing times. Not only was dismissal an ever-present possibility, but 'voluntary' quitting was also influenced by the control regime: a worker given a couple of warnings, or who found the work pace intolerable, might find leaving the only option. Such quitting helped to reinforce managerial authority because those who might question it did not stay long. More generally in these plants, discipline was used openly to enforce work standards in a way that had many coercive elements. This illustrates the point that the conduct of discipline cannot be separated from overall patterns of workplace relations, and that the niceties of corrective discipline and proceduralism are not necessarily followed on the shopfloor. The following section elaborates on this argument.

## DISCIPLINE IN ACTION

*Types of Rules*

Prescriptive treatments of discipline start from the assumption that all organizational rules have the same status, being statements of agreed norms whose violation is likely to lead to disciplinary action. There are in fact different sorts of rules, which have different origins and are treated differently by people in organizations, and which need not stem from shared interests or perspectives.

In his classic study of a gypsum mine and factory Gouldner (1954) identified three types of bureaucratic rule. 'Mock' bureaucracy covers rules that are ignored by all; Gouldner's example is a no-smoking rule that management made no attempt to enforce except when agents from the insurance company visited the site. 'Representative' bureaucracy was exemplified by safety rules, to which management devoted considerable attention and against which workers expended few energies, the result being that safety matters were highly bureaucratized and rules were enforced. 'Punishment-centred' bureaucracy involves rules that are enforced by one party against another, with sanctions being imposed for disobedience, an example being the rule against absenteeism, which managers wished to enforce rigidly and which workers resented. Breaches of different rules will be treated very differently in practice. Mock rules are ignored. Representative rules are important to all, so that a worker disobeying a safety rule is likely to be seen, by work mates as well as management, as careless and as deserving no support. Punishment-centred rules are imposed, and the group on whom they are imposed may well feel that they are unfair, and may react by trying to evade them, supporting those who are punished, and questioning their relevance.

Rules are not, then, all of a piece. But there are also some other, less frequently cited, aspects of Gouldner's discussion. First, he stresses (1954: 205) that his types are not fixed: in another organization a safety rule might have a punishment-centred and not a representative character. Second, he makes an important but implicit qualification about representative bureaucracy. Why was management bothered about safety? Safety can assist in production by reducing costly accidents. But safety rules can also be used to control workers: management introduced a rule that was justified on safety grounds and therefore hard for workers to resist, preventing movement between parts of the factory, but its real purpose was to strengthen managerial control over what workers were doing. In addition, management neglected safety interests where these conflicted with the demands of production, a point which has also been made by other writers (e.g. Nichols and Armstrong, 1973; Nichols, 1975). Even 'representative' rules may not serve everyone's interests, and they can be used as a cloak for other things.

Rules, together with the sanctions that go with their breach, are part of wider relations of conflict and control within workplaces. Mellish and Collis-Squires (1976) develop this point in their critique of the 'consensus approach' as represented by the work of Anderman (1972) and Ashdown and Baker

(1973). There is a tendency to concentrate on procedures and not on the substantive rules that the procedures are intended to enforce. Procedures say little about actual processes and may be ignored or altered. The stress on formalization, moreover, ignores evidence from factory case studies (Brown, 1973; Terry, 1977) that informal rules may supplant formal ones. Managers may grant concessions to workers in order to meet production demands, but concessions can rapidly grow into precedents and then into relatively well-established custom and practice rules. These rules will reflect the reality of bargaining power on the shopfloor, and attempts to codify and formalize procedures are unlikely to have much effect on behaviour. A further criticism is the inadequate view of management that is adopted. It is assumed that management has the will and the freedom of action to institute reform. But in cases where union organization is weak, there may be little felt need among managements to reform, while, where unions are strong, managers may be unable to institute reform that effectively alters behaviour. In addition, the concentration on management leads to the neglect of discipline that can be imposed by unions and work groups. The question of workers' collective discipline leads to the final criticism: the tendency to individualize what may be a collective issue. In situations where workers are organized collectively, discipline ceases to be an individual matter but involves bargaining. And the distinction between the two may lie not in the intrinsic nature of an issue but in the approach taken by the parties in respect of any issue. That is, an apparently individual act such as theft may, in fact, stem from collective norms and understandings.

Mellish and Collis-Squires outline an alternative view based on their research on the docks. They found that formal rules on time-keeping were ignored, with gangs of workers deciding when to start work and how many workers would be working at any one time. In addition, systematic overtime was worked on a 'task and finish' basis, so that, although workers were supposed to be present for all the overtime period, in practice they went home when the job was finished. Such practices would involve breaches of formal rules such as leaving work without permission and associated clocking offences. The actual rules governing attendance and work conduct were very different from those inscribed in formal rule-books and procedures.

Some of these points require elaboration and qualification. One important elaboration concerns the activities of production managers and supervisors. The reformist approach neglects these, while writers such as Mellish and Collis-Squires see workers and shop stewards as the main authors of rule-bending. But the demands of the productive system itself must be given attention. Armstrong et al. (1981) studied three small firms. They found that managers had to juggle a large number of competing demands: orders from customers, the supply of raw materials, and the flow of goods through the production process all created conflicting pressures. The costs of setting up a run of a particular size or style of product, for example, create pressures for long runs. But a long run of one part may create shortages of others and put pressure on other sections of the factory; and customers' demands may also call for rapid and costly change-overs between styles. Nichols and Beynon

(1977: 33) studied the apparently more ordered world of a chemicals factory, but they also found that managers faced unremitting pressures of scheduling production so as to try to meet cost and delivery targets. In trying to balance different objectives, managers are unlikely to pay close attention to formal rules about workers' behaviour. It is easy to see how they can permit practices such as task and finish to emerge: managers need workers' co-operation to attain production requirements, and may be willing to buy this co-ooperation with concessions.

But how universal is this tendency? Mellish and Collis-Squires imply that all work groups tend to develop collective norms that undermine managerial rules and, while admitting that the docks are in many ways exceptional, they treat their research material as illustrative of a more general phenomenon. But, as the authors themselves note in criticizing the corrective approach, there are also circumstances in which workers' shopfloor organization is weak and in which firms have little incentive to bring their disciplinary arrangements in line with the corrective model. Informal practices do not necessarily emerge to challenge formal rules. And, even where such practices exist, they need not pose a direct threat to managerial rules. That is, they may form part of a set of shopfloor understandings about appropriate forms of workplace behaviour, but they may not be so strong as to replace the formal rules; instead formal and informal practices may have an uneasy co-existence.

### Varieties of Shopfloor Relations

To develop this point about the range of circumstances in which discipline operates, it will be useful to look in some detail at different cases. The discussion cannot cover every eventuality, but will concentrate on four patterns that illustrate differing ways in which disciplinary rules and shopfloor practices are related. These patterns are obviously not free-standing entities: they have histories, and there are important differences within each. But a simplification of their characteristics is sufficient for the purpose of exploring the links between discipline and behaviour. (For a more extended discussion, see Edwards, 1986: 224–81.)

The first pattern is that characteristic of the docks and other areas where informal rules are highly developed. As Mars (1974) shows in his study of dockers, there are strong work group standards of behaviour, and members of the group display a high degree of commitment to these standards. The norms have both a positive and a negative aspect: positive in that certain behaviour is prescribed, and negative in that there are powerful sanctions for non-conformity. A member of a dockers' gang who told management about illicit practices would find himself severely penalized. Among the main practices involved are what is known in some ports as 'welting' (that is, the practice of organizing work such that half the crew works while the other half rests, sometimes right away from the workplace) and the systematic pilferage of cargo. There are strict rules on the latter concerning what types of goods should be pilfered and how much should be taken. Attempts to enforce the formal rules are likely to be met with a collective response. Gangs of workers are self-governing and self-regulating. Just how typical such arrangements are, even within the docks themselves, is of course an open question. It is likely that containerization and the growth of small independent ports have altered the dockworkers' tradition in important respects, but the example remains important as an extreme case of the strength of social norms.

These are not limited to the docks or to other traditional strongholds of illicit practices such as the printing industry. Edwards and Scullion (1982b) found that in two of their seven plants, shopfloor organization had developed to such a point that many areas that were supposedly managerial prerogatives were in fact either jointly controlled or subject to an effective veto by the shop stewards. The two plants, owned by the same engineering firm, were given the pseudonyms of the Large Metals Factory and the Small Metals Factory. In both, shop stewards had developed powerful controls of manning levels, the allocation of work, and the amount and distribution of overtime. A foreman could not, for example, move a semiskilled production worker from one task to another without the steward's agreement. Managerial attempts to impose formal rules were met with organized resistance, as disputes in both factories graphically revealed.

There were, however, some important differences in the way in which matters that go under the heading of discipline were handled. In the Small Metals Factory there was a relaxed and informal approach. Workers could slip out of the factory for a short time with the foreman's agreement, and the making of 'foreigners', that is goods produced illicitly in the firm's time and with the firm's materials, was well known. As long as workers did not go beyond some vaguely defined but understood notion of what was acceptable, no one was very bothered. Senior managers were certainly highly concerned about productivity and manpower utilization, but they saw this issue as a general one of regaining control and not as something specific to indiscipline on the shopfloor.

In the Large Metals Factory, by contrast, there was a significant disciplinary problem. Most significant were two related practices, mass leaving before the end of the shift and members of work gangs taking it in turns to absent themselves for periods of up to half a shift. The latter was often highly organized, and in some sections rotas for time off were openly displayed. An important feature of such arrangements was that they did not conform to the standard model of custom and practice in which supervisors tolerate the growth of informal rules in order to gain co-operation. Foremen were certainly aware of the arrangements, and tolerated them in the sense of treating them as a fact of life. But they were neither their authors nor their supporters.

The reasons for the contrast between the two factories relate to the degree of trust that existed between foremen and workers and to the specific form of work organization: in the Large Metals Factory workers were organized into relatively autonomous gangs which allocated work between gang members, the result being that there was little respect for foremen and that gangs felt that it was reasonable to decide when gang members should be present in the factory (Edwards and Scullion, 1982a: 338; 1982b: 138–40). Strong shopfloor organization appears to be a necessary condition for the emergence of social norms that directly challenge formal rules; by this is meant not just the presence of shop stewards but also the growth of a particular kind of organization, namely, one that seeks control of the work process. But organization is not a sufficient condition, as the contrast between these two strongly organized factories shows. Small and independent work teams also seem to be required. In such circumstances managerial attempts to impose control are likely to be resisted.

A second pattern can usefully be contrasted with the first. This is one of very great managerial power which is in many ways the mirror image of strong work group organization. But a crucial similarity is the irrelevance of reformist models of discipline, for here management has no need for reform, and movements in that direction might well prove to be counterproductive. The three plants studied by Armstrong et al. (1981) were characterized by a high degree of managerial control such that the pricing of piecework jobs and the movement of workers within the factory depended on unilateral managerial decisions. A few informal customs emerged, but they did not attain the status or stability of rules, being instead covert practices on which management could clamp down with confidence. Management could, moreover, use custom to its own ends; for example, in one of the factories managers successfully argued that unqualified workers should continue to drive fork-lift trucks because this had always been the custom. It was not a matter of formal and informal rules being in conflict or even clearly separable. Instead, the formal rules were a resource, and management, because it had by far the greater power, was able to use the resources in its own interests. The implication is that management will choose to use its formal procedures at times and in a fashion which suits itself. Disciplinary procedures are not separate from day-to-day life on the shopfloor but are interpreted in the light of shopfloor realities. In view of the evidence on the growth of procedures reviewed above, it is likely that plants such as these will have formal disciplinary procedures. But their operation will reflect not the unstated assumption of the corrective model, namely that managements can afford the luxury of carefully monitoring behaviour and giving workers a chance to improve their performance, but the realities of shopfloor power. Managers can impose their own interpretations of the rules, which are not a statement of the rights of the worker as an industrial citizen, but are instead a set of political resources.

Further evidence comes from the clothing plants studied by Edwards and Scullion. As above, discipline was tightly enforced and highly visible. Managers explained this in terms of the need to control costs in a competitive industry. Discipline was not a means of pulling an aberrant minority back within shared standards but was central to the whole operation of the business.

Within this situation, there were significant variations. Male workers who tended the machines that knitted the basic fabric were subject to a less severe form of discipline. Their work was less closely supervised, and they were allowed to move around and talk to each other; a few breaks to go outside for a smoke were also tolerated. Among the reasons why the men were treated differently from the women were managers' beliefs that the men's skills were more important and harder to replace; the fact that the men worked night as well as day shifts, and were thus difficult to oversee; and the nature of the technology, with the effort put in by the women having a direct result in more output, while the men had to set up their machines which then ran automatically, the result being that the men could legitimately spend time doing no more than keeping an eye on their machines. The application of disciplinary rules varied accordingly.

A further important feature of these plants was the way in which authoritarian methods were combined with paternalistic ones. Managers claimed to know their workers by name, and to be sympathetic to those who were ill. Such claims were not mere rhetoric: there was a degree of concern for the workers' personal welfare, and some groups of long-serving women doing the more skilled tasks were valued. The conventional contrast between authoritarian and corrective approaches fails to grasp such subtleties, and also implies that authoritarian methods apply to all aspects of workers' work lives. It is certainly true that some firms adopt an unrelievedly authoritarian style. Hoel (1982: 86) reports that employers in small clothing plants in Coventry interfered with every aspect of their female employees' work lives, for example by telephoning absentees and asking why they were absent, and telling those who said that they were ill to report for work. Such practices are likely to be limited to particular types of very small firms. Those studied by Hoel employed on average 25 workers, while those studied by Edwards and Scullion had 650 and 350 workers. It is conceivable that the contrast with Hoel's factories reflects a relative insulation from market forces in the larger plants and also an appreciation that trying to prevent absenteeism could provoke resentment on the shopfloor itself, whereas managers in the smaller plants were less concerned with long-term stability. What is certain is that disciplinary practices reflect the problems that managers see as most pressing, and that 'authoritarian' methods are not homogeneous.

Before leaving the case of strict managerial control, it should be stressed that 'authoritarian' methods are not limited to small and medium-sized firms. Cavendish (1982: 84) reports an incident while she was working on the assembly-line in a firm employing 20,000 people. A young woman was doing a particularly difficult job and expressing her dissatisfaction by working slowly. She was taken to the supervisor's office and told to work properly or hand in her resignation; she did the latter, and was thus recorded as having left voluntarily. The niceties of disciplinary procedures are a long way from a reality in which workers are weak and uncertain of their formal rights. Pollert (1981) describes very similar experiences of women working in one of the subsidiaries of the Imperial Group. And Lawson (1981) reports a case study of the large electronics firm of Pye, which, despite its size and technical sophistication, relied on low wages and paternalism. In such cases, the power of management is likely to mean that, although formal rules exist, the operation and meaning of the rules will reflect the realities of this power and not the bland model of some of the prescriptive tests, which treat procedures outside their organizational context.

A third pattern shares with the second the characteristic that management has a great deal of power and shopfloor organization is weak or non-existent. The difference is that the nature of the work task encourages a variety of illicit practices, the result being that there is a sharp divorce between everyday practices and the operation of discipline. A good example is provided by Ditton's (1979) study of the despatch department of a bakery. As noted in an earlier study of the roundsmen who delivered the bread to the customers (Ditton 1977: 19) illicit practices were endemic. These included a range of fiddles against the customer, such as delivering less than had been ordered and supplying stale bread as fresh. Management encouraged the practice, and supervisors taught trainees how to fiddle. They adopted a different approach to fiddles against the company, which they termed 'stealing' when it was individual-istic and 'dealing' when it involved collusion with others. Managers were well aware that stealing and dealing took place, and occasionally acted when the situation seemed to be getting out of hand. But, as Ditton (1979: 101) stresses, the sackings had only a temporary effect. Without changing the whole organiza-tion of work, identical practices would reappear: 'sacking one workforce and then replacing it with another is merely expensive in recruitment and training'.

In such circumstances, disciplinary rules are not, and cannot, be operated even-handedly between different offences and different offenders. Since everyone was involved in fiddling, it was arbitrary and accidental as to who would be punished. Again, the model of discipline as applying to the small minority who do not accept managerial rules is inappropriate. Discipline is an external threat, imposed on work situations in which fiddles are endemic and in which, although there are understandings among workers about how and when to fiddle, workers lack strong collective organizations that could make their own definitions of the situation effective against managerial power. Other examples include the hotel and catering industry (Mars, 1973) and retailing (Mars, 1982: 66–75).

A final pattern falls between this situation and one of strong work group control. Here, workers have established some degree of collective control over their own efforts and they are neither so weak that discipline can be imposed on them nor so strong that they can enforce their informal rules against the formal ones. The classic studies of pieceworkers in engineering factories (e.g. from Britain, Klein, 1964; Lupton, 1963; and from America, Roy, 1954; Burawoy, 1979) fit here. Workers often develop a series of fiddles to attain 'loose' times and to limit the variability of earnings; examples include the book-ing of output from one job when running another and running machines more rapidly than work study standards state. Although each worker is struggling to 'make out' on his or her own, there are collective norms about behaviour, of which the most important is a ceiling on the amount of piecework bonus that can be earned. The contrast here with the first pattern of powerful organiza-tion is instructive, for here the norms are likely to be more firmly enforced; for example, when the Small Metals Factory had been on piecework there was a factory-wide earnings ceiling, enforced by periodic inspections by stewards of workers' pay slips, together with fines on rate-busters.

The key point about these fiddles is that they are accepted by everyone on the shopfloor and are often necessary for production to continue. They do not just oppose the formal rules but also represent ways in which management's aims are attained despite and not because of the rules. Burawoy (1979: 171–6), for example, describes the cycle of crack-downs that occurred in his factory: from time to time senior management, concerned about costs and profits, tried to impose the formal rules, but the rules had the unintended consequence of making it impossible to produce effectively, with the result that shop management soon relaxed them and permitted informal practices to re-emerge. The actual rules, as opposed to the formal ones, represent a negotiated compromise between different interest groups. To see the rules as clear and objective entities that reflect the organization's purpose is to misunderstand their role and character.

This raises the question of how discipline can work in such a situation. A distinction needs to be made between practices which are central to workers' control of the effort bargain and those which are not. A crack-down on running machines too fast or on clocking offences related to the control of time might provoke resentment on the shopfloor, whereas the imposition of discipline for excessive absenteeism might be accepted and even welcomed. Much will depend on the details of the situation and on workers' perceptions of the formal rules and the understandings that govern actual behaviour. A careful management would investigate the operation of the rules and the politics of the situation before acting to enforce a rule, for otherwise it might spark off some unexpected and unwelcome reactions.

*Rules and Power*

The four patterns described above indicate some of the different ways in which discipline can work. They do not cover every eventuality. It should not, for example, be thought that all small firms employ the authoritarian practices described by Hoel. Goffee and Scase (1982) have identified a very different principle of employment relations in small building firms, that of 'fraternalism'; the employer works alongside his employees, he has often worked in the trade before becoming an employer, and he treats his workers on the basis of fraternal and not hierarchical rights and obligations. And Swaffin-Smith (1982) studied 24 British firms and 12 American ones each with fewer than 200 employees. He found that discipline was conducted in an informal and personal way, concluding that in many respects employees had rights greater than the legal minimum; an employer might be willing to give a worker 'a last chance' instead of sticking to the letter of a disciplinary procedure.

This illustrates the general point that formalization may operate against the interests of the individual worker, if managers feel constrained to be consistent and are unable to make exceptions and to exercise discretion in individual cases (Dickens et al., 1985: 257). In their study of small firms, Evans et al. (1985: 36–7) included discussions with employees. They found that, although some favoured procedures, others felt that flexible and informal relationships would be damaged. The contrast between firms of similar size also illustrates the point that a firm's employment relationships reflect its product and labour-market circumstances, the character of the work tasks, the nature of union organization, and a range of other contingencies. There is no single model which applies to all small firms, or all large ones. The practice of discipline has to be understood in terms of the overall pattern of control of the work process and not reduced to the operation of rules and procedures.

Disciplinary rules are, moreover, not just impersonal regulations to be applied to cases of disobedience but resources that can be deployed in a wider political struggle. Identical disciplinary procedures would work very differently in the different situations described above. It follows that the operations of disciplinary procedures by personnel managers is not just a technical matter. It will depend on the broader objectives of management and the situation in which it finds itself. Consider for example the discussion by Strauss and Sayles (1980: 225) of a case in which a disciplinary suspension was withheld because there was a rush of jobs and management needed the worker in question. The authors criticize the decision, arguing that there should be consistency and that the employees learned that the relevant rule would not be enforced. Similar practices have been reported by Henry (1983: 114) and by Cunnison (1966: 94), and appear to be quite common. They may be necessary in particular circumstances, and a personnel manager who insisted on procedural correctness in all circumstances would not be popular with other managers trying to meet delivery dates. The point is general: the application of rules must reflect organizational necessities and the demands and interests of different groups within management, as well as the reactions of workers on the shopfloor. A disciplinary policy which tries to ride roughshod over these realities will be resisted or ignored.

## WHITHER DISCIPLINE?

An attempt has been made above to indicate how industrial discipline works in practice. Without an understanding of these matters, attempts to develop a workable disciplinary policy will be based on false assumptions. This is not, however, to suggest that policy changes are inherently unworkable. There has plainly been a massive reform of procedural arrangements in Britain. But there remains the question of what substantive effect this reform has had. There appears to be some uncertainty on the aims of the reform, with the ultimate purpose being assumed to be the improvement of morale and performance (however measured) and yet with practical achievements being limited to much narrower questions concerned with the benefits of clear and consistent procedures. Such benefits may well exist and should not be neglected, but the broader gains of reform have been assumed and not demonstrated. The actual content of discipline may have been affected far less than procedural reform might suggest. And, to the extent that changes have been made, for example in the prevalence of informal practices in sectors such as the docks and printing, the origin of 'reform' may lie not in disciplinary arrangements themselves but in broader managerial policies concerned with payment systems, effort levels, and the control of worker behaviour.

In assessing the role of discipline, it is necessary to have a view of the relationship between employers and workers. Prescriptive approaches tend to assume a harmony of interest. 'Radical' views stress power, inequality and conflict. The present account draws on some aspects of a radical perspective, but does not follow such a perspective to the conclusion that is commonly reached, namely that workers and managers have totally opposed sets of interests and that all reforms of disciplinary procedures are mere shams designed to mislead the workers. Several writers have begun to develop a more subtle approach which stresses that there are shared as well as conflicting interests and that such things as formal grievance procedures can produce real benefits for workers (e.g. Burawoy, 1979; Cressey and MacInnes, 1980). In the case of discipline, there is evidence that workers are prepared to accept some rules and not others, that the general need for discipline is widely accepted, and that workers are often less tolerant of what they see as slacking than are managers. This is not to suggest that their interests in discipline are the same as, or even broadly congruent with, those of management. It is, rather, to argue that there are some principles, such as doing a job in which one can have some self-respect and not shirking one's responsibilities, which are common among work groups and which may limit challenges to management's rules. There may not be total acceptance of the rules or of the logic that they reflect, but there may not be the will or the alternative logic to challenge them.

Disciplinary developments in the past should not, then, be seen as a smooth and natural drift to a corrective approach. Policies based on the approach have certainly been adopted, but they should not be seen as the working out of needs that are common throughout the organization. To the extent that they have undermined custom and practice, they have harmed certain interests. And to the extent that they have made managerial policy more coherent and deliberate, they have merely made the disciplining of a worker a more certain and effective action than it was in the past.

As the previous chapter intimated, current developments are often seen in terms of a shift towards self-discipline. Thus, from a relatively conventional standpoint, Torrington and Chapman (1979: 245) argue that managerial thinking is moving away from a reliance on penalties and towards self-discipline. And, from a radical perspective, Henry (1982: 378–80) discerns a shift from coercive discipline, through the corrective approach, to a use of peer-group discipline based on notions of participation and employee responsibility: participative discipline is the ultimate form of capitalist control. Little evidence is adduced in support of these large claims, and it is doubtful whether there is one dominant trend. There was probably never a wholesale shift to the corrective approach, and self-discipline may be no more than one among a number of emerging principles. Changes are occurring but, as has been stressed above, new forms of what Henry calls disciplinary technologies cannot be separated from broader trends in the control of work. A full consideration of the question is impossible here, but some points can be made.

It is clear that, over the past decade, the recession and a new managerial assertiveness have challenged many traditional assumptions about British industrial relations. At the end of the 1970s it was still possible to counterpose formal and informal rules and to suggest that, in well-organized sectors such as printing, the docks, and the car industry, the latter would triumph. The picture now has to be substantially modified. It remains true that informal practices are important. But the power relations in which they are embedded have altered as managements have reasserted their own authority. The style associated with Michael Edwardes of BL (as it then was) or Ian MacGregor in the steel and coal industries is not one that stresses the niceties of a corrective approach, let alone self-discipline. Yet it is widely argued that overtly 'macho' managers are in the minority (Batstone, 1988: 192) and that change has been less dramatic than many observers claim (MacInnes, 1987). There probably is no one trend in the use of discipline, but three possibilities may be identified.

First, there is the direct managerial attack on existing shopfloor rules and demarcations which is often summarized in the phrase 'macho management'. The implication for discipline is that management begins to insist on its own rules and to put a 'corrective' approach rigorously into effect. The content of such correction is likely to be rather different from that presupposed in discussions of the approach during the 1970s. The emphasis then was on the development of joint regulation, with proper rules and procedures replacing the disorder of informality: substantively, the approach implied a fairly 'soft' application of the rules. In the current climate, the same formal rules may have a much harder practical edge, with management insisting that the rules must be followed and insisting that, in the event of a failure to agree, management must manage and has the right to insist on making changes. In quite large parts of the public sector there appear to be moves in this direction, with traditional understandings based on harmony and consensus coming under challenge as management, often under pressure from the state, become increasingly concerned with efficiency (Winchester, 1983). In addition to the cases of BL and British Steel, management in the Post Office and British Telecom has adopted a tougher 'commercial' logic (Batstone et al., 1984), and in areas such as education and the local authorities similar pressures are evident.

Second, there is a drift towards a more openly authoritarian style. In many firms, particularly small ones, 'correction' has never had much substantive effect. The growth of part-time work and subcontracting, and the privatization of services in the public sector, suggest that there may be a rise in the types of work which are subject to close supervision and strict discipline. To these trends must be added the continuing challenges to the Wages Councils and other attempts to 'make labour-markets work' at the lower end of the hierarchy of jobs. It is hard to assess how much effect such things will have, either on the number of jobs or on the types of control to which they are subject. But it is plain that the logic underlying them is one of restoring or strengthening managerial authority and not encouraging participation and self-discipline.

Finally, and most interestingly, there is the question of the overall regime practised in firms where self-discipline is stressed. There is no doubt that many managements have begun to use the language of participation and human resource management (Storey, 1987; Edwards, 1987). A key question, however, is what this means on the shopfloor. Are workers given more autonomy, and do both punitive and corrective discipline fade into the background, or is there a hard edge to 'self-discipline'?

Some recent studies support the latter view. American car firms have been in the lead in developing quality-of-work life and employee involvement programmes. Yet Wood (1986: 442) concludes his review of them by saying that there are 'many features of the current strategy which increase management's control and reduce individual autonomy'. A case study of a plant relocation by General Motors argued that

> the code of conduct is pleasingly philosophic, yet disturbingly imprecise. In contrast to the prior rules [in the old plant], the new ones leave GM with a much more unrestricted hand in meting out penalties. (Zipp and Lane, 1987: 75)

In a survey of workers, 14 per cent saw the rules as more lenient, whereas 50 per cent said that they were tougher.

British evidence on new disciplinary regimes is limited. Peter Wickens (1987), Director of Personnel at Nissan, has, however, provided an account of that firm's approach. It is based on 'flexibility, quality, and teamwork'. On lateness, Wickens (1987: 100) argues, 'if the Supervisor and his staff have the right relationship and everyone is properly motivated, good time-keeping does not depend on a mechanistic form of time recording but on the self-generated discipline within the group'. Absenteeism, he goes on, can similarly be controlled by promoting interest in the job and commitment to the company, and not by mechanistic controls; he cites an absence rate of 3 per cent at Nissan, as against a motor industry average of 10 per cent.

A critic might, however, point to his recognition that this low figure reflects 'the fact that the workforce is young and all have undergone a stringent medical examination' (Wickens, 1987: 107): some problems of health-related absence have been organized out of the system. More fundamentally, Wickens says nothing about the pressures to work hard and to conform at Nissan, and there is no reliable evidence as to what the workers thought about the system, though stories abound of a strict regime and unremitting demands for hard work (Briggs, 1988). It is arguable that, while teamwork has promoted some commitment and trust, it has also reduced workers' freedom to generate their own standards of discipline. 'Self-generated discipline within the group' has, after all, to be consistent with the demands of production, and, with the strong emphasis on productive efficiency in firms like Nissan, the demands on workers are likely to be considerable.

Evidence consistent with this view can be found in Trevor's (1988) study of another Japanese firm associated with the 'new industrial relations', Toshiba Consumer Products, where again teamworking and responsibility are stressed. As an independent analysis, Trevor's account is particularly useful. It points to two features of managerial practice which have to be set alongside self-discipline. First, there was a very strong orientation to the task: achieving high quality production was made central to the whole activity of the plant, and any self-discipline that workers generated was directed to this end. Second, in a recruitment video the managing director made it very clear that strict standards of attendance were required: 'we're trying to say right from the word go to anyone who may have a problem looking after a child with a cough or cold at home ... that perhaps you should think again about coming to Toshiba' (Trevor, 1988: 124). Trevor also did a survey of workers' opinions. From a list of twelve factors important to 'getting on at TCP', workers did not choose 'taking an interest in the Company', or 'getting on well with other people at work'. Instead, they stressed hard work, attendance, and good time-keeping. Interviewees, while accepting a need for discipline, also felt 'that the manner of ensuring regular and punctual attendance had deteriorated' and that 'the manner of enforcing discipline was heavy-handed' (Trevor, 1988: 194–5, 210).

Similar points emerged from the author's current research mentioned above. There appears to be growing managerial concern about absenteeism and time-keeping, although as would be expected with their reliance on informality, small firms are less affected by this tendency. There has been a move towards closer monitoring of attendance and the enforcement of standards. In one firm subjected to case-study analysis, absence control was high on the managerial agenda. Although some efforts were being made to increase communication with the shopfloor, workers were more aware of pressures to work harder and tightening discipline. One-third reported that they had been subject to some form of disciplinary action, and there was some feeling that control was unduly stringent (Edwards and Whitston, forthcoming).

This is not to disparage efforts to increase motivation. It is to argue that the term self-discipline should not be taken to imply that workers have a new freedom to make their own choices. Neither is the need for change necessarily being questioned. The firms tightening absence controls were not doing so out of whim (although neither was this a response to growing rates of absence). They stressed that staffing levels were being tightened and that, as a result, absence had more direct consequences than was previously the case. There was widespread concern about the need to keep absence in check. Again, the means of doing so were consistent with a corrective approach: standards were identified, and the initial approach to workers exceeding them was through counselling and not punitive discipline. But the tightening of control points to the tougher aspects of disciplinary regimes. The strong task orientation of firms such as Nissan and Toshiba also indicates that the context of self-discipline is one of meeting specific requirements, with workers' freedom to exercise initiative being set within very clear parameters.

The present argument is not that this is in any simple way against the interests of workers. Wickens argues that standard forms of time control such as clocking not only hinder management by being bureaucratic but also generate bad feeling among workers; new systems based on trust can benefit everyone. The present aim is not to evaluate such arguments, but merely to underline the fact that underlying them is a control dimension. In a celebrated article, Walton (1985) spoke of a move from control to commitment. It might be better to say that control through bureaucratic rules is being replaced by control through commitment.

One way of characterizing the situation might be to identify an area of self-discipline bounded by coercion if workers step beyond acceptable limits. This would, however, be too simple. The limits are not purely coercive: they are enforced in a corrective manner, in some respects workers accept rules, and overt coercion is rare. And what goes on inside the limits is not separate from control aspects: self-discipline is directed towards set ends. Disciplinary regimes are complex wholes. As Evans et al. (1985) suggest, three forms of discipline can be identified: normal control, where employees' behaviour is seen as broadly legitimate and rewards are used to maintain this state of affairs; corrective discipline, used to return workers deviating from standards to normalcy; and critical discipline, where such a return was seen as difficult, and dismissal is contemplated if improvements are not made. The key point is that such forms operate simultaneously. A corrective approach does not exist in isolation from the possibility of punishment, and self-discipline is not divorced from correction and punishment. Discipline is part of an overall set of control mechanisms. To understand how discipline was created and sustained at Toshiba, for instance, requires attention to systems of reward, the type of commitment sought, and recruitment policies (for careful policies aimed at selecting 'flexible' workers are important ways in which managements can shape shopfloor relations), as well as formal discipline.

In firms such as this, there appears to be a carefully integrated package. In other firms, a growing question is the congruence between different aspects of policy. There are indications that the message of commitment and that of tighter standards of performance are seen as conflicting. There may be no logical contradiction between saying that proper standards need to be enforced and that workers are encouraged to use initiative, but in practice the overtly disciplinary aspects of the former may reduce the credibility of the latter. The different strands of formal disciplinary arrangements need to be seen in relation to each other, to the 'third face' of the practical understanding and rules of behaviour, and to business aims more generally.

# Bibliography

Anderman, S.D. 1972. *Voluntary Dismissals Procedure and the Industrial Relations Act*. London: PEP (Political and Economic Planning).

Armstrong, P. 1983. 'Class Relationships at the Point of Production: A Case Study'. *Sociology*, 17: August, 339–58.

—— Goodman, J.F.B. and Hyman, J.D. 1981. *Ideology and Shop Floor Industrial Relations*. London: Croom Helm.

Ashdown, R.T. and Baker, K.H. 1973. *In Working Order: A Study of Industrial Discipline*. Department of Employment Manpower Papers 6. London: HMSO.

Bagwell, P. S. 1963. *The Railwaymen: The History of the National Union of Railwaymen*. London: Allen & Unwin.

Batstone, E. 1984. *Working Order: Workplace Industrial Relations over Two Decades*. Oxford: Blackwell.

—— 1988. *The Reform of Workplace Industrial Relations: Theory, Myth and Evidence*. Oxford: Oxford University Press.

—— Boraston, I. and Frenkel, S. 1977. *Shop Stewards in Action: The Organization of Workplace Conflict and Accommodation*. Oxford: Blackwell.

—— Ferner, A. and Terry, M. 1984. *Consent and Efficiency: Labour Relations and Management Strategy in the State Enterprise*. Oxford: Blackwell.

Beach, D. S. 1975. *Personnel: The Management of People at Work*. 3rd edn. New York: Macmillan.

Briggs, S. 1988. 'The End of the Nissan Honeymoon'. *New Statesman and Society*, 15 July: 25–6.

Brown, W. 1973. *Piecework Bargaining*. London: Heinemann.

Burawoy, M. 1979. *Manufacturing Consent: Changes in the Labor Process under Monopoly Capitalism*. Chicago: University of Chicago Press.

Cameron, D. 1984. 'The When, Why and How of Discipline'. *Personnel Journal*, July: 37–9.

Cavendish, R. 1982. *Women on the Line*. London: Routledge & Kegan Paul.

Child, J. and Partridge, B. 1982. *Lost Managers: Supervisors in Industry and Society*. Cambridge: Cambridge University Press.

Clifton, R. and Tatton-Brown, C. 1979. *Impact of Employment Legislation on Small Firms*. Department of Employment Research Paper 6. London: HMSO.

Clinton, A. 1984. *Post Office Workers: A Trade Union and Social History*. London: Allen & Unwin.

Collins, H. 1982. 'Capitalist Discipline and Corporatist Law'. *Industrial Law Journal*, 11: June and September, 78–93 and 170–7.

Cressey, P. and MacInnes J. 1980. 'Voting for Ford: Industrial Democracy and the Control of Labour'. *Capital and Class*, 11: Summer, 5–33.

Cunnison, S. 1966. *Wages and Work Allocation: A Study of Social Relations in a Garment Workshop*. London: Tavistock.

Daniel, W.W. and Millward, N. 1983. *Workplace Industrial Relations in Britain*. London: Heinemann.

—— and Stilgoe, E. 1978. *The Impact of Employment Protection Laws*. London: PSI.

Deaton, D. 1984. 'The Incidence of Dismissals in British Manufacturing Industry'. *Industrial Relations Journal*, 15: Summer, 61–5.

Dickens, L., Jones, M., Weekes, B. and Hart, M. 1985. *Dismissed: A Study of Unfair Dismissal and the Industrial Tribunal System*. Oxford: Blackwell.

Dilts, D.A., Deitsch, C.A., and Paul, R.J. 1985. *Getting Absent Workers Back on the Job: An Analytical Approach*. Westport, Conn.: Quorum.

Ditton, J. 1977. *Part-Time Crime: An Ethnography of Fiddling and Pilferage*. London: Macmillan.

—— 1979. *Controlology: Beyond the New Criminology*. London: Macmillan.

Edwards, P.K. 1985a. 'Myth of the Macho Manager'. *Personnel Management*, April: 32–5.

—— 1985b. 'Managing Labour Relations through the Recession'. *Employee Relations*, 7: 2, 3–7.

—— 1986. *Conflict at Work: A Materialist Analysis of Workplace Relations*. Oxford: Blackwell.

—— 1987. *Managing the Factory: A Survey of General Managers*. Oxford: Blackwell.

—— and Scullion, H. 1982a. 'Deviancy Theory and Industrial Praxis: A Study of Discipline and Social Control in an Industrial Setting'. *Sociology*, 16: August, 322–40.

—— and Scullion, H. 1982b. *The Social Organization of Industrial Conflict: Control and Resistance in the Workplace*. Oxford: Blackwell.

—— and Scullion, H. 1984. 'Absenteeism and the Control of Work'. *Sociological Review*, 32: August, 547–72.

—— and Whitston, C. Forthcoming. 'Industrial Discipline, the Control of Attendance, and the Subordination of Labour'. *Work, Employment and Society*.

Edwards, R. 1979. *Contested Terrain: The Transformation of the Workplace in the Twentieth Century*. London: Heinemann.

Evans, S., Goodman, J.F.B. and Hargreaves, L. 1985. *Unfair Dismissal Law and Employment Practice in the 1980s*. Department of Employment Research Paper 53. London: HMSO.

Glasbeek, H.J. 1984. 'The Utility of Model Building: Collins' Capitalist Discipline and Corporatist Law'. *Industrial Law Journal*, 13: September, 133–52.

Goffee, R. and Scase, R. 1982. '"Fraternalism" and "Paternalism" as Employer Strategies in Small Firms'. *Diversity and Decomposition in the Labour Market*. Ed. Day, G. et al. Aldershot: Gower, 107–24.

Gouldner, A.W. 1954. *Patterns of Industrial Bureaucracy: A Case Study of Modern Factory Administration*. New York: Free Press.

Henry, S. 1982. 'Factory Law: The Changing Disciplinary Technology of Industrial Social Control'. *International Journal of the Sociology of Law*, 10: November, 365–83.

—— 1983. *Private Justice: Towards Integrated Theorising in the Sociology of Law*. London: Routledge & Kegan Paul.

Hoel, B. 1982. 'Contemporary Clothing "Sweatshops", Asian Female Labour and Collective Organisation'. *Work, Women and the Labour Market*. Ed. West, J. London: Routledge& Kegan Paul, 80–98.

Hudson, K. 1970. *Working to Rule. Railway Workshop Rules: A Study of Industrial Discipline*. Bath: Adams & Dart.

Institute of Personnel Management. 1979. *Disciplinary Procedures and Practice*. London: IPM.

Klein, L. 1964. *'Mulltiproducts Ltd': A Case-Study on the Social Effects of Rationalised Production*. London: HMSO.

Lawson, T. 1981. 'Paternalism and Labour Market Segmentation Theory'. *The Dynamics of Labour Market Segmentation*. Ed. Wilkinson, F. London: Academic Press, 47–66.

Littler, C.R. 1982. *The Development of the Labour Process in Capitalist Societies*. London: Heinemann.

Lupton, T. 1963. *On the Shop Floor: Two Studies of Workshop Organization and Output*. Oxford: Pergamon.

McCarthy, W.E.J. 1966. *The Role of Shop Stewards in British Industrial Relations*. Research Paper 1, Royal Commission on Trade Unions and Employers' Associations. London: HMSO.

—— and Parker, S.R. 1968. *Shop Stewards and Workshop Relations*. Research Paper 10, Royal Commission on Trade Unions and Employers' Associations. London: HMSO.

MacInnes, J. 1987. *Thatcherism at Work: Industrial Relations and Economic Change*. Milton Keynes: Open University Press.

Mars, G. 1973. 'Chance, Punters and the Fiddle: Institutionalized Pilferage in a Hotel Dining Room'. *The Sociology of the Workplace: An Interdisciplinary Approach*. Ed. Warner, M. London: Allen & Unwin, 200–10.

—— 1974. 'Dock Pilferage'. *Deviance and Social Control*. Ed. Rock, P. and McIntosh, M. London: Tavistock, 209–28.

—— 1982. *Cheats at Work: An Anthropology of Workplace Crime*. London: Counterpoint.

Mellish, M. and Collis-Squires, N. 1976. 'Legal and Social Norms in Discipline and Dismissal'. *Industrial Law Journal*, 5: September, 164–77.

Millward, N. and Stevens, M. 1986. *British Workplace Industrial Relations, 1980–84*. Aldershot: Gower.

Newby, H. 1977. 'Paternalism and Capitalism'. *Industrial Society: Class, Cleavage and Control*. Ed. Scase, R. London: Allen & Unwin, 59–73.

Nichols, T. 1975. 'The Sociology of Accidents and the Social Production of Industrial Injury'. *People and Work*. Ed. Esland, G., Salaman, G. and Speakman. M.-A. Edinburgh: Holmes McDougall, 217–29.

—— and Armstrong, P. 1973. *Safety or Profit: Industrial Accidents and the Conventional Wisdom*. Bristol: Falling Wall.

—— and Beynon, H. 1977. *Living with Capitalism: Class Relations and the Modern Factory*. London: Routledge & Kegan Paul.

Plumridge, M.D. 1966. 'Disciplinary Practice'. *Personnel Management*, September, 138–41.

Pollard, Sidney. 1965. *The Genesis of Modern Management: A Study of the Industrial Revolution in Great Britain*. London: Arnold.

Pollert, A. 1981. *Girls, Wives, Factory Lives*. London: Macmillan.

Prude, J. 1983. 'The Social System of Early New England Textile Mills: A Case Study, 1812–40'. *Working-Class America*. Ed. Frisch, M.H. and Walkowitz, D.J. Urbana: University of Illinois Press, 1–36.

Reid, D.A. 1976. 'The Decline of Saint Monday, 1766–1876'. *Past and Present*, 71: May, 76–101.

Roy, D. 1954. 'Efficiency and "The Fix": Informal Intergroup Relations in a Piecework Machine Shop'. *American Journal of Sociology*, 60: November, 255–66.

Sokolik, S.L. 1970. *The Personnel Process: Line and Staff Dimensions in Managing People at Work*. Scranton: International Textbook.

Storey, J. 1980. *The Challenge to Management Control*. London: Kogan Page.

—— 1987. 'Developments in the Management of Human Resources: An Interim Report'. Warwick Papers in Industrial Relations 17. Coventry: Industrial Relations Research Unit, University of Warwick.

Strauss, G. and Sayles, L.R. 1980. *Personnel: The Human Problem of Management*. 4th edn. Englewood Cliffs, NJ: Prentice-Hall.

Swaffin-Smith, C. 1982. 'Small Businessmen and Disciplinary Issues'. *Employee Relations*, 4: 1, 27–31.

Terry, M. 1977. 'The Inevitable Growth of Informality'. *British Journal of Industrial Relations*, 15: March, 76–90.

Thomason, G.F. 1978. *A Textbook of Personnel Management*. 3rd edn. London: IPM.

Torrington, D. and Chapman, J. 1979. *Personnel Management*. Englewood Cliffs, NJ: Prentice-Hall.

Trevor, M. 1988. *Toshiba's New British Company: Competitiveness through Innovation in Industry*. London: PSI.

Upton, R. 1987. 'What Makes a Disciplinary Procedure Appealing?'. *Personnel Management*, December, 46–9.

Walton, R.E. 1985. 'From Control to Commitment in the Workplace'. *Harvard Business Review*, 53: March–April, 77–84.

Welch, B. 1978. 'Keeping the Discipliners in Line'. *Personnel Management*, August, 21–4.

Wickens, P. 1987. *The Road to Nissan: Flexibility, Quality, Teamwork*. London: Macmillan.

Winchester, D. 1983. 'Industrial Relations in the Public Sector'. *Industrial Relations in Britain*. Ed. Bain, G.S. Oxford: Blackwell, 155–78.

Wood, S. 1986. 'The Cooperative Labour Strategy in the US Auto Industry'. *Economic and Industrial Democracy*, 7: November, 415–47.

Zipp, J.F and Lane, K.E. 1987. 'Plant Closings and Control over the Workplace'. *Work and Occupation*, 14: February, 62–87.

# PART VI
Participation and Involvement

# 14 Employee Communication Programmes

*Barbara Townley*

It is generally true to say that British management has not placed a strong emphasis on employee communication programmes, despite many prescriptive statements that communication is of central importance for the effective functioning of an organization. A survey conducted in the mid-1970s found that 80 per cent of employees did not feel that their company kept them informed of corporate developments (CBI, 1976: 32). Reasons advanced for this apparent neglect include the limited demand for information from employees and a lack of employee interest in the company (BIM, 1975: 24; CBI, 1976: 40; Marsh and Hussey, 1979: 13). In some cases the charge that there has been a failure to communicate with employees is not acknowledged – 'many a manager has had a couple of pints with the shop steward and assumed there is an effective communications system'.

There is evidence, however, that British management is beginning to take the area of employee communication more seriously, with a growing awareness of the role a formal programme may play within the organization. An IPM survey indicated an increasing financial commitment to such programmes, from an average expenditure of £8 per employee in 1977 to an estimated £15 in 1983, although a third of the organizations did not undertake systematic costings of their programmes (IPM, 1981a: 54–5). This is paralleled by an increase to 42 per cent in those companies having appointed individuals with sole responsibility for employee communication at senior management level, and an increase to 40 per cent in those having written policy statements (IPM, 1981a: 6). Significantly, the number with written policy statements is more than twice earlier estimates of 13 per cent (Knight, 1979) and 21 per cent (Reeves and Chambers, 1978).

Within general management and personnel literature, communication programmes have often been prescribed as a universal panacea for a variety of ailments: low employee morale, high absenteeism and turnover rates, low productivity, resistance to change and, perhaps most frequently, labour conflict. Where recognized, the communication 'gap' is seen as bridgeable. The 'content and technique' approaches to communication programmes have exhorted management to 'identify your audience', 'know your objective', followed by discussion of the relative merits of the various methods available to communicate what employees 'ought to know'. The aim of this chapter is to locate corporate communication systems in a broader context. In doing so, it considers the extent to which companies have taken prescripts concerning the need for effective communication to heart, and examines the rationale for, and the implications of, their introduction. Although recognizing the importance of communication at all levels in the organization, the emphasis here will be on *direct* communication between management and individual employees.

## COMMUNICATIONS IN PRACTICE

*Downward Communication – from Employer to Employee*

Table 14.1, which draws on a wide range of surveys, suggests managements' communication systems are likely to use a number of different methods, although with a preference for written rather than oral presentation. Employee notice boards still remain the most favoured method, though increasingly these are being supplemented by house newspapers, magazines and special reports. The latter, however, tend to be the prerogative of larger multi-establishment enterprises. Oral presentations – conferences and seminars – are also becoming more popular, supplementing the more traditional method of direct communication via line management (IPM, 1981a: 28). Audio-visual methods, such as videos, closed circuit television (CCTV), are used by a minority of companies, 22 per cent, largely reflecting cost considerations. Where they are used, they tend to be integral to training programmes and the introduction of new working arrangements. A number of larger companies, Rolls-Royce, IBM, Dunlop, Ford, Shell and ICI, have introduced videos in this context (Maude, 1977: 118).

Rather than indicating the superiority of one particular method over another, the surveys point to the reliance of a series of interlocking channels as the basis of a communication system or network. Some methods, however, are considered to have greater impact, especially face-to-face communication where it is a component of organized line management communication. Employee newspapers, reports, conferences and seminars have a more supportive role: 'useful but not vital' (IPM, 1981a: 34). Research into the extent to which the various methods are appreciated by employees, in that they would be missed if not used, indicates that communication through line management is the most popular method of receiving information (IPM, 1981a: 58).

Two methods in particular have gained prominence recently: employee reports and team briefings. Employee reports, which are the equivalent of shareholder reports, are 'statements produced at least annually, in written form, especially for all employees, which provide information relating to the financial period of the undertaking' (Hussey, 1979: 9). Some of the larger companies have issued these for several years. A survey of the Financial Times 30 Share Index found that 27 of the companies prepared them (Holmes, 1977). The more general surveys indicate an increase in the companies issuing them. From the relatively low levels of 22 per cent reported by BIM (1975)

TABLE 14.1 *Communication channels, companies reporting use (%)*

| | BIM 1975 | CBI[a] 1976 | ORC 1978 | IOD 1981 | IPM 1981[a] | Hussey[b] and Marsh 1983 |
|---|---|---|---|---|---|---|
| *Written methods* | | | | | | |
| House journals | 54 | 21 | 50 | 10 | 71 | — |
| Notice boards | 66 | | 65 | 15 | 95 | — |
| Written communications direct to individuals | 52 | 12 | 37 | — | 35 | — |
| Employee reports | 22 | 6 | 19 | — | 62 | 59 n. 1033 |
| Shareholders' report | — | — | 7 | — | — | — |
| Notices in pay packets | — | — | 24 | — | — | — |
| Notices at home | — | — | 8 | — | — | — |
| *Oral* | | | | | | |
| Briefing groups | 51 | — | — | 58 | 43 | 30 |
| General meetings of employees | 30 | 14 | 28 | — | 24 | — |
| Conferences/seminars | — | — | — | — | 62 | 20 |
| Immediate boss | — | 5 | 46 | 56 | 73 | — |
| Senior management | — | 5 | — | 30 | — | 40 |
| Shop steward | — | 5 | — | 6 | 65 | 23 |
| TU official/national officer | — | 1 | — | 1 | — | — |
| Works/staff council | — | — | 22 | 10 | 71 | 20 |
| Loudspeaker | — | — | 7 | . — | 25 | — |
| CCTV/video | — | — | 6 | 2 | 22 | — |
| Audio-visual | — | — | 2 | | 26 | — |
| *Other* | | | | | | |
| Grapevine | — | 9 | 26 | 3 | — | — |
| Newspapers/radio/TV | — | 16 | — | — | 11 | — |
| None | — | — | 3 | — | — | — |
| | n. 391 | n. 1038 | n. 1524 | n. 115 | n. 145 | n. 371 |

*Notes*: [a] for communication of profit only
[b] financial information only

and 25 per cent by Opinion Research and Communications (ORC, 1978), a later survey by Hussey and Marsh (1983) reported 41 per cent of companies issuing such a report, sometimes on a quarterly or monthly basis. In the IPM survey this figure rises to 62 per cent, with a 21 per cent growth in the years 1977–80, although much of this was in 1979 (IPM, 1981a: 29).

Companies producing employee reports tend to be larger, multi-establishment, public companies with 500 or more employees. Single establishment private companies, employing fewer than 500, make less use of them, although there are some indications that this could change in the future. Marsh and Hussey (1979: 10) conclude that 'the practice of employee reporting is now well established and unlikely to recede'. In some cases employee reports have been supplemented by employee annual meetings, paralleling shareholder meetings, where the company elaborates on the state of the company and future plans (Fenn and Yankelovich, 1972).

Of all the communication methods in use, team briefing is perhaps the most systematic in the provision of 'top-down' information to employees. Information is disseminated, or 'cascades', through various managerial tiers, being conveyed by the immediate superior to a small group of employees, the optimum number being between four and twenty, where employee queries are answered. This takes place throughout all levels in the organization eventually to be conveyed by supervisors to shopfloor employees. On each occasion the information received is supplemented by 'local' news of more immediate relevance to those being 'briefed', usually in the ratio of 70 per cent local information to 30 per cent detail from senior management levels (for examples, see Toole 1983; Parr, 1983; IRRR, 1986b). Actively promoted by the Industrial Society, which estimates that it has helped introduce such arrangements in 400–500 organizations, these groups have the advantage of face-to-face communication, increased contact with immediate supervision and involvement of all layers of management, for whom communication becomes a 'normal part of the job' (Garnett, 1980 and 1981). An early survey found that 51 per cent of firms regularly used briefing groups or variations on this method (BIM, 1975). Later studies indicate that this figure has probably increased (IOD, 1981; Batstone, 1984: 268). The Second Workplace Industrial Relations Survey found that 62 per cent of organizations made use of communication systems which relied on the team briefing principle (Millward and Stevens, 1986: 153).

Organizations employing 5000 or more are more likely to have formal employee communication systems, although this is more associated with the structural complexity of the organization rather than size *per se*. Foreign ownership is another factor correlated with the existence of such schemes (Purcell et al., 1987). They are also more common where there is a specialist personnel function, the latter usually providing the impetus toward the introduction of such schemes (IPM, 1981a: 8).

Table 14.2 gives a summary of the nature of information disclosed to employees. This is based on employer estimates which, as a number of surveys have shown, may give a more favourable impression than employee or trade union estimates (Daniel and Millward, 1983: 148; Millward and Stevens, 1986: 154). Separate information classification systems may also result in some overlap of figures. Nonetheless, some generalizations are possible. Generally, issues relating to pay and conditions (wages, salaries, fringe benefits, payment systems and pension schemes) are the subject of more communication to the workforce than manpower requirements (issues affecting job security, maintenance of employment), although personnel data (number of employees, labour turnover, absenteeism and redeployment) are usually divulged. Information communicated on production issues (productivity,

TABLE 14.2  *Information disclosed, companies reporting disclosure (%)*

| | BIM 1975 | ORC 1978 | IPM 1981 | Recommended by CBI* | Recommended by TUC* |
|---|---|---|---|---|---|
| *Pay and conditions* | | | | | |
| Pay scales salaries/wages | 73 | 81 | | * | * |
| Make up of pay | 80 | | | * | * |
| Directors' fees | 9 | | | * | * |
| Executive salaries | 2 | | | | |
| Holidays/hours | | 89 | | * | |
| Pension schemes | 79 | | | * | |
| Canteen/welfare | 64 | | | | |
| *Manpower/Personnel data* | | | | | |
| Turnover/absenteeism | 20 | | | * | * |
| Manpower plans | 14 | | | | |
| Changes in senior management | | 53 | | | |
| *Performance/Production issues* | | | | | |
| Strike levels | | 33 | | * | |
| Organizational change | | 40 | | * | |
| Market share | | 27 | | | |
| Exports | | 25 | | * | |
| Unit costs | 8 | | 49 | | * |
| Order book position | | | 46 | * | |
| Changes affecting working conditions | | 81 | | * | |
| Productivity/efficiency | | 64 | 57 | | |
| New plant/equipment/new tech. | | 55 | 68 | | |
| Sales levels | | 48 | 77 | | * |
| Product quality | | 46 | 53 | | |
| *Future plans* | | | | | |
| Employment prospects 3–6 months | | | 69 | | |
| Expansion policy | 30 | | | | |
| Mergers/takeovers | 18 | 27 | | | |
| Factory or unit closures (including redundancies) | 38 | 54 | | | |
| New investment | | 36 | | | |
| *Financial information* | | | | | |
| Sales revenue | 25 | | | | * |
| Before/after tax profits | 30 | | | | * |
| Profit and loss | | 48 | 84 | * | |
| Government grants/subsidies | 7 | | | | * |
| Rate of return on capital | 16 | | | | * |
| Value of company | 21 | | | | * |
| Investments abroad | | 17 | | | |
| Investments | | | 50 | | |
| Profits of operating units | | | 56 | | |
| | n. 391 | n. 1524 | n. 145 | | |

work scheduling, unit costs, etc.) varies widely. Equally, future plans and prospects (expansion, closure, merger, investments, etc.) are also disclosed to varying degrees. In the IPM (1981a: 43) survey 40 per cent of companies supplied all employees with production and employment prospects for the following six months. Financial information (details of company finance before and after tax, turnover, etc.) is the subject of least communication, although there is some indication of a slight movement away from the traditional pattern of management jealously guarding this type of information (Moore, 1980). A more recent survey reported a high percentage (86 per cent) of companies with a stated policy of communicating information on financial matters and performance to employees (Marginson et al., 1988). When it does occur, disclosure of information on financial issues relies on the use of briefing groups and employee reports. The Second Workplace Industrial Relations Survey (Millward and Stevens, 1986) confirms the patterns of disclosure reported in the earlier surveys. Terms and conditions of employment and major changes in working methods or work organization were the two areas which were more frequently communicated to employees. Staffing or manpower plans were the next most common topic for disclosure. The financial position of the establishment and the organization as a whole, together with investment plans, were the least likely subjects for communication (Millward and Stevens, 1986: 154–60).

Not all information is disclosed to every employee. Status within the organizational hierarchy usually determines the amount of information received. Management also draws a distinction between the type of information disclosed and the forum for its disclosure. The BIM survey (1975: 10) found a preference for consultation committees as the medium for disclosure of general performance indicators, on the grounds that this forum was seen as being inherently less conflictual and membership was not just restricted to unionized employees. Information disclosed in this forum is then circulated to other employees usually via written minutes for non-manual employees or notice boards for manual employees, or informal oral communication (Daniel and Millward, 1983: 138). Expansion plans were also released in joint consultation forums, whereas closures and information on income were usually restricted to union channels.

A greater disclosure of information is reported by larger enterprises, nationalized industries and foreign-owned companies (Millward and Stevens, 1986: 155–6). Companies where there was a personnel or industrial relations specialist represented on the board were also more likely to disclose more information, as were those companies recognizing a number of trade unions, although no systematic disclosure of routine personnel and income data was found in 25 per cent of companies where bargaining took place (BIM, 1975). Another influential factor is the level of pay negotiations. Where negotiations take place at establishment level, disclosure on pay and financial information was highest (Daniel and Millward, 1983).

One of the reasons given for limited disclosure of information is the difficulty it is assumed employees will have in understanding it. Even so, the BIM survey (1975) revealed that training in information handling was provided by only 35 per cent of companies and even here was usually restricted to managerial and supervisory employees. Limited training was also confirmed in the IOD survey (1981), but case study material reveals that some companies see training as a serious adjunct of a communications system (IPM, 1981b).

*Two-way Communication*

Having given details of the communication methods used to convey information from management to employees, the methods used to ascertain the views of employees will now be examined. Obviously, not all the schemes outlined above are purely 'one-way'. They are, however, primarily designed as a means of imparting information from management to employees and are limited in the extent to which they provide the opportunity for employee feedback, in particular in the opportunity they present for individuals to voice opinions on issues not directly related to a predetermined agenda. In an attempt to address this, companies have devised a number of 'two-way' communication systems. The Second Workplace Industrial Relations Survey shows that of the initiatives introduced in the 1980–4 period, two-way communication is the most frequently cited (Millward and Stevens, 1986: 165). Twelve per cent of establishments reported such schemes, from a base of 5 per cent in 1980. The most common forms of two-way communication are 'speak out' programmes, suggestion schemes, attitude surveys, and employee appraisals.

In 'speak out' or 'speak up' schemes, employees are able to contact a counsellor or ombudsman with a grievance or query. Assured of the strictest confidence, grievances are passed on, anonymously, to whoever has responsibility for the issue concerned, with the individual usually guaranteed a response within a set time period. Where the point is thought to be of general relevance, replies may be printed in company newspapers. In the USA, such schemes have for some time been a feature of communication programmes of large, mainly non-union, corporations such as Caterpillar, Xerox, Polaroid and Raytheon, where they usually function as useful 'warning devices' in potential litigation cases, for example sexual harassment cases (Fenn and Yankelovich, 1972; Berenbeim, 1980; Foulkes, 1980). In the UK, the IBM 'speak up' system, which is supplemented by an 'open door' programme allowing an employee to appeal against a manager's decision, handles approximately 1000 cases a year covering a range of issues (IDS, 1984). Although in theory it is possible for an employee to take an issue to the UK Chairman's office, most are resolved at middle or senior management level (Bassett, 1986: 168–70).

Employee suggestion schemes are also a prominent feature of North American communication programmes. Beneficial in terms of improved employee participation and 'identification', there is also the advantage of increased efficiency and financial savings which can be gained from such schemes. In the UK, a suggestion scheme introduced in Jaguar Cars was estimated to have made savings of 20 per cent in its first year and to have given 'rewards' to employees ranging from £5 to £1250 (IRRR, 1982). IBM records savings of approximately £0.5m in 1984 (Bassett, 1986: 168). Evidence of cost savings, estimated to be over £8m in a recent survey of 125 companies, has resulted in the increased adoption of suggestion schemes in the UK (Industrial Society, 1986). The Second Workplace Industrial Relations Survey showed 25 per cent of establishments had such schemes (Millward and Stevens, 1986: 153).

A more systematic means of obtaining feedback is the attitude survey. Dating back to the 1930s, when the National Institute of Industrial Psychology started experimenting with such surveys in studies on labour turnover, their use has since been expanded to include surveys into attitudes held on supervision, remuneration and working conditions, as well as on specific aspects of personnel policies, such as pension or incentive schemes (IPM, 1981b). Although the Second Workplace Industrial Relations Survey shows that only a small percentage of companies (8 per cent) make use of surveys (Millward and Stevens, 1986: 153), some companies place great store by them. IBM, for example, started using attitude surveys in 1962 and so has access to information on a long-term basis. In biennial surveys, which usually receive a high response rate (99 per cent), employees are asked over 100 questions covering aspects of job satisfaction including evaluations of managers (Bassett, 1986: 168). The surveys have played a key role in the development of effective personnel policies and have enabled the company to gauge how change has been received (IPM, 1981a; IDS, 1984).

Although surveys are a valid method of achieving a systematic measure of employee attitudes (Keohane 1971; Cross, 1973), their agenda is circumscribed to particular areas of management interest and as instruments of communication they remain very passive. One way in which they have been used to enhance the element of participation is in conjunction with project teams or taskforces. Areas highlighted by surveys as being of concern to employees are given as 'problems' to project teams of a small number of employees and supervisors who attempt to devise 'solutions'. Usually confined to job-related tasks, employees are released from work to follow up particular issues and make recommendations.

Another potential area of feedback is the employee appraisal system discussed in chapter 7. Its value in a communication programme is very much dependent on the perceived function of appraisals within the organization and the success with which the often conflicting objectives of appraisals are managed. Its use as a communication channel requires the assessment and overt control function of appraisal to be highly modified to a more open, developmental approach, with discussion of achievements, aspirations, values and, in addition, grievances (see, for example, IPM, 1982). The survey of appraisal systems by Long (1986) reveals that there has been an increase in the trait rating methods, which is not in itself conducive to a more open appraisal style (Meyer et al., 1965) and probably indicates that the use of the appraisal review as a fully integrated component of a communication system remains rather undeveloped.

## THE IMPETUS TO INCREASED COMMUNICATION

The 1970s saw great emphasis being placed on various forms of employee involvement and participation, requiring provisions for the disclosure of information and greater sophistication in channels of communication. The IPM survey (1981a: 6) showed that the trend to the formalization of employee communication policies, which began in the 1970s, doubled in the years 1976–9. The following section considers some of the changing political and economic factors which prompted the gradual move away from 'management by concealment' that had earlier characterized British management (Moore, 1980).

### *The Legislative Imperative*

Several statutes have been enacted in the past two decades which have had as their purpose, both implicitly and explicitly, the increased dissemination of information to employees, either individually or through recognized trade unions. Although having the same intent, it is possible to distinguish two different underlying rationales which prompted their enactment. The first, the 'democratic imperative', placed an emphasis on access to information as the essential prerequisite to greater participation in decision-making. The second stressed the 'educative' function of disclosure which, by making employees more aware of the financial circumstances of companies would, it was hoped, contribute to the 'reform' of industrial relations through modified wage demands.

The Labour government's unsuccessful 1969 Industrial Relations Bill first proposed the statutory disclosure of information, although it was not an area in which unions were actively seeking assistance, nor was it recommended by the Donovan Commission (BIM, 1975). This provision was subsequently taken up by the incoming Conservative government's Industrial Relations Act 1971, influenced partly by the desire to 'reform' industrial relations, but also with a view to Britain's entry into the EEC. Under section 57 of the Act, any company with more than 350 employees had to 'issue in respect of that financial year a statement ... to persons employed in the undertaking'. Although this section had not come into effect by the time of the Act's repeal in 1974, attention was focused on the importance of the provision of financial information to employees and trade union representatives for the purposes of collective bargaining.

The 1974 Labour government took a number of legislative steps to increase the flow of information. The 1974 Health and Safety at Work Act placed an obligation on employers to publish a written safety policy and required disclosure of information on health, safety and welfare arrangements to be provided to employees and included in-company annual reports. The disclosure provisions of the 1975 Employment Protection Act, coming into effect in 1977, placed a duty on employers to disclose information, albeit unspecified, to trade unions for the purposes of collective bargaining. Reference was restricted to information without which bargaining would be impeded to a 'material extent'. ACAS, following its predecessor the CIR (Commission on Industrial Relations), produced a Code of Practice listing areas of relevant information but, in keeping with the 'voluntarist' tradition, the subjects disclosed were to be determined through collective bargaining (ACAS, 1977).

The legislation with the most far-reaching consequences in terms of the potential extent of disclosure, though not the number of companies affected, was the 1975 Industry Act. An enabling statute, it required those companies making a 'significant contribution' to an important industrial sector of the economy to disclose upon request to the Secretary of State detailed economic and financial information which, at the Minister's discretion, could also be made available to recognized trade unions. The statute was devised to supplement Labour's economic strategy and to facilitate the development of planning agreements and, had it been enforced, would have required major disclosures of information (Hussey and Marsh, 1983).

Further developments taking place during the final years of the Labour administration came with the establishment in 1975 of the Bullock Committee of Inquiry on Industrial Democracy which led to the government's White Paper on Industrial Democracy issued in 1978. Although considerably diluting the majority of Bullock's proposals, the recommendation of worker representation on a participatory company board required detailed consideration of policies on disclosure and channels of communication (Elliot, 1978). A further White Paper on the Future of Company Reports recommended that companies with more than 500 employees should send them annual reports and accounts, giving a detailed breakdown of company activities (Hussey and Marsh, 1983). The controversy surrounding the industrial democracy proposals, division within trade union ranks and the pressure of other events resulted in both legislative initiatives being shelved. Three years of continuous debate and the prospect of imminent legislation, however, did much to focus attention on the whole area of disclosure of information and communication.

The legislative concerns of the subsequent Conservative governments did not place a high priority on information disclosure. However, a Liberal amendment to the 1982 Employment Act obliged employers of both public and private companies employing more than 250 to include in the company's annual report a statement indicating action taken to 'introduce, maintain or develop' arrangements aimed, amongst other things, at 'providing employees systematically with information on matters of concern to them'; 'consulting employees or their representatives on a regular basis' to ascertain their opinions; and 'achieving a common awareness on the part of all employees of the financial and economic factors affecting the performance of the company' (Rochester, 1982; Wates, 1983). With no legal obligation to consult or communicate, only to report, the only tenuous sanctions which apply are enforceable through the Companies Act.

Legislative initiatives have not only been confined to Britain. A number of EEC proposals, principally the Fifth Directive on Harmonization of Company Law and the Directive on Procedures for Informing and Consulting

Employees (the Vredeling–Davignon proposals), are designed to increase access to information. The former proposes employee directors on a company supervisory board, whilst the latter obliges multinationals to consult on closures, mergers and major company changes. As the result of political manoeuvrings, both directives have undergone a number of changes, with the final outcome being difficult to predict, except to say that any enactment will have serious implications for communication channels and access to information (IRRR, 1984b and 1984c; EIRR, 1985).

Although the increased incidence of communication policies and programmes coincides with the legislation of the 1970s, as table 14.3 indicates, this is not often cited by management as a reason for the introduction of such schemes. This may be because the impact of law is diffuse, being absorbed via seminars and employer association reports into management thinking, or due to a reluctance by management to admit to a reactive stance. The direct impact of specific statutes is difficult to assess, and where evidence is available it is ambiguous.

Both the Brown (1981: 75) and the First Workplace Industrial Relations surveys (Daniel and Millward, 1983: 144) indicate that the health and safety legislation was influential in establishing committees. This did not, however, necessarily translate into increased communication and dissemination of information. The BIM survey (1975: 23) found that only 12 per cent of respondents had improved information arrangements to conform with the requirements of the Act, and a later survey indicated that two-thirds of representatives were failing to receive accurate and comprehensible information (Labour Research Department, 1984). The majority (65 per cent) of companies in a survey by Dickens (1980) reported that the disclosure provisions of the Employment Protection Act (EPA) had had no effect on company policy, although a minority (24 per cent) had increased provision. Information agreements were rare. Generally, the impact of the EPA provisions have not been as extensive as might be supposed. Failure to specify the information to be disclosed, the lack of legal obligation on the employer, the onus on trade unions to identify information, the narrow interpretation of the statute and the clumsy enforcement procedure have all contributed to this (Hussey and Marsh, 1983; Gospel, 1978; Gospel and Willman, 1981; Bellace and Gospel, 1983).

There does, however, seem to have been a rapid rise in the publication of employee reports. Although a few companies in the Marsh and Hussey (1979) survey (4 per cent), issued reports prior to 1971, a rapid growth took place in the period 1975–7, leading the authors to conclude that companies, faced with the threat of imminent legislation, were anxious to introduce their own schemes before being obliged to do so by law, a conclusion which is in part substantiated by the sharp fall in companies issuing reports in 1978 when legislation appeared less likely. Company response to the 1982 obligation to report employee involvement has varied. Few companies anticipated the introduction of the legislation (Wilding and Marchington, 1983) and, once introduced, positive action in response appears limited (Mitchell et al., 1986; IRRR, 1984e).

TABLE 14.3  *Reasons given for the introduction of communication schemes (%)*

| | IOD[a] 1981 | Hussey and Marsh[b] 1983 | IPM 1981[a] |
|---|---|---|---|
| *Participation and Involvement* | | | |
| Involve employees in company affairs | | | |
| – participation and involvement | 18 | 84 | – |
| Motivate employees/improve morale | 6 | – | 66 |
| *Production Benefits* | | | |
| Motivate employees towards higher | | | |
| productivity | – | 14 | 51 |
| Make the organization work better | – | – | 78 |
| Gain acceptance of change | – | – | 66 |
| Increase work flexibility | – | – | 16 |
| *Educative Purposes* | | | |
| Encourage sense of responsibility | – | 46 | – |
| Improve employees' understanding of | | | |
| company policy and business generally | 64 | 23 | – |
| *'Industrial Relations Purposes'* | | | |
| Moderate wage demands/influence | | | |
| negotiations | 3 | 4 | 20 |
| Reduce work disruption | 3 | – | 31 |
| Minimize trade union influence | 4 | – | – |
| Make managers manage | – | – | 42 |
| *External Pressures* | | | |
| Employee pressure | – | 4 | 10 |
| Trade union pressure | – | 2 | 14 |
| Legal requirements | – | 4 | 18 |
| Pre-empt expected legislation | – | – | 13 |
| *Broader 'Political' Considerations* | | | |
| General social trend | – | – | 21 |
| Discharge responsibilities of company/ | | | |
| 'right to know' | – | 42 | 60 |
| | n. 115 | n. 371 | n. 145 |

*Notes*:  [a]  First reason taken
       [b]  Relates to publication of employee reports only

To see the increased emphasis given to communication systems solely as a response to legislation, although it undoubtedly provides a backcloth against which to view company policies, would be to place too great an importance on the role of law. It would also underestimate some of the more significant changes which have been taking place in approaches to personnel management, in addition to failing to explain why communication is still considered important when the legislative underpinning and formal proposals for increased participation have been removed.

As was argued earlier, two rationales underlay the legislative initiatives of the 1970s: the right to greater participation in decision-making and the 'educative' function of increased disclosure. Whilst the former may not have been readily espoused by management, despite lip-service being paid to democratic principles, the second rationale of reform of industrial relations had a more direct relevance and may be seen as the basis of some of the moves towards increased communication in the period.

## Communication as a Process of Education

The basis of this approach can be seen in the CBI report *Priorities for In-Company Communications*. Critical of British management for failing to explain the economic context in which companies operate, it identifies several 'objectives for education' aimed at making employees more aware of economic 'reality'. Widespread ignorance of levels of company profitability and the tendency of employees to overestimate this were identified as leading to unrealistic expectations contributing to the 'rampant inflation and breakdown of free collective bargaining' occurring in the 1970s (CBI, 1976: 19). The report states, 'if communications are to be relevant they must be designed in such a way that employees' action in response to particular situations is better informed . . . not merely that employees should understand the theory of how the market economy works . . . but also that they should be aware of how it is working in practice at that particular time in their own workplace' (CBI, 1976: 6). Communication which makes employees more aware of their contribution to the creation of wealth through increased productivity and to its distribution through wage bargaining is seen as contributing to more 'informed' or 'realistic' bargaining. It should include a recognition of the importance of investment and the return to shareholders in dividends, the role of entrepreneurs in wealth and job creation, and the importance of the managerial role (CBI, 1976: 36).

Communication in this sense bears a close resemblance to the role ascribed to it by Drucker (1970), that of propaganda. With its emphasis on the workings of the free market system, it is aimed at producing a greater degree of consensus on macroeconomic and political issues, giving the logic of managerial decisions a greater legitimacy. In abdicating the task of communicating to the workforce to the trade unions, management was unable to counter these alternative sources of information concerning the economic performance of the company. Not only had management lost a major source of influence, it had also contributed to its own loss of credibility and status. The CBI survey found that employees had little understanding of managers' contribution to the organization or the complexity of the issues with which they were called upon to deal. Thus, a complementary function of the 'educative' approach was to reassert the role of management, particularly line management, and emphasize the importance of leadership.

The programme introduced at Austin Rover (then BL) was indicative of this type of approach. It represented, in Edwardes's (1983: 164) terms, 'taking over the driving seat for the first time in twenty years'. The changes to be implemented were 'too important to the recovery programme to be passed on through shop stewards at factory floor meetings' (1983: 257). Hence a newly-styled communication programme was introduced including factory briefing sheets, posters, face-to-face meetings between employees and managers, communication to employees through national newspaper advertisements, and writing to employees at home. Central to this communication programme was line management whose role was strengthened *vis-à-vis* both shopfloor representatives and the employee relations department. No longer defined in narrowly operational terms, the supervisors' role and involvement in the communication programme was seen as being the means to increase the status of an increasingly marginal role. This aggressive reassertion of management's role was held to have contributed directly to the successful handling of collective negotiations and industrial disputes which threatened.

Other studies reveal that for the majority of companies the introduction of communication schemes was also in response to a crisis (Batstone, 1984: 263; IDS, 1984). In this respect support is given to Legge's (1978: 93) view that only in times of crisis are aspects of personnel policy seriously considered. In most cases the precipitating factor was the serious financial circumstances of the company or an unenviable industrial relations record. The brewery industry experimented with the introduction of such schemes following changes in consumer demand and the impact of the recession. In conjunction with the major rationalization of its production sites in the 1970s, Greenall Whitley introduced a communication programme consisting of detailed monthly briefings and annual slide presentations on the company's financial situation, in addition to training in handling financial information and a share option scheme. Attitude surveys revealed that both were favourably received (IRRR, 1981b). Similarly, consultation, harmonization and profit-sharing schemes were introduced at Vaux Breweries in an attempt to counter the effects of the recession (IRRR, 1984a). Communication schemes were seen as an integral part of a major reinvestment programme introduced at Cadbury Somerdale (IRRR, 1984d), and a major restructuring at Babcock Power (IRRR, 1986a). At Jaguar Cars an overview of its communication programme led to the introduction of quality circles in an attempt to reverse declining sales figures which were attributed to problems with reliability and quality. Suggestion schemes, broadsheets, meetings, and videos were also part of the communications system, in addition to schemes designed to promote broader involvement, including family nights, open days, social and sports events (IRRR, 1982).

Given that the economic circumstances of the companies in themselves would have been sufficient to secure the changes required, the question arises as to why communication and involvement programmes should have been introduced. The 'cycle of control' thesis presumes that such programmes only gain prominence when economic conditions render employee compliance difficult and decline in periods of recession (Ramsay, 1977). The prevalence of 'bad news', however, may reduce the element of risk involved in information disclosure, and function as an implicit threat which reinforces compliance. There is some evidence to support this interpretation with the tendency of information disclosed to emphasize 'bad news' (Daniel and Millward, 1983; 159), and for companies with below average performance to disclose more information than average performers (Millward and Stevens, 1986: 159).

As an approach, however, reliance on communication programmes to convey 'bad news' items may prove counterproductive. The IPM survey (1981a: 16) found that high levels of unemployment and the recession increased feelings of insecurity and with this a resistance to organizational change – feelings which would only be reinforced by negative disclosures. The survey identified an acknowledged need to improve employee morale. This latter aspect perhaps highlights the main reason for the introduction of such schemes – the recognition that employee compliance is no longer sufficient and there is a necessity to secure *commitment* to organizational change. The need to improve overall organizational effectiveness in highly competitive and adverse market situations, discussed in chapter 2, has been the main factor behind this 'commitment' strategy. Increased competition and the need to retain a competitive advantage have stimulated approaches which stress increased involvement and identification, prompting some companies to review their personnel policies and implement and develop those which indicate a 'human resource' ethos.

## *Communication as a Strategy of Commitment*

Premised on a theory of motivation which holds that employees have an interest in work beyond the mechanics of the task in hand, the emphasis of this approach is on securing normative compliance by paying attention to these wider needs. Lack of a formal communication programme, especially in circumstances which encourage rumours of mergers, rationalizations and redundancies, is seen as fostering low morale, low trust and the pursuit of disparate goals – all detrimental to organizational effectiveness and not conducive to the acceptance of change. With the satisfaction of individual needs projected as a prerequisite of achieving organizational objectives, a communication programme is seen as fulfilling the role of both increasing the individual's identification with the company and the acceptance of organizational goals. The advantages are held to be more favourable employee attitudes, informed involvement and increased productivity. In this respect a developed communication system is usually seen as an integral part of a range of personnel policies which may include profit-sharing, greater job discretion, harmonization and single status, and merit pay schemes, all of which are designed to reinforce the overriding strategy of individual identification with and commitment to the organization.

The importance of increased motivation through employee communication is reinforced by international comparisons, particularly with the role model of the 1980s, Japan. The latter's impressive productivity record, it is frequently held, results from the greater identification employees have with their company. Although many factors contribute to this, the 'Monday morning assembly' of employees and senior management, daily section meetings with foremen, quality circles and briefing groups have been identified as prominent features in this (IRRR, 1981a and 1981c; IDS, 1984). The USA also provides examples of companies which attribute their success to personnel policies with emphasis on well-developed employee communication and identification programmes (Peters and Waterman, 1982; Foulkes, 1980).

The role of communication as a 'motivator' or 'hygiene factor', increasing organizational commitment, has featured in managerial orthodoxy since the popularization of the human relations school (Rose, 1975). Increased international competition and the changing nature of production systems, however, have given this strategy of commitment, and the role of communication in this, a more immediate relevance (Walton, 1985). Communication which concerns itself only with the narrowly defined task in hand is no longer considered adequate for competitive strategies which rely on increased product quality, or where manpower reductions or the introduction of new technology requires greater task flexibility. As the literature espousing this approach remarks, 'the commitment to quality cannot be achieved simply by passive information provision or exhortation' (NEDC, 1986: 27). What is required is the active participation and closer identification of employees with the company, products and markets. 'Many firms have concluded that a significant step forward lies in developing systems of communication and consultation which enable employees to participate to the greatest measure of their skills, experience and responsibilities in decisions about the work they do' (NEDC, 1986: 4). It is not unusual that one of the principal functions of upward communication programmes is the opportunity to tap the accumulated knowledge and experience of employees.

In many respects communication as an element in a commitment strategy can be seen as developing from the 'educative' approach outlined earlier. The individual is taken to be the unit of response in each case. The underlying objective, that of safeguarding or improving economic performance, remains the same. Both are premised on the view that management and labour are mutually dependent. Neither perceive communication to be the simple transmission of data but are in Walton and McKersie's (1965) terms an exercise in 'attitudinal restructuring'. Communication in this instance is 'the process by which an idea is transferred from a source to a receiver with the intention of changing his or her behaviour. Such behaviour may encompass a change in knowledge or attitude as well as in overt behaviour' (Rogers and Rogers, 1976: 9).

Although the underlying objectives remain the same, there is a distinction between the 'educative' and 'commitment' rationales in terms of their emphasis or tone. They differ in their views of motivation, the means of achieving compliance and the concepts of managerial prerogative. The 'educative' view can be seen as more reactive in its approach, stemming from the attempt to fill a perceived vacuum left by the retreat of trade union power. Nor is it as integrated into a comprehensive package of personnel policies designed to achieve organizational objectives. The 'commitment' or 'human resource' approach eschews the more overt reference to the nature of the power relationship between management and workforce and functions more as an integrative mechanism, aimed at influencing perceptions held of the organization and stressing a commonality of experience. It displays a greater commitment to the view that management can only manage effectively with the active co-operation of its workforce and is more conducive to an integrative problem-solving approach. The degree to which each is emphasized will vary according to economic circumstances and the variety of factors which influence management's approach to the handling of labour relations. The two approaches may also be in evidence in the same organization, with divisions within management reflecting different views of the communication system. Supervisors, for example, tend to see communication as a means of getting a job done more efficiently and quickly, while amongst senior management there is a tendency to view it as a means of instilling confidence and motivation (Reeves, 1980).

## RESPONSES TO COMMUNICATION SCHEMES

It is difficult to estimate the impact of a communication programme, not least because of the problem of isolating its effects from other aspects of both personnel and organizational policies which may accompany its introduction. Perhaps because of this, systematic data are limited. Certainly very few of the companies surveyed undertook an evaluation of their communication system's effectiveness. Although 61 per cent of respondents in the IPM survey carried out some assessment, this relied heavily on informal feedback and other factors generally taken to be indicators of organizational health. Only 22 per cent of respondents used attitude surveys as a source of evaluation, with only 10 per cent using them on an annual or more frequent basis (IPM, 1981a: 50). Thirty-nine per cent of companies using employee reports conducted assessments of employee responses (Marsh and Hussey, 1979: 50). Table 14.4 gives

TABLE 14.4  *Results reported from the introduction of communication systems (%)*

| | |
|---|---|
| Increased productivity | 65 |
| Fewer industrial disputes | 68 |
| Less time lost through absenteeism | 41 |
| Reduced employee turnover | 46 |
| Improved morale/loyalty | 80 |
| Better customer relations | 47 |
| No improvements | 3 |
| Difficult to evaluate | 8 |
| | n. 115 |

*Source:* IOD, 1981

management's views of responses to the introduction of communication programmes. These positive results also find support in the case studies, although reported unsuccessful cases are difficult to find.

Employee responses to communication schemes tend to be mixed. The move toward increased information is generally treated with suspicion when communication has been neglected in the past. The assumption is usually that the news is bound to be 'bad news'. After initial scepticism, however, communication systems are more favourably received (CBI, 1976: 31). This is more likely to be in response to the company having 'shown the trouble', with the move toward increased communication being taken as indicative of a change in attitude toward the workforce. It is the expressive nature of the communication rather than the factual content *per se* which is valued. As Marsh and Hussey (1979: 35) conclude, 'it may be that these external messages are sometimes more important than the actual contents'.

This is not to deny, however, the importance of the factual information given. Employees appear to show a preference for 'local' information dealing with prospects for the plant or that part of the organization with which there is daily contact, reflecting the most immediate concerns with security of income and employment. This includes reference to staffing policies and job prospects, departmental performance and future plans (CBI, 1976: 25; Marsh and Hussey, 1979: 32; Hussey and Marsh, 1983: 115–22). In other areas – finance, profit and loss, new investments, exports, mergers and takeovers – employees do not report the desire for more information, largely because this is not perceived to be of direct relevance to their immediate concerns. Satisfaction of demands for 'basic' information (for example, decisions about salaries, holidays and hours of work and changes affecting working conditions) however, leads to a greater demand for disclosure on how these issues are arrived at.

On the whole, employees give a favourable rating to the credibility of information disclosed, although this is heavily influenced by job status, with manual workers showing a much greater distrust of company information than managers. This is particularly true of financial information, especially profits, with a strong belief that figures had been 'fiddled' (CBI, 1976: 32). Scepticism tended to be highest amongst young, male skilled manual employees in the private sector (ORC, 1978: 62). There is also a discrepancy between the two groups in terms of access to information, particularly employee reports, with managerial grades having the most access (Hussey and Marsh, 1983: 115–22). The issue of credibility highlights the tension inherent in communication systems between the desire to influence behaviour and the need to provide 'objective' information. Where the 'educative' element becomes too prominent, is seen as controversial or inappropriate, it detracts from the credibility of the other information (Marsh and Hussey, 1979: 37). Even where there is a degree of consensus on the exigencies of market requirements, this does not necessarily lead to unquestioning acceptance of some managerial decisions. 'Acceptance of the system does not necessarily constitute an unconditional mandate for companies to redeploy capital and pursue growth targets as they please', as the CBI recognizes (1976: 21).

Although the most frequently cited response to a communication system is that of improved employee morale, concrete evidence from the surveys on this is ambiguous. The 1976 CBI survey reported a high correlation between those employees regarding themselves as well informed and generally accepting as credible the information disclosed by the company, and those reporting a high degree of job satisfaction. Those considering themselves to be ill-informed and disbelieving of company information reported greater dissatisfaction with their job. The Second Workplace Industrial Relations Survey found that the industrial relations climate, both with trade unions and the workforce as a whole, was more favourably assessed when a lot of information was given to employees (Millward and Stevens, 1986: 159). There are several difficulties in assessing the significance of these claims, however. The causal relationships between the benefits of a communication system and its impact on well-established predispositions, the industrial relations 'climate' and the amount of information disclosed, are difficult to distinguish. As to responses to increased communication, the CBI report concluded 'we found no conclusive evidence that behaviour at work has actually changed and teamwork functions of individuals improved' (1976: 36).

For management, communicating directly to employees, rather than through established trade union channels, has the obvious advantage of being able to promote a commonality of interests between employee and organization. For the trade union representative, there is sometimes the advantage of not having to convey to the workforce the company's position on a particular issue, thus avoiding a possible loss of credibility and workforce acceptance that this dual role may bring. In these circumstances the trade union channel functions as the principal means of reporting back employee sentiment. However, the development of a separate channel of employee communication deprives unions of an important source of power, that of the control over information, and it is perhaps in the implications for established trade union representation that communication programmes have their greatest impact. The development of a channel for management's view paralleled with that of the 'trade union' view works to promote the idea of a 'third' constituency – the workforce – the 'electorate' forced into choosing between differing interpretations. In a context where this is fully developed, trade unions are no longer the natural voice of the work group, but become increasingly distanced: another constituency in a pluralist association of interests or, in more extreme cases, an outside influence disturbing a harmony of interests.

The potential for communication systems being used as a means of undermining trade union representation has aroused considerable distrust and, not unnaturally, provoked some resistance from trade unions to their introduction, particularly in those sectors where union presence has been strong, for example printing and engineering (BIM, 1975: 12). Other surveys, however, have noted limited or no resistance from trade unions (IOD, 1981: 36). Responses to the introduction of communication programmes have varied. From initial 'veto' responses of attempting to implement boycotts, there has been an increasing tendency for trade unions to respond in like manner by improving communication to their members. In general, trade union response has been highly contingent upon the nature of the existing relationship with the employer, the extent to which they have been involved in the new systems, and on the attitudes of key individuals such as convenors (IDS, 1984: 3).

There is no evidence from the surveys to indicate that communication programmes are being introduced as a tactic in a strategy of 'union substitution', that is, in reducing employees' perceived needs for a union. Non-unionized firms do not communicate more regularly or systematically to individuals than unionized firms, nor are they more likely to have a formal communication policy (IPM, 1981a: 7; BIM, 1975: 11). Neither are industrial relations criteria – minimizing trade union influence, reducing work disruptions, assisting in wage negotiations – regarded as the primary objectives of such policies except in a small minority of companies (IOD, 1981: 20). Rather than being a weapon in an armoury of managerial attacks on established trade union representation, communication systems function more as a means of bypassing union influence rather than explicitly confronting it (Batstone, 1984: 235). Management is still willing to talk *to* unions though not *through* them (Edwards, 1985). However, this is not to deny that in specific instances, especially where shop steward resistance has combined with severe economic problems, communication and involvement policies have been aimed at reducing the trade union role (Batstone, 1984: 271–2). Equally, elaborate communication programmes often feature as an important component of personnel policies designed to minimize the need for union organization, usually associated with some of the large, non-union, American companies (Foulkes, 1980).

The impact of communication programmes on collective bargaining is difficult to gauge. There has been an effect on the *conduct* of bargaining. Whereas previously management abstained from communicating directly with employees (because this was seen as undermining the authority of trade union negotiators) for some, management communication in the form of fact sheets distributed through all stages in negotiation is now an integral part of their strategy. However, the impact of increased dissemination of information on bargaining *outcomes* is ambiguous. While increased access to information may lead to a more 'realistic' bargaining stance possibly based on a more integrative, problem-solving approach, as the 'educative' approach holds, it may also significantly alter the balance of power in favour of unions as information concerning one sector is used as a bargaining counter in another. Again, the information is inconclusive. Bellace and Gospel (1983: 58) conclude 'although information is obviously a power resource in industrial relations the effects of disclosure are by no means clear cut'. Trade union representatives reported that the information disclosed, particularly financial information via employee reports, was of limited value (Moore, 1980; Gill, 1979). Where bargaining takes place at plant level, information required includes operating accounts, costing information, stock levels, transfer prices, and orders. Information disclosed through any of the communication channels is rarely this specific. Financial information, when disclosed, tends to refer to the group level, with the IPM survey (1981a: 43) showing that only 26 per cent of companies provided information specific to the operating unit.

The effect of increased information has to be seen in the context in which bargaining takes place and the nature of the existing bargaining relationship. Supporting the results of early research (Mellinger, 1956) that increased information only aids the accuracy of opinions held if it takes place within a high trust relationship, evidence from the First Workplace Industrial Relations Survey indicates that it is the pre-existing relationship which is the determinant both of the amount and value of the information disclosed (Daniel and Millward, 1983: 152).

The view that information will automatically be translated into 'rational' decision-making in bargaining is, however, based on several dubious assumptions. The ability to pay, although becoming more influential, has never been the only or, indeed, the major factor in determining pay levels (Sisson, 1984). Other factors such as cost of living and comparability have featured strongly (Daniel, 1976). In some respects the role ascribed to information denies the very nature and process of bargaining (Hussey and Marsh, 1983: 124). While information may lead to a more sophisticated bargaining, as claims and counterclaims are more fully prepared and substantiated, by itself information cannot invalidate the division of interest which necessarily accompanies the bargaining process. 'If we look at the central problem in industrial relations – the struggle between labour and capital for higher returns for their respective inputs – there is no communications problem at all . . . no amount of paper, no quantity of briefing sessions will counter the basic disparity of interest' (Gill, 1979: 8).

## CONCLUDING REMARKS

A formal communication programme may have both different underlying rationales and equally different implications for managerial styles which accompany it, as well as for the respective roles of personnel and line management. Communication programmes cannot, therefore, be viewed from a simple systems framework, as is often the case in the literature recommending its use, as 'inputs' to bring about reduced levels of conflict or higher levels of trust. To view communication as a universal panacea for organizational 'ills' leads to both unwarranted expectations in its introduction and qualified failure in its implementation (see, for example, Thomson, 1983; Hyman, 1982). Increased communication remains ineffective when there is resentment against new management; the introduction of employee reports is no compensation for dissatisfaction with other aspects of personnel policies (Marsh and Hussey, 1979: 18, 34). Equally, communication cannot be viewed merely as the reflection of a pre-existing relationship – the often held view that 'good' communication is the logical outcome of 'good' industrial relations. Rather than being viewed in isolation, communication programmes have to be evaluated in relation to the overall strategy of management towards its workforce. IBM practices cannot be divorced from other elements of a policy which have stressed a high degree of job security, harmonization of terms and conditions, and an emphasis on the individual, etc. (IPM, 1981b). Nor can the Japanese system be adequately assessed apart from the whole panoply of policies which emphasize product quality.

This obviously renders any generalized statements on the significance or likely future developments of communication programmes difficult to make. One factor which may be isolated, however, is the extent to which such programmes have been integrated into corporate personnel policies. Any comment on the significance of such schemes must distinguish between those which have been introduced as the result of a well-considered philosophy or policy, and those which are an *ad hoc* pragmatic response to a number of different stimuli, reflecting little of a conscious, strategic analysis – the distinction between those companies, such as IBM, where communication programmes have been a long-established component of corporate personnel policies and those more recently established as part of a crisis management approach.

Generally four 'types' of companies may be identified: the pro-active – those companies where communication is a well-established practice; pre-active – where schemes are 'voluntarily' introduced but usually in response to perceived threats, usually legislation; re-active – where their introduction corresponds with an organizational crisis; and those companies where communication systems are not developed and control is much more overt. Where programmes are a component of a fully integrated 'human resource' policy, a well-developed communications programme is likely to be considered an essential feature of future personnel policies designed to secure employee commitment. Communication programmes in such companies are seen as both allied to competitive advantage and an integral component of facilitating organizational change (IPM, 1981a: 18; Sieff, 1984). The communication systems of reactive companies, however, are much more volatile, with the possibility that they may fall into disuse once the 'crisis' – labour unrest, poor organizational performance, industrial relations problems – has passed. It cannot be certain that the management of these companies will have recognized some of the implications of a comprehensive communication policy, or have introduced the support mechanisms necessary to sustain it.

The move towards increased communication potentially has major implications both for management style and concepts of prerogative. One requirement is for the development of a more 'open' style of management. This is not a framework within which British management is prone to work, prompting fears of managing in a 'goldfish bowl' and a concomitant dilution of managerial authority. There are also implications for the nature of managerial job definitions, no longer narrowly task-oriented but with an emphasis on the role of manager as facilitator, particularly at supervisory level. At its most practical level, the criteria used in managerial selection, appraisal and recommendations for promotion, as well as management training and development requirements, would have to be seriously reviewed. Where communication programmes are an important component of personnel policies, managerial selection and appraisal procedures give serious weight to the individual's ability to handle personnel (Foulkes, 1981: 153–5). Nor is it surprising that three quarters of IBM's annual training programme for managers concentrates on 'people management' (Bassett, 1986: 167).

The implications of a move towards improved communication, not least in terms of resources, may make management wary of steps in this direction. Another factor which may add to circumspection lies in what may be termed the inherent ambiguity involved in the process. Despite being largely conceived of in terms of a process by which management wishes to direct or dominate the behaviour of the workforce, communication, by definition, also implies dialogue: the reciprocal exchange of ideas with a view to influencing opinion or bringing about change. Although inequality in power renders communication as a process of equal exchange invalid, the expectation is created, and a communications programme to maintain its credibility must bring about a degree of change. It is perhaps in the expectations to which communications gives rise, in particular, the desire to influence decision-making, that management's main difficulty lies. As the CBI (1976: 35) recognizes, there is an 'irreversible current' flowing strongly in the direction of participative management – 'modified ... rules for bargaining, for consultation, and for management decision taking' – stimulated by such programmes. Any systematic move toward increased communication inevitably raises the issue of the increased accountability of management and may require a redefinition of the basis of managerial authority. It is this ambiguity involved in communication programmes which has led the CBI (1976: 7) to counsel management to identify 'the maximum price to be paid for successful communications'.

The evidence points to a dramatic rise in the number of companies introducing formal communication programmes. It is too early to tell, however, whether these are in response to the exigencies of the recession or herald a significant change in the handling of labour–management relations. One indication of the seriousness of management's approaches will be seen in its response in different economic conditions. Management may well be more cautious when an upturn in economic conditions renders news more palatable. Evidence from present practice is not a good indication of future response, and in all probability management itself is unsure of its approach in such a context.

## NOTE

The material in this chapter draws upon four principal surveys: Smith (1975) for the BIM; Arnott et al. (1981) for the IPM; Brandon and Arnott (1976) for the CBI; and the Institute of Directors (IOD, 1981). Although not strictly comparable – being conducted at different times and varying in their range of respondents and research objectives – they are cited because of the paucity of systematic survey data on the nature and extent of communication systems. In the interests of brevity the surveys will be referred to by their sponsoring body. Where relevant, this material will be supplemented by documented case studies of current company practice.

# Bibliography

Advisory, Conciliation and Arbitration Service (ACAS). 1977. *Disclosure of Information for Collective Bargaining Purposes*. Code of Practice 2. London: HMSO.

Bassett, P. 1986. *Strike Free*. London: Macmillan.

Batstone, E. 1984. *Working Order: Workplace Industrial Relations over Two Decades*. Oxford: Blackwell.

Bellace, J.R. and Gospel, H.F. 1983. 'Disclosure of Information to Trade Unions: A Comparative Perspective'. *International Labour Review*, 122: January–February, 57–74.

Berenbeim, R. 1980. *Non-Union Complaint Systems: A Corporate Appraisal*. Report No. 770. New York: The Conference Board.

British Institute of Management (BIM). 1975. *Keeping Employees Informed: Current UK Practice on Disclosure*. Management Survey Report No. 31. London: BIM. (Prepared by R. Smith).

Brown, W. Ed. 1981. *The Changing Contours of British Industrial Relations: A Survey of Manufacturing Industry*. Oxford: Blackwell.

Confederation of British Industry (CBI). 1976. *Priorities for In-Company Communications*. London: CBI. (Prepared by M. Brandon and M. Arnott).

Cross, D. 1973. 'The Worker Opinion Survey: A Measure of Shopfloor Satisfaction'. *Occupational Psychology*, 47: 3, 193–208.

Daniel, W. 1976. *Wage Determination in Industry*. London: PEP.

—— and Millward, N. 1983. *Workplace Industrial Relations in Britain*. London: Heinemann.

Dickens, L. 1980. 'What are Companies Disclosing for the 1980s?'. *Personnel Management*, April, 28–30, 48.

Drucker, P. 1970. 'What Communication Means'. *Management Today*, March.

Edwardes, M. 1983. *Back from the Brink*. London: Collins.

Edwards, P.K. 1985. 'The Myth of the Macho Manager'. *Personnel Management*, April, 32–5.

Elliot, J. 1978. *Conflict or Co-operation? The Growth of Industrial Democracy*. London: Kogan Page.

*European Industrial Relations Review* (EIRR). 1985. 'EEC: A New Approach on Vredling'. No. 133. February.

Fenn, D.H. and Yankelovich, D. 1972. 'Responding to the Employee Voice'. *Harvard Business Review*, 50: March/June, 83–91.

Foulkes, F. 1980. *Personnel Policies in Large Non-Union Companies*. Englewood Cliffs, NJ: Prentice-Hall.

—— 1981. 'Large Non Unionized Employers'. *US Industrial Relations 1950–1980: A Critical Assessment*. Eds. Stieber, J., McKersie, R.B. and Quinn Mills, D. Madison: Industrial Relations Research Association, 129–57.

Garnett, J. 1980. *The Manager's Responsibility for Communications*. London: Industrial Society.

—— 1981. 'Team Briefing'. *Industrial Society*, 63: September, 29–30.

Gill, K. 1979. 'Employee Reports under Attack'. *Industrial Society*, 61: May/June, 8–9.

Gospel, H. 1978. 'The Disclosure of Information to Trade Unions: Approaches and Problems'. *Industrial Relations Journal*, 9: Autumn, 18–26.

—— and Willman, P. 1981. 'Disclosure of Information: The CAC Approach'. *Industrial Law Journal*, 10: March, 10–22.

Holmes, G. 1977. 'How UK Companies Report to their Employees'. *Accountancy*, November, 64–8.

Hussey, R. 1979. *Who Reads Employee Reports?*. London: Touche Ross.

—— and Marsh, A. 1983. *Disclosure of Information and Employee Reporting*. Aldershot: Gower.

Hyman, J. 1982. 'Where Communication Schemes Fall Short of Intention'. *Personnel Management*, March, 30–3.

Incomes Data Services (IDS). 1984. *Employee Communications*. Study No. 318. London: IDS.

*Industrial Relations Review and Report* (IRRR). 1981a. 'The Japanese Approach to Employee Communication'. 241: February.

—— 1981b. 'Employee Involvement and Disclosure at Greenall Whitley'. 246: April.

—— 1981c. 'Toshiba Consumer Products (UK) Ltd – New Start, New Industrial Relations'. 253: August.

—— 1982. 'Quality Circles at Jaguar Cars'. 277: August.

—— 1984a. 'Involving Employees at Vaux Breweries'. 312: January.

—— 1984b. 'EEC Proposals on Employee Involvement. Part 1'. 318: April.

—— 1984c. 'EEC Proposals on Employee Involvement. Part 2'. 320: May.

—— 1984d. 'Cadbury Somerdale – The Management of Change'. 328: September.

—— 1984e. 'Involving Employees: Companies Report'. 328: September.

—— 1986a. 'Babcock Power – Long Term Survival Plan'. 367: May.

—— 1986b. 'Team Briefing: Practical Steps in Employee Communication'. 361: February.

Industrial Society. 1986. *Successful Suggestion Schemes*. London: Industrial Society.

Institute of Directors (IOD). 1981. *Communications at Work: The Challenge and the Response. A Survey of Communications within Britain's Medium-Sized and Larger Companies*. London: IOD and Bolton Dickinson Associates.

Institute of Personnel Management (IPM). 1981a. *Employee Communication in the 1980s: A Survey Covering 145 Organisations Conducted for the IPM 1980 Conference*. London: Charles Barker Lyons. (Prepared by M. Arnott, C. Minton and M. Wilders).

—— 1981b. *Practical Participation and Involvement 1: Communications in Practice*, London: IPM.

—— 1982. *Practical Participation and Involvement 3: The Individual and the Job*. London: IPM.

Keohane, J. 1971. 'Methods for Surveying Employee Attitudes'. *Occupational Psychology*, 45: 3 & 4, 217–31.

Knight, I.B. 1979. *Company Organisation and Worker Participation: The Results of a Survey*. London: HMSO.

Labour Research Department. 1984. *Safety Reps in Action*. London: LRD Publications.

Legge, K. 1978. *Power, Innovation and Problem Solving in Personnel Management*. Maidenhead: McGraw-Hill.

Long, P. 1986. *Performance Appraisal Revisited: Third IPM Survey*. London: IPM.

Marginson, P., Edwards, P.K., Martin, R., Purcell, J. and Sisson, K. 1988. *Beyond the Workplace: Managing Industrial Relations in the Multi-Establishment Enterprise*. Oxford: Blackwell.

Marsh, A. and Hussey, R. 1979. *Survey of Company Reports*. Croydon: Company Secretary's Review.

Maude, B. 1977. *Communications at Work*. London: Business Books.

Mellinger, G.C. 1956. 'Interpersonal Trust as a Factor in Communications'. *Journal of Abnormal and Social Psychology*, 52: 304–9.

Meyer, H., Kaye, E. and French, J.R.P. 1965. 'Split Roles in Performance Appraisal'. *Harvard Business Review*, 43: January–February, 123–9.

Millward, N. and Stevens, M. 1986. *The Second Workplace Industrial Relations Survey 1980–1984*. Aldershot: Gower.

Mitchell, F., Sams, K.I. and White, P.J. 1986. 'Research Note: Employee Involvement and the Law: Section 1 of the 1982 Employment Act'. *Industrial Relations Journal*, 17: Winter, 362–7.

Moore, R. 1980. 'Information to Unions: Use or Abuse?'. *Personnel Management*, May, 34–8.

National Economic Development Committee (NEDC). 1986. *Communicating for Change*. London: NEDC.

Opinion Research and Communications (ORC). 1978. *A Survey of Employee Attitudes to Special Employee Reports and to Other Management Communication Techniques*. London: ORC.

Parr, D. 1983. 'Facing up to the '80s'. *Industrial Society*, 65: September, 15–16.

Peters, T.J. and Waterman, R.H. 1982. *In Search of Excellence*. New York: Harper & Row.

Purcell, J., Marginson, P., Edwards, P. and Sisson, K. 1987. 'The Industrial Relations Practices of Multi-Plant Foreign Owned Firms'. *Industrial Relations Journal*, 18: Summer, 130–7.

Ramsay, H. 1977. 'Guides to Control: Worker Participation in Sociological and Historical Perspective'. *Sociology*, 11: 3, 481–506.

Reeves, T.K. 1980. *Information Disclosure in Employee Relations*. Bradford: MCB Publications.

—— and Chambers, B.P. 1978. *Employee Communications – An Act of Faith? A Report on the Use of Mass Media Techniques to Communicate with Employees*. London: Business Decisions Ltd.

Rochester, Lord. 1982. 'The 1982 Employment Act'. *Industrial Society*, 64: December, 8–9, 14.

Rogers, E.M. and Rogers, R. 1976. *Communication in Organizations*. New York: Free Press.

Rose, M. 1975. *Industrial Behaviour: Theoretical Development since Taylor*. Harmondsworth: Penguin.

Sieff, Lord. 1984. 'How I See the Personnel Function'. *Personnel Management*, December, 28–30.

Sisson, K. 1984. 'Changing Strategy in Industrial Relations'. *Personnel Management*, May, 24–7.

Thomson, F. 1983. 'The Seven Deadly Sins of Briefing Groups'. *Personnel Management*, February, 32–5.

Toole, B. 1983. 'Talking Things Through'. *Industrial Society*, 65: June, 12–13.

Walton, R. 1985. 'From Control to Commitment in the Workplace'. *Harvard Business Review*, 63: March–April, 74–84.

—— and McKersie, R. 1965. *A Behavioral Theory of Labor Negotiations*. New York: McGraw-Hill.

Wates, J. 1983. 'Reporting on Employee Involvement'. *Personnel Management*, March, 32–5.

Wilding, P. and Marchington, M. 1983. 'Employee Involvement Inaction?'. *Personnel Management*, December, 32–5.

# 15 Quality Circles

## *Ron Collard and Barrie Dale*

For most of the post-Second World War period, British management has been concerned with securing effective employee participation and involvement as a means of improving performance, efficiency and service. The emphasis has varied between those who have sought greater involvement as a way of satisfying more fundamental requirements, such as job satisfaction and better working relationships, with improved performance as a spin-off, and those who consider that better employee participation can itself make a direct contribution to improved performance. The nature and extent of involvement has also varied between, for example, improved communication of information through briefing groups and other media, as discussed in the previous chapter; indirect or representative participation involving consultation through joint councils at departmental, plant and company level, as discussed in the next chapter, or the employee directors associated with the Bullock Committee of Inquiry (1977); and more direct or individual participation in the immediate task.

In Britain, the participation and involvement of employees has generally been associated with indirect or representative participation such as joint consultation or collective bargaining. Certainly these forms of participation and involvement have been the subject of most discussion and debate. Developments in direct or task participation, by contrast, have received relatively little attention, even though there is evidence to suggest that it is participation in the immediate task situation that is of most concern to individual employees.

The focus in this chapter is on one particular form of direct or task participation, namely, quality circles, to use the generic term. A typical quality circle is a voluntary group of between six and eight people from the same workplace who meet for an hour every week under the leadership of their supervisor to solve work-related problems in their department. Members of the circle select the problems they wish to tackle; collect the necessary data; apply systematic problem-solving techniques in working towards solutions; present their findings and proposed solutions to management for approval; implement their solutions where practicable, and monitor their effect. In undertaking these activities, it is argued, people learn new skills and develop their abilities, while the team approach also helps to engender a spirit of trust and respect for one another's abilities. The organization benefits, both directly and indirectly, by tapping the knowledge and experience of its employees at all levels; employees make a direct contribution to real problems and they develop commitment to the organization.

There are several related reasons for singling out quality circles for special attention in any discussion of task participation in Britain. First, there has been a very considerable growth in the number of organizations practising quality circles. The first major example reported in Britain, involving Rolls-Royce of Derby, was introduced as recently as 1978; the company copied the ideas from Lockheed in the USA, where quality circles had been 'rediscovered' in the mid-1970s after the successful development in Japan of what was an idea that originated in the USA (IPM, 1982: 80–2). Within a short space of time the number of organizations in Britain with quality circles had grown significantly. In 1981 Lorenz suggested that about 100 organizations were involved; in 1985 Incomes Data Services estimated that the number had grown to 400. Significantly, too, as the next section will show, quality circles involve non-manual as well as manual employees; they are also to be found in the service sector, as well as manufacturing. The development also led, in 1982, to the formation of the National Society of Quality Circles (NSQC), whose aim is 'to encourage the healthy development of quality circles in the UK by combining the experience and energy of people from its member organizations'. In 1988 the NSQC had 120 organizations in membership and their newsletter is circulated to some 240 work locations.

The other reasons for singling out quality circles concern the availability of research evidence. The growth in the number and spread of quality circles has given rise to a considerable number of research studies. Unlike some of the other areas of direct or task participation, then, such as job enrichment schemes, there is a fair amount of systematic data from which to draw conclusions. What these data suggest, moreover, is that a study of quality circles, as will become evident from later sections, illustrates very clearly many of the underlying issues involved in attempts to promote participation and involvement at work. This is above all true of management attitudes. The inability of British managers, largely for structural reasons, to develop more participative styles emerges as perhaps the biggest single obstacle to further developments.

The chapter, which draws on consultancy as well as research experience, discusses the reasons why British managements have introduced quality circles and describes how quality circles operate in practice. It also examines the reasons for the success and failure of quality circles and the reactions of employees, trade unions and managers. The final section offers an initial evaluation of the experience of quality circles.

## WHY DO MANAGEMENTS INTRODUCE QUALITY CIRCLES?

In discussions of quality circles there have been a number of popular misconceptions which bear on this question. One is that quality circles are very much, if not exclusively, a manufacturing phenomenon. It is true that quality circles first appeared on the shopfloor in manufacturing, and most of the early ones involved manual employees in machining, assembly, packing and warehouse activities, stores and quality control (Dale, 1984). Increasingly, however, quality circles have spread their net. Thus, there are many examples to be found in white-collar areas of manufacturing, including production engineering, technical departments, laboratories, general offices, accounts and finance departments, and even among groups of managers themselves (Temple and Dale, 1985). There are also many examples in the service sector involving hospitals, transport, finance and travel (Lees and Dale, 1985).

A second misconception, which is understandable in view of the title they have been given, is that managements introduce quality circles primarily, if not exclusively, in order to improve quality. Certainly many organizations have introduced circles as part of a drive on quality improvement, but this has not necessarily been the only or even the main reason for their introduction. Indeed, a number of organizations have deliberately gone out of their way to emphasize the more general character of their groups' problem-solving nature by giving them a different name. Austin Rover, for example, calls them 'zone circles'; Sainsbury's calls them 'job improvement committees'. It is perhaps significant, too, that in Japan the quality revolution was well under way prior to the widespread introduction of quality circles; there is also evidence (Dale and Lees, 1986) that those managements in Britain that have seen quality circles as a panacea for the organization's quality ills have been sadly disappointed.

The detailed survey evidence suggests that managements have had a number of objectives reflecting specific situations. In the case of manufacturing the main reasons given, in rank order, were to improve employees' job satisfaction; to improve quality; to improve communication; to develop employees; and to make cost savings (Dale, 1984). In the case of the service sector, the main reasons given, again in rank order, were to develop employees; to improve employees' job satisfaction; to improve the quality of service; to improve communications; and to improve competitiveness (Lees and Dale, 1985). Not only, then, was there little difference in the reasons given for the introduction of quality circles in the two sectors, but also development, involvement and quality (of service as well as manufacture) were said to be the primary reasons, while cost savings and improved competitiveness were regarded as less important.

Typical examples would be Prestwick Circuits (in manufacturing) and American Express (in services). At Prestwick Circuits, circles were introduced to develop the communication abilities of employees and to improve their problem-solving skills and quality of thought process, which it was hoped would eventually lead to making employees more quality conscious. At American Express, the objectives were to provide a supportive atmosphere which encompasses the active involvement of employees in all aspects of the work process; to improve quality and increase overall productivity; to promote improved communications and teamwork between all levels of the organization; and to foster the development of employees in the skills of problem-solving and management presentations.

In some organizations quality circles have been introduced with the 'problem' of supervision discussed in chapter 9 very much in mind. Quality circles, in other words, have been seen as a way of enhancing the leadership role of supervisors, of giving opportunities to develop their leadership and problem-solving skills, and of helping them to improve relations with their immediate work groups (IPM, 1982: 84).

In short, although there is evidence to suggest that some managements are primarily interested in instrumental benefits to the organization (Bradley and Hill, 1987: 71–2) and have not been slow to emphasize the cost benefits or quality improvements, most seem to have introduced them for reasons relating to participation and involvement rather than specific and measurable changes. When questioned, they tend to concentrate on intangible benefits such as improvements in relations, communications, morale and involvement. The overall view seems to be that a technique which helps to resolve problems, enables employees to gain a better understanding of their job and related systems, and provides a forum for open discussion is likely in the longer run to produce a climate in which cost savings and quality improvement will follow.

At first sight, then, the considerable increase in the number of organizations introducing quality circles would appear to be evidence of a significant shift in practice: British management, it might be argued, has indeed been persuaded of the human relations thinking discussed in chapters 1 and 4. Such a conclusion, however attractive it may be to those anxious to find signs of change, would be premature. It is extremely difficult, of course, to establish whether the reasons given for the introduction of quality circles, especially in questionnaire surveys, are genuine, or whether they are simply *post hoc* rationalizations or answers which they think people expect them to give. The suspicion must be, as the evidence produced later on the success and failure of quality circles will confirm, that a number of managements have not acted out of conviction – and certainly not out of a genuine conversion to the human relations thinking which lies behind the concept. In some cases the apparent success of US and Japanese companies with quality circles was enough to persuade their British counterparts to follow suit. In others it is likely that they acted out of a desire not to be seen to be out of line with current fashion; such has been the momentum that no self-respecting organization could say that it did not have quality circles (Collard, 1981).

## QUALITY CIRCLES IN PRACTICE

There has been a tendency to dismiss quality circles as an initiative which involves no more than marginal changes. In fact, as this section will seek to show, quality circles do involve significant organizational and structural changes in the traditional pattern of authority relations. Before the quality circle is set up, for example, a number of preliminary issues have to be sorted out, including the overall direction and resourcing of the programme. In operation, quality circles raise important issues of decision-making and implementation. Each of these will be considered in turn.

*Preliminaries*

*Steering committees*. As the brief prepared by Incomes Data Services (1985: 2) points out (although not all organizations with quality circles have such a brief) there is likely to be a steering group whose main function is to guide, publicize and manage circle activities and progress. Typically, it is made up of representatives of various functions such as personnel, training, production and finance; it is also likely, depending on the level of commitment, to involve key senior line managers, as well as staff specialists, supervisors and circle members. In those organizations which do not have steering groups (examples would include Young's Seafoods and Gardner Merchant in contract catering) the programme is usually controlled by senior managers or comes under the control of an existing body such as a joint works committee. The point that advocates of quality circles are unanimously agreed on, is that there is a need for a highly visible source of authority for quality circles to develop, otherwise the resistance to change will be too powerful.

*Facilitator*. The facilitator or co-ordinator has been described as the 'linchpin' of a quality circle programme (IDS, 1985: 2). Usually a middle manager working full-time or released from normal duties for a significant part of the time, the facilitator is responsible for the day-to-day administration of the quality circle programme, its performance and development. This usually involves arranging facilities and access to specialist advice, training, supporting and counselling circle members, organizing presentations to senior managers and monitoring progress.

The experience of quality circle programmes in Britain suggests that the facilitator plays a vital role in the establishment and success of any programme. Indeed, it is no exaggeration to suggest that the success of quality circles is proportional to the input made by the facilitator. This emerges very clearly from the two studies on quality circle 'failures' by Hayward (1983) and Frazer (1984). In answer to the question, 'what, if anything do you think can be done to prevent quality circle failures?', the importance of the facilitator was emphasized with comments such as:

> pick your facilitator very carefully;
> make the facilitator appointment full-time;
> the full-time support of a facilitator;
> a very enthusiastic facilitator;
> a lot of effort and hard work on the part of the facilitator can in some circumstances overcome the problems;
> a facilitator who is alert to the problems of declining interest or developing frustration and able to intervene to revitalize circle activity.

Significantly, too, of the 32 respondents reporting a 'failure' of their quality circle programme, no less than ten had not appointed a facilitator (Frazer and Dale, 1985).

*Training*. The idea of training in participation may seem rather odd, but as in the case of the facilitator, the evidence suggests that it is vital to the effectiveness of quality circles. Otherwise, the circle will only be able to deal with superficial problems and there is the danger that meetings quickly turn into 'tea and toilet' discussions or simply 'management bashing'. Typically, the training involves explanation of the background to quality circles – their objectives; the reasons why the organization is introducing them; the specialist techniques involved (discussed below); the processes of data collection; statistical analysis; presentation skills; and interpersonal skills involving group dynamics, teamwork and leadership styles. Both initial and follow-up training is involved.

Two main approaches to training may be identified. One is to begin by training those who are going to lead the circles and then to train the circle members with a consultant or facilitator assisting the circle leader. The alternative is for the circle leaders and members to be trained as a group, either by the facilitator or consultant. Clearly, the first helps to establish the position of authority of the circle leaders.

*Pilot programme*. Experience with a range of initiatives in industrial relations and personnel management from productivity bargaining through to job enrichment suggests that there are dangers in claiming too much too quickly. Quality circles are no exception. Thus, the approach adopted by many organizations has been to develop quality circle programmes through an initial pilot project lasting a period of months. The pilot programme would normally involve a small number of circles (probably no more than half a dozen) and would involve 'appropriate' departments. Likely criteria in deciding 'appropriateness' would be, first and foremost, the interest and commitment of the managers in the department, the likelihood of sufficient volunteers coming forward, and the size and the representativeness of the activities. Less obvious, but usually of paramount importance, is the choice of departments where there is a strong likelihood of success. In the case of Young's Seafoods, for example, following the successful completion of a pilot study, the board supported the progressive extension of quality circles to other sites in the company, using the experience of the first to justify their interest.

Not all organizations with extensive quality circle programmes, it needs to be emphasized, have used pilot programmes as the foundation for their programmes. Indeed, some of the well-publicized examples did not. For example, Wedgewood did not undertake any form of pilot study and within 20 weeks had 24 quality circles up and running. Similarly, Mullard Hazel Grove introduced their first circle in December 1980 and a year later had 51 circles in operation. In both cases, however, there was a very high level of commitment to the introduction of quality circles on the part of senior managers and substantial resources, in terms of both time and money, were invested in making the initiative a success.

*Organization of Quality Circles*

Not surprisingly, there is no standard format for the operation of quality circles. There are a number of issues that have to be resolved, however, and they include the leadership of the circle, the conduct of circle meetings, the choice of circle projects, and the implementation of circle recommendations. Each of these will be considered in turn.

*Circle leaders*. Each circle has a leader whose role is to disseminate information about quality circles to the department; to seek volunteers for membership; to organize circle meetings; to chair circle meetings and make sure they run smoothly; to allocate tasks among circle members; to develop circle members; and to liaise with the facilitator and other managers as necessary.

The supervisor or first line manager is usually, but not invariably, the quality circle leader. Supervisors, it is argued, are likely to have more experience than individual workers of chairing meetings, making presentations and briefings, and establishing liaison with other departments; they are also more likely to be experienced in the politics of the organization. But this is only part of the story. By leading the circle, it is argued, the supervisor is put in a position where he or she can develop their leadership skills and can enhance their authority in the eyes of their work group. Indeed, as indicated in the previous section, underpinning the role of the supervisor is often a major reason why organizations introduce quality circles or briefing groups in the first place. By contrast, if the supervisor is not made quality circle leader, at least to begin with, there is the danger that he or she will become alienated from the process.

Even so, supervisors are not circle leaders in every case. For example, at the Clayton Analine company, a major manufacturer of synthetic dye-stuffs, there was considerable suspicion, especially among the craftsmen, of supervisors becoming quality circle leaders. In such cases it is not unusual to have a deputy leader who is a non-supervisory employee. In other cases it has been found that the responsibilities of quality circle leader have developed to a point at which it is sensible for the supervisor, even if he or she remains in the circle, to relinquish the post in favour of another member. An advantage of this, it is claimed, is that other members of the group can develop some of the skills associated with the circle leader.

Circles led by non-supervisory employees can, it needs to be emphasized, be very effective. For example, the gear and rocker lever circle at Leyland Engines completed its training in January 1983 and after a period of approximately one month, the leadership passed to a machine setter on the supervisor's promotion. The circle continued to function effectively, and by the middle of December 1984 had achieved savings of some £180,000.

*Circle meetings*. Quality circles usually meet in paid time and members receive their normal rates of pay; in the case of workers on incentive systems, it is usual to exclude from the bonus calculation those hours spent on quality circle activities. In those cases where they meet outside normal hours – in the service sector, for example, or where manual workers are involved in a continuous manufacturing process and complex rotas – quality circle members are usually paid overtime.

The length and frequency of meetings depend on circumstance. At Honeywell Control Systems, for example, office-based circles meet for about an hour each week, while field staff meet for two to two and a half hours a month; at Black and Decker for about one hour a week; at London Life for about 16.5 hours each week; at Jaguar's Castle Bromwich plant and at Tioxide for one hour or so each fortnight (IDS, 1985: 3). Overall, the evidence from the questionnaire surveys (Dale, 1984; Lees and Dale, 1985) suggests that circles in both manufacturing and services meet for about an hour at a time; in manufacturing meetings are usually weekly and in services fortnightly.

*Circle projects.* Ideas for quality circle projects come from a number of sources; from circle members, from their colleagues in the department, and, albeit usually covertly, from management. Normally there are only two conditions restricting the consideration of projects: the 'problem' or 'issues' to be tackled must relate to the immediate department, and a project will not be considered if it involves criticisms of an individual or, especially where trade unions are recognized, issues which are deemed to be the subject of collective bargaining. With regard to the type of projects, the evidence from the questionnaire surveys (Dale, 1984; Lees and Dale, 1985) suggests that the five main themes in manual circles were quality, productivity improvement, cost reduction, waste and production processes; in service circles, they were quality, administration, productivity improvement, communication, and service processes. In general, it would seem that the first projects a circle tackles are to do with immediate work problems and the work environment, after which they move on to issues relating to product quality.

*Techniques.* Some ideas of the techniques used in quality circles will have been gained from the discussion of training above. They include checksheets, histograms, statistical process control 'cause and effect' analysis, Pareto analysis (which is a way of separating the 'important' from the 'not so important'), 'force field' analysis (which looks at the pressures 'for and against' things happening), 'brainstorming', and action planning. Indeed, the quality circle manual of Nissan Motor Manufacturing (UK) Ltd contains descriptions of no less than 17 tools and techniques. In practice, however, the evidence (Dale and Lees, 1986) suggests that it is rare to find all these techniques used; typically it is a question of cause and effect analysis, brainstorming and action planning, and in some cases only brainstorming.

*Implementation.* This is the critical step. The culmination of the quality circle's activity is usually a presentation to management which describes the nature of the problem, seeks to demonstrate the negative effect of current practice, suggests a solution, and outlines a way forward. Thereafter, although some companies such as Honeywell have a procedure for monitoring the outcome which enables circle members to keep some track of developments, the responsibility for implementation rests with management. This is where many a quality circle has come to grief. If the ideas of the quality circle are not implemented, or circle members are not given very good reasons why they are not going to be implemented, enthusiasm can very quickly wane.

*Conclusion*

It is easy to dismiss quality circles as a gimmick or as a marginal activity. If the starting point is the structures and patterns of authority of the traditionally-run work organization, however, quality circles can represent a radical departure. To quote from the IPM survey:

> The introduction of quality circles into an organization . . . has implications going far beyond the establishment of a few shopfloor groups looking at ways of improving quality. It challenges existing arrangements for quality control and appears to pose a challenge to middle managers responsible for the quality of output. It also challenges the relationship between managers and managed, with managers and other technical specialists becoming a resource upon which work groups can draw. Quality circles therefore call for a shift in management style and willingness to accept a devolution of the level at which problem-solving can take place. Finally, it requires some investment in training and therefore the establishment of appropriate training budgets to meet this cost. These are therefore matters which require top management consideration and agreement prior to any development of a quality circle programme. (1982: 85)

That a number of these challenges are experienced as real, especially by middle managers, will become clear in the next two sections.

## SUCCESS AND FAILURE

Defining what is meant by 'success' and 'failure' in the case of quality circles is no easy task. Certainly few commentators on quality circles are very clear on the definitions that are appropriate. Others, for example Imberman (1982) and Goodfellow (1981) in the USA, are clear; but the definition used – quality circles are a success if the measured benefits are greater than the costs of operation – is far too narrow. Quality circles, supporters argue, have many intangible benefits which, over the long term, can have results that can be greater than the immediate cost savings associated with quality circles. The following comment made by a facilitator to Frazer (1984) during the course of his research reflects this view:

> I feel that any circle which has met more than a half dozen times can never be deemed a failure. The benefits of the training and also the comradeship and team spirit built up during the meetings does not suddenly fade. It's rather like painting a house – even if you stop partway, the bits you have covered last for a long time.

For the individual organization, of course, the task of establishing whether or not quality circles have been a success is slightly easier: some attempt, however rudimentary, can be made to measure the actual practice of quality circles against the specific aims and objectives set on their introduction. For example, in addition to estimating the costs of operating a circle programme and comparing these costs with project savings, the management at Mullard Hazel Grove made a serious attempt to establish whether the programme is achieving some of the more intangible benefits that they hoped for. This was done by providing managers with guidelines to support the programme, by encouraging circle leaders to assess the performance of their circles and, perhaps most importantly, by systematically measuring changes in attitudes by an annual questionnaire survey of all employees.

Even so, problems remain. In determining success or failure, is reference to be made to individual circles or the programme as a whole? Is success, for example, to be measured in terms of change in attitude or individual development or group attitudes and teamwork? And how are these and similar variables to be measured? Is 'failure' deemed to have occurred when the facilitator recommends the circle stop meeting or when the circle members themselves decide to stop? Is a quality circle a 'failure' if a significant number of members express a willingness to join a new or a revised circle?

In the light of these problems, all that this section can hope to do is to point to some of the key issues that would appear to affect the success and failure of quality circles. To do so, it draws on a number of surveys.

*Success*

Potentially, the introduction of quality circles can benefit the employees, managers and the organization. In the case of the large-scale survey in manufacturing which has already been quoted (Dale, 1984), 11 different categories of benefit to circle members were claimed, of which the most often cited were increased job satisfaction, an opportunity to become involved in the organization, and better teamwork within the department. The two main benefits for managers were the resolution of problems at shopfloor level, which made it possible for managers to concentrate on issues of more strategic importance, and the enhancement of the leadership role of supervisors. The three most claimed benefits to the organization were the increased involvement of employees, better communications, and improvements in quality and productivity.

Generally speaking, those who had introduced quality circles appeared to be reasonably satisfied (Frazer and Dale, 1985). Certainly this was true of the organizations where circles were in operation. Even where a programme had not been implemented or had collapsed, the concept of quality circles itself had not been rejected. For example, eight of the 17 respondents who had not implemented a quality circle programme proposed to reconsider the issue at a later date; only five organizations had positively rejected the idea. Similarly, the majority of those organizations whose programmes might be said to have failed proposed to reconsider resurrecting the programme at a future date.

Following a two-year project, which involved both questionnaire surveys and interviews with a range of individuals, Dale and Lees (1986) felt confident of reporting that the overwhelming majority of people interviewed 'are positively in favour of quality circles. Criticism has not been of the concept itself, but rather of the way circles have been introduced and operated, and the lack of management commitment to making them work.'

The attitudes of management will be explored in more detail in the next section. As far as the introduction of quality circles is concerned, the evidence suggests that, for quality circles to be effective, senior managers must be convinced of the benefits; provide the necessary resources for the setting up of the programme; be actively involved; and accept from the outset that quality circles are a long-term commitment. The issue of a policy statement expressing these positions also seems to be important. Other important prerequisites for successful introduction include the involvement of middle managers and supervisors at the beginning of the programme, and adequate consultation with trade unions where they are recognized. Additionally, many of the issues referred to in the previous section would also appear to be critical: the setting up of a steering committee or similar body: the appointment of an appropriate person as 'facilitator'; and the training of circle leaders and members. The careful selection of departments in which to conduct pilot studies of the initial projects is also important: circles need to be composed of voluntary members in areas where there is interest, especially on the part of the managers, and where there is a good chance of progress in the short run. There also needs to be recognition and publicity to be given to circle activities in order to maintain interest and momentum.

Even so, Dale and Lees (1986) have argued, organizations cannot rely solely on what might be described as a 'check list approach'. It is important, they suggest, to capture 'the spirit of quality circles' and this means, above all, ensuring that individual quality circles are conducted in an appropriate manner to engage the energy and enthusiasm of members.

*Failure*

Even if many of the definitional problems are set aside, it is important to distinguish between three basic categories or types of failure: the failure, after due consideration, to implement quality circles; the suspension of a pro-gramme as a whole; and the suspension of individual circles. Drawing these distinctions, the postal questionnaire surveys referred to above (Hayward, 1983; Dale and Hayward, 1984; Frazer, 1984; Frazer and Dale, 1985), which involved a total of 127 organizations, suggest that only a minority of organizations which have introduced quality circles have not experienced a failure of an individual quality circle, if not the programme as a whole.

*The failure to implement quality circles*. Seventeen respondents out of the total number of 127 organizations in the surveys said that they had given considera-tion to, or taken steps towards, introducing quality circles, but had not yet proceeded at the time of the survey. Where the decision had been taken not to proceed, the average time taken was nine months; the decision had not been taken at the time of the survey in seven organizations.

In the final analysis, the main reasons for not proceeding had to do with either trade union opposition, which will be considered in more detail in a later section, or the belief that quality circles were unnecessary in the particular organization. In some cases there was a feeling that there were more pressing issues facing the organization. In others, it was claimed that the management style already allowed a forum for open discussion and solution to problems. The following response from one of the organizations effectively encapsulates these views:

> On investigating quality circles in depth some three years ago it was decided by the company that they were unsuitable for us and would not be fruitful in any way. Our company is a small efficient organisation with short lines of communication and set procedures. We are also extremely flexible and promote modern techniques throughout the company at all levels.

There is no way of knowing whether or not such complacency was justified. Such views, however, are not unusual.

*Programme suspension*. Altogether, no less than 32 of the 127 organizations in the surveys reported the suspension of their quality circle programmes. The average length of time a programme ran before suspension was 14.7 months, and all the suspensions took place within three years of their introduction. A variety of reasons was offered for the failure of programmes. Five, however, stood out: the economic situation, causing redundancies and restructuring; problems or obstacles confronting one or more circles which gradually led to the suspension of the programme as a whole; management saw little or no advantage in continuing the programme; lack of management support; and the opposition of trade unions, leading to a withdrawal of support.

Overall, the most commonly quoted reason for programme suspension in the two surveys was redundancy or restructuring. Redundancies and restructuring, not surprisingly, not only break up circle membership, but also have an adverse effect on morale and enthusiasm to continue participation. In particular, circle members are likely to be reluctant to make suggestions which might do themselves or their colleagues out of a job, or which, in their view, will not be implemented because of restructuring.

*Individual circle suspension*. Seventy-eight out of the 127 organizations reported that, although they were continuing to operate a quality circle programme, they had experienced the suspension of individual circles. In total, they reported the failure of 370 circles, which amounted to 25 per cent of the number of circles that had been set up. The number of individual circles ceasing operation reported by each company varied between 1 and 50. The average failure rate for all 78 organizations was nearly one third, but only about half the organizations reporting a failure said that more than two circles were affected. If the 42 organizations who did not experience any circle failures are taken into account, this means that the average failure rate in the surveys as a whole falls to approximately 20 per cent, which compares favourably with experience in the USA and Japan. In the USA Ambler and Overholt (1982) claim that, although many organizations have successfully introduced quality circles, over half the total number have ended in failure. In

Japan, according to Cole (1980), one third of quality circles make no contribution.

As in the case of overall programmes, the first eighteen months would appear to be the most critical period in the life of individual circles, since the majority (91 per cent) of suspensions occurred within this period. The average life of a circle which was suspended was 9.4 months.

It is also interesting to note that quality circles involving non-manual employees would appear to be more difficult to sustain than those involving manual employees. The average duration of a suspended circle involving non-manual employees was 6.5 months as compared with 10.5 months for those involving manual employees. Temple and Dale (1985), in a later study devoted exclusively to non-manual employees, reached a similar conclusion, although there did not appear to be any evidence to suggest that quality circles involving this group were more difficult to initiate.

Why do individual quality circles fail? In the postal questionnaires organizations were asked to list no more than four main reasons for the failure of individual circles. The 20 most common reasons are listed in table 15.1 together with the number of quality circles failing and the number of organizations quoting the reason.

Two points stand out. First, as in the case of the programme suspensions discussed earlier, redundancies and restructuring were the most common reasons cited for suspension of individual circles, followed closely by labour turnover (including transfers, promotions and retirements). Second, if the total number of reasons involving management is added up, it becomes very clear that in most cases they must bear the bulk of the responsibility for the failures that take place. In particular, it would appear that the lack of co-operation from middle managers and first line supervisors was especially important.

*Obstacles to Quality Circles*

Before leaving this section, it is instructive to consider the views of the respondents to the postal questionnaires on the main obstacles hampering the operation of quality circles. The main obstacles given by respondents in manufacturing, in rank order, were suspicion about circle activities; delay by managers in responding to quality circle recommendations; lack of support from managers; over-ambitious projects; circles spread over too wide an area; the timing of the introduction of circles; the inadequate training of circle leaders and members; the closed style of management; the lack of recognition for quality circle activities; and the unilateral action of circle members (Dale, 1984).

In services, the main obstacles, again in rank order, were problems of maintaining initial impetus; lack of management support; labour turnover and company reorganization; delay by managers in responding to quality circle recommendations; the closed style of management; circle leaders not having enough time to carry out activities; over-ambitious projects; the multi-site nature of the organization which made circles difficult to implement and

TABLE 15.1  *Failure of quality circles*

| Reasons for failure | Number of quality circles failing ( N = 370) | Number of companies quoting the reason (N = 54) |
|---|---|---|
| Redundancies and/or restructuring caused by the economic situation | 98 | 35 |
| Labour turnover (transfers, promotions, retirements, etc.) | 83 | 34 |
| Lack of co-operation from middle management | 78 | 31 |
| Circle leaders lacked time to organize meetings | 59 | 32 |
| Circles ran out of projects to tackle | 51 | 23 |
| Lack of co-operation from first-line supervisors | 42 | 16 |
| Delay in responding to circle recommendations | 36 | 19 |
| Circle members disillusioned with quality circle philosophy | 33 | 16 |
| Circle members lacked time to carry out activities | 23 | 16 |
| Over-ambitious projects tackled | 20 | 10 |
| Lack of recognition | 20 | 10 |
| Groups spread over too wide a work area | 19 | 18 |
| Leader not following through initial training | 19 | 2 |
| Failure to get solutions implemented | 19 | 11 |
| Inadequate training | 18 | 8 |
| Lack of extrinsic rewards/motivation | 17 | 6 |
| Lack of support from facilitator | 16 | 6 |
| Poor circle leadership | 13 | 2 |
| Lack of co-operation from functional specialists | 13 | 4 |
| Management change | 10 | 1 |

maintain; and lack of support from first line supervisors (Dale and Lees, 1986).

## REACTIONS TO QUALITY CIRCLES

One clear conclusion can be drawn from this discussion. While what might be called 'technical' reasons are not unimportant in the success and failure of quality circles, much more important is the question of attitudes. This section will therefore examine in more detail the reactions to quality circles. In particular, it examines the attitudes, first, of employees, then of trade unions, and, finally and most crucially, of managers.

## Employees

In considering the attitudes of employees, it is important to distinguish between those who are circle members and those who are not. In general, the evidence (see, for example, Bradley and Hill, 1983: 299–302) suggests that circle members are enthusiastic. Not only do they feel that quality circles lead to better understanding and better communications, but also that they provide working people with an opportunity to have some influence, however marginal, on the immediate work situation. Those who are not members of quality circles, however, do often express opposition. As Bradley and Hill observe, however, this is largely because such individuals can be made to feel 'outsiders'; there is little or no evidence to suggest that they are opposed in principle to the concept of quality circles.

## Trade Unions

The attitude of trade unions at national level has been ambivalent. The TUC, for example, while recognizing that quality circles could potentially be an opportunity for working people to influence their immediate work situation for the better, was lukewarm in its reaction as manifested in its guidelines produced in 1981:

> Trade unions have been urging employers for decades to give workers more control over the jobs they do. QCs are a belated recognition of employees' expertise and knowledge and the need to put them to use. At the same time trade unionists may be understandably sceptical about the merits of the latest in a succession of 'vogue' management techniques. (TUC: 1981)

Although the electricians' union has come out in support, other unions have adopted a similar position to the TUC (see, for example, Hammond's foreword to the Department of Trade and Industry's publication prepared by Tyrell and Dolan, 1985). In particular, the Transport and General Workers' Union (TGWU) and the then Association of Scientific, Technical and Managerial Staffs (ASTMS), as reported by Wintour (1987), have expressed reservations. Understandably from their point of view, there is a fear that the introduction of quality circles may, at the very least, serve to undermine the authority of the shop steward and the union in the workplace, as well as worsening the terms and conditions of employment. The result is that in some organizations trade unions have opposed the introduction of quality circles, or have withdrawn their support after they have been introduced.

Such opposition does not necessarily manifest itself in the workplace, however. It is true that in five out of the 14 cases of organizations failing to implement a quality circle programme in the surveys referred to in the previous section, trade union opposition was quoted as an important consideration. Overall, however, the evidence does not suggest that, in practice, trade union opposition has been a major consideration. Thus, only five of the 32 organizations which had suspended their quality circle programmes said that trade union opposition was a serious consideration; while only 13 out of a total number of 370 quality circle failures in 78 organizations could be attributed to the withdrawal of trade union support. Perhaps part of the explanation is that quality circles are not seen by trade union members as undermining trade unions. Indeed, there is some evidence (Bradley and Hill, 1983: 320) that quality circles, in giving managerial legitimacy to the principle of participation, actually enhance the position of trade unions.

In general, in the workplace the evidence suggests that trade union opposition is unlikely providing two main conditions are satisfied: first, that they are properly briefed about quality circles and are involved in their introduction and development through, for example, a steering committee; and, second, that there are guarantees that there will be no redundancies or worsening of pay and conditions directly arising from the introduction of quality circles.

The experience of Young's Seafoods, which had contrasting experiences on the three sites where it introduced quality circles, is instructive. On one site, management failed to brief the shop stewards properly or to involve them, and this nearly led to the suspension of the programme. Only after they had been fully involved did the stewards adopt a more positive attitude. On the other two sites, having been fully briefed in advance, the shop stewards were not only more positive in their attitude, but also a number of them actually became quality circle members.

In a number of organizations, Clayton Aniline for example, shop stewards have become quality circle leaders. At Leyland Engines, the terms of reference for quality circles state that each circle should include a shop steward. In both Clayton Aniline and Leyland Engines shop stewards have played very active roles as circle members.

*Management*

One thing emerges very clearly from the evidence, both of the surveys and of the case studies, and it is that managers are the major obstacles to quality circles. To repeat, many circle programmes and individual circles fail because of a lack of management support, the poor response to circle initiatives from management, a closed management style, and lack of recognition given to circle activities.

In unravelling the attitudes of managers, it is important to distinguish between different groups (Bradley and Hill, 1987). Senior managers are usually in favour of them and think they are a good thing. Crucially, however, they very rarely make the kind of changes necessary to support the development of quality circles. The position is different as far as middle managers and supervisors are concerned. Here there is considerable evidence of opposition (Bradley and Hill, 1983, 1987; Klein, 1984).

Two sites belonging to Gardner Merchants, both in city locations providing a very similar vending service to clients in their catchment area, show how middle managers can influence the performance of quality circles. On one side, middle managers were extremely positive towards quality circles; they helped circle members to organize meetings within the working day and responded to circle recommendations for change. On the other site, however, while professing to support the idea of quality circles, the middle managers repeatedly found reasons why it was impractical for quality circles to meet or for quality circle recommendations to be implemented. The result was that, whereas on the first site quality circles continued to thrive three years after their introduction, on the second site they had all but collapsed.

In their survey of middle managers in a range of both UK and US organizations, Bradley and Hill (1987: 74–5) found three common factors. First, initial reactions had been unfavourable and senior managers had to exert pressure. Second, there was a consensus that good management was synonymous with the efficient use of technical and human resources, and that participation was unnecessary if managers were doing their job properly. Third, there was concern about managerial prerogative; not only was there a desire to restrict circle activity to research and consultation, but there was also a complete rejection of democratic leadership.

Another crucial consideration was the time factor. To quote Bradley and Hill:

The burdens involved in operationalising participative management are usually ignored by its advocates. The middle managers, however, complained that these were unwelcome additional burdens in jobs that were already taxing. They asserted that quality circles dealt with minor problems, most of which managers had already recognised but had been prevented from solving for reasons of cost expediency; that rank-and-file employees were not competent to help on the important problems because of their limited formal education and job knowledge that was based on a narrow range of tasks; that regular circle meetings jeopardised departmental production targets; that managers had to give up time to deal with quality circle business which would have been better spent on more pressing issues. Quality circles were therefore seen to add to managerial workloads for comparatively small returns. (1987: 75)

Lying behind these objections are often more basic considerations. By definition, quality circles do challenge traditional notions of authority in the work organization; the comments and suggestions of quality circles are seen by many managers as an implicit, if not explicit, criticism of their performance, and dealing with them is not as easy as many of the pundits assume. Supervisors, in particular, may be fearful that quality circles are the thin end of the wedge, leading to more advanced forms of employee decision-making, such as autonomous work groups, with the result that they may be out of a job.

Many organizations have sought to overcome these and similar problems by extensively briefing managers and by holding series of specific in-house workshops. For instance, Young's Seafoods held a number of one-day workshops for its managers at each of the three locations which introduced quality circle programmes. The objective was to help managers to understand more fully the rationale for having quality circles, to understand how meetings should be conducted, to be aware of the techniques to be used, and to make them familiar with the crucial importance of their own role in the operation of quality circles. Similar workshops have been arranged by Gardner Merchant, Sony (UK) and Clayton Aniline, suggesting that there is widespread recognition, both in manufacturing and services, of the potential problems in management attitudes.

A further way in which the attempt has been made to overcome management resistance has been to introduce quality circles among the ranks of managers. This, it is argued, has a double effect. Managers become more aware of the problems and the potential of quality circles; simultaneously, the fact that managers are involved demonstrates that the organization is firmly committed.

Two key findings also emerge from the detailed comparison of two companies each in the UK and USA undertaken by Bradley and Hill (1987), which used the same consultants' package and which experienced similar levels of initial opposition from managers. First, in the USA company the performance of managers in dealing with quality circles was incorporated into their appraisal system, whereas in the UK company it was not. Second, existing structures of responsibiity were extremely important. In the UK companies managers had little scope to implement initiatives because of their inability to spend even comparatively small sums of money or reorganize work without senior management approval. In the US companies, by contrast, managers already enjoyed sufficient authority to take action. Consequently, whereas the UK managers felt that the credit for improvements might go to their superiors, the US managers believed they would earn the credit. In the words of Bradley and Hill:

> Thus, Usacorp's managers had a double incentive to respond constructively to quality circles. First, they were appraised on the perceived success of their circles. Second, they personally gained credit for any efficiency gains arising out of quality-circle activity. Therefore, despite the reservations they shared with Ukayco's managers about the principle of participative management, they accepted quality circles as part of their jobs. Ukayco's managers, however, continued to regard quality circles as alien bodies belonging to the coordinating team and not as the 'property' of line management. (1987: 76)

There would appear to be important lessons here for British companies generally.

## AN INITIAL EVALUATION

In the early days of quality circles in Britain, questions were asked about their suitability to the manufacturing environment in this country. It is a measure of their durability that today the questions are more about how to evaluate quality circles, how to make the best use of them, how to overcome the difficulties experienced in running them, how to maintain enthusiasm, and how to integrate quality circles with other quality management tools and techniques. In other words, it can be argued, the novelty has worn off and quality circles have become a permanent feature of many organizations.

As far as their contribution to improving quality is concerned, there is evidence to suggest that quality circles have made some impact. Moreover, the contribution has not only been direct, in the form of savings and improvements, but also indirect by generating a much greater awareness of quality issues. Equally, however, the evidence suggests that they work best where they are considered to be one element in total quality management: they cannot be expected, as some managers seem to think, to succeed in isolation.

The problem here is that, until recently, very few organizations in Britain have developed a total approach to quality. Indeed, in many cases circles were introduced before the organizations began to take the issue of quality seriously. Thus, in the course of their research Lascelles and Dale (1986) found only one organization which had seriously considered quality circles as a launch·pad for the development of groups as part of a company-wide improvement initiative. In the absence of such an approach there must be the likelihood that, having reached a plateau, quality circles will wither and die.

The evaluation of what for many observers has been the prime interest of quality circles, namely to improve the participation and involvement of employees, is more difficult to make. Clearly, quality circles have been among the most important, if not the most important, experiments in participation and involvement in recent years; few other developments can match their widespread coverage, the range of issues discussed and their duration. What is especially difficult to establish precisely, however, is whether they have made a significant contribution to participation and involvement or whether they have had a marginal effect; even where management is convinced that they have made a contribution, there are usually many other variables, such as an improvement in communications, which may also be important. An interim, let alone final, judgement of this issue would, to say the least, be speculative.

Some issues are a little clearer, however. On the face of it, the experience of quality circles has not led to demands for more far-reaching participation and involvement in the wider affairs of the organization, as some observers suggested it might. The lack of such pressure could be construed as evidence to confirm the view that it is task participation in the immediate work situation that individual employees are most concerned with and, indeed, that they are not interested in issues, such as business planning, which are much more remote from their immediate work situation. It could be, however, that reticence is not necessarily a function of lack of interest on the part of employees; the individual and workplace focus of quality circles, it can be argued, is itself a constraint on the development of a wider horizon, while the economic and political context discussed in chapter 2 has not been supportive to demands for wider involvement. It could also be a question of time: quality circles, extensive and durable as they may have become, are still relatively in their infancy.

Perhaps, more immediately, the importance of quality circles lies in their commentary on attitudes to change in traditional ways of work organization. Employees, it seems, have generally welcomed the opportunity to make a contribution to their work situation offered by quality circles. Trade unions, perhaps understandably, have been more suspicious and, in some cases, hostile; quality circles pose, potentially, a challenge to working arrangements won through collective bargaining and even, in the long run, to jobs; they also, in targetting individuals, can be a threat to collective action.

Especially revealing, however, is what the experience of quality circles tells us about the attitudes of managers. Senior managers, generally speaking, are very enthusiastic and much of the initiative has come from them. Middle managers and supervisors, it emerges, have taken a very different view. Indeed, there is a considerable body of evidence to suggest that middle managers and supervisors are the biggest single stumbling block in the introduction of quality circles, and that they are largely responsible for many of the quality circle failures. The explanations that have been put forward to account for this reaction – middle managers and supervisors feel threatened by quality circles; they are unable to cope with the more participative style of management involved; and they remain unconvinced of the need to concede what they perceive to be managerial authority – speak volumes for the hold that traditional authority relations have over people who are usually regarded as the major change agents. If nothing else, then, the experience of quality circles points to one inevitable conclusion: there have to be very considerable changes in the managerial structures which underpin these authority relations before there can be any significant developments in the participation and involvement of people at work in Britain.


## NOTE

Barrie Dale is indebted to Theresa Ball, Mark Frazer, Selwyn Hayward, Jayne Lees and Ian Temple for their invaluable assistance in carrying out the UMIST quality circle survey work, and for allowing some of their individual survey results to be used in this chapter. He also wishes to thank the management of American Express, Leyland Engines, Mullard Hazel Grove, Prestwick Circuits and Wedgewood for allowing their experiences with circles to be quoted. Barrie Dale wishes to thank the National Society of Quality Circles, Manpower Services Commission (TDS175/ST5/19/1984) and the Economic and Social Research Council (FOO 23 2020) for supporting the UMIST research on quality circles.

Ron Collard wishes to thank the management of Clayton Aniline, Gardner Merchant, Sony (UK) and Young's Seafoods for allowing his experiences in these companies to be used.

# Bibliography

Ambler, A.R. and Overholt, M.H. 1982. 'Are Quality Circles Right for Your Company?'. *Personnel Journal*, 61: November, 829–31.

Bradley, K. and Hill, S. 1983. '"After Japan": The Quality Circle Transplant and Productive Efficiency'. *British Journal of Industrial Relations*, 21: November, 291–311.

—— and Hill, S. 1987. 'Quality Circles and Managerial Interests'. *Industrial Relations*, 26: Winter, 68–82.

Bullock. 1977. Committee of Inquiry on Industrial Democracy. *Report*, Cmnd 6706. London: HMSO.

Cole, R.E. 1980. 'Will QC Circles Work in the US?'. *Quality Progress*, 13: 7, 57–66.

Collard, R. 1981. 'The Quality Circle in Context'. *Personnel Management*, September, 26–30 and 51.

Dale, B.G. 1984. 'Quality Circles in UK Manufacturing Industry – A State of the Art Survey'. Occasional Paper No. 8402. Manchester: School of Management, UMIST.

—— and Hayward, S.G. 1984. 'A Study of Quality Circle Failures'. Occasional Paper No. 8403. Manchester: School of Management, UMIST.

—— and Lees, J. 1986. *The Development of Quality Circle Programmes*. Sheffield: Manpower Services Commission.

Frazer, V.C.M. 1984. 'Quality Circles: An Examination – Pass or Fail?'. MSc dissertation, UMIST.

—— and Dale, B.G. 1985. 'Quality Circle Failures: An Update'. Occasional Paper No. 8501. Manchester: School of Management, UMIST.

Goodfellow, M. 1981. 'Quality Control Circle Programs – What Works and What Doesn't'. *Quality Circle Papers – A Compilation*. American Society of Quality Control.

Hayward, S.G. 1983. 'An Investigation as to Why Quality Circles Fail'. MSc dissertation, UMIST.

Imberman, W. 1982. 'A Managers Guide: Making Quality Control Circles Work'. *Data Management*, 20: 11, 54–9.

Income Data Services (IDS). 1985. *Ever Increasing Circles*. Study No. 352. London: IDS.

Institute of Personnel Management (IPM). 1982. *The Individual and the Job*. Vol. 3 of *Practical Participation and Involvement*. London: IPM.

Klein, J.A. 1984. 'Why Supervisors Resist Employee Involvement'. *Harvard Business Review*, 62: September–October, 87–95.

Lascelles, D.M. and Dale, B.G. 1986. 'How Change Agents Can Effect Quality Improvement'. *Proceedings of the Second National Conference for Production Research*. Edinburgh: Napier College, 132–45.

Lees, J. and Dale, B.G. 1985. 'A Study of Quality Circles in the UK Service Sector'. Occasional Paper No. 8511. Manchester: School of Management, UMIST.

Lorenz, C. 1981. 'Learning from the Japanese – Quality Circles'. *Financial Times*, 26, 27, 28 and 30 January; 2, 3, 4, 5 and 6 February.

Temple, I.A. and Dale, G.G. 1985. 'White Collar Quality Circles in UK Manufacturing Industry: A Study'. Occasional Paper No. 8510. Manchester: School of Management, UMIST.

Trades Union Congress (TUC). 1981. 'Quality Circles'. TUC Circular No. 311.

Transport and General Workers Union. 1984. *Employee Involvement and Quality Circles*. London: TGWU.

Tyrrell, R. and Dolan, P. 1985. *Quality Circles*. London: Department of Trade and Industry.

Wintour, P. 1987. 'Japanese Quality Control Idea a Threat to Unions'. *Guardian*, 10 January.

# 16 Joint Consultation in Practice

## Mick Marchington

It is perhaps indicative of the interest in joint consultation in Britain today that the subject once again justifies a chapter all to itself in a text such as this. In Flanders and Clegg (1954: 323–64), joint consultation was treated on an equivalent basis with collective bargaining, but recent texts have either overlooked it altogether (Bain, 1983) or have accorded it no more than a few pages within a general chapter on participation, management techniques or regulatory processes (see, for example, Armstrong, 1977; Clegg, 1979; Thomason, 1984). Stimulated by a variety of pressures, the institution appears to have become rather more widespread over the last decade, and there is now a more vigorous academic and practical debate about its role, its character, its potential and its drawbacks. Depending upon the source, joint consultation has recently been regarded as a mechanism capable of achieving a variety of aims, such as promoting more extensive employee involvement at work, preventing the need for European legislation on participation, strengthening managerial prerogatives in employee relations, incorporating workers more effectively into unitary conceptions of enterprise goals, or marginalizing contacts between managers and worker representatives. Whatever the view, however, joint consultation is considered to be worthy of discussion and analysis.

It is the purpose of this chapter to cast some more light on the subject, and to provide a framework for continuing analysis. It begins with a brief history of joint consultation based on published data, before examining competing definitions, and breaking these down into component parts. It will be argued that joint consultation can take any one of a number of different forms, depending upon the objectives of the parties involved and the climate within which it takes place. In the third section, it will be suggested that four different models of consultation may be seen in operation within British industry, in terms of the links with collective bargaining and employee representation. In some organizations, joint consultation may be used by managements to *prevent* the establishment of independent trade unionism. In others, it may be *marginal* within the enterprise, to either employer or employee, and come to be characterized as 'tea and toilet' committees. The most recent departure from the traditional pattern is where management seek to *upgrade* joint consultation as a substitute for collective bargaining. Finally, especially where unionism is strong and well developed, it may be seen by both sides as a valuable *adjunct* to collective bargaining.

Interesting though these descriptions may be in themselves, they are also valuable in helping to isolate the factors which may lead to the adoption of one form rather than another. Broadly, these can be broken down into four types of influence: management or employer philosophy and strategy in employee relations; employee (or specifically trade union) strength and organization at the level at which consultation takes place; the nature of trust between the two parties; and the degree to which the external environment (and notably the product market) creates unity or division between the two parties. To some extent, all of these factors are inevitably tied in with one another, and all can change over time, thus producing the dynamics of joint consultation in practice.

## HISTORY AND DEVELOPMENT

### Early Roots

Joint consultation has a long and somewhat chequered history in Britain. Although there are examples of committees on which managers and employees sat to discuss issues of so-called 'common interest' in the nineteenth century, this only became a regular occurrence during and after the First World War. The Whitley Committee, set up towards the end of the war, devoted considerable attention to joint consultation, and proposed the establishment of three tiers of involvement from national to works level. Whilst, in part, these were to be concerned with utilizing the knowledge and experience of workpeople, a primary consideration was to secure a permanent improvement in relations between employers and employed. According to Brannen (1983: 41–2), 73 joint industrial councils were started between 1918 and 1921, and there were over 1000 local councils by 1922. None were formed in industries such as mining, the cotton industry or in engineering, where trade unionism was already well developed and there was a high degree of workplace control. Although many of the councils fell into disuse during the depression of the 1920s, some were maintained or developed on the Whitley model in 'progressive' companies such as Rowntrees, Cadbury and ICI. The system of works councils in the latter came into operation in 1927 and was designed to promote communication between management and the workforce; Roeber (1974: 25) notes that the unions thought the councils sinister from the start since they were not based upon union channels, and he acknowledges that there may have been an element of an attempt to compete with the unions. The sophisticated paternalism of the company was also obvious in that one purpose of the councils was to encourage loyalty to a company 'which paid them better than others in the industry, provided all sorts of fringe benefits and was concerned enough about their welfare to provide a channel through which their worries and problems could be discussed'. It was not until 1970 that the joint consultative system in ICI came to be based upon unions and shop steward representation (Roeber, 1975: 221–3).

During the inter-war years, it was felt that the extent of joint consultation declined, except in the largest companies. Even where consultative committees did continue in existence, there was still a separation between consultation and collective bargaining based upon union channels. The Second World War changed this situation, and consultative bodies were revived 'initially on a voluntary basis, but later with government encouragement and the blessing of the TUC' (Hawes and Brookes, 1980: 354). This wave of interest was centred around the practice of joint production committees, and their agendas covered items relating to production, efficiency, productivity and the like, but excluded anything to do with negotiable issues such as pay. Most sources indicate that consultation remained a significant element of British industrial relations throughout the 1940s, especially in engineering, mining, shipbuilding and construction (Clegg, 1979: 152). During the nationalization phase following the end of the Second World War, obligations were placed upon the new publicly owned industries to agree with unions upon joint machinery for consultation on matters of mutual interest. At the end of the 1940s, a postal survey of management respondents by the National Institute of Industrial Psychology found that 73 per cent claimed to have some form of joint consultation within their establishments (Brannen, 1983; 46).

During the 1950s and 1960s, the conventional wisdom is that joint consultation went into decline. A variety of surveys provide evidence to support this point of view. Marsh and Coker (1963: 183–4) estimated, on the basis of steward responses, that the number of consultative committees declined in engineering by a factor of one-third between 1955 and 1961. Brannen (1983: 46) reports the results of an unpublished inquiry by the Ministry of Labour in 1957 which suggested that only about one-third of plants employing 500 or more had some form of permanent consultative machinery. Clarke et al. (1972: 73) found that only 32 per cent of their private sector respondents had a formally constituted consultative body. McCarthy (1966: 33–4) argued that the decline in joint consultation was directly related to the development of shop floor organization, because shop stewards preferred negotiations, and would either boycott committees or change their character so as to make them indistinguishable from negotiating bodies. It was felt that consultation would only retain a primary place in workplace relations where union and shop steward representation was weak or non-existent. Whilst there has been some criticism of this view in relation to recent developments (Marchington and Armstrong, 1983: 24), it was generally accepted (Hebden and Shaw, 1977: 78–81; Guest and Knight, 1979: 143; Poole, 1975: 79) that joint consultation was in a state of terminal decline, particularly in well-organized workplaces.

## The Recent Resurgence

The 1970s and 1980s, however, seem to have produced a rather different outcome, and this has led to a new debate about employee involvement and joint consultation. The evidence comes from a variety of sources and not simply from the reporting of developments in Japanese subsidiaries and on 'green-field' sites (see, for example, Bassett, 1986). Brown (1981: 78) reported that consultative committees existed in about 40 per cent of manufacturing establishments, and their coverage had more than doubled in the previous five years. The Workplace Industrial Relations Survey (Daniel and Millward, 1983: 130–3) found that 37 per cent of public and private sector workplaces operated with formal consultation, and of these almost half had come into existence during the late 1970s. Consultative committees were also four times more likely to exist alongside collective bargaining than on their own. Batstone (1984: 254) found that the extent of union-based consultation was even greater than had been reported in the earlier Warwick survey (Brown, 1981), and a similar result emerges from the sample of private sector companies investigated by Joyce and Woods (1984b: 3–4). Edwards' (1985: 34) survey of chief executives indicates that consultation continued to grow in large private sector organizations up to 1984. Finally, the most recent British Workplace Industrial Relations Survey (Millward and Stevens, 1986: 139) indicates that consultative committees have become more extensive in the public sector since 1980, although there has been a slight fall in the private sector, due primarily to the shifting pattern of employment and to the greater significance of smaller establishments.

Although most analysts would agree that consultation has become more extensive since the early 1970s, MacInnes dissents from this position. He argues (1985: 93) that 'the statistical evidence available does not in fact provide evidence of expansion in consultation, and the qualitative evidence suggests that it has not changed its role either. It appears that the "renaissance" of consultation is an illusory phenomenon.' His case primarily rests upon methodological shortcomings and the fact that in different surveys, different people (managers and/or stewards) were asked questions about different concepts (formal and/or informal consultation) based at different levels within the organization (establishment and/or company-wide). This has led to a tendency for some surveys probably to overstate the extent of consultation, whereas others have tended to understate. Thus, he suggests that the aggregate coverage of joint consultation has been remarkably stable since the war (1985: 98).

Precisely because of the lack of standardization in survey design and operationalization, it is difficult to contest some of the earlier findings, and there might well be some truth in MacInnes's criticisms. The recent evidence, however, is less open to question for the simple reason that all of the surveys have asked for information about growth as well as coverage. Even if they cannot be compared with each other due to differences in respondents, sector, level of operation or type of committee, all the authors cited previously report a growth over the period leading up to the survey date. There is a consistency in reported increases which can only partially be explained by the fact that people remember the birth of committees better than they remember their demise, a point which is central to MacInnes's explanation of stability (1985: 106). Further evidence to support the notion of growth over the last decade is provided by the Daniel and Millward survey; after acknowledging that their results may slightly overstate the growth in consultative machinery, they report that 'with establishments with newly introduced committees outnumbering those that have abandoned them by about nine to one, we can be sure that some growth has taken place' (1983: 133).

## COMPETING DEFINITIONS AND INTERPRETATIONS

### Theories of Growth and Decline

If we accept that the period since 1970 has actually witnessed a growth in the extent of consultation, whatever its nature, we are then left with two competing interpretations of this growth; one, the major proponent of which is Ramsay (1977, 1983), is that participation comes in waves and reflects cycles of control in the management of labour. In broad terms, this means that participation (and with it joint consultation) may be seen as an attempt to sustain the status quo, as well as to defuse trade union power by incorporating their representatives into the management of the organization. In Ramsay's view (1983: 204), 'managements have been attracted to the idea of participation when their control over labour has been perceived to be under pressure in some way. This perception has coincided with periods of experience of a growing challenge from labour to the legitimacy of capital and its agents.' Thus, one would expect variations in the extent of consultation over time, and also in its nature even if its extent did not alter very much. The alternative conception is one of evolution towards a new and permanent era, in which a variety of forms of participation may co-exist, or one in which more radical and all-embracing forms may be introduced into the enterprise. This argument rests upon the notion that subordinates expect to be consulted by their superiors, and the latter believe that this is the right and proper way to conduct their business. Due to the growth in education, rises in living standards and an erosion of deferential attitudes, coupled with opinions from abroad (e.g. Japan) about better ways of managing people, the rest of the century is likely to see a continuing development in employee involvement.

An alternative, and potentially more productive, interpretation is to follow the line of reasoning promulgated by Joyce and Woods (1984a: 2–8), who argue that fluctuations in the extent of consultation can be explained by one of three approaches. First, the McCarthy thesis implies that the extent of joint consultation can be inversely related to the strength of union organization. This means that joint consultation should have declined during the 1970s, since unions grew in strength over that period, and it should have been increasing in significance throughout the first half of the 1980s because the opposite conditions existed. Second, the 'incorporation' thesis assumes managements see less need to consult in the climate of a recession for much the same reasons as those put forward by Ramsay and discussed above. Third, what they term the 'external threat' thesis is one which anticipates growing popularity for joint consultation in the current climate because both sides are willing to collaborate in order to ensure the survival of the enterprise.

None of these approaches seems able to provide a total explanation which can account for developments over the period 1975–85, across a wide range of industries, sizes of establishment, variations in union power, and pressure from the environment. Reasons for wanting to introduce consultation may have varied over the decade to 1985, such that accommodating relatively powerful unions was important for the first phase, whilst countering the external threat has been rather more crucial in the second. Small firms may be using consultative mechanisms as an alternative to unionism, whereas larger establishments may be using it as an adjunct to collective bargaining; that is, a mixture of 'accommodation' and 'external threat' theses. What is also important, however, is to move beyond a discussion relating solely to the extent of consultation – that is, its mere absence or presence – and begin to examine the nature of consultation in practice.

## Definitions and Components

There have been a number of attempts to define exactly what is meant by the term 'joint consultation', and it is from these that we can isolate its primary components. For the Whitley Committee in 1917, joint consultation was seen as a means of improving the utilization and practical knowledge and experience of workpeople, and was particularly concerned with improvements to decision-making, especially at a time of change, and with ways to increase employee commitment to agreed courses of action. Clegg and Chester (1954: 342–3) refer to a 1947 Ministry of Labour pamphlet in which the function of joint consultation was defined as 'the regular exchange of views between employers and workers on production matters'. The process of interaction therefore becomes two-way and the content is specifically related to production. Clegg and Chester also raise questions about the extent to which unions alone should be involved in consultation, and whether or not it is desirable to place some limitation on the powers of joint consultation in order that it should not overlap with collective bargaining (1954: 323–6). The Ministry of Labour in its evidence to the Donovan Commission is clear about the 'generally understood' meaning: 'discussion between management and workers in an establishment of matters of joint concern which are not the subject of negotiation with trade unions'. Thus, there is reference to processes (discussion), parties (management and workers), subject matter (those of joint concern) and limitations on responsibilities and scope of interaction, although there is no mention of objectives or anticipated outcomes. The idea of common interests or joint concern, or ideas of an integrative nature, has been central to most other definitions of joint consultation (for example, see Armstrong, 1977; 311), and has also been the focus of criticisms about its likely achievements (for example, see McCarthy, 1966: 36; MacInnes, 1985: 101–6).

Aware that the quest for an all-embracing definition may be ill conceived, Farnham and Pimlott (1983: 329–32) come up with three alternatives: the *managerial* approach, which is highly protective of prerogatives and seeks to advance industrial harmony to the exclusion of power-based employee representation through trade unions; the *traditional* approach which involves a 'process by which management seeks the views, feelings and ideas of employees through their representatives, prior to negotiating or making a decision'; and *advanced* joint consultation in which the aim is to promote industrial democracy at work, and in which the artificial distinctions between consultation and negotiation become blurred.

Putting all of these definitions together, it seems that there are at least five primary components which may vary between different schemes and from one time period to another. The *objectives* for joint consultation may be clear from the constitution of a committee, or they may be hidden and/or implicit in the processes which take place. Published objectives tend to refer to the benefits in terms of improved output, greater efficiency, and enhanced employee commitment to organizational decisions. Quite clearly these are employer objectives, although there may well be incidental (and sometimes quite substantial) benefits for employees if these are realized. Equally, however, greater efficiency may also mean tighter work controls, and that is less likely to be seen as an advantage by employees. Nonetheless, some constitutions actually go as far as to highlight mutual benefits to employees and company, and to stress this as one of the underlying philosophical aspects of the scheme. At the other end of the spectrum, there are also instances in which consultation may be developed and extended in order to prevent union intervention and recognition, but it is hardly likely that such objectives will be committed to paper and disclosed to employees.

Whilst most definitions tend to agree that consultation is about issues of common interest, *the subject matter* of joint consultative committees is also likely to vary. Some concern themselves with parochial matters of relatively minor importance, such as social and welfare activities, the quality of the canteen tea or reports on personnel, whilst others have as their agenda items issues relating to production and order statistics, commercial matters of business and investment decisions. Again, the range of subject matter depends to some extent upon the intentions and stances of the parties, and the extent to which each wishes to operate in an open manner. Indeed, one of the recent claims is that joint consultation is now concerning itself with matters of strategic importance to the plant or company (Terry, 1983: 56). This vision of rejuvenation contrasts somewhat sharply with the image of trivia conveyed by Nicholson (1978: 42).

Thirdly, the *processes* which accompany consultation can also vary quite considerably, and the flow of information can be perceived as either predominantly upward or downward, or both. The upward flow idea focuses on the contribution of employees to improvements in the quality of decisions – using shopfloor experience, collecting all ideas prior to making decisions – and this is well illustrated by Dowling et al. (1981: 186) when they suggest that 'there is a broad measure of agreement between the parties that consultation is a process which enables the views of employees to be expressed, discussed and taken into account before management makes a final decision on a proposal'. Others assume the flow to be mainly downward and to have the aim, as per Section 1 of the 1982 Employment Act, of encouraging a common awareness of economic and financial factors which can affect company performance; in this view, therefore, consultation has an educative role, one which may help to achieve employee commitment to management decisions, and one in which managers' primary training needs are those of improved selling techniques. For many consultative committees, however, two-way communication is more usual, and each side may use the machinery to feed information to the other in an attempt to structure their expectations prior to bargaining, or to prevent bargaining altogether (Marchington and Armstrong, 1981: 13–14).

The *powers* of a consultative mechanism may be stated quite explicitly in constitutions, or they may be left rather loose and ill defined. If they are stated explicitly, there is usually some reference to what may not be discussed, and the places to which such issues should be referred for resolution. The clarification of this distinction between consultative and negotiable items may be equally desired by both parties, and both may act as custodians of collective agreements within the consultative machinery. Consultation does not generally involve decision-making and, especially if unions are well organized and strongly represented on the committees, this is not necessarily a source of weakness. On the contrary, it may actually be viewed as advantageous, and as an arrangement which allows both parties to expose ideas and test the water before entering the more competitive collective bargaining arena. Conversely, machinery with no explicit clarification of powers may produce a vagueness within constitutions which can either reflect, or result in, a greater *inequality* of power between management agents and employee representatives. It is the fluidity which probably most worries the opponents of consultation since this arena can be used by management to impose their views on employees in situations where employees are not independently represented. The use, by both sides, of joint consultation as an *adjunct* to collective bargaining is more likely when unions are relatively strong, and in these instances the fluidity may be beneficial to employees as well as to employers.

Finally, the *parties* to consultation may vary, and the employer may be represented and led by line or personnel management. The 'employee' side could consist of manual or staff workers alone, a combination of the two groups, and even some relatively senior managers. As Daniel and Millward found (1983: 134), it was more likely for there to be two separate committees than it was for the manual and non-manual employees to be combined on one committee. There were also likely to be multiple committees in cases where there was recognition of more than one union. Representation of employees could be based on union channels alone or by department irrespective of union membership. The character of consultation may be radically different depending upon the presence of unions within the workplace and the degree to which contentious items can be channelled through separate negotiating committees.

Overall, therefore, it can be seen that joint consultation can take a variety of forms and serve a number of interests, depending upon the context in which it operates. If it has been introduced specifically for the purpose of preventing the development of trade unionism, it is likely to function somewhat differently from the context in which both parties use consultation as a valuable adjunct to, or preliminary process for, collective bargaining. If managements see advantage in contributing to the success of consultative meetings as one element of their employee relations policy, it is likely to be very different from a situation in which both sides feel unwilling to expose their thinking to each other, and where joint consultation is marginal to the management process. Consequently, the search for a universal definition of joint consultation is ill founded; researchers who write of a renaissance of interest and activity through high-level bodies are right in certain circumstances, though not all. Those who regard consultation as a marginal exercise which is used to confirm management's powers are also quite correct in certain circumstances, though not all. And so, too, are those who believe consultation to be an adjunct to collective bargaining, not its competitor. The point is that the recent growth in the extent of joint consultation is due to different reasons depending upon a variety of influences, and each 'theory' may be true in certain situations. Before examining the contextual factors which help to account for the nature of consultation, four different models will be described so as to place the interpretations in perspective.

## DIFFERING MODELS OF JOINT CONSULTATION

*An Alternative to Collective Bargaining?*

Hawkins (1979: 40–1) suggests that employers might set up and develop consultation in order to resist collective bargaining since this has the potential of allowing for representation of employee views and the conveying of information from management to workforce. That this has been successful in the past is well documented; Clegg and Chester (1954: 329–30) report on a number of incidents during the earlier part of the twentieth century, and it still remains a fear on the part of unions. Certain areas, such as private services or small firms, are more likely to be prone to this usage of consultation than others.

The stance adopted by employers in this model is essentially unitarist both in philosophy and practice, but it is more sophisticated than that of the traditional anti-union owner-manager; the latter would see no need for any recognition or formalization of employee goals, whereas the former would feel it was their duty to persuade employees of the benefits of management policies. The company will be likely to devote considerable time and energy to the process of consultation, the central objectives of the system being to promote industrial harmony and the willing acceptance of management decisions. The process will be one-way and fundamentally educative, although the system will also have value in highlighting areas of employee concern since this provides senior management with the facility to monitor the effectiveness of their communications and indeed their own subordinates. Thus, apprehension or dissent will be seen, in a typically unitarist fashion, as evidence of inadequate communications or influencing skills on the part of managers, and is likely to be met with a search for better ways in which to present data to employees. It is not the message which is wrong, but the medium.

Since employees lack independent representation, and may well be dubious about its benefits in any event, there is likely to be little overt challenge to managerial prerogatives. The desire for more information is either met, or refused on the basis of confidentiality, complexity or inappropriateness. Meeting with senior managers on a regular basis, and perhaps spending more time discussing issues in an informal social environment before or after the meeting, confirms the belief that these people are essentially reasonable and committed to the overall benefit of the organization and its employees. Perhaps employees are also likely to be impressed by these senior managers, and either share their beliefs or values about current affairs or defer to them due to their status and assumed expertise. Either way, there is acceptance or acquiescence of one's place in society, and the fruits of joint consultation do not conflict with prior expectations.

The experience of involvement may lead, however, to increasing awareness of the ambiguities, limitations and contradictions in the system, and eventually to its downfall. Participants may begin to realize, especially if controversial issues surface within the committee, due to difficult trading conditions or other externally imposed factors, that they are powerless in relation to managers. This can cause increasing criticism of the system and its proponents, and may ultimately lead to demands for independent union representation. Cressey and MacInnes (1984: 24–5) point to the experience of some Scottish companies involved in their study which became more authoritarian in response to external pressures and internal dissent, and suggest that this exposed the fragile nature of consultation forged out of such circumstances. Marchington and Armstrong (1985: 23) similarly cite the way in which managements may redouble their efforts to prevent unionization by a mixture of threats and inducements, and which in one of their case studies led to the evaporation of interest in both the idea of unionization and the role of consultation. Management accusations of disloyalty merely served to convince employee representatives of the futility of their resistance, and equally reduce their commitment to co-operative ventures.

This need not be automatic, however, and a combination of successful trading circumstances and expressions of concern and interest on the part of employers may reinforce individualistic values and engineer a commitment to corporate goals. But consultation itself may have had little to do with this state of affairs, in that any system can be well regarded if the organization is performing well in the market-place and prospects for job security look rosy.

### *Marginal to Collective Bargaining?*

This describes the situation in which joint consultation achieves little or nothing for the parties, is marginal to any activity in the workplace, and is in the process of stagnation leading perhaps to the eventual collapse of the system. It is the type of joint consultation which is usually described by critics as typical of machinery in general, but it certainly does not provide a total picture. It is more likely to operate in organizations where there is little trust, where management or union is prone to the use of opportunistic tactics to undermine each other, and where there is little management commitment to joint arrangements which have emerged under duress. Depending upon the relative power imbalance, managements may not consider it to be worth the time or effort to go through the motions of the consultative process, and starve the committees of either information or indeed key personnel. Unions may lack the strength or the motivation to object. It is the kind of situation in which the fluidity, flexibility or vagueness which may surround consultation is its primary source of weakness and, given the fact that most committees lack decision-making powers in any event, this is fertile ground for the critics. Clegg and Chester (1954: 346) note that 'the formal machinery of consultation may remain in existence for a time or even permanently, but the manager will conduct the meeting without interest . . . the most capable workers are likely to resign, and the rest may be suspected by their fellows as seeking promotion or other favours'. For MacInnes (1985), consultation is fundamentally contra-dictory since it cannot possibly meet the conflicting objectives sought from its exercise by managements and stewards. It is beset by internal tensions and, in addition to being marginal to any regulatory processes, it is also unstable. He feels that the nature of consultation is best described in terms of a circular pattern, in which the initial enthusiasm for consultation is enough to overcome the looseness of its definition. As time goes by, it achieves less and less for the parties until one day it eventually peters out, only to be resurrected by a new manager at some future date. The death of consultation is described thus:

> Eventually either one of the parties decides the effort is not worthwhile and the attempt is abandoned, or consultation becomes a very marginal activity, going through the motions on a diet of trivial issues. There is rarely a dramatic end. Usually committees become progressively less regular and meaningful as members fail to turn up or have more pressing priorities. Eventually someone not only forgets to organise a meeting, others forget that they have even forgotten. (MacInnes, 1985: 104)

This is a vivid description, and one which is probably familiar to some readers. MacInnes' primary mistake, though, is in confusing the specifics of consulta-tion in the organizations with which he was involved with a generally observable pattern of decline and renaissance. The companies which formed the basis of his study were those in which unions were either not recognized by employers, or were relatively weak in organizational terms, and were also those which faced significant trading difficulties. Cressey and MacInnes (1984: 29) note that 'in the context of poor results, quick action might be deemed necessary without the luxury of securing agreement in advance. Parti-cipation meetings were cancelled or postponed as managers were called away to more urgent tasks'. Furthermore, even when meetings were held, the effect of the recession was to emphasize the different courses of action that could be taken and the prospect of very divergent results from common interests.

In one of the companies investigated by Marchington and Armstrong (1985: 19–22) consultation collapsed due to an increasingly hostile approach by senior management towards the unions, and a desire to exclude the senior stewards from any interaction with them. This also coincided with a greater emphasis on communicating direct to the workforce, and a harsh process of rationalization. The multi-union organization was not able to resist these moves since it lacked the cohesion to operate together centrally against the employer. Joint blaming sessions increasingly characterized joint consultative meetings, and the actual demise of the system came as no great surprise to any of the participants.

### Competing with Collective Bargaining?

Within this perspective, joint consultation is seen as being in direct competition with collective bargaining, although in this instance the objective of management is to upgrade consultation such that negotiations become less necessary or meaningful. This is the view of the recent renaissance theorists, and it is founded on the continuing role of union representation in workplace arrangements. As Terry indicates:

> Part of the strategy is an intention to involve stewards ... more closely in an understanding of the problems and issues confronting the company and hence of the logic and inescapability of the conclusions and policies proposed by management. But it is important to note that the logic of this strategy rests upon the maintenance of the representative structure of the workforce, and of its authority and legitimacy, rather than upon their destruction. (1983: 56)

The subject matter of consultation has therefore to be of substance rather than concern with trivia, and put across in the essentially co-operative climate of consultation rather than the competitive environment of negotiations. According to Terry (1983: 56), 'investment plans, the development of new products, problems of productivity and competitiveness, national and international, amalgamation, takeover and rationalisation are their agenda items'. Previously, these may or may not have been dealt with during negotiations, but now they come before the consultative committee for discussion. Support for this view of rejuvenation comes from Chadwick (1983: 6) and Edwards (1985: 35).

Combined with this upgrading of consultation, there is often development of other forms of employee involvement, designed to convince employees of the reasons for managerial actions, and also perhaps to apply a brake on steward activity. Some of these have been well publicized and have already been discussed in the two previous chapters: quality circles, briefing groups, toolbox talks, company presentations and videos, and employee reports. As Batstone (1984: 264) notes, 'management have been attempting to use a variety of techniques to win worker and steward co-operation where steward organization is strong, and market and other pressures have forced management to take a series of harsh decisions'. But it should be noted that there does not appear to have been an explicit attack on steward organization *per se* in these companies; nonetheless, there can be little doubt that this may be fostered in order to weaken unionism by the back door. Such an approach relies upon the expenditure of a good deal of time and effort on the part of management, which is presumably regarded as necessary in order to encourage co-operative relations at work. Employees and their representatives need to be persuaded, not bludgeoned, into compliance with managerial plans.

There is certainly anecdotal evidence to support the notion of revitalized arrangements and extensions to include other more direct forms of employee involvement. Joint consultative arrangements will have more extensive items on their agendas in such companies, but it is too early to assess whether the process of consultation is actually more meaningful than it was previously, or whether the powers of consultative committees have in any way been extended. Business plans may be unveiled, but they are not open to change. Decisions about rationalization may be communicated to the employee representatives after they have been taken, but they may still be contested in the negotiating arena. The success of managements who aim to use upgraded consultation in order to undermine collective bargaining depends upon the nature of the crisis confronting the company and the ability of the union organization to resist managerial intentions. Both of these will be dealt with in more detail in the final section, but there is no doubt that the perception of pressures emanating from the external environment can have a critical impact upon employee relations.

Working through established networks of employee representation is, of course, one way in which to seek an upgrading of consultation in order to displace collective bargaining. Another is to operate the two systems – consultation and negotiation – alongside but independent of each other. Bargaining will be conducted by union representatives, whereas representatives on consultative committees will be on the basis of expertise, function or department irrespective of union membership. Upgrading the significance of consultation can therefore have the effect of divorcing the union from its members, particularly if successes in the negotiating arena are few and far between. The union can come to be seen as less 'real' in the eyes of its members, only raising anxieties about the future, complaining about lack of influence or information, or fighting to preserve the position of employees under threat of disciplinary action. Committee members may be able to enthuse about future prospects, provide information about top-level issues or help to involve employees in contributing to the improvement of work-related matters (for example, helping to de-bug a new machine). That such arrangements exist is made apparent from research by Marchington (1980), Bate and Murphy (1981) and Cressey and MacInnes (1984), although once again the fragility of this machinery, especially from the employee side, is also made clear. In addition, managements can also find such arrangements time-consuming and potentially counterproductive, in that splits within the workforce may not automatically be to their advantage. Putting union and non-union representatives, perhaps from different levels within an organization, together on a consultative committee may serve to expose contradictions in management processes more effectively rather than lead to adoption of management goals, and may also have the effect of hardening union stances in collective bargaining.

### An Adjunct to Collective Bargaining?

The previous models assumed that joint consultation and collective bargaining are competing processes of regulation in the workplace and, depending upon the climate, one or the other will provide the primary focus in employee relations. Within this model, the two can be seen as operating in conjunction with each other, and the two processes are kept strictly separate, although the representatives on each committee will be the same people. Collective bargaining is used for matters concerning wages, working conditions and aspects of a distributive nature, whereas joint consultation fills in the gaps, focuses on issues of an integrative character and helps to oil the wheels of industry. If asked to choose between them, shop stewards would have no doubt about which to go for: collective bargaining. But the two are not seen in competition, and both can provide benefits for employees and the organization for which they work. Contrary to the stance taken by McCarthy and his adherents, there has recently been increasing support for the possibility of this model, especially in well-organized workplaces (Marchington and Armstrong, 1981: 15; Daniel and Millward, 1983: 134–5).

Indeed, strong workplace organization may be regarded as a necessary prerequisite for this model, since stewards will be keen to occupy the places on both consultative and negotiating machinery, and will have the potential power to prevent any attempts to undermine the role of the latter by upgrading the former. Stewards argue that by sitting on both types of body, their centrality to regulatory processes is protected, and not only do they receive information relevant for bargaining purposes but they can also use the consultative forum as a way in which to convey their attitudes to management. In this way, stewards may be able to influence managerial actions prior to decisions being made by management. Of course, managements may also make use of the consultative machinery in order to test employee reaction and influence the thinking of employee representatives. Unlike the previous two models, therefore, this conception is not based upon the inability of shop stewards to resist management preferences and actions. Experienced stewards are unlikely to be hoodwinked by elaborate management tactics designed to indoctrinate or confuse them, and are likely to resent any attempt by management to use consultation for this purpose. The notion of trust relations is also central to this model, as too is the upholding of a jointly agreed set of rules as to what is and is not legitimate behaviour in the consultative forum.

Such managements are unlikely to use consultation to undermine trade union organization, and indeed see great value in operating the two systems alongside one another. Some companies, such as ICI, pride themselves on their consultative approach to employee relations and, it could be argued, such systems have become synonymous with the overall approach of the employer to personnel issues. Therefore managements who wish to use consultation alongside collective bargaining will do all they can to protect the unions as a bargaining agent provided they are well organized and in tune with the wishes of their members. There is also support for the provision of facilities, time-off, the check-off, access to new recruits and all the other factors which go along with management commitment to trade unionism in the workplace.

In multi-plant companies, there is likely to be a hierarchy of committees for progressing issues up or down the system. Stewards are just as likely as managers, perhaps more so, to sit on higher-level committees beyond the immediate establishment, and to have access to a good deal of information and a wide range of contacts within the company. There may even be sub-committees which are set up to investigate more complex or detailed issues, and these will usually be jointly staffed by management and employees. The actual practices which accompany consultation will probably differ from one company to another, but may include a range of procedural mechanisms to ensure that the committees are run on a joint basis or proceed as smoothly as possible. Management and stewards might have joint control over the agenda and minutes, a chair which rotates between members, an action list to identify the appropriate person to investigate an issue, a date for reporting back, pre-meetings for stewards, statistics packs providing information on business and production matters, and other practices which are illustrative of an open and co-operative approach to managing. If possible, information will be provided in advance, although companies may be anxious about committing confidential information to paper. In addition, there are likely to be regular reviews of progress and monitoring of activities which may involve the use of outside independent consultants. Much of this reads like a check-list for achieving successful consultation (as produced in either Guest and Knight, 1979: 267–86 or Thomason, 1984: 490–8), but the lists in themselves are probably without value unless seen in the context of the system – for example, one of high union membership and the co-operative attitudes of the employer towards employee relations. None of these would be of any value if the employer is using consultation to prevent unionization, of course.

The state of the external environment, and the perceptions held by both sides of its influence, are also likely to exert some pressure on the state of consultation. Perhaps this description is more easily recognized from organizations operating in expanding or stable product markets, but there are also examples of consultation taking this form in organizations which have been confronted with crises of traumatic proportions, and which have sought greater unity in the struggle to fight for corporate survival (Purcell, 1981: 232–8). Nonetheless, the spectre of product market collapse may still hover over the parties.

## THE CONTINGENT FACTORS

A major concern in this chapter has been to emphasize the variety of forms which joint consultation can take in British industry, and that no one model is sufficiently flexible to account for these different situations. Each of the models may be appropriate and observable in certain circumstances, which need to be analysed and explored in a rather more direct fashion. Basically, these contingent factors can be subdivided into four broad areas, and each of these will be considered in turn.

### Management Philosophy

Central to textbook prescriptions for success is the notion that managements must be committed to consultation, and be willing to invest time and energy in improving the process. Of course, this is based upon the assumption that managements actually want consultation to be successful, and that they will be open and participative in their approach to involving employees. In some instances this is plainly not true, particularly in the case of the models in which consultation is marginalized or trivialized in its operation. Underlying the commitment to consultation, however, is also the wider question of management philosophy in employee relations, and it would be wrong to envisage consultation in isolation from other processes in the workplace.

Employee relations philosophy can be analysed using Friedman's (1977) distinction between 'responsible autonomy' and 'direct control'. Under the first two models described in the previous section, managements are keen to tackle the unions head on, and maintain their power by opposition or confrontation. Under the 'adjunct' model, the anticipation is that working with the unions in strongly organized workplaces will produce co-operation rather than confrontation. Indeed, some companies ascribe the maintenance of industrial peace to their underlying co-operative philosophy as evidenced by their desire to make consultation work. The model of upgraded consultation is, on the surface, similar to the notion of responsible autonomy, that is in persuading employee representatives of the benefits of management's pre-ferred options by exposing them to extra information about the performance of the undertaking. But there is also a hidden motive, and that is to weaken the hold of the unions by undermining collective bargaining, which places the model more firmly in the adversarial camp. Of course, this may lead to the view that joint consultation is the 'joint con!' (Dowling et al., 1981: 189). In consequence, therefore, management philosophy exerts a crucial influence over the nature of joint consultation in practice, particularly since most schemes are initiated by managements.

The discussion of employee relations philosophy leads to a consideration of management strategy. Recently it has become more customary to talk of 'management strategy' as if employers had carefully devised pro-active policies for the management of labour which were not only important to them but were also capable of being put into practice. Again, there are certain questionable assumptions behind this point of view, notably the extent to which managements actually do have grand plans or merely muddle through from one crisis to another. A decision which may appear to have a particular meaning when examined with the benefit of hindsight may have been made for very different reasons at the time – in order to deserve the label 'strategy' intentions have to be obvious at the outset. Policies and intentions may exist in the minds of senior managers but fail to be interpreted thus by supervisors or actually implemented in accordance with original expectations; the significance of custom and practice for industrial relations bears testimony to this observation. And, finally, labour relations policies may not even be considered by senior managers in setting targets at strategic levels in the organization, although this does not mean that there are no explicit consequences for employees because of this. These features are analysed by Child (1985: 122) in relation to the introduction of new technology. He suggests that corporate strategies 'at the least establish certain parameters within which implementation and actual changes to jobs, and employment relations take place. The transition to implementation is subject to intervening processes and actions. In short, actors, processes and contextual conditions all have to be taken into account'. Thus, it is quite possible for two consultative committees within the same company to operate in different ways, even though both are guided by the same set of philosophical judgements by senior management and subject to the same structures. It is for this reason that the management process – from initiation through to refinement and implementation – is such a crucial variable in analysing the development and operation of joint consultation.

### Union Organization and Worker Resistance

The focus on management strategy creates the temptation to overlook any resistance to employer action, especially in the context of recession when unions are less overtly powerful. This has been a recurrent criticism in recent analyses of the labour process (see, for example, Thompson, 1983: 122–52), and it is also a relevant consideration with regard to joint consultation. In the situations in which consultation was used by managements in order to prevent or undermine union organization, it is clear that there was a lack of effective resistance to management plans. Staff associations or in-house unions tend to be less capable of defending workers due to their lack of independent organization and their reliance upon the employer's goodwill for the provision of facilities and resources. Managements are therefore more likely to be able to impose their views on employees. Similarly, if consultation is being used to undermine union organization, the ability to exclude union representatives from the consultative process, or to channel issues through consultation rather than the negotiating arena, must reflect a substantial shift in the balance of power. Perhaps, in the past, the strength of unions had been built upon their ability to exploit product market demands by the use of sectional activity, and their lack of centralized resources now acts as a restraint on their powers. In summarizing the operation of their committees, Cressey and MacInnes (1984: 20) point to a substantial power imbalance when they declare that 'it was up to management to determine what information to take to the committee and when, what subjects were proper matters for discussion, what form that discussion should take and finally what would result from discussion. In practice, management control of participation often extended to unfettered control of the agenda and direction of discussion'.

This observation has to be contrasted with that pertaining to the situation in which consultation is seen, by both parties, as an adjunct to bargaining. Here, union representatives are likely to have joint ownership of a number of aspects of the constitution and, like management, the right to refer matters to the negotiating committee should that be deemed appropriate. The separation of the two committees may be rather easier to maintain if unions are well organized and able to combat managerial actions centrally. It is because of this that Marchington and Armstrong conclude their assessment of the links between steward organization and joint consultation with the following statement:

> where stewards were well organised they seemed to value joint consultation, albeit with limited powers, and where they were poorly organised they were generally negative or neutral about it. In addition, there would also appear to be a strong similarity of views between stewards and management about consultative success when steward organisation was strong. There was less similarity where stewards organisation was less well developed. (1983: 31)

Once more, the explanation for events in the 'marginal' schemes is somewhat more complex, depending upon which party expresses least interest in consultative affairs. If unions are relatively powerless, they may not be able to challenge managerial attempts to marginalize activity not only in the consultative but also in the negotiating area. If unions are relatively powerful, they may withdraw from consultation if they feel that management is not taking it seriously, for fear that they may weaken their oppositional stances in collective bargaining.

*Trust and Co-operative Relations*

The notion of trust and concern for the processes of interaction has been the subject of investigation in a number of studies in recent years. Drawing upon the work of Fox (1974), Purcell (1981) has developed the theme of trust relations between managers and stewards, as too did Batstone and his colleagues (1977) in their analysis of shop steward activity in the engineering industry. It is probably best summarized in Brown's (1973: 135) quote from a convenor who said 'without trust you're like a conger eel on ice'. The conception of Batstone et al. (1977) of a strong bargaining relationship involves a willingness to 'drop one's guard' and trade confidences with the other party, safe in the belief that these will not be used against you. Part of the rules of the game insist on this respect for the position of the other party, and the willingness to work together to reduce uncertainty in the workplace.

Although much of the work cited here (see also Walton and McKersie, 1965) is concerned with bargaining relationships rather than the consultative arena, it is likely to be the latter in which trust may be more easily developed and sustained. Thus, one major advantage of consultation cited by stewards and managers is the way in which it can lead to better relations between the two parties, which can then spill over into the bargaining area. This is not to go along with the argument that, as implied by the 'competition' or 'prevention' models, the structuring of attitudes is simply a one-way process. There is considerable evidence of stewards in well-organized workplaces using consultation meetings to try and influence management opinion – giving notice, so to speak, of what the reaction will be should management attempt a certain line of action. And, of course, managers also use the consultative machinery to test the water about future issues. What binds all of these issues together is the fact that both parties can use consultation to trade information, and that each has sufficient trust in the intentions of the other to want to do this rather than spring a surprise on the other party when it may be off guard. As the personnel manager at one of the sites typical of the adjunct model argued, the consultative committee is important because, amongst other things, it 'gives us a chance to develop a mutual trust and understanding of each other' (Marchington and Armstrong, 1981: 11).

This is perhaps to be expected, as is the absence of trust at the sites where consultation achieved little for either party; the blame for delays in the consultative machinery is immediately put at management's door and is symptomatic of low trust; at a poorly organized site, management's use of the consultative committee to structure the expectations of the representatives is seen as an underhand use of this machinery and leads to a lack of trust of anything which management says. In either of these cases, previous events can be interpreted in different ways depending upon the level of trust between the parties.

Nevertheless, trust is harder to maintain than it is to lose, and because it is such an imprecise commodity it is difficult, if not impossible, to define it exactly. As Purcell (1981: 246–7) comments, 'a relationship built on trust is a risky investment. The complexity of the future is reduced by placing trust in the other party on whom you are dependent. Should that vulnerability be violated, the reaction is liable to be fierce, particularly since previous higher trust actions are now no longer reciprocated'. The maintenance of high trust may also be dependent upon continued certainty in the market-place or on the shopfloor, and on the ability of the other party to keep its promises. If trust seems to have resulted in the prospect of a brighter future, perhaps demonstrated in the form of new building work or a continued willingness to consult no matter what the message, then previous open behaviour could be seen as being repaid. Neither party would wish to damage this. But, again, a sudden and unforeseen deterioration in market share may provoke management responses which shatter the basis upon which the trust has been built up. Thus it is quite feasible for there to be shifts in consultative behaviour from one model to another – say, as an adjunct to bargaining to one where it is a marginal or unstable activity – due to shocks in the external environment.

## The External Environment

Whilst it would be nonsense to conceive of employee relations without reference to the environment within which it takes place, one also has to be careful not to go too far in the opposite direction and imply a direct causal and deterministic relationship between factors in the environment, say the economic or political climate, and processes such as consultation. There is a danger that this has occcurred, perhaps implicitly, in recent publications on the subject, and this obscures the degree to which managements may be able to make choices in *how* to respond to external pressures and deal with industrial relations issues. This is central to the more sophisticated discussions on the implementation of new technology which argue for greater consideration to be given to the politics of the change process, and the junctures at which managements can and do intervene to choose between options (Wilkinson, 1983: 21). Purcell (1981: 190–1) also warns against the adoption of a deterministic perspective when he states that 'to suggest that product market pressures forced a change in management's handling of industrial relations is too simple. It implies there was no choice when in fact a lengthy and often bitter debate took place between senior managers ...' (1981: 187). 'Product market pressures predicated the need for action, but not unilateral action which was bound to trigger resentment from the unions' (1981: 190–1). However, it can sometimes look this way since managements may tend to *legitimize* non-participation by reference to market or other external constraints on the organization (Marchington and Loveridge, 1983: 74–8).

The nature of the economic recession and the product market can have different effects on consultation depending upon its place within the employee relations framework. If employers are attempting to prevent or marginalize unions, a tight economic climate makes consultation less necessary since unions are further weakened, and time for involvement is less available. In the 'upgrading' model, the recession creates the need for more extensive consultation if both sides are to unite and fight off the common enemy. To some extent, this is also the case for the adjunct model in that management will aim to work even harder to ensure that co-operative and trust relations are sustained in the face of external pressures. Although a specific link can be found, this also demonstrates the lack of determinism *per se*, and the need to consider carefully the motives and philosophies of the parties as well.

The structure and process of decision-making within the company itself can also have a significant effect on consultation, although the 'prevention' model would depend less upon company structure than upon philosophy. If all decisions are taken centrally, then there is little that consultation can achieve beyond the communication of information at local level. Conversely, if all are taken at local levels, or the consultative machinery operates at several tiers within the organizational structure, then the potential for involvement, though not necessarily the practice, is much greater (Warner and Peccei, 1977: 10). It is more likely that the 'adjunct' and 'upgrading' models will operate in the latter circumstances, whereas the 'marginality' model would be more likely to fit the former. There is also the prospect of dynamism here since companies shift the locus of decision-making for a variety of reasons, and consultation could therefore become more or less important depending upon the direction of the shift, or upon the willingness of the employer to devise new arrangements which more adequately fit the new structure.

Clegg and Wall (1984: 439–40) cite the degree of uncertainty in the environment as another factor which may influence the potential for consultation within an organization. Basically, they argue that organizations functioning in a relatively predictable context provide little scope for involvement, and that 'the impediment to participation is one of impoverished content'. This may fit with conceptions of the marginality model in which consultation degenerates into discussions about trivia. Conversely, organizations in a more uncertain environment offer greater scope for involvement because more decisions have to be taken and changes effected. However, the degree of differentiation between different groups in this kind of organization is more pronounced, and 'the principal impediment to participation in this context is thus one of process'. Again, this may fit with the marginality school if the processes do not work well, but it is more likely to be observed in the adjunct or upgrading models in which efforts are put into making the system work.

## CONCLUDING COMMENTS

The principal purpose of this analysis has been to expose the inadequacies of any attempt to explain recent developments in joint consultation with reference to one all-embracing theory. The institution, like most in the sphere of industrial relations and personnel management, is considerably more complex than previously conceived by students of the subject. The motives of the parties and their philosophical approach to employee relations are mixed; managements may wish to use consultation to prevent or compete with unionism, or they may wish to use it as another plank in their essentially co-operative approach to managing people. Employee representatives may be suspicious of collaboration or powerless to make consultation work, or they may trust management sufficiently – and have the muscle to sustain their position – to use consultation as an adjunct to bargaining. And, without doubt, the nature of the external environment (and perceptions of its influence) can exert a significant pressure upon the potential for involving employees through joint consultation.

It is more difficult to assess whether this complexity of arrangements is a recent phenomenon, since much of the historical analysis is based upon problems of growth and decline – that is, the *extent* – of consultation rather than upon variations in its *nature*. Thus, it is quite possible for consultative arrangements to degenerate without actually going out of operation, or to be revitalized without being considered as a new initiative and consequently not be accounted for in the figures of growth and decline. Joint consultation may remain in existence, and be transformed as the recent case studies of both Marchington and Armstrong (1985) and Cressey and MacInnes (1984) demonstrate. It is in the purposes and the processes of consultation, affected as they are by changing external and internal factors, that one can begin to appreciate the consequences of consultative efforts in a more dynamic way. The models outlined above, whilst identifying certain ideal-type situations, should not be seen in a static fashion, and it is quite feasible for there to be shifts between them. Before analysing the dynamics of consultation in greater detail, however, one needs to be able to describe current arrangements rather more accurately and fully than has previously been the case.

Over 30 years ago Clegg and Chester (1954: 344) posed the following question about joint consultation, 'why should a device which is given almost universal public approval meet with such limited success?'. Whilst that may have been the picture in the early 1950s, the question for the late 1980s needs to be framed rather differently: why should a device which is given almost universal academic disapproval meet with such continuing success, especially in large workplaces? Academics have traditionally been sceptical of consultation because it does not challenge the status quo, but operates in a flexible way. Practitioners on both sides of industry, conversely, have become accustomed to working within the status quo, and will make use of any institution which helps them in the process of managing their people or best representing their members' interests no matter how messy or ill-defined that arrangement.

# Bibliography

Armstrong, M. 1977. *A Handbook of Personnel Management Practice*. London: Kogan Page.

Bain, G.S. Ed. 1983. *Industrial Relations in Britain*. Oxford: Blackwell.

Bassett, P. 1986. *Strike Free*. London: Macmillan.

Bate, S.P. and Murphy, A.J. 1981. 'Can Joint Consultation Become Employee Participation?'. *Journal of Management Studies*, 18: 4, 389–409.

Batstone, E. 1984. *Working Order: Workplace Industrial Relations over Two Decades*. Oxford: Blackwell.

—— Boraston, I. and Frenkel, S. 1977. *Shop Stewards in Action: The Organization of Workplace Conflict and Accommodation*. Oxford: Blackwell.

Brannen, P. 1983. *Authority and Participation in Industry*. London: Batsford.

Brown, W. 1973. *Piecework Bargaining*. London: Heinemann.

—— Ed. 1981. *The Changing Contours of British Industrial Relations*. Oxford: Blackwell.

Chadwick, M. 1983. 'The Recession and Industrial Relations: A Factory Approach'. *Employee Relations*, 5: 5, 5–12.

Child, J. 1985. 'Managerial Strategies, New Technology and the Labour Process'. *Job Redesign*. Eds. Knights, D., Willmott, H. and Collinson, D. Farnborough: Gower, 107–41.

Clarke, R., Fatchett, D. and Roberts, B. 1972. *Workers' Participation in Management in Britain*. London: Heinemann.

Clegg, C.W. and Wall, T.D. 1984. 'The Lateral Dimension to Employee Participation'. *Journal of Management Studies*, 21: 4, 429–42.

Clegg, H.A. 1979. *The Changing System of Industrial Relations in Great Britain*. Oxford: Blackwell.

—— and Chester, T. 1954. 'Joint Consultation'. *The System of Industrial Relations in Great Britain*. Eds. Flanders, A.D. and Clegg, H.A. Oxford: Blackwell, 323–64.

Cressey, P. and MacInnes, J. 1984. 'The Relationship between Economic Recession and Industrial Democracy'. Glasgow: Centre for Research in Industrial Democracy and Participation, University of Glasgow. Unpublished paper.

Daniel, W.W. and Millward, N. 1983. *Workplace Industrial Relations in Britain*. London: Heinemann.

Dowling, M., Goodman, J., Gotting, D. and Hyman, J. 1981. 'Employee Participation: Survey Evidence from the North West'. *Employment Gazette*, April, 185–92.

Edwards, P.K. 1985. 'Myth of the Macho Manager'. *Personnel Management*, April, 32–5.

Farnham, D. and Pimlott, J. 1983. *Understanding Industrial Relations*, 2nd edn. London: Cassell.

Flanders, A.D. and Clegg, H.A. Eds. 1954. *The System of Industrial Relations in Great Britain*. Oxford: Blackwell.

Fox, A. 1974. *Beyond Contract: Work, Power and Trust Relations*. London: Faber.

Friedman, A. 1977. *Industry and Labour*. London: Macmillan.

Guest, D. and Knight, K. 1979. *Putting Participation into Practice*. Farnborough: Gower.

Hawes, W.R. and Brookes, C.C.P. 1980. 'Change and Renewal: Joint Consultation in Industry'. *Employment Gazette*, April, 353–61.

Hawkins, K. 1979. *A Handbook of Industrial Relations Management*. London: Kogan Page.

Hebden, J. and Shaw, G. 1977. *Pathways in Participation*. London: Associated Business Press.

Joyce, P. and Woods, A. 1984a. 'Joint Consultation in Britain: Towards an Explanation'. *Employee Relations*, 6: 2, 2–8.

—— and Woods, A. 1984b. 'Joint Consultation in Britain: Survey Evidence During the Recession'. *Employee Relations*, 6: 3, 2–7.

McCarthy, W.E.J. 1966. *The Role of Shop Stewards in British Industrial Relations*. Research Paper 1, Royal Commission on Trade Unions and Employers' Associations. London: HMSO.

MacInnes, J. 1985. 'Conjuring up Consultation: The Role and Extent of Joint Consultation in Post-War Private Manufacturing Industry'. *British Journal of Industrial Relations*, 23: March, 93–113.

Marchington, M. 1980. *Responses to Participation at Work*. Farnborough: Gower.

—— and Armstrong, R. 1981. 'A Case for Consultation'. *Employee Relations*, 3: 1, 10–16.

—— and Armstrong, R. 1983. 'Shop Steward Organisation and Joint Consultation'. *Personnel Review*, 12: 1, 24–31.

—— and Armstrong, R. 1985. 'Joint Consultation Revisited'. Glasgow: Centre for Research in Industrial Democracy and Participation, University of Glasgow. Unpublished paper.

—— and Loveridge, R. 1983. 'Management Decision-Making and Shop Floor Participation'. *Industrial Relations and Management Strategy*. Eds. Thurley, K. and Wood, S. Cambridge: Cambridge University Press, 73–82.

Marsh, A.I. and Coker, E.E. 1963. 'Shop Steward Organization in the Engineering Industry'. *British Journal of Industrial Relations*, 1: June, 170–90.

Millward, N. and Stevens, M. 1986. *British Workplace Industrial Relations 1980–1984: The DE/ESRC/PSI/ACAS Surveys*. Aldershot: Gower.

Nicholson, N. 1978. 'Can Consultation Work?'. *Personnel Management*, November, 42–6.

Poole, M. 1975. *Workers' Participation in Industry*. London: Routledge & Kegan Paul.

Purcell, J. 1981. *Good Industrial Relations: Theory and Practice*. London: Macmillan.

Ramsay, H. 1977. 'Cycles of Control: Worker Participation in Sociological and Historical Perspective'. *Sociology*, 11: September, 481–506.

—— 1983. 'Evolution or Cycle? Worker Participation in the 1970s and 1980s'. *Organisational Democracy and Political Processes*. Eds. Crouch, C. and Heller, F. London: Wiley, 203–25.

Roeber, J. 1975. *Social Change at Work*. London: Duckworth.

Terry, M. 1983. 'Shop Stewards through Expansion and Recession'. *Industrial Relations Journal*, 14: Autumn, 49–58.

Thomason, G. 1984. *A Textbook of Industrial Relations Management*. London: IPM.

Thompson, P. 1983. *The Nature of Work*. London: Macmillan.

Walton, R. and McKersie, R.B. 1965. *A Behavioral Theory of Labor Negotiations: An Analysis of a Social Interaction System*. New York: McGraw-Hill.

Warner, M. and Peccei, R. 1977. 'Problems of Management Autonomy and Worker Participation in Multinational Companies'. *Personnel Review*, 2: Autumn, 7–13.

Wilkinson, B. 1983. *The Shopfloor Politics of New Technology*. London: Heinemann.

# Index

*Index by Jackie McDermott*